# How Hampstead Heath was saved

## a story of 'people power'

ISBN 978 1 913213 00 8

Cover: Figures on
Hampstead Heath C19,
Herbert William Piper
(1846-1921);
from the collection
of the late Nigel Winder

Printed and bound in Great Britain
by Marston Book Services Ltd, Oxfordshire

THE FIR AVENUE,
HAMPSTEAD HEATH.

JOTTER.

# How Hampstead Heath was saved

## a story of 'people power'

*by* Helen Lawrence

*Edited by* David A Hayes
*Designed by* Ivor Kamlish
*Published by* Camden History Society

*With the generous financial support*
*of the* Heath & Hampstead Society

**CAMDEN
HISTORY
SOCIETY**
L O N D O N

# Contents

Foreword                                                              5
Introduction                                                          6
Acknowledgements                                                      9

PART 1: SETTING THE SCENE
1. The origins of the manor and village                              10
2. The Heath shrinks; the village grows                              23
3. The rise of the Romanticks                                        38

PART 2: LET BATTLE COMMENCE
4. Enter Sir Thomas Maryon Wilson                                    49
5. The lungs of London                                               60
6. Private versus public interest                                    68
7. What price the Heath?                                             80
8. The turning point                                                 92
9. The end of the beginning                                         105

PART 3: THE HEATH EXPANDS
10. The new campaigners                                             114
11. Kenwood redivided                                               121
12. O Gardeners spare our heat                                      132
13. Into the 20th century                                           140
14. Kenwood – the last chapter                                      151

PART 4: THE DUTY
15. Heath restored                                                  163
16. The management dilemma                                          176
17. Three into one – another London shake-up                        187

PART 5: THE HEATH IN LIMBO
18. The abolition of the Greater London Council                     195
19. The Heath divided                                               203
20. The final settlement                                            209

PART 6: PRESERVING THE RURAL ILLUSION
21. The rise of town planning                                       217
22. The Fringes of the Heath – planning battles                     234
23. The constant vigil                                              245

Appendix : Roll of honour                                           254
Bibliography                                                        255
Index                                                               257

# Foreword

*by* Lord Hoffmann, President
of the Heath & Hampstead Society

Est. 1897

Alexis de Tocqueville, writing of American democracy in 1840, noted the tendency of the people to form associations. "If it be proposed to advance some truth, or foster some feeling by the encouragement of a great example, they form a societyI have often admired the extreme skill with which the inhabitants of the United States succeed in proposing a common object to the exertions of a great many men and getting them voluntarily to pursue it." In a country with a powerful aristocracy, such as the England of his day, he said "the principle of association was by no means so constantly or adroitly used."

As the tide of democracy in England rose, the importance of associations grew. They became, as in the United States, a powerful instrument by which people, powerless as individuals, could get useful things done or prevent damaging things from happening. This book is largely the story of one such association, the Hampstead Heath Protection Society, now called the Heath & Hampstead Society, and its ceaseless efforts over more than a century to preserve Hampstead Heath as a fragment of original countryside within the urban sprawl of London. It was the product of a nineteenth century movement, associated in particular with John Ruskin, to preserve and even revive the values, architecture and countryside of old England, and to resist the industrialisation and urbanisation which was destroying the opportunities of ordinary people for creativity in both work and leisure. And it became a model for similar preservation societies in every town and village of the country.

The functioning of such associations depends, as de Tocqueville said, on getting people voluntarily to pursue its objects. This book chronicles the efforts of many public-spirited men and women to protect the character of Hampstead Heath. It has not been an easy matter: powerful interests of money and bureaucracy are often deployed to justify some nibble at the perimeter or "improvement" of the landscape and the defenders of the Heath sometimes receive brickbats as well as bouquets. But Hampstead and the Heath have been fortunate in the expertise and dedication of the people who have served the Society since its inception. Not least among these is the author of this book, who has given many years in various capacities to working for Hampstead and now has erected a fine monument to her colleagues and predecessors.

Leonard Hoffmann

# Introduction

There are a great many histories of Hampstead Heath mostly focused on the achievement of the 1871 Hampstead Heath Act. None of them deals in any depth with how it grew from 220 acres to 800, or with the continuation of its history in the 20th century. Between Barratt (1912), and F.M.L. Thompson (1974), Farmer (1984) and the Victoria County History (1989), there was a gap of many years. But none of the latter three books says much more about what happened after 1871, and Kit Ikin's short booklet commissioned by the Greater London Council for the Act's 1971 centenary, did not have the space for it. All were written before the abolition of the GLC.

The battle for the Heath did not happen in isolation - it was not unique but it was emblematic; it was "where the seeds of national awareness were sown".[1] There is scarcely a parliamentary debate on open space in the 19th century in which it is not mentioned, forming a vital background not just to the Heath campaign but to the growth of the whole movement to conserve open spaces. As David Sullivan remarked: "For a true historical perspective we should not focus on Hampstead in isolation".[2] I have sought to place events in the larger context of cultural and socio-political developments, and rediscover the people who played their part in that history, piecing together a few more strands of this tangled and fascinating story. It is also the story of a community and its deep attachment to place, handed down through generations.

There is no one saviour of the Heath as has been suggested – each generation produced new people who continued the task, and trying to understand what motivated them often throws light on the events themselves. For instance, it was not until John Carswell researched the Kenwood story in 1994 that it became clear that the real unsung saviour of Kenwood was Sir Arthur Crosfield, supported by dozens of local residents, and not, as had been generally accepted for decades, Lord Iveagh. His lordship's role was just the icing – albeit the most delectable icing – on that particular cake. More has also come to light about Sir Thomas Maryon Wilson, the leading antagonist, about whom very little is known. A recent discovery in Camden's archives is the Journal kept by Henry Sharpe when he first went to live in Hampstead in the 1840s. Acquired from Sharpe's grandson in the 1980s, by Malcolm Holmes (Camden Borough Archivist until 2007), it throws fascinating new light on Maryon Wilson's character.

The completely new element in this account is the story of the Heath & Hampstead Society (H&HS), which mostly concerns 20th-century events. No previous history has given much, if any, attention to their work, without which the Heath would be a very different place. John Richardson, Camden History Society Chairman, asked in his book *Hampstead One Thousand*: "...why are so few of the reliable people who helped to save the Heath and its extensions for us ...so badly remembered?".[3] Founded over a century ago in 1897 the Hampstead Heath Protection Society grew out of the 19th-century campaign to save Hampstead

Heath as a public open space and several of its founders were involved in that 40-year campaign. Now the Heath & Hampstead Society, it has responded to changing times with changes to its name. It is the oldest continually active civic society in London and its archives are full of important material giving new insights into the story of the Heath. The Society played a significant part in the development of modern democratic accountability, pioneering the role of civic, as opposed to political representation. Many of its past committee members were eminent and interesting people worth a book to themselves.

One of them was E.V. (Evoe) Knox (editor of *Punch* until 1949), who was on the Society's committee from 1947 to 1960. In 1959 Sir Colin Anderson, then Chairman, tried to get him to write a history of the Society but alas this project never got any further than a nine page typescript which is in the H&HS archives. Sir Colin wrote: "until [he] gets busy on a history of our Protection Society itself I don't feel he has even started the great work, for histories of the Heath are already fairly common and that in effect is all he has dealt with so far. ... The only difference is that he has written them entertainingly whereas they are usually rather dull".[4]

I have felt it necessary to deal with certain elements of Professor F.M.L. Thompson's book *Hampstead: building a borough, 1650-1964*,[5] commissioned by Hampstead Borough Council on its abolition in 1965, and published in 1974. His account, especially the two chapters on Hampstead Heath, one of which is headed 'Character Assassination', is an astonishingly revisionist version of events in which he, uniquely, casts Maryon Wilson as a hard-done-by victim. It is Professor Thompson, however, who does the assassinating, maligning and denigrating the Heath campaigners. His thesis is that a couple of dozen copyholders in Hampstead were able, by "deceit, fraud and misrepresentation", to delude both Houses of Parliament, the Law Lords, the whole of the press establishment and the rising cadre of radical social reformers, through "surreptitious and dishonest means" over a period of forty years, simply for their own personal "private" reasons and financial benefit.[6]

None of this accords with the documented record and Thompson also makes several errors of fact. He tells the story almost exclusively from the Maryon Wilson point of view, despite admitting that Sir Thomas was capable of perjury.[7] He appears never to have looked at the copyholders' minutes (deposited in the Greater London Record Office in 1962), or the astonishing family correspondence in the Maryon Wilson archive, all of which contradict his narrative. His indiscriminate condemnations leave no-one unscathed: Lord Denman, Thomas Barratt, and a whole generation of philanthropists including Lord Shaftesbury, Octavia Hill, Robert Hunter and Lord Eversley. As Sir Simon Jenkins has commented, Thompson "turns aside from a scholarly account of the town's nineteenth-century expansion to deliver a sustained attack over two chapters on Sir Thomas's critics".[8]

Kit Ikin dealt with some of these errors and omissions in an article in the *Camden History Review*[9] soon after the Professor's book was published. I have found a great many more. I have addressed a few of them by way of endnotes in this text, as they arise, and will write a fuller rebuttal for the *Review*.

## NOTES to Introduction

1. EH listing, Gainsborough Gardens (historicengland. org.uk/listing/the-list/ list-entry/1392570)
2. *H&HS Newsletter,* Oct 1994
3. Richardson (1986), p 103
4. Typescript notes: E.V. Knox, 'The records of the Hampstead Heath Protection Society' (c.1959); Sir Colin Anderson, memorandum (H&HS archive:A/1048/5/4/1, also A/1048/3/11/1)
5. Thompson was Professor of Modern History at the University of London.
6. Thompson (1974), pp 167, 179, 162
7. Ibid., p 171
8. Jenkins & Ditchburn (1982), p 99
9. C.W. Ikin, 'The battle for the Heath', *CHR 4* (1976)

## NOTES AND REFERENCES

are at the end of each chapter.
Table of picture credits [tbc]
Abbeviations used:

*CHR*   *Camden History Review*
CHS   Camden History Society
CLSAC   Camden Local Studies & Archives Centre
EH   English Heritage
GLC   Greater London Council
H&HS   Heath & Hampstead Society
H&OHS   Heath & Old Hampstead Society
HAHS   Hampstead Antiquarian & Historical Society
*Ham & High   Hampstead & Highgate Express*
HBC   Hampstead Borough Council
HC Deb   House of Commons debates
HHPS   Hampstead Heath Protection Society
HL Deb   House of Lords debates
LBC   London Borough of Camden
LCC   London County Council
LMA   London Metropolitan Archives
MBW   Metropolitan Board of Works
VCH   Victoria County History

# Acknowledgements

I would like to record my gratitude and appreciation to the organisations
and people who have assisted in the production of this book.

I particularly thank David Hayes, Publications Editor of Camden History
Society, for his help, interest, advice and assiduous attention to detail in preparing
this text for publication; and to Ivor Kamlish for his, as ever, superb design.

I am deeply grateful to Lord Hoffmann, President of the Heath & Hampstead
Society, for writing the foreword, and to Marc Hutchinson, Chair, for his
invaluable support and encouragement, meticulous proof-reading, and many helpful
suggestions; and facilitating the collaboration of the Society with generous financial
support for the book.

I am indebted to Malcolm Holmes, former Camden Borough Archivist, not
only for reading through the first draft and making helpful suggestions and corrections,
but for suggesting further invaluable research directions in the Camden archives.

My warmest thanks to staff at the various archives: Tudor Allen and
his unfailingly helpful team at the Camden Local Studies & Archives Centre,
producing obscure sections of archive for me and scanning various maps and
photos; various departments at the London Metropolitan Archive, in particular,
Louise Harrison for drawing my attention to uncatalogued files and making them
available to me, and staff who conserved documents which otherwise could not be
accessed; and the Archivists at Scone Palace for helpfully answering my queries.

Pauline Sidell's translations of the Hampstead Manor Court Rolls (from Latin
to English) for the Camden History Society have been invaluable, as has been the
research by many fellow CHS members recorded in the Camden History Review.

Special thanks to Julius Bryant for sparing time to share his recollections
of his experiences at Kenwood, as Chief Curator and Director of Museums
and Collections at English Heritage (1990-2005); and to Frank Kelsall for
enlightenment about English Heritage in the 1980s.

I am most grateful to Shirley Brihi of the Metropolitan Public Gardens
Association, Dr Peter Barber, former Head of Maps, British Library, Jeremy Wright,
Ruth Hayes, Roger Seaton, William Johnstone (Assistant Archivist, Westminster
Diocesan Archives), and Michael Hammerson, who have all made information or
research material available and helped in my quest to track down original sources; and
to Ian Layzell-Smith of Hunters-solicitors for kindly facilitating permission from Lord
Gough for me to reproduce material from the Maryon-Wilson Estate in the LMA.

I was particularly fortunate to have 'inherited' some of Kit Ikin's archives,
which included much hitherto unpublished research into primary sources. I am
glad to be able to repay his generosity by using them throughout this book.

This book is dedicated to all those in the H&HS, past and present, who have
worked so hard to conserve and enhance Hampstead and its Heath, in particular
my immediate predecessors, David Sullivan, Peggy Jay, Kit Ikin, John Carswell
and Gerald Isaaman, with whom it was my pleasure and privilege to work.

# PART 1 SETTING THE SCENE

## Chapter 1

# The origins of the manor and village

I t is an extraordinary thing to find a piece of apparently wild countryside so close to the centre of a great city like London. Hampstead Heath today now seems such a permanent part of our lives it is hard to imagine that the land originally

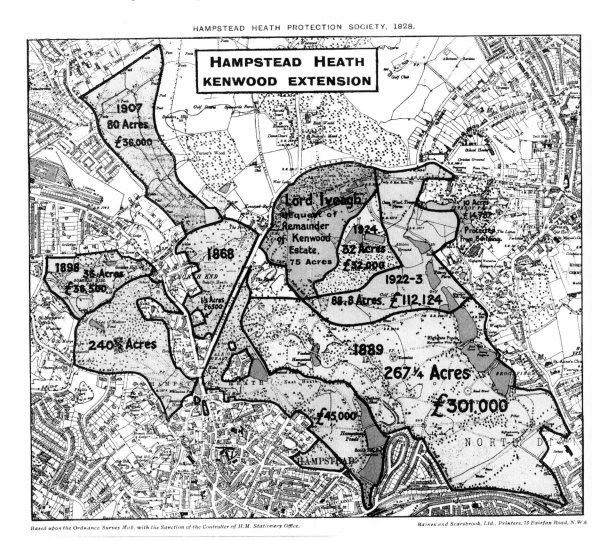

1. The main acquisitions of the Heath at 1928; map drawn by Sir Lawrence Chubb (1873-1948) after Kenwood House and grounds were added to the Heath. First published in the Hampstead Heath Protection Society annual report 1928

10

saved by Act of Parliament in 1871 was only a fraction of what we have now. The story of that first 40-year battle with the Lord of the Manor, Sir Thomas Maryon Wilson, culminating on 5 May 1869 with his death, is well known: Sir Walter Besant likened it to "guerilla warfare".[1] But in 1871 only 220 acres – all that remained of the original 500-acre Heath – were saved. Now Hampstead Heath is even larger with over 800 acres of wonderfully varied landscape: hills and valleys; meadows and woods, and ponds. The story of how that happened – the coming together of social, political, economic and artistic events all at the right moment to make this achievement possible – is a remarkable one.

It is a story of 'people-power', the fruit of many large and small campaigns over a period of a hundred years. The Heath has been wrested from destruction, piece by piece, by the actions of local people, ceaselessly lobbying Parliament and government. Nor did the campaigners stop after that 1871 triumph; generation after generation of Hampstead residents worked for over 50 more years to add further land and reclaim lost areas of Heath, increasing it to the 800 acres that we have today. And it goes on expanding. Is it perhaps the only inner city green space to have done so?

During the long course of that first campaign a new understanding of the value of open space developed so that by 1871, when the people of Hampstead finally got their Act of Parliament, a real movement had been established. A group of formidable people had joined the campaign for the Heath and went on to be at the heart of what became the new conservation movement. They set up the Commons Preservation Society in 1865 (now the Open Spaces Society, Britain's oldest national conservation body), and the National Trust in 1895; and they were all involved in the founding of the Hampstead Heath Protection Society in 1897– today's Heath & Hampstead Society, the oldest continuously active civic society in London. The movement was strongly supported throughout by the press, led by *The Times* newspaper. By the 1830s the paper had earned the nickname 'The Thunderer', and thunder it did.

Following the Hampstead Heath Act, in quick succession, Wandsworth Common was purchased by a body of conservators; Earl Spencer gave 700 acres of Wimbledon Common as a park; Clapham Common was acquired from its lord of the manor by the Metropolitan Board of Works in 1877; and the Earl of Dartmouth waived his manorial rights over the 275 acres of Blackheath, which went to the Board at no expense.

But, of all of them, the story of Hampstead Heath is the most extraordinary, involving legal stratagems of every kind, in and out of Parliament, national press campaigns, vitriolic character assassination, perjury, wholesale misinformation, and even accusations of bribery and blackmail. So how did it all begin? Why did Hampstead with its Heath – just one of the many such commons that surrounded London – become so prized?

## Back to the beginning

Its early history follows a pattern typical of such villages, and its records go back to Saxon times. King Ethelred the Unready granted it to Westminster Abbey in 986. After the Norman Conquest large swathes of the Abbey's land were given to various Norman knights and followers of William the Conqueror. Hampstead was recorded in the Domesday Book and the Knights Templar held land around Watling Street (the Shoot-up Hill area). By about 1280 the Abbey had managed to regain control of most of its Hampstead lands again, and the Heath itself was first recorded by the Westminster monks in 1312 as "a certain heath". Sir Roger de Brabazon, Chief Justice of the Court of Common Pleas, owned estates in the Belsize area in the 1300s, which he bequeathed back to the Abbey when he died. In one of those curious quirks of history he was an ancestor of Lord Brabazon who, hundreds of years later, in the 19th century, did so much to help rescue Hampstead's open spaces.

Until the 16th century it was largely wooded country, prized for hunting. In 1536 Henry VIII issued one of his notorious (and widely quoted) proclamations, reserving the hunting of game from his palace at Westminster, to Hampstead Heath, "for his owne disport and pastime".

The village of Hampstead was of no great significance and its residents were mostly farm labourers. It did not even have its own parish church to begin with but was an annexe of St. Mary's Church at Hendon, although by the 1250s it had a chapel. In the 15th century the Hampstead tithes went to the rector of Hendon,[2] but from 1540 it had its own vicar.[3]

At the dissolution of monasteries, Westminster Abbey became a protestant bishopric and briefly held on to its land, but its first and only bishop, Thomas Thirlby, managed to alienate nearly all the Abbey's property during his nine years in office and it was reduced to a deanery. In 1550, under Edward VI, the Hampstead estate reverted to the Crown thus bringing to an end monastic rule in Hampstead, although Belsize remained with Westminster. Edward then granted Hampstead, with the lordship of the manor, to one of his favourite courtiers, Sir Thomas Wroth in 1551. It was not considered a particularly important estate – many lords held several such manors – and when Wroth's grandson squandered the family inheritance it was sold in 1620, to pay the debts, to Sir Baptist Hicks, later Viscount Campden, a wealthy City silk merchant who counted among his clients King James and his courtiers.[4] It then passed, through Hicks' daughter, to the Noels, who became the Earls of Gainsborough. They sold it in 1707 to Sir William Langhorn of Charlton in Kent, a wealthy East India merchant. Passing then through various complicated female lines of extended family, by way of daughters and nieces, it descended by marriage to General Sir Thomas Spencer Wilson, and then to his son Sir Thomas Maryon Wilson in 1798.

None of these families ever lived in Hampstead so there was no resident lord of the manor, or manor house, to provide a focus for village life or social hierarchy. The main Maryon Wilson home was Charlton House near Greenwich and the

Hampstead estate was managed on their behalf by stewards.[5] But there was a substantial farm with a "Manor place" at Frognal, mentioned in 1543 in the Act which gave the City the right to pipe water from the Heath springs. There was a medieval Hall on the corner of Frognal and what is now Frognal Lane, and a complex of farm buildings with a dairy, and a pond, rented out to various tenant farmers. The Manor Court book[6] records a windmill at 'Ostend', the area where Fenton House now stands, further up the hill near Windmill Hill. Some of these old buildings were still there as late as 1790.[7]

By the 19th century the other major landowners around Hampstead Heath were the Earls of Mansfield at Kenwood, Lord Southampton on the Highgate side (and to the south), and Eton College to the north. Most of what we now call Hampstead Heath includes farm or meadow land preserved from these various estates.

## The role of 'commons'

Commons or 'wastes' were the "bleakest and most distant lands of a township or village, too poor to grow crops on" and therefore left uncultivated.[8] Relics of a feudal (and even pre-feudal) agrarian past, their origins lost in time, they were nevertheless a vital part of the rural economy, providing a source of timber, fuel and common pasture for the villagers of the manor. The Hampstead waste included not just the Heath with its steep slopes and many waterlogged boggy areas, but other parts of the manor at Kilburn and West End. Such land could be enclosed to extend gardens or to build new houses, but a series of time-honoured procedures had to be gone through. The lord of the manor, or more usually his steward, would convene annual hearings of the Customary Court, at which the request for enclosure would have to be agreed by a jury called the 'homage' – made up of villagers who were already copyholders – and the appropriate 'fines' would be paid. The new copyholder's grant would be formalised by giving him a copy of the court roll showing his holding, hence 'copyholder'. Originally copyholders performed services for the lord in return for their tenancy, but by the 16th century these had generally been converted into money payments, involving large 'entry' fines and nominal annual rents.

Ownership of such land was governed by a complicated series of laws and procedures underpinned by the ancient 1235 Statute of Merton. Even in the 19th century this antiquated law with its ambiguities still applied: "the owner of the soil of a common is owner of everything upwards to the heavens and downwards to the centre of the earth, except such thing as custom, usage, or grant has conferred upon the commoners". This created in effect a joint or divided ownership; the lord of the manor could not do just as he pleased.[9]

Most copyhold land could be bought and sold, inherited by descendents, left in a will, and mortgaged, provided the copyholder went through the prescribed procedures and payments, which had to be done through the lord of the manor. Many landholdings were held by the same family for generations. From the 16th

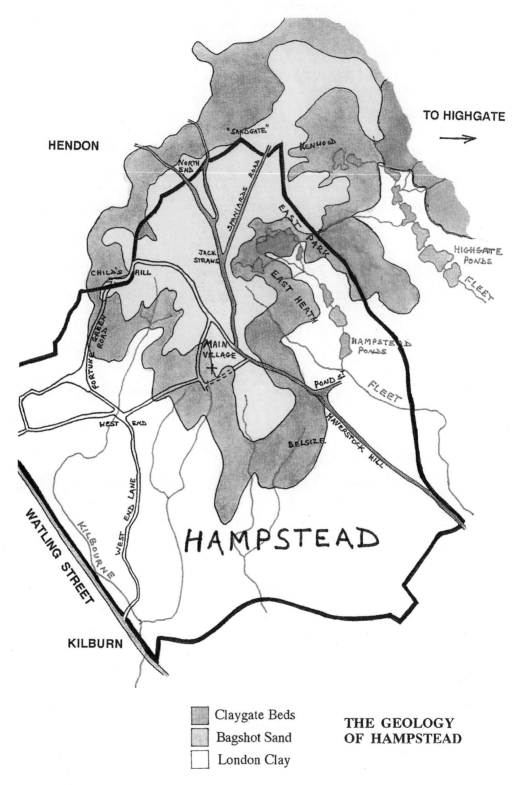

TO HIGHGATE →

HENDON

"SANDGATE"

KENWOOD

NORTH END

SPANIARDS ROAD

EAST PARK

HIGHGATE PONDS

JACK STRAWS

CHILD'S HILL

EAST HEATH

FLEET

PORTUNE GREEN ROAD

MAIN VILLAGE

HAMPSTEAD PONDS

POND S.

FLEET

WEST END

HAVERSTOCK HILL

BELSIZE

WATLING STREET

KILBOURNE

WEST END LANE

HAMPSTEAD

KILBURN

■ Claygate Beds

■ Bagshot Sand

□ London Clay

**THE GEOLOGY OF HAMPSTEAD**

2. Geology of the Heath, David Sullivan (*The Westminster Corridor*, Map E)

14

century copyhold began to be replaced by leasehold agreements, and freeholds could be acquired by being 'enfranchised' through various further payments or 'fines', with the consent of the other copyholders. It is notable that nearly as many women as men came before the Manor Court – daughters and wives, who were equally eligible to inherit or own property in their own right. Indeed, as already noted, the lordship of the manor of Hampstead itself passed through the female line during the 17th and 18th centuries.

The main ancient rights of common were connected with agricultural use: pasture for certain specified animals; estovers, the cutting and taking of wood (but not timber); turbary, the digging of turf or peat for fuel; 'in the soil', the right to take sand, gravel and stone; and piscary, the right to take fish from ponds and streams. But trying to establish just what the customs and rights were was fraught with difficulty and varied from manor to manor. There were differences between demesne lands, 'land reserved by the lord for his own use and occupation', freeholders' rights, commoners' rights and copyholders' rights. And added to the mix were Crown rights, and 'lammas' lands, which forbade use as pasture, or agricultural cultivation during the closed season of April to August, but allowed common grazing and other rights during the rest of the year. It is a history rich with conflict. Commoners' rights could help protect commons but not guarantee public access to them. Some rights could be lost by lack of use but others not, depending on different kinds of tenure. In some cases commoners could actually stand to gain if a common was built on because they could claim compensation; in others they were quite willing to agree to the lord's plans, but, as happened in Hampstead, he could not rely on them to co-operate.

### What makes a heath: geological structure

"How few of the multitudes of people, who every year visit Hampstead and enjoy its breezy Heath, remember that their pleasure and the beauty and characteristics of the place and its surroundings are due to the internal structure of the hill, and the character of the ground below their feet." So said Professor Logan Lobley in 1889[10] and, he might have added, the ongoing concern of local people to preserve that beauty and those characteristics.

Sand is the most important element of the underlying geological structure which gives rise to the landscape and character of heath land. The summit of the Northern Heights, running from Hampstead to Highgate along Spaniards Road and Hampstead Lane, is a ridge of Bagshot Sands about 80 feet deep. Its curious name comes from the fact that it is an outlying portion of the Bagshot Sands, found in the district around Bagshot in Surrey, extending to Chertsey and Weybridge and giving rise to the heaths and commons of Woking, Aldershot, Frimley, and Sandhurst. It is thought to have been deposited 40 million years ago by a giant river system in the Thames basin which extended over the greater part of southern England, washing the sands along its length.[11] The 'Hampstead Outlier', as it is called, is one of the best examples because it is so distinct from the surrounding beds, so limited in area and so well exposed.[10] Bagshot Sands are sterile, therefore the ground is of little or no agricultural value, but the sand is of a high quality, useful to both builders and iron founders, and it brought in a certain amount of income to the lord of the manor. The Bagshot layer is surrounded by Claygate Beds, a belt of sandy clay about 50 feet deep. Underlying it all and forming the great bulk of the hill, is a lower bed, or 'Formation', an immense mass of London Clay.

The whole area is criss-crossed by springs and streams – some of which were later dammed to create the ponds. From the summit, valleys radiate in every direction, each giving rise to springs. The sculpturing produced by water action is beautifully seen around the Heath.[12]

It is this combination of specific underlying geology, hilly terrain and man's activity – digging and quarrying, tree planting, damming of streams and often sheer neglect – that has contributed to what we now admire as its great wild and natural beauty. As can be seen from Constable's many paintings of the Heath, when it was a real heath with few trees, its appearance was originally much bleaker than it is today.

## The Heath's utility

Its early attraction was its utility rather than its scenic beauty. Apart from free grazing, it provided clean water, and high-quality sand and material for building and making roads. Some of the dozens of carts collecting materials for road-building by the Turnpike Trust are depicted in Constable's paintings. One of the witnesses at the 1869 Chancery case (see p 98), a sand-digger called Charles Morgan, said that the quantity of sand dug increased by about 20 times from the 1800s.[13]

3. Hampstead Heath, 1825 to 1830; one of Constable's many pictures depicting the Heath as the 'plain' described by Defoe

Hamfted Mills

Hamfted

S.'Brides

4. Hampstead's windmills: small section of the Claes Visscher panorama
of London first published in Amsterdam in about 1616

## Windmills, laundresses and fairs
18th-century Hampstead still had a stocks, a whipping post and a cucking pond.[14]
There was a maypole, and fairs were held in the summer in Flask Walk. Windmills
can be seen in Visscher's 1616 View of London, and of course it was famously
the home of laundresses. With so much water available, there was a large laundry
business, and the slopes of the Heath provided good drying grounds right up
until 1871. What is now Holly Bush Hill was called Cloth Hill. On a visit to
Hampstead in 1833, a Mrs Jane Tilt describes encountering washerwomen with
their children, in the wildest most open part of the Heath, "attending to the clothes
drying on the furze". Their covered carts were parked nearby and "they presented
the appearance of so many gypsy camps".[15]

## Water - the creation of the ponds
Three tributaries of the Thames flow from Hampstead Heath's numerous springs:
the Fleet, the Westbourne and the Tyburn; all have a long history of providing
fresh water for London. Hampstead was originally full of small ponds, many of
them shown in the plans of properties in the Manor Court records. The Clock

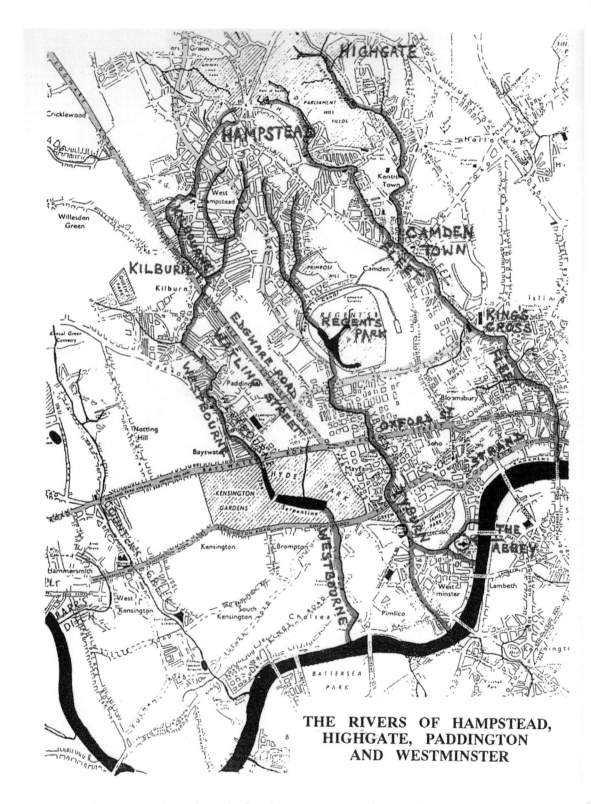

## THE RIVERS OF HAMPSTEAD, HIGHGATE, PADDINGTON AND WESTMINSTER

5. River sources on the Heath, David Sullivan (*The Westminster Corridor*, Map H)

House (now Fenton House) had its own pond; Frognal Hall had one; and the site of Red Lion Pond is now the entrance of Thurlow Road. By Tudor times getting fresh water to the City of London was becoming a problem and Hampstead's abundant springs were seen as a solution. In the London Conduit Act of 1543, Henry VIII granted the City of London Corporation power to explore "dyvers great and plentifull springs ... and dyvers places within fyve miles of the said Citie". "Hampstede hethe, Marybon, Hakkney [and] Muswell Hill" were mentioned.[16] In 1589 conduits were built by the City to channel water from the Hampstead Heath springs to the centre of the city. These sufficed for another hundred years. Then in 1692 William Paterson, better remembered as the founder of the Bank of England, formed the Hampstead Water Company, with a lease on the springs from the City. The company began to create reservoirs – today's Heath ponds – to meet London's growing need for clean water. Beginning on the Hampstead side, it dammed the Hampstead brook, one of the sources of the Fleet, creating the Hampstead Ponds. By 1703 it had completed two ponds on Lower Heath. It then bought Millfield Farm and created the Highgate Ponds from the streams forming the other source of the Fleet. The pond in the Vale of Health was added in 1777.

There is some question as to whether the Leg of Mutton Pond on West Heath was made, or whether it was an existing natural pond that was dammed to enlarge it. An 1816 newspaper report[17] mentioned plans "to make an artificial piece of water on the north-west side of the Heath", but neither the Manor Court or Vestry records mention the making of any pond.

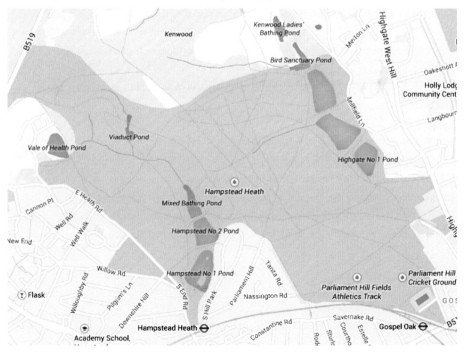

6. Map section showing the main reservoir ponds on the Heath

By 1835 demand for drinkable water was so great that an additional well was sunk at the southern end of the Heath. But a depth of nearly 400 feet had to be dug before good water was found and a steam-engine was required to raise it to the surface. This engine house was still standing in 1890 and can be seen in prints of the time.

7. The Old Engine House at the bottom of East Heath Road, looking towards South End Green

In 1853 the Hampstead Water Company was taken over by the New River Company, which built the covered reservoir at the top of the Heath in Hampstead Grove in 1856. The nearby Whitestone Pond, originally a small dew pond known as the horse pond was enlarged in 1875 by the Vestry, which made footpaths, repaired the sides and the bottom, and by 1890 arranged for it to be filled artificially with water from the mains. Its present name derives from the white milestone to be seen in the shrubbery next to it, which is ancient and is referred to frequently in the Manor Court rolls.

The Branch Hill Pond, much painted by Constable, was filled in around 1889. Of two other lost ponds, one was at the bottom of Pond Street, now South End Green; the other, at the bottom of Keats Grove, was filled in to form the grassed approach to the Heath from Hampstead Heath Station in 1892. All the remaining Heath ponds are now ornamental and not used for water supply since new purpose-built reservoirs were constructed by the West Middlesex Water Company: that in Platt's Lane in 1868, and the Grand Junction Reservoir in Mill Lane in 1875.[18]

### The botanists' favourite
The Heath's rich ecology was prized very early. The heath offered such varied habitat, ranging from marshes to quite barren places, all within easy reach of London, that it became "a most favourite spot with the botanists" and plant

hunters, "a luxurious spot to them".[19] John Gerard, the Elizabethan botanist, gave us the earliest descriptions of the flora of the Heath in his *Herball, or General History of Plants* of 1597. He made "herborising excursions" and described the wide variety of plants to be found there. He was followed by Thomas Johnson, dubbed 'The father of British field botany', whose *Iter Plantarum* of 1629 describes a visit to Hampstead Heath, and who in 1633 brought out a new edition of Gerard's *Herball*.

The Apothecaries' Company, incorporated in 1617 and based at Blackfriars, continued the tradition. They "very seldom miss coming to Hampstead every spring and here have their herbarizing feast";[20] and a trip to Caen Wood was also popular "for the purpose of botanizing, after which they retired to Jack Straw's Castle Hotel or the Bull and Bush, and there spent the remainder of the day in the manner peculiar to London Companies".[21]

John Keats discovered Hampstead as an apprentice apothecary when William Salisbury, his lecturer in medical botany at Guy's Hospital, brought his pupils to the Heath on field trips. Like Gerard before him, Salisbury published lists of the plants he found. Professor Lobley still prized the Heath's qualities in 1889: "... although now joined to London, it still possesses many of those charms of Nature usually sought much further afield, and remains a happy hunting-ground for the naturalist. Its structure, surface features and characteristics, are so interesting and instructive that the locality has become "classic ground for London ecologists".[22]

## Military manoeuvres

The Heath had immense military value: commanding the view over London, the Northern Heights provided a natural line of defence to protect the City. The beacon warning system was ancient and unique to England. Its high period was the 16th and 17th centuries.[23] A beacon in an iron cresset, which stood in the area of the later Flagstaff, was part of a chain of beacons as far as Plymouth which was to signal a warning of the invasion by the Spanish Armada.

8. The Telegraph cottage, 1808 (Telegraph Hill). According to Barratt (vol. II) this was from a watercolour drawing by J.J. Park (1795-1833) when a boy, and owned by E. E. Newton.

In the Napoleonic Wars when a French invasion was feared, an Admiralty telegraph relay station was installed on high ground at what is now the junction of West Heath Road and Platt's Lane (today's Telegraph Hill). One of a line of twelve such stations from the Duke of York's Headquarters at Chelsea to Yarmouth on the East Coast, it operated between 1808 and 1814. Volunteer corps were being set up all over the country and the Volunteers of the Loyal Hampstead Association, under their captain Major Josiah Boydell, took part in the review held in June 1799 in Hyde Park before King George III. The Association was composed of "Gentlemen and respectable Tradesmen of the Vicinity", and the Heath provided valuable training and exercise ground. A rifle range known as the Battery was created on the Upper Heath between Spaniards Road and the Vale of Health, where the volunteers performed "their exercise in a manner highly honourable to themselves, and satisfactory to a numerous body of spectators".[24] Their ceremonial drum can still be seen at the Hampstead Museum, Burgh House.

George William Potter, builder, estate agent, surveyor and keen local historian, who lived at Gardnor House, recounts an amusing story told by an old Hampstead volunteer of 1812, Sir William Bodkin.[25] Of target practice by his company at the Battery on the Heath, he recalled: "after a long practice only one man throughout the day hit the centre of the target at sixty yards, and he was seen to shut his eyes when he fired".[26] But such was the men's enthusiasm that residents began to complain that the military exercises on the Heath were disturbing ordinary users and causing a danger, and started campaigning to get it stopped. Eventually the ground was levelled.[27]

### Notes, Chapter 1

1. Besant (1902), p 7
2. VCH (1989), pp 91-111
3. For a detailed study of this period, see Sullivan (1994); see also Kennedy (1906).
4. The philanthropic Hicks built a new Session House at Clerkenwell (Hicks Hall), repaired the old Hampstead Parish Church and made many charitable gifts. In 1642 his widow, Lady Elizabeth Campden, established the Campden Charity "for the perpetual benefit of the poor and needy of the Parish of Hampstead", with a bequest of £200; it was used to buy land in Child's Hill and existed till 1880, when it merged with the Hampstead Wells Charity.
5. Charlton House, a magnificent Jacobean mansion, was the home of the Maryon-Wilson family until 1916. It was sold to Greenwich Borough Council in 1925 (and is managed today

by the Royal Greenwich Heritage Trust). On the death of Sir Spencer Maryon-Wilson in 1944, the Charlton Estate went to his only daughter, Viscountess Gough, while the baronetcy and the Hampstead property passed to his nephew, Sir Percy Maryon-Wilson.
6. Hampstead Manor Court Book (LMA: E/MW/H/219 1726)
7. Sullivan (1994), p 123
8. Baines (1890), ch. 2: 'The Manor of Hampstead'
9. Halsbury's Laws of England, 4th ed. (1973-87), vol. 6, para. 639
10. Lobley (1889), p 35
11. 'Geology in the Vale of Health', paper by Dr Eric Robinson, Dept of Geological Sciences UCL, geological adviser to the H&HS, 1990-2001; see also Sullivan (1994), ch. 2
12. Lobley (1889), p 54. Professor Lobley points out, that the stretch of Heath between East Heath Road and Heath Street enclosed for building was from this

Bagshot Sand layer. A consequence of this – not widely enough understood – is the inherent instability of the sandy foundations giving rise to regular collapses of roads in modern times.
13. Transcript of court case, Gurney Hoare v Maryon Wilson: analysis of Affidavit filed on the part of the Plaintiffs by P.H. Lawrence, 17 Jun 1867 (CLSAC: ST2/ID/14)
14. A ducking or cucking pond was the same thing; in Hampstead it was always referred to as a cucking pond.
15. 'A month in Hampstead – from the Journal of Mrs Jane Tilt', CHR 17 (1992)
16. Cited in Sexby (1898), p 399. Lieut-Col Sexby was Chief Officer for Parks, LCC.
17. London Courier & Evening Gazette, 18 Dec 1816
18. Howitt (1869), p 121
19. Park (1812, 1818), p 22
20. Soame (1734), p 27
21. Address by Sir Walter Besant, President, to the

1st General Meeting of the newly formed Hampstead Antiquarian & Historical Society, 23 Mar 1898 (HAHS)
22. Lobley (1889), preface
23. 'The Hampstead Beacon', unpublished paper by Kit Ikin (author's collection), citing Frank Kitchen's book Fire over England: the Armada Beacons, 1988
24. 'A forgotten Hampstead worthy: Josiah Boydell, artist and alderman', paper by E.E. Newton, HAHS meeting, 13 Dec 1899. Newton attributes this description to a newspaper of the period (1798), but does not say which.
25. Assistant Judge at the Middlesex Sessions, and MP, Bodkin lived on Highgate West Hill.
26. Potter (1904), p 91
27. Hampstead Manor Court Rolls and copyholders' minutes (LMA)

## Chapter 2

# The Heath shrinks; the village grows

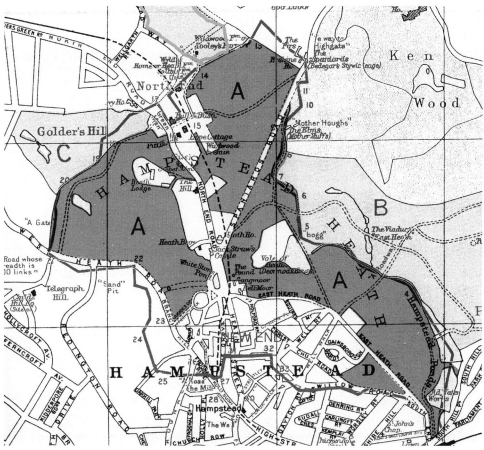

9. The extent of the Heath in 1680, outlined in red; from Barratt's *Annals*

A
t the beginning of the 17th century Hampstead was still a village of poor
labourers and washerwomen. Its Heath was useful but its village was not
of any particular interest. Enclosures, either of the Heath or of other land,
were mainly for farming purposes. All this was about to change. As living conditions
in the City became increasingly cramped and unhealthy, City merchants began
looking outside its walls to nearby villages. Hampstead's healthy situation and fine
outlook, relatively close by, was seen as an attractive alternative, at first for country
houses but soon for more permanent residences. By the time of the parliamentary
survey of 1646 there were already 68 large houses as well as 78 cottages.[1]

## The Hampstead Dissenters

Quite a number of these City men were Dissenters. The City of London was
strongly Presbyterian and Parliamentarian in the Civil War, as were some of the

wealthiest Hampstead residents. In the aftermath of the Civil War religious schism provoked the Five Mile Act of 1665, which barred nonconformist ministers from preaching within five miles of any town. Hampstead was just beyond that five mile limit from the City, only an hour's journey. By the time the 1689 Act of Toleration allowed them to set up places of worship, there was already a quite large community of Dissenters of various denominations in Hampstead, meeting in each other's houses. Several of the first trustees of the Hampstead Wells Charity were Dissenters, including the Foleys, the Honeywoods, and Sir Thomas Lane who was Lord Mayor of London in 1694.

Gradually, portions of the Heath were enclosed to build fine houses for this steadily rising population of wealthy gentry. By 1680 it had shrunk to 337 acres and in Georgian times, during the height of its first wave of popularity as a spa, demand for enclosures for building increased still further. There was not much concern at these piecemeal encroachments for single houses or gardens; such grants provided income for the lord of the manor. There was little other income from the 'waste' of the Heath, and it was the obvious place from which to take any land for building, rather than from useful and profitable farmland. Daniel Defoe noted that: the "uneven Surface, inconvenient for Building, uncompact and unpleasant ... does not check the appetite for building", so that in addition to the spa area around Well Walk, high ground at the top of the Heath around Whitestone Pond was also enclosed.[2] The Heath once stretched to Hampstead High Street, but now it was gradually enclosed for building and what was once called Middle Heath Road became instead East Heath Road.

The Manor Court provided a rudimentary form of planning control. Copyholders were reprimanded for allowing properties to fall into disrepair or for leaving holes on the Heath where they had dug out turf for their gardens. Grants of 'waste' often came with prohibitions on building and, where this was permitted, stipulations were made as to the minimum amount of money to be spent on a house, so as to ensure quality; a licence from the Lord was needed to erect or to pull down a building. As pressure to enclose the Heath increased, a range of restrictions were added to protect its amenity and beauty, which in those days was perceived to be its openness and views. There were injunctions against planting trees or putting up high walls or fences that would spoil the views, and clauses to encourage and preserve the growth of furze and gorse, rather than cut them. Many of the complaints at Manor Court sessions were because the beauty of the Heath was being destroyed.[3]

## Squatters

Squatters were an ever-present problem, but in earlier times the attitude towards them was fairly relaxed. The lords of the manor of Hampstead were not resident, and neither were their Stewards[4], who were usually London solicitors, so there was no-one to keep an eye on things. The population was still quite small and there was plenty of land available. Baines describes how they "acquired a title from

merely sitting down or squatting on a corner of the waste of the manor".
It would begin with some sort of tent which became a more permanent hut,
"and lastly perhaps a brick and timber structure. ..... In other cases, the
squatter's claims have been extinguished by ejectment or compromise".[5]

Moreover, it suited villagers to be able on occasion to enlarge their
holdings by enclosing small pieces of the surrounding Heath, legally or
otherwise; there was always plenty of ground left to satisfy grazing rights.
Copyholders frequently enclosed much more ground than they had been
granted by the Manor Court, and the lord stood to gain financially by simply
legalising these incursions. G.W. Potter wryly observed: "The fences round
the gardens of some of these small houses on the heath were said to possess
the peculiar property of movement and expansion, always in an outward
direction, and only at night".[6]

If steps were not taken immediately to remove squatters they were
able to establish themselves and become copyholders. An application to the
'homage' with a small payment usually secured the encroachment to the
squatter, although these tenants did not always have rights of common.

NEAR JACK STRAW'S CASTLE, HAMPSTEAD HEATH.

10. Rustic cottage on the Heath – perhaps a squatter's cottage – near Jack Straw's Castle; by John Thomas Smith (1766–1833) (known as Antiquity Smith), Keeper of Prints for the British Museum, mentor and friend of Constable and author of a life of the sculptor Joseph Nollekens. From *Remarks on Rural Scenery*, 1797

But from 1684 the system began to unravel. It started with an "accidental" fire at the steward's house that year, which destroyed the Court rolls recording who legally owned what. Even though there were various copies, applications to the Manor Court throughout the late 1680s were frequently accompanied by the observation that ownership of land could not be established, because "they could not discover anything remaining in the Rolls of the Court".[7] Moreover, this coincided with the period when the fashion for water-cures was gathering pace, and it was discovered that Hampstead had a chalybeate well.[8] It quickly became popular and attracted large numbers of would-be new residents and tradesmen. There was constant buying and selling of copyholds and many of the copyholders were absentee landlords. The problems multiplied.

## The extraordinary days of the Wells

In December 1698 the Lady of the Manor, the Hon. Susanna Noel, mother of the Earl of Gainsborough, granted six acres of Hampstead Heath surrounding the well to a trust, for the benefit of the poor of Hampstead. The well's supposed medicinal properties were probably already known; Potter suggests that the chalybeate water may have been discovered as far back as the reign of Henry VIII, during the search for a new water supply for the City of London.[9] The new Wells Charity was headed by Sir Thomas Lane, the former Lord Mayor, who lived in a grand house called Aldenham in Pond Street. Local entrepreneurs saw their chance and in 1701 the Trust leased out some of the land to one John Duffield, who built a Long Room and a Pump Room in Well Walk, where Gainsborough Gardens now is. (The present gardens are the remnants of its pleasure grounds, which included a bowling green, an ornamental pond with boathouse, and an ice house of which there are still remains.) Daily entertainments were provided to draw the crowd: concerts, dances, plays and gambling. "Crowds flocked to Hampstead; and for those who were unable to come to the waters, the owners of the rival springs sent the water every morning to London".[10] Hampstead Wells became enormously popular, rivalling Tunbridge Wells and other well-known spas.

The much quoted Daniel Defoe description[2] noted that "Hampstead indeed is risen from a little Country Village, to a City, not upon the credit only of the Waters. Though 'tis apparent its growing Greatness began there; but Company increasing gradually, and the People liking both the Place and the Diversions together. On the Top of the Hill indeed, there is a very pleasant Plain, called the Heath, which on the very Summit, is a Plain of about a Mile every way; and in good Weather 'tis pleasant airing upon it. But it must be confest, 'tis so near to Heaven, that I dare not say it can be a proper Situation, for any but a race of mountaineers, whose lungs have been used to a rarify'd air, nearer the second region, than any ground for 30 miles round it."

Attracted by Hampstead's lively social scene and beautiful situation, the Kit-Cat (or Kit-Kat) Club – an assemblage of formidable power and patronage established in 1690 to promote Whig political objectives – began to hold its summer meetings at the Upper Flask Tavern, which stood in extensive grounds at the top of Heath Street on the corner with East Heath Road. The Club's curious name is said to have come from a noted mutton-pie-man called Christopher Katt, in whose house near Temple Bar the Club first met. His pies were called Kit-Kats and were the regular dish at the Club suppers. Its distinguished membership included no fewer than nine dukes – leading Whig politicians – and the leading writers and artists of the day, such as William Congreve, John Locke, Sir John Vanbrugh, Joseph Addison, Richard Steele and Sir Robert Walpole. Another member, Sir Richard Blackmore, one of the Court Physicians to William III – and a minor, somewhat derided poet – went so far as to compare Hampstead to Parnassus in a poem about the Kit-Cat meetings: "Or when, Apollo-like, thou'rt pleased to lead Thy sons to feast on Hampstead's airy head – Hampstead, that, towering in superior sky, Now with Parnassus does in honour vie".[11]

The artist Sir Godfrey Kneller established the tradition of painting members' portraits.[12] The extraordinary gatherings, which lasted until the 1720s, laid the foundation for Hampstead's literary fame and artistic associations.

Hampstead was now 'on the map' and for the next few years it was the place to be seen, the presence of the Kit-Cat luminaries setting the seal of approval.

11. Upper Flask when it was the residence of George Steevens; it ceased to be an inn around 1750. Drawing by John Thomas Smith, originally published in *Johnsoniana*, 1836

A play put on at Drury Lane in 1706 gave a vivid picture of daily life at the Hampstead Spa. This much quoted comedy, called *Hampstead Heath*, part of a genre of 'spa drama', was a revised version of a banned play, *An Act at Oxford* by Thomas Baker. In Act I, Scene 1, the characters Bloom and Smart are discussing Hampstead, which "for a while assumes the day. The lively season o' the year; the shining crowd assembled, and the noble situation of the place … gives us the nearest show of Paradise". But more lurid passages signal problems: a "variety of diversions feast our fickle fancies, and every man wears a face of pleasure. The cards fly, the bowl runs, the dice rattle; some lose their money with ease and negligence, and others are well pleased to pocket it. … We have court ladies that are all air and no dress;

city ladies that are overdressed and no air; and country dames with brown faces like a Stepney bun; besides an endless number of Fleet Street sempstresses that dance minuets in their furbeloe scarfs and their clothes hang as loose about them as their reputations".[13]

The Spa became a victim of its own success. The entertainments became increasingly licentious, attracting gamblers, raffling shops and card sharpers. Crowds of disreputable visitors, drawn by these dubious diversions, arrived by the coachload. "Its Nearness to London brings so many loose Women in vampt-up old Cloaths to catch the City Apprentices, that modest Company are asham'd to appear here".[14]

There was horse racing on West Heath near Jack Straw's Castle, which became the centre of a racing fraternity. The horses had amusing names such as Drowzy Jenny and Creeping Kate, according to adverts in the *Daily Courant* quoted by Park, with prizes of 10 and 20 guineas.[15] "Hampstead came in for its full share of folly and indecorum. ... The general dissoluteness of the period must be a matter of lamentation and disgust to every refined mind".[16] Hampstead's good name suffered: "... you see sometimes more gallantry than modesty: So that the ladies who value their reputation, have of late more avoided the wells and walks at Hampstead, than they had formerly done".[2]

John Gay is said to have based events in the *Beggar's Opera* on this gaudy Hampstead scene, which he witnessed when he was recuperating there. He had invested his considerable earnings in South Sea Company stock, and lost everything when the notorious South Sea Bubble burst in 1720. So overwhelmed was he by this loss that he became seriously ill. His friends Pope and Arbuthnot took him off to try the air and the waters of Hampstead, where Pope looked after him until he recovered.

It could not last. There was a spectacular breakdown of control both of the Spa, and the Manor which had had several different owners in quick succession, two of them minors: the Earl of Gainsborough in the 1700s, and in the 1730s William Langhorn Games. By all accounts the Steward, Robert Sherrard, appointed in 1707 when the 3rd Earl of Gainsborough sold the Manor to Sir William Langhorn, was failing to provide supervision. With no oversight from the lord of the manor or his steward, problems mounted on all sides, exacerbated by the influx of unruly revellers. Sherrard seemed incapable of keeping order. According to G.W. Potter, "Among the records of the manor there is a paper giving an account of the *Several Misbehaviours of Mr. Sherard*, steward and receiver of the rents of the Manor of Hampstead." They included failing to hold regular general Courts, charging extravagant and arbitrary fees and not collecting the quit rents.[17]

The Wells Charity itself fell into difficulties. Trustees were negligent: rents were not collected, no money was distributed to the poor or proper dues paid, and by 1719 it was heavily in debt. The magistrates took action: the Wells activities were halted and new trustees appointed; the races were put down, the gambling dens were closed, and the Long Room was converted into a chapel.

Meanwhile, one of the aggrieved copyholders, a Mr Harrison, attempted, unsuccessfully, to dislodge Sherrard and set himself up as steward. With no authority whatsoever, he appointed a deputy steward called John Ditchfield, who saw his opportunity amidst the chaos. Around 1720 Ditchfield began holding bogus 'Courts' in rivalry to the official steward, handing out fraudulent copyholds by the dozen, mostly to local tradesmen or craftsmen, in response to the unmet demand. Sherrard took legal advice on at least three different occasions and several cases were taken to the Court of Chancery.[18]

It took until 1737 for the Manor Court to bestir itself to deal with the problem. Now under the firmer control of Mrs Margaret Maryon, Courts held in 1737 and 1738 ruled that "all such grants or pretended grants as were made ... to any person at any Court held or pretended to be held for the said Manor by one Ditchfield, and commonly called Ditchfield Courts, were made without any lawful right, power or authority and were or are Incroachments".[19] Several dozen people were summoned before the Court and a compromise was reached whereby most of them were admitted retrospectively as legal "customary tenants"; but the fines payable were to go towards the rebuilding of the Parish Church, and in future would be fixed at more reasonable terms. Ditchfield grants were still coming to light in the 1740s. Outlying hamlets such as North End, Littleworth (the area behind Jack Straw's Castle) and Heath End near the Spaniards Inn, began or grew as a result of these events, as did Pond Street, New End and the area of Heath around the Wells Charity land.

But the water cures were not forgotten. By 1730 things had settled down again sufficiently for a new start to be made at the Wells by John Soame, a local doctor, who revived the idea. But rather than "a place of crowded and fashionable resort, teeming with amusements, folly, and dissipation ... it has at length subsided into a much better thing, the permanent residence of a select, amicable, respectable and opulent neighbourhood".[20] The race-course must still have been there because George Whitefield, the 'prince of preachers' who, with John and Charles Wesley founded the Methodist movement, mentioned it when he preached on the Heath in 1739. A renowned 'field' orator, accustomed to vast audiences, he recorded his Hampstead visit in his Journal: "Preached, after several Invitations thither, at Hampstead-heath, about five miles from London. The Audience was of the politer Sort, and I preached very near the Horse-course, which gave me Occasion to speak home to their Souls concerning our spiritual Race. Most were attentive, but some mocked".[21]

The Spa's disreputable days forgotten, the good Dr Soame now carefully promoted the Heath for its pleasant walks and curious and useful plants. Its recovered reputation was accompanied by a growing appreciation of the Heath as a place of beauty in its own right. The "fine heath to ride out and take the air on" became part of the attraction.[22]

With all that earlier fame and notoriety it is not surprising that Samuel Richardson set some of the scenes in his novel *Clarissa*, published in 1748, at the

Upper Flask. The book was an international best-seller and Hampstead became a tourist attraction. Contemporary readers travelled to the Upper Flask Tavern especially to see where Clarissa and Lovelace stopped, foreshadowing modern-day curiosity about buildings mentioned in popular novels and television series! According to Anna Barbauld, "a Frenchman paid a visit to Hampstead, for the sole purpose of finding out the house ... where Clarissa lodged".[23]

A wealth of poems, songs and other literary tributes date from this period, such as *The Beauties of Hampstead*, by Abiel Wichello:[24]

> Here where lovely Hampstead
> stands
> and the neighb'ring vale
> commands
> What surprising
> Prospects rising
> All around adorn the lands.

Another song,[25] *Hampstead* by Mr Seedo, enthused over

> Hampstead delight
> of ev'ry sense
> and bliss of ev'ry ravished eye.

Pleasure gardens were one of the new more sedate attractions, with one at the Spaniards Inn, and another at Turner's Wood called the New Georgia. They offered sham reptiles, curious topiary and practical jokes such as chairs which sank into the ground if you sat on them. One of the old buildings at

12. The present chalybeate well head, built in 1872

13. *The Beauties of Hampstead* by Abiel Wichello, from *Bickham's Musical Entertainer*, ca.1737

14. The so-called Chinoiserie outhouse at Spaniards Inn, J.T. Wilson, 1869

15. Jack Straw's Castle tea garden still in use around 1835

the Spaniards, called a Chinoiserie outhouse, survived until 1934. The H&OHS noted its demolition, which was reported in *The Builder*, with regret, saying they heard about it too late to take action.

Bowling greens continued to be immensely popular and almost every tavern or inn had one, including Jack Straw's, the Spaniards, the Bull and Bush, and the Upper Flask Tavern which after 1750, when it became a private home, was called Bowling Green House.

A new Long Room was built in the 1730s further along Well Walk, near to Burgh House, with a Great Room or Pump Room, and these became meeting places for local "good company", in the words of contemporary writer Robert Seymour. He remarked particularly that "such care has been taken to discourage the meaner sort from making it a place of residence that it is now become, after Scarborough and Bath and Tunbridge, one of the Politest Public Places in England, and to add to the Entertainment of the Company there is, besides the long room in which the Company meet publicly on a Monday evening to play at cards, etc., a new Dancing Room built this year".[26]

## A desirable country retreat

Hampstead was firmly re-established as a highly attractive and fashionable country retreat for well-to-do City men, lawyers and gentry, with easy access to London. It drew a remarkable number of eminent people, and the list of lawyers and politicians who settled in Hampstead from the 18th century onwards is as impressive as the list of artists: Sir Henry Pollexfen, Thomas Clarke, Lords Alvanley and Wedderburn (later Lord Loughborough), and Edward Montagu, some of them commemorated in today's street names. Howitt thought that "the contemporary residence of three great lawyers, Loughborough, Mansfield, and Erskine, in Hampstead, is one of the most remarkable associations of the place";[27]although "whether Hampstead was good for the law or the law good for Hampstead, is not entirely clear".[28] The most famous of them and the most significant for the story of the Heath was Lord Chief Justice William Murray, the 1st Earl of Mansfield, who bought Kenwood in 1754. Hampstead also attracted prime ministers: Spencer Perceval, (a relative of Sir Thomas Maryon Wilson, who enjoys the unfortunate distinction of being the only British Prime Minister to die at the hands of an assassin in 1812), Lord Grenville, and the Earl of Chatham.

The demand for elegant residences soon led to the transformation of some of the old squatter cottages, and the new copyholders would enlarge their holdings by regularly applying for extra grants of land until they became small country estates. Littleworth, for example, the stretch of Heath from Jack Straw's Castle down North End Way to North End, begun by Ditchfield's squatters,

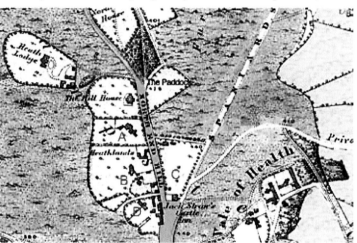

was particularly popular in the 1800s, and with fine new villas it became a wealthy enclave. One of the first to arrive was William Oram, architect, landscape painter and Master Carpenter to the Board of Works (often referred to as 'Old Oram'

16. The Littleworth enclave, from an 1860s map: A, Cedar Lawn; B, Fern Lodge; C, Heath House; D, Heath Brow (formerly Crewe and Camelford Cottages)

to distinguish him from his son Edward, also a landscape-painter); he built Heathlands in 1764. In 1777 his widow sold the copyhold to Sir Francis Willes, who played an active role in Hampstead life. But did Hampstead realise it had a government spy living in its midst? His grandfather, Rev. Edward Willes, had been head of the Post Office Secret Decyphering Branch from 1716, intercepting mail, and especially despatches sent to foreign governments from their representatives in Britain. He turned it into a 'family' business, his sons and then his grandsons working for it.[29]

Five old cottages directly behind Jack Straw's Castle, rebuilt as two dwellings, became the centre of a glittering social scene, as members of the Whig political set moved in. One was rented to Lady Crewe, celebrated beauty and Whig hostess, between 1792 and 1807; and next door, Lady Camelford, widow of Thomas Pitt, 1st Baron Camelford (whose younger brother was William Pitt, the 1st Earl

17. Heathlands, home to Old Oram, Sir Francis Willes (1735-1827), member of the copyholders' committee; Hugh Mackay Matheson (1821-98), founder of the Rio Tinto Company and Heath campaigner in the 1860s; and Howard Figgis, chairman of the H&OHPS in the 1920s

of Chatham) took up residence in 1799. Her son the notorious 2nd Baron lived there for a short while until he was killed in a duel. Lady Camelford's son-in-law William Wyndham, Lord Grenville, then took over the copyhold.[30,31] As prime minister in 1806, Grenville headed the Ministry of All the Talents which saw the abolition of the slave trade. He left Hampstead around 1813. Fanny Burney left an account of an evening at Lady Crewe's where among the other visitors were Edmund Burke, Charles Fox, and Sheridan. The cottages later took the names of their famous residents: Camelford and Crewe Cottages.

Heath Lodge, the most northerly of the houses, was built in 1775 in highly controversial circumstances, demonstrating just how sought after the area had become. Jane Hemett,

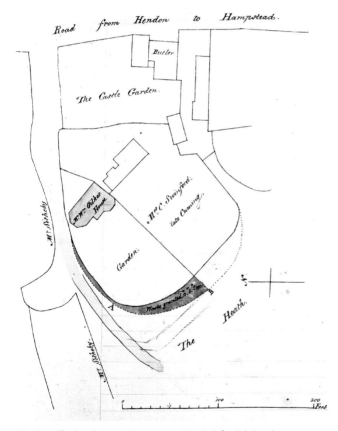

18. Camelford and Crewe Cottages; a plan in the Manor Court book just after the Ladies Crewe and Camelford had left. It shows how copyholders acquired strips from the Heath: the strip coloured green has been requested by Mr Gilkes and a map a few pages on shows Mrs Swinford doing the same on her side. Later the 'cottages' were turned into one house called Heath Brow, by Sir Richard Temple. The boundary with Mr Sotheby's Fern Lodge property is marked on the left of what is now the roadway, Heath Brow

33

an actress also known as Mrs Lessingham, had set her heart on having a house in fashionable Hampstead. "This lady has assumed a prominent place in the history of Hampstead, from a hotly litigated case of enclosure on the Heath". She was, according to Howitt, "an actress of secondary parts at Covent Garden, but also an actress of other parts which gave her a greater notoriety".[32] She was the mistress of Sir William Addington, a magistrate, who persuaded the Lord of the Manor to grant her an unusually large two acre portion of the waste at Littleworth. However, according to Park, one of Hampstead's 'customs', "peculiar to a few manors in England", was that such a grant could be made only to someone who was already a copyholder. When it was discovered that Mrs Lessingham was not a copyholder, "a violent opposition" was raised. "A battle," says Park, "of a very sanguinary nature is reported to have taken place between the bricklayers and the constables; and the public papers of the day teemed with communications on the subject of 'the riot on Hampstead Heath', the parties to which were attacked and defended with considerable warmth".[33] They proceeded to demolish the enclosure and destroy the building, and legal proceedings were begun. Park mentions a "metrical pamphlet" in which "the whole affray was depicted in a ludicrous form", called *The Hampstead Contest*:

> 'Two acres!' bawl'd he in a rage,
> 'And to an actress on the stage.
> A single rood too much is.'
> Yet mind rash fools what you're about
> Got into law, who'll get you out?
> The Courts love litigation.[34]

By the time the case came up Mrs Lessingham had managed to purchase a copyhold cottage, thus overcoming the objection. But in any case the judge's ruling was that, as the land was waste and therefore of no value, the copyholders had not lost anything. Mrs Lessingham triumphed, and built her house. Others who lived there after her were Lord Byron, the poet's uncle and, from 1843, David Powell one of the Heath campaigners. The house is long gone but the garden is now the Hill

19. Heath Lodge, pulled down by Lord Leverhulme in 1914 (see p 165); from an original 1910 drawing by A.R. Quinton

Garden, part of Hampstead Heath, of which more, later. Hill House, next door, which became John Gurney Hoare's residence, was begun as a Ditchfield grant by William Seville, who paid his dues and became a legitimate copyholder.[35] It was probably Lewis Allen who during the 1770s replaced the cottage with the house that the Hoares knew. Next to that was Cedar Lawn, where several more little tenements were replaced by a house with stables, around the 1780s.[31]

## The 'grandfathers'

Across the road on the summit of the Heath was Heath House, the home from 1793 of the Hoares, the philanthropic Quaker banking family who became "a landmark in the history of Hampstead"[36] and of the anti-slavery movement. Descended from a family who had gone to Ireland with Cromwell's army and become Quakers, and having prospered as a successful merchant in Cork, Samuel

20. Hill House 1780; later the residence of Samuel and John Gurney Hoare

Hoare senior came to London in the 1740s and joined one of the leading Quaker merchant firms in the City, Jonathan Gurnell & Co. It was his son, Samuel II, who established the family in Hampstead. Destined for the wool trade, he had been apprenticed to Henry Gurney, a Norwich woollen manufacturer. He married Gurney's daughter Sarah in 1776, beginning the long and enduring friendship cemented by ties of marriage between the two families (which eventually saw the Hoare family moving permanently to Norfolk). Samuel II, however, decided to go in for banking rather than wool and became a partner in another Quaker bank, Bland and Barnett of Lombard Street.[37] The young couple set up home

21. Heath House, 1910; drawing by A.R. Quinton

in Stoke Newington, the centre of a lively Quaker community, where Samuel was involved in the anti-slavery movement from its inception in 1783 and was a founder member of the Committee for the Abolition of the Slave Trade. His wife died young, and in 1790 he moved with his four children and second wife, Hannah, to Heath House[38] on medical advice, because of its higher and drier situation.

Samuel Hoare considerably enlarged the property to accommodate his family and it became renowned as a centre of philanthropy and literary life in Hampstead. Many meetings of the abolition movement were held there – perhaps Lord Grenville walked across the road from his 'cottage' behind Jack Straw's Castle to attend. Other visitors included an array of distinguished political and literary figures, in particular the poet George Crabbe, who was a frequent guest, and Wordsworth, who was a particular friend of Mrs Hoare. Samuel's other great preoccupation was the importance of education for the poor; he helped set up the first pauper's school in Hampstead.

As his children married locally, an extended family was established which became the backbone of the Hampstead community in the first half of the 19th century, "known during several generations for their high ideals of service, coupled with practical achievements in many fields".[39] They left the Society of Friends and joined the Church of England, but retained many of their Quaker friends. Samuel served on the Hampstead Vestry and the Copyholders' Committee, and was chairman of the Wells Charity. His sons-in-law, Robert Pryor (who lived on East Heath in the house later called the Pryors after him), and David Powell (at Heath Lodge), were also Vestrymen and copyholders and were prominent in the Heath campaign. Samuel's son, referred to in the manorial records as Samuel Junior, married Louisa Gurney, the daughter of John Gurney, his old friend from Norwich, and he bought Hill House at Littleworth for them. Their son John Gurney Hoare, born there in 1810, would also play a crucial role in the Heath campaign from 1840 to the1860s. Viscount Templewood, Gurney Hoare's grandson, made an interesting comment that it was the wives who pushed their husbands into public roles. This is not surprising when one remembers that Louisa's

22. Samuel Hoare (1751-1825), by Joseph Slater

23. Samuel Hoare Junior (1783-1846)

sister was Elizabeth Gurney Fry, the great prison reformer; another sister married Fowell Buxton, who was also involved with the abolition movement, and for a time in the 1800s lived at Myrtle Lodge, North End (also known as Myrtle Cottage or Grove, and now as Byron Cottage).[40]

In the absence of a resident lord of the manor, these men were regarded as the 'Squires' of Hampstead, which was "in a sort of indirect way, governed by a few leading citizens known as the 'grandfathers', to whom each public question was referred for decision".[41] Dickens' journal *All the Year Round* also alludes to this: "But, two or three families, the great bankers and others, were still looked up to as its natural heads, and when they agreed to a thing as right, and for the public good, he'd have been a bold man who said them nay".[42]

**Notes, Chapter 2**

1. Barratt (1912), vol. III, Appendix 3, p 359
2. Daniel Defoe, *Tour through the whole island of Great Britain (1724)*
3. Hampstead Manor Court books, *passim* (LMA)
4. Except for John Stride, who in 1814 took the copyhold of the Old Court House – perhaps the reason for its name; Court book J (LMA: E/MW/H/227)
5. Baines (1890), p 160
6. Potter (1907), p 37
7. Hampstead Manor Court Rolls, 1685-1689 (LMA: E/MW/H/8)
8. Chalybeate water has a high iron content, and was believed to have health-giving properties; it tasted so unpleasant that it could not have been used for everyday drinking.
9. Potter (1904), p 30
10. James Thorne (1876), *Handbook to the Environs of London*, p 280
11. Sir Richard Blackmore (1708), *The Kit-Kats, a poem*, published by the notorious Edmund Curll
12. Kneller's 48 pictures painted over a period of 20 years now hang in the National Portrait Gallery and the National Trust's Beningbrough Hall in Yorkshire.
13. Howitt (1869), p 17
14. Macky (1722)
15. Advert in *Read's Weekly Journal*, 8 Sep 1716, cited in Park, pp 235-236
16. Park (1812, 1818), pp 245, 250
17. Potter (1904), p 61
18. Transcripts of court case, Gurney Hoare v Maryon Wilson (CLSAC: ST2/ID/4)
19. Court roll, May 1738 (copy at CLSAC)
20. Park (1812, 1818), p 242
21. *George Whitefield's Journals*, 3rd journal, p 321. According to Christopher Wade (2000), p 34, this meeting took place on the site of what is now Summit Lodge (formerly Hawthorne House and before that Tudor House) and once the Speakers' Corner of Hampstead.
22. Macky (1732), i.89
23. Barbauld, Anna L, ed. (1804), *The correspondence of Samuel Richardson* (Richard Phillips), p cix
24. Published in *Bickham's Musical Entertainer, 1730s*
25. Jerry & Elizabeth Shields, 'Musick for Beaux and Belles', *CHR 3* (1975)
26. Seymour (1735), vol. 2, Appendix, p 870: 'The village of Hampstead'
27. Howitt (1869), p 82
28. Thompson (1974), p 30
29. It was abolished in 1844 after the scandalous revelation that the British Government, at the behest of the Austrians, had opened letters sent to the Italian nationalist Giuseppe Mazzini, then resident in London.
30. Hampstead Manor Court books (LMA: E/MW/H/226 1803-08, book I
31. Ibid., book J
32. Howitt (1869), pp 108-109
33. Park (1812, 1818), pp 130-132
34. Lost for many years, this satirical account of the events in verse was found in Birmingham Reference Library by Alan Farmer just as he was writing his book *Hampstead Heath* in 1983-84; it was reprinted for the first time as an Appendix to his book.
35. Transcripts of court case, Maryon Wilson v Gurney Hoare (CLSAC: ST2/ID/14)
36. Baines (1890), p 448
37. John Bland had lived at North End, Hampstead.
38. Heath House was built by Christopher Arnold, who was one of the earliest arrivals acquiring the copyhold of three cottages and some land in 1744. He replaced the cottages with a fine house, stables, coach house, pleasure grounds and garden. Curiously he was a director of the other Hoare's Bank (at the sign of the Golden Bottle in Cheapside) and, according to the Court Rolls, Arnold and Richard Hoare were already in Hampstead in the 1690s. According to Edward Hoare, who researched the genealogy of the Hoare families in 1883, both branches descended from the same ancestor.
39. Obituary of Margaret Hoare, *The Times*, 4 Mar 1936
40. Viscount Templewood (1949), *The unbroken thread* (Collins)
41. C.E. Maurice, note about life in Hampstead, in Barratt (1912), vol. III, p 315
42. Joseph Charles Parkinson, 'Hampstead Heath', *All the Year Round*, vol. XVII, no 409 (23 Feb 1867), p 198

# The rise of the Romanticks

24. View City of London, Westminster and Highgate from the Heath near the Spaniards 1780; by George Robertson (1748?-1788), who had Hampstead associations through the Boydell family. An early romantic depiction of Heath landscape; later used for the front of the H&HS Heath Vision booklet (see p 216)

(see p 216)

Hampstead Heath was made for the Romantic era. Almost every artist of note either lived in Hampstead at some point or visited it and, as part of the Romantic ideal, its beauty – and that of other such open spaces – was an important element in changing attitudes towards them. A new appreciation of the value of countryside had grown throughout the 18th century, and the idea of preserving landscape for its own sake was promoted by the great 'nature' poets: Wordsworth and Blake (who both knew Hampstead), John Clare and others. Gainsborough celebrated not only the subjects in his portraits of landed gentry, but the 'picturesque' landscapes of their estates as they were transformed to reflect the romantic idealisation of the 'natural' look. As Hampstead's popularity revived in the 1750s, a golden age began, this time with the Heath as the centre of attention, and again painters and writers flocked to it, finding in its scenery and views just the romantic inspiration they wanted. According to the artist John Thomas Smith, Keeper of the Prints department of the British Museum, Hampstead was considered by landscape painters in the late 18th century as "the most salubrious and beautiful of all the Montpeliers of England". He reels off a list of artists, including Wilson, Gainsborough, Loutherbourg, and Kirk, who for several years had lodgings at Hampstead and "made that spot the seat of their morning and evening study".[1] The writers soon followed. As well as in countless paintings, the Heath's charms were celebrated in literature, song, and poetry: "a whole 'nest of singing birds' collected there – Keats and Shelley and Hunt in the Vale of Health, while on the heights above, at the house of Mr. Hoare, were to be seen from time to time Rogers, Coleridge and Crabbe, Campbell and Wordsworth".[2]

25. Leigh Hunt (1784-1859)

The most famous of the writers were drawn to Hampstead by Leigh Hunt, poet and essayist, an important figure in the Romantic movement and in local iconography, whose cottage in the Vale of Health briefly became the centre of a glamorous poetic circle. Born in 1784, he made his name, not as a poet, but as a literary and political critic, in the ferment of radical ideas emerging in the early 19th century. His ancestors had fled Cromwell's England and settled in Barbados, but his father found himself on the wrong side in the American Revolution, and fled back to England where he became a Church of England minister. He led a somewhat rackety, nomadic life, and Leigh Hunt inherited from him not only this tendency, but a "Zeal for the public good [which] was a family inheritance"; later both his parents became Unitarians.[3] Hunt, who knew Hampstead from his childhood when his father lived there for a short while, first settled locally around 1811. His greatest passion was for literature and poetry but it was through the quality of his journalism rather than that of his poetry that he became a central figure in literary London. "He was not, as he wished to be and knew he was not, one of its great poets".[4] He made his name with a radical weekly newspaper, *The Examiner*, established in 1808 with his brother John, which became a leading intellectual journal. It campaigned against repressive legislation, and political and journalistic corruption, and for Reform in Parliament, while Hunt's theatre reviews introduced a new tone of critical independence. Also writing for *The Examiner* were such leading reformers as Hazlitt, Charles Lamb, Henry Brougham; and Thomas Barnes, Hunt's lifelong friend from their schooldays together at Christ's Hospital[5] and later to become the campaigning editor of *The Times*.

The Hunt brothers were repeatedly prosecuted by the government for their outspoken views in *The Examiner*. In 1813 they were imprisoned for two years for a supposedly libellous attack on the Prince Regent. Leigh Hunt served his term in Surrey County Gaol, but it was no ordinary imprisonment. He was allowed to decorate a set of rooms in the most flamboyant manner - Lamb described these as something not found outside a fairy tale - and have the use of a small garden. His reputation was by now such that he had a constant stream of eminent visitors: Lord Byron, Thomas Moore, Brougham, Jeremy Bentham and others came to cheer and support him. It was there that he wrote the first three of his seven 'Sonnets to Hampstead', expressing his deep attachment to the place: "the Hampstead fields had ever been my delight".[3] Longing to be back there, he invokes the

> Sweet upland, to whose walks, with fond repair,
> Out of thy western slope I took my rise
> Day after day, and on these feverish eyes
> Met the moist fingers of the bathing air ; —
> If health, unearned of thee, I may not share.
> Keep it, I pray thee, where my memory lies,
> In thy green lanes, brown dells, and breezy skies.
> Till I return, and find thee doubly fair.

After Hunt's release from prison, his cottage in the newly developing Vale of Health became a magnet from 1816 for some of the most eminent names in English literature, led by Shelley, Keats and Byron, who sought him out, drawn by his enthusiasm and support for their work, as well as his great personal charm. In *The Examiner* Hunt championed this rising young 'second wave' of Romantic poets (the first having been the Lake poets). Charles Lamb, in a famous letter to Southey, described him as "the most cordial-minded man I ever knew, and matchless as a fireside companion".[6]

But having survived the attack from the State, he was now subjected to a literary onslaught by *Blackwood's Magazine*, which in 1818 viciously attacked Hunt and his circle of poets, in particular Keats, sneeringly dubbing them the "Cockney School" – a term chosen to deliberately disparage the class background of these new young 'upstart' poets of the lower 'plebeian' classes, and their champion, even though Shelley and Byron were aristocrats. The *Blackwood's* essays are considered to be among the most notoriously malevolent pieces of invective in English literature.

Hunt's biographer, Cosmo Monkhouse, suggested that perhaps those two years in prison took the spirit out of him. He resigned from *The Examiner* and withdrew from political writing. On his return to England from a stay in Italy in 1825, he lived briefly at Highgate, where, he said, "I took possession of my old English scenery and my favourite haunt with delight – beloved Hampstead was near with home in its churchyard as well as in its meadows", a reference to the fact that his mother was buried there.[3] Much is made of his attachment to Hampstead, but in fact he spent very little time there. By the time the Heath battle had begun in 1829, Hunt had moved away from Hampstead Heath, never to return. Having renounced his youthful firebrand views, he spent the rest of his life constantly on the move, living a hand-to-mouth existence. Notwithstanding his oft-repeated love of the Heath, his voice was entirely absent from the campaign and he took no part in the saving of it.

## Popular appeal

Just as important as the contribution of the artists was the Heath's popularity with ordinary working people: a piece of open countryside within walking distance of the old City, which they could visit for the day. There was a long tradition of commons as public meeting places, used for political demonstrations and meetings as well as to mark great events and local festivities. Hampstead Heath was the place where great social occasions, entertainments, and public gatherings took place. Elections for the county of Middlesex were held there until 1700, when they were transferred to Brentford.[7]

Occasional fairs had been held in Hampstead since the 17th century. Park reprints an advert that appeared in *The Spectator* in 1712, for a four-day Hampstead Fair to be held in the Lower Flask Tavern Walk on 1 August.[8] There were fairs on the Heath at South End Green in the 1830s, but it was only around the middle of the century that they began to become fixtures, gradually growing into major visitor attractions. Baines describes steam roundabouts as having been "revived, and [carrying] on the tradition in a neighbouring field in a very emphatic and not wholly acceptable way".[9]

A particularly notable event was a visit by King William IV, who drove through Hampstead in 1835 on his way to dine at Kenwood House. Spirited accounts of the event in both *The Times* and Barratt's *Annals* describe the whole of Hampstead decorated with greenery and variegated lamps. "On the heath an immense temporary triumphal arch little inferior to Temple-bar in dimensions" was put up across the road at Whitestone Pond, draped in crimson cloth and decorated with flags, flowers, coloured lamps and gilded shields, with grandstands for the spectators on either side of it. The King and Queen halted under the arch to listen to a loyal address from Colonel Bosanquet, chairman of the organising committee, and 21 cannons were lined up on the green beside the pond to fire a royal salute. "The royal party then proceeded on their route, amidst the almost deafening cheers of the immense population which thronged the road".[10]

The official Heath-keeper, John Stevenson, who had to clear up afterwards recorded on 23 July (with his original spellings and punctuation): "The Triumphant Arch left for inspection it was reported a ball to tak place under the Arch on Tuesday night, it brought company to Hampstead, but no Dancing, therefore if it ad not bene well watched would a been Burnt Down, it was threatened. One man lost life at averstock Hill by Coach goin over

26. The Triumphal Arch in honour of the visit of William IV and Queen Adelaide, 1835; from a contemporary lithograph

41

him. July 28: Taken the Triumphant Arch Down".[11]

Henry Sharpe mentions another grand fete, at Kenwood in 1844, with a string of carriages from 3 pm onwards: "all Hampstead was out looking at them". He also records encountering people coming from the Heath one evening after a meeting of teetotallers: "there must have been many thousands".[12] According to press reports it was an annual occurrence, people "arriving in vans and afoot, with bands of music and banners, and taking up their abode in marquees. A vanful of people represented the Chartist Teatotalers [*sic*]; rumours of whose attendance caused a somewhat needless display of police".[13]

Donkeys became an indispensible part of any visit to the Heath, inspiring cartoons and drawings, and many descriptive articles. Evoe Knox quipped that "there seemed to be an uncontrollable desire to ride donkeys".[14] They are first recorded in the 1820s, although they probably arrived earlier. By the 1830s there were said to be 100 donkeys daily on the Heath. Amongst those for whom a picnic on the Heath and a donkey ride was a favourite outing was the family of Karl Marx; he apparently rode "with more fervour than skill". His friend and colleague, Wilhelm Liebknecht, remembered that "the greatest treat was a general donkey riding. There was a mad laughing and whooping! And those ludicrous scenes! And how Marx amused himself and us by his primitive art of riding!"[15]

27. Quiet times – a sketch on Hampstead Heath 1875, by Edwin Buckman (1841-1930)

But with the donkeys' rising popularity came increasing problems. Unfortunately, the donkey-men did not look after their animals or control them adequately. Complaints began as early as 1825, when the Vestry minutes record that the steward of the manor was to take counsel's opinion on how to deal with the nuisance caused by them. By the 1840s there were determined moves by the leading gentry to get them stopped on Sundays under the Lord's Day Observance Act. Newly arrived in Hampstead, Henry Sharpe felt it unfair that "poorer classes should be deprived of the pleasure of a ride" on a Sunday, the only day of the week when they could enjoy it: "It is a monstrous thing that a poor man should not be allowed to take a 6d ride on a donkey when a rich man may ride on his horse". Neither did he think much of the old Hampstead gentry – the Hoares and the Pryors – whose attitude to the donkey-men he considered unduly harsh. He recounts his efforts to help them in his *Journal*, seeking legal advice on their behalf, but lecturing them about their "riotous behaviour", and readily admitting that "They are such a set of vagabonds, ... almost too bad a set for me to undertake to manage ...". Sharpe risked falling out with his new neighbours over it, in particular the Hoares and Pryors; but he won his battle: the magistrate threw out the case against the donkey-men, and he managed to mend relations with his neighbours.[12]

Dickens' journal *Household Words*, while evincing sympathy for the animals, excoriated the donkey-drivers. They were "absolutely brutal", and had a "pleasing uncertainty respecting fares. An hour's ride, or a half-hour's ride, on Hampstead Heath are the same facetious fictions as eightpenny and one-and-fourpenny fares are in London. Of a truth, donkey drivers know as little of practical arithmetic as some bishops".[16] The nuisance greatly increased after 1860 with the coming of the railway. The lord of the manor was asked by the copyholders to put a stop to the donkeys: "they do not respect the object of the Lords of the Manor"; their owners were not local residents; they rode "cruelly and wantonly", used "offensive and improper language" and were rude and ill-behaved.[17]

G.W. Potter remembered Queen Victoria's frequent visits to Hampstead in the early days of her reign, "coming morning after morning from the Finchley Road to the Heath, and then back via Heath Street or Holly Hill to London. Two or three of her young children were generally with her in the carriage".[18]

Thus Hampstead and its Heath had built up a very special place in the affections of London people, treasured by everybody from the Queen herself to the working man. In the space of that crucial century between 1700 and 1800, the locality had been transformed

28. Plate with view of the Long Room and Burgh House; part of the Wedgwood 'Green Frog' service made in 1774 for Catherine II, Empress of Russia

from an insignificant village of farm labourers to a place of renown and a tourist attraction, inhabited by men of wealth and status, its "extensive and picturesque view, the admiration of foreigners and the delightful study of our artists".[19] Such was its fame that when, in 1773, Wedgwood was commissioned by Catherine, Empress of Russia, to create a grand dinner service decorated with views of British castles, palaces and landscapes, no fewer than twenty-seven of the 952 pieces were views of Hampstead and its Heath.[20] It was the combination of a community of affluent and influential local residents, already conscious of the distinctiveness their home, enthusiastic artists, and enormous popularity amongst the public at large, which helped save the Heath.

## Changing attitudes

But the other crucial factor was the rise of new political sensibility in response to the gathering pace of industrialisation, the problems caused by social change, and the uncontrolled expansion of London that it brought in its wake. Hampstead remained popular with a new generation of City merchants and bankers, self-made men, closely involved with the City guilds, many of them Dissenters – Presbyterians, Quakers and Unitarians – men of high social conscience and philanthropic ideals.

Parliamentarians became increasingly concerned by the effects of enclosures in the countryside, which provoked widespread protest as the poor were seen to be further dispossessed. The realisation grew that, in addition to their value as places of beauty, open green spaces contributed to peoples' health and wellbeing. As early as 1808, in a significant debate about proposals to build houses in Hyde Park, the idea of parks as 'the lungs of London' was referred to by William Windham MP.[21] He maintained that it was already "a saying of Lord Chatham", thus placing the earliest known use of the expression in the late 18th century.

Commons, also, were beginning to be valued for their amenity, but such ideas clashed with equal concern about the backward state of agriculture and the perception that uncultivated common land was wasted. Sir John Sinclair MP, a somewhat derided figure, tried unsuccessfully to promote a more scientific approach to agriculture. He established a new Board of Agriculture, was its first President, and appointed a Select Committee to look at how the cultivation of wastes and commons could be improved. Between 1793 and 1817 he instigated the first national agricultural survey of Great Britain, conducted county by county, examining every facet of farming practice. Its findings, in complete opposition to the Romantic view, were that common and heathland were being wasted. John Middleton of Merton, a land surveyor and farmer, who reviewed the County of Middlesex in 1807, considered that "The many barren and uncultivated wastes … remained a mark of disgrace to the spirit and character of Britain", and should be "changed into a permanent resource of wealth and prosperity to the nation". He was not unsympathetic to the plight of the poor, recommending that wherever enclosures were made they should be with "due attention to the interests of the poor (as they ought always to be)". But he shared the view that letting good agricultural land on commons go to waste did not help the poor. He also saw no harm in using such land where it was not cultivable to be "adorned with elegant villas".[22]

Commons and heaths were also notorious as dangerous places infested with highway robbers. Hounslow and Finchley were the worst, but Hampstead Heath had its full share of such robberies (although its legendary association with Dick Turpin is probably apocryphal). Louisa Cathcart, the future wife of Lord Stormont, heir of Kenwood, wrote after returning safely from a visit to Lord Mansfield with her father in the 1790s: "Papa and I dined at Caen Wood ... and came home after nine o'clock without being robbed, which I think was a lucky escape".[23] In 1803, against the background of the Napoleonic Wars, Sir John Sinclair used comically warlike language in his widely quoted call for more enclosures to address these problems: "Why should we not attempt a campaign also against our great domestic foe? ... Let us not be satisfied with the liberation of Egypt, or the subjugation of Malta, but let us subdue Finchley Common; let us conquer Hounslow Heath, let us compel Epping Forest to submit to the yoke of improvement". Finchley Common was enclosed in 1812, and little remains of Hounslow Heath, but Epping, like Hampstead, was saved by a long drawn-out campaign.

As London's inexorable sprawl spread to villages formerly regarded as quite separate from the City, commons around London acquired new value as potential building land. Several other London commons were already under threat: enclosures of Stanmore, Willesden, Enfield Chase, Harrow and Hornsey were all taking place by 1820; and a public protest meeting about Wandsworth was reported in *The Times* in 1827. More and more of them were being swallowed up, not for agricultural enclosures but to provide large scale lucrative housing developments. Such developments were already lapping at the edge of Hampstead's boundaries.

## The Finchley Road

The Crown Estate had begun to sell off land in St John's Wood. The Eyre family, who had the largest holding on the boundary with Hampstead Manor, were making plans to develop their land in 1819, but they needed a road to make the new estates viable. They assumed that the Maryon Wilsons would welcome their plans to extend a road into Hampstead, which would create frontages that could be profitably developed. But they misjudged. At that time the Maryon Wilsons' policy was still to preserve Hampstead's seclusion and the "special charm on which the value of [their] lands depended".[24] They fought the Eyres in their several attempts to get private road bills through Parliament.

The Wilsons won the first round, against a road along Belsize Lane, but the Eyres switched their route to what was to become the new Finchley Road. When his father died in 1821, young Sir Thomas continued the fight: the new road, which would have cut through the middle of the Manor Farm (called Hall Oak Farm), was, he said, not planned for any public good, as was claimed, but simply for private profit, "with a view to benefit certain individuals engaged in building speculations".[24] He pointed out that while these new frontages might be very beneficial to Colonel Eyre, they were no use to him because his father's will prevented him from granting building leases. As part of his written evidence to Parliament against the new Finchley Road, young Sir Thomas made a special point of the several codicils added to his father's will just before he died, granting the power to make building leases for 99 years on his other estates, but not at Hampstead. He claimed that, when asked specifically if he would grant 99-year leases at Hampstead, his father had "said no; and expressed his sentiments for leaving that as it was".[25] But it was all to no avail. He was finally defeated, and the Act to enable the building of the Finchley Road was passed in 1825. By 1826 Eton College had obtained an Act enabling 99-year building leases to be granted on the Chalcots estate and building was already taking place on the Bliss estate in Belsize.[26]

Was this lost Finchley Road battle a critical event that provoked a change of mind for young Sir Thomas? Newly come into his inheritance at a relatively young age – only twenty when his father died – he was enjoying life as an eligible young baronet, following the usual course of the affluent young man about town, and abroad. The *Morning Chronicle* reports a "brilliant fête" given by him in Genoa, which was then popular with "distinguished English Families".[27] He had done his duty by his father and, having seen all his arguments in favour of preserving Hampstead swept aside, why should he not examine the possibilities of development instead? It would not have been unreasonable to think of profiting by selling to builders, as his neighbours and scores of other landowners were doing, especially those on the edge of large towns.

Or were the Wilsons already attacking the copyholders' rights to try to extract more profits from the land in Hampstead? Friction had developed even before 1800 between the Hampstead copyholders and the lord of the manor. Copyholders had always assumed that it was their right to take turf and gravel from the waste for use in their gardens, but in 1781 this was challenged by the then Lord of the Manor, General Sir Thomas Spencer Wilson (young Sir Thomas's grandfather), who took a case to the Court of King's Bench against Lady Riddell and the copyholders for digging loam. Led by a Mr Henry White, a builder, they won a famous victory which was celebrated in glowing terms in the *Gazetteer and New Daily Advertiser* and the *Westminster Journal*. The Lord's action, they said, was "no more than a despicable remain of feudal law, a relique of tyranny that disgraces a free country". Mr White "may be regarded as, to quote Gray,[28] 'a village Hamden who with dauntless breast the little tyrant of his fields withstood'". General Wilson gracefully accepted his defeat: "Well White you have beat me." "Yes Sir Thomas we have and I am glad of it." Sir Thomas: "I don't blame you. I like a man of spirit. I thought it was my right but I find it is not".[29]

## The Copyholders' Committee

However, it was not until Sir Thomas's grandmother took control after the General's death that the atmosphere appeared to change. In 1801 and 1802, Dame Jane – who continued in charge of the estates, even though Maryon Wilson's father was of age – renewed the attack on the copyholders' rights, serving writs for trespass on Edward Page and Sir Francis Willes for cutting turf. According to the Manor Court book, Willes was actually imprisoned in the Marshalsea for a while![30] The leading copyholders were no longer small tradesmen but affluent landed gentry and City merchants, several with aristocratic connections. The Holfords, Lord Erskine, Sir Francis Willes, Samuel Hoare, Sir Thomas Neave and the Pryors probably

46

considered themselves equal in social class to the Maryon Wilsons and were not going to be treated in this way without challenge. They took forceful concerted action, forming a Copyholders' Committee in 1801 to "ascertain our several rights … to cut and dig turf, marle, sand, gravel and loam from any part of the Waste of the Manor". They sought to have it "absolutely confirmed by … legal and equitable proceedings", and to defend themselves and their property "against any encroachment or attack that may be made by the Lord or Lady of the Manor in any way whatever".[31] They accused Dame Jane of infringing and violating "divers ancient customs" and of demanding and receiving excessive fines and fees on admission. Significantly, they appear to accuse her of "digging, selling and disposing of … sand, gravel and loam" from the Heath herself. There was polite but determined opposition and her Ladyship appeared to back down a little in the face of it. The Steward, John Stride, assured them that the dispute was only about cutting turf that damaged the green sward, and they would "meet the

29. Sand Pits, Hampstead Heath, 1849, by John Linnell (1792-1882), who lived at Old Wyldes, 1824-1828

copyholders in the most amicable manner[32] and with the least possible expense" to settle the matter.[31]

But this time the verdict was a disappointment. In March 1806 the judges found against the copyholders' case, because it "was so unlimited that it might operate to the destruction of the Right of Common and was therefore an unreasonable right".[31] The copyholders accepted the ruling but were then angered when they saw that no-one else appeared to. They accused Lady Wilson of being inconsistent and "in opposition to the united wishes of her tenants" when she "declined to put a final stop to any further depredations upon the Heath". Thenceforward the copyholders were on their guard, alert to any perceived abuse of their rights.[33]

## Notes, Chapter 3

1. Smith, J.T. (1828). The bronze bust of Lord Mansfield at Kenwood is by Nollekens.

2. Review of *The Hampstead Annual,* in *The Spectator,* 29 Jan 1898

3. *The autobiography of Leigh Hunt* (1850, Smith, Elder & Co.)

4. www.poetryfoundation. org/poems-and-poets/ poets/detail/leigh-hunt

5. Today, two of the school's Houses are named after Barnes and Leigh Hunt.

6. Cosmo Monkhouse (1893), *Life of Leigh Hunt* (Walter Scott Ltd)

7. Sexby (1898) cites adverts in such newspapers as the *True Protestant Mercury* (Mar 1681) and the *Flying Post* (Oct 1695).

8. Park (1812, 1818), p 246; *The Spectator, No.443* (29 Jul 1712). This was the daily publication which lasted from 1711-12, founded by Joseph Addison and Richard Steele, both Hampstead residents at various times.

9. Baines (1890), p 227

10. *The Times,* 24 Jul 1835; Baines (1890), pp 265-267

11. *The diary of a Heath-Keeper, 1834-39* (CLSAC)

12. Henry Sharpe, Journal 1841-47 (uncatalogued collection, CLSAC)

13. *The Spectator,* 10 Jun 1843, p 2

14. E.V. Knox, 'Memorandum: the records of the Hampstead Heath Protection Society' (H&HS archive: A/1048/5/4/1); Knox was the editor of *Punch* and a Society member.

15. Wilhelm Liebknecht (1896), *Biographical memoirs* (Chicago. C.H. Kerr)

16. Theodore Buckley, 'Hampstead Heath', *Household Words,* vol. IV, no. 79 (27 Sep 1851), p 15

17. A Presentment (complaint) made by the copyholders in 1862 at the General Court; transcripts of the Case in Chancery, Gurney Hoare v Maryon Wilson (CLSAC)

18. Potter (1907), p 97

19. *London Courier & Evening Gazette,* Dec 1816

20. The Green Frog Service in the Hermitage museum, St Petersburg. All this contradicts Professor Thompson's assertions that there was "little evidence of any explicit appreciation of the Heath on aesthetic or therapeutic grounds ... or as an invigorating exercise ground", or that it "only had a cultural history and importance from the early 1800s"; Thompson (1974), pp 152-154.

21. HC Deb 30 June 1808 vol 11 cc1122-6; not, as Professor Thompson asserts, during the 1829 debate on Wilson's Estate Bill, an error he has unfortunately repeated in his 2004 ODNB entry for Sir Thomas Maryon Wilson

22. John Middleton (1807), *View of the agriculture of Middlesex,* 2nd ed., (Board of Agriculture)

23. E. Maxtone Graham (1927), *The beautiful Mrs Graham and the Cathcart Circle* (Nisbet). Lady Louisa Mansfield, Lord Stormont's second wife, was the daughter of Lord Cathcart

24. Petition of Sir T.M. Wilson against the Bill for a new road at Belsize Lane, May 1820; Statement of grounds of opposition by Sir T.M. Wilson (LMA: E/MW/H/03/038/015)

25. The Case of Sir Thomas Maryon Wilson against the [Finchley Road] Bill, now before Parliament 17 May 1824 (LMA: ibid.)

26. *The Times,* 29 Sep 1827

27. *Morning Chronicle,* 30 Jan 1824

28. Thomas Gray (1750), *Elegy written in a country churchyard*

29. Transcript of court case, Gurney Hoare v Maryon Wilson: analysis of Affidavit filed on the part of the Plaintiffs by P.H. Lawrence, 17 Jun 1867 (CLSAC: ST2/ID/14)

30. Hampstead Manor Court books (LMA: E/MW/H/227), book J, pp 528-536

31. Minutes of the Copyholders' Committee, 27 Mar 1801 (LMA: M 81/8-9)

32. *Ibid.* An 'amicable suit' was an action to secure clarification on a point of law, in concord and in the mutual interest of the parties involved.

33. Ref. 31, May 1807

Chapter 4

# Enter Sir Thomas Maryon Wilson

The Hampstead estate of about 2,000 acres was but a small part of the Maryon Wilson holdings. Hampstead Heath took up about 250 acres on the north and east of the village, and 356 acres of the old demesne farmland – Hall Oak Farm – stretched south from Frognal. But it was a much smaller block of 60 acres on the other side of the Heath, between East Heath and Lord Mansfield's Parliament Hill, that was to become the source of contention. Then known as the brickfields, and later as East Park, it was originally a wood called Whytebirch, and was cleared by the lord of the manor for farmland in the 17th century. Although not part of the Heath, local residents regarded it as indistinguishable from it when it came to walking, riding or admiring the view, and the only access to it was across the Heath. For

30.  Sir Thomas Maryon Wilson, Bt (1800-69), Sotheby & Co. catalogue 1993

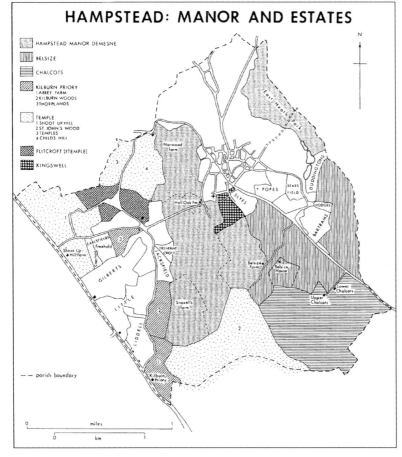

31. Map of Hampstead Manor estates

young Sir Thomas Maryon Wilson, the nature of his inheritance and his father's will presented a major obstacle to any plans for development.

The estates were 'entailed' (setting out the order of succession) under a strict 'settlement', the system of inheritance designed to preserve and control a family's possessions and protect the rights of future heirs over a number of generations. Wilson's father had divided his extensive holdings between his eldest sons, Thomas, who inherited the Hampstead, Kent and Sussex estates with grand houses at Charlton and Searles; and his second son John who inherited 1,500 acres in Essex with a fine mansion, Fitzjohns, at Great Canfield. But young Sir Thomas inherited only as a 'tenant for life'; he could not grant leases for longer than 21 years, or lasting beyond his life, or from which he might benefit at the expense of his successors, and neither could he sell any part of the estate. A 21-year lease was not a commercial proposition: no builder would take land on these terms, and to build houses himself Sir Thomas would require ready cash. If he had married and had a son, he and his heir-apparent could have agreed to the cutting-off of the entail, but Sir Thomas never married. On his much larger estates in Kent and Sussex, some 4,000 acres, codicils to his father's will allowed him to grant 99-year leases, but no such codicil had been made for Hampstead. This omission, which he used to his advantage at the Finchley Road hearing (see p 45), was to prove the main stumbling block; but he could overcome it by applying to Parliament for a private estate act to change the terms of the will. Such applications had become frequent, as the new industrial economy changed attitudes to land use, and they were standardised in form and content. The first step was a Petition to the House of Lords, setting out the reasons for the application, for consideration by the Law Lords.[1] But it was laborious and expensive, and the consent of other parties involved in the settlement had to be obtained. It was rare for them to be contested, but Maryon Wilson and his estate bills were to be a remarkable and notorious exception to the rule.

Sir Thomas lodged his first Hampstead Estate Bill in the House of Lords in 1829 and set in motion the forty-year "guerilla war". In March, the Bill went through the usual scrutiny procedure by two judges, Barons Park (a leading judge of the day) and Littledale, who found "nothing objectionable", and that it was a "proper bill to be passed". At that stage the significance of the different codicils was evidently not appreciated. The Bill was successfully given its first and second readings in the Lords and only then was the alarm raised, thought to have been by Lord Mansfield, in a letter to a local resident. After all the family's efforts to preserve the neighbouring land from building, Mansfield would have been appalled at the possibility of buildings within sight of Kenwood.

It was the first anyone in Hampstead had heard about it and a public meeting was called immediately, chaired by James Fenton of the Clock House (now Fenton House). There was dismay that Sir Thomas had not had the courtesy to inform copyholders of his plans, and concern over two particularly controversial elements – firstly, the schedule of land included reference to the Heath and the Waste of the Manor; and, secondly, a clause to 'enable' copyholders to buy building licences for 99-year leases. These were seen as an attack on the copyholders 'immemorial' rights.

The Copyholders' Committee, a recognised part of the Manor procedure since it was formed in 1801,[2] was deputed to take action on behalf of the 350

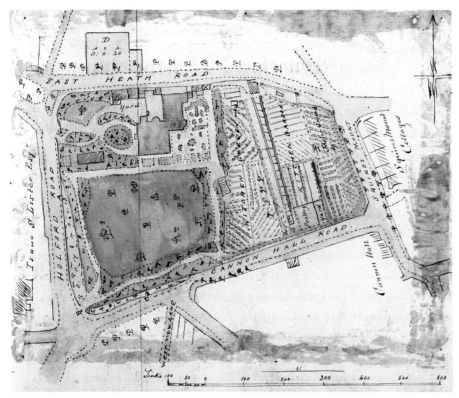

32. The Holford estate on East Heath Road, in the 1850s. On the left is the boundary with Bowling Green House (the old Upper Flask), then owned by Isaac Solly Lister (Manor Court Book P, p 438)

or so copyholders, led by Charles Holford.[3]

Apparently anxious to avoid a direct confrontation with Sir Thomas, they first approached the solicitor for the Bill, seeking to get it altered rather than to stop it, by asking him to remove the objectionable clauses relating to building licences and the Heath. But their request was refused. Two petitions, one from the copyholders and one from their lessees and other residents, were therefore sent to the House of Lords in May 1829, and Lord Shaftesbury was asked to present them. They protested that "... the Lord of the Manor has assumed that all questions at issue between himself and the copyholders are in his favour", including "a right to enclose parts of the Heath on his own authority over which the copyholders claim and exercise certain rights and privileges. He now seeks the right to issue licences on payment of a 40s fine to the Lord and £3.3 fee to the Steward for each license", something that had always been done before without payment, "thereby assuming that the copyholders have no rights." "The copyholders are desirous only that their rights should be left undisturbed and

they do not seek to prevent the Lord, who had a life interest in the Manor from obtaining Powers under this Bill which the law would have given him."
They were aggrieved that "no adequate reason can be offered" for the solicitor's refusal to make the requested changes to the Bill.[4]

They wrote directly to Sir Thomas, in a conciliatory vein, assuring him "that the opposition to your Bill does not arise from any hostility to you or from any desire to infringe on your right or prevent you ... from increasing the value of your property". But they pointed out that even though the Steward and the Solicitor had recently attended two Hampstead Manor Court meetings, not a word had been mentioned about the Bill, leaving them to feel that the information had been deliberately withheld from them.[4] Ignoring the substance of their objections, Sir Thomas simply replied that "The clauses in my bill are intended for the benefit of the copyholders. I am sorry you should view them in any other light. ... I assure you it was never intended they should ... injure anyone".[4]

However, the copyholders at last secured a meeting with Sir Thomas, whose perverse responses left them in little doubt about the character of the man they had to deal with. The Bill was proceeding smoothly through Parliament and he saw no need to concede anything. Again the copyholders request for alterations was refused and Sir Thomas repeated that the power to grant licences was intended as a benefit to the copyholders; furthermore he expressed annoyance that they did not come straight to him with their objections rather than "adopt the course they had of writing to him". In reply they pointed out that these supposed "benefits" had always previously been available as a right and without payment, and that "it would not have been businesslike" or courteous to simply turn up to see him without giving notice.[5]

Eventually, assisted by Lord Shaftesbury, the copyholders' solicitor attended a Lords Committee hearing on 27 May and got a clause inserted, exempting existing copyholders from the new measures. On 30 May it was publicised in *The Times*, in a letter from one W.H.J., headed "Enclosing of Hampstead-heath". It spelled out the copyholders' stance: that their rights were being breached and that no notice was given to them of the Bill, but also making clear that they had no wish to prevent the Lord from obtaining other powers under its provisions.[6]

In this amended form the Bill was passed by the Lords on 1 June, and that might have been the end of it. But when Charles Holford reported back to a meeting of the copyholders on 16 June, that the Bill was now satisfactory and they would drop their objections, some of them were furious – "a very stormy discussion took place".[7] The Copyholders' Committee split; Holford and his colleagues resigned and one William Ripley took up the cause.

### The mysterious Mr Ripley
Quite why William Ripley became so concerned about Wilson's Bill is a mystery, but were it not for his intervention, there would probably now be no

52

Hampstead Heath. His connection to Hampstead was through his older half-brother, Rev. Thomas Hyde Ripley, who had inherited a 50-acre copyhold of farmland in Kilburn called Gilberts, which the family had held since the 1750s; he also inherited the incumbency at Wootton Bassett Parish Church in Wiltshire, from his father in 1813. None of them lived at Hampstead; the farm

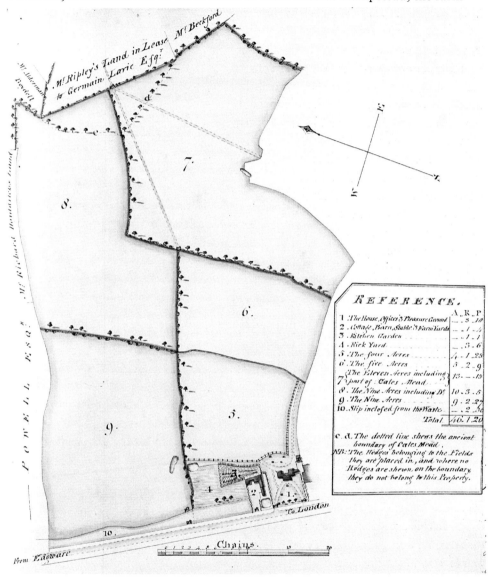

33. The Ripley estate (Manor Court Book J, 1808-1815, p 475);
'Gilberts' lay east of the north end of today's Kilburn High Road

was rented to a John Taylor. William Ripley[8], a solicitor with rooms at Gray's Inn, took charge of the family's affairs, acting on behalf of his reverend brother.

There was no time to lose: the Bill was due to go to the Commons on 19 June. He sought counsel's opinion, which was that the changes to the Bill got by the copyholders would not have protected their rights.[9] The national press rallied to the cause with editorials as well as letters from the protesters. Maryon Wilson had gravely underestimated the significance of Hampstead Heath. On 17 June *The Times* published two letters, together with its own article giving them its full backing. In an impassioned outburst, it reminded readers of its previous campaign against building in the London parks, placing the emphasis firmly on the perceived threat to the Heath: "We trust that Parliament will have virtue – nay, humanity – enough to throw out the bill for giving Sir Thomas Maryon Wilson a right to annihilate Hampstead- heath ... [and] as has been done with so many other places of healthful recreation for the smoke-dried inhabitants of London – surround or cover it with rows of brick-built houses. Hampstead-heath, that spot so animating, so accessible to the crowd, so refreshing to the imprisoned population of those narrow districts of the metropolis. It is frightful to think of Hampstead-heath becoming the subject of a bill of enclosure".[10]

The first of two strongly worded letters accused the promoters of the Bill of proceeding "irregularly, as well as uncourteously", forcing "its insidious way ... through the houses of Parliament, under false pretences". It only reached the knowledge of the Hampstead copyholders by accident, when a peer wrote to a resident at Hampstead, "expressing his regret at finding such a bill before the house". The writer considered that "as it approaches to the nature of an enclosure bill, it ought to have originated in the House of Commons, and to have been preceded by notices of the intention to introduce it, to all the parties interested".[11]

The second letter,[12] a *cri de coeur* on behalf of the "oppressed of all classes of the community", is an interesting portent of things to come. It exhorted the editor to "assist the copyholders of Hampstead in forming the vanguard of the battle on behalf of the public", to preserve "the open and beautiful prospect" and "the quiet and greenness of the country." The writer brought a wider perspective, referring to the "alarm ... sounded for Epping Forest" and "the fate of 'Wandsworth-common", asking "Where will they stop?" Another letter, thanking the paper for its support, described the Bill as having been "smuggled into Parliament at the fag end of the session for smuggling Hampstead Heath from the public".[13] *The Spectator* took the same line, with "a Bill for Enclosing Hampstead Heath", which was "quietly stealing its way through Parliament, till ... an active local opposition was organized";[14] as did the *Morning Herald*, which felt that "The comforts of the lower classes are too much neglected by the Aristocracy of this country...."[15] The *Morning Chronicle* launched an attack on the very idea of private bills, "enacted in stealth", that removed public rights: "that Parliament should retain the power of making private laws; ... setting aside the law in favour of individuals is of itself a very great evil".[16]

Ripley made sure that MPs were put "in possession of the real facts of the case".[17] There was to be no tinkering with clauses; the Bill had to be stopped. His brother had political connections at Wootton Bassett and it was probably through them he approached Robert Gordon, MP for neighbouring Cricklade,[18] and Ralph Bernal, MP for Rochester, both on the side of reform. A curious and unpredictable man, Gordon was known for frequently presenting petitions on local legislation and private matters. Sometimes nicknamed 'Bum Gordon' Henry Brougham caricatured him as 'Bombastes Furioso'; but he was considered a "damned good-natured fellow".[18]

Ripley had chosen the right man for the task. In Parliament, having presented the Hampstead copyholders' petitions, Gordon launched straight into a demolition of the Bill, as being "objectionable in every point of view". It professed to be an estate bill but looked more like an enclosure bill; notice had not been served on the copyholders who had an interest in the matter; it sought powers for the steward to collect money by way of licence, and therefore assumed the shape of a money bill, and ought to have originated in the Commons not the Lords. It would deny the copyholders their rights. He then turned to the issue of the Heath, going well beyond the copyholders' interests, declaring that: "even if all the copyholders had consented to the measure, he should object to it on behalf of the public of this great metropolis, because it professed to encourage the copyholders to build on the Heath. It was not the fashion of the day to think much about the amusements or comforts of the poorer classes of society"; but Gordon nevertheless contended that "the House was bound not to do anything that might tend to abridge those comforts or amusements." Ralph Bernal quoted the counsel's opinion obtained by Ripley, that the copyholders' rights would not have been protected by the changes to the Bill.

John Stewart, MP for Beverley, agreed that: "the Heath at Hampstead was a common source of good to all classes in the metropolis and even artists were in the habit of going to Hampstead Heath to draw sketches of the metropolis". He also raised the significance of the codicils to old Sir Thomas's will, pointing out that they indicated "he never intended any part of it to be parcelled out" in the way proposed. Sir Joseph Yorke (Reigate) made an impassioned plea for preserving Hampstead Heath as an open space, on the grounds of people's health and enjoyment. London would soon be hemmed in on all sides at the will of a few private individuals.

The landowners' view was put by Sir Charles Burrell, who "could not see why the lord of the Manor should not have the same power and privilege over his property at Hampstead, as in any other part of the country". However, he was in a minority and the general feeling of the House was so against the Bill that it was withdrawn by its sponsor, Spencer Perceval, Sir Thomas's cousin, who said that, from the turn which the debate had taken, he would save the House the trouble of dividing by withdrawing it.[19]

Ripley now asked Holford to call another meeting of the copyholders. Finding his requests ignored, he called a meeting himself in August 1829, advertising it in the press. It was not well attended – only 22 people were there, including seven reporters from the morning papers. With Mr Fenton again in the chair, Ripley launched into a criticism both of Sir Thomas, and of the Copyholder's Committee, which he accused of going behind the backs of the copyholders. Perhaps his description of Sir Thomas's actions goes to the heart of the matter, explaining why the copyholders had been so anxious not to challenge him: "The endeavour to carry that Bill was an infamous attempt to bully upwards of two hundred most respectable copyholders out of their rights". Ripley forcefully reminded them that if it had not been for the action taken by him and his brother, the Reverend Ripley, in getting another petition drawn up and briefing the MPs, the Estate Bill would now be an Act of Parliament. He questioned the committee's authority and right to act on behalf of all the copyholders, asking how they were elected; all they had done was get a clause inserted which was of no use. He declared that a number of "the most respectable freeholders and copyholders were strongly opposed to the bill [and] dissatisfied with the kind of opposition which was offered ... last year". He moved that a subscription be raised for funds to oppose "any bill that may be brought forward in the next session of Parliament". He read a letter from Lord Mansfield, offering to subscribe £50, and said he had also been in touch with Lord Clifton, Thomas Neave and others.[20] He was supported by Mr Kelly, who said they were all indebted to Ripley for his exertions in opposing the Bill and the resolution was carried.[21]

Sir Thomas, presumably surprised and annoyed at this unexpected setback to his plans, offered to meet the copyholders to ascertain their grievances, either at Charlton House, or at his Steward's house in Carey Street, London. Deputed to meet him and report back to the copyholders were Thomas Sheppard, who lived at Bowling Green House and became MP for Frome in 1832; Henry White, son of the builder who had faced down old General Wilson in 1781; and C. H Winfield.[22]

If the copyholders were under any remaining illusion that Sir Thomas might offer some sort of conciliation, they were in for a rude awakening. "Considerable discussion" took place between them, and Sheppard and White sent him a transcript of it for approval to make sure they had not misrepresented or misunderstood his words; he sent it back with his corrections in red. Citing the Statute of Merton, he categorically denied the right of the copyholders to get materials from the waste of the manor without his consent, and claimed he had the right to enclose any part of it: "No exception is made of the Manor of Hampstead ... in the Statute of Merton". Neither did he admit "that the copyholders generally have rights of pasture", although he conceded their right to improve their copyholds and would willingly give consent to a reasonable but limited extent, so long as his rights and interests were not compromised. He and his Steward even went so far as to deny that any copyholder had the right to attend the Court Baron unless they were summoned; to claim that it was not unusual to summon the same persons repeatedly; and to assert that it was his right to appoint who he wanted to the Homage and the Jury on the Court Leet. He declared that he had every intention of applying to Parliament again, but because of the "misstatements and false alarms which arose from a misconstruction" of his first Bill, he would strike out all the clauses respecting the copyholders and would not include the Heath or any part of the Waste in his schedule. In effect, far from conciliating the copyholders Sir Thomas had declared war.[23]

## A new Bill

The new Bill was introduced in Parliament and another public meeting was called in May 1830. This time the copyholders were united and the meeting was packed; Charles Holford was back in the chair and the Earl of Mansfield's solicitor and agent were in attendance. Despite Wilson's removal of the objectionable clauses, it was essentially the same Bill, and still highly injurious to their interests. Dissatisfaction was widespread and grievances were aired that must have been brewing for some time, in particular that the Steward packed the Homage meetings with copyholders who were likely to agree with the Lord's views (as Sir Thomas had claimed was his right): "none of the large and independent copyholders were ever summoned ... although they held copyholds of considerable value". A petition against the Bill would be sent to the House of Lords, which had postponed the second reading to allow the copyholders time to object; and a committee was appointed to organise the opposition, consisting of Samuel Hoare (the second), Holford, Smith, Paxon, and Colonel Bosanquet, Esq. who lived at The Firs, Spaniards End.[24]

Two large petitions were presented, and again *The Times* gave valuable support, printing letters, and appeals for funds to fight the case. Sir Thomas was again supported by his relatives the Percevals, now by Lord Charles Arden, another cousin. But this time his Bill got no further than the House of Lords. Attention now focused on the legal implications of old Sir Thomas's will and its codicils. Lord Mansfield (the 3rd Earl) asked "whether Parliament would ... alter the avowed and express object of the testator" unless there were "such an altered state of circumstances as rendered it imperatively necessary to make new arrangements". In his view, no such reasons were given "and it was plain, from the fact of his father allowing him to let one estate for ninety-nine years, and restricting his power in another, that he did not intend that Hampstead Heath should be let in the manner desired by the present tenant for life. ... the House ought not to interfere for the purpose of altering the will". Lord Tenterden, the Lord Chief Justice, who lived in Hendon and rode across the Heath on his way into town, agreed: "... by such a power having actually been given to the present Sir T. Wilson over his Woolwich estates, while no such power was conferred over his estate at Hampstead Heath, it was to be presumed that he ought not to have it given to him. ... the Bill ought not to pass." It was defeated by 23 votes to seven.[25]

Sir Thomas, "having found how strong and obstinate was the opposition of Lord Mansfield, ... obtained with some difficulty an interview with him at his house in Pelham Place". He challenged him as to why he was so opposed to his Estate Bill when he never opposed other private estate bills, and had not assisted him in fighting the Finchley Road plans. Mansfield's reply, according to Sir Thomas, was that: "other Estates for which private bills come before Parliament are not at Hampstead and the new road through your property does not come near Caen Wood".[26]

Sir Thomas retired, momentarily defeated. But he was soon on the attack again, now aiming directly at those who had thwarted him: if he could not develop the land he would start extracting profits from it. He opened hostilities against the copyholders in 1834, informing them "of his intention to prevent them ... from taking loam or soil from the waste for the improvement of their copyhold gardens, a privilege which they have heretofore enjoyed". They met to decide whether to submit to his demands or "defend any action at law which may be brought by the Lord".[27] They enquired about precedents and evidence of past usage and asked Mr Lyddon, the Steward, to spell out what the new arrangements might be. Lyddon, while admitting there had been a custom for the copyholders take loam and soil from the Waste, contended that it was a bad custom and that no more than 8 loads of loam or earth at 1 shilling and 6 pence per load would be permitted in future. On enquiring further afield, the copyholders discovered that at Wimbledon copyholders were indeed charged for these privileges by the lord of the manor. Therefore, although they felt that the evidence showed that the custom still existed in Hampstead, they wrote to Sir Thomas setting out their own proposals for charges. They were clearly reluctant to challenge him, recording that it was "inexpedient ... to defend any action which may be brought by the Lord". They would have to rely on his promises that he was willing allow them to continue these customs so long as they sought permission and were willing to pay.[27]

Perhaps the post of Heath-Keeper was introduced as part of this new regime. John Stevenson's diary appears to begin in 1834 and offers a glimpse of the rudimentary way in which the Heath was regulated: "Mrs. Heavens [Evans] sent for me, with Mrs. Heavens' compliments, hoping Mr. Lydden [the Steward] will not allow any trees to be planted on the hill where the people dry their close, as it will hinder them having the morning her [air]." Stevenson regularly chased cows and their owners off the land: "Hoping it will meet with the Lord's approval. I drove fifty-nine cows off the Heath, belonging to Mr. Veale". Sometimes he stayed up at night to catch thieves, putting himself in danger in the line of duty and often being abused for his pains. Village boys were troublesome, setting light to furze bushes or cutting them to use for bonfires. On one occasion he "Met boys with furze, boys ran away but two Young Gents of the swell mob stopt and struck at me with fork. I rescued the fork and have got it at my house, they ran away, I after them but they outrun me, fork marked L.R." On another occasion he was accosted by a home-owner in the Vale of Health who accused him of telling the lord of the manor that the home he was building encroached on the open land: "Mr Munyard came from the garden ... Called Stevenson, said you darned old rascal, aren't you a pretty fellow to tell Lyddon I have encroached on the Lords ... I have not ....". [28]

58

**Notes, Chapter 4**

1. Dan Bogart & Gary Richardson, *Parliament, property rights, and public goods in England: 1600 to 1815*

2. The Copyholders' Committee was set up in 1801 – not, as Professor Thompson erroneously states, "in 1819 to help the Maryon Wilson side against the Finchley Road project" – Thompson (1974), p 141. In fact, its purpose was to oppose the then Lord of the Manor, Dame Jane, who was seen to be attacking their rights. Some of the most eminent residents served on the Committee, including Lord Erskine and Samuel Hoare. Far from helping Maryon Wilson, the Vestry minutes of 1825 show that residents were in two minds about whether to oppose the Finchley Road at all.

3. Holford lived in the area where Holford Road now is.

4. Copyholders' report and petition, 14 May 1829 (LMA: M 81/8-9)

5. This account of events by the copyholders in their Report of 14 May 1829 completely undermines Professor FML Thompson's contention that: "The Heath campaigners deliberately sowed confusion" (Thompson (1974), p 147); that they presented "their case in the terms of the Heath alone" (p 150); and that it "had

to be preserved by the deceit fraud and misrepresentation which portrayed these grounds as being public property already" (p 167). They clearly did nothing of the sort; indeed, their original response was rather tepid, concentrating almost entirely on their rights, and fizzled out altogether after their effort in the Lords.

6. *The Times*, 30 May 1829

7. *Morning Chronicle*, 18 Jun 1829

8. In a garbled account of events Professor Thompson disparages William Ripley, implying that he had a personal grudge against the Steward because he was a Roman Catholic (Thompson (1974), p 143, footnote), citing no evidence of this whatsoever. In fact, Ripley had a solid C of E background, both his father and brother being vicars; he was involved with setting up Christ Church, Hampstead, and wrote a widely quoted textbook about Church of England tithes. In pursuance of his theory Thompson conflates events that happened a dozen years apart, quoting the Steward's words that Ripley had a "pique" against him. But the Steward made this remark in 1844, not 1829, possibly referring to Ripley's having asked about the possibility of enfranchisement and been told No. – letter from Ripley to Lyddon,

5 Jun 1844 (LMA: E/MW/H/03/038/014, formerly E/MW/H/III/38/14).

9. Minutes of copyholders' meetings 1801-29 (CLSAC); *Morning Chronicle*, 18 Jun 1829

10. *The Times*, 17 Jun 1829, p 2

11. *Ibid.*, p 3: letter signed "Ariel"

12. *Ibid*: letter signed "T. Gray's-inn"

13. *The Times*, 20 Jun 1829

14. 'Hampstead Heath Inclosure', *The Spectator*, 20 Jun 1829

15. *Morning Herald*, 16 Jun 1829

16. *Morning Chronicle*, 18 Jun 1829

17. *Ibid*, 6 Aug 1829

18. A staunch supporter of opposition and a maverick reformist, whose mentor was Henry Brougham, Gordon defended the agricultural distress petitions, and an inquiry into child labour in factories; he opposed the curtailment of civil liberties in 1817. www.historyofpar-liamentonline.org/volume/1820-1832/member/gordon-robert-1786-1864

19. Hansard, 19 Jun 1829; *The Mirror of Parliament*, a weekly record of debates in both Houses of Parliament, founded and edited by John Henry Barrow, Charles Dickens's maternal uncle, as a competitor to Hansard (1828–41). Between c.1831/32 and 1834, Dickens filed his reports from the Reporters' Gallery

at the Houses of Parliament for *The Mirror*.

20. Viscount Clifton was a copyholder who later owned Squire's Mount, Court Books M & N (LMA: E/MW/H/230, 231); Neave had a large holding at Branch Hill.

21. *The Times* and the *Morning Chronicle*, 6 Aug 1829

22. *The Times*, 5 Oct 1829

23. Report of meeting with Sir Thomas to General Copyholders' meeting, by Thomas Sheppard and Henry White, 2 Jan 1830; Copyholders' minutes (CLSAC: UTAH 706)

24. Meeting of the copyholders, *The Times*, May 5, 1830, p 1. Again, contrary to Professor Thompson's contention, their chief concern was clearly stated to be that the value of their property would be greatly depreciated, and their interests damaged. No mention is made of Hampstead Heath other than that the land around it would be built on.

25. HL Deb 5 May 1830, vol. 24 cc 423-4

26. Sir Thomas Maryon Wilson (1843), hand written account of events of 1830 (LMA: E/MW/H/03/038/014)

27. Copyholders' meeting, 1 Feb 1834 (CLSAC: UTAH 706)

28. *The diary of a Heath-Keeper, 1834-39* (CLSAC)

# Chapter 5
# The lungs of London

There was a gap of a decade before Wilson returned to the attack, due, it is suggested, to a recession in the building industry. But in that time much was to change. The Great Reform Act of 1832 created three new parliamentary boroughs in Middlesex, where before there were just two MPs for the whole county. One of these was St Marylebone, which included the Parish of St Pancras, and Marylebone's two MPs were to become staunch allies of their Hampstead neighbours in the Heath campaign.

The case against commons enclosures gathered increasing force as the condition of the "labouring classes" grew ever worse. Led by MPs and the press, there were more and more calls for protection of open space for exercise and recreation which might help to alleviate these problems. The very idea of fresh air was an important issue of long standing dating back as far as Tudor times. As long ago as 1661, John Evelyn's polemic, *Fumifugium*,[1] remarkably ahead of its time, suggested there should be a green belt of parks around London. Open spaces as the 'lungs' of London were now regularly alluded to in many of the debates.

34. Thomas Barnes (1785-1841), editor of *The Times* 1817-41

A significant element in the campaign, not just for Hampstead Heath, but for the wider issue of open spaces, was the stance taken by the press in general and *The Times* in particular. In 1817 Thomas Barnes, one of Leigh Hunt's circle of radical writers, took over as editor of the paper. He reshaped it with an emphasis on analysis of events and strong leading articles, and by the 1830s it was a powerful advocate of Reform, earning the nickname 'The Thunderer'. Barnes's successor, John Delane, who took over in 1841, continued its reforming stance, and the paper devoted many columns to the issue of open spaces, supporting their preservation and setting the tone for decades to come; its arguments still have resonance today. Its role as opinion-former in supporting the campaign to save the Heath cannot be overstated. In 1825 an article of nearly 2,000 words introduced the idea that the 'Hampstead hills' must remain a barrier to the expansion of London: "The toil of getting to the verge of the town on any side of it is unspeakable, and increases daily; ... the Hampstead hills on the north, and the Surrey range on the south, remain very perfect, and form the only hope of an impassable barrier to the unbridled rage of building. ... It particularly behoved [the Government] not to part with any space which was at all calculated to better the common atmosphere. The Parks were called the lungs of the capital".[2]

As the paper of record, *The Times* reported almost every vestry, parish and public meeting, the various deputations, and the parliamentary debates. It published letters and, where Hampstead Heath was concerned, wrote its own forceful commentaries and editorials. Later, the weekly proceedings of the Metropolitan Board of Works and the London County Council were fully recorded. It is therefore possible to follow events and ideas as they happened.

LONDON going out of Town. — or — The March of Bricks & Mortar.

35. *London going out of town - or the march of bricks & mortar!* (1829); George Cruikshank's cartoon comments on the frenzy of construction that was taking place in London in the 1820s.

And there was plenty to report. Cruikshank's 1829 satirical cartoon, 'London Going Out of Town or the March of Bricks and Mortar', with its signpost pointing to Hampstead and said to be provoked by Sir Thomas's estate bill, reflects the growing concerns about the never-ending expansion of London. Industrialisation was causing immense problems of overcrowding and disease in rapidly growing cities, and the frenzy of building was eating up the surrounding countryside. A movement to provide allotments for the poor had begun as far back as the 1790s. Against a background of economic depression and rural unrest which resulted in the Swing Riots in the 1830s,[3] MPs regularly deplored "the rage for enclosures" which if it "had been more tempered with discretion, the country would not at that moment have been burthened with such a mass of poor as now existed".[4] The whole population "were injured by these enclosures".[5]

In 1833, at the urging of Robert Slaney MP,[6] Parliament appointed a Select Committee on Public Walks, "to consider the best means of securing open spaces in the immediate vicinity of populous towns, ... to promote the health and comfort of the inhabitants" and ameliorate "the miserable condition of the poor".[7] Significantly, Slaney pointed out that "there were in the neighbourhood of some large towns commons which might be advantageously used" to create public walks. They were often the only land freely available to the public and were being rapidly enclosed, often (as with Maryon Wilson's Hampstead estate bills), in a secretive and misleading way. The Committee particularly recommended that the Government should take steps to preserve Primrose Hill, as open space.[8]

A Common Fields' Enclosure Bill, in 1834, purporting to be about agricultural fields rather than commons, aroused great opposition because it was seen in reality to be an attempt to give even more powers to landowners to enclose commons. MPs were very concerned that it would "deprive the poorer classes of society of that healthful recreation ... obtained by having free access to unenclosed common lands".[5] *The Spectator* emphasised the threat it posed to the London commons: "Few of our readers are aware that a Bill for facilitating the Enclosure of Open and Arable Fields in England and Wales has reached almost its last stage in the House of Peers having been hurried through the House of Commons with little or no discussion. Under this bill, Hampstead and Putney Heaths, Blackheath, Wimbledon, Roehampton, Wandsworth, and Clapham Commons, in the neighbourhood of London ... may be enclosed." The article deplored "the deceit and subterfuge" with which many of these bills were promoted through Parliament: "Had the measure been avowedly for the enclosure of heaths, the alarm would have been sounded, and the bill would have been arrested in its earlier stages: but the contrivers artfully describe it as a measure for facilitating the enclosure of 'open and arable fields'".[9]

However, two important provisions were secured: one was a clause exempting common fields near towns from enclosure, and, where London was concerned, within ten miles of the city.[10] The other, secured by Joseph Hume, MP for Middlesex,[11] was a resolution: "That in all Inclosure Bills provision be made for leaving an open space sufficient for the ... exercise and recreation of the neighbouring population".[12] This radical reformer regarded any enclosure bill as "a landed proprietors' Bill; ... it would take away from poor men ... the enjoyment of air and exercise on these commons".[13] The great Sir Robert Peel himself agreed that: "It was most desirable that the neighbourhood of manufacturing towns, and indeed of all towns, should have some place where the population might find the means of innocent recreation. Such an arrangement would have a most beneficial effect ... on their health".[12] Debates on the provision of open space and allotments raged on well into the 1840s, often invoking events at Hampstead Heath.

## The Portland scandal

In a curious episode of just the sort described in *The Spectator*, a surreptitious attempt was made to enclose Hampstead Heath under the guise of creating a cemetery on Primrose Hill. The Portland Cemetery Company introduced a Bill in 1837, seeking power to enclose not just land at Primrose Hill, but fifty acres anywhere within ten miles of North London. Moreover, it included clauses referring to a power for the Lord of the Manor of Hampstead to sell his interest in the Heath. As seemed to happen with so many of these bills, it passed two readings in the Commons and its committee stage before the public found out about it. An article in *The Observer* and letters to *The Times* revealed that it was, in fact, a bill to establish a building company to enclose and lease out Primrose Hill.

The Hampstead Vestry invited the parliamentary counsel for the rival London Cemetery Company, a Mr. S. Motte, to a meeting to explain the provisions of the bill, in particular those that gave power to enclose Primrose Hill or Hampstead Heath. Thomas Toller, the Hampstead Vestry Clerk, reminded everyone of how in 1829 and 1830, the parish had similarly not been given notice of bills which affected their rights. The House of Commons was petitioned against it and Paddington and St Pancras Vestries also protested. St Marylebone went further and demanded that Primrose Hill be bought for the public. But the matter then descended into scandal as it transpired that several members of the parliamentary committee who had allowed the Bill to proceed were also trustees, directors or shareholders of the Portland Company, revealing a serious conflict of interest. Amid calls for an inquiry into the conduct of the clerk to the committee, the Bill was thrown out.[14].

St Marylebone followed up its call for Primrose Hill to be acquired with a delegation directly to the Prime Minister, Lord Melbourne, with the eventual result that it was secured for the public in 1842 by the Government. Gratifyingly, for ever cost-conscious ministers, it was achieved through an exchange of land between the Crown and Eton College rather than any capital outlay. It was one of the first public parks in London and was followed by Victoria and Battersea Parks in 1845 and 1846.

Thus, since 1803, when Sir John Sinclair called so memorably and forcefully for wastes to be enclosed, circumstances had completely changed. The movement to create public parks was now well under way, and preserving green open space for public amenity and outdoor recreation, especially in increasingly overcrowded and polluted towns, was firmly on the agenda.

## New perspectives

Hampstead too was changing. New families had arrived, many of them self-made City men, merchants and lawyers, who brought new vigour and perspectives to the campaign. As the City changed from a place of residence to one of offices and businesses, Hampstead, like other suburbs within a convenient distance, became ever more popular as a London residence. And with the new Unitarian Chapel establishing itself on Red Lion Hill (the Rosslyn Hill Chapel),[15] it continued to attract Dissenters who brought with them a strong sense of civic responsibility. They included in particular two families closely connected by marriage, friendship and professional ties: the Fields, who went on to found the Hampstead Heath Protection Society, and the Sharpes.

Edwin Field – whose family was descended from Oliver Cromwell through his grandmother, and one of whose ancestors, Richard Cromwell, was a Hampstead resident in the 1750s – was a distinguished lawyer who devoted much of his life to law reform. He was instrumental, as Secretary of the Royal Commission in the 1860s, in getting the present Royal Courts of Justice built, and his statue still stands in the building today. He was involved, too, in legislation to improve the position of Dissenters, giving his services *pro bono* (his father having been a Unitarian minister). Field was also a keen artist and painter and took a leading part in campaigning for the Fine Arts Copyright Act of 1862, and in setting up the Slade School of Art in 1871. He got to know

36. Edwin Wilkins Field (1804-71); from *A Memorial Sketch* by Thomas Sadler

the Sharpe family when he and William Sharpe were articled in the same City law firm and then went into partnership together. He married Sharpe's sister Mary. William's brothers, Henry and Daniel, set up H&D Sharpe, a City merchant house trading with Portugal. Henry and Edwin Field both moved to Hampstead in the 1840s. Henry lived first in Heath Street and then from 1865 at The Grove (now Admiral's House), while Edwin established himself at Squire's Mount.[16]

These were men who had no particular attachment to the old cause of copyholders' rights. Their lives were characterised by a new kind of social awareness manifesting itself in a generous concern for others, and their concern for the Heath was as a public amenity for those less privileged than themselves. Sharpe and Field both devoted much spare time before work and in the evenings to teaching classes for young working men: Sharpe helped establish the Hampstead Reading Rooms in 1842, and Field set up the Hampstead Conversazione Society which met at his home, providing lectures on science and art for them. Sharpe installed the first drinking fountain in Hampstead in 1859,[17] and seats on Haverstock Hill and on the Heath. But he "lived his active ...

HENRY SHARPE,
MERCHANT,
BORN AUGUST 21ST 1802, DIED APRIL 27TH 1873.

THIS MONUMENT IS RAISED
BY THOSE WHO, DERIVED BENEFIT IN THEIR YOUTH
FROM HIS DISINTERESTED EFFORTS FOR THEIR INSTRUCTION
AND IMPROVEMENT AND WHO, THOUGH SCATTERED THROUGH THE
WORLD GRATEFULLY UNITE TO PERPETUATE THE MEMORY
OF A LIFE DEVOTED TO THE GOOD OF OTHERS.
*"None of us liveth to himself."*

37. Henry Sharpe as depicted on a memorial plaque in St John's Church, Hampstead

useful life quite out of the public eye" and "shrank from any public recognition" of his remarkable public spirit and devotion to the "service of man". His name is now forgotten but there is a quiet memorial to him in Hampstead Parish Church, placed by those he helped, to remember "a life devoted to the good of others".[18]

In 1858, Isaac Solly Lister, another City solicitor, came to live at Upper Heath (the once fashionable summer rendezvous of the Kit-Cat Club). Another Unitarian, like the Sharpes and the Fields, he taught classes of boys after work[19] and devoted much time to other charitable causes.

Thomas Turner and Philip Hemery Le Breton were both barristers. Turner came to live at Fenton House in the 1840s and was to become Hampstead Vestry's first representative on the Metropolitan Board of Works in 1855. He played a hugely significant role in the Heath campaign, leaving his own record in an informative account of events in the 1850s.[20] He was followed as Hampstead's representative on the MBW by Le Breton, a member of the Inner Temple. Also a Unitarian, he was born in Jersey in 1806 and was educated at Westminster School. He married the authoress Anna Laetitia Aiken, niece of Mrs Barbauld (who had known the Hoare family in their Stoke Newington days before they moved to Hampstead), and in 1851 he settled in John Street (now Keats Grove). Le Breton served on the Vestry from 1855 until 1880 and took over from Turner at the MBW in 1859, later playing a leading role as chairman of its Parks Committee. Other lawyers who played a role in the campaign were W.J. Strickland Cookson, a colleague of Edwin Field, and Henry Ray Freshfield, member of a City law firm that still bears his name today.[21] The Hampstead Vestry was not short of legal expertise!

A new generation of the old-established families had grown up and were prepared to take a much more forceful line. Thomas Toller, involved from the

38. John Gurney Hoare (1810-75)

beginning as clerk to the Copyholders' Committee from 1827, now began to play a more assertive role. A solicitor from a respected family of lawyers long established at Hampstead, he gave a lifetime of service to the community, serving as Vestry Clerk, as Clerk to the Guardians of the Poor, and as Superintendent Registrar. His father Edward lived at Admiral's House from 1830 to 1848, while Thomas lived in Well Walk. They were related to the Holfords by marriage.

John Gurney Hoare inherited his father Samuel's mantle from the 1840s. A popular figure, he was chairman of the bench of magistrates, a vestryman and a supporter of numerous local philanthropic causes.

Henry Crabb Robinson, a lawyer and *Times* correspondent, who had many friends among this Hampstead circle, was full of praise for their qualities. Of Le Breton he wrote: "He has no prejudices and no antipathies, but manifests a generous love of goodness." And Strickland Cookson, who was also active in law reform, was "one of the most able and safe counsellors. ... In judgment, among our common friends, I do not know his equal".[22]

But support for Hampstead Heath also came from another more unexpected quarter: the Grosvenors. The Grosvenor family was extraordinarily philanthropic, each generation instilling a strong sense of moral principle in their children, believing that along with position, power and prestige came civic responsibilities. Sir Robert Grosvenor (1st Baron Ebury) and his nephew Hugh Lupus, Grosvenor, 1st Duke of Westminster, devoted their lives to meeting that obligation in a host of public positions. Both men actively supported efforts to save the Heath at various stages and gave generously of their time and resources to the campaign for it. The Duke, who may have been aware of his uncle's involvement in the campaign to save the Heath in the 1850s, later played an important role in saving Parliament Hill and in the founding of the Hampstead Heath Protection Society.

Sir Robert had followed Joseph Hume as MP for Middlesex in 1847 and shared his concern for the condition of the poor. He knew and worked with Dr Thomas Southwood Smith, another Unitarian, physician, social reformer, and tireless campaigner for decent living conditions for the poor. The two men were involved in setting up the Metropolitan Association for the Improvement of the Dwellings of the Industrious Classes.[23] Leigh Hunt, Smith's patient for a time, eulogised him in his autobiography[24] as his "old and distinguished friend", and "the Physician to Mankind". Significantly for the story of Hampstead Heath, Southwood Smith lived in Fitzroy Park, Highgate, in a Victorian villa called Hillside,[25] and was the grandfather of Octavia Hill, of whom more anon (p 115).

39. Sir Robert Grosvenor (1801-93), 1st Baron Ebury, MP for Middlesex 1847-57

**Notes, Chapter 5**

1. *Fumifugium, or, The inconvenience of the Aer and Smoak of London Dissipated* (1661)
2. *The Times,* 24 Aug 1825
3. Rural workers in south east England rose in violent demonstrations demanding higher wages and an end to the threshing machine which destroyed their winter employment.
4. Bucklebury Enclosure Bill, HC Deb 8 May 1834, vol. 24 cc 748-53
5. Common Fields' Enclosure Bill, HC Deb 31 Jul 1824, vol. 25 cc 787-93
6. Whig MP for Shrewsbury; he later went on to promote the Recreation Grounds Act of 1859 to promote the provision of parks.
7. HC Deb 21 Feb 1833, vol. 15 cc 1049-59
8. *The Times, 7 Sep 1833*
9. *The Spectator,* 13 Aug 1836
10. Common Fields'Enclosure Bill,HC 19 Aug 1836 vol. 35 1328-30

11. A Scottish doctor and reformer, who worked with other philanthropists, to help improve the condition of the working classes,
12. Enclosure Bills - Public Recreation, HC 9 Mar 1837, vol. 37 cc 162-4
13. Commons Enclosure, HC 4 Jul 1845, vol. 82 cc 15-52
14. HC Deb 8 Jun 1837, vol. 38 cc 1247-9; *The Times,* reports and letters May 1837
15. Legal constraints on Unitarianism had gradually been lifted, beginning with Doctrine of the Trinity Act 1813.
16. Edwin Field's daughters - Emily and her sisters - lived at Squire's Mount until 1921, finally leaving the whole estate, which included two "shepherds' cottages" on East Heath Road, to the National Trust.
17. For more detail about Sharpe's fountains, see David A.Hayes, 'Drinking fountains and horse troughs …', *Camden History Review* 27 (2003)

18. P.W. Clayden (1883), *Samuel Sharpe, egyptologist and translator of the Bible* (K. Paul & Trench). Sharpe's nieces founded Channing School. The memorial plaque is in the East Gallery of Hampstead Parish Church, surveyed by CHS in the 1970's (www.hampsteadparishgchurch.org.uk)
19. All three men were involved in the Lancastrian (or 'Monitorial') system schools for the education of poor children, started by Joseph Lancaster in Southwark in 1798, but which later fell out of favour.
20. Turner became Treasurer of Guy's Hospital and later left Hampstead.
21. Freshfield's father had joined the City firm of solicitors Winter & Kaye, established in the 18th century, and the Freshfield name was incorporated in its title. Both Henry and his brother, Charles Kay Freshfield, lived in Hampstead and Henry Ray was also closely involved in saving Ashdown Forest.

22. Robinson, Henry Crabb, *Diary, reminiscences, and correspondence … 1775-1867*
23. Southwood Smith worked closely with Edwin Chadwick and Robert Slaney MP (who campaigned for the Public Walks Committee); he helped establish the Health of Towns Association, which led to the model dwellings movement
24. *The autobiography of Leigh Hunt* (1850, Smith, Elder & Co.), Preface, p X; 'Physician of mankind' is from his poem *Our Cottage.*
25. Demolished in the 1950s and since replaced by six houses called the Hexagon; see David A. Hayes, 'From Southwood Smith to Octavia Hill', *Camden History Review* 33 (2009).

# Chapter 6

# Private versus public interest

It was against this background of a reformed Parliament, a rising tide of antagonism towards enclosures in towns as they affected the plight of the poor and dispossessed, and loss of green space in general, that Sir Thomas Maryon Wilson, oblivious to all these developments, tried again in the spring of 1843. He launched his third attempt with an Estate Bill similar to that of 1830, and again without letting anyone in Hampstead know about it. He claimed that he had informed Thomas Toller, who hit back firmly in a letter sent to all the copyholders, making it clear that, as in 1829 and 1830, "no communication whatever was made to me either by Sir T.M. Wilson, or his Agent"; yet "a Bill interfering with the interests" of the copyholders "could not with propriety be introduced into the House unless [they] were parties to it".[1]

A war of words broke out between Toller and Sir Thomas, who bombarded the area with printed circulars explaining that he did not intend to interfere with the copyholds and that he had no intention of enclosing the Heath. Sharpe thought these letters "very silly, ... not stating out boldly what it is that he is doing; and he loses character by the transaction, and I should think will not carry his bill". Sir Thomas was "very sore about it" and was already "furious against Hoare and the Hampstead Gentry for their opposition, abus[ing] them in good round terms". "He is evidently not the man to carry a difficult point; he could not, even to me, talk of it without getting out of temper." Sharpe thought it would be very sad "to see the surrounding fields built upon", but realised that, because the land was demesne land, "we have not so much grounds for opposing."

The Copyholders' Committee was reconvened and, at a public meeting chaired by Samuel Hoare and addressed by Rev. Allatson Burgh, Toller read out the Bill; it was resolved to send a petition against it to Parliament.[2] They also did some research, discovering papers from the 1824 Finchley Road Bill showing that Sir Thomas was now contradicting what he had said then about building at Hampstead. They pointed out that the Steward of the Manor, Lyddon, had been one of the witnesses to all the codicils. However they did not, apparently discover Sir Thomas's 1824 statement that his father did not grant a power to make building leases at Hampstead because he wanted that "left as it was"; a missed opportunity that would have revealed Sir Thomas as a liar. Had the Lords known of this statement, none of his estate bills would have been countenanced; Parliament would not flout a testator's expressed wishes or intentions. Even today lawyers are wary of doing so.

Attention now shifted to the terms of the will and the implication of codicils that gave power for building leases at Woolwich and Charlton, but not for Hampstead. Even without knowing about Sir Thomas's 1824 statement,

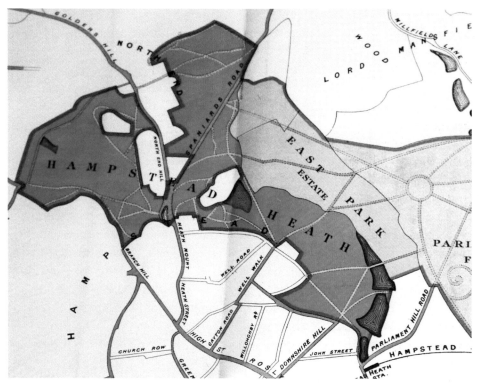

40. The East Park estate in relation to East Heath; building on it would drive a wedge into any plans for saving the adjoining lands. From 'A plea for the extension of Hampstead Heath' and the preservation of Parliament Fields', St Pancras Vestry, July 1885

peers and MPs drew that conclusion for themselves from what was implied in the codicils to the will. It is striking that even Sir Thomas's supporters in Parliament were anxious to make clear their support for the preservation of the Heath.

The danger to East Heath from Wilson's plans also began to be understood by everyone. Even if he was not technically trying to enclose the Heath, any development on the East Park fields would effectually "inclose" it, because East Heath would be surrounded by houses and "must be cut up ... in order to form roads to the new buildings".[3] Wilson described Toller's claims as absurd, nevertheless admitting that "a single road on some part of the Heath would be required"; he accused Toller of unfairness and "an abuse of language" and continued to deny that he had not informed the copyholders.[4]

Two remarkable letters appeared in *The Times,* written as though the author was Hampstead Heath itself and spelling out the true nature of the threat:

"My complaint against you, Sir Thomas is, not that you seek by an enclosure bill to appropriate me to your own use ... but that you want to spoil ... all my beauty, so that I shall no longer be as I now am.... That done, I may be thrown as a worthless weed away".[5] "Sir Thomas Wilson seeks ... to build me round and brick me in. For beauty and health there is nothing in the neighbourhood of the metropolis to be compared to me. I am public property, and I throw myself upon your protection in the full confidence that you will not suffer me to be sacrificed to a greediness of gain, a selfish desire to accumulate wealth, than which there is not another assignable or imaginable reason for the bill which Sir Thomas Wilson seeks to obtain".[6]

The paper followed this up with its own vigorous 1000-word report recounting the history of events in detail, the terms of old Sir Thomas's will of 1806 and the significance of its codicils, repeating verbatim some of Toller's statements from the letters sent to all the copyholders.[7] The Bill was withdrawn.

The next year Wilson tried a new tack, with a Bill to give him power to sell the whole Hampstead estate, including the lordship of the manor. But now he found himself opposed from an entirely unexpected quarter: his own family. Extraordinary letters from his brother's trusted family solicitor at Dunmow, William Thomas Wade,[8] reveal the state of dissension between the two brothers. As Sir Thomas's heir, John Maryon Wilson would have to be party to any plans for the estate and he made it clear to Wade that he did not approve of his "brother's wishes as to the sale of the Hampstead Estate ...". Wade agreed with his reservations: "You have arrived at years of discretion to judge for yourself as to the propriety of joining in the proposed application to Parliament; ... you will not, I conceive, do an act which may possibly prejudice those who may come after you, and are now incapable of acting for themselves." He censures Sir Thomas's plan as an "ill-advised and unprofitable measure, half digested and arising more from caprice and whim than from any sound judgement or discretion. ... Your brother seems to point at me, as if I was influencing your mind in this matter ..." These last significant words are underlined.

Wade informed the Steward, Lyddon, on 3 February 1844 that "Mr Wilson has an objection personally to the proposed application to Parliament for the sale of the Hampstead Estate". Lyddon became obstructive and difficult, refusing Wade's request to see Sir Thomas's petition for the Bill, and, in reply to a request for sight of his brother's will appearing to make covert threats, perhaps implying that the will might be changed if John does not co-operate.[9] But John Wilson and William Wade (who were related by marriage) were clearly at pains not allow this fraught relationship with Sir Thomas to become public knowledge. Wade writes that they were anxious to avoid "a rupture which you would be so unwilling to create as I was to recommend",[9] so they acceded to Sir Thomas's demands and the Bill was introduced in the Lords by his cousin the Earl of Egmont, another member of the Perceval family.

Told that his arguments - that there was no residence in Hampstead, or that it was far from his estates in Kent and Sussex, and that money raised from such a sale could be used to purchase other estates – would not secure the passing of the Bill, Sir Thomas even sought legal counsel. On being advised that his case would be strengthened if he could show that an advantageous opportunity had arisen to invest in an estate near Charlton, he began scanning the sales columns![10]

The long and carefully considered report to the Lords by the judges who scrutinised the Bill – Mr Baron Parke (later Lord Wensleydale) and Mr Justice

41. Wyldes Farm, by John Wood, 1857.
A popular summer retreat for many artists and writers,
among them Linnell, Dickens and Collins (the father of Wilkie)

Cresswell – sowed seeds of doubt: "it is reasonable that such bill do pass into a law unless it should appear to your Lordships that the testator, by giving a power to grant long leases of part of his estates only, intended that none should be granted of the residue, and that by this act such intention may be evaded".[11]

Lord Chief Justice Denman, who often stayed at Wyldes Farm, but who was "not in the habit of giving his opinion without grave deliberation",[12] said he was pained to have to oppose "a Gentleman with reference to the disposal or appropriation of his own property. This, however, was a very peculiar case." He fully understood that while the Bill was not technically an attempt to inclose the Heath, in effect it would give power to any builder to build around it. On the subject of the will, "it was a direct overruling and altering of the intentions of the testator" and would be wrong. He quoted his predecessor, Lord Tenterden, who had said of a previous application "If we pass it, it is making, in Parliament, a will for a man after his death". The newly succeeded 4th Earl of Mansfield naturally also spoke against it. The Bill was rejected.[13]

Following this decision, *The Times* published an interesting letter, focusing on what now began to emerge as the crucial issue that set the Heath case apart from other estate bills. Although praising the Lords' decision to reject, it pointed out that their claims about the will were inconsistent: Parliament constantly disregarded the intentions of testators in almost every estate bill they passed, unfettering entails or overriding wills, "enabling the sale of a property the testator never intended should be sold". But, the letter pointed out, there was a crucial distinction between all those cases and that of Sir Thomas Wilson. In other cases the result would affect no-one but the parties concerned; in the case of Sir Thomas Wilson, granting his wish would inflict damage on the wider public "and, as guardians of the public interests, it was their duty to have regard to those interests and to refuse to aid a purpose from which the public would suffer". The letter-writer also suggested: "It may therefore be worth the while of the Commissioners for Woods and Forests to treat for the Purchase of the Heath, and give it for ever to the London public".[14]

After this fourth defeat Maryon Wilson changed tack altogether and began to consider the possibility of developing East Park; he could not grant long building leases to someone else, but he was free to build houses on it himself. He commissioned plans for 28 large villas along the lines of those in Regent's Park and started work in October 1844. Consequently, he visited Hampstead a good deal at this time, usually staying at Jack Straw's Castle Hotel.[15]

At first it was thought that the ground was being prepared for a cemetery, perhaps because of the Portland episode in 1837, and a report to that effect appeared in *The Times*. But it soon became clear that Sir Thomas had something else in mind. In fact, he was laying out the ground for a new road to the proposed villas, requiring a viaduct to be built across a swampy valley which was to be drained to form an ornamental pool. But the excavations repeatedly collapsed and it took until 1845 just to get to the point of laying a foundation stone, for which, with his customary bravado, he staged an extravagant ceremony. *The Times* relented from its critical stance for the occasion, to give a rather

42. Jack Straw's Castle as it may have looked in the 1840s when frequented by both Sir Thomas Maryon Wilson and Charles Dickens. Dickens' friend and biographer John Forster recounts an invitation to meet him there for dinner: "You don't feel disposed, do you, to muffle yourself up and start off with me for a good brisk walk over Hampstead Heath? I knows a good 'ous there where we can have a red-hot chop for dinner, and a glass of good wine' which led to our first experience of Jack Straw's Castle, memorable for many happy meetings in coming years."

43. The Viaduct built by Sir Thomas Maryon Wilson

jolly account of proceedings. A large crowd was entertained by a band of musicians who had marched to the ground playing "a variety of lively airs, not forgetting the never tiring polka. They were followed by a party of amateur 'artillery', who mounted their pieces on the heights, ready to announce the auspicious event by a discharge of cannon".[16]

Wilson arrived with a party of relatives and friends, and his sister, Mrs Drummond, laid the first stone to a hearty burst of cheers, accompanied by the playing of the national anthem. Dinner was then provided for the workmen in a marquee on Parliament Hill, at Sir Thomas's expense.[17] Hampstead tradesmen also celebrated the event. The project, which at first was unpopular was now seen by them as something that would benefit Hampstead by increasing the trade of the town. *The Times* rather mistakenly added: "and it must, in justice to Sir Thomas Wilson, be stated that the East-park does not in any way whatever encroach upon the heath or any of those portions of Hampstead to which the public are in the habit of resorting for recreation".[16] However, Henry Sharpe recorded in his *Journal* that he refused his invitation to the event and that none of the Hampstead gentry attended. It took three years to complete the viaduct, which was long known as Wilson's Folly.

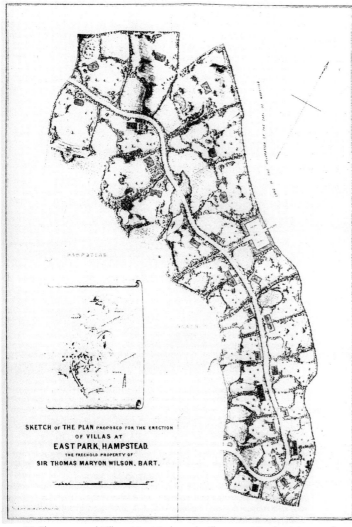

SKETCH of THE PLAN PROPOSED FOR THE ERECTION
OF VILLAS AT
EAST PARK, HAMPSTEAD.
THE FREEHOLD PROPERTY OF
SIR THOMAS MARYON WILSON, BART.

When Wilson began to clear East Park fields for the proposed villas, Sharpe confided to his *Journal:* "I am so grieved at seeing it done"... "The public should buy the fields but I fear it cannot be managed". Wilson had admitted "that it was done to spite Lord Mansfield and the Hoares". He "is evidently spoiled by living entirely with people who are dependent upon him and are obliged to laugh at his jokes. He is a pretty instance of how little riches contribute to a man's happiness; here he is with perhaps £10,000 a year going to put himself

44. The proposed Villas at East Park; each villa was set in about 1 acre of ground on either side of Sir Thomas's new road, with lodges at the entrances

to all manner of trouble and vexation, probably for the rest of his life, in order to add perhaps a couple of thousand to it, having all the while no family to spend it on, or to leave it to."

A more sensible man would have come to some mutually agreeable arrangement over East Park. But only a few courses of brick foundations were laid for the first villa – Sir Thomas got no further, perhaps realising that such a scheme was beyond his resources. He also planted several thousand trees including willows, firs and Turkey oaks on East Heath itself to provide an "ornamental" park for his proposed new houses.[18] Charles Dickens's journal *Household Words* took a pot shot at him: "We have noticed a number of infantile trees cased in with wooden hurdles. ... Who planted them? Had he any business to do so? They are an eyesore. Where will they end? Did not someone once say, that somebody, we forget, and do not care who, tried to enclose Hampstead Heath? If he does so, may his heirs find a quick road to their inheritance! It must have been some half-fledged baronet, the second of the family, who, having a half title to his own property, fancied that no title at all might suffice for appropriating that of the public. Whoever he was, may his dreams be redolent of Smithfield, may nightmare tread with donkey hoofs on his chest, and may visions of angry laundresses scald his brain with weak tea!" [19]

It was becoming ever clearer that the only sure way to protect the Heath and the adjoining lands was to try to buy them, and suggestions began to be voiced that the wealthy Hampstead residents should get together to do it. That was easy to say, but who would then look after it? It would have been beyond the capacity of the Vestry. Could the Government be persuaded to take action? Primrose Hill had been declared a public park by the Government; why not Hampstead Heath? The exasperated Earl of Mansfield was said to have threatened to line Spaniards Road with a row of terraced housing in retaliation, and both he and the Hoares had tried to buy East Park. But the real problem, as they were to

discover, was Sir Thomas's obstinacy and greed – he insisted on demanding the inflated prices that building land could attract, rather than the reasonable amount it could be expected to fetch as 'waste' land. When the copyholders offered to withdraw their opposition if Sir Thomas would agree not to build near the Heath, he dismissed it as "bribery". He was not prepared to cooperate or compromise in any way.

Nevertheless, a first attempt to persuade the Government to consider buying the land began – the curious

45. Charles Robert Cockerell (1788-1863)

74

and little-known episode of the Cockerell plan of 1853. Charles Robert Cockerell was a distinguished architect, surveyor of St Paul's Cathedral and Architect to the Bank of England. He lived at Ivy House, North End (later the home of Anna Pavlova), from 1838. His elaborate scheme proposed creating a large park, including not only the Heath, but the adjoining lands of East Park, South Hill Park, Telegraph Hill, Parliament Hill, and part of Golders Hill; and linking the whole thing to Primrose Hill by means of a curved, tree-lined boulevard, part of which was the Belsize avenue – in all about 350 acres. The plan was published in *The Builder* with an enthusiastic description of its features: "Parks we have it is true, but none to compare with what this would be". But, it warned, that as some of the land was already let out for building, by next year it may be too late.[20]

The Copyholders' Committee had, unsurprisingly, now faded away and leadership of the campaign had passed to the Vestry. A public meeting on 22 June 1853 to discuss the Cockerell plan unanimously resolved "... that it is important to the interests of the inhabitants of the metropolis, and of this parish and neighbourhood that the use and enjoyment of Hampstead-heath as a place of Public Recreation should be secured through the purchase by the Government of the said Heath together with such portions of the adjoining ground as are essential to its beauty".[21] It was thought that Cockerell's scheme could cost about £100,000 but the principal obstacle remained Sir Thomas's extortionate price for the Heath of £600 per acre. A large committee was appointed to carry the matter forward.[22] The resolution was sent to the to the Commissioners of Woods and Forests and Land Revenues, and a deputation was made to the prime minister. He was willing to recommend a contribution from government but made it clear that the whole expense could not be born without some local contribution. The plan fell through.

At the same time they were fighting off renewed attempts by Sir Thomas to get estate bills through Parliament, beginning in May 1853 with his fifth bill. His new solicitor, William Loaden, called a public meeting in Hampstead but, if his aim was to placate the opposition, he only made things worse. That notice of the meeting was given only the previous evening was described by Gurney Hoare as "rather sharp practice". Yet again the Bill was already before Parliament, whereas the meeting ... "should have been summoned before the Bill was brought in (cheers)." Loaden tried to explain at length why everyone was wrong. In reply Hoare told him: The meeting would not be hoodwinked" by his recitation of the will and codicils and his assertion that the judges "did not understand" – they were not stupid. The meeting could judge for itself who was right: Mr Loaden, who was an interested party, or the judges whose job it was to be disinterested.[23]

Dickens's weekly journal *All the Year Round* also described a public meeting attended by Sir Thomas's agent, at which a compromise proposal was discussed. "But the agent refused to make any such engagement; for him it was all or nothing, 'the whole hog, bristles and all'". Whether this was the same meeting, or perhaps a fictionalised account, it certainly rings true.[24] St Marylebone and St Pancras backed Hampstead with petitions against the new Bill.

Sir Thomas also faced further hostility from his brother John, who was clearly becoming increasingly annoyed by his conduct. John's solicitor, William Wade, told Loaden that "Sir Thos M. Wilson should write to his brother [Wade's underlining] as to what he wishes him to join in doing at Hampstead". But there was a further more serious complication: John's eldest son, a lieutenant serving with the 33rd West India Regiment, was now of age, and as a 'remainderman'[25] his support too had to be secured. But he had been posted to Kingston, Jamaica, and Sir Thomas was demanding that he provide an unlimited power of attorney in his absence. The young lieutenant found these demands excessive. He had to find solicitors in Jamaica to act for him and a letter from them makes quite clear that he was not disposed to give "aid to the passing of a Bill that shall contemplate more than the mere extension of the power to grant building leases, and that being the case we think the Power of Attorney should be restricted in its language to that particular object".[26]

The lieutenant spelt out his irritation at his uncle's demands in no uncertain terms in a letter to Wade from Kingston: "I have not the remotest idea of risking my life for anybody's Bill, unless it were something to my own advantage and that something tangible. I hope there is an end to deeds for a few years. ... I wrote to Sir Thomas last mail and told him I had objected to sign an unlimited power of attorney but that I would sign his deed ... also that if he wants anything of the sort in future he'd better make arrangements for payment of expenses out here. I don't mince matters. If he don't like it, I don't consider I owe him much or anyone else at the same time".[27] Eventually the duly signed document was sent and the bill proceeded. But in his desperation Sir Thomas resorted to subterfuge, trying to deceive the scrutinising judges by withholding the codicils. The House of Lords had to order him to produce them.[28]

Lord Shaftesbury led the opposition, now focused firmly on the public interest. Nobody, he said, was depriving Sir Thomas of his rights. He "had the full benefit of the property devised to him by his father's will, and no one wished to disturb him in it", but "Their Lordships ... were bound to inquire whether the powers asked for would, if granted, be beneficial or injurious to the public". He emphasised that "... the inhabitants of Hampstead and the neighbourhood would have no objection to Sir Thomas Wilson building on either side of [the Finchley] road." The Bill was stopped at the second reading.[29]

For once Sir Thomas appeared to have listened. His sixth application in 1854 was called the Finchley Road Estate Bill and concentrated on that part of the estate only. It was a semantic subterfuge and no-one was fooled. *The Times* called it "but a piratical craft. Her master showed his real colours in 1829".[30]

Lord Chief Justice Campbell pointed out that if this application was granted there was no reason why it would not also apply to the whole of Hampstead Heath. Lord Clanricarde, moving the second reading, made the point that Sir Thomas's brother and nephew had not objected to the Bill, obviously unaware of the family dissension on the matter. John Wilson had clearly been at pains not to allow the fraught relationship with his brother to become public knowledge. Clanricarde's perfectly valid argument that old Sir Thomas would probably have changed his mind if he could have known about the making of the Finchley Road, was countered by Lord Brougham: one should not set aside a will on a speculation that some possible change in the testator's intention might have occurred had he lived longer. The Bishop of Oxford warned that a Hampstead resident had written to him saying that not only would Sir Thomas not be satisfied with what this Bill sought, but that he considered it as "only the first instalment of what rightfully belonged to him, and that he was determined to have the whole of Hampstead Heath as soon as he could get it".[31] But despite the judges' advice that "there were no reasonable grounds for applying for the powers which are sought", the Bill got through the Lords.

In a wide ranging debate in the Commons, led by Lord Robert Grosvenor, the emphasis was decisively on the public interest. Grosvenor told the House of Sir Thomas Wilson's refusal to co-operate: ten years ago he had rejected the copyholders' offer to withdraw their opposition if he would agree not to build on East Park. Grosvenor revealed that he himself had been to see Wilson's agent just two days before and his refusal to contemplate any compromise "had been confirmed". He pointed out that if, as "was indeed said … Sir Thomas Wilson had no intention to build upon Hampstead Heath", it was remarkable that he refused all such offers.[32] He went on to dismiss all Sir Thomas's accusations of "exaggeration" and "misrepresentation", or that the public were being misled, or that the House was unfairly prejudiced. He considered that "the case was so plain against the measure that it required no amount of dressing up". He hoped to persuade the House that, not only as legislators, but as trustees for the public, they ought to put an end at once to any further attempt at legislation on this subject". [32]

Bernal Osborne – the son of Ralph Bernal who had spoken in 1829, and also a Middlesex MP – reminded the House of Sir Thomas's previous attempt to mislead the judges by withholding the codicils from them. "As Sir Thomas Wilson would give no pledge that he would not build on Hampstead Heath, it was clear that he had an eye … to building on that space at some future time. … by agreeing to this Bill, you conceded the whole principle." He was not much concerned with the rights of the copyholders: "the main point was the question as it related to the poorer and middling classes, who had a vested interest in the preservation of Hampstead Heath." He urged the Government to take up the matter.[32]

Sir Benjamin Hall, MP for Marylebone, who was at that very moment drawing up legislation to reform London government, suggested that it would be premature to pass this Bill just as a new governance was to be established in the metropolis.[33] He declared that "if Sir Thomas Wilson did not intend to build on Hampstead Heath let a clause be introduced in the Bill to that effect".

Robert Lowe, MP for Kidderminster, introduced a rather more cynical tone, asking why such a wealthy community did not simply raise the money to buy the land: "no doubt it was very desirable that Hampstead Heath should be preserved to the public; but, if so, let the public purchase it, and let them not employ the power given them of rejecting this Bill as a means of saving their money, or of making better terms with Sir Thomas Wilson. They were rich enough to be able to afford to be honest". Perhaps he was unaware of Sir Thomas's extortionate demands. Nevertheless, he admitted that as a lawyer he was swayed against the Bill by the matter of the codicils. The Bill was voted down by a large majority of 97 to 43.[34]

Lowe was also leader writer for *The Times* and it was not long before his views on the Hampstead community found their way into the paper, marking a notable change of stance. It now urged: "Is not this, then, a proper time for both parties ... to endeavour to arrive at an understanding calculated to promote the real interests of both? Sir T. Wilson is stalemated for the moment; the time will shortly come when the public will be checkmated on the matter of Hampstead-heath." It was becoming a race against time and something had to be done. The writer wished "to see ... negotiation conducted in a spirit of fairness on either side; ... there is no reason why the Wilson family should be expected to sacrifice their interests in the long run to the public convenience. They are entitled to a fair and reasonable price for the property, which we wish to see purchased for the sake of the public, and we have little doubt but that the public would be prepared to pay such a price. We have spent already large sums of money on parks in different quarters of London; but there is no open spot so frequented as Hampstead-heath."

This was all very fine, but the sticking point was that of making any "reasonable" terms with Sir Thomas Wilson at all, fair or otherwise. The Hampstead community had tried from the beginning; Hoare, Mansfield and Robert Grosvenor had tried; but the problem was Sir Thomas's obduracy. He was not being asked to give the land away – simply not to build on it. He refused all offers of compromise, regarding them as attempts at blackmail, and the sort of sums he demanded were in the realms of fantasy. Indeed, the article acknowledged that: "He is, however, a pertinacious partisan of his own interest. ... If five rebuffs could not dispirit him, neither will six; and so we must make up our minds every two or three years to fight this battle over again as we have fought it before. The enclosure of Hampstead-heath is with Sir T. Wilson the absorbing, idea of his life".[35]

Sir Thomas's response was to continue twisting the truth in a reply to *The Times,* yet again claiming: "I never desired either to enclose or build on Hampstead-heath; nor have I ever attempted to do so", as though that Heath clause in the 1829 Bill had never existed.[36] However, the mounting pressure must have had some effect, because in a draft for a seventh Bill in 1855, was a clause stating "that nothing in this Act shall in any wise empower or be construed to empower the said Sir T M Wilson to enclose or build upon, or let for building purposes any part or parts of Hampstead Heath, or build upon, or let for building purposes any parts of the lands on the east or west sides of the said Heath." But it was too late and Sir Thomas was perhaps now too notorious. Following yet another adverse report by the judges the Bill was withdrawn.[37]

**Notes, Chapter 6**

1. Thos. Toller, Letter to the copyholders of the Manor of Hampstead, 12 May 1843 (H&HS archive: A/1048/3/2/1/1)
2. The reports of this meeting, and Henry Sharpe's comments, further refute Professor Thompson's contention that the Heath campaigners "deliberately" used "deceit fraud and misrepresentation" to present their case in the terms of a threat to the Heath. They were perfectly frank, publicly stating their views, which were reported in the press: "no man was at liberty to build houses for his own advantage to the prejudice of the copyholders". "Most … inhabitants were induced to reside there solely on account of its beautiful heath." "They and the public had one common interest in the preservation of Hampstead Heath whilst on the other hand it was an individual interest". "The public no doubt would look after their own rights and interests but it was the duty of every copyholder to resist these encroachments". (Excerpts of the report of the public meeting, *Morning Post*, 16 May 1843)
3. Toller, letter to the copyholders, 12 May 1843

4. Sir T M W, letter to copyholders, 15 May 1843
5. Letter to *The Times*, 31 May 1843, signed "Sir Thomas, I have not the honour to be entirely yours, HAMPSTEAD HEATH"
6. Ibid., 23 May 1843, signed "Yours, etc. Hampstead Heath"
7. *The Times*, 2 Jun 1843
8. Executor and trustee of the estate from 1853 and later the Steward
9. Letters 3 Feb 1844, Wade to Lyddon; 9 Feb 1844, Wade to John Maryon Wilson (LMA: E/MW/H/03/026/054)
10. John Ruddall's opinion on the Bill for sale of the Manor, Oct 1843 (LMA: E/MW/H/III/38/14)
11. The Judges' report, 3 Jun 1844
12. HL Deb 7 Jul 1853, vol. 128 cc 1357-61 Lord Campbell. According to a later resident, Mrs Arthur Wilson, Denman "had the cottage for several summers" (HAHS, talk, 1902-03, 'Wyldes and its story').
13. HL Deb 6 Jun 1844, vol. 75 cc 312-8
14. *The Times*, 11 Jun 1844
15. Account of Sir T.M. Wilson with the Castle Hotel 1844-50 (LMA: E/MW/H/IV/28)
16. *The Times*, 4 Sep 1845
17. Since this was Lord Mansfield's land, one wonders how this was achieved. Was he trespassing?

18. Maryon Wilson evidence to Select Committee, 29 May 1865, 6068. He asked Sharpe about importing them from Portugal (Henry Sharpe, *Journal* (CLSAC)
19. Theodore Buckley, 'Hampstead Heath', *Household Words*, vol. IV, no. 79 (27 Sep 1851), p 18
20. *The Builder*, 2 Jul 1853
21. Hampstead Vestry minutes, 22 Jun 1853
22. The committee included Gurney Hoare, Le Breton, Turner, Toller, Joseph Hoare, Rev. Ainger, Clarkson Stanfield, Henry Ray Freshfield, General McInnes, Robert Pryor, Edwin Field and Cockerell.
23. *Morning Herald*, 3 Jun 1853,
24. Joseph Charles Parkinson, 'Hampstead Heath', *All the Year Round*, vol. XVII, no 409 (23 Feb 1867), p 200. It has only recently been discovered that the author of this article was Parkinson; a journalist, civil servant and social reformer, he took over as editor of *All the Year Round* when Dickens died in 1870. The account is so detailed that one suspects that Parkinson, or even Dickens himself, attended some of these meetings.
25. A person entitled to inherit, in due course, property in an estate
26. Hill Airey, solicitors, Kingston, Jamaica to Lieut. Wilson,

21 Apr 1853 (LMA: E/MW/H/03/026/039)
27. Ibid., Lieut. Wilson to W.T. Wade, 21 Apr 1853. His reference to "risking his life" is because yellow fever was rife on the island. In fact, young John never lived to receive his inheritance – he and his wife succumbed to the fever at Up Park Camp, Kingston in August that same year; J.H Lawrence-Archer (1875), *Monumental inscriptions of the British West Indies* (Chatto & Windus)
28. 'The case of Hampstead Heath', by a member of the Metropolitan Board of Works [Thomas Turner], 1857 (H&HS archive: A/1048/3/2/1/3)
29. HL 7 Jul 1853, vol. 128 cc 1357-61
30. *The Times*, 26 Jun 1854
31. HL 27 Jun 1854, vol. 134 cc 733-41
32. HC 27 Jul 1854, vol. 135 cc 806-21
33. Hall steered through Parliament the 1855 Act that set up the MBW; as its first Commissioner of Works, he was responsible for many environmental and sanitary improvements in London.
34. Second Reading, HC 27 Jul 1854, vol. 135 cc 806-21
35. *The Times*, 28 Jul 1854
36. *The Times*, 24 Jul 1854
37. Finchley Road Estate Bill 1855 (LMA: E/MW/H/III/26/14 / 53; 38/ 16-18)

# Chapter 7

# What price the Heath?

**1**855 turned out to be a momentous year, with reforms to London governance and changes in the law which opened up new possibilities for saving the Heath. Sir Benjamin Hall's Metropolis Management Act established the Metropolitan Board of Works (MBW) with the power to raise money from Londoners for the benefit of the capital. This provided at last the mechanism through which to save the heaths and commons. Municipal Corporations in England and Wales, had been established in 1835, but reform in London had met with opposition. However, the cholera epidemics of the 1830s and 1840s forced the government into action and the MBW was primarily set

up to do something about the sewer system following Dr John Snow's work proving that cholera was a waterborne disease.[1]

Appointed rather than directly elected, the MBW was not universally welcomed and despite its many good works it was never a popular body. Each vestry chose one member as its representative and the City of London sent three members. Its first Chairman was John Thwaites, a vestryman of wide experience of local government and strict philanthropic religious principles. Vestries themselves were reformed by the introduction of elections; the political landscape was transformed.

46. The MBW logo

Preserving the remaining commons had now become just as important as the creation of parks. It had also become urgent in London because while their value for agricultural purposes was receding, their value as building land and for the development of railways was posing a far greater threat. Thomas Turner, newly elected by Hampstead Vestry as its representative on the MBW, now led a five-year campaign to try to persuade the Board

47. Sir John Thwaites (1815-70), first chairman of the Metropolitan Board of Works

to buy the Heath, and the adjoining lands – East Park, Parliament Hill and Telegraph Hill. He worked closely with fellow vestrymen John Gurney Hoare and Philip Le Breton, with their MP Lord Robert Grosvenor, and with neighbouring vestries who supported their aims. Week by week, at almost every meeting of the MBW between 1855 and 1859, Turner lost no opportunity to emphasise "the importance ... of securing Hampstead Heath and vital adjoining land as a place of public recreation for the inhabitants of the Metropolis", with a regular stream of memorials and deputations from the Hampstead Vestry, backed by strong support from St Pancras and St Marylebone.[2]

But at the same time there arose a new and unexpected threat to the Heath in the shape of the Leases and Sales of Settled Estates Bill. It had been under discussion for some time, and was designed to ease the problems caused by restrictive settlements and entails of just the kind that afflicted so many families in Jane Austen's novels, and that Sir Thomas Maryon Wilson was facing. Taking an estate bill through Parliament was enormously costly, with lawyers tending to drag out the proceedings for financial advantage. The new Bill would allow these cases to be dealt with by the Court of Chancery, supposedly simplifying the process and reducing the cost – a somewhat optimistic aspiration, even allowing for the fact that a series of reform measures had been enacted in recent years, culminating in the Suitors in Chancery Relief Act 1852; notorious for its inefficiency, it was famously ridiculed by Dickens in *Bleak House*. However, it was Lord Campbell who asked: "Would the powers of enclosure sought for by the heir of Sir Thomas Wilson be granted under this Bill? He hoped not"; or "that they should not unhappily live to see Hampstead-heath covered with houses, streets, and squares".[3]

As realisation dawned of the threat this Bill posed, neighbouring London vestries called a meeting at the St Marylebone Court House in April 1856, the first of several, to consider what steps could be taken both to preserve the Heath and deal with the Bill. Lord Grosvenor was asked to present a petition to Parliament against the Bill being passed in its present form. Strenuous efforts began to stop it altogether and debates focused a great deal on how it would affect Hampstead Heath. A huge campaign built up, with keen public interest locally. Turner was petitioning the MBW on two fronts: to oppose the Leases and Sales of Settled Land Bill, and to urge them to act swiftly to buy the Heath. Meetings were held by residents in St John's Wood, Camden Town and other nearby districts, to discuss how the Heath might be secured: would a metropolitan rate of 2d in the pound be adequate; would the other metropolitan parishes contribute; could a "compromise" with Sir Thomas be found; would a sum of £100,000 be enough to buy the land?[4] *The Times* turned out a stream of editorials and reports, discussing how it might be achieved and making its own recommendations. One senses again the hand of Robert Lowe in the question "who is to pay for this park?" While praising the campaign, and agreeing about the danger of the proposed Leases and Sales of Settled Land Act, one article suggested that "... the Metropolitan Board of Works cannot do everything at once. [It] has enough to do in the metropolis without driving away to Hampstead to purchase a suburban park. ...The people of Hampstead, who are most interested in this matter, are a very wealthy community; and if, instead of requesting the Board of Works to rate the whole metropolis for the purchase money of the Heath, they would rate themselves, or subscribe among themselves, they might easily do not a little towards effecting a Purchase, and could then, with some show of reason, ask Parliament for a grant. ... we are pretty confident that the House of Commons will meet them in the same liberal spirit".[5] In Parliament, Lord Grosvenor assured MPs that the Hampstead community "were desirous of paying its fair value" and that "arrangements were now in progress which he ... hoped might lead to the purchase of the property upon just and equitable terms".[6]

Eventually a highly controversial solution was found to the problem of the Settled Estates Bill. A clause was devised that barred anyone who had previously applied to Parliament, and been refused, from being eligible to make use of it. Described as an extraordinary piece of unconstitutional discrimination, the notorious Section 21 was obviously aimed at Sir Thomas, and it was said that he was the only man in England to whom it applied. Debates on it continued into the 1860s, Sir Thomas making several attempts with amending bills to get the clause removed. He was supported in Parliament by the Irish MP James Whiteside, whose hyperbolic exaggerations in defence of Sir Thomas – who "no more intended to build on the Heath" than "to build in the moon" – impressed no-one. Edwin James (Marylebone) said "he could only suppose that the right hon. Gentleman was engaged to conduct the Bill [to amend Section 21] through the House because no English Member would undertake it".[7]

A majority of MPs realised that, aside from the Wilson case, there were wider issues at stake, in particular concern about giving the Court of Chancery power to overrule a decision made by Parliament; or to authorise the overriding of wills; and about the lack of adequate publicity for any such application. Although Section 21 remained on the statute book, it was well understood that it could only protect the Heath during Sir Thomas's lifetime; his heirs would not be bound by it and a more permanent solution had to be found. There were more calls "for the people of the Metropolis to make some arrangements with Sir Thomas Wilson to secure Hampstead Heath as a place of public resort". "... if the public wanted it they should buy it" – words which were later echoed by Sir Thomas.[8] "Rich and benevolent persons, in conjunction with the owners of property in the neighbourhood" should raise the money themselves. But all these looked increasingly unrealistic in the face of Sir Thomas's stance.[9]

As a new body with as yet untested powers, the MBW was hesitant. Under great pressure from the rising demand for new parks and open spaces, it made favourable noises about "the advantages which Hampstead Heath presents for promoting the health of the Metropolis, and ... the beauty of its site as an ornament to the capital", but did nothing. It was pointed out that the Heath should be purchased as soon as possible because, if delayed, it might involve a much larger expenditure.[10] But the Board dithered. Moreover with the new enthusiasm for saving open spaces, Hampstead was not the only contender: the MBW was also being petitioned for a new park in southeast London, and Islington Vestry was pressing for one in Finsbury.

A committee was appointed to consider how to provide more parks for the metropolis. One of the first excuses was whether it actually had the power under the Metropolis Act to tax the ratepayers for such objects; it only authorized the Board to apply to Parliament if it felt that further powers were required.[11] By August the Government, acting uncharacteristically swiftly, passed an amending Act, giving the Board "ample powers" to provide "parks, pleasure-grounds and open spaces", subject to parliamentary approval. So that concern was disposed of.[1]

However, the MBW's members were vestrymen from across London each with their own parochial concerns. Although the Works and Improvements Committee "acknowledged ... the great advantage that would accrue ... by the purchase of Hampstead Heath", there was not universal support for it. Some thought "that improvements of a much greater necessity ... are more urgent and desirable". The Bethnal Green representative declared that they were not "at all interested in the preservation of Hampstead-heath, seeing that they had already a fine, spacious park of their own. (Hear, hear.) What they wanted the Board to do was to construct sewers for them".[14]

With staunch support from neighbouring and other vestries, Turner intensified the pressure with more deputations, and Lord Grosvenor arranged deputations to Government. The possibility of a compromise with Sir Thomas Wilson, to let him build on the Manor Farm, if he would surrender rights to the Heath on moderate terms, was discussed with Sir Benjamin Hall (now First Commissioner of Works). But he, no doubt remembering that debate in Parliament, pointed out that this had already been attempted without success. He referred them back to the MBW and expressed surprise at its lack of action; if it would reconsider he would be willing to recommend a grant from the Government's Consolidated Fund to help purchase the Heath.[15] Lord Grosvenor, together with Sir Benjamin, then took a deputation with several members of the MBW and the supportive vestries, to the Chancellor of the Exchequer, to find out if the Government was indeed prepared to help. While the Chancellor agreed that the preservation of Hampstead Heath "would be of the highest advantage to the public, ... the great difficulty was to find the funds." He said he could not give any promise upon the subject.[16]

The matter was tossed back and forth for months: some MBW members were concerned as to "whether they ought to vote away the money of the people living in the metropolis for such objects", while others felt, not only that "the question of securing Hampstead Heath was most pressing and urgent", but that preserving the surrounding land was also vital; without it, its "beauty would be entirely annihilated and they knew not how soon that land might be built upon. It would be to the eternal disgrace of the board if they were to suffer that spot to escape from their hands. Parliament had given them the power, and now was the time for action." Marylebone Vestry urged the Board to start negotiations with

Sir Thomas to try to discover on what terms he might dispose of his rights.[17]

All this activity provoked an exceptional intervention by Sir Thomas, whose solicitor William Loaden wrote directly to the MBW in 1857, accusing those trying to persuade it to buy the Heath of perpetrating a "fraud upon the public" because the Lord of the Manor was not applying for an Act to enclose it. Loaden was invited to address the Board, and he assured them that "Sir T.M. Wilson does not wish to enclose it; that he is desirous that the Heath should remain in its present state, and does not wish it to be made into a prim park, and that the public need not fear any enclosure of the Heath till a Bill for that express purpose shall be brought forward".[18] This is all disingenuous to say the least, completely ignoring Sir Thomas's intentions to build on East Park, but the pusillanimous Board was duly frightened off and decided that further consideration of "forming a Park for Hampstead" be postponed. They put their support behind the Finsbury Park proposals.

The Hampstead Vestry took matters into its own hands, informing the MBW that they were drawing up their own private Bill to Parliament for the purchase of the Heath and the adjoining lands. They "prayed that the Board would be pleased to prosecute the Bill ... subject to such alterations or modifications ... as to the Board might seem fit" or to introduce its own bill if preferred. It was advertised in *The Times* on 23 November 1857, with a detailed description of all the adjoining lands including East Park, Parliament Hill and Fields, Telegraph Hill and South Hill Park, which it was thought necessary to acquire, clearly based on the Cockerell plan.[19] Marylebone Vestry congratulated the Hampstead Vestry, "expressing their admiration of the manner in which the Parish of Hampstead and several of the inhabitants thereof in their private character, are using their endeavours to preserve Hampstead heath to the public".[20]

Turner continued his bombardment by deputation to the MBW which agreed to seek a meeting with Sir Thomas to discuss a basis for negotiations about the Heath, and that the Clerk of the MBW Committee of Works would visit Hampstead to view the Heath and the adjoining lands.[21] The approach to Sir Thomas got nowhere; he clearly had no intention of co-operating. His first reply was a simple refusal "to make any appointment for an interview". After five weeks of correspondence he finally replied that if the Metropolitan Board declined to adopt the proposed [Hampstead Vestry] Bill then it would not be in any position to negotiate with him.[22]

Several of the south London vestries made it clear to the MBW that they objected to support for the Bill and the MBW instructed its solicitors to oppose it. Without the Board's support the Parliamentary Private Bill Committee rejected it on the grounds of its financial implications: by seeking to impose on the Board the duty to provide funds for the purpose, a precedent would be set that the principle of representation and taxation in the Metropolis Act could be overridden by Parliamentary power. However, the Parliamentary Committee was

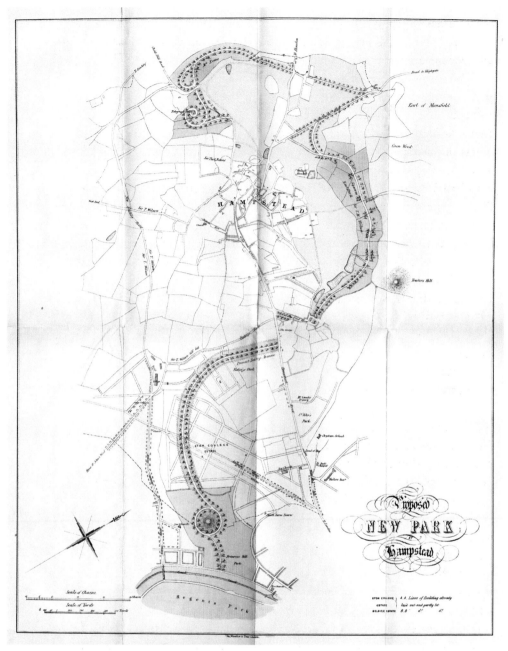

48. Proposed New Park at Hampstead – the plan, based on Cockerell's plan, drawn up by the Vestry to accompany their Bill in 1857

not only "strongly impressed with the public utility of the proposed purchase of Hampstead Heath for the purposes of the recreation and health of the labouring classes of the Metropolis", but made a special report to Parliament to the effect that "securing Hampstead Heath to the public was a measure which should be carried out." The report urged the Board to give the matter its serious attention without delay because the price would increase if deferred much longer.[23]

Thus, although the Vestry's attempt had failed, it marked a significant step forward. The MBW felt unable to ignore the Parliamentary Committee's advice and duly voted to take steps for the preservation of Hampstead Heath as soon as possible: to "confer with any persons they may think desirable" and to ascertain whether the Hampstead Vestry would contribute to the cost. The idea of raising funds to save the Heath was given formal recognition by referring it to the MBW's Finance Committee, but there the matter rested, while the Board timidly continued to hesitate and prevaricate for several more years. Turner stepped down as the Hampstead representative and his place was taken by Le Breton. Having tried every avenue – the MBW, Parliament, Government, and direct approaches to Sir Thomas himself – the campaigners paused for a brief period and turned their attentions to the problem of the new railways. But Sir Thomas, after 30 years of frustration, prevented, as he saw it from capitalising on his inheritance,

49. Spaniards Road, by Captain Thomas Hastings, in 1823 before the sand was dug out on either side

and now blocked by the notorious Section 21, escalated his war of attrition.

The article in Dickens's journal *All the Year Round*[24] (see p 75) describes how Wilson began to exploit the Heath for commercial gain in every way he could for whatever he could get, in defiance of local opinion. If he could not build houses on his East Park fields, he turned them instead into an unsightly brickfield. A 21-year lease for a brickmaker was no problem. Sand and gravel was carted away to be sold in ever larger quantities from the Upper Heath on either side of Spaniards Road, turning it into a raised causeway.

Those who hung washing out to dry on the Heath, or ran geese, or let their donkeys on it, were made to pay. He negotiated a deal with London

Dyeing Company to cover large areas with ugly wooden beating frames, which created dust and nuisance to local residents. He even managed to turn a penny from the Heath's growing popularity, by licensing an Italian ice-cream vendor to put up a temporary refreshment room called the Rotunda near Downshire Hill.[25] From 1865 he regularised the fairs on the Heath that were again becoming popular, and charged stallholders for their pitches, so that he could profit from the crowds brought by the opening of the railway in 1860; Hampstead Heath station provided a direct route from the East End.

As Sir Thomas's continuing attempts to get Section 21 repealed failed, he began to examine other legal stratagems to see if he could indeed find a way to build on the Heath itself – an intention he had always previously denied. He threatened to make grants of 'waste' without any covenants to prohibit

50. Hampstead Heath Station around 1900 (postcard)

building. Using the recent Copyhold Enfranchisement Act of 1852, and granting copyholds to his own nominees, he could acquire freeholds on the Heath strip by strip which could then be sold as building plots. His assertions that he had never intended to build on the Heath looked increasingly hollow.

For the campaigners, the need to buy the land became ever more urgent; the question was how? Merely assuming that the rich men in Hampstead could afford to buy it was simplistic. As pointed out in an article from the *Solicitors Journal*, reprinted in *The Times*: "If the inhabitants of the locality are patriotic enough to lay down the money themselves the difficulty may be overcome, or if they are powerful enough to collect it among their friends they may succeed; but they may with good reason ask why they, a very small portion of the public should be left to do what is in reality for the benefit of the public at large, and more immediately of a very different class of people than that of which they are as a body composed. ... It appears, indeed, only reasonable, if the heath be necessary for the public that the public should pay for it, and that the public money should be devoted to this purpose".[26]

## Motives, claims and counter-claims

While the copyholders were careful not to denigrate Sir Thomas, he showed no such scruples, frequently resorting to personal abuse. He flung accusations at all and sundry with complete disregard; everyone except him was a liar; Toller's claims were "absurd", unfair and "an abuse of language". Mansfield and Gurney Hoare had waged a deliberate campaign against him – an accusation he had been making since the 1840s. Thomas Turner, Hampstead's MBW representative, felt obliged to deal with Wilson's relentless barrage of misinformation. Turner lived in Hampstead for only about fifteen years and appeared to have no particular attachment to the place. He could therefore be described as a disinterested witness; moreover he was a lawyer.

In *The Case of Hampstead Heath*, in 1857, he set out a strongly argued account of events giving the legal and historical background, the motives of both sides, and the case for public purchase.[27] He marshalled all Sir Thomas's arguments and powerfully demolished them one by one. He pointed out that it was Sir Thomas's friends who "succeeded in producing an impression upon a considerable number of people, that he has been hardly used". "... it is not attempted to deny that the residents at Hampstead have an interest ... The writer may, however, with confidence affirm, that the trouble which has been taken by many of those residents, to say nothing of the expense which they have incurred, is much more than the amount of personal interest at stake would have induced them to undergo. It has been and is urged by them as a public question. It may be emphatically said, it is a poor man's question." While the public were instrumental in publicising the objections, it was "the intrinsic force of those objections, and not the influence of those who have urged them, which has produced the decisions that have been come to". Moreover, "the advantage of personal influence, so far as it exists, ... is with the Baronet ... and his family connexions in the Upper House,[28] and not with the untitled commoners who resist it."

Lord Grosvenor also, from the floor of the House, comprehensively dismissed accusations by Sir Thomas and his supporters of attempts to "impose upon the public", or that MPs were unfairly prejudiced. In 1855, during the debate on the Leases and Sales of Settled Estates Bill, he said he "must deny being under the influence of popular clamour on the present occasion, as no tumultuous meetings had taken place on Hampstead Heath".[29] Edwin James (Marylebone) pointed the finger firmly back at Sir Thomas and his supporters, accusing them of attempting "to hoodwink the House by introducing, in the guise of a public Bill, a measure which Parliament had over and over again rejected as a private Bill".[30]

What emerges most clearly from all the evidence is that it was the MPs and the press, rather than the copyholders, who led the way in focusing on the value of the Heath as a public amenity, contrary to Professor Thompson's assertion that the copyholders exaggerated the threat to the Heath as a cover to protect their own interests.[31] Concern about preserving open spaces for the underprivileged of society had already been the subject of press articles, and debates in Parliament well before any campaign had begun in Hampstead. They understood the issues perfectly and were not "hoodwinked" by anyone. And as the record shows, the copyholders' opposition had collapsed until Ripley intervened. Every aspect of the case, for or against, was given a fair and public hearing and no-one was prevented from airing their view.

Perhaps Sir Thomas's real misfortune was to arrive on the scene too late; times had changed and new ideas about preserving public space had evolved which he seemed incapable of understanding. He was mystified and aggrieved that the Hampstead copyholders did not share his desire to "improve" their estates by building on them, and refused to believe his assurances that he had no intention of enclosing the Heath. He believed building villas at East Park would add to the beauty of the Heath, and protect it because "their value will depend on keeping the Heath as a heath", ensuring that his successors would preserve it in their own interest, and at no cost to the public. But preserving the Heath simply to enhance your building development is a very different matter from preserving it for the wider public benefit; with hindsight we can safely say that it was highly unlikely that this would have lasted long. His claims that he had no intention of enclosing or building on the Heath were not credible in the face of the exorbitant price he demanded for it, based on building land value. The Heath needed legal protection.

But what it got at this point was a highly provocative intervention by the newly established *Hampstead Weekly Express* (later to become the *Ham & High*). It ran a series of articles throughout 1861 and 1862 supporting Sir Thomas's line that Lord Mansfield, John Gurney Hoare "and other wealthy men living in sight of the East Park" were to blame for putting the Heath at risk because of their opposition to his plans. The articles only survive because they were collected together into two pamphlets, called 'The Heath in danger' and 'Sir T. Maryon Wilson and Gurney Hoare Esq., on Hampstead Heath'.[32]

In the first pamphlet, spanning July 1861 to March 1862, the paper set out a mischievously distorted, sly and partial account of events, simply repeating the claims of Sir Thomas and his Steward, that "misleading assertions of a few interested persons ... had firmly settled a false conviction on the public mind, which had embittered Sir Thomas Wilson". His plans to "beautify" the Heath "had been thwarted by certain persons owning property on the Heath, who feared it would become a spot of choice public resort and thereby their privacy would be disturbed." This is of course nonsense, because it already was a "spot of choice public resort" and part of the whole point of the campaign was to preserve it as such. And Gurney Hoare did not live "in sight of the East Park".

It appears to be a deliberate attempt to discredit the campaigners under the guise of concern for the Heath. The paper reported a speech given by the Steward, William Loaden, at the annual Court Baron dinner in which he claimed that the campaign has "so much diminished [Sir Thomas's] long sustained desire to preserve the Heath from building, that it was not improbable he might make grants of portions of the Heath for building, as his last chance of making the Wilson Hampstead estate profitable." Loaden's scurrilous accusation to the MBW of "the deception practised on the Metropolitan public" is repeated. There is no mention of Sir Thomas's 1829 Bill, which, with its inclusion of Hampstead Heath, set the whole controversy going, or of the real threat to East Heath that Sir Thomas's plans to build there posed: it would be cut up by roads, and surrounded by buildings, effectively enclosing it.[33]

Most interestingly, a copy of a letter written by Sir Thomas in April 1854 is also reprinted, confirming that in the 1840s Lord Mansfield not only offered to buy East Park, but parts of the Heath itself, but would pay only its agricultural value. According to Sir Thomas, Mansfield opposed the Bill seeking to allow the sale of the whole estate, because had it passed the price of the land would have been higher. When the Bill was lost, Mansfield's agent then proposed he should introduce a bill to sell parts of the estate "to his lordship" and that "if I would be so obliging, there would be no difficulty as to the rest of my wishes". Sir Thomas concludes by blaming Mansfield for having "been at the bottom of the whole outcry against me".[34]

The second pamphlet covers April and May 1862 and is subtitled 'to amend the Leases and Settled Estates Act'.[35] It begins with an account of a public meeting in April – chaired by Donald Nicoll of Oaklands Hall, West Hampstead, himself ironically, a developer – at which John Gurney Hoare again proposed an offer of a compromise to Sir Thomas. If he were to "pledge himself not to seek further building powers" for the East Park Estate and build only on his Finchley Road Estate his application would not be opposed. Informed of this offer by Nicoll, Sir Thomas wrote back dismissing it, saying that he was ready to meet them in court but was not "ready to pay a bribe". This letter too was passed to the newspaper and included in the pamphlet. Sir Thomas did not thank the newspaper for its intervention, describing the articles as "an interference" in his affairs. He hurled further insults at Hoare and Le Breton, implying that they were deceiving Parliament: "If they have an honest case to submit, why should they influence members of Parliament to keep the Court of Chancery shut against me". The newspaper then embellished this accusation against Hoare with an even more outrageous one of their own, that he had "systematically made false statements to members of Parliament", and demanded that he explain himself. Hardly surprisingly, Hoare ignored them.[36]

The newspaper takes at face value everything Sir Thomas and his steward claimed, without any attempt to examine the other side of the story.

Even more reprehensible, the paper admitted that it received many letters protesting at its stance but these are not reprinted in the pamphlets, and unfortunately the earliest editions of the newspaper are no longer available to be checked. Set against the Hansard reports of the Parliamentary debates, these accounts bear no relation to reality and simply sound like mischief-making. One can only suppose that the paper's founder thought he would increase sales for his new venture and make his name by stirring controversy.

**Notes, Chapter 7**

1. Dr Snow famously convinced sceptical officials to take the handle off the Broad Street pump in Soho, because he believed it was the source of contaminated water. His point was proved when the outbreak of cholera in the area almost immediately died down.
2. Deputation from the Vestry of St John, Hampstead, including Le Breton, Gurney Hoare, Cockerell, Freshfield, and Toller, report in *The Times*, 8 Mar 1856
3. HL Deb 11 May 1855 vol 138 cc397-401
4. *The Times*, 23 Apr 1856
5. *The Times*, 10 Mar 1856
6. HC Deb 15 Jul 1856 vol 143 cc945-6, Settled Estates Bill
7. HC Deb 5 Mar 1860 vol 156 cc2286-90
8. HC Deb 4 Aug 1857 vol 147 cc1078-81, Sir Henry Willoughby
9. *The Times*, 19 Jun 1856
10. Sexby (1898), pp 379-380
11. Metropolis Management Act 1855, section 144; Sexby (1898), Introduction
12. MBW minutes, 8 Aug 1856
13. Ibid., 31 Oct 1856
14. MBW debate, report in *The Times*, 17 Mar 1856

15. *The Times*, 12 Apr 1856
16. *The Times*, 3 Jul 1856
17. MBW meeting, *The Times*, 1 Nov 1856
18. Letter from Loaden to MBW, 27 Jun 1857; MBW minutes, 29 Jun 1857
19. This is another of Professor Thompsons misrepresentations used to defame the campaigners: he states wrongly that the Vestry "forbore to say how much of the adjoining lands ought to be secured" and that their "extreme vagueness" was a "routine forensic trick". In fact, the public notice in *The Times* is minutely detailed, and Vestry and MBW minutes record that maps were issued with the Bill.
20. Hampstead Vestry minutes, 22 Jan 1858
21. MBW minutes, 19 Mar 1858
22. Ibid, letter from Thos Maryon Wilson to MBW, 16 Mar 1858
23. Letter from Smith & Son to MBW, reporting on the outcome of the Parliamentary Committee's deliberations on the proposed Hampstead Heath Act; MBW minutes 7 May 1858

24. Joseph Charles Parkinson, 'Hampstead Heath', *All the Year Round*, vol. XVII, no 409 (23 Feb 1867)
25. LMA: E/MW/H/III/38/16
26. *The Times*, 24 Dec 1866
27. 'The case of Hampstead Heath', by a member of the Metropolitan Board of Works [Thomas Turner], 1857 (H&HS archive: A/1048/3/2/1/2)
28. The Wilsons were connected to the Perceval family, the Earls of Egmont, by marriage, two of Sir Thomas's aunts having married the sons of John, 2nd Earl of Egmont. His Aunt Jane's first husband was the Rt Hon Spencer Perceval, the assassinated Prime Minister, who had lived at Belsize House for a time. His cousins sponsored and supported most of his Bills.
29. HC Deb 9 Aug 1855 vol 139 cc2052-60, Leases and Sales of Settled Estates Bill
30. HC Deb 5 Mar 1860 vol 156 cc2286-90
31. Thompson (1974), chapters 3 and 4 *passim*, in particular, pp 141, 147, 150, 155
32. Articles from the *Weekly Express* bound into two pamphlets (H&HS archive: A/1048/3/2/1/3)

33. Ibid.: 'The Heath in danger' July 1861 to March 1862'
34. Ibid. James Whiteside MP also alluded to Wilson's account of these approaches from the Mansfields during an early debate on the Leases and Sales of Settled Land Act (HC Deb 9 Aug 1855 vol 139 cc2052-60).
35. Ref. 32: Sir T. Maryon Wilson and Gurney Hoare Esq., on Hampstead Heath, April & May 1862
36. Ibid. Prof. Thompson's animus towards John Gurney Hoare appears to be based solely on this pamphlet. He repeats verbatim many of its accusations which originated with Sir Thomas (Thompson (1974), pp 176-179). But he undermines his argument by admitting: "The evidence as to Hoare's complicity in this plotting and this deliberate distortion of the facts is purely circumstantial" (p 179). There is in fact no evidence to substantiate Thompson's accusations in any of the archives or in the vestry minutes.

## Chapter 8

# The turning point

However, all these recriminations faded into the background as Parliament itself now took action. In June 1864, Frederick Doulton, MP for Lambeth and Metropolitan Board of Works (MBW) member, called for a resolution "on the necessity of preserving open spaces in and around the metropolis. ... the difficulties of obtaining control over them were increasing ... whether in reference to Hampstead Heath" or other places; "there was almost unanimous opinion in favour of their preservation." Importantly, he emphasised that "His object was to have them preserved in all their wild and uncultivated condition", not "transformed into neatly trimmed and laid out gardens and parks". Henry Cowper, MP for Hertfordshire, suggested that it would even better if a select committee were appointed to inquire into the whole subject. This was agreed, and the formal inquiry "into the best means of preserving for the public use the Forests, Commons, and Open Spaces in and around the Metropolis" was to be a significant turning point. It also brought to notice a major new figure in the campaign for the commons.[1]

## George Shaw Lefevre and the Select Committee

George Shaw Lefevre, a barrister, was elected Liberal MP for Reading in 1863. He was born into the world of politics; both his father and his uncle were parliamentarians.[2] Over the next 20 years he held various posts in Gladstone's cabinets but his greatest contribution to public life was his work to preserve open spaces. He founded the Commons Preservation Society and was involved in every campaign for Hampstead Heath from its first triumph through all the major additions, including Kenwood. It is notable that Barratt dedicated his *Annals of Hampstead* to him for his "lifelong, unceasing and successful achievements in the national crusade for securing open spaces for the people and as a special tribute to his distinguished services in the various historic struggles for

51. George Shaw Lefevre, MP (1831-1928), Baron Eversley 1906, founder of the Commons Preservation Society, later President of the Hampstead Heath Protection Society

the saving, protection, and extension of Hampstead Heath". John Carswell observed that if anyone deserves a memorial on the Heath, he does.[3]

Shaw Lefevre played a leading role on the Select Committee, identifying "about seventy commons and greens of various sizes within fifteen miles of London, which were all in jeopardy; ... the state of the law as regarded public rights was very embarrassing and unsatisfactory. ... the rights and customs of the public in respect to recreation had been almost refined away to nothing." In his view one of the most important duties of the Committee would be "to investigate what the rights of the public really were".[4]

The Committee began its hearings in the spring of 1865, summoning witnesses from all over London, including Sir Thomas's land agent Frederick James Clark (a solicitor), and Philip Le Breton and Thomas Turner from Hampstead. Asked whether Hampstead residents were prepared to pay extra rates to acquire the Heath, Le Breton and Turner replied that they were. But, they pointed out, it would not be fair if they alone were expected to pay for it. Hampstead ratepayers contributed to the purchase of Finsbury and Southwark Parks; and the same principle should apply.[5] One person who spoke well of Sir Thomas was Colonel Alcock, whose militia used the Heath for drilling and parading. The military was Sir Thomas's abiding interest and he was "always most gracious and kind in offering to us every facility", giving permission to create more level surfaces on the Heath for their drilling activities.[6]

Sir Thomas himself appeared, revealing his true colours, his replies to questions curt and hostile, and obsessed with making the most profit. His truculent tone and stance had not changed since that encounter with the copyholders thirty years before. He told the Committee that the public had no rights on Hampstead Heath; it was private property and they must have permission to go on it, and pay, although when pressed he admitted that there were no notices to warn the public of this.[7] "If the public chose to prevent me or to make any bargain that I am not to inclose it, they must pay for the value of what they take from me".[8] When asked whether he wished to make any proposition to settle the dispute about Hampstead Heath, he replied "No, I have no proposition to make".[9] Nor was he was willing to dedicate a portion to the public in exchange for the right to build upon another part: "No, I make no compromise and no promise". His only aim was to "... turn the heath to account, and get what I can. By the outcry that has been made against me, I am deprived of about £50,000 a year. My property would have produced me that without the slightest injury to the public".[10] If his latest Finchley Road Bill was thrown out, he "should consider the most profitable mode of building on Hampstead Heath proper".[11]

He rejected his steward's claim that he had been authorised to say that if Parliament granted power to build on the Finchley Road he would agree not to touch Hampstead Heath:

"I never gave him any such authority".

Q: Therefore the 1862 Bill was based on a false assumption?

A: Quite so. Mr Loaden asked me if I would ever
agree to anything of the kind and I told him No.[12]

Shaw Lefevre put it to him: "You are aware that very frequently in Bills that are brought into Parliament a bargain is made with private individuals"; to which all he could reply was "It may be so".[13] Of course, he regarded all such attempts to bargain as bribery or blackmail. He mentioned again the offers that had been made to him but which he had rejected: "There were other parties who wanted to possess my property. Mr Samuel Hoare wanted it, and offered a price for it; and Lord Mansfield was also anxious to have it, and so they wanted to come poor Poland over me".[10]

Wilson also gave a new version of the story about the codicils to his father's will: "My father was very ill when Mr Lyddon came down to Charlton to add that codicil about that property at Woolwich and Charlton and Mr Lyddon suggested that the same thing should be done with regard to Hampstead. My father said, 'I am too tired now to do it; I must put it off until tomorrow'".[14] One is left wondering which version is true? Was he lying in 1824 when he said his father did not want there to be building at Hampstead? Or was that the truth and this version a perjury? Either way, he was obviously capable of inventing facts to suit whichever version of events would advance his cause. From 1829 he stuck to the new version, that his father's failure to make a codicil for Hampstead was mere oversight and the estate bills hardly more that a legal formality to remedy it. Even Professor Thompson has to admit: "It cast a curious light on the character of the man who spoke easily of the dishonourable conduct of others".[15] Although no-one discovered this discrepancy at the time, the implication of the differing codicils was so strong that people looking at them drew the 1824 inference for themselves.

## The Commons Preservation Society

The publication of the Select Committee's report with its recommendation, that the Statute of Merton should be repealed and the rights of the public strengthened, caused a furor; the lords of the manor were most unwilling to admit any general public right to exercise and recreation which "promotes health and happiness". Many moved swiftly to enclose their commons before action could be taken to stop them. George Shaw Lefevre, together with the Hampstead campaigners, acted equally swiftly, founding the Commons Preservation Society (CPS) in the autumn of 1865 to resist these enclosures.[16] Its founding members included Philip Le Breton, John Gurney Hoare, Octavia Hill, Robert Hunter, John Stuart Mill (who played a leading role in the campaign for Epping Forest), and many of the MPs who had spoken in the debates on enclosures in general and Hampstead Heath in particular, including Cowper, Doulton, Charles Buxton, Thomas Alcock, Sir William Fraser, Alderman Mr William Rose, and John Locke. Hampstead Heath was to be the first of the CPS's legal battles.

The CPS had backing at the highest level: one of its first meetings was hosted by the Lord Mayor at Mansion House in January 1866. It was keen that the rights of the lords and the commoners should be acquired rather than extinguished. In London it was extremely difficult to ascertain who the commoners were, or what were the rights of the lord of the manor. Action was urgently needed to define them and the Metropolitan Board of Works should be empowered to purchase these rights. It was acknowledged that some lords of the manor were disposed to act generously (Lord Spencer at Wimbledon and the Earl of Dartmouth at Blackheath, for example); and also that it would not be fair to expect them all to lay out money for the benefit of the public. However the idea of selling off portions of the open spaces in order to meet the expenditure was considered most objectionable.[17] The CPS was also greatly concerned about the increasing threat to commons from the new railways. Unenclosed commons were the easiest places to build the tracks, and lords of the manor welcomed the money they received in compensation. At least three lines were being proposed across Hampstead Heath (see p 140).

The Select Committee's recommendations became the Metropolitan Commons Act on 10 August 1866, giving power for schemes of management of commons, even if the lord of the manor did not consent, although disappointingly, the recommendation to repeal the long outdated Statute of Merton was not followed. No enclosures in London were to be allowed within fourteen miles of Charing Cross, and a new five-member Board of Commissioners was set up, including a representative of the MBW, to oversee the new management schemes. Many of them were disputed and already being referred to the Court of Chancery. Thus Hampstead Heath now became part of a wider movement to save the London commons. The Act, although an important milestone, did not solve all the problems, and went on being debated and amended for several years. But it was a start.

## Sir Thomas, villain or victim

Five main groups of protagonists were now in play: the MPs, who were on a clear mission to save London's commons; the MBW which was given the powers to do so, but was failing to use them; the Hampstead campaigners backed by several other vestries; the press; and the newly formed CPS. Standing against them all, holding out for his perceived "rights" was Sir Thomas Maryon Wilson Bt, entrenched in his uncompromising attitude, and even, on occasion opposed by his own family.

With the discovery of Henry Sharpe's *Journal*, his claim that he had become "imbittered" over the years because of opposition to his plans, does not stand up to scrutiny. There can be no further doubt that he was a difficult and hot-tempered bully, the cause of his own misfortunes. Sharpe's most intriguing disclosure is that he was at school with both the Wilson brothers.[18] Sharpe was invited to dine at Charlton soon after moving to Hampstead, and his comments about Sir Thomas are revelatory. "He is very little altered from what he was at school; reserved and cold though apparently very kind-hearted.

The circumstances of his father having been of a bad character having probably prevented his being introduced into the society of his equals in rank when young, appears to have had a great influence on him and prevents his feeling at his ease in company". His brother John was also there and Sharpe's comment about him is even more startling: he "is as thorough a blackguard as he used to be at school".

Little is known about Sir Thomas's family background – is there another more nuanced and intriguing side to this story? His family tree shows that both his parents died young, within three years of each other: his mother in 1818 when her son was only 18, and his father in 1821, aged only 48. The obituaries of his father – the 7th Baronet – speak of an invalid who died after a long illness, although there is no hint that he was a "bad character". However, the late Janet Semple, historian, tells us that he was "deranged" and "subject to a morbid melancholy".[19] Unfortunately she gives no source for this statement. G.E. Cokayne's *Complete Baronetage* (1903) makes a point of providing the curious information that the 7th Baronet "was owner of a private menagerie of wild animals, some of which were allowed to run loose about his house, Charlton". All these hints, that something was amiss or odd in Wilson's family background, certainly fit with Sharpe's comments. What effect might all this have had on his character?

Sharpe met Sir Thomas often in the 1840s, when he was staying at Jack Straw's Castle to oversee the building of the viaduct.[20] Sharpe used his longstanding acquaintance with him to intercede on various matters such as the row about the donkeys and the attempt to build over West End Green. He always endeavoured "to be on good terms with him", as he felt he could do more good in that way, and was also anxious to find some good in Wilson where he could. He paints a picture of a lonely "shy person glad to find somebody to be sociable with". He thinks that Wilson "evidently does not mean to spite Hampstead in what he is doing but to do what good he can to it by draining, opening courts etc." He remarks that it is curious "... what a different view of life such a man must have, looking down upon all the great merchants as people in trade. His is not a happier position, and he makes it still worse by quarrelling with the world about this unfortunate estate bill." Sir Thomas simply could not see that he was no longer dealing with small tradesmen, but with men who probably regarded themselves his social equal – they were also landowners with rights.[21] And indeed his own ancestors had been City merchants.

There is also ample other evidence of Sir Thomas's combative nature. He was embroiled in various disputes over the years. The reference to "their many grievances" at the copyholders' meeting in October 1829 suggests an already festering problem. There was a long drawn-out court case with the Hampstead Wells Trust, which he was trying to overcharge for renewal of their copyholds; and another for trying to deny a local copyholder his rights of inheritance. He behaved in a similarly high-handed manner at his Charlton estate where, in 1829, riding roughshod over public opinion and "despite verbal and physical objections", "he gradually annexed Charlton village green", fencing it off from the villagers to add to his park at Charlton House.[22] As Barratt suggests: "Much of the old feudal spirit seems to have survived in Sir Thomas".[23] Unfortunately, he emerges as stubborn and arrogant, obsessed with mercenary values and cavalier with the truth.

Meanwhile, having once said that he would continue to promote estate bills until Parliament got tired, Sir Thomas did just that, with yet more applications in 1865 and 1866. The first Bill again dealt only with the land at Finchley Road and for the first time contained a grudging acknowledgement that "some public interest might be prejudiced" by what he had asked for previously; but it was immediately nullified by the declaration that "Sir T. Maryon Wilson considers that there is no public interest".[24] It did not get past the Lords.

The second Bill passed in the Lords but was voted down by the Commons, where the emphasis had now shifted to urging Sir Thomas to agree to sell. Harvey Lewis, MP for Marylebone, suggested: "The wisest course for Sir Thomas Wilson would be to enter into negotiations with the metropolitan authorities with a view to handing Hampstead Heath over to them on terms that would be mutually advantageous to himself and the public". Alexander Beresford-Hope, MP for Stoke-on-Trent, agreed: "Let Sir Thomas Wilson come forward with a fair offer to cede his rights in Hampstead Heath to the Metropolitan Board, or some other authority, getting if he pleased a just price for it".[25] But

52. Sand digging on the Heath next to Spaniards Road, 1860s

Sir Thomas had no intention of doing any such thing and instead stepped up his depredations of the Heath. In 1866-67 he sold huge quantities of sand from either side of the Spaniards Road to the Midland Railway Company for their extension to St Pancras, turning it into the 'raised' causeway we know today.

Pressure began to mount on the MBW: Hampstead's vicar, Rev. Charlton Lane, wrote to *The Times*, asking why so many years had been allowed to pass by the MBW without carrying out the 1858 House of Commons Committee recommendations.[26] It came under increasing fire from the vestries: what steps had been taken with a view to securing Hampstead Heath and the adjoining lands? Why had negotiations with Sir Thomas not been started?[27] Hampstead, Marylebone, Islington, and St Pancras Vestries made a deputation to the MBW in November, urging it to use the new Open Spaces Act to "come to some fair and just arrangement with the Wilson family ... as expressly recommended by the House of Commons Committee in 1858". One of the deputation, vestryman and church warden Mr Barber, who lived at The Grange, West Heath Road, appealed in *The Times* for pressure to be put on the MBW to act; Sir Thomas had started building at the flag-staff; brickmaking activities had been extended, and enormous quantities of sand were being removed by the railway contractors. But Barber was at pains not to cast blame on Sir Thomas: "He is in a difficult position, ... as his Bill for building on the Finchley-road estate was again rejected last Session".[28]

Sir Thomas boasted of his building near the Flagstaff at Whitestone Pond in a letter to Henry Sharpe: "I have commenced building a dwelling house which I intend to convert to my own use, or the use of my agent. ... I build the first house where everybody can see it, so that it may be known what I intend to do".[29] Legend has it that locals would go at night to pull down the walls as fast as they went up, perhaps invoking the old practice of "abating an inclosure" by physical removal, to demonstrate an assertion of right.[30]

The vestries stepped up their demand that Sir John Thwaites, the MBW Chairman, seek a meeting with Sir Thomas. But in the meantime the Hampstead campaigners had sought advice from the CPS, which recommended legal action. Shaw Lefevre therefore wrote to Thwaites (now knighted for his services to London), advising him against meeting Sir Thomas or offering any large sum of money for his manorial rights until the outcome of the case might be known, as it might hinder "the settlement of many others of the numerous commons around London".[31] The Hampstead case was to be taken to the Court of Chancery to determine just what were the rights of the lord of the manor and of the copyholders, and to consider if it was possible to put a value on the Lord's rights so as to decide the means of purchase or compensation.

A Hampstead Heath Protection Fund Committee was formed to raise money for the costs. Led by Gurney Hoare as Chairman and Treasurer, it included W.J. Strickland Cookson (who now lived at the Pryors), Isaac Solly Lister of The Heath (formerly Upper Bowling Green House), Edwin Field, Charles Knight of Rosslyn Park, James Marshall of Cannon Hall, Richard Ware of North End, and Charles Hathaway of Montague Grove who acted as Honorary Secretary. Four MPs who had defended the Heath in Parliament were also on the Committee: William Cowper, and three members of the CPS: Shaw Lefevre, Thomas Hughes and Charles Buxton.

A circular was sent to local residents requesting subscriptions towards expenses and advising that: "The Lord of the Manor of Hampstead is proceeding actively to build over and enclose the Heath; he is also stripping the turf, and digging and selling about sixty loads of sand daily. The Copyholders, Owners, and other Inhabitants, are advised that these acts are wholly illegal, and are therefore taking measures to protect the Heath." They disclaimed any intention "to deprive Sir T.M. Wilson of his legal rights", but the Lord of the Manor had made such preposterous claims in reference to the Heath that there was no alternative but to test the matter in court. The circular included the exchange of letters between Gurney Hoare and Sir Thomas:

Hampstead, Dec. 6th 1866

Dear Sir, My neighbours, as well as myself, much regret that
you have commenced building on the Heath. Several gentlemen
interested in the matter met last night, and were advised that
the only course open to them was an appeal to law.

I can assure you that they will do this with reluctance, as they
have no hostile feelings towards you; and it would give great and general
satisfaction in this place if you would consent to stay all proceedings
and to obtain a legal decision on the real or supposed rights of yourself
and the copyholders, by an amicable suit. In this manner a long and
costly litigation, as well as much irritation, may be avoided.
Believe me, Your very obedient Servant,

J. Gurney Hoare[32]

Sir Thomas, in his famous reply,[33] simply threw down the gauntlet:

Sir, take your own course".

I am, Sir, Your obedient Servant,

Thos. Maryon Wilson

It was his view, as he had written to Henry Sharpe, that "if the Publick want the Heath, they may have it by paying for it", which of course they had made plain that they were prepared to do. But he had made that impossible and he now upped the price again, claiming that "I find the mineral value is about ten thousand pounds per acre".[34]

The vestries continued to demand action from the MBW Chairman. An angry meeting of Marylebone Vestry asked why he had not yet met Sir Thomas Maryon Wilson, and criticised him for being off-hand in his approach. He had written to Sir Thomas to give him "permission to call upon him" at his office, to which Sir Thomas had replied sarcastically that it was "a privilege I am not likely to avail myself of".[35] Thwaites reminded them that Shaw Lefevre himself had advised that he should wait until after the Hampstead Heath case came before the Master of the Rolls; but under the circumstances, he said, he was willing to meet Sir Thomas. After much to-ing and fro-ing in exchanges of letters, Thwaites eventually had to travel to Charlton House for the meeting on 24 January 1867 where, Thwaites records, "he was very courteously received by Sir Thomas with his solicitor Mr. F.J. Clark in attendance".[36]

But it was a most difficult encounter. Sir Thomas's opening gambit was that until Section 21 of the Leases and Settled Estates Act was repealed, he could not sell or even treat for the sale of the Heath. Sir John Thwaites refuted this, but made an offer to Sir Thomas that if he would agree to an arrangement for the purchase of the Heath, the Board would be willing to support him in his application to Parliament for the power to grant building leases on adjoining lands that the Board might not require. Sir Thomas answered that he saw no reason why "he should sell his property at Hampstead for the purpose of gratifying and benefiting certain parties who had for years opposed him in obtaining his rights". Asked what value he would put on the land, he stuck to his astronomical claim of between £5,000 and £10,000 per acre. In reporting all this to the Board's committee, Sir John expressed his astonishment, as well he might; such a price – a possible £2½ million – was out of the question, and the committee was in full agreement. While expressing their regret at such an outcome, they now had the perfect excuse to defer any further consideration of the matter until they knew the result of the lawsuit. [37]

In June 1868 the Hampstead Copyholders' case came before Lord Romilly, Master of the Rolls, who was by now highly experienced in these cases, having already dealt with several since the 1866 Metropolitan Commons Act. John Gurney Hoare, Isaac Solly Lister and Richard Ware were the three appellants, although in the event the Master of the Rolls was satisfied for Gurney Hoare to represent all the copyholders – perhaps the origin of his designation as the "man who saved the Heath". They received wide publicity and strong support.

53. Sir Robert Hunter (1844-1913), co-founder and "inventor" of the National Trust; advisor to the Heath campaigners; later Vice-President of the Hampstead Heath Protection Society

P.H. Lawrence, Solicitor to the Commons Preservation Society, acted for the Hampstead campaigners and Sir Robert Hunter, also of the CPS, helped prepare the case. They dug up every possible document going back to the original 1560 grant to Wrothe from the King. Every 'Presentment' to the General Court on Nuisance or abuse of the Customs of the Manor was mustered: encroachments, the donkeys, the Volunteers' target practice –where interestingly Lord Erskine's name appears as one of the complainants – unwarranted tree planting, digging of loam, and building in defiance of the restrictive covenants. The case of Mrs Lessingham, the actress, was included, and also the turf-

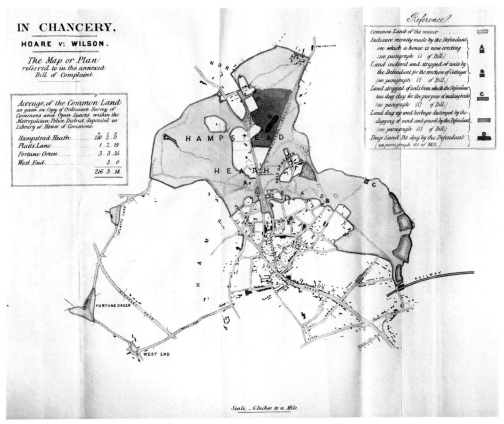

54. The Rogers Field map of the Heath, one of several he prepared for the court case based on the Ordnance Survey and other original plans, and his own survey work: "This whole has been carefully examined and checked on the ground by myself and my assistants so that ... I am now enabled to say from my personal labour bestowed on it and my work on the ground during several months that it is substantially accurate."

digging of Sir Francis Willes, the spy. There is a detailed explanation of the illegal Ditchfield Courts in the 1720s. Gurney Hoare, Lister, Ware, Thomas Toller and Rogers Field, the engineer son of Edwin Field, all prepared evidence, as did various local tradesmen and gardeners who affirmed that some of the copyholders did indeed still keep cows and turn them on the Heath for grazing.

In his written evidence to Lord Romilly, Sir Thomas continued to assert his right to do almost anything he wished, including building upon the Heath, although he does concede that he is "not entitled to exercise my said rights ... further than is consistent with the due preservation of the customary privileges". He denied that the plaintiffs had any right to use the Heath for enjoyment or recreation or that they were entitled to the various copyholders' rights. His heirs, his brother and his nephew, and his steward also gave evidence.[38] Romilly adjourned the case until facts concerning these disputed issues – and the particular way in which these rights were applied by custom in Hampstead – could be tried by a special jury.

Sir Thomas continued his spiteful retaliations to the end, using the 1852 Copyhold Enfranchisement Act to force some of his chief antagonists to

enfranchise their copyholds at great expense, presumably, in an attempt to
deprive them of their right to give evidence as copyholders. In 1865 he told
Isaac Solly Lister he was "desirous that [your] property should be enfranchised"
before the court case.[39] And he also "compelled" Gurney Hoare to enfranchise
his remaining copyhold property, including the Paddock. Gurney Hoare
had objected strongly, but "he had no choice" and "it was very costly".[40]

However, the final act of the drama came upon them a great deal sooner
than anyone expected; in Thomas Barratt's tactfully worded phrase, "another
mediator intervened", Sir Thomas Maryon Wilson died suddenly on 5 May
1869. A vestryman is said to have remarked rather more unkindly: "the hopes
of Hampstead people were brightened by the death of Sir Thomas".[41]

With the succession of his brother John, the community's fears proved to be
quite unfounded. He turned out to be reasonable and open to compromise.
In fact, it was Frederick James Clark, Wilson's solicitor and surveyor for 27
years, who initiated proceedings, as he later told the Parliamentary Select
Committee who scrutinised the Hampstad Heath Bill: "It was always a
matter of conversation between him [the late Sir Thomas] and myself. I tried
to see what I could do, and found him impracticable. The moment he died I
made use of my position, as one of his executors to see the present baronet,
and ascertain whether some arrangement could not be made". [42] Clark was
actually a local resident, living at Oak Lodge on the Edgware Road opposite
Willesden Lane. This statement indicates that he must have cared about
the Heath and found himself in a difficult situation with his employer.

With Clark's assistance, negotiations were underway by January 1870
between Sir John and his son Spencer, and Sir John Thwaites and Philip Le
Breton (as the Hampstead representative on the MBW). An initial suggested
price of £50,000 for the manorial rights in the Heath was reduced to £45,000,
a very far cry from Sir Thomas's notional £2½ million. The agreements
included the lord's right to make roads across East Heath to access East
Park but the demand to retain four acres by the flagstaff for a residence and
offices was opposed by the MBW. The alacrity with which Sir John reached
agreement probably reflected a longstanding distaste and embarrassment over
his brother's conduct, and relief to be shot of these confrontations. But in
truth all were glad to be spared further potentially costly litigation. Sir John
and his son Spencer also immediately initiated proceedings to disentail the
estate, which were completed in August, freeing it up for development.

In September the necessary parliamentary notices were given and the
MBW began drawing up the Bill, to be introduced in the next parliamentary
session by Sir William Tite MP (Bath) and Dr William Brewer MP (Colchester),
also a member of the MBW for the St George's Hanover Square Vestry.

Select Committee hearings began on the Metropolitan Board of Works
(Purchase of Hampstead Heath) Bill on Monday 30 March 1871 and their
deliberations provide more revealing insights. Clark's concern for the Heath

did not stretch as far as East Park, which he still saw as a valuable development prospect: "Q: Do you propose to sell it? A: Directly I can. If I could sell it tomorrow I dare say I should be able to get £2000 an acre for it". [42] There were some petitions against the Bill, from Islington and Battersea Vestries, Eton College (who were worried about how their access to the Wyldes Estate would be affected), and also the Commons Preservation Society which feared that paying for the Heath would set a bad precedent. However, all these objections were overcome. Philip Le Breton, as a member of the MBW, was an important

55. A Heath Keeper's cottage that used to stand near North End; Section 18 of the Act gave the MBW "power to build Heath keepers lodges ... ornamental buildings of an elevation not more than twenty feet".

witness, and Henry Ray Freshfield, solicitor to the Bank of England, was also called, although he no longer lived in Hampstead. He described his role in the campaigns, working with Sir Benjamin Hall and Lord Ebury against "Sir Thomas Wilson's Friends" to secure Section 21 in the Leases and Settled Estates Act. [43]

There was rigorous questioning and much discussion of how the money to buy the Heath would be raised, how it would affect the rates, and how the arrangements compared with those at other parks purchased by the MBW, such as Finsbury and Southwark. Interestingly it was stated that £900 per acre was paid for Southwark Park while for Hampstead Heath it was only £200 per acre. There was concern about the clause empowering the MBW to borrow the funds needed, described by one MP as "robbing Peter to pay Paul", and about the precedent that might be set. On just who the users of the Heath were – whether they really came from across "the metropolis" – the point was particularly made that the majority of people who "derive the chief benefit are of the poorer classes" and are not the sort of people who would be able to pay for it. [44] The Select Committee was satisfied with the answers, the preamble was approved, and on 29 June 1871 the Hampstead Heath Act was passed with its now famous declaration:

*"It would be of great advantage to the inhabitants of the Metropolis
if the Heath were always kept uninclosed and unbuilt on, its natural
aspect and state being, as far as may be, preserved."*

### Notes, Chapter 8

1. HC Deb 28 Jun 1864 vol 176 cc431-7
2. His father, Sir John Shaw Lefevre, was the Clerk of the Parliaments; his uncle, Charles Shaw-Lefevre, Viscount Eversley, was Speaker of the House of Commons.
3. Carswell (1992), p 58 footnote
4. HC Deb 21 February 1865 vol 177 cc502-15
5. Select Committee on Open Spaces (Metropolis) 1865, section 2115
6. Ibid., section 2198
7. Ibid., section 6104
8. Ibid., sections 6182, 6183
9. Ibid., section 6067
10. Ibid., section 6068
11. Ibid., section 6096
12. Ibid., section 6089
13. Ibid., section 6114
14. Ibid., section 6107
15. Thompson (1974), p 137
16. Professor Thompson erroneously states that "The Commons Preservation Society "played a large part in obtaining the 1865 inquiry" (Thompson (1974), p 189). It was not founded until after the inquiry.
17. *The Times*, 25 Jan 1866
18. Manor House School, newly established by Rev. John Bransby at Stoke Newington, then in the country near London, was considered a better and more expensive school. Its chief claim to fame was that Edgar Alan Poe went there, but quite why the Wilson brothers should have been sent all the way from Sussex to Stoke Newington for their schooling remains a mystery.
19. Janet Semple (1993), *Bentham's Prison: a study of the Panopticon Penitentiary*. Bentham corresponded with Lady Wilson, and John Stride the Steward, hoping to buy some Maryon Wilson land near Charlton for his model prison.
20. Account of Sir T.M. Wilson with the Castle Hotel (E/MW/H/IV, 1844-50)
21. Henry Sharpe Journal (CLSAC)
22. J.G. Smith. *History of Charlton*, vol. 3, p 221
23. Barratt (1912), Vol. II, p 208
24. 1865 Wilson's Estate Act 28 Vict session (Maryon Wilson archive, LMA)
25. HC Deb 9 Jul 1866 vol 184 cc752-5
26. *The Times*, 9 Jun 1865. Lane was a descendant of the 17th-century Lord Mayor, Sir Thomas Lane.
27. MBW minutes 1866, *passim*
28. *The Times*, 28 Nov 1866, p 4
29. H&HS: A/1048/3/2/2/5, 13 Dec 1866. It would be fascinating to know what Henry Sharpe thought of this but alas his *Journal* stopped in 1847.
30. Lord Eversley (1894), *English commons and forests* (Cassell); he amusingly describes how this ploy was used at Berkhampstead, to where a force of 120 navvies was sent down from London overnight by train to remove newly placed iron railings on the common.
31. Shaw Lefevre, letter to Sir John Thwaites, 27 Dec 1866 (MBW files, LMA]
32. Professor Thompson misquotes and misinterprets Gurney Hoare's letter to Sir Thomas, substituting the word 'friendly' for 'amicable', and then suggesting "Gurney Hoare presumably with his tongue in his cheek" (Thompson (1974), p 180). He appeared not to be aware that in this context 'amicable' had a specific legal connotation and purpose, as indicated by the last line of the letter: "In this manner a long and costly litigation ... may be avoided".
33. H&HS: A/1048/3/2/2/5
34. Ibid.: letter to Henry Sharpe, 13 Dec 1867
35. *The Times*, 11 Jan 1867
36. Frederick J. Clark was the manager of Wilson's estates for 25 years; his brother William was, for a short while, the Steward of Hampstead Manor.
37. Report of Sir John Thwaites to the Committee (MBW minutes, 1 Feb 1867)
38. Transcripts of court case about the ownership of Hampstead Heath; Field's evidence, 17 Jun 1867 (CLSAC: ST2/ID/14)
39. Documents - motion for decree (ibid., ST2/ID/2)
40. Hampstead Vestry minutes, 1895: letter of Sir Samuel Hoare, 20 Jun
41. Ikin (1985), p 18
42. Select Committee hearing on the MBW Purchase of Hampstead Heath Bill, 25 April 1871; evidence of Frederick James Clark
43. Ibid., evidence of Henry Ray Freshfield
44. Ibid., evidence of Philip Hemery Le Breton

# Chapter 9
# The end of the beginning

Even before the ink had dried on the Hampstead Heath Act, the eagle-eyed Hampstead campaigners had spotted several discrepancies between the map lodged with the bill and the map referred to in the Act. Several bits of land thought to be part of the Heath were left out. In December 1871, the vestryman Mr Barber again wrote to *The Times* to point these out and he, together with Rogers Field, John Gurney Hoare and Thomas Turner, pursued the matter with the Metropolitan Board of Works (MBW). They met Colonel James McGarel-Hogg, the new Chairman,[1] to point out the mistakes: "the Lord of the Manor had sold land which was not his to sell" and "important portions of the Heath had been omitted from the purchase, notably Judges Walk, and the avenue at North End". They were met with irritation and condescension by Colonel Hogg, who replied that "these were only very small" errors and that "the brush drawing up the map may have gone a little too far"[!] He testily pointed out that to have to alter the terms at this stage would delay the finalising of the contract.[2] The Hampstead Vestry established a Heath Committee to pursue the matter and a list of the pieces of overlooked land appears in the Vestry minutes in January 1872. The MBW did later buy in Judges Walk, and Wildwood Avenue at North End; according to Samuel Hoare, in a letter to the Vestry in 1895, his father John Gurney Hoare had arranged for Wildwood Avenue to be transferred to the MBW.[3] But disputes over land and footpaths near Whitestone Pond, and in particular the Vale of Health, were still running a century later.

The MBW took formal possession of the Heath on 13 January 1872. Members of the Board, headed by Colonel Hogg, with Mr John Pollard, Secretary, and Mr Mackenzie, landscape gardener, were met at Hampstead Heath station by Philip Le Breton with the churchwardens and members of the Hampstead Vestry. They were supposed to "perambulate on foot the boundaries of the heath", but of course it was pouring with rain, so this part of the programme had to be abandoned. Instead they proceeded in "covered conveyances", and various points of interest, such as an area that would make a "most extensive cricket ground, and two new donkey rides" were pointed out, as were some recent encroachments and enclosures, "which gave rise to a generally expressed opinion that the Metropolitan Board had not stepped in ... a day too soon".

At the summit of the Heath by the Flagstaff, Colonel Hogg made "a few graceful observations", dedicating the Heath to the free use and recreation of the people for ever, and "the company adjourned to Jack Straw's Castle where a *déjeuner* had been provided at the expense of the Hampstead Vestry", presided over by the vicar, Rev. Charlton Lane. He proposed Hogg's health, comparing the acquisition of the Heath with some of London's other great achievements, and stressed that it was not for Hampstead alone, but the whole metropolis, that this had been done. Colonel Hogg in reply could not resist alluding to the "fancy price of the heath" demanded by its previous owner, and assured the assembled company that the "beauty of the heath consisted in its wild and unsophisticated appearance, and as such they intended to keep it." Mr. Clark, Surveyor to the Lord of the Manor equally could not resist stating once more that it was never the late lord's intention to build on one inch of the Heath. When it was pointed out "that by some mistake" the Lover's Walk had been withheld, the new baronet, Sir John, responded "God forfend that it should be done; we know nothing of it", and he "surrendered all his rights to the public" there and then![4]

And then there started the complaints. Sir Thomas had left the Heath in a shocking state. George Vulliamy, superintending architect to the MBW, described it as being "much changed for the worse, the surface being denuded of the gorse and broom which [once] covered it", and great holes had been left along the sides of Spaniards Road where sand had been dug out.[5] The MBW was supposed to repair some of this damage and were "charged to enclose and plant certain specified portions as ornamental grounds". The Board naturally preferred not to spend money if it could help it, so benign neglect was the order of the day. Six months later *The Times* complained: "we see no evidence of any eagerness to enter upon the task." Moreover encroachments were still taking place, public property being appropriated to private use: "Gipsies and idlers" were still using fences for firewood; "bird trapping and shooting are unchecked. Trees and shrubs are damaged without hindrance or restraint." The paper accused the MBW of having "a very inadequate conception of the duty which has devolved upon [them]".[6]

Philip Le Breton, now Chairman of the MBW Parks and Open Spaces Committee, defended the Board, saying there had been no delay in carrying out the necessary arrangements. The Act of Parliament stated that they were not "in any way to interfere with its present natural appearance" and that "the inhabitants of the district required nothing better than that it should remain in its present condition". But clearly opinion was divided. Some local people wrote in hearty agreement with *The Times*: "the state of the Heath at present is a disgrace to the community", wrote one correspondent,[7] while another bemoaned the pruning of the willows "shorn by the monsters of Heath rule".[8] James Thorne, however, writing in 1876, thoroughly approved of the MBW's parsimonious approach: "The Board of Works have happily done little in the way of improvement, and nothing towards rendering the Heath prim or park-like. Under their 6 years of judicious neglect, Nature has begun to reassert her rights. Hampstead Heath, in fact, looked better in the summer and autumn of 1876, than it had looked for the previous thirty years".[9]

For the first time the Heath was in the charge of a bureaucracy, with powers given in 1877 to make byelaws and regulate activities; these became the subject of cartoons lampooning their efforts. But one in particular ended up in the law courts. In 1882 the MBW took it upon itself to begin regulating sports and games, and prohibited the playing of cricket on West Heath. W. Strickland Cookson offered £1,000 to the MBW to lay out a cricket ground for the use of the cricket club on the old Trap-ball ground at the end of Well Walk, opposite Foley House, but this turned out not to be practical and nothing came of it.[10] However, the MBW designated eighty acres to be set aside for cricket, football and other sports. But cricket had been played on West Heath 'from time immemorial' on a ground below the Flagstaff that had been laid out in 1822. Henry Sharpe records in the 1840s that people were out playing cricket every evening, amongst them many of the lads he taught, and the ground was still in use in the 1870s, although no longer in good condition.

Now notices appeared forbidding cricket, football and all other games on West Heath, with a penalty of 40 shillings. This was considered inordinately high-handed and the Hampstead Vestry sent a resolution to the MBW, calling on it to withdraw the prohibition. They also tartly expressed the opinion that it would be in the public interest for the Board to consult the Vestry before promulgating any order affecting the public enjoyment of Hampstead Heath.[11]

A Hampstead Heath Defence Association sprang up, led by the redoubtable George Potter, to "vindicate the public right"; if this "attack on their privileges were to pass unchallenged, other rights might be threatened". It was suggested that in seeking to enforce its byelaw the MBW was possibly acting *ultra vires*. The Board contended that the 1877 Act gave them power to over-ride all pre-existing rights, such as the customary right of common,

56. Three cartoons: 'The pleasures and pains of Hampstead Heath' (*Punch*, 11 Nov. 1882)

56 a. Detecting an offender

56 b. Don't sit on the grass

56 c. In possession

for the purpose of regulating games. Letters of protest, two deputations to the Parks and Open Spaces Committee, and a public meeting asking for the repeal of the obnoxious byelaw, were met with a direct refusal by the MBW.

But Potter was not prepared to let it go. An appeal was made for funds and an affidavit was obtained from a William Greening, who, it was said, had laid out the Cricket Ground in 1822. Potter informed the head Heath constable that he intended to play a game of cricket on West Heath at seven o'clock the next evening, and warned him to be there. Accompanied by his two sons, he led a team onto the old ground in a deliberate challenge. As Barratt described it: "They were rather scratch teams ... but they were equal to the occasion and the game was duly played. The score was not recorded".[12] As expected, they were hauled before the Hampstead magistrates, charged with having broken the byelaws. But the magistrates found in their favour, deciding that the customary right must override the byelaw, which they declared to be invalid, and they dismissed the summons. The MBW appealed; Chief Justice Coleridge in the Court of Queen's Bench upheld the magistrates' ruling. But the MBW made very heavy weather of the matter, insisting on pursuing it. Eventually, after another referral back to the Hampstead magistrates, and then again back to the Queen's Bench, in December 1883, Lord Coleridge said that the magistrates were perfectly right in their decision because the Act of 1877 gave power to regulate games, not to prohibit them.

*The Times* reported the case in full, saying it raised a question "of universal application to the many wastes or commons on the whole matter of customary rights". In particular, rights of recreation were a subject of frequent

**57.** Bank Holiday 1907, with the old engine house on the left; postcard in the Oilette series of miniature oil paintings produced by Raphael Tuck & Sons

dispute; were they "a profitable right of common" or an easement? Significantly it was a rare legal affirmation of a right of recreation over a common.[13]

Many years later, F.R. D'O Monro, Clerk to the Wells Charity, a member of the H&OHS committee in the 1940s, a keen cricketer and, like Potter, an historian of Hampstead, paid this tribute to him: "May there always be stalwarts in Hampstead of the type of Mr. G.W. Potter ... who will fight if necessary to preserve the Heath as an open space for the use of the public".[14]

## The great Holiday destination

1871 was also the year when Sir John Lubbock's Bank Holiday Act was passed, creating three holidays for working people in the summer months and bringing even more visitors to the Heath. Visitor numbers had begun to rise after the opening of the Hampstead Heath railway station in 1860, when they came in their thousands. But now, with the legal seal of approval as a public open space, they began arriving in the tens of thousands. It was estimated there could be as many as 100,000 on a Bank Holiday: "Perhaps there is no spot around the Metropolis which is more identified with the holiday life of the Londoner than the Heath, and on Bank Holidays the northern heights become uncomfortably crowded".[15] Generally the crowds were well-behaved, but on one occasion this popularity was the indirect cause of a dreadful fatal accident. On Easter Monday 1892, two women and six boys were suffocated by the dense crowd descending the stairs at Hampstead Heath station.[16]

58. Jubilee bonfire 1897, by Robert Finlay Mcintyre (c.1846-1906)

Queen Victoria's Golden and Diamond Jubilees (1887 and 1897) were celebrated with bonfires near the Flagstaff with fireworks, and salutes fired by the Hampstead Volunteers. Guy Fawkes night was marked for many years with an annual bonfire and procession organised by the Hampstead Bonfire Club; and the Rosslyn Hill Band regularly provided music on the Heath on Saturday evenings in the summer. Henry Sharpe records skating on the Vale of Health Pond in the 1840s, and in the 1870s a skating club was

HAMPSTEAD: BUILDING THE BONFIRE ON THE HEATH.

59. Guy Fawkes bonfire, Hampstead Heath, 1860s

established.[17] Beacon Fires near the Flagstaff were lit to celebrate the end of the Crimean War; and for King Edward VII's marriage and his Coronation.[18]

Although the donkeys were one of the biggest attractions, they had become more and more of a nuisance, and one of the MBW's first initiatives was to introduce measures to control the donkeymen. The traditional donkey stands by Whitestone Pond, dubbed the 'Ponds Asinorum' by George du Maurier, were earmarked in the 1871 Act to be enclosed and 'planted as ornamental grounds'. The introduction of a licensing scheme was welcomed by *The Times*: "They have at length put an end to the nuisance of the donkey-boys who use to ply their trade so noisily and offensively". The drivers now had to wear numbered badges, "conspicuously displayed", on pain of a fine under new byelaws.[19]

By the 1880s the fairs were famous. Hampstead had its own Pearly King and Queen, Bert and Becky Matthews, who were fixtures

*Donkey Island near the Pound*

60. The uniformed heathkeeper at the donkey pound; photo by Thomas Barratt

61. Swinging Boats – all the fun of the fair

62. Donkeys for hire

at the fairs, selling jellied eels, cockles and whelks. Bert was born in Hampstead and lived there all his life. He was married at the Parish Church, worked for the Council, and is buried in the Parish Church yard.[20]

The *Hampstead Express*[21] painted a lively picture of a Bank Holiday Monday: "the holiday makers began to arrive very early ... and by midday ... presented a most animated appearance. There was ample provision for [their] enjoyment in the shape of swings, cocoa-nut shies, skipping, pony and donkey riding, and in the Vale of Health a steam roundabout and a switchback trapeze". There were "tea and coffee stalls, ice barrows, and hot fried fish

63. 'Appy 'Ampstead on Bank Holiday, by Phil May (1864-1903)

booths ..., all of which attracted many patrons. The holiday-makers seemed to come from all quarters of the metropolis". After some heavy showers [nothing much has changed!], "holiday-makers speedily returned to such amusements as kiss-in-the-ring, al fresco dancing, &c. 'Ladies' tormentors [squirts charged with scent], peep-shows, curiosity exhibitions, the camera

64. The Lost Children's Shelter, Hampstead Heath 1897

obscura, conjurors, Punch and Judy shows, and a variety of other amusements all helped the pleasure-seekers to spend a long and pleasant day".

"A strong body of police, in uniform and plain clothes, under the direction of Inspector Collis, S division, assisted the Heath constables to maintain order, and the officer of the Hampstead Society for the Protection of Animals was on the alert to prevent cruelty. As usual, seven or eight lost children came under the care of the Hampstead police"

By the time the London County Council took over the Heath, they reckoned it was London's most popular open space: "bank holiday pleasures at other London parks were mere 'modifications' of those at Hampstead".[22] The cartoons of Phil May, who lived in Hampstead, provided a pictorial record.

It was the heyday of the Music Hall. The 18th-century tradition of songs eulogising the Heath's charms continued. It was now *'Appy 'Ampstead'* that was immortalised in a song by Albert Chevalier, and became a nationally known phrase. Another earlier piece, even before the Heath was saved, was Watkyn Williams' *Hampstead is the Place to Ruralise, of* 1861, sung by Miss Annie Adams, a popular London singer (who is buried in Highgate Cemetery):

> Hampstead is the place to ruralize,
> ri-ti-ruralize, extra-muralize
> Hampstead is the place to ruralize
> On a summers day.

Another song was *The Cockney Riviera:*

> Oh give me a breath of its air
> A stroll o'er the heath when tis fair
> A cosy nook a pleasant book
> and a sweet-heart the joy to share
>
> The rich go to MonteCarlo
> or spend their weekend by the sea
> But I'll stick to good old Hampstead
> The Cockneys riviera for me

And, of course, the most famous of them all was *Down by the Old Bull and Bush.*

## An unfinished task

But although there was much congratulatory talk publicly, privately the Heath campaigners were well aware that there was much left to be done. So far from being the end of the story, the events of 1871 were just the first step on the way. They had won the legal Heath – what was left of it – but the long-drawn-out campaign had served to emphasise just how important the adjoining lands were: none of them was secured and important bits of Heath were compromised. A strip of land at West Heath, which provided valuable frontage on West Heath

HAMPSTEAD IS THE PLACE TO RURALISE.

SUNG WITH IMMENSE SUCCESS BY

MISS ANNIE ADAMS,
COMPOSED BY WATKYN WILLIAMS.

LONDON, H D ALCORN 8 RATHBONE PLACE OXFORD ST.W.

65. 'Hampstead is the place to ruralize': song sheet

Road, was retained by the Wilsons, cutting historic Telegraph Hill off from the Heath. Most damaging of all, East Park, the preservation of which had been as important as that of the Heath itself, was still in danger and posed a threat to East Heath. The agreement with the new lord of the manor, Sir John Wilson, contained permission for access roads 60-foot wide across the narrow strip of East Heath; if he took up the building options to develop it, East Heath would be destroyed. The restrictions specified in the 1806 Will no longer applied: Sir John and his son had disposed of them. Section 21 of the Settled Estates Act had become irrelevant.

Notes, Chapter 9

1. Sir John Thwaites had died in 1870 just before the Act was finalised in Nov 1871.
2. Manuscript memorandum of meeting with Lt Col Sir James MacNaughton Hogg, Nov 1871 (H&HS: A 1048/3/2/2/4)
3. Hampstead Vestry minutes, 20 Jun 1895
4. *The Times*, 15 Jan 1872
5. Report by Vulliamy to MBW Works & General Purposes Committee, 28 Feb 1870
6. *The Times*, 12 Dec 1871
7. *The Times*, 14 Dec 1871
8. *The Times*, 15 Mar 1873
9. Thorne, James (1876), *Handbook to the environs of London* (Murray), p 292
10. *Ham & High*, 18 Aug 1874
11. *The Times*, 18 May 1882
12. Barratt (1912), vol. II, ch. XIX
13. *The Times*, 12 Dec 1882; Court of Appeal, Potter's own account in Baines (1890), pp 156-159. The protagonists placed a formal account of the event on the Court Rolls of the Manor to ensure there was a permanent record of their "struggle".
14. F.R. D'O Monro (1949)
15. Sexby (1898), p 377
16. For a detailed account, see Robin Woolven, 'The Hampstead bank holiday crush of Easter Monday 1892', *CHR* 36 (2012).
17. Baines (1890), ch. XVI
18. Ikin (1985), p 23
19. *The Times*, 14 Apr 1873
20. www.tombwithaview. org.uk/abg-people/bert-matthews/
21. Cited in Baines (1890), p 228
22. LCC annual report, 1898-99, p 127

# The new campaigners

The Commons Preservation Society was disappointed that the Chancery action had to be abandoned. Had it been won – and Shaw Lefevre was confident that it would have been – the price paid for the Heath might have been less, and the general cause of preserving commons furthered. His view was that if Sir Thomas "cannot inclose without the consent of the copyholders, his rights are worth little or nothing beyond the value of the sand or gravel which he is entitled to dig".[1] And, with the new Metropolitan Commons Act, was it really necessary to have paid the Maryon Wilsons for the Heath at all? At Wimbledon, Earl Spencer had voluntarily dedicated the greater part of the common to the public in 1864. At Blackheath the Earl of Dartmouth consented to a scheme of management, as did Sir John Lennard at Hayes Common in 1869. Shaw Lefevre feared that paying for the Heath might compromise the principle that commons were now protected by law from being enclosed.

Hampstead was now a thriving small town, still surrounded by open fields to the north and not quite engulfed by London from the south. The generation of the 'grandfathers' was fading. When John Gurney Hoare died in 1875, the *Ham & High*'s strange accusations were forgotten, replaced with praise for a blameless life devoted to public service. He was "distinguished for his benevolence and the warm interest he took in religious and philanthropic movements; ... he was also one of the most earnest workers for the preservation of the Heath as a recreation ground for the people".[2] Edwin Field died tragically in 1871, trying to save a friend from drowning, and Henry Sharpe died in 1873. Thomas Turner had left Hampstead and Thomas Toller died in 1879.  Philip Hemery Le Breton retired from the Metropolitan Board of Works in 1880 owing to ill-health and died in 1884.

With the rising population came a new generation of campaigners. Vestries grew larger and, with the reorganisations of 1855 and 1873 – when the parish was divided into wards and the number of vestrymen doubled – they acquired greater powers. Hampstead became a parliamentary constituency in 1885 with its own MP. City lawyers and businessmen continued to make it their permanent home, and devote time to service on the Hampstead Vestry, which was highly thought of: "I don't think there's been a better board of guardians, or a parish more fairly managed, than ours, ... gentlemen who'd rather put their hands in their own pockets than let any one suffer for want of proper help and comforts in time of sickness or distress".[3] Charles Booth concurred, finding "good business-like management. ... Men of high character are willing to serve, party politics are little regarded. In the administration of the Poor Law also, there is at Hampstead no lack of people of character and leisure willing to serve as Guardians. The tone is sympathetic, but careful".[4] Money was found for various town improvements including a fine new Vestry Hall,[5] which began to host a wide variety of cultural events such as the Hampstead Popular Concerts, featuring an extraordinary array of leading artists of the day. "Art was rampant on the Northern Heights at the end of the century" recalled Sir Arnold Bax. "There were literary clubs, book societies, annual exhibitions of paintings by Hampstead artists", and Brahms's favourite violinist, Joachim, at the Town Hall.[6]

The "men of high character" included Sir Henry Harben, chairman of the Prudential Assurance Company who lived in Fellows Road, a vestryman from 1874 to 1900 and the first mayor of the new Borough of Hampstead. Frederick E. Baines, a Post Office assistant secretary, and E.E. Newton, a tea merchant, both keen amateur historians,[7] served as vestrymen in the 1880s and 1890s. Thomas Barratt, who was born in St Pancras in 1841, came to live at Bellmoor, opposite Whitestone Pond around 1877.[8] The chairman of A. & F. Pears, the soap manufacturers, he has been called 'the father of modern advertising', his most famous stroke being the purchase of Sir John Millais's picture *Bubbles* for 2,000 guineas, in order to turn it into a poster to advertise his soap.[9] Barratt made an enormous contribution to the enlargement of the Heath, helping to raise money for several of the campaigns, and he was a devoted Hampstead historian, leaving us his superb, gossipy 3-volume *Annals of Hampstead*.

66. Sir Henry Harben (1823-1911), knighted in 1897

Another strand of newcomers were people involved with the wider movement for social reform and conservation, who gathered around Octavia Hill towards the end of the 19th century. Although she never lived in Hampstead, many of her family settled there, becoming her "beloved Hampstead circle".[10] Hampstead Heath had been part of her childhood on her frequent visits to their maternal grandfather, Dr Thomas Southwood Smith, in Fitzroy Park (see p 66). The Howitt family were his close neighbours at Highgate West Hill.[11]

67. Thomas J. Barratt (1841-1914), fervent campaigner for the Heath

115

Octavia's parents came to know the family of Rev. F.D. Maurice, a prominent Christian Socialist theologian, social reformer and pioneer of adult education, through her mother's work with the Ladies' Cooperative Guild based in Russell Place, Fitzrovia.[12] Maurice settled in Hampstead at Rosslyn Hill in 1873 and was a mentor to Octavia Hill.[13] By the 1870s two of her sisters, Gertrude and Emily, were living at 25 Church Row, with Margaret Gillies, a noted artist who had been Southwood Smith's companion for many years after the death of his wife. Gertrude married Charles Lewes (the son of George Lewes, the lover of George Eliot), who later served on the London County Council. The couple lived for a while at Elm Cottage on

68. Octavia Hill (1838-1912), co-founder of the National Trust

the corner of Downshire Hill, before moving to Southwood Smith's old address at Hillside, Fitzroy Park (although the house had been rebuilt). Emily married F.D. Maurice's son Charles; they lived for a time at Squire's Mount and then at Eirene

69. *Work*, by Ford Madox Brown (1821-93), who lived in Heath Street in 1852. A 'social realist' painting representing the different classes of workers in Victorian society: intense physical labour contrasts with two 'educated intellectuals' on the right. F.D. Maurice, far right, is depicted conversing with Thomas Carlyle. It has been linked to the widely discussed initiatives to build new sewerage and drainage systems as a response to the cholera epidemic. A copy of the painting, commissioned by the Heath & Hampstead Society, can be seen at Burgh House

70. Dame Henrietta Barnett (1851-1936) and Canon Samuel Augustus Barnett (1844-1913); the plan is probably of the Hampstead Heath Extension on the Wyldes estate

Cottage (now No. 9A Gainsborough Gardens), newly built for them.[14] On the Highgate side was the philanthropist Angela Burdett-Coutts, with whom Dickens collaborated on various projects to alleviate poverty. All were involved with the campaign to buy Parliament Hill.

Octavia Hill's own personal life was not to be so happy. She was briefly engaged in 1877 to Edward Bond, of a long-established Hampstead family, with whom she worked closely on many of her own projects.[15] But his mother objected – Octavia was six years older than him – and she broke off the engagement. Both remained unmarried.

It was through Octavia in the 1860s that two other future Heath campaigners, Henrietta Rowland, daughter of a wealthy businessman, who devoted her life to charitable work, and Samuel Augustus Barnett, co-workers on Octavia's various social projects, were brought together, and an enormously important partnership was born. All were inspired by the Christian Socialism of F.D. Maurice.

Octavia and her sister Miranda founded the Kyrle Society[16] in 1876 as part of their work to improve living conditions in the overcrowded slums. Now long forgotten, it was a forerunner of the conservation movement, and laid the foundation for the National Trust later founded by Octavia Hill and Robert Hunter. Its aim was to "Bring Beauty Home to the People": besides the provision of better housing, the quality of life should be enhanced with art, books and open spaces. The Kyrle Society had branches all over the country and attracted support from a remarkable range of influential and eminent people, the 'great and good' of the day. They included William Morris, the Duke of Westminster, Lord Brabazon, George Shaw Lefevre, Robert Hunter, Sir Frederick Leighton, the Duke of Argyll, Robert Browning, and the Deans of Westminster and St Paul's. Prince Leopold, Queen Victoria's youngest son, was its President, Octavia Hill its Treasurer and her brother-in-law Charles Maurice its Secretary.[17] The Society's most influential and active section was its Open Space Committee, originally formed to restore London's disused and overgrown burial grounds so as to provide some open space for the poor. With Robert Hunter as its Chairman, it soon widened its remit to support campaigns for the preservation of commons and open spaces generally, and had a branch in Hampstead. *The Times* regularly reported meetings of the Kyrle Society, which had enormous influence on other organisations.

These included Ebenezer Howard's Garden City movement, and the Metropolitan Public Gardens Association (MPGA) which Lord Brabazon (later the Earl of Meath) went on to establish in 1881. The MPGA was launched in the *Pall Mall Gazette* with an article, 'The social wants of London' by Walter Besant,[18] another Hampstead resident who lived at Frognal End, off Frognal Gardens. Like the Grosvenors, Lord Brabazon was a descendant of an ancient aristocratic family, and he used his position to campaign for urban reform. His Vice-President at the MPGA was the public health reformer and medical journalist, Dr Ernest Hart,[19] who had set up the National Health Society to promote the improvement of public health through, for example, the smoke abatement campaign. Brabazon invited Hart to merge his National Health Society with the MPGA and it was Hart who initiated moves to save Golders Hill Park. As the Kyrle Society declined, the MPGA, a far more activist group,

71. Lord Brabazon, 12th Earl of Meath (1841-1929), founder of the Metropolitan Public Gardens Association; first Chairman of the Parks Committee, London County Council 1889-92

72. Sir Walter Besant (1836-1901), who lived at Frognal End, Frognal Gardens. His grave at Hampstead Parish Church is a listed monument.

supplanted it; and the Commons Preservation Society also grew in importance.

Another leading member of this circle was Lawrence Chubb, an Australian who came to London as a student in 1887. A keen walker, he was soon drawn into the open spaces movement by Octavia Hill after she heard him speak at a debate. He became the first Secretary of the National Trust from its foundation in 1895, then Secretary of the Commons Preservation Society, where he worked closely with Shaw Lefevre and Robert Hunter, founded the Ramblers' Association, and played an instrumental role in saving Kenwood. All saw the provision of green open space and fresh air as part of the solution to the problems of the poor, and all had links to the campaign to extend Hampstead Heath.

The new Lord of the Manor, Sir John Maryon Wilson, and his son Spencer, wasted no time in starting on the development of the Hampstead estate, but fortunately had the sense to leave East Park alone, letting it to local builder John Culverhouse for brick-making, and concentrating instead on the Conduit Fields behind the Finchley Road. Octavia Hill, launched a brief but unsuccessful attempt to save some of the latter, persuading the Wilsons to allow time for an appeal to be made to buy some fifty acres at about £1,100 an acre. *The Times* thought this "very moderate ... considering the market value of adjacent land". Strickland Cookson – still looking for a cricket ground – promised £1,000 if part of it was used to provide one. Octavia Hill appealed in *The Times* for support: it is "of so much importance to the poor of London" that funds should be raised to save the fields. But, she warned: "The owners ... cannot, of course, keep that offer open long".[20]

Barely three weeks later Edward Bond had to write to the *Ham & High*, saying that although £8,000 had already been raised and promises were coming in daily, the campaign had to be abandoned. The Wilsons appeared to have simply played along with the idea while they were having difficulties negotiating arrangements with the Hampstead Vestry for the new road which became Fitzjohn's Avenue. These had suddenly been resolved and, wishing to press ahead, the offer was withdrawn. The *Ham & High*'s view of the Wilsons was now somewhat modified from its support for Sir Thomas a decade earlier: this "explanation certainly detracts considerably from what appeared to be the generosity of the Wilson family".[21] Amongst the flurry of correspondence in the *Ham & High* was a letter presciently suggesting that the campaigners would be better advised to turn their attention to saving Parliament Hill.

Sir John died in 1876, but it was not until the 1880s that his son Sir Spencer began to advertise the East Park property – still being ravaged as an unsightly brickfield – as available for building. If "Sir Spencer Wilson's .... East-park, on the one side of the heath, and Telegraph-hill, on the other, were covered with houses, the prospect from the heath would be spoiled," said *The Times*.[22] And it was not just East Heath which was at risk, but the Mansfield land as well. Stretching from Hampstead Lane across Parliament Hill to Gospel Oak, it was all still open country ripe for development, and London's expansion was continuing all round it: "... it is singular to how great an extent the heath depends for its attractiveness upon the preservation of the hills and slopes which surround it ... It is therefore, peculiarly dependent upon the mode in which these fields [Parliament Hill and Lord Mansfield's park] are used. Hitherto, as we have said, the hills around the heath have been covered with green sward. But if bricks and mortar take the place of turf, visitors to the heath will hardly recognize their old acquaintance".[22]

That concern was widely shared: "If [Kenwood] were ever sold to speculative building contractors, along with the adjacent grassy fields, including Parliament Hill and Sir Spencer Maryon Wilson's brickfields, the East Heath would lose all its attractions ... and would become a mere ugly playground".[23]

**Notes, Chapter 10**

1. Letter to Sir John Thwaites at MBW prior to the Chancery hearing, Dec 1866
2. 'Death of Mr. J Gurney Hoare', *Ham & High,* 20 Feb 1875
3. Joseph Charles Parkinson,'Hampstead Heath', *All the Year Round*, vol. XVII, no 409 (23 Feb 1867), p 198
4. Booth (1886-1903), p 212
5. Famously condemned by Pevsner in 1952 as crushingly mean and a disgrace to so prosperous and artistic a borough
6. Arnold Bax (1943), (later Master of the King's Music) *Farewell, my youth* (Longman & Green), p. 9
7. See Bibliography
8. By around 1800 there were several copyhold cottages on this site, one of which was later called Bellmoor, and another Harrow Lodge, where Basil Champneys lived from 1869. Barratt converted them into one large house.
9. Barratt married Francis Pears' eldest daughter, Mary, in 1865 and became a partner in the firm.

10. Letter to Miss Harris, 7 Dec 1893 (*Life of Octavia Hill as told in her letters*, Arkose Press, 2015)
11. Originally of a Quaker family, Hampstead historian William Howitt lived in Highgate between 1854 and 1870, and was also part of the social reform movement.
12. A Christian Socialist initiative to help poor 'ragged school' children; Octavia would take them on Sunday outings to Hampstead Heath.
13. Maurice established the Queen's College for Women (1848) and Working Men's College (1854); he is buried in Highgate Cemetery.
14. David A. Hayes, 'From Southwood Smith to Octavia Hill'; and Isabel Raphael, 'Southwood Smith, his extraordinary life and family', *Camden History Review* 33 (2009)
15. Bond had been involved with the CPS, later represented Hampstead on the LCC, and became MP for East Nottingham.

16. Named after John Kyrle, the 18th century benefactor of Ross-on-Wye, amateur architect, physician and lawyer, who spent much of his fortune improving the town's amenities. He was lauded by Pope as the 'Man of Ross'.
17. *The Times*, 28 Jan 1881: report of Kyrle Society 1st meeting
18. Sir Walter Besant (1836-1901), novelist, antiquarian and social reformer; wrote a 10-volume survey of London, and his socially conscious novel, *All sorts and conditions of men*, prompted the establishment of the People's Palace in Mile End; founded the Society of Authors to protect their legal rights; deeply interested in Hampstead matters, and an active committee member of the Hampstead Antiquarian Society and, later, of the Heath Protection Society. Eminent in his day, he is now almost completely forgotten.

19. Ernest Abraham Hart (1835-98), ophthalmic surgeon and medical journalist; wrote for *The Lancet*, and in 1866 was appointed editor of the *British Medical Journal*; his second wife (1872) was Alice Marion Rowland, the sister of Henrietta Barnett.
20. *The Times,* 15 & 20 Jul 1875; Professor Thompson entirely misrepresents this, ascribing to Octavia Hill the opposite sentiment: "it was hardly in the minds of the chief promoters of this preservationist move that indiscriminate gaggles of the poor should be invited into the bosom of Hampstead" (Thompson (1974), p 306).
21. *Ham & High*, 21 Aug 1875
22. *The Times*, 2 Feb 1884
23. *Illustrated London News*, 24 Apr 1886, cited by Ikin (1985), p 20

## Chapter 11
# Kenwood redivided

Originally a Church property, the Caen Wood estate was divided in 1525 when its owners, Holy Trinity Priory, Aldgate, fell into debt. The southern part, which we know today as Parliament Hill, became Millfield Farm; the northern part consisting of Caen Wood and Gyll Holt was for a while held by the Crown. After the Reformation the two halves of the estate were sold separately. Millfield Farm went to the Hampstead Water Company, while the northern lands and woods passed through several hands before being bought in 1616 by John Bill, the King's Printer, who built the first house on the site. Several more upheavals, including a bankruptcy caused by the South Sea Bubble, brought it into the ownership of the Earl of Bute, a noted amateur botanist who oversaw the creation of Kew Gardens and was prime minister under George III. He sold it to fellow Scot, William Murray, a younger son of the Stormonts of Scone Palace who had acquired title and position through service to King James VI of Scotland at the end of the 16th century. Educated at Westminster School and Oxford, Murray reached the top of his chosen profession as a lawyer, becoming Solicitor General in 1742, Attorney General in 1754, the year he bought Kenwood, and two years later succeeding to the highest judicial office, Lord Chief Justice, taking the title of the 1st Earl of Mansfield. He famously reformed the law of evidence, of insurance, of slavery and of religious disability.[1]

When he acquired Kenwood it was not a particularly important estate and at first he used the small villa only occasionally for entertaining.[2] Ten years later he employed Robert Adam to redesign and enlarge it, and after the fateful night in June 1780, when his London home in Bloomsbury was attacked and destroyed by Gordon rioters, Kenwood became his permanent residence. He set about improving and enlarging the estate by acquiring the surrounding lands whenever they became available, freehold to the south and leasehold to the north, in order to protect its rural feel and the wonderful views over London. In effect,

73. William Murray (1704/5-93), Lord Chief Justice of England and Wales, 1st Earl of Mansfield. Line drawing by Eric Wade, one of several artists who contributed to the Heath & Hampstead Society newsletters over the years (*Newsletter,* autumn 1979

121

he reinstated the Priory's original medieval estate. He bought up Millfield Farm when Hampstead Water Company's lease expired in 1789, thus securing the land up to the summit of Parliament Hill. Northward he extended the estate beyond Hampstead Lane by leasing 700 acres of farm land and woods, including Highgate Woods, from the Bishop of London, which provided income to finance the improvements to the house and to create the beautiful parkland to the south.

Although he did not live to see his plans completed, Murray's Scottish heirs continued his policy of buying up land to protect the estate, which ultimately covered over 1,500 acres, and his far-sighted management plan enabled them to maintain it through five generations. He had no children, so Kenwood, together with the Mansfield title, was left to his nephew Viscount Stormont, heir to the Scottish estates, who became the second Earl in 1793.[2] He continued the first Earl's cherished plans, even leaving a sum of £20,000 in his will for their completion.[3] In the 1790s he got Hampstead Lane, which originally ran right in front of the house, re-routed further away, bringing North Wood into the estate. He rebuilt the farm house to the octagonal design seen today and built the dairy for his wife, Louisa.

Tending a dairy in the manner of the French queen, Marie Antoinette, had become a fashionable hobby for aristocratic ladies. The Earl's neighbour, Lord Southampton at Fitzroy Farm, a 100-acre estate bordering Kenwood on the Highgate side, had built a house with landscaped grounds, sometimes described as a *ferme ornée*,[4] which was considered to rival Kenwood. Anna Lætitia Barbauld, the poet and writer, left an amusing picture of the rivalry between the two Ladies in a letter to her brother: "Lady Mansfield and Lady Southampton, I am told, are both admirable dairywomen, and so jealous of each other's fame that they have had many heartburnings, and

74. The Kenwood Dairy. In 2012 The Heath & Hampstead Society contributed £5,125 towards the restoration of the windows in Lady Mansfield's tea room as part of refurbishments by English Heritage, helped by National Lottery funding.

have once or twice been very near a serious falling out on the dispute which of them could make the greatest quantity of butter from such a number of cows".[5]

It was the third Earl of Mansfield (1796-1840) who supported the battle to save the Heath in the 1830s, speaking against Wilson's estate bills in Parliament and subscribing £50 to the campaign. Some time before 1803 he bought the rest of the Parliament Hill land down to Gospel Oak from the canons of St Paul's Cathedral, extending the southern boundary to the banks of the Fleet River. The land was run as a dairy farm by Edward Austin of Kentish Town Green.[6] In 1823, following the death of Lord Erskine who had lost his money and left Hampstead, Mansfield bought Erskine's estate, Evergreen Hill, which stretched along the frontage of Spaniards Road, including Old Mother Hough's (or Huff's), then called the Shakespeare's Head; it later became a private house called Nine Elms. He also tried unsuccessfully to buy the East Park Fields from Sir Thomas, as various accounts relate.

The fourth Earl (1840-98) bought up the Fitzroy Park farm and meadow-land from the Southamptons when they were selling up in 1840. The Southamptons had lost interest in their Highgate estate by the 1830s, and sold off land profitably for the new London to Birmingham railway line. In 1840 they put the rest of the estate up for auction with plans, it is said, for rows of terraced housing next to Kenwood to force Mansfield's hand. He bought 25 one-acre plots bordering Kenwood by private treaty prior to the auction, to protect the Kenwood estate.[7] To the south, the Kentish Town Green farm was bisected by the Hampstead Junction Railway in 1854. St Pancras Church still owned various separate parcels of land including, curiously, a 4-acre field right in the middle of Mansfield's land. He owned a field the other side of the railway and in 1871 an exchange was agreed to tidy up this anomaly.[8]

For a century and a half, therefore, Kenwood remained in the hands of one family, who continued to respect the wishes of the first Earl.[9] As John Carswell

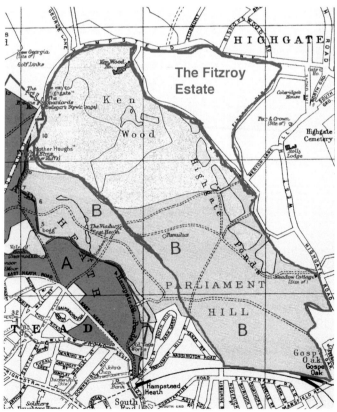

points out, he created no entail such as the one which so hampered his neighbours the Maryon Wilsons, simply entrusting "those who are nearest and dearest to me" to care for it "according to events and contingencies which it is impossible for me to foresee ... through the many labyrinths of time and chance".[10] And so they did. The magnificent unintended consequence of this long-term vision enabled the Heath to come down to us today protected on every side. It owes more than

75. The Kenwood estate by 1880

most people realise to the first Earl's carefully thought-through management arrangements. However, from the 1850s onward, although still cared for meticulously, it became an increasingly secondary possession for the family.[10]

William Howitt railed against the way Kenwood House stood empty in the 1870s, as being "one of the worst features of the continued feudal system; ... thousands of the most beautiful parts of [this island] which God created for general pleasure, are, in a dog-in-the-manger style, shut up for the greater part of the year, and seen only by a few bailiffs and labourers. During six months of spring and summer, ... houses and grounds are closed to human enjoyment; ... there is something grossly out of joint here".[11] The view from Parliament Hill was not open to the public: people sometimes broke through the hedges in order to walk over the Hill, and the Mansfields had to employ someone to watch the boundary and keep people out.[12]

The beginning of the end came in 1884, when Kenwood's long-standing leases on the woods and farm lands to the north were called in by the Ecclesiastical Commissioners with a view to development.[13] This struck at the self-sustaining system so carefully preserved by Murray's descendants. As compensation, the Commissioners were persuaded to concede the freehold of North Wood between the house and Hampstead Lane in return for the surrender of the other leases, but the land beyond the Lane, including Highgate Wood, was gone forever and with it the income that made the estate viable.[14]

Until then it was assumed that Lord Mansfield had no idea of selling any part of his Kenwood property. But now, at just the moment when the Heath campaigners wanted to buy it, it had become expedient for the Mansfields to think of selling the Parliament Hill lands. "Lord Mansfield [the 4th Earl] was already of a great age, and his heir, Lord Stormont, made no secret of his intention to realise the building value of the land whenever he should come into possession of it".[15] Moreover, as Carswell points out, from the Mansfields' point of view such a transaction had a double benefit: a capital sum would provide income to replace that lost from the leased lands taken back by the Ecclesiastical Commissioners; and it would preserve the treasured view south just as effectively as when they owned the land themselves.[16]

### The campaign for Parliament Hill

Charles Maurice called a meeting on 23 January 1884, under the auspices of the Kyrle Society, at the Holly Bush Inn, Hampstead. Cornelius Walford (the insurance expert) took the chair and many influential residents attended. Shaw Lefevre and Robert Hunter from the Commons Preservation Society were there and the gathering was addressed by Hunter, Maurice and John W. Hales (Professor Emeritus at King's College, London, and later Vice-President of the Hampstead Antiquarian Society).

The Hampstead Heath Extension Fund Committee was formed, its list of members reading like the index of the *Dictionary of National Biography*, and a national campaign was launched. It was headed by the Archbishop of Canterbury, no less (although he seemed to have dropped out by 1889), and Cardinal Manning. There were two dukes, three earls (including Lord Brabazon, the Earl of Meath,), two viscounts, a marquis and 21 MPs. The goal was to persuade the Metropolitan Board of Works (MBW) to buy East Park from Sir Spencer Maryon Wilson, and Parliament Hill and Fields, and part of the Elms Estate (part of Erskine's old garden) from Lord Mansfield.

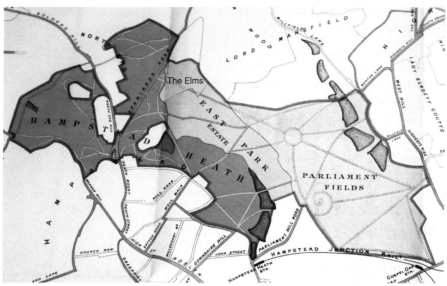

76. 1885 map showing all the land to be acquired. From 'A plea for the extension of Hampstead Heath and the preservation of Parliament Fields', St Pancras Vestry, July 1885

The indefatigable Shaw Lefevre was the Chairman, Octavia Hill's two brothers-in law Maurice, and Lewes were Honorary Secretaries and Octavia herself, by now renowned for her campaigning work for the poor, was the Treasurer. The 1st Duke of Westminster, nephew of Lord Robert Grosvenor, the Middlesex MP who had been such a staunch supporter a generation before, became President. Among the active members of this large Committee were Angela Burdett-Coutts and her husband William Burdett Coutts, MP for Westminster; Edward Bond; Sir Spencer Wells of Golders Hill House (Queen Victoria's surgeon, and President of the Royal College of Surgeons); and leading Hampstead vestrymen Sir Henry Harben, Baines, E.E. Newton and Mr H.F. Pooley (later the Honorary Secretary of the Heath Protection Society).

It was a more difficult proposition financially than the 1860s campaign, because it was not common or 'waste', but good private agricultural land and therefore more expensive. £350,000 was the initial asking price, putting the £2½ million for the same acreage dreamt of by Sir Thomas Maryon Wilson thirty years earlier into perspective. Furthermore, having to deal with two different landowners and with the MBW, which was to be the official purchaser, added complications. The negotiations were tortuous and, as before, it became a campaign of national significance, with *The Times*, and other newspapers there to report on every detail with long, often verbatim accounts. A stream of impassioned letters from Octavia Hill, Angela Burdett-Coutts, Shaw Lefevre, and the Duke of Westminster – whose "princely liberality" was particularly noted by Frederick Baines[17] - were published, exhorting the Board not to fail in its duty.

One of the points widely made was that, compared with south London, "North London, curiously enough, is very badly off for open spaces. There is no common-land, except the Heath, between Hackney, and Wormwood Scrubs at Fulham. Nor are the Hackney Commons, except the Marshes, of any great extent or beauty, while Wormwood Scrubs are flat and dull, and mostly used for military purposes. Epping Forest ... is distinctly an East-end outlet, being cut-off from North London almost as completely by the Lea".[18]

Moreover, the Heath was special: that it "should be thus singled out from other London commons is not surprising. It is on the immediate edge of the metropolis. And, further, it is on the top of a hill. Englishmen (whatever may be the case with other nations) like to get to the top of a hill. The sense of trouble taken is a distinct addition to the enjoyment of the view which rewards exertion. On the top of the heath there is the sense of being lifted above London, being a little clear of the smoke and human breath and exhausted air of the huge, closely-packed city. ... There is, however, great danger. ... The Wilson estates have now come into the hands of an absolute owner, and are being rapidly covered with houses".[19] As the paper said at the end of the campaign: "To have allowed such a spot to be covered with houses would have been to build a high wall on the north of London, and to deprive the residents in the crowded districts of Camden and Kentish Towns of their nearest natural outlet".[20]

There were problems on all sides, not the least of which was that the MBW was in no position to make so expensive a purchase and was not at all anxious to do so. "Hampstead was already endowed with its Heath; why should it have another open space at the expense of the metropolitan rates, when other parishes had no common at all? Such was the question asked by many members of the Board".[20]

George Shaw Lefevre's own account of events interestingly reveals that they had hoped to secure the whole of the Kenwood property, but the Mansfields were not quite ready to relinquish the House and were unwilling to sell anything but the 200 acres of Parliament Hill. "The whole of 1884 and the best part of 1885 were occupied in difficult and delicate negotiations with the two landowners. Sir Spencer Wilson agreed to hold his hand for a time. Lord Mansfield, after much discussion, consented to entertain a definite proposal for the purchase of 200 acres of his land, though he specially excluded Ken Wood and the land nearest to his residence".[21]

The next step was a deputation to the MBW urging it to take up the negotiations with the two landowners to purchase the 260 acres. Shaw Lefevre told them: "The time is now come when this question of enlargement must be faced. The common is now too small for the enormous number of people who use it; it will be seriously injured, if not destroyed in value if building takes place on the adjoining land." But the Board flatly refused, "alleging that the amount of money involved in the purchase was too large to justify it in imposing the burden on the ratepayers". It refused even to discuss with Shaw Lefevre's Committee, the possibility of reducing the cost by obtaining contributions from other sources.[21]

This was a disappointing rebuff, flying in the face of public opinion which was strongly in favour of the extension. Nothing daunted, Shaw Lefevre and his Committee arranged a huge garden party with a thousand guests on Parliament Hill to demonstrate the importance and beauty of the site. There were marquees "gaily encircled with flags" and more flags marked out the extent of the whole site. The guests were received by Baroness Burdett-Coutts, Lady Constance Lefevre and Lady Holland (wife of Hampstead's first MP), and among them were Sir James M'Garel-Hogg, chairman of the MBW, and many other members of the Board. The band of the Coldstream Guards played and several thousands of the general public gathered to watch.[22]

That same month St Pancras Vestry demonstrated its enthusiasm for the cause by publishing its own appeal, *A plea for the extension of Hampstead*

77. The Garden Party on Parliament Hill; illustration for *The Graphic*, 8 August 1885

*Heath*, recounting the history and especially the difficulties with Sir Thomas Maryon Wilson, including the unwarranted attempts to malign Gurney Hoare.[23] The Duke of Westminster wrote to *The Times*, deploring the MBW's lack of action, saying he had Lord Mansfield's authority to state that he was willing to entertain any proposal.[24]

Negotiations with the two landowners, aided by Robert Hunter and William Burdett- Coutts, were re-opened. If they could get the price reduced, perhaps the MBW might reconsider; they succeeded in getting a reduction of £50,000. At the same time the Extension Committee hit upon the device of preparing an enabling Act (the Hampstead Heath Enlargement Act,) empowering, but not compelling, the MBW to buy the land, and providing a legal framework for the vestries, district boards and the City of London Parochial Charity Fund to contribute. Burdett-Coutts helped steer the Bill through Parliament, the MBW did not object, and it was given Royal Assent in September 1886. The Committee then set about ensuring the support of the St Pancras and Hampstead Vestries and the City Parochial Charity Fund, which, with perfect timing had just been reformed to ensure that its money could be used to benefit the whole of London, with a specific remit to provide open spaces and recreation grounds. All were persuaded to contribute, with promises amounting altogether to £100,000.[25]

Having secured all this by the autumn of 1886, the Committee went back to the MBW, pointing out that they had not only got the landowners to reduce their price to £302,000, but had also secured promises of donations from several other quarters, thus reducing the amount required of the MBW to £205,000. Still the Board declined to take action. The Vestries, discouraged by the Board's reluctance, began to waver on their promises, making objections to having to contribute to a scheme which would benefit the whole of London and which therefore should be funded by the MBW. There was deadlock and another year went by, as Shaw Lefevre and his Committee tried to find a solution.

They went back to the two Vestries to stiffen their resolve by getting wider public backing. Committee member Frederick Baines, a Hampstead vestryman, organised a public meeting at the Vestry Hall on Haverstock Hill. He was supported by, among other local residents, Sir Spencer Wells, Professor Hales, Herbert Asquith (the future prime minister), the Maurices, and Miss Frances M. Buss (the founder of North London Collegiate School who lived in King Henry's Road). The meeting passed a resolution that the Hampstead Vestry should give £20,000 and it duly obliged.[26] A similar strategy was implemented at St Pancras, where stronger opposition had developed within the Vestry. This time William Burdett-Coutts led, and again it was a public meeting that saved the day. Enthusiastic and unanimous support for a grant of £30,000 was followed up with deputations and memorials "from all classes of the ratepayers", to the Vestry meeting which took place the next day, and Burdett-Coutts made a powerful speech in support. The sum was voted by a large majority.[27]

At last, in October 1887 after long hesitation, the MBW came to a decision: it would contribute, but only half of the total cost, not the £200,000 the campaigners had hoped for. In so doing it was signalling that it regarded the scheme not as a Metropolitan one but as only a "local improvement". The Extension Committee had to accept the compromise and launched a public appeal to raise the remaining £50,000. Several large London landowners, no doubt urged on by the Duke of Westminster, gave liberally; £46,000 was raised and the St Marylebone Vestry came to the rescue by voting for a £5,000 donation to fill the remaining gap. *The Times* published several lists of subscribers, from which it can be seen that the Duke of Westminster and the Duke of Bedford each gave £3,000, and the Burdett-Coutts £1,500. Other donors included the Duke of Devonshire, several members of the Rothschild family, Barings and Hoare Banks, and Sir Frederick Leighton. Many Hampstead residents subscribed generously, including most of the vestry members; Henry Harben and his daughter contributed £1,150. Frank Debenham,[28] the store owner, who went on to be active in local civic matters and in the campaign to save Golders Hill, also contributed.

Even then the problems were not yet over. There were further hold-ups over legal matters: about how the vote was taken, and when the money was to be paid. The MBW demanded that all the money be paid up front, whereas some of it had been promised to the Committee only in installments. Then, just as had happened in 1871, discrepancies between the plans agreed with Lord Mansfield and those deposited with the Act in the House of Lords, caused yet further delay. At the last minute St Pancras had a further loss of nerve, and tried to wriggle out of its agreement, even calling another public meeting, hoping that the ratepayers would support them in saving an addition to the rates – an extraordinary *volte face*. But the St Pancras ratepayers stood firm in support of the scheme.

By now Shaw Lefevre was becoming extremely worried that the two landowners would lose patience and back out. But at last all these difficulties were settled, and on 6 March 1889 the contracts were finally exchanged. On 25 March, *The Times*, which had kept faith throughout, with leaders, reports and letters in support, devoted 3,000 words to the achievement in addition to a leading article giving an account of the whole campaign, and a full report of the meeting hosted by the ever-generous Duke of Westminster in the music room of Grosvenor House, Park Lane, to receive the final report of the Extension Committee. The size of the Heath was now doubled to 481 acres. The Times pointed out that the "addition to the rates [was] so trifling as to be practically inappreciable. For the next fifty years the inhabitants of the metropolis will pay an increased rate of one-sixteenth of a penny; the ratepayers of Hampstead will pay an additional one-third of a penny; and those of St Pancras a farthing. For such payments a tract of nearly 500 acres is preserved".[20]

Barrett observed that in the end the Lord of the Manor had done pretty well out of Hampstead Heath: £45,000 for the manorial rights in 1871 and a further sum of £100,000 for East Park. He recounts one rather intriguing story told by Charles Maurice, of an old gentleman who wished to remain anonymous, who "went to the bank and paid in £200 in gold" and later paid two more sums of a similar amount. "He gave a different name each time and from that day to this the identity of the mysterious donor has remained undiscovered".[29]

The Extension Committee was wound up and a small surplus of £600 was divided between the Kyrle Society and the Commons Preservation Society, who had helped so much to achieve this successful outcome. It was one of the last acts of the MBW before being abolished and replaced by the London County Council (LCC).

## New governance for London – farewell to the MBW

The possibility of a reorganisation of London Government had been under discussion throughout the 1880s, and the Local Government Act of 1888 brought a complete shake up, with the LCC replacing the MBW and taking over responsibility for the Heath. Hampstead had two representatives on the new LCC.

It started well. One of its first initiatives in 1890 was to add two acres to the Heath by buying up some abandoned land on the Highgate Road, opposite Croftdown Road, for £6,500. It was the site of an old well, owned by the New River Company but disused since 1853.[30] Next, in May 1893, a Highgate Bathing Pond (now the Highgate Men's Pond) was opened to the public – until then only the Hampstead Pond (now the Hampstead Mixed Pond) had been open to swimmers – and several improvements were made, including changing rooms, hitherto unheard of! It had the first diving stage in England and the Royal Life Saving Society staged the first National Graceful Diving Competition there in 1895.[12]

78. LCC coat of arms

But it was not long before problems emerged, this time over management of the land; the new Council could not leave well alone. After the MBW's 20 years of benign neglect, the LCC's Parks Department took charge of the Heath, "a logical move on the face of it, but one which was to lead to endless conflict between the tidy floral aspirations of that Department and the [Heath Protection] Society's desire to preserve the wildness of the Heath".[31] They began to build roads. Octavia Hill wrote twice to *The Times* in January 1890

79. The new high diving board at Highgate, 1900s

to protest. Although the Department stopped making a road across Parliament Hill, it carried on at the Viaduct, "... though the road leads nowhere. ... Surely it was not for this that the land was purchased."[32] Then there were schemes "for planting Parliament-hill, the East-park, and ... Spaniards-road", approved and carried out in 1895-96.[33] Hedges on Parliament Hill were removed; there was cutting and burning of gorse, filling hollows and small ponds, and clearing away waterside plants from the margins of ponds. What especially annoyed people was the planting of 2,000 more trees, many of them along Spaniards Road, which would block the view.

There was a horrified outcry; the LCC was tidying up the Heath and 'parkifying' it; objections poured in. The LCC recorded that "They received many communications and petitions from residents ... who took a keen interest in preserving the natural features and beauties of the heath, ... and several deputations came to them and personally laid before them their views on the subject." So far from stopping, the LCC justified these works, saying they were approved "with a view to enhancing the attractiveness of those pleasure-grounds"; "willow trees planted by the lord of the manor 40 years ago were fast decaying", while the trees "near the Spaniards-road were ornamental and were intended to check the scour of the fine sand". The LCC claimed that "they had laid strict instructions on the officials not to interfere in any way with its existing features" and that "they had received the unanimous approbation of the vestries of Hampstead and St. Pancras".[34] These explanations served only to confirm the objectors' worst fears: the Heath would lose its wild, rustic character and its views, and be turned into a prim suburban park.

### Notes, Chapter 11

1. John Carswell, 'New light on Kenwood', *H&OHS Newsletter* (May 1991)
2. Carswell (1992), p 6
3. Summerson (1962), p.10
4. A farm designed for both utility and beauty, the buildings treated decoratively and contributing to the aesthetic effect within a picturesque landscape (www.oxfordreference.com)
5. *Memoir of Mrs Barbauld: letters and notices of her family and friends*, by her great-niece Anna Letitia Le Breton (G. Bell, 1974), p 63
6. *Mansfield Conservation Area appraisal and management strategy* (LB of Camden, 2008)
7. Two large houses were built where Southampton Lodge had stood: Beechwood and The Elms, both now listed.
8. Michael Ogden, 'Old St Pancras Church and its fields', *CHR* 21 (1997). The fields had been bequeathed by an anonymous donor sometime before 1189 to provide income for the repair of the parish church.
9. Carswell (1992), p 5
10. Ibid., p 22
11. Howitt (1869), p 335
12. Dermot Green, 'Highgate Men's Pond: a short history', *CHR* 33 (2009)
13. The Ecclesiastical Commission, appointed in 1835 to reform Church finances, gradually took over responsibility for the administration and management of the Church Estates.
14. Carswell (1992), p 28. Highgate Wood was acquired by the City of London Corporation from the Ecclesiastical Commissioners in 1886 after a campaign by Henry R. Williams, Chairman of the Hornsey Local Board and School Board. He was supported by Hunter, Shaw Lefevre, Octavia Hill, and *The Times*, which regularly published their letters. The wood was publicly dedicated under the Highgate and Kilburn Open Spaces Act 1886, as 'an open space for ever', on 30 Oct 1886 by the Lord Mayor, Sir John Staples.
15. Eversley (1894), p 55: 'Hampstead Heath'
16. Carswell (1992), p 28
17. Baines (1890), p 155
18. *The Spectator*, 19 Jul 1884
19. *The Times*, 2 Feb 1884
20. *The Times*, 25 Mar 1889 (leader)
21. Eversley (1894), p 56, (Ken Wood is now called South Wood) Prof. Thompson sneers at this eye-witness account, as, written "in the stirring tones of a general reliving the incidents of a recent victory ... it is characteristically partisan" (Thompson (1974), p 190).
22. *The Times*, 30 Jul 1885
23. Burgh House archive
24. *The Times*, 14 Nov 1885
25. Concerns about use of money raised by City of London parishes, many of which were moribund and depopulated, led to the Parochial Charities Act 1883. The five largest City parishes continued to administer their own charitable endowments, but the rest were to be administered by a new body, the City Parochial Foundation.
26. *The Times*, 2 Dec 1886
27. Final report of the Hampstead Heath Extension Fund Committee
28. Of Debenham & Freebody; lived at 1 Fitzjohn's Avenue, now part of South Hampstead School
29. Barratt (1912), vol. II, p 220
30. Sexby (2014), p 415; Charles E. Lee, 'Plentyfull Sprynges at Hampstead Hethe', *CHR* 3 (1975)
31. Woodford (1998), foreword
32. *The Times* 7 & 30 Jan 1890
33. LCC Parks & Open Spaces Committee report, *The Times*, 19 Feb 1898
34. Ibid., 25 Jan 1897

## Chapter 12

# O Gardeners spare our heath

Yet another campaign began. Letters appeared in the press and Hampstead shops put up cards in their windows with the slogan "save the meadow paths".

By 1896 things came to a head. Two memorials – petitions in modern parlance – were got up, the first in February by the artist Walter Field, son of the lawyer Edwin Field, who now lived at The Pryors. It was not a large petition but the signatories included the President of the Royal Academy and some of the most eminent "Artists and other admirers of the wild and picturesque beauty of the Heath". Sir John Millais was joined by Hubert Herkomer, vice-president of the Royal Watercolour Society, Norman Shaw, Octavia Hill, George du Maurier, Charles Santley the opera singer, Sir Walter Besant and Herbert Beerbohm Tree, and the petition was reported in *The Times*. Field personally presented it to the London County Council's Parks and Open Spaces Committee, with a highly emotional speech. He reminded them that this was his third petition to them and informed them that "we artist professors know more than you business gentlemen as to the matter of what makes our English landscape so lovely". He entreated them "to protect the Heath as your petitioners require".[1]

80. Hampstead Heath, by Walter Field {1837-1901}

Two months later Hampstead residents presented another petition in a deputation to the Parks Committee. Sir Walter Besant wrote with bitter irony: "The London County Council are certainly doing their best to secure the love and respect and gratitude of the people whose city they are protecting. Their attempts to convert the greater part of Hampstead Heath into a smug little park ... have gone a long way to endear the Council to all Hampstead People".[2,3] The outcry reached not only the national press, the weeklies and the specialised journals, but such papers as the *Liverpool Mercury, Birmingham Post,* and *Pontefract Advertiser,* which had clearly not forgotten the battles of the 1860s. A letter published in the *Pall Mall Gazette,* in March 1896, gives an idea of the passion and vehemence of the protest:

Sir,– Is it possible to interest you in the subject of Hampstead Heath? Some kind of action has been taken in the shape of a memorial to the London County Council Committee of Parks and Open Spaces, praying that they refrain from any further mutilation and damage of the Heath. But they make no allusion to the gigantic error and mountain of bad taste displayed in the indiscriminate way in which the unfortunate Heath has been studded with trees without the slightest regard to fitness.

If anyone will take the trouble to walk along the Spaniards' Road, he will see one of the worst specimens of the furore of tree-planting which has possessed this committee. This particular bit of the Heath was, until the other day, one of the wildest and most enchanting bits, to a lover of nature, to be seen. Now, there are over a hundred trees newly planted, and its distinctive character is completely ruined. There are other instances quite as bad as this, but I must not exhaust your patience. South African questions, the Cuban insurrection, and all other ephemeral subjects must come to an end some time.[4] Hampstead Heath, however, we shall always have with us, and as it is the choicest bit of open country so near to London, it behoves us all to do what we can to prevent its being completely blotted out as such, and transformed into a sort of Bois de Boulogne *a la mode de* London County Council.

I remain sir, yours faithfully,
Tree Lover, BUT Not Tree Worshipper.[3]

Another submission was a splendid piece of doggerel verse in the *St James's Gazette,*[5,3] purporting to represent the other end of the social spectrum:

No! I don't set up for a artist, and I ain't a culchered bloke.
Though I keeps my barrer tidy and takes a pride in my moke;
My tastes aren't eddycated; but I think I knows wot's wot,
An' I know that 'Ampstead's lovely, and the Old Kent Road is not.

I loves the sights, the sounds, the scents, an' I'll see the Council blowed
Before they spile the picter with their paths and lamps and road.
"Ands off" sez I, "good genelmen; you've better work to do
Than a cuttin' up of lanskips" - an' my missis sez so too.

Another verse protest pleaded:

> O Gardeners spare our heath
> Lop not another bough!
> We always liked it wild,
> Why, then, 'improve' it now?
>
> Throw down your spuds and spades,
> Your shears put in their sheath!
> Nor try again to make
> A garden of our Heath [6, 3]

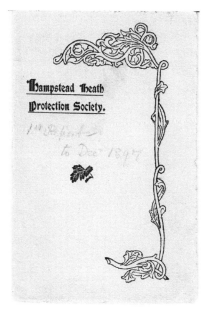

81. Front cover of the Hampstead Heath Protection Society's 1st annual report

## Hampstead Heath Protection Society

A public meeting was called on 7 April 1897 at the Drill Hall in Heath Street. The local community realised that the safeguarding of their precious Heath could not be left to the authorities. It was going to be necessary to maintain an "eternal vigil" to ensure that those in whom management of the land was vested did not betray the trust. A permanent Committee was required and it was inaugurated at the meeting as the Hampstead Heath Protection Society (HHPS). It has adapted its name over the decades in response to changing times, and is now the Heath & Hampstead Society. There was even one dissenter at the meeting, duly reported by *The Times*, and his words strike a curiously modern note: Mr J.B. Wilkin of the Hampstead Ratepayers' Association said that the resolution was "too artistic" for him. He considered that "great credit was due to the London County Council for the work they had done in making the heath and Parliament-Hill-fields accessible to the public".[7]

The founder members of the HHPS included several of the 1869 campaigners: Richard Ware and Isaac Solly Lister who, with Gurney Hoare had been the original defendants at the Chancery hearing before Lord Romilly. Gurney Hoare's two daughters and his son Samuel Hoare, MP for Norwich, were there. His nephew E. Brodie Hoare, Hampstead's second MP, presided over the inaugural meeting and became the new Society's first President, while the Duke of Westminster continued his support for the Heath by becoming its first Patron. Emily Field, whose entire family campaigned in the 1860s, was the driving force in founding the HHPS, and was its first Honorary Secretary; all ten of her family joined. Other founder members included Norman Shaw, the artists Carl Haag and David Murray RA, Charles Santley, the first singer to be knighted (in 1907), Canon and Mrs Barnett, and Frank Debenham. The Bishop of Exeter, Edward Henry Bickersteth, who had been the much-loved Vicar of Christ Church, Hampstead, for thirty years from 1855, lent his name in support as an Honorary Member. He knew the Hoare family well: John Gurney Hoare and three of his

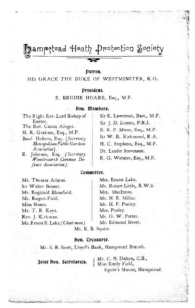

82. The first committee; from the 1st annual report

83. Brodie Hoare (1841-1911), MP for Hampstead and the Society's first President

84. Hugh Lupus Grosvenor, 1st Duke of Westminster (1825-99), first Patron

brothers helped to found Christ Church.

It is a mark of the significance of the Heath and the extraordinary battle for its survival and extension that so many prominent Hampstead residents not only joined, but were prepared to be active committee members in support of this new civic society. They were a veritable 'who's who' of the arts and the burgeoning conservation world. The first Committee included Emily Field's brother Rogers Field the engineer, and John Gurney Hoare's daughters Miss Margaret Hoare and Mrs Anna Maria MacInnes. They were joined by Sir Walter Besant; the architect Reginald Blomfield RA, and Cornelius Dalton, a lawyer, patents expert and highly experienced civil servant[8] (both later knighted); and George Potter the estate agent, who had already shown his mettle over the cricketing incident. And later, Basil Champneys, Lady du Maurier, architect Clough Williams-Ellis, artist E.S. Nevinson, and Sir J.C. Lamb, a civil servant, all served on the committee.

The roster of distinguished Honorary Members (or who today would be called Patrons) included Sir William Thistleton Dyer, the Director of Kew Gardens, and Mr Samuel Parsons, former Superintendent of Planting of the New York Parks. From the arts world Sir William Richmond, Sir James Linton, Sir Ernest Waterlow (nephew of Sir Sydney Waterlow), Arthur Severn and George Aitchison RA, President of the RIBA, lent their names. Several local MPs were on the list: the two St Pancras MPs, Edward Moon and Robert Webster; H.C. Stephens, MP for Finchley (who left Avenue House, Finchley to the public when he died); Thomas Milvain, MP for Hampstead from 1902-05; the Hon. Sydney Holland (whose father, Henry Holland, was Hampstead's first MP); and the Rt Hon. Lord Hobhouse, lawyer and politician, who was one of the first Aldermen on the London

County Council. Both the Earl of Mansfield and the Lords of the Manor, the Maryon Wilson family (all animosity now forgotten), played their parts as honorary committee members, and Mansfield became Patron on the death of the Duke of Westminster in 1899. Later, members of the Guinness family, the 2nd Earl of Iveagh and Lord Moyne, showed their support by becoming members. George Shaw Lefevre maintained his connection and was President from 1908

85. Ernest Lake (1844 -1917) the first chairman of the HHPS

(elevated to the peerage as the 1st Baron Eversley in 1906).

The Society's first Chairman, Ernest Lake, a solicitor with a practice at Lincoln's Inn, had come to Hampstead in 1872 on his marriage to the daughter of Dr Dyne, headmaster of Highgate School, and lived at East Heath Lodge. He was well versed in local matters, having served as a vestryman for nine years, as a trustee of the Hampstead Wells and Campden Charity, and as a churchwarden of Hampstead Parish Church. He was so well regarded that when Hampstead became a borough, a deputation from Town Ward tried to persuade him out of retirement in 1903 to return to political life. Although he told them "he felt he had done his bit and had earned the right to stay by his fireside", such was his sense of duty and public spirit that, by then in his sixties, he served as an Alderman, and as Mayor of the Borough in 1908. At his funeral the Vicar described him as "an upright English Gentleman of the old school".[9] He laid down two principles for the Society, the second of which was probably due to his political acumen and has stood it in good stead over the last 121 years:

"interfering as little as possible with the natural beauty plants, shrubs and bird life – on the heath" and "the necessity for working in harmony with the London County Council".

The HHPS formed links with other like-minded organisations, keeping in close touch with *The Architect and Building News*, the Royal Institute of British Architects, the Society for the Protection of Ancient Buildings (founded 1877), and the National Trust, founded only a year earlier in 1896 by Octavia Hill and Robert Hunter who were, of course, closely involved in saving Parliament Hill and the founding of the Society. The Secretary of the Wandsworh Common Defence Association, a Mr Johnson, was an Honorary Member in the early years, and the Honorary Secretary of the Norfolk Broads Protection Society was a founder member of the HHPS. In particular, they worked closely with Lord Meath the Chairman, and Basil Holmes the Secretary, of the Metropolitan Public Gardens Association (MPGA), which had long been a keen supporter. Holmes later became a Vice-President of the Society and remained involved until his death in 1939. Later on they welcomed new groups such as the Council for the Preservation of Rural England (CPRE) in 1926, the Georgian Group in 1937 and the Civic Trust in 1957.

The Hampstead Heath Protection Society was the first Civic Society in London and others slowly began to follow. The Wimbledon Society was founded in 1903, Hampstead Garden Suburb Residents' Association and the Kew Society in 1911, and the London Society in 1912. In the 1930s the HHPS welcomed the fact that more local societies like theirs were being established,[10] and their advice was sought on how to start a society by new groups such as the Hammersmith and Chiswick Improvement Society in 1932.[11]

The history of Hampstead Heath from this point is almost inseparable from that of the HHPS. Its first annual report welcomed a resolution taken in 1896 by the London County Council to reduce the number of gardeners employed on the Heath to three. "This, of course, is quite in accord with the views of the Hampstead Heath Protection Society, which strongly deprecates any gardening operations on the Old Heath".[12]

In a nice touch, the Society's first Chairman and Secretary were Mr Lake and Miss Field, and one of its later secretaries was a Mr Heath, thus almost creating reality out of that letter from 'Hampstead Heath' to *The Times* in 1843.

## Golders Hill Park estate

Almost immediately the new Society was thrown into battle to save the Golders Hill Park estate, which came on the market and was due to be auctioned that same year, 1897, on the death of Sir Spencer Wells, who had been a keen supporter of the campaign for Parliament Hill. The estate dates from the 1750s and the house is thought to have been built by Charles Dingley, who also owned North End (or Wildwoods), later known as Pitt House.[13] Politically ambitious, he had invited the prime minister, William Pitt the Elder (1st Earl of Chatham), to stay at North End and took the Golders Hill property while Pitt was in residence in 1766. Later, Golders Hill was owned by John Coore, who hired Humphry Repton to landscape the grounds and who also built Ivy House next door.

In the 1890s developers were closing in and there was a boom in urban flat-building. As a writer to the local newspaper spelled out, Golders Hill would be "overlaid by mountainous monstrosities of glaring red brick such as now line the sides of the once-beautiful Finchley Road"[14] (a description somewhat hard to credit today)

It was Ernest Hart of the MPGA who began fundraising in the summer of 1897; among those who contributed were Samuel Figgis, Rogers and Emily Field, and Thomas Barratt. One of the new Protection Society's first acts was to send a resolution to the Hampstead Vestry, urging it to encourage London County Council to acquire "such a portion of the Golders Hill Estate as will preserve the trees [and] add so much to the value and natural beauty of the Heath", if it could be obtained at a reasonable price.[12] Unfortunately, Hart died soon after and now speedy action was required. The first auction failed to sell the estate but it was put up again in 1898. Samuel Figgis, who had come to Hampstead from Dublin in 1884 and was a founder member of the

HHPS, took up the campaign, and the willing auspices of *The Times* were again engaged to publicise and support it at every stage. Through the paper's letters columns, in June 1898, Figgis informed anyone who was interested that a meeting would take place at his home, Wildwoods (Pitt House), to form a special committee to take action; his neighbour, Mr Walter Smith of Ivy House, would also be there. It was a reconvening of many of those who had been involved in the Parliament Hill extension a decade earlier, and were already members of the new Society. With Sir Henry Harben as chairman, they formed themselves into a fifteen-strong guaranteeing committee, including Thomas Barratt, Frank Debenham, Rogers Field, Harold Harmsworth (later the 1st Lord Rothermere), and Ernest Hart's widow, Alice. They agreed to become collectively responsible up to a limit of £35,000, which it was supposed was the most that would be bid at the impending auction. If they were successful they would then launch a fundraising appeal to cover the cost. But the speculative builders competing for the land took the price above this agreed amount. Thomas Barratt did not need to think twice: he continued bidding on his own account and saved the day by securing the property for £38,000.

Fundraising began in earnest, and at the highest level, with a public meeting at the Mansion House hosted by the Lord Mayor. Among those present was Lord Knutsford (Hampstead's first MP), and letters expressing sympathy

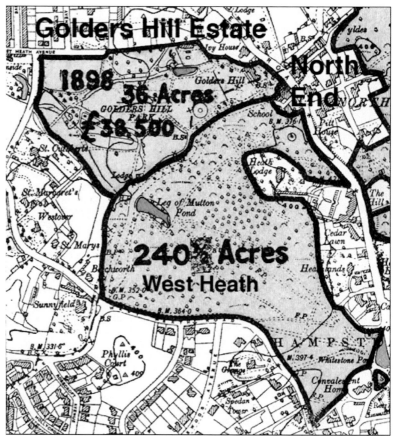

86. The West Heath (blue) and Golders Hill Estate (green); detail of the map drawn by Lawrence Chubb (see p 10)

with the campaign were read from the Bishop of London, Lord Carrington, Mr Asquith MP, and Sir Lawrence Alma-Tadema. The Marquis of Lorne (the future Duke of Argyll) moved a resolution supporting the endeavour to preserve the beauty of Hampstead Heath and extend its area. Two days later a great garden party, as had happened at Parliament Hill, was held in Golders Hill Park, to show off its beauties, and was attended by some 10,000 people.[15]

87. Golders Hill mansion, 1900s

By October Henry Harben was able to inform readers of *The Times* that the public appeal, generously supported again by the Duke of Westminster and Shaw Lefevre, had successfully raised the required sum.[16] A deputation to the LCC secured a contribution of £12,000; Hampstead Vestry had voted £10,000, and Marylebone, St Pancras and Paddington Vestries all gave support, as did the City of London Corporation, Middlesex County Council and the City Parochial Foundation. Contributions from 700 private individuals amounted to £13,000. Eventually over £41,000 was raised and the surplus was donated to the MPGA as the nucleus of a fund for some further extension of the Heath: possibly, the HHPS hoped, Telegraph Hill, should it come up for sale. But it was in the end used to purchase a small plot of land opposite the Old Bull and Bush.

1899 saw another change to local government, which was to prove positive for future campaigns for the Heath. Under the London Government Act 1899, Hampstead Parish became a Metropolitan Borough with a Mayor, seven Aldermen, and 42 Councillors. Many of them, besides Ernest Lake, were members of the HHPS, and some of them were on its Committee, thus enabling it to work closely with the Borough in the local interest. Charles Booth expressed the view that the change from Vestry to Borough Council was unlikely to make any difference to Hampstead Vestry's long-enjoyed reputation for good management.[17]

**Notes, Chapter 12**

1. H&HS archive: A/1048/3/2/2/6
2. *The Queen*, 20 Feb 1897
3. Contained in a booklet, 'Extracts from the Public Press, showing the widespread interest in the case which the Society has taken up', published by the HHPS (author's archive)
4. The Boer Wars and the Cuban War of Independence (1895-98)
5. 'L.S.', in *St James's Gazette*, 2 Mar 1896;

'moke'– a donkey.
6. From *Truth*, a periodical founded in 1877 by the diplomat and Liberal politician Henry Labouchère
7. Report of inaugural meeting of the HHPS, *The Times*, 9 Apr 1897
8. (Sir) Cornelius Neale Dalton (1842-1920) became Comptroller General of Patents, Designs & Trademarks in 1897. He lived successively on Downshire Hill, at 11 Heath Rise, Willow Road (in the 1880s),

and at 'Eskhaven', East Heath Road from 1899; then at 26 Belsize Lane (by 1911), and finally at 57 Belsize Avenue.
9. *Ham & High*, 7 Oct 1917
10. HHPS annual report, 1936
11. It was not until after WWII with the establishment of the Civic Trust that dozens of Societies began to form.
12. HHPS annual report, 1898
13. The North End estate was begun in

1727 by his father Robert Dingley, partly with Ditchfield encroachments; when Charles inherited in the 1760s he transformed the cottage into a mansion.
14. Cited by Farmer (1984), p 132, but with no attribution
15. *The Times*, 20 Jul 1898
16. *The Times*, 7 Oct 1898: 'Hampstead-heath extension scheme'
17. Charles Booth (1886-1903), p 212

## Chapter 13

# Into the 20th century

### The coming of the Tube

The next problem which faced the Society was the coming of the underground tubular railway – the Tube. Commons, with empty land that could be got cheaply, were the favoured routes of railway promoters. In the 1860s the Metropolitan & St John's Wood Railway Company[1] had tried to purchase 29 acres of Hampstead Heath to make a tunnel under it. Residents strongly opposed it, backed by the newly formed Commons Preservation Society. MPs saw off this attempt to push through a private bill that, as Frederick Doulton reminded them, would have reversed its own decision not to give Sir Thomas Wilson power to build on the Heath. He pointed out that at Wandsworth Common a railway company that got land in this way had used the surplus for building purposes.[2] "Since then", wrote *The Times* in 1900, "no promoters have dared to touch the heath".[3] In 1893, however, the Charing Cross, Euston & Hampstead Railway Company, financed by the American Charles Yerkes, had obtained powers to make a deep underground railway from King William Street, Strand, to Hampstead. "Hampstead was much perturbed by the vision of an electric railway burrowing mole-like under the heath, and throwing up stations here and there to mark its track".[3] A terminus at Holly Hill (the present Hampstead Underground station) was already authorised and power was being sought to extend to Golders Green, tunnelling directly under Whitestone Pond, with stations on the Heath near Jack Straw's Castle and at North End.

The Hampstead Heath Protection Society Committee watched these developments anxiously. They were not against the construction of the railway to Hampstead, as they made clear in letters to the press, but they strongly opposed any tunnel under the Heath, and any stations on it which would urbanise and destroy the very characteristics that made it so valued. A tunnel laid under the Heath might act as a drain and cause loss of moisture to its vegetation.[3] As Samuel Figgis pointed out, the proposed Hampstead Station is within three minutes' easy walk of the top of Hampstead-heath – another station was not needed.[4] The HHPS had heavyweight support from the MPGA, the Commons Preservation Society and the National Trust; and also from the *Municipal Journal* and *The Builder*. Figgis again took the lead setting up a special Committee to fight the tunnel. The campaign was given full coverage in the press and *The Times* published a list of some forty names headed by the Earl of Mansfield as President. All the old supporters contributed funds: Asquith, Besant, Bond, Debenham, Harben, the two Hoare MPs, E. Brodie and Sir Samuel, David Murray, and Norman Shaw. Others included Mrs Allingham, Sir Lawrence Alma-Tadema and Lord Iveagh.[5]

Lord Mansfield (the 5th Earl) presided over a packed protest meeting at Hampstead Town Hall (the old Vestry Hall on Haverstock Hill), at which it was pointed out that there was an alternative route to Golders Green without needing to tunnel under the Heath. A supporter of the pro-'tube' party was shouted down with cries of "Bogey!" and "Rot" "from the bulk of the audience".[6] The Borough Council firmly sided with the HHPS and a joint petition was presented to Parliament. A letter circulated to the press made it clear that they did not oppose the new railway, only the proposals to tunnel under the Heath and build stations there.[7] However, in May 1902 the *Daily News* reported that the Lords Committee examining the bill refused the HHPS *locus standi* to appear before it, and its counsel was not even allowed to argue the question.[7]

Later in the year a second railway was announced from Edgware, via Hendon, to Hampstead, again tunnelling under the Heath. Figgis and Ernest Lake wrote a joint letter of protest to *The Times*; they had tried to persuade the promoters to go round the Heath via Platt's Lane and Child's Hill, to no avail. They appealed for "the support of all Londoners in our efforts to preserve for future generations this splendid lung of London".[8]

This brought a reply from a Mr J.H. Hiley of the railway company, whose sneering tone showed just how novel a concept it was that local residents should band together to protect their environment. Referring to the "self-styled 'Hampstead-heath Protection Society'", he claimed that "Hampstead-heath is not under the 'protection' of any society" and that "no station is proposed under or on the heath", which was not strictly true. His ill-informed assertion that the Heath was "originally purchased and maintained by the Metropolitan Board of Works out of money charged upon the rate-payers" was only half the truth.[9] It did not seem to occur to him that, in any case, the people of Hampstead were the "rate-payers" and therefore fully entitled to a say.

They lobbied Parliament against the plans and in 1902 their persistence resulted in the matter being referred to a Select Committee to examine whether the proposed railway would cause damage to the Heath. Although the Bill could not be stopped, clauses for the protection of the surface of the Heath were strengthened and the proposed station on the top of the Heath was abandoned. But the one at North End remained a threat, as it became clear that Eton College intended to take advantage of the new railway to sell the Wyldes Farm fields adjoining Sandy Heath for development. As *The Times* pointed out: "… if care is not taken, the additional means of enjoyment may involve the destruction of that which is enjoyed".[10]
A small postscript to these events is to be found in Sir Arnold Bax's memoirs: the family's house, Ivy Bank on Haverstock Hill subsided and began to collapse after the tube tunnel was built.[11]

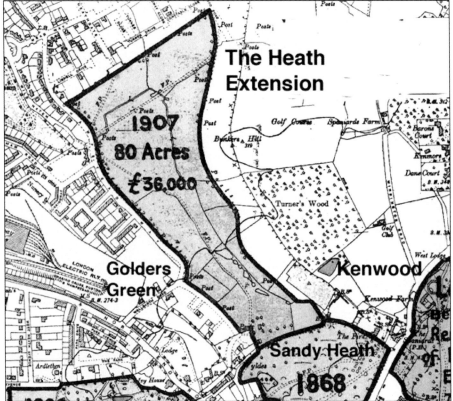

88. The Chubb map again, showing the Hampstead Heath Extension

## The Heath Extension

It was in response to the threat from the railways that another new campaigner entered the fray, the formidable Henrietta Barnett, along with her husband Canon Samuel Barnett, both old friends of Octavia Hill and founder members of the Heath Protection Society. They had a country retreat at Heath End House, Spaniards End and realised that with the Tube extension to Golders

142

Green on its way, and a proposed station at North End, Wyldes Farm would all be swallowed up for building. Working with the Society's secretary Emily Field, Mrs Barnett set up a Hampstead Heath Extension Council to persuade Eton College to sell 80 acres of the open space to add to the Heath. She "mobilised a formidable group of gentlemen – Eton being unwilling to negotiate with a lady", to persuade the College to sell them the land.[12] A price of £48,000 was agreed.

Henrietta Barnett did not do things by halves. The lists of members of the 179-strong Council headed by the Princess of Wales, and the names of those who donated, make astonishing reading. The Archbishop of Canterbury and Cardinal Manning are again at the head, and this time, no doubt due to her husband's connections – Canon Barnett had risen up the Church hierarchy to become a Canon of Westminster Abbey in 1906 – they were joined by four bishops. There were 12 peers of the realm, including Shaw Lefevre, now Lord Eversley, who was President, and the Earl of Meath, of the MPGA, who was Vice-President. Sir Robert Hunter and Edward Bond were the Treasurers. Local notables included Ridley Bax (who lived at Ivy Bank next to Hampstead Town Hall, the father of the composer Arnold Bax, later Master of the King's Music); and William Garnett (who built 'The Wabe' in Redington Road, and was the grandfather of Peggy Jay). Many of the people who had contributed in 1884 did so again: Debenham, Harmsworth, the Burdett-Coutts and Lords Rothschild and Iveagh; they were joined by the Earl of Mansfield, Canon Rawnsley of the National Trust, and Joseph Beecham of Beecham's Pills, who lived in Arkwright Road (also a director of Barratt's firm A. & F. Pears and father of Sir Thomas Beecham the conductor).

Despite this backing, the public-minded readiness of Eton College to sell the land at a fair price, and firm support from *The Times*, it was no easy task. Just as in previous campaigns, the local authorities had to be persuaded and cajoled. Application to the London County Council was first met with an absolute refusal, unlike their ready and generous response at Golders Hill Park. The land was outside the County of London and they had been attacked for extravagance – money had recently been given at Brockwell, Wandsworth and Springfield Parks, and Marble Hill – and the money market was in a bad condition for raising loans. It was only after "great exertions on the part of the Extension Council that a promise of £8,000 was at length extracted".[13] The LCC's parsimony was criticised in *The Times*.[14]

Hampstead Borough Council reluctantly contributed £5,000 after much debate, and other local boroughs – Hendon, Finchley, Islington and St Pancras – were even more cautious. With only £17,500 in public subscriptions there was a large gap in the finances. Mrs Barnett persuaded Eton College to reduce the price from £48,000 to £36,000 by changing the shape of the 80-acre area under consideration – extending further north into their estate but giving the College more scope for attractive building frontages – although with the added complication that new roads would have to be built.

But even with a grant from Middlesex County Council and increased contributions from Islington and St Pancras, in 1904 the Extension Council was still £5,000 short. Thomas Barratt once again stepped up to the mark. He recounts in his *Annals of Hampstead* that "a little private meeting took place at the Reform Club between Lord Eversley, Sir Robert Hunter" and himself, when they agreed to guarantee the necessary amount, "finding their satisfaction in having completely secured the property for the public".[15]

There were then further delays while the final agreement and legal matters were settled, and it was not until 1907 that the Hampstead Heath Extension was actually conveyed to the LCC. The final cost was £43,955, about half of it found by public bodies and City companies, and the rest from private subscriptions.[16]

And of course Mrs Barnett did not stop there. Following Ebenezer Howard's ideas for new garden towns, she set up the Hampstead Garden Suburb Trust Limited, in 1906, supported by members of the Extension Council, to buy the remaining 240 acres of Wyldes Farm and ensure that whatever was built would not spoil the rural setting.[17] She commissioned Raymond Unwin, designer of the first Garden City at Letchworth in 1903, to create her visionary scheme, the social experiment that became Hampstead Garden Suburb. As *The Times* put it: "The entire scheme is so free from the sordid spirit of speculative building".[18] Unwin lived in part of Wyldes Farm while he supervised the building

of the new suburb, and stayed there for the rest of his life.[19]

Mrs Barnett's campaign effectively put a stop to the planned North End (or Bull & Bush) tube station in Hampstead Way; deep underground, it remains a ghost station to this day. Various narratives circulate as to its uses since then: as one of four secret underground government 'war rooms' during the Cold War should London be hit with a nuclear bomb; or as part of the London Underground's civil defence preparations in case of flooding. It now functions as an emergency escape route for

89. The Walter Field fountain on the Heath extension near Hampstead Way: Emily Field presented the Portland stone fountain in memory of her brother Walter, the artist who had set in motion the protest that led to the founding of the Hampstead Heath Protection Society.

London Underground passengers should a train become stranded; a little hut that looks like a transformer building still gives access to the station below.[20]

## Hatches Bottom

This curious little relic of the days before the Vale of Health, a quarter-acre garden glorying in the name of Hatches (or Hatchett's) Bottom, remained enclosed on the Heath for many years after 1871. Samuel Hatch, a horse-harness maker, first appears in the Court Rolls in 1688 as a copyholder at Littleworth next to Jack Straw's Castle; in 1714 we find him with his workshop, the sole inhabitant on the slopes of the Heath on the other side of the road, above the stagnant bog called Gangmoor, where the Vale of Health now is. He was joined by the parish cottages for the poor, also relocated from Littleworth, and they were the only inhabitants until the Hampstead Water Company drained the marshy ground to enlarge the pond in 1777. The name stuck even after the area was renamed Vale of Health, but eventually came to refer only to this little piece of garden.[21]

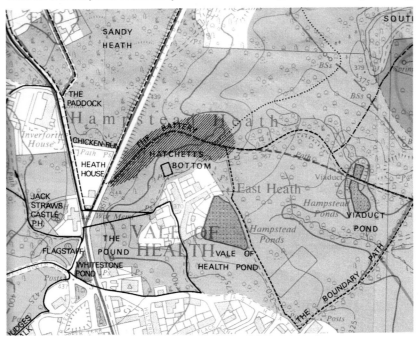

90. Hatches Bottom and also the Battery firing range (see p 22), shown on a GLC map

According to Sir Samuel Hoare (the son of John Gurney Hoare), the land was originally acquired by his great-grandfather when he came to Hampstead in the 1790s, and was let by him as a "friendly act" to one of his neighbours, although he gives no further explanation. Its 999-year lease, with a strict proviso that it was to be used only as a garden, was renewable every 21 years at an annual rent of £2.[22] It was kept fenced with a hedge and ditch as a wild bird enclosure, but no-one seemed to care for it and the fence had deteriorated into an unsightly state. Protests about its continuing enclosure began around 1905. The HHPS urged Hampstead Borough Council to acquire the lease from Sir Samuel. Now living in Cromer, Norfolk, he readily deferred to the Society's wishes and proposed to hand over the freehold as a gift to the Borough Council for the benefit of the public.[23] He also offered to pay for a shelter with seating to protect people from the rain, but everyone – including Vale of Health residents and the Hampstead Branch of the London Council for Promotion of Public Morality – objected to that as inappropriate, and Sir Samuel gracefully withdrew. The Borough Council decided to repair the fence and preserve it as a wildlife enclosure, sub-leasing it to the LCC on the same 21-year basis.[24] However, the LCC began using the enclosure as a rubbish dump, causing further annoyance. The situation was only finally resolved in 1942, when the Borough Council conveyed the freehold of the land to the LCC to be incorporated into the Heath.[25]

## Telegraph Hill

In 1912 efforts were made to secure the five acres of land at Telegraph Hill for the Heath. It had been withheld from the 1871 handover and was now put on the market by the Wilson family. However, the Wilsons gave the HHPS the opportunity to raise money to buy it to add to the Heath and, led by Sir Robert Hunter, the Society opened negotiations. Having obtained a valuation, they canvassed the LCC, Middlesex County Council, Hampstead and Hendon Councils, and the MPGA, and secured substantial contributions and pledges. In April 1913 an offer was made, but the sum demanded by the Wilsons so greatly exceeded the value put on it by the HHPS's advisers that negotiations were abandoned, and the money raised was returned. The HHPS Committee greatly deplored the loss of this opportunity. It was Robert Hunter's last service to the Society; he died in November 1913 and Telegraph Hill with its historic associations was lost.[26]

## Wartime

The Heath, with its long tradition of use by the military, was commandeered for many activities in both World Wars and the Society, patriotically, fully approved of its use to support the war effort. Indeed, the framers of the 1871 Hampstead Heath Act even made provision for such activity: Section 24, which is still in force, forbids any byelaw that might prohibit military drill without the sanction of the Secretary of State for War.

During the Great War there were allotments at Gospel Oak and the King's Meadow, on the Heath Extension and the Highgate slopes, and on the old allotments near the Vale of Health Pond, used by Hampstead tradesmen and known as 'Soldiers' Allotments'. With the crop failure of 1916 and the U-boat blockade, these became part of a vital supplyline.

There were patriotic recruitment, and anti-war pacifist, meetings and sometimes they clashed: at one peace meeting, a well organised opposition knocked the speaker off the platform and tried to throw him in the Whitestone Pond. "In some places, ... you have a recruiting meeting in one corner and a short distance away you hear someone denouncing the War in all the moods and tenses. I do not suggest any interference with liberty, but at a time like this ... I suggest that there should be stricter supervision with regard to the character of those speeches which are made on Hampstead Heath".[27]

There were at least 13 brigades training on the Heath, among them the Queen Victoria Rifles, the Royal Engineers Signal Service, the Artists' Rifles, and the 1st City of London Royal Field Artillery. The undulating terrain, and tree and shrub cover, were ideal for training for manoeuvres and for digging trenches, and the Heath was close enough to London to be easily reachable for the volunteers. Sir J.D. Rees MP praised their efforts: "We have in the City of London National Guard some 2,000 men. Surely it is a good thing that those men are willing ... to spend their Sunday in tramping over Hampstead Heath!"[28]

A volunteer Hampstead Howitzer Brigade was formed, based in Golders Hill Park, using Golders Hill House for offices, and camping next to the bandstand. Yet through it all the park and the zoo were still open to the public. The YMCA put up a marquee to provide refreshments for the officers, catering for 400 men every day, and the British Women's Temperance Association

91. 183rd (Hampstead) Howitzer Brigade, Golders Hill 1915    92. YMCA workers: group picture

93. Brigade gun team with horses

opened a hut to provide cheap refreshments for troops drilling on the Heath.

In 1915 the Mayor of Hampstead raised another volunteer brigade, the 138 Heavy Battery, Royal Garrison Artillery, who also trained on the Heath. They soon became known as the Hampstead Heavies and were on active service in France and Belgium from 1916 to 1918.[29] A mobile anti-aircraft brigade was stationed at Kenwood until 1916 and was in action several times at an emergency site on the top of the Heath.[30] The Hampstead Mixed Bathing Pond was used as a munitions dump. Much damage was done; in the 1916 air raids several bombs fell on the edges of the Heath, leaving large craters.

At first the troops' training sessions attracted crowds of spectators but, as the war increasingly took its deadly toll, enthusiasm waned. "The presence of wounded soldiers became more frequent on the Heath" and "the MPGA provided twelve seats for them by Jack Straw's Castle; the YMCA organised a gymkhana for wounded soldiers on East Heath and there were Historic Heath rambles for them guided by local antiquarian E.E. Newton".[29] Entertainment was not forgotten: concerts were given and, according to the HHPS annual report, a band played for dances held for a nominal charge on Thursday evenings at a temporary enclosure made on part of the old brickfields which had been levelled by the unemployed.[31]

Among the volunteers were some of Hampstead's eminent artists. The composer Edward Elgar came to live in Hampstead in 1912 and was there throughout the war. He was sworn in as a special constable and staff inspector to the corps at Hampstead Police Station, and also attended a meeting at which it was proposed to form an Artists' Corps.

August 1914: Sir Edward Elgar, Staff Inspector (lower left) with the Hampstead Special Constabulary.

94. Elgar (lower left) on parade with the Hampstead Special Constabulary in the grounds of University College School

148

He left his own description of his help for the war effort: "I am sure others cd. do the work better but none with a better will. I was equipping & taking receipts & registering my men for hours last night: this morning at six I inspected the whole district".[32] But his friend William H. Reed "trembled at the thought of him going out to perambulate the streets at any hour of the day or night ... firmly grasping his truncheon and looking about for German spies...".[33] Elgar later joined the Hampstead Volunteer Reserve, which involved him in shooting and rifle practice for the only time in his life. Lady Elgar recorded that after spending some time at a rifle range: "E. much excited about shooting – Hit target at 600 yards, wonderfully good as he never tried a rifle before".[34]

His music room at Severn House, Netherhall Gardens (a Norman Shaw house long since demolished) was used for small private fundraising concerts in aid of Belgian refugees. Elgar, at heart a countryman, chose Hampstead for a London residence because of the Heath. He walked there frequently and often mentioned it in his letters. He was keenly interested in life sciences and new technology, and made frequent expeditions across to the Highgate Ponds to collect material for slides for his microscope. Judges' Walk, the ancient avenue of trees at Branch Hill where Constable had frequently painted, was one of Elgar's favourite haunts: "We saw Judges Walk transfigured by the evening sun from miles away thro' my field glasses ...".[35] He immortalised it in a postscript on the manuscript score of *The Music Makers*.

The poet John Masefield , who lived in Well Walk, was rejected on medical grounds  when he went to enlist, but was accepted for the reserves. In a letter of December 1914, Rupert Brooke said Masefield was drilling hard in Hampstead, "and told me with some pride ... that he was a Corporal".[36]

95. Judges' Walk, 1860s, by George Clarkson Stansfield (1828-78)

Perhaps the most unusual reminder of these war years is the darkly satirical opera by Havergal Brian, called The Tigers, based on his own experiences as a conscript, the prologue of which takes place on Hampstead Heath on an August Bank Holiday. [37]

At the end of the war, various army service corps "held a torch-lit procession to the flagstaff on the heath where an effigy of the Kaiser was burnt on a bonfire, watched by thousands of spectators and fireworks and fire balloons were set off." The following year there were more celebrations with a procession of massed church choirs and bands up to the Heath for a dedicatory service. [29]

**Notes, Chapter 13**

1. The company built the first section of what became part of the Metropolitan underground line, north from Baker Street to Swiss Cottage, opened in 1868. An extension to Hampstead was authorised by an Act of Parliament in 1864, but the scheme was abortive. When the original line was eventually extended in 1879, it veered westward, well clear of the Heath.
2. The Times, 16 Feb 1866
3. The Times, 25 Dec 1900: 'The tunnel under Hampstead-Heath'
4. The Times, 2 Jul 1901
5. The Times, 11 Jan 1901
6. Opinions of the Press on the proposal to tunnel under Hampstead Heath published by the HHPS (author's archive)
7. HHPS, annual report, 1901
8. The Times, 20 Dec 1901
9. The Times, 8 Jan 1902
10. The Times, 29 Jun 1903

11. Arnold Bax (1943), Farewell, my youth (Longman & Green), p 10
12. Barnet Council, Area D character appraisal, Hampstead Garden Suburb, Heath Extension
13. Extension Committee final report (H&HS archive)
14. The Times, 3 Aug 1904
15. Barratt (1912), vol. II, p 228
16. Extension Committee final report (H&HS archive: A/1048/3/3/3/2)
17. Ebenezer Howard (1898), To-morrow: the peaceful path to real reform (later reissued as Garden cities of to-morrow). Howard founded the Garden City Association in 1899.
18. The Times, 27 Dec 1904
19. David Sullivan, 'Old Wyldes and Wyldes', Camden History Review 37 (2013)

20. More information and photographs are available on the following webpages: underground-history. co.uk/bullbush.php; abandonedstations.org. uk/North_End_station. html; subbrit.org.uk/sb-sites/sites/n/north_end_ station/index.shtml
21. Hampstead Vestry minutes, 25 Sep 1855
22. Letter from Sir Samuel Hoare in HBC minutes, 6 Jul 1905
23. HBC minutes, 11 May 1905, p 463
24. HHPS annual report, 1910
25. LCC Parks Committee, 8 Mar 1942
26. HHPS annual report, 1913
27. HC Deb 17 Jun 1915, vol 72 cc815-91
28. HC Deb 1 Mar 1915, vol 70 cc624-36
29. Carrie Cowan, 'The First World War on Hampstead Heath', The London Gardener, vol. 20 (2015-16)
30. Gwynydd Gosling, 'The Grand Duke at Kenwood', Camden History Review 5 (1977)

31. HHPS annual report, 1915
32. Jerrold Northrop Moore (1984), Spirit of England: Edward Elgar in his world (Heinemann)
33. Reed, William H. (1936), Elgar as I knew him (Gollancz)
34. Robert Anderson (1993), Elgar (J.M. Dent, Master Musicians series)
35. Jerrold Northrop Moore (1989), Edward Elgar, the Windflower letters: correspondence with Alice Caroline Stuart Wortley and her family (Clarendon)
36. Cited on the webpage, fantastic-writers-and-the-great-war.com/ war-experiences/john-masefield/
37. First performed on BBC Radio 3 in 1983 but only reissued on disc in 2015 (H&HS newsletter, Nov 2015; The New Grove Dictionary of Music)

## Chapter 14

# Kenwood – the last chapter

The last major piece of the jigsaw was the remainder of the Kenwood Estate. Under the 5th Earl of Mansfield the lights shone briefly at Kenwood again and he supported community life in Hampstead and Highgate. When the Duke of Westminster died, the Earl took over from him as Patron of the Hampstead Heath Protection Society, and opened Kenwood House for entertainments and charitable causes. But he died young, and the era when the Mansfields did all they could to preserve the surrounding land from development was long gone. The 6th Earl, who inherited in 1906, did not have much use for it, living wholly in Scotland and rarely leaving Scone. Mounting land taxes, and a massive increase in death duties in Lloyd George's 'People's Budget' of 1909, were turning the estate from an asset into a liability. With the southern half – Parliament Hill Fields – already sold off, it lay like a sleeping beauty, closed off from the public, and gradually becoming a nature reserve with a rich and varied wildlife supporting many rare plants and animals.

But its potential value as building land was rising as London expanded. A notice of a possible sale appeared in *The Times* as early as 1908, but it did not reach its reserve price and was withdrawn. The Earl of Meath, the Metropolitan Public Gardens Association (MPGA) Chairman, approached Lord Mansfield and extracted a promise from him that if he decided to sell he would give first refusal to a public body. In the meantime the house had been rented to the Grand Duke, Prince Michael Romanov of Russia, who had been forced into exile in 1891 because of a morganatic marriage. His wife was, in fact, a great-granddaughter of Russia's national poet, Pushkin – good enough for anyone, one might have thought – but she was not of noble birth and the Russian royal family were obsessively strict about such protocol.

96. Prince Michael (1861-1929)

97. Arthur Crosfield (1865-1938)

151

Prince Michael was persuaded to come to Kenwood by his friend Arthur Crosfield, the northern industrialist, whom he had known for some years, and who himself was eying up what was to become the nearby palatial mansion, Witanhurst. Liberal MP for Warrington for five years from 1906, he and his brothers had built up an enormously successful chemical firm in Warrington (one of its products was Persil) from their father's small soap manufactory. The company was bought out in 1913 by their rival, William Lever of Sunlight soap, making Crosfield a wealthy man. (Later, the two men became friends and both built fine mansions on the edge of Hampstead Heath.) Freed from company responsibilities, Crosfield devoted his life to good causes, in particular to providing access to open space for working people; he was Chairman of the National Playing Fields Association and a governor of Highgate School. He travelled widely and had met and become a close friend of Prince Michael at Cannes golf club. The Prince was installed at Kenwood in 1909 on a 21-year lease. He took an interest in the local community, gracing public occasions, and joining local societies such as the Hampstead Heath Protection Society and the Highgate Literary and Scientific Institution. He opened the new high-diving board at Highgate Pond, and in 1913 he threw a grand Ball at Kenwood for 800 guests, presided over by King George and Queen Mary. When the Zeppelins began to fly after 1914, he allowed anti-aircraft guns to park on Kenwood's front drive.

98. Anti-aircraft guns at Kenwood

A further attempt to sell the estate was made even as war loomed in 1914, with a report that a building syndicate was already drawing up plans for a network of streets with terraced housing. Lord Eversley, now 80 years old, was still Vice-President of the HHPS. (He had resigned as President in 1911 and moved to Winchester, but the Society did not let him go so easily.) He and Lord Meath went to see Lord Mansfield, reminding him of his 1908 pledge. Mansfield's reply was that such an offer would be made but the price would be £550,000 – far more, even, than the price which building land commanded at that time. Steps were taken to form a purchasing committee, but all was swept away by the outbreak of the Great War. It was one of Eversley's last involvements with active campaigning; from now on he took a back seat.

With the Russian revolution in 1917, Prince Michael's funds dried up and out he had to go. A wealthy American widow took up the remainder of the lease, but after the war Mansfield terminated it and the fears of development of the estate again loomed. An announcement of the proposed sale duly appeared in *The Times* in July 1919, commenting that "Its development as a building estate is a thing hardly to be thought of". The paper's Estates correspondent, who supported the campaign to save it throughout, did his best to pour cold water on the idea, writing that it was "hardly a practicable proposition in present circumstances. The prospects to a speculator for development are not very attractive at the present time".[1]

It was of more than just local concern: Lord Curzon asked the Prime Minister in a parliamentary question whether "he has any information as to the intended sale of the Ken Wood estate, at Hampstead, and, if so, can any steps be taken to acquire this property for the country and to prevent the woods" – still haunted by badgers, as *The Times* pointed out – "being cut down?"[2] The newspaper kept up the agitation: "the pressure of public opinion is wholly in favour of the conservation of the land". It also made a wider point, evoking Howitt's outburst of 1869: "... mishandling of the problem ... would raise many questions which have lain dormant, as regards the duties and privileges of ownership. ... opinion has for a long while inclined towards insistence that there are obligations resting upon owners of certain classes of property, and Ken Wood is such a property. It is hoped that Lord Mansfield will come forward with a reasonable proposition, conceived with due regard to the public welfare".[3] Barely a year later, on the opposite side of Hampstead Lane – formerly the Bishop of London's park – villas were already rising where before there had been pasture and woodland. "Anything is better than that the speculative builder should get a foothold there; ... the beauty and value of the Kenwood estate ... is inestimable".[4]

Crosfield took up the cause and made the saving of Kenwood his great purpose in life. He set up the Kenwood Preservation Council in 1919, with a distinguished collection of names, following the pattern of previous campaigns. There were thirteen peers (Lord Eversley, of course, among them) with Lord Plymouth as President, a duke, a marquis, former PM Arthur Balfour, and five MPs. As John Carswell suggested, some of them could have bought the estate single-handed yet as time would show, very few of them gave more than a few pounds at best.[5] Even Prince Michael supported the cause, from more modest premises in Cambridge Gate, Regent's Park, which had been found for him. Other notabilities with Hampstead connections included prominent newspaper men such as Cecil Harmsworth[6] of the *Daily Mail*, James Garvin of *The Observer* and St Loe Strachey[7] of *The Spectator*. They also had backing at national level from the Royal Society, the Royal Society for the Protection of Birds, and the Commons Preservation Society.

99. Sir Robert Waley-Cohen of Caen Wood Towers (1877-1952)

The active core of the Council were Crosfield's neighbours: Sir Robert Waley-Cohen of Caen Wood Towers (now Athlone House), and Henry Goodison who lived at Hillside, Fitzroy Park, Southwood Smith's old address, as Treasurer. Others were Alderman Frank Howard, of Hampstead Borough Council, and Sir Lawrence Chubb, who provided solid legal and administrative help. Beatrice Osmond, who had set up a separate Hampstead committee, was persuaded to amalgamate with the Council and became its Honorary Organising Secretary. She brought in Sir Herbert Nield, MP for Ealing and Middlesex County Councillor, who lived in The Bishops Avenue. The Hampstead Heath Protection Society was represented by committee member Mr Pooley, and Mr Pease, its Secretary. The public appeal for funds was launched in the summer of 1920, supported by a poster campaign on the Underground. A curious diversion occurred to begin with, when Professor Flinders Petrie the Egyptologist, who lived in Cannon Place, suggested Kenwood could be acquired by the University of London, then looking for somewhere to build a permanent home. Crosfield was not against this idea, and there was a brief flurry of correspondence about it in *The Times*, but in the end nothing came of it and the public appeal went ahead.[8]

John Carswell observed that Crosfield and Lord Mansfield never seem to have met face to face;[9] the negotiations were carried on with the Earl's agent

100. C.B. King's offices on the corner of Church Row, Hampstead

Charles Bean King, a long-established local builder of some substance.[10]

The first task was to get the price reduced. After protracted and difficult discussions, Crosfield, Sir Robert Waley-Cohen and Sir Herbert Nield got it down to £340,000, but with a time limit of one year ending on 1 September 1921. This seemed to be an encouraging start, and Queen Mary gave public support with a visit in 1920. But the campaigners had gravely miscalculated. As Crosfield admitted by the end of the year, the time-honoured method of launching such appeals by persuading wealthy men to promise large contributions no longer worked.[11] In fact, it took a six-year bitter struggle, haggling with Lord Mansfield through his agent, every inch of the way, and dogged by a lack of support, both from the relevant local authorities and the public. The aftermath of the horrors of the Great War was not a propitious time for such fundraising, with industrial unrest and a national coal strike leading to severe financial depression. There was also local competition: the Burdett-Coutts's Holly Lodge estate was on the market and there was talk of a similar campaign to preserve that. It also emerged that the London County Council was not that keen to accept responsibility for this new tract of land with its onerous maintenance costs.

During the summer and autumn of 1921, a series of receptions and garden parties held at Kenwood (by permission of the Earl) aroused public interest and warm support in the London and provincial press, but raised very little money. With time on the option running out and only £16,000 raised from private subscriptions, Crosfield changed tack and approached the borough councils and other local authorities for support. Deputations met with enthusiasm – Hampstead and Islington voted £20,000 each, and St Pancras £30,000, and Hendon and Hornsey agreed to contribute – but they were only promises and would have taken more time than Crosfield had left to him to turn into hard cash. The Committee had to go back to Mansfield and ask for the option to be renewed. They were given, first another month, and then another three weeks, but Mansfield refused to renew any further unless a non-returnable deposit of £34,000 was put down. The sum raised was nowhere near enough even for that, and the Council began to come in for some criticism; questions were asked about just how much had been raised and how the price had been arrived at. Even *The Times* sounded a dispirited note, suggesting that "there are parts of the estate which could probably be developed without detriment to the use of the remainder as an addition to the Heath". But it also queried whether Mansfield actually had any buyers: "... we should like to see a new valuation of the estate, for the price of building land is not what it was before the war. ... Kenwood may not at the present time prove to be so marketable for the purposes of development as it seems".[12]

In his report to the Kenwood Council in January 1922, a defeatist note crept in; as the option expired, Crosfield had to admit sadly: "if it is impossible to put forward any alternative plan acceptable to Lord Mansfield the attempt to save Ken Wood must be suspended or abandoned".[13] There was even dissention within the Council over tactics: Harold Spender, Liberal politician, author and journalist (father of the poet Stephen Spender), resigned very publicly with an announcement in *The Times* because he was dissatisfied with the Committee's conduct of the negotiations. He believed that its correspondence with Lord Mansfield should have been published, so as "to bring to bear on that gentleman a force of public opinion which he could not have resisted". Otherwise the Council should "honestly tell the public that Lord Mansfield is asking for a price which we cannot honestly, as their trustees, advise them to pay".[14]

But Crosfield was not so easily beaten. Acknowledging that it was not going to be possible to buy the whole estate in one go, he drastically changed his strategy. He went back to his roots in the North, where his Quaker family were well-remembered as large and popular employers, who had endowed schools, public buildings and the first free library.[15] This had earned lasting good will and his appeal for support received a generous response. Three large donations

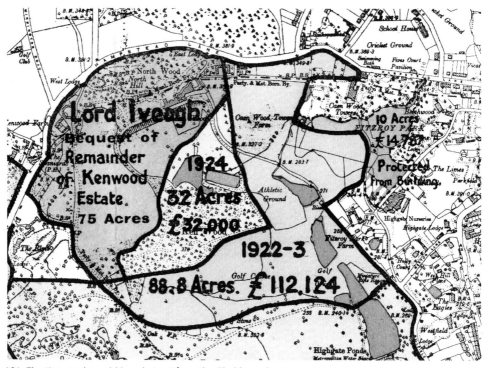

101. The Kenwood acquisitions (extract from the Chubb map)

came from fellow northern industrialists, William Whittingham of Harrogate, who gave £50,000; and F.C. Minoprio of Liverpool and T.W. Wilkinson of Carnforth, who each contributed £20,000. An anonymous donation of £25,000 was annotated "introduced by Sir A Crosfield", and Carswell suggests this may have been Crosfield himself.[16] A smaller gift came from a Mr Muir MacKean of Paisley who gave £4,000.

In London, the City Parochial Foundation gave £3,000, the Poulter Trust for Open Spaces £2,500, and Lord Glendyne of Branch Hill Lodge, Hampstead,

£3,050. By July 1922 Crosfield had raised £132,000 and was able to announce triumphantly in the press that sufficient funds had been raised to buy 95 acres – nearly half the estate - comprising the land between Parliament Hill Fields and the woodlands, the three northernmost Highgate Ponds, and the meadows between Hampstead Lane and Fitzroy Farm, the farm itself having already been sold privately by Lord Mansfield.[17] And because the land was sloping and difficult to develop, it was got at a reduced price of £140,000. Moreover, "this important result has been achieved without ... imposing any burden upon the ratepayers".[18]

The LCC rejected ten acres of remote land next to Fitzroy Park as being too expensive to maintain and patrol, but it was of great visual importance to the Heath. One and a half acres were sold on to St Pancras Borough Council for allotments, but an unusual solution was found to preserve the remaining nine acres: local residents whose land bordered Kenwood, including Kenwood Council member, Waley-Cohen, bought them under stringent covenants

103. Detail of the Chubb map showing its relation to Kenwood

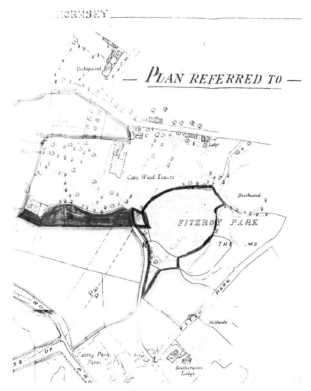

102. 1926 map of the 10 acres rejected by LCC (author's archive)

restricting building or any use other than as private gardens, to preserve the natural beauty of the hillside. They became part of the grounds of Caen Wood Towers and The Elms, Highgate, causing controversy and accusations of self-interest. In fact, the residents paid the full development price for land they would not be allowed to develop, and thereby helped the Kenwood Council's cash flow: the money they paid went towards the funds for the Kenwood acquisitions. Nearly a century later these generous actions paid off as the Waley-Cohen land at Caen Wood Towers was acquired for the Heath – although another legal battle arose when a tramp was allowed to squat on, and acquire title to part of the land (see p 251).

It took the whole of 1923 to complete the complicated legal arrangements, while the land was temporarily vested in three trustees, Crosfield, Herbert Nield, and Lawrence Chubb, before it could be transferred to the LCC. The point was re-emphasised that this was "the first occasion on which a large metropolitan open space has been acquired without calling on the ratepayers for assistance".[19]

With this achievement under their belts, the reinvigorated Committee turned their attention to the 30 acres that included South Wood. Charles Bean King, Mansfield's agent, had produced a new plan to build some thirty villas here. Alderman Howard of Hampstead Borough Council now led the negotiations; a

104. Frank Howard (1859-1935), civil engineer, and Alderman and Mayor of Hampstead (*Hampstead Year Book* 1929).

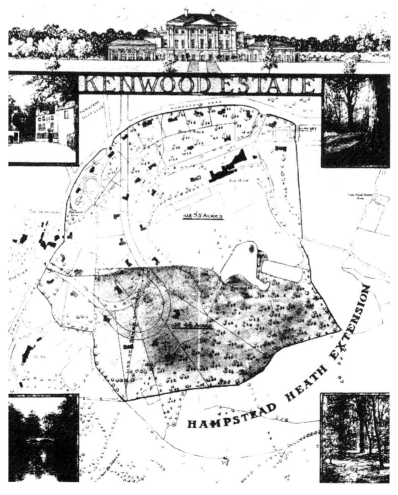

105. C. B. King's plan for an estate of villas at Kenwood

committee member of the Hampstead Heath Protection Society (later its Vice- President) and the Kenwood Preservation Council, he was several times Mayor of Hampstead and represented it on the LCC from 1926 to 1934. A man of prodigious energy and a skilled politician, he was "a man who got things done", typical of those "the value of whose services to London it is difficult to over-estimate, … who modestly and unobtrusively give freely of their leisure and business ability in the service of the public".[20]

Howard also served on the Metropolitan Water Board, and he realised there was a fatal weakness in King's development plan – drainage;  a new drain would be needed but where was it to come from? Howard, who must have well understood the inscrutable ways in which a local authority could be seen to be granting permission while actually denying it, masterminded the stratagem which was instrumental in saving the rest of the estate. The nearest sewer was the Hampstead Borough Council pipe in the Vale of Health, but that would mean running a connection under the Heath and permission would have to be got from both the LCC and Hampstead Borough Council. The alternative – running it uphill across Kenwood land to Millfield Lane – would be prohibitively expensive and involve damaging the woods. The LCC said no; the Borough Council urged it to reconsider.[21]

After tortuous negotiations between the three parties, with access to the Vale sewer and the preservation of the wooded skyline as bargaining chips, Mr King was persuaded to cede seven acres of the woodland to the LCC to protect the foreground view of Kenwood in return for supposed access to the Vale sewer. Too late, King realised that what he had agreed to in effect sterilised South Wood, as far as any development was concerned, and made it impossible to build the projected villas. He had been outmanoeuvred by Howard. Part of the deal had included permission to remove the old Toll Gate House and widen Spaniards Road to create access to the new development. Howard was able to report triumphantly to the HHPS in 1923 that eight acres of South Wood were to be handed over to the LCC at a bargain price extracted by the drainage concession. King, on the other hand, had to advise Mansfield to sell the remaining land for what it would fetch because the building scheme would not work. South Wood was secured and at a lower price, and the Toll Gate House was saved.

On 21 April 1924 Crosfield announced this success in *The Times*, with details about the funding. This time it was the local authorities who were providing the means, making good their earlier pledges, but with much reduced amounts: £7,500 from St Pancras and £5,000 from Hampstead. Islington promised £2,500, Stoke newington £1,000 and Kensington £500. Hornsey, Finchley, Hackney, and the Middlesex County Council also offered support, and the Kenwood Council had £12,000 in hand from the subsale of the covenanted nine acres unwanted by the LCC.

On 18 November *The Times* announced the completion of the purchase, with a paean of praise for Crosfield and his Committee in both an article and

106. Edward Cecil Guinness (1847-1927), 1st Earl of Iveagh

an editorial. Crosfield, in turn, wrote the following day to express his appreciation of "the invaluable support *The Times* has given us throughout the whole of our work and which has so largely contributed to our success". He paid special tribute to the role of the Mayor of Hampstead, and to Lawrence Chubb, the value of whose work, "soundness of judgment, ... wide technical experience and legal equipment" it would be "difficult, indeed, to exaggerate".

This left only 74 acres and Kenwood House itself, now an empty shell after all the contents, preserved almost unaltered since the 1st Earl's time, had either been auctioned off or removed to Scone Palace in 1922. It is curious that the name of Edward Cecil Guinness, Earl of Iveagh did not feature in this saga before. He had bought Heath House in 1909 and must have been well aware of all that was going on. Indeed, he had donated to Henrietta Barnett's Heath Extension appeal, and given £500 to the HHPS's appeal to buy the Paddock.[22] Behind the scenes, however, there was highly significant but secret activity, hinted at obliquely in a letter to *The Times* by Councillor Howard: "The most that one can hope for is that someone may purchase the house and remaining part of the property, enjoy it during life, and at death bequeath it to the nation", which is of course exactly what happened.[23] This was followed up more positively two days later by Crosfield: "Although I am not at liberty to say more at the present time, it can now be definitely stated that not a yard of the remaining 76 acres of Ken Wood will ever be sacrificed to the builders".[24] By January 1925 the secret was out and it was the *Ham & High* that got there first, leaving *The Times* to report, on 12 January

107. The opening of Kenwood to the public, 18 July 1925

that following an announcement that Kenwood House "had been bought by a peer, who promised that the land should never be built upon, the Hampstead and Highgate Express states:- We are informed that the peer referred to is the Earl of Iveagh".[25] He acquired the house and the remaining 75 acres for £107,900,[26] and

108. King George V in the grounds of Kenwood

it would all be bequeathed to a Trust for the benefit of the public after ten years, or at his death if sooner.

That summer, attended by crowds from far and wide, the new addition to the Heath received the royal seal of approval from King George V and Queen Mary, who formally declared it open to the public. Prayers were said by the Bishop of Willesden, and the King referred to the movement that had created Hampstead Heath, saying it was "the happy conclusion of more than half a century's efforts to preserve this line of heights so that their beauty ... and their wide expanse serve as a recreation ground for a crowded city population". In words that sound more as though they might have come from the Parks Department at County Hall, he gave a majestic warning against litter – which was apparently heartily applauded – and enjoined the need for discipline among the public, to whose "use and enjoyment it was his great pleasure to dedicate this lovely spot for all time". [27]

Lord Iveagh died not long after, in 1927. Kenwood House was duly bequeathed to the nation with an endowment of £50,000, and opened to the public in 1928. The Iveagh Bequest (Kenwood) Act 1929 specified how both the house and land were to be used and managed, the grounds going to the LCC to become part of the Heath. The mansion, with Lord Iveagh's priceless art collection – which the art dealer Sir Joseph Duveen, his neighbour at The Elms, Spaniards Road, had helped him assemble[28] – was placed under the curatorial responsibility of the National Gallery, whose director would always be one of the six Trustees.

109a. Recording the Kenwood Council's achievement: the Goodison Memorial fountain designed by the Liverpool sculptor Tyson Smith; traces of chalybeate iron can still be seen in its rust-coloured water.

109b. Plaque to Sir Arthur Crosfield at Kenwood House; commissioned by the H&HS, 2000

As Julius Bryant recounts in his history of this period,[29] it was no easy task: "the situation of Kenwood, on clay, involving as it does a large variation of humidity, is very bad for pictures". It lacked its own curator before 1950, having only a general manager, who on one occasion reported that "… another small piece … has fallen off the picture of Lady Louisa Manners since yesterday. I have searched for the piece but regret it cannot be found, I expect it has been swept up with the dust". As Bryant comments this would be "almost farcical if [it] were not so frightening".

The 1929 Act also required that if the trustees found the continuation of the Kenwood Trust impracticable, they should invite the LCC to become trustee in their place. At the end of the Second World War the endowment income was no longer sufficient for the trustees to continue, and in 1949 the LCC agreed to become the administrative trustee. It appointed Anthony Blunt, Director of the Courtauld Institute and Surveyor of the King's Pictures, as their advisor.[30]

So, after 100 years of campaigning the 800 acres of the Heath we know today were finally secured. As *The Times* put it: "The addition of Ken Wood will crown the achievements of those who have sought to enrich the most diversified, picturesque, and popular of London's pleasure grounds".[29]

**Notes, Chapter 14**
1. *The Times*, 17 Jul 1919
2. Ibid., HC Deb 17 Jul 1919 vol 118 c593. Curzon was an early enthusiast for heritage protection and one of the sponsors of the Ancient Monuments Consolidation and Amendment Act 1913; he saved Tattershall Castle, Lincolnshire, and Bodiam Castle, Kent, which he restored and bequeathed to the National Trust. Carswell (1992, p 63) suggests that Crosfield was behind his intervention.
3. *The Times*, 18 Jul 1919
4. 'The estate market', *The Times*, 17 Jul 1920
5. Carswell (1992), p 74

6. The Harmsworth family had lived in Hampstead since the 1870s. Alfred Harmsworth, Lord Northcliffe, began his career as a reporter on the *Ham & High*; he bought *The Times* in 1908 and also owned *The Observer* and *Daily Mail*. His brother Harold became the 1st Viscount Rothermere.
7. St Loe's uncle was Lytton Strachey, a one-time Hampstead resident; his daughter Amabel [*sic*] married the architect Clough Williams-Ellis, who owned Romney's house and was on the committee of the HHPS (1931-39)
8. *The Times*, reports & letters, 16, 17, 20, & 23 Jul 1920
9. Carswell (1992), p 61
10. Founded in 1746 and with offices at 28 Church Row, the King firm built many houses in the Well Walk area and at Gainsborough Gardens. www.tombwithaview.org.uk.

11. Letter to *The Times*, Jan 1921
12. *The Times*, 31 Aug 1921
13. *The Times*, 21 Jan 1922
14. *The Times*, 4 May 1922
15. Carswell (1992), p 35
16. Ibid., pp 87-88: Whittingham was connected to shipbuilding; Wilkinson dealt in reinforced concrete; Minoprio was a cotton merchant and respected philanthropist with a social conscience; William Muir Mackean's firm made (edible) starch.
17. *The Times*, 1 Aug 1923
18. *The Times* 18 Jul 1922
19. *The Times*, 1 Jan 1923
20. Obituary, *The Times*, 15 Jul 1935
21. Hampstead Borough Council minutes, 20 Sep 1923
22. HHPS annual report 1925, list of donors (author's archive)

23. *The Times*, 4 Dec 1924
24. *The Times*, 6 Dec 1924; Carswell (1992, p 2) suggests that "there is evidence to show that in the final stages Crosfield and Iveagh were acting in concert"
25. *The Times*, 12 Jan 1925
26. Summerson (1962), p 12
27. *The Times*, 20 Jul 1925
28. Duveen added the Turner wing to the Tate Gallery (now Tate Britain).
29. Julius Bryant, 'Kenwood's lost chapter: the forgotten story of the National Gallery's management of the Iveagh Bequest, 1928-49', *Apollo*, 159 (1 Mar 2004), pp 40–46
30. *The Times*, 18 Nov 1924

Chapter 15

# Heath restored

K it Ikin asked: "Is Hampstead unique in feeling a duty to add to the Heath? Did the duty become an obligation because of the 40 year guerilla war with the Lord of the Manor?" He pointed out that "the great additions to the Heath were not the work of the Society. It was however the Society which kept the duty alive. There was no grand design but only the pressure of the Duty when the opportunities arose".[1] For the Hampstead Heath Protection Society (HHPS) and its members, this duty to add land to the Heath became a guiding principle and a crucial part of their work from the moment it was founded in 1897. They inherited "the responsibilities of those who had fought the Lord of the Manor for the continued enjoyment of the Heath – Gurney Hoare, Henry Sharpe, Edwin Field, Richard Ware amongst many others".[2] The Society's first chairman, Ernest Lake, was also keenly aware that "it was the duty of this society to give the Council their advice as to the method to be adopted in order to keep the heath in its wild state, and to prevent it assuming a park-like appearance".[3]

Their vital role in watching over the Heath, defending it and adding to it, is perhaps too little known. As Peter Woodford observed, few are aware of "just how much has been spared through the Society's efforts for our present enjoyment".[4] The 20th-century histories give it no more than passing mentions; it is only when one reads the Society's own reports that one begins to appreciate just how important its role has been.

Another aspect of "the Duty" is the extraordinary number of prominent people who felt it incumbent upon them to give of their time to serve the community through the Society's committee. Viscount Knollys, for example, who only lived in Hampstead for a couple of years before going off to be Governor of Bermuda, is to be found on the committee in 1938.

Ernest Lake was succeeded in 1917 by Howard Figgis, the son of Samuel Figgis (who had launched the campaign for Golders Hill). He and his father were City men who ran their own firm, Figgis & Co. Produce Brokers. According to Howard's obituary in *The Times*: "He will be long remembered as, for half a century, one of the commercial leaders of the City of London, but many will have known him better as one who never turned a deaf ear to anything which did good. ... he believed in organized but unostentatious charity".[5] A keen gardener, he opened his garden at Heathlands for the National Garden Scheme. In 1918, Emily Field, Mr Pooley and Cornelius Dalton (by then Sir Cornelius) were still active on the Society's committee, and had been joined by, among others, James Thursfield, journalist and leader writer for *The Times*, and first editor of the *Times Literary Supplement*; an authority on naval history, he was knighted in 1920 and lived in Golders Green.

The Society's role in the Golders Hill, Heath Extension and Kenwood campaigns set the pattern for the 20th century. They also watched for any new opportunity to rescue small parcels of land from surrounding estates whenever possible, mostly by persuading the authorities to act, but on two occasions raising money to buy land themselves. These additions, sometimes restoring to the Heath what had originally been part of it, were achieved through the dogged persistence of the HHPS and its members. In 1903, working with the Northern Heights Footpath Association,[6] they persuaded the London County Council (LCC) to purchase a small piece of freehold ground opposite the Bull and Bush at North End, to prevent building on it.[7]

Even as the Kenwood campaign was being launched, Samuel Figgis was busy in 1919 saving the small green at the bottom of North End Avenue from building. He had moved from Wildwoods (Pitt House) in 1899. Sir Harold Harmsworth (later Viscount Rothermere) lived there for ten years and sold it to Valentine Fleming (father of the James Bond creator, Ian Fleming) in 1909. Figgis, meanwhile, had moved to Montagu Grove in Frognal (named after Edward Montagu,18th-century Master in Chancery). But he joined his erstwhile neighbours – Mrs Fleming, and Lady Fanny Byron (a cousin by marriage of the poet) who lived at Myrtle Grove (now Byron Cottage) – in buying the green, which was on sale for building in 1919, and presenting it to the LCC as an addition to the Heath.

**The Hill – and The Paddock**

In 1925, the year that the campaign to save Kenwood culminated, the Society itself secured a tract of land called The Paddock, a curious enclosure of the Heath belonging to Hill House – sometimes called The Whinns – in North End Way, after long drawn-out and sometimes rancorous negotiations with Lord Leverhulme. Following the Ditchfield encroachment in the 1730s, it had been sold on to various different 'gentry' owners between 1748 and 1793, one of whom, Thomas Gattaker, had a drawing made of the charming villa with coach house and stables. The next owner was William Fawkener, who began acquiring more land, and it was he who got permission to enclose 150 rods of Heath on the opposite side of the road in 1805, which became known as The Paddock, accompanied by the usual condition that the land would never be built on.[8] In 1807, Samuel Hoare the elder, of Heath House, bought what was by then a small estate, for his son Samuel the younger, on his marriage. John Gurney Hoare was born at Hill House in 1810, and it was for nearly a century one of the Hampstead homes of the Hoare family. While they presided, The Paddock was made freely available for use by the community, regularly used for cricket matches; and in 1859, following another invasion scare, the Hampstead Rifle Volunteer Corps, which Gurney Hoare helped to set up, used it as a training ground.

But when the Hoares left everything changed. John Gurney's son Sir Samuel, MP for Norwich, had made his permanent home at the family's estate in Cromer, Norfolk, and in 1895 he put the Hampstead property up for sale. The Hampstead Vestry sent a deputation led by Henry Harben, to his London house in Hereford Gardens, asking him to withdraw The Paddock from the sale to allow time for it to be acquired for the public. This he did, in a most interesting letter to the Vestry, giving the history of the family's Hampstead holdings. It would appear that the *Ham & High* had revived its attack on John Gurney Hoare over the matter of The Paddock. This clearly rankled and Sir Samuel was at pains to spell out that the family had never themselves sought to enclose any Heath land – The Paddock having been enclosed by the previous owner – and that his father, Gurney Hoare, had worked selflessly for Hampstead and the Heath. He recounted how, as a result of the 1869 court case, Sir Thomas Maryon Wilson had forced his father to enfranchise (viz: buy the freehold of) his remaining copyhold property, including The Paddock. Gurney Hoare had objected strongly – "it was very costly" – but was "given no choice".[9] He remarked that it seemed strange that no public body had shown any interest in acquiring The Paddock before. He hoped that whoever bought it would follow his family's example of keeping it open, but pointed out that this must entail a heavy loss on someone – ratepayers or possibly subscribers. After much consideration he decided to undertake the loss himself and withdrew The Paddock from the sale.[9] It does rather prompt the question as to why he did not feel able to give the land to the Heath himself, as he had done with the Hatches Bottom enclosure.

Hill House was bought by George Fisher, a fine art dealer, who rebuilt it and, in turn, sold it on in 1904 to William H. Lever, the industrialist, later the 1st Viscount Leverhulme, who also bought The Paddock. He transformed the house into the grandiose mansion it is today, adding two wings and a ballroom under the terrace, and had apparently also intended to build on The Paddock. In a letter to Hampstead Borough Council, Lever complained that the largest share of the purchase money was for The Paddock which he had bought with a view to building there. But clearly the stipulation that the land would never be built on was still in force, and he agreed to refrain while Sir Samuel Hoare was still alive.[10] He turned instead to enlarging the property. He bought up the two neighbouring houses with the intention of demolishing them and adding their grounds to his garden. He began with Heath Lodge – Jane Hemett's old house of 1776 – and in 1911 called in the expert Thomas Mawson to turn the whole into an elaborate landscape. Mawson extended the pergola and created a stone bridge over the public footpath onto the Heath, to link the two gardens.

Lever's next step was to try to get the public right of way under the new bridge closed altogether, using The Paddock as a bargaining chip. In 1913 he wrote to the HHPS, of which he was a member, asking if it would approve of an exchange of land which would include closing the right of way, in return for The Paddock. But the Society felt that although this would have resulted in an extension to the Heath, the footpath was too important to public enjoyment to be lost they could not recommend it. In 1914 Lever turned his attention to the other side of Hill House where he bought Cedar Lawn, another estate originally put together from squatters' cottages, to complete the enlargement of his garden. But its temporary use as maternity home, founded by Queen Mary for the benefit of wives and children of servicemen, delayed his plans. Lever returned to the issue of the right of way in 1915 with a revised proposal that the HHPS Committee accepted, but which the membership voted so heavily against at the Annual Meeting, that Lever withdrew. There were many letters of protest to the *Ham & High*. Clearly aggrieved, in 1919 and now a peer of the realm as Lord Leverhulme, he offered The Paddock to Queen Mary for a permanent maternity home.[11] But a Mr Ernest Seymour, of Heath Street, sent the whole correspondence and the articles that had appeared in *The Times* and the *Ham & High* to the Palace,[12] so that the Queen was made well aware of the "opposition on the part of the residents of Hampstead to the Paddock being built upon".[13] "The injury to the Heath would outweigh the benefit of such a home, and in deference to what appeared to be the general wish of Hampstead, Her Majesty declined Lord Leverhulme's offer".[11] Instead he donated the site of the old Upper Flask Tavern of Kit Cat Club and *Clarissa* fame, on the corner of East Heath Road opposite Bellmoor, which had to be demolished to make way for the new Queen Mary's Maternity Home. It opened in 1922.

Leverhulme tried again in 1923, as work on the extension to his garden was being finalised. A new proposal for an exchange of land was accepted by Hampstead Borough Council but turned down by the Society which called a special general meeting at Hampstead Town Hall to consult the membership. A letter from the now exasperated Lord Leverhulme was read out, threatening that if his suggestion was not agreed to he would allow building operations to begin on The Paddock – a move hardly likely to win support; a resolution against the proposal was strongly supported. Howard Figgis and Alderman Howard led a deputation from the Society to the Borough Council, urging it to raise a public subscription to buy the land. But there was division within the Council itself; a motion that any bargaining with any part of Hampstead Heath was opposed to the public spirit which inspired its acquisition by Act of Parliament, and that Lord Leverhulme should be informed that any building on The Paddock would "arouse the anger of the people of London", was voted down, and nothing further happened.[14]

The HHPS decided to try to raise the funds itself, to buy the land outright, but Leverhulme demanded a prohibitive price. However, he then suggested another exchange on much more favourable terms, offering extra land as well as The Paddock; this was agreed by the Council and the Society but this time foundered on LCC intervention. It carried on negotiations and inserted new terms without informing the Borough Council, resulting in Leverhulme breaking off negotiations. Finally, at the beginning of 1925, all the parties agreed, but Leverhulme died in May before he could sign the contract. This enabled the HHPS to go ahead and launch an appeal in the *Ham & High* to buy the land

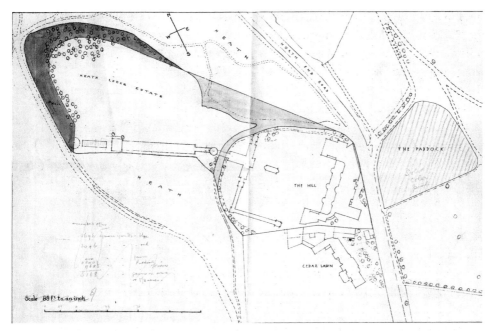

110. Plan of the amended Paddock offer, showing Lever's acquisitions at The Hill, and the proposed exchange of land.

The strip coloured red and The Paddock were to be exchanged for the strip with the footpath, coloured blue.

outright. The £6,500 needed was soon raised – three-quarters of it from members of the Society – and the deal was finalised without the loss of any heathland or rights of way. A small granite tablet at the side of the road marks the event.

Leverhulme's conduct in this matter contrasts greatly with his benevolence as an employer,[15] and generosity and public spirit elsewhere, donating to local causes and often lending his house and garden for charitable events. After Leverhulme's death, the Hill estate was bought by Scottish shipowner Andrew Weir, Baron Inverforth, who left it to Manor House Hospital when he died in 1955. They gratefully renamed the mansion Inverforth House in his memory.

## The ghosts of Littleworth

"When the town takes it only rarely gives back"; the land at North End between Jack Straw's Castle and The Hill was one of those rare exceptions.[16]

By 1900 there remained seven large houses set in their own grounds between Jack Straw's Castle and North End village. Heath Lodge and Cedar Lawn were subsumed by Leverhulme into the grounds of The Hill as described above. Heathlands (Oram's and Willes's old house) had been bought in 1855 by Hugh Mackay Matheson (nephew of the co-founder of the trading company Jardine Matheson), who lived there until 1898. A Scottish Presbyterian, he was a man of tremendously strong religious conviction and had refused to join his uncle's company on principle because of its involvement in the Opium Wars; he founded his own company, the Rio Tinto mining group. Although he spent much of his time travelling – often performing missionary work – he served

167

briefly as a Hampstead vestryman between 1866 and 1869 and was involved in the efforts to persuade the Metropolitan Board of Works to secure the Heath for the public. The last owner of the house was Howard Figgis, the second Chairman of the Hampstead Heath Protection Society, who lived there from the 1930s until he was bombed out in the Second World War. He moved out of London and died shortly afterwards.

Next to Heathlands was Fern Lodge, built around 1800, in place of a squatter's cottage, by Samuel Sotheby of the auctioneering firm. He went bankrupt twice and finally lost his Hampstead estate in 1841. By the end of the century, it was the home of the MacInnes family, relatives by marriage of the Gurney Hoares.[17] They still owned it when it was demolished by the wartime bombing raid. Crewe and Camelford Cottages, behind Jack Straw's Castle, were amalgamated into one house, Heath Brow, and another cottage, Heath Brow Cottage, was built in its grounds. It was a school in the 1870s, and then rented until 1902 by Sir Richard Temple, politician and government administrator in India, active member of the Hampstead Antiquarian & Historical Society and founder member of the HHPS. Sir Hall Caine, the writer, bought Heath Brow for his wife in the early 20th century, and in the 1930s it was acquired by the Air Ministry (see p 219).

On 19 March 1941 a parachute mine destroyed the area and "for once the encroaching bricks began to recede".[16] The extensive bomb damage provided the opportunity to restore more land to the Heath; as Kit Ikin wryly observed: "the work of the Luftwaffe ... should not be overlooked".[18]

## The post-war Committee

The Society, with its now rather cumbersome new title, the Hampstead Heath and Old Hampstead Protection Society (HH&OHPS) fielded a formidable committee

111. Geoffrey Hutchinson MP, later Baron Ilford (1893-1974)

in the post-war years. It was then still perfectly acceptable to serve on its committee and be involved in both local and national politics. Geoffrey Hutchinson, who became Chairman in 1948, was a barrister (whose main practice was in the field of local government), and also a politician. Born in 1893 in Lancashire, he settled in Hampstead in the 1920s and lived in Church Row from 1926. He fought in both World Wars (with the Lancashire Fusiliers) and was awarded the Military Cross in 1919. He served as a Hampstead Borough councillor and also represented Hampstead on the LCC. He became MP for Ilford in 1937, was knighted in 1953 and elevated to the peerage in 1962. He served the Society for over forty years, as

Secretary, Chairman, and from 1954 as President, until his death in 1974. He never allowed the holding of political office to influence his judgment in matters of democratic accountability. In an early Chairman's report he sharply reminded the LCC (of which he was a member) that "they should remember that the Heath and its various additions were not secured for the people of London by their initiative, or that of their predecessors, nor solely at their expense. They should therefore be scrupulously careful to observe the conditions upon which the Heath was vested in them and to avoid anything which may seem to infringe these conditions".[19]

Several eminent public figures joined Hutchinson on the committee. Architect Maxwell Ayrton (1874-1960), who lived in Belsize Park Gardens, and

112. John Fremantle, Baron Cottesloe (1900-1994)

113. Oswald Milne (1881-1968)

later Church Row, designed the old Wembley Stadium and the National Institute for Medical Research at Mill Hill. Oswald Milne started, like Ayrton, as an assistant to Lutyens before setting up his own practice. He served on Hampstead Borough Council between 1937 and 1953, as Mayor in 1947 and 1949, and was later Vice-President of the Royal Society of Arts. The politician Henry Brooke, who joined the Society's committee in 1935, served on the Borough Council and the LCC, of which he was Conservative leader until 1951. Like Hutchinson, he entered Parliament, serving as Hampstead's MP from 1950–66, and was later Home Secretary. He continued to serve the Society for nearly fifty years, lastly as Vice-President, until his death in 1984. John Fremantle, later Lord Cottesloe, who also served on the Society's committee for over forty years, came from an illustrious naval family, one ancestor having been a close friend and colleague of Admiral Lord Nelson. His life was devoted to public service: he, too, served on the Borough Council and represented Hampstead on the LCC, from 1945-55. He was Chairman of the Arts Council of Great Britain (1960-65) and of the South Bank Theatre Board. Lady du Maurier (1876-1957), the former actress Muriel Beaumont, was the wife of Sir Gerald du Maurier and mother of the novelist Daphne; the family lived at Cannon Hall for many years and she was on the Society's committee for ten years. Leo Bonacina, on the committee from 1947 to 1961, was a Fellow and sometime Vice-President of the Royal Meteorological Society. E.V. (Evoe) Knox,[20] one of the most successful editors of *Punch*, lived at 110 Frognal, and joined the committee in 1947, and Dr Oliver Plowright, a much loved local GP, was a committee member throughout the 1950s.

## Seizing the opportunity

When the last of the MacInnes family of Fern Lodge died in 1946, her executors offered the bombed-out property to the Society for £3,500, giving them the opportunity to add it to the Heath. It became their second outright purchase. Geoffrey Hutchinson launched an appeal for funds to buy both Fern Lodge and Heathlands (Howard Figgis's house), strongly backed by the *Ham & High*, which praised the Society's efforts and urged people to donate. Although the austere period after a devastating war was a difficult time to raise funds, the appeal brought in about £4,000, enough to buy Fern Lodge but not both properties. It was then discovered that Heathlands had already been bought by C.B. King, the local building firm, which was still going strong, with the intention of restoring or redeveloping it.[21] King was extremely put out when the Society persuaded Hampstead Borough Council to acquire the property with a compulsory purchase order. After lengthy negotiations, and much haggling over the price, a deal was struck to compensate King with £10,000. The LCC only contributed £5,000, rather less than had been hoped, but the neighbouring local authorities – Middlesex County Council, St Pancras, St Marylebone, Paddington, Hendon and Hornsey – all once again generously supported with donations. The deeds of both properties were at last handed over to the LCC at a special ceremony in 1952.

There was also talk of commandeering some of the land to create car parks, something which had been under discussion since 1939. In 1947 the Society called a special general meeting which unanimously resolved: "That no part of Hampstead Heath ought in any circumstances to be set aside to be used as a car park". They urged the LCC to resist such proposals, but there was increasing pressure on the LCC from other authorities and it was

114. Two granite slabs marking the Society's acquisitions: (a) The Paddock and (b) Fern lodge, "This area of approximately half an acre was added to the Heath in 1952 by the Hampstead Heath and Old Hampstead Protection Society"

eventually agreed to create a car park on the lower fairground site on East Heath; the Society reluctantly accepted this as a reasonable compromise. In 1953 the LCC bought the ruins of Heath Brow behind Jack Straw's Castle and turned that site also into a discreet car park for Heath visitors. The pub itself was not rebuilt until many years later, in 1965, by Raymond Erith.

## Pitt House

Further down North End Way was Pitt House, formerly called Wildwoods or North End, a large estate built up from 1727 by the Dingleys.[22] Robert Dingley was a City goldsmith and his son Charles, a would-be politician, made a fortune out of trade with Russia. By 1769 there was a coach house, stabling, and a fine garden with a summer-house, grotto and wilderness. It was Charles who invited William Pitt the Elder to the house in 1763 for his famous melodramatic sojourn, giving rise to its 20th-century name of Pitt House; he was in residence there between 1765 and 1767 during the period when he became prime minister.[23] Following the Figgis, Harmsworth and Fleming families (see earlier), in 1924 the Earl of Clarendon bought the house. He became President of the HHPS in 1928 and lived at Pitt House until 1938 when, as he explained in a letter to the then Chairman, Howard Figgis, he had been appointed Lord Chamberlain and needed to move into London; (although he remained President of the Society until 1954). He did his best to "to try to find an individual purchaser so that this old house may be preserved", but feared it would be difficult and that he might have to sell to a developer.[24] His fears were alas confirmed. The house was requisitioned by the Army during the Second World War, but together with North End village, it was severely damaged by a parachute mine leaving it a wreck past repair; it was sold off for development and demolished in 1952. The Society campaigned for several years to get the LCC to acquire the whole site and add it to the Heath as had happened at Fern Lodge. At one stage the local authorities were prepared to act, but the Minister of Housing refused consent for a bridging loan. Geoffrey Hutchinson wrote furiously to MPs saying: "The wishes of the LCC and 5 Borough Councils in such a matter should

115. Pitt House garden; ghostly relics of garden features can still be seen.

not be brushed aside".[24] However, the Society's efforts were partially rewarded when, after a local inquiry, three acres of the garden were at last added to the Heath in 1953. Hutchinson remarked in the Society's Annual Report that if the LCC had acted when first approached two years before, it could have bought the whole site from Lord Clarendon for £12,000.[25]

## The Hill again: the Pergola

Once Manor House Hospital took over the massive grounds of the Hill estate, the gardens and the extraordinary Pergola, went into a slow decline. The Hospital, established by the War Office in 1916 to treat injured servicemen, had been given the Manor House estate on the corner of Hampstead Way opposite Golders Hill Park, once briefly the site of Hendon Manor House (hence its name).[26] From 1919 it housed the Industrial Orthopaedic Society, specialising in treating victims of industrial accidents. In 1952, in need of space to expand, they bought Ivy House, opposite, for £12,000 with a view to building in the grounds, but there was wide objection and permission was refused. Then, as described above, Andrew Weir unexpectedly gifted Hill House to the Hospital in 1955. There followed a series of planning applications to build in the gardens of both Hill House and Ivy House, all of which were refused. Realising that they would not be allowed to build, the Hospital trustees then offered part of the garden – the old Heath Lodge property annexed by Lord Leverhulme – to the LCC, which bought it with part of the Pergola in 1959. It was restored and opened it to the public in 1963 as the Hill Garden. However, by 1970 the structure of the Pergola had deteriorated to such an extent that it was closed as unsafe and only opened intermittently to the public over the next ten years.

Peggy Jay, having joined the Society's committee in 1961, had become Chairman in 1968. Like Hutchinson, Brooke and Fremantle, she was deeply involved in politics. Her husband was Douglas Jay, a minister in the Wilson government (see Chapter 21). She herself had served for many years as a councillor on the LCC, and then on the Greater London Council (GLC) which replaced it, becoming Chairman of the Parks and Smallholdings Committee in

116. The Pergola

117. Peggy Jay (1913-2008) in 1965

1965. However, on losing her GLC seat in 1967, she became more involved with the Society, succeeding Sir Colin Anderson as Chairman. Peggy, too, was of that old breed who saw service to the community, given freely, as a duty. Her formidable political skills and contacts were put at the service of the Hampstead community for over four decades. One of her many achievements was getting the Pergola restored and opened to the public, bit by bit, brokering deals between the GLC and Manor House Hospital, and then later the City of London Corporation. She persuaded the Hospital to agree to the GLC taking over maintenance of the Pergola in 1972, but this caused legal problems over the divided control between the Hospital and the GLC.[27] In 1982, she succeeded in persuading the Hospital governors, and the Industrial Orthopaedic Society to gift the whole garden with the Pergola, its undercroft and the old Kitchen Garden beneath it, to the GLC which agreed to accept it. More protracted negotiations ensued, including a High Court ruling, because the Hospital Trustees could not under charity rules legally give the Pergola away. Then any idea of restoration was thrown into further doubt by the abolition of the GLC in 1984 (see Part 5); the decision of the Hospital, which was by then running into financial difficulties, to sell Inverforth House; and the long hiatus before the City was appointed to take over from the GLC. It was to be another ten years before the legal tangle was sorted out, during which the Pergola had to be closed at various times for safety reasons. The London Residuary Body made some improvements and, under continuing pressure and persuasion from the Society, a deal was struck whereby the City bought the Pergola from them for £1. Once the City took over in 1989, Peggy Jay worked closely with Peter Rigby, who was Chair of the City's Policy and Resources Committee and then of its Hampstead Heath Management Committee, with the result that the City spent over £1 million from its own funds to carry out a complete and most generous restoration. It is now one of the glories of the Heath.

### Lord Erskine's garden

Like Lord Mansfield his mentor, Lord Erskine was a younger son of a Scottish aristocrat, the 10th Earl of Buchan, and was sent off to London to make his own way in the world. Perhaps it was this friendship that drew Erskine to Hampstead. He took the copyhold of what was called the Blue House next to the Spaniards Inn, begun as an illegal encroachment by one John Pratt, who was granted a retrospective copyhold by the Lord of the Manor.[28] By 1762 it belonged to John Sanderson, the architect who rebuilt Hampstead Parish Church in Church Row; he had enlarged the property to nearly an acre, with a coach house and stable, and a garden on the other side of Spaniards Road taken from the Heath. There were

173

stringent conditions against
building or planting trees
which might obstruct the
view from the public highway.
It then passed to John Stubbs
from whom Erskine acquired
it in 1795. He renamed
the house Evergreen Hill
and began acquiring still
more land, some copyhold
and some freehold, until
his estate stretched along
Spaniards Road to include
the old Mother Huff Inn,
by then rebuilt as the
Shakespeare's Head.[29]

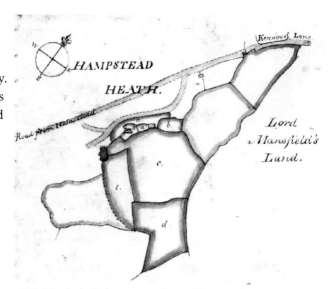

118. Map in the Indenture recording Erskine's acquisitions

For centuries this tavern was the only building along Spaniards Road
between Heath House and Spaniards End. Much frequented in the days of the
Wells, it is said to have been there by 1680, and is mentioned in Thomas Baker's
play *Hampstead Heath* (see p 27). Kit Ikin estimated that Erskine's freehold and
leasehold acquisitions eventually amounted to about 25 acres. A tunnel under
Spaniards Road linked his house to the gardens – some say the tunnel was
already there; others that it was Erskine who constructed it.[30] The tunnel still
featured on an LCC map of Kenwood c.1925 and the door to it is apparently still
visible in the garden of The Cottage.

However, Erskine made some disastrous financial decisions and had to
sell up just before he died in 1823. The 3rd Earl of Mansfield acquired the whole
estate, copyholds and freeholds, as part of the family policy to protect Kenwood.
Thus the frontage of Spaniards Road was protected from development, except for
the old tavern which later became a private residence called Nine Elms. A family
called Hodgson rented the property in 1851 and turned the old Inn buildings into
a house which later became simply The Elms.[31] From the 1880s much of Erskine's
25-acre estate was returned to the Heath, beginning in 1889 with nine acres of
the garden included as part of the acquisition of Parliament Hill (see Ch. 11).

In 1894, still an estate of 12 acres, the house was rented from Lord
Mansfield by the art dealer and benefactor Sir Joseph Duveen, who richly
embellished its mock Jacobean-style interior (now listed).[32] The family took an
interest in the local community; his son Edward lived at Gangmoor until 1933
and served on the Society's committee until 1938. On Sir Joseph's death in
1908, The Elms was acquired by Sir Joshua Kelly Waddilove[33] and then in 1920
was sold to the American businessman Clarence Warren Gasque, a financial
director of Woolworths. His daughter, who married John Roland Robinson,
MP for Blackpool (later Baron Martonmere), inherited the property and they

lived there until the outbreak of the Second World War. She went to America with their children and stayed with the Woolworth family, while Robinson served in the RAF.

After the War, seeing an opportunity to capitalise on this valuable property in the context of the new Plan for London, Robinson applied for planning permission from the LCC in 1952, to develop the site at a density of 100 persons per acre. But the Society's lobbying had got the land designated as private open space in the new Plan and permission was refused (see Part 6). Fortunately, St Columba's Hospital came to the rescue. In need of new premises and with the support of the local authority, not only did the Hospital buy The Elms, but they sold another 4½ acres of the grounds to add to the Heath, for £1,500 – a price that today seems astonishing. The GLC was persuaded by Kit Ikin in 1972 to buy a further strip of land from the Regional Hospitals Board to open up a new footpath for the public from Spaniards Road to Kenwood.[34] For the time being, The Elms was safe.

**Notes, Chapter 15**

1. *H&OHS Newsletter*, May 1996
2. Sir Colin Anderson, 1st report as Chairman, H&OHS annual report 1959
3. HHPS, 8th annual meeting, *The Times*, 20 Feb 1905
4. Woodford (1998), foreword
5. *The Times*, 15 Sep 1944
6. Formed in Hampstead in 1888 to protect the public rights over footpaths, roads, and bridleways, on open lands in the neighbourhood.
7. LCC Parks and Open Spaces Committee, report 30 Jan 1903, minutes 10 Feb 1903
8. Hampstead Manor Court Book 1802-08 (E/MW/H/226). A rod is roughly 18ft x 15ft.
9. Sir Samuel Hoare, letter to HBC, 1895 Hampstead Vestry, minutes 1895, vol. 34, p 221, report no. 2 T&OS cttee; deputation to Sir Samuel Hoare at Hereford Gardens, 19 June. Sir Samuel was not entirely correct – manor

records show that the Hoares, like everyone else, had enclosed strips of waste in the early 1800s to enlarge their gardens.
10. HBC minutes, 2 Feb 1905, p 216
11. HHPS annual report, 1919
12. Report, *Ham & High*, 15 Nov 1919
13. *The Times*, 4 Dec 1919
14. HBC minutes, 20 Oct 1923
15. Lever built the model garden village Port Sunlight on the Wirral to give his workers decent housing.
16. David Sullivan in *Ham & High*, 25 May 1979
17. John Gurney Hoare's daughter Anna Maria married Captain John Reynolds MacInnes, who died young of diphtheria in 1865.
18. *H&HS Newsletter*, May 1996
19. H&OHS annual report, 1950
20. His daughter, the novelist Penelope Fitzgerald, wrote a fascinating account of this intriguing and

remarkable family, *The Knox Brothers* (1977).
21. The C.B. King who had been Mansfield's agent died in 1928 and is buried in the Additional Burial Ground, Hampstead Parish Church.
22. See note 12, ch. 12
23. Pitt wasn't quite the recluse there as has been made out; the *Newcastle Courant*, 26 Jul 1766, reports: "the Earl of Sherbourne had a long conference with Mr. Pitt at Mr. Dingley's at Hampstead".
24. Letter, Clarendon to Figgis, 17 Jun 1938 (H&HS archive: A/1048/3/8/7/4)
25. H&OHS annual report, 1952
26. In the 1790s, John Bone, Lord of the Manor of Hendon, built a new Manor House there; it ceased being the manor house after his death, but the name stuck (www.barnet.gov.uk/citizen-home/libraries/local-studies-and-archives/pocket-histories.html)

27. HH&OHS *Newsletter*, Spring 1978
28. Hampstead Manor Court Roll 8, 1685-89. Its name varies from Blue to Blew in different documents.
29. Indenture, Lord Erskine (LMA: E/MW/H /III/31/8)
30. Kit Ikin, 'Three younger sons' (unpublished paper, author's archive)
31. J. Hodgson is listed in *Shaw's Hampstead Directory* at Nine Elms in 1854. Mrs Hodgson is listed at The Elms in the directory of 1885.
32. Indenture of Lease between the Earl of Mansfield and J.J. Duveen, 1895; Refurbishment report 1899; Archives, Scone Palace
33. Waddilove established the Provident Clothing & Supply Co. Ltd, which still exists today as Provident Financial.
34. Ikin (1985), p 32

## Chapter 16

# The management dilemma

And having got the Heath, what was to be done with it? Management has been contentious throughout its history and has been the Society's biggest preoccupation. Of all the issues, trees – to plant or not to plant have been the most controversial. The old manorial prohibition against tree planting, so that views should be preserved, is now long forgotten. As long ago as 1816, protest was raised at "improvers" of the Heath when a programme of relief work for the poor was carried out, because they were "shaving, levelling, embanking and turfing Hampstead Heath". "...these extensive and picturesque views, the admiration of foreigners and the delightful study of our artists, are in danger of being reduced to a tame, formal, vapid smoothess, by the rash hands of tasteless improvers".[1]

As well as the many paintings and drawings of the Heath, we have contemporary descriptions of it from its earliest years when its moorland character was very different from its appearance today. Gerard and Johnson, the herbalists; Lysons, Defoe, Park, Patmore, Thorne – the list of writers who left descriptions is a long one (see Bibliography). Howitt, for instance goes into detail about "an interesting swampy hollow and quaking bog" near the Leg of Mutton Pond, "But the spring which fed the bog was drained by the Metropolitan Board of Works a few years ago, to the distress of lovers of semi-aquatic plants".[2]

Two of the different kinds of Heath habitat

119. Hampstead, view of the open fields from the Viaduct, 1897, by David Murray, a founder member of the Hampstead Heath Protection Society

120. West Heath sandy moorland, 1885, John Steeple

In fact, only a quarter of the area we now call Hampstead Heath is actually heathland; the large additions made after 1871 were originally either farmland or parkland. Its landscape has been greatly altered over the centuries by man's activity. Digging for sand, quarrying and brickmaking provided income for the lord of the manor, leaving huge pits. The creation of the ponds by damming up streams, levelling mounds, and Sir Thomas Maryon Wilson's tree planting, road and Viaduct of the 1840s – all have contributed to the uniquely varied landscape.

It is, of course, a common mistake to suppose that a 'wild and natural' appearance does not require management. The Society understood from the beginning that not only did it need management but it had to be a very particular kind, and its concerns about how this should be done have been a constant theme of its deliberations. Its crucial role in seeing that the Heath continues to be managed as a piece of countryside, not a park, cannot be overstated. But its aim was also to influence how the Heath was managed by working harmoniously with the authorities, as its first Chairman spelled out.

In 1871 it was clear that some landscaping was needed, if only to repair the harm done by all of Maryon Wilson's depredations, but the scale of interference by the London County Council (LCC) when it took over in the 1890s was something quite different. Within weeks of its formation, the Society commissioned the great William Robinson, pioneer of promoting the natural look in gardens, and author of *The English Flower Garden*, to give advice. He believed firmly in creating a natural-looking Heath that should appear "open [and] breezy". His recommendations to the Society, presented in a report in 1898 on how the Heath should be managed, are exceedingly forthright.

121. William Robinson (1838-1935)

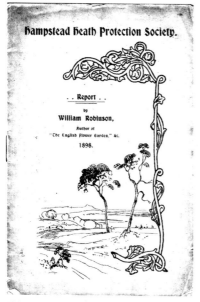

**Hampstead Heath Protection Society.**

. . Report . .
by
**William Robinson,**
Author of
"The English Flower Garden," &c.
1898.

122. Front cover of
William Robinson's report

"The existence of stupid planting and jerry building is no proof that there are not better ways, and it is just as practicable and with a little thought, as easy to group and mass in picturesque ways the vegetation most suitable for Hampstead Heath, as to plant trees like lampposts, and attempt to adorn it with mere samples of the conventional shrubbery.

"At the edge of the Viaduct Pond trees and shrubs from many parts of the world are thrown together as in a shrubbery in a St John's Wood villa, without regard to anything but their size as they left the nursery, and so jumbled together that they can but kill each other and never produce any good effect." Robinson felt "strongly that this is a place for our native shrubs and trees, which are very much neglected in ordinary planting.

"In the fine series of ponds at Hampstead, a mistake has been made in destroying the water plants, and disfiguring the margins by forming them into hard, ugly lines – the result of thoughtless cleaning of the ponds, when not only the native plants were taken up, but the ground lines characteristic of the margin of water destroyed. The result is as ugly and unnatural as anything could be, and a loss not only of the effect of the vegetation natural to the waterside but also as regards food and cover for the fish and water birds. When I last walked round these ponds at the end of May there were several miles of bare, ugly margin (in some cases three feet high) hard over the water. ... such a state of things is deplorable in a place which is supposed to be kept in a natural state".[3]

As Kit Ikin remarked, "it is ironical that the LCC were busy 'gardening' on the Heath, but the great gardener, Robinson, abjured their works".[4] "... Over time many of Robinson's recommendations for the Heath were carried out, and much of the way that the Heath is experienced today is down to his opinions and beliefs".[5] Robinson remained associated with the Society as an Honorary Member of its committee for its first 20 years, and since then the Society has been fortunate in being able to call upon a wide range of expertise both locally and further afield.

## The battle to be heard

The Society's early committee members, under the chairmanship of Alderman Ernest Lake, were a determined bunch: the Field and Hoare families, who had been involved in the 1860s campaign and the 1868 Hampstead Copyholders' Court case, Sir Walter Besant, Reginald Blomfield RA, Cornelius Dalton, and the redoubtable George W. Potter, were undaunted by their task. In 1899, with the support of Lord Meath of the Metropolitan Public Gardens Association (MPGA), they pressurised the LCC to have a resident Superintendent Ranger and they got one: a Mr George Palmer. In 1901 the Society reported that its recommendations for improving planting round banks of ponds were being followed, and in 1902 it persuaded the LCC to build a shelter for birds. In 1903 it objected to "shows" being held close to East Heath Road, in particular a large Wild Beast Show: the Heath is an "entirely unsuitable place for noisy shows or exhibitions in tents or booths covering a large area of ground".[6]

The Society was, in fact, in the vanguard of the development modern democratic accountability. It was one of the first such societies in London and it was, as its Chairman said in 1936, a "pioneer in the movement for providing organised means of expressing the views and wishes of the residents".[7] Indeed, in 1897 there were only two other local amenity societies in the whole country, both in Devon, which, like the Society, still exist today.[8]

They were dealing with an entirely new situation: the LCC was a new concept and so was any idea of consulting the wider public; even the universal franchise was still some way off. The LCC must be made to consult and it was the Society that established this principle. And their concern did not stop there: they were also keenly aware of their own obligation "to ensure that there should be an interchange of views between the Society members and the Committee with regard to what policies should be followed by the Society".[9] They suggested in 1904 that the Boroughs of Hampstead and St Pancras should be directly represented on the LCC Parks and Open Spaces Committee.

There now began a battle to get the LCC to accept this principle of consultation, and the Society was not going to be deflected. Their first attempt to get the new Superintendent to confer with them – about work to trees – was rejected by the Parks Committee, although it conceded that if work was undertaken of which the Society did not approve "the Committee would be prepared to give immediate attention to any representation which the Society may communicate to them".[10] Undeterred, Society committee members devoted increasing amounts of time to every aspect of management, whether putting up fencing, scything of nettles, correct treatment of bogs, fencing cotton grass to help preserve it, how saplings should be planted, or the problem of the dreaded sycamores. One of their earliest and most consistent concerns was with overplanting, beginning with the trees along Spaniards Road which was one of the reasons the Society came into being. Both the Hampstead Borough Council and the LCC had also to be continuously restrained from their urge to make regulation footpaths; when they tar-paved the path on Spaniards Road the Society persuaded them to remake it with gravel.

They complained about the unsatisfactory condition of the water in Whitestone Pond, especially after a public holiday. In 1905 they complained to the Metropolitan Railway about black smoke emanating from their chimney at Neasden, because "it could be seen from the Crest of the Heath". With the help of the Coal Smoke Abatement Society, formed only two years after the HHPS itself, they got the company fined.[11] The Society's concern for wildlife was evident from the beginning. In 1902 they got a shelter for birds built and planted with shrubs, and reported that it "was frequented by many song birds".[12] They objected to "the imprisoning of wild animals" when the zoo enclosure was formed at Golders Hill Park: "it was not the intention of the purchase of the estate".[13] At their request, grazing of sheep was temporarily stopped on East Heath because of the danger to the animals. They persuaded the LCC Parks and Open Spaces Committee to meet Society committee members at North End to discuss the future of the new Heath Extension.[14] In 1908 they strenuously objected to an LCC idea to make a "Serpentine Lake from the Vale of Health Pond to the lowest Hampstead Pond", which would have required "a 100ft dam near the east end of Downshire hill road". The next year they managed to scotch an LCC plan to cement over the bottoms of the ponds and make them a uniform depth.

The Society constantly complained to local schools about the "thoughtless acts of children" who destroyed shrubs, flowers and grasses on the Heath. In 1910 it sent over a hundred letters to local schoolmasters, asking them to point out to their pupils that there were legal penalties for such behaviour.[15] Vandalism remained an ongoing problem; on a bank holiday in 1911, the damage done by fires was so bad that the Society wrote to the London newspapers to draw attention to it. An unremitting stream of deputations, letters, and requests for meetings, information and consultation was kept up. But it was an uphill struggle, as borne out by a letter to *The Times* in 1909 from "An old resident, Hampstead Heath", pleading for "its guardians to show more loving care of the beauty committed to their charge". The writer complained that nothing was being done about rubbish being dumped on the Heath, especially builders rubble from "constant building going on close by", and "unnecessary mutilation" of trees, to all of which "the constables are indifferent and inefficient".[16] And *The Times* noted the Society's efforts: "Complaints have recently been raised by the Hampstead Heath Protection Society against the way in which the Heath has been administered by the Parks Committee of the London County Council, and the alleged disregard of that body for the characteristic features which distinguish [it]".[17]

Discontent was widespread and the polite niceties of written communications hide real anger. Willows at the Leg of Mutton Pond had been cut down for no apparent reason. The Society's committee wrote to the LCC, and its Honorary Secretary, Mr Pooley, called personally at the LCC offices to reinforce the message. At the suggestion of Walter Reynolds, the LCC member for Hampstead, nine Society committee members made a deputation to the Parks Committee and "pressed upon them the desirability of information being given to our Society before operations of this kind were carried out". They "suggested the appointment of a sub-committee, acting in consultation with our Society, to deal with the management of the Heath".[15] The LCC loftily replied that "they did not see their way ... to adopt [the Society's] suggestion of a special sub-committee". They did say, however, that arrangements had been made for Hampstead Borough Council LCC members "to be notified of all important proposals affecting the Heath", so that "the Council would be kept in close touch with local feeling" and that "representations made from time to time by [the] Society would be carefully borne in mind by the Council when considering questions relating to the management of the Heath".[15]

The Society called in another expert, William Goldring – a distinguished landscape architect and naturalist, in charge of the Herbaceous Department at Kew Gardens – to draw up a report on the correct way to treat old elm trees. He too, became an Honorary Member of the Society's committee. His paper was circulated to the LCC Parks and Open Spaces Committee and to Hampstead and St Pancras Borough Councils.[18]

The Society's AGM in 1910 was attended by some of its most eminent supporters, including Sir Robert Hunter, Basil Holmes, Sir Edwin Durning-Lawrence[19] and Sir Cornelius Dalton. A resolution was passed, reprimanding the LCC: "...this meeting desires to impress upon the London County Council the imperative necessity of strictly carrying out their statutory duties, under Section 16 of the Hampstead Heath Act 1871, viz., To preserve at all times, as far as may be, the natural aspect and state of the Heath, and to that end, to protect the turf, gorse, heather, timber and other trees, shrubs and brushwood thereon".[15] This seemed to have an effect, and in June there came a breakthrough: "the Parks Committee would be pleased to meet two members of the Society's Committee on the Heath". Sir Cornelius Dalton and Mr Pooley, the joint Honorary Secretaries, met four members of the Parks Committee and discussed the problems with them.[15]

## The arrival of Major Maud

But it was with the arrival in 1911 of Major Maud as Chief Officer of the LCC Parks Department, that a new era opened.[20] His response was quite different. When the committee called his attention to any problem, he, remarkably, seemed more than willing to listen, writing on one occasion that "he would be much obliged if any member would report such matters to the council staff". He met members of the Society's committee with other officials from the LCC, and visited various parts of the Heath with them, thus establishing the idea of regular walks to discuss its management. He even promised to consider the possibility of clearing a vista through the much disliked trees on Spaniards Road.[21]

As the Great War started in 1914, the Society was waging its own local war on the carrion crows which were destroying and driving out other birds. They even wrote to Prince Michael at Kenwood, asking him to shoot the crows when the opportunity arose. In 1917 they recorded that the LCC granted permission for "a gentleman residing in Hampstead to shoot carrion crows on the heath subject to proper provision for safeguarding the public".[22] (One wonders whether it was the Prince!) Later, in the 1930s, they railed against jays and the growing incursion of grey squirrels – there were still red squirrels on the Heath then – and advocated shooting them too! Maud was called up again in 1914 and served with distinction, mentioned in dispatches, throughout the War, returning to his work at the LCC as a Brigadier-General. Progress continued: one of the first things he did on his return was to meet members of the HHPS committee and consider some of their suggestions for the much needed post-war restoration.

Emily Field – acknowledged by all as being the prime mover in founding the Society – died in 1918, but lived long enough to hear that the Parks Committee was at last going to cut down some of the trees planted along Spaniards Road that had so angered everyone.

This steady improvement continued. The Society's committee was "in frequent communication with Major Maud," and by 1933, despite the financial crises of the interwar years, the Society was able to record that its "relations with the authorities responsible for the management of the Heath have remained excellent", and that their representations and suggestions had been received with courtesy and consideration, and had in most cases been acted on.[23]

However, that turned out to be the high point. When Brigadier-General Maud retired in 1935, it was already apparent that management of the Heath was going downhill. The economic crisis set off by the 1929 Wall Street Crash and the Great Depression forced the slashing of budgets. Yet some of the LCC decisions seemed perverse: funds to provide adequate management dried up, while money was spent on widespread overplanting of trees. The deterioration on the Heath became ever more noticeable, with large areas now too densely wooded. At the same time other trees, such as those in Ken Wood, (the original medieval Caen Wood, now referred to as South Wood) were not receiving adequate attention, and fine views were being lost. With Maud gone, the Society's complaints went unheeded. The Heath was no longer a tongue of wild country penetrating into the built-up area of London; it had become an island in the centre of a growing densely populated urban area, and with a hugely increased number of visitors the strain was showing. It was enormously popular for every form of outdoor activity and facilities increased accordingly. Running (the Highgate Harriers had started in 1879) and swimming (the Highgate Lifebuoys had begun in 1894), along with cricket, hockey and skating, were joined by athletics and football.

In 1936 there was an upset over the Heath ponds, and even a threat that they might be drained. The City Corporation still owned the freeholds, and the 1871 Hampstead Heath Act had permitted them to continue leasing them, first to the New River Company and then to its successor, the Metropolitan Water Board. However, modern filtration systems had rendered the ponds redundant as a source of water and the Water Board would have been happy to fill them in when the lease expired. Unsurprisingly, there was a public outcry at such a suggestion, and also against a proposal to turn one of the ponds into a lido; the whole point of the Heath ponds was that they provided natural facilities, unlike purpose-built swimming pools. By 1939 the LCC accepted its responsibility for the maintenance of the ponds as public swimming areas.[5] But presumably as a result of this incident, the idea of a lido took hold: the Parliament Hill Lido was built in 1937 and opened the following year. The Society incurred criticism for not opposing it, but they felt that it would have been "churlish to stand in the way of the health and legitimate pleasure of thousands of Londoners, especially children".[24]

## Post-war decline

Unfortunately, the story after the Second World War is one of continuing decline, financial constraint and the lack of political will to devote either sufficient resources or expertise to the Heath's care. In addition, increasing party-political partisanship began to get in the way of what might actually be the right thing for Heath management. The Society's annual reports, minutes and archives tell a tale of frustration and disappointment.

It needed a body of remarkably determined men and women to maintain the 'constant vigil' and refuse to take 'no' for an answer. The Society's committee began calling for a new approach to management, with a special report on the problems. Levels of staffing, and methods of management and public supervision, which had not been necessary in the past, were now needed. But the LCC's response reverted to the lofty irritation of its early years. When in 1947 the Society sent notes and suggestions on bird sanctuaries – by V.R. Garrett (Society member and keen bird recorder) – the LCC replied that, whilst these were desirable, they could not be given precedence. The Society's tart response was that "the protection of the sanctuaries is of more importance that many of the other purposes for which fencing is required".[25]

In the midst of increasing concern and damage to trees, shrubs and birds, the Chief Officer of the LCC Parks Department felt impelled to attend the 1949 AGM. He tried to reassure the Society that the LCC was fully aware of problems, claiming that they were due to shortage of material and staff. The Society was well aware of the economic problems, but the fact was that the LCC continued unnecessary expenditure on overplanting and other projects. One of these was an extraordinary event staged on the Heath in 1950 and 1951, giving the Society further anxiety about the LCC's intentions. An 'Anglo-Norwegian' skiing competition was held on the Heath, promoted by the Central Council of Physical Recreation in association with the Oslo Ski Association. The Society's annual report recorded that it was difficult to reconcile the statutory obligations of the LCC with an event that involved the closing of parts of the Heath for several days, "attracting vast crowds and innumerable motor cars" which "detract from the value of open space".[26] But it was enormously popular with the public and over 100,000 were thought to have attended. *The Times* gave it enthusiastic support, calling it an unqualified success: nowhere "could be more appropriate to this sport of the mountains" than Hampstead Heath. The Society had to bite its collective lip. 45 tons of snow were brought all the way from Norway, and an immense artificial jump, some 60 feet high, was built on scaffolding near the Vale of Health, giving the skiers a run of 100 feet to a jumping point about 12 feet above the ground. The skiers were all amateurs, mostly from Norway, but some from Oxford and Cambridge Universities also competed.[27]

123. The ski jump (photo: Ben Brooksbank)

124. John Hillaby (1917-96)

A rather more charming addition in the 1950s was the Buckland caravan, which was on display in the grounds at Kenwood for a time. It was an old Romany caravan built about 1900 for the country showground family of Mr and Mrs Buckland, beautifully painted and with hand-carvings. It had been brought regularly to the fairs on Hampstead Heath until 1935, and was then rescued and restored and presented to the LCC. It is currently kept in the Kenwood stables.

There was no improvement as the 1950s unfolded, and by 1958 matters reached a crisis point. John Hillaby, naturalist and travel writer, joined the Society's Committee

184

in 1956. He was science correspondent for the *New York Times* and later for the *Manchester Guardian* and the *New Scientist*, a lecturer at Yale University, and a member of the Council for Nature. He walked daily on Hampstead Heath, to which he was devoted, and used his influence and extensive contacts to try to get something done. He took a leading role in setting up a special Heath Sub-Committee of the Society, chaired by Lena Townsend (Hampstead representative on the LCC), and invited a panel of eminent experts to take stock of the problems and draw up a series of reports as a matter of extreme urgency.[28] They included Professor W.H. Pearsall, Quain Professor of Botany at the University of London and specialist in plant ecology; Professor Eric Warmington of Birkbeck College; Dr Palmer Newbould of University College London, a leading ecologist; Julian Huxley who lived in Hampstead; and, most eminently, Dr Francis Rose of Bedford College Botany Department, regarded by many as possibly the greatest British field botanist of the 20th century.[29]

Their first report concentrated on Kenwood, which had been managed as a separate park unit by the LCC since it opened to the public in 1925. It needed "immediate and unremitting attention", particularly the West Field bog which was highlighted as "one of the most interesting habitats within 10 miles of the City of London".[29] The LCC paid little attention. However, a second report and a letter from Dr Rose, saying that the Heath needed "rehabilitation", could not be ignored, especially after *The Times* publicised it in May 1959 in a report of the Society's AGM: "Mr. Reginald Stamp, chairman of the parks committee went himself to the annual meeting to tell members about his committee's problems and intentions regarding Kenwood and the Heath." He told *The Times* that the LCC had a 10-year programme for its parks and open spaces.[30] But behind the scenes another difficulty emerged: it became apparent that the LCC was reluctant to take advice or help from 'outsiders', whether professional or volunteers, the attitude being that the LCC had its own. In addition, the very idea of using unpaid voluntary labour "transgressed an ideological barrier" and the Society felt it must "be careful not to tread on toes". Privately, doubts were expressed about whether the LCC had either the resources or the ability to carry out the advisers' recommendations.[31]

Nevertheless, the Chief Officer of the Parks Department and his team did visit the Heath and hold discussions with committee members, whose hope that this might become an annual event appeared to be fulfilled when the visit was repeated in 1959. Reginald Stamp agreed to implement new planting methods in response to Society criticism, and at last a meeting was arranged in 1960 with Dr Rose, John Hillaby and Leo Bonacina. Stamp, a Hampstead resident, now began to attend the Society's annual general meetings and took a more conciliatory tone. In 1961 several of the Society's suggestions were adopted and the Society's Heath Sub-Committee disbanded itself, thinking it had fulfilled its objective. But the improvement was short-lived. The LCC refused to send an officer to accompany the Society's new advisers in a walk on the Heath saying only that they would read a report if one were sent. Perhaps the LCC knew its days were numbered. The Society's committee arranged their own walks across the Heath and sent the LCC their reports.

**Notes, Chapter 16**

1. London Courier & Evening Gazette, 18 Dec 1816. This could be referring to a scheme instigated by Henry White to provide employment for the poor by improving old roads and footpaths on the Heath, recorded in the Court Book K Feb 1816-Nov 1822 (LMA: E/MW/H/228), see Chapter 1.
2. Howitt (1869), p 155
3. Report by William Robinson 1898 (author's collection) and H&HS archive: A/1048/3/6/1/1
4. 'Hampstead Heath – past and present', unpublished paper by Kit Ikin (author's archive)
5. 'Hampstead Heath Ponds: an historic environment assessment' (Museum of London Archaeology; London Borough of Camden, 2013)
6. HHPS annual reports, *passim*

7. HH&OHPS, annual report, 1936
8. The Sid Vale Association the oldest civic society in Britain, founded 1846 "to conserve the charm and attractiveness of Sidmouth and the Sid Valley"; and Dartmoor Preservation Association (1883), founded in similar circumstances to the HHPS.
9. HHPS, annual report, 1909
10. Ibid., 1904
11. Following the Public Health (London) Act of 1891, in which Ernest Hart played a significant role, the Coal Smoke Abatement Society, like the HHPS, was an early example of community protest on behalf of the environment; they mobilised taxpayers to bring pressure on their local authorities to prosecute offenders.

12. HHPS, annual reports, 1902 & 1904
13. Ibid., 1905
14. Ibid., 1906
15. Ibid., 1910
16. Letter to *The Times*, 17 Sep 1909
17. *The Times*, 29 Mar 1910
18. William Goldring, 'Trees on Hampstead Heath'; various reports on preservation of trees on the Heath 1907, 1909 & 1911 (H&HS archive: A/1048/3/6/1/19/1)
19. Sir Edwin was MP for Truro, and a lawyer; another Unitarian who devoted much time to philanthropy, he was briefly a member of the MBW, and an Honorary Member of the HHPS.
20. Brigadier-General Philip Maud (1879 -1947) saw distinguished military service in Abyssinia, for which he was awarded the CMG; obituary in *The Times*, 3 Mar 1947

21. HHPS, annual report, 1912
22. Ibid., 1917
23. HH&OHPS, annual report, 1933
24. Ibid., 1937
25. Ibid., 1947
26. Ibid., 1950
27. Various reports, Ski-jumping on Hampstead Heath, *The Times*, Jan-Mar 1950 & 1951
28. HH&OHPS, annual report, 1958
29. Dr F. Rose, 'Conservation on Hampstead Heath' (H&HS archive: A/1048/3/6/1/11)
30. 'LCC answers Kenwood criticisms', *The Times*, 19 May 1959
31. Correspondence in H&HS archive: A/1048/3/6/1/11

## Chapter 17

# Three into one – another London shake-up

I n 1965 there came yet another shake-up of London governance. Under the London Government Act of 1963, the ancient historic boroughs were absorbed into new 'superboroughs', artificial administrative constructs with little connection to the old communities they were supposed to serve. The LCC was replaced by the Greater London Council (GLC). The Borough of Hampstead was merged with those of Holborn and St Pancras into the new London Borough of Camden.

125. The Society's tree logo first appeared on the annual report of 1961

126. The shield of the GLC

127. Camden Council logo

At first the merger seemed to pass without much upset, but what the Society could not have anticipated was the insidious effect of the abolition of Hampstead's borough status. Swept away with the borough was a working relationship that had developed over the course of decades, focused on the interests of Hampstead and its residents. As Charles Booth had said so many years before, "party politics were little regarded" and, according to Enid Wistrich, a Camden GLC councillor who lived in Hampstead, this was still the case in 1965: "Hampstead Council retained a sedate quiet image. Up to 1945 it was dominated by councillors sponsored by the Ratepayers and Municipal Electors Associations," with a tradition that candidates would not accept a whip or consider local affairs from a party political viewpoint. "Even by 1962 party politics still played little part in the Council's deliberations".[1] By contrast, Camden Council was from the beginning "a highly political borough at both Council and staff levels".[2] The new borough name was a subject of much debate. Wistrich lists some of the various ideas that were rejected, such as Fleetside and Heathfleet, suggested because the River Fleet links all three boroughs. But other more bizarre suggestions were Panhamborn, St Hamborn, Bornham, and Bornhamcras.

On Hampstead Heath, matters did not improve under the new GLC, and from now on there was no local administration to which the Society could turn for support. Crucial changes of management saw the Kenwood estate amalgamated with Parliament Hill Fields and managed from the depot on Parliament Hill; the emphasis changed from managing it as an historic landscape to managing it more as an urban park, and its deterioration continued.[3] Then, out of the blue, the Heath's status as a London wide regional open space was questioned; it had been taken for granted that under the 1963 London Government Act the Heath had been transferred intact to the new GLC. But a closer reading of the Act finds that it contains powers under which the GLC could transfer parks to the Boroughs. Following an Act of 1967 dealing with Greater London Parks and Open Spaces, it was revealed in *The Times* that negotiations had been going on between the GLC and the London Boroughs Association, for parks of "only local importance" to be handed over to the boroughs as a cost-cutting measure, and that Camden was keen to take over the Heath. As *The Times* put it: "Hampstead Heath is not – amazing to relate – apparently considered a park 'of more than local importance'".[4] There was talk of dividing the Heath, with Kenwood going to the GLC, the Heath Extension to Barnet, and the remainder to Camden.

Horrified, the Society's big guns fired a broadside. Lord Ilford, Sir Colin Anderson and Peggy Jay wrote to express their dismay at this wholly unexpected turn of events, reminding the powers that be that the Heath belongs to London, as specified in the 1871 Hampstead Heath Act, and that splitting it up between three different authorities would be deplorable.[5] A public outcry, revelations about running costs, and the legal chaos that the three-way split would have led to, stopped the plan in its tracks. Hampstead Heath remained intact in the care of the GLC.[6]

But management under the GLC continued to deteriorate; the Society's 1969 annual report recorded that the Heath was turning into a jungle. And added to anxiety about the state of the Heath were increasing planning threats to the fringes of the Heath. The Society's energies were already fully stretched by proposed building at Ivy House, Mount Tyndal on Spaniards Road, the Russian trade delegation block of flats overlooking the Heath at Highgate, the Vale of Health public house and fairground site, the siting of a radio mast, the future of the old Toll Gate House, and constant attempts to widen roads which would have destroyed Hampstead and taken land from the Heath. It was clear that the GLC had no management policy for the Heath or Kenwood and appeared to have no plans to formulate one. As for any idea of conservation, they all but destroyed a sphagnum peat bog in the valley below the dairy at Kenwood – one of the few such bogs in southeast England - using it to provide moss for thousands of municipal hanging baskets and allowing it to become choked with scrub.[7] As Peggy Jay wrote despondently in her 1973 annual report: "Each defeat, even though the proposal may be trifling in itself, represents an inexorable erosion of what the Heath is, or of what it might have been." There was even a proposal to stop the Royal Horse Artillery from using Whitestone Pond.

Kit Ikin, solicitor and Hampstead historian, had lived in a house on the edge of Sandy Heath all his life. He had been a member of the Society for many years and joined its Committee in 1965, having become increasingly concerned

that the planning side of its work now took
up too much of its time, and that insufficient
thought was given to the Heath. "Relations
with the [GLC] Parks Department are good
but contacts with the two superintendants
who make day to day decisions are few".
It was clear to him that, as a start, there
needed to be a policy document for the
Heath agreed with the Department.[8] He
suggested that there were at least four different
environments to take into consideration: the
former heathland, the meadow, the forest,

128. C.W. ('Kit') Ikin, d.1998

and the parks, each needing a specialised kind of care. The Heath described
by Defoe and painted by Constable – open landscape with furze, heather,
broom, blackthorn, bilberry and whortleberry – was gone. West Heath and
Sandy Heath were now woodland, having lost all their heather and almost all
of their open space, gorse and other shrubs. The upper part of East Heath
was also heavily wooded as a result of Maryon Wilson's tree planting in the
1840s, and continued by the LCC from the 1890s. This had destroyed the
former heath and other kinds of ground cover.[9] Kit lamented the fact that "the
Sandy Heath, West Heath and Upper East Heath are no longer moorland;
... woodland can easily be found round London and moorland cannot".[10]

James Kennedy, Chief Officer of the GLC Parks Department, gave a
Centenary address to the Society's 1971 annual general meeting. One of the
Department's most experienced staff, with 21 years at the LCC, he spelled
out the underlying problem of lack of finance, which was causing all the GLC
functions to be cut back, and admitted that money which might have been spent
on improving the Heath was being diverted to provide better facilities in other
boroughs. The GLC was unable to look after the Heath as it would wish.[11] But
yet again this claimed lack of finance for Heath management did not stop the
GLC from coming up with other elaborate and expensive schemes, such as the
Parliament Hill athletics stadium,[12] a widened East Heath Road, a proposal for
a plastic toboggan track on Branch Hill,
the radio mast in the shrubbery next to
Whitestone Pond, the building over of the
Branch Hill estate, and the proposal to turn
Whitestone Pond into a traffic roundabout.

The Heath sub-committee was reconvened in 1974, led by Kit Ikin and David
Sullivan, to try to build a working relationship
with the GLC Parks Department so as to
improve the GLC's management of the Heath.
Sullivan, a distinguished QC, authority on the

129. David Sullivan (1926-2015)

painting of John Constable and historian of medieval Hampstead, also had a wide knowledge of topography and geology. He cared passionately about the Heath and for many years lived at Wyldes Farm on the Heath at North End. Ikin summed up the management challenges, especially with regard to trees, with his usual wry humour: the birdwatcher wants plenty of trees and bushes, preferably fenced off; the wildflower man wants fewer trees; the law-abiding man wants trees that children cannot climb; the law-and-order man wants no bushes or hedges behind which villains can skulk; some want only native trees; others want them felled to return the Heath to a proper Heath; some bewail the lost views; others want country meadows with rough grass. What was certain was that whenever the GLC felled a tree someone would complain![13]

In the absence of any written GLC strategy, the Society's sub-committee decided to prepare their own survey. They studied the Heath in detail sector by sector, and issued a seven-point policy summary which they hoped would be put up for public discussion and become a management blueprint. It is a mark of just how much the Heath had been allowed to deteriorate that such basic recommendations were not already in force:

- get rid of sycamores
- save the gorse
- retain and restore old heath habitat
- save remaining open spaces
- restore some views
- get some groundcover back
- thin the woods

This summary, with a letter of complaint from Peggy Jay to Desmond Plummer, Leader of the GLC, led to a brief period of improvement. GLC officers agreed to meet the sub-committee regularly to develop a closer working relationship, and to work towards producing an appropriate policy. But the GLC's centralised approach to maintenance, dealing with all the parks from head office rather than having dedicated local teams, meant the policy never materialised. Set against a background of political turmoil in the 1970s, further cutbacks to the GLC budget in 1975 led to more staff reductions and things began to slide again. In addition, the GLC now appeared to be reluctant to work with the Society at all, failing to communicate or reply to letters; plans agreed between them were delayed.

David Sullivan, as Chairman of the Heath sub-committee in 1976 and 1977, wrote hard-hitting reports: "The question is are the GLC willing and able to tackle properly the growing conservation issues on the Heath. The Heath needs country maintenance not urban park maintenance. ... the Society's concerns and recommendations have been forcefully presented to the GLC ... the country–like qualities of the Heath demand special staff who are devoted whole time to the Heath and not diverted to other 'park-like' duties such as tennis courts, bowling greens and playing fields". "It is extraordinary, not to say lamentable, that in 1977, over one hundred years since the Heath originally became public property, we should still be having to urge this. ... a proper policy decision by the GLC is about 105 years overdue".[14] Enid Wistrich, the local GLC member, raised the matter at a GLC committee meeting, asking whether the GLC accepted the need for a conservation plan for the Heath, and would the Parks Department officers be preparing a survey and programme of action? Assurances were given that, following a meeting with David Sullivan and Kit Ikin, action would be taken.[15]

At last some progress was made. Two new superintendants were appointed and GLC committee members took part in a walk with members of the Society to see the problems for themselves.[16] But, as the Society wearily commented, "It would be cynical to think that May 6th [the local elections 1977] had anything to do with this" and, indeed, after the elections, which saw big changes, the verdict was "we have gone back to square one".[14] But not entirely. Dave King, one of the new superintendents, took over responsibility for Kenwood and Parliament Hill and began a determined programme of scrub clearance with encouragement from the Society.

## The Society under fire

But this much-needed work introduced two years of controversy about management of the Heath, both within the H&OHS, and between the Society, its members and the wider public. For the first time the Society itself came under fire, and was made acutely aware of the potential for public misunderstanding of their aims. The nature of the conservation work that was being carried out was completely misunderstood. The work had been neglected for so long and needed such drastic action that to many Heath users, and even some H&OHS members, it looked more as though the "wild and natural Heath", which the Society was supposed to protect, was being eradicated in a deliberate attempt to turn the Heath into a park; and the Society was encouraging these efforts rather than opposing them. In particular, efforts to save West Field stream and bog, with their designated SSSI status, from being blocked and dried out by birch trees and saplings, met with "an emotional attack in the press".[17]

A Heath Action Group (HAG) was formed, and hostilities broke out in the pages of the *Ham & High* and in the Society's *Newsletter*. In April 1978 a whole edition of the latter was devoted to angry letters from members complaining about its policy. The controversy even reached the pages of *The Times*, which reported the affair with a humorous gloss: "Axes are being noisily ground again in Hampstead, home of impassioned causes".[18]

It put the GLC in an awkward position: even though it was inundated with letters of objection from the public to the conservation work, in all honesty it had to acknowledge that the H&OHS was right about the need for it, and did so publicly at a GLC question time. In reply to a question asked in July 1978 by an Islington councillor, Arthur Wicks – "Are there any proposals to act on the criticism in the H&HS Annual Report?" – Sydney Ripley, Chairman of the GLC Open Spaces Committee (and a member for Kingston upon Thames), admitted:

"I cannot disagree with the general tenor of the Society's comments ... there are insufficient resources to do all that is necessary". Quoting passages of what the Society had said, he went on: "Of all the 5,350 acres in the charge of the Parks Department, Hampstead Heath is, I believe the most difficult. When local staff embark on conservation work public disquiet is often expressed." He was going to visit the Heath and had offered to meet representatives of HAG. If necessary he would consider the possibility of allocating more resources.[19]

Kit Ikin knew that such dissention was bad, not only for the Society but for the well being of the Heath itself. He also believed that the difference of opinion with HAG was not fundamental; it was more a matter of degree and balance. Malcolm Holmes (former London Borough of Camden Archivist) recalls members of HAG visiting the archives in search of pictures to prove their point, that clearing the scrub and bramble and thinning trees was an attack on the Heath's historic "wild and natural" habitat, and being astonished when they realised that, in fact, historically the Heath had few trees and little vegetation. But many objectors quite reasonably pointed out that "opening up vistas just enables us to see buildings and traffic" – shades of a letter written by A.E. Housman in 1898 (see Chapter 19)! As Ikin told *The Times*, "It's a pity, really, because we have so many ideals in common". He made overtures to the three HAG protagonists, met them for walks on the Heath to discuss their concerns and invited them onto the Society's committee. Differences were resolved and the controversy faded away.

But perhaps this episode brought home to the GLC the necessity of looking after the Heath in a more coherent and timely fashion. At the 1978 Spring walk with GLC officers it was agreed that the Society would prepare a paper, to include a detailed map, showing an agreed policy on Heath management. Ikin and the Heath sub-committee looked at the Heath section by section, starting with Parliament Hill and Fields. Their detailed proposals were published in the Society's *Newsletter* and circulated to the membership for comment.[20]

In 1979 Kit Ikin was succeeded as Chairman of the Heath sub-committee by Ray Softly, a retired bank official and keen amateur entomologist. In his quiet but persistent fashion he continued to make a progress. Despite widespread public cynicism that the GLC did not really look after the Heath and that the Society could not do much about it, and as the controversy died down, he galvanised Heath sub-committee activity, pressing the GLC for greater commitment to management and conservation. Dave King now set up a special team of six 'Heathmen' to deal with the arrears of conservation work, and representatives of the Society held regular meetings with officers at County Hall to discuss working arrangements and priorities. At last real progress began to be made. "Quarterly meetings with GLC staff, the traditional Spring walk, and the site meetings with the superintendents and foremen ... all continued amicably", and an experiment took place to create a wildflower meadow in a little-used field near the stock pond.[21] These efforts certainly did not go unnoticed at the GLC: "Hardly ever before can there have been a situation in which a small part of the activities of a department ... has been subjected to virtually day to day scrutiny as provided by the [Society's] sub-Committee. ... How many organisations could live with this intense scrutiny and still maintain a happy relationship?"[22]

The Society also took great care to consult, inform and survey its membership. Ray Softly provided a constant stream of detailed articles about the committee's efforts in the Society's newsletters, with maps and work schedules; and consultative meetings for members were held at Burgh House. The committee was gratified to find that members replying to surveys now agreed with the Society's proposals, although they were also still critical of the GLC – there was still too much 'parkification'. In the few years of its existence the GLC's new Heath conservation unit showed what valuable work it could do, although the frustrating limitations of its inadequate size were equally apparent.[23] But just as this painstaking progress had been made and a productive working relationship had at last been established with the officers, all was thrown into doubt again: government plans to abolish the Labour-controlled GLC were announced in the Conservative Party manifesto for the 1983 general election campaign, and were confirmed in the Queen's Speech.

## The gypsies

One last skirmish erupted before the GLC was swept away: the arrival of a gypsy encampment on the Heath in June 1984. It began with one caravan on the East Heath car park. The GLC's response was curious to say the least; instead of taking action, it took advice from its Ethnic Minorities Unit. By the end of the month a hundred caravans, cars and lorries had arrived, parking far beyond the car park right up towards The Pryors buildings, and cars and motorbikes were being driven across the Heath. The rescue boat on the Hampstead swimming pond was vandalised, fencing was broken and the pond had to be closed. The mounting litter was a health hazard and park staff, who were being stoned by travellers' children, refused to handle any more rubbish collections. But it became clear from GLC responses that it had no intention of doing anything about it: GLC officials expressed concern only at the 'harassment' of the travellers and it emerged that Heath staff were actually prevented from removing the caravans by the Ethnic Minorities Unit at County Hall. Instead the Unit "provided skips and mobile toilets to minimise the public health risk" and followed that up with a visit from an 'outreach worker' who advised the travellers that "their case would be helped if they kept the area clean and kept nuisance to a minimum".[24]

The Society threatened County Hall with legal action if the caravans did not leave immediately and the matter reached the pages of the national press, especially when it was apparent that two left-wing leading lights were at loggerheads with each other over the matter. Michael Foot, lately Labour Party leader, who had lived in Pilgrim's Lane for decades (but had only just joined the Society), was famous for his daily walk on the Heath with his dog Dizzie. He called for the gypsies to be removed, and the *Evening Standard* made it their front-page headline, portraying it as a spat with Ken Livingstone the leader of the GLC.[25] Foot, they reported, was said to be furious at this "contravention of the Heath Act".

The Society followed up with a solicitor's letter threatening legal proceedings. Peggy Jay commented: "It is particularly unfortunate because last week our society delivered a petition to Mrs Thatcher asking that the GLC be saved to continue looking after the Heath".[26] In the Society's *Newsletter*, she described the GLC's negligence as "the irresponsible intervention of one GLC department in the duties and responsibilities of another" and suggested that the Ethnic Minorities Unit budget be used to pay the enormous bill for cleaning up the mess the travellers left behind when they were eventually removed.[27] This provoked an extraordinarily petulant letter to Peggy Jay from Peter Pitt, Chair of the GLC Arts and Recreation Committee. The Society was at that time hoping to republish Kit Ikin's 1971 booklet about the saving of Hampstead Heath and had asked the GLC to let them have the copyright.[28] Pitt now replied that because of the damaging remarks and Peggy Jay's "abusive and offensive" behaviour, he would not do so.[29]

The gypsy encroachment happened again the following February, and, as a local resident wrote to the *Ham & High*: "once again the Ethnic Minorities Committee is preventing immediate steps being taken to remove them. ... the GLC has abdicated as Guardian of the Heath". Peter Pitt said he must by law seek an eviction order but refused to say when this might happen, adding a highly pejorative and inappropriate remark about Hampstead residents for good measure: "the trouble with people living in Hampstead is they forget travellers are human beings. ... Adolf Hitler had a policy of exterminating travellers but I am not prepared to do that". But even as he wrote, the GLC's fate was sealed.

**Notes, Chapter 17**
1. Wistrich (1972), p 6
2. Richardson (1985), p 142
3. Bryant & Colson (1990), p 29
4. 'Diary', *The Times*, 16 Sep 1968
5. *The Times*, 21 Sep 1968
6. 'Diary', *The Times*, 21 Oct 1968
7. Bryant & Colson (1990), p 30; H&OHS minutes, *passim*
8. H&OHS *Newsletter*, Autumn 1971
9. Kit Ikin, 'Hampstead heath - past and present', unpublished paper (author's archive)
10. Ikin (1985), p 31
11. Report of AGM, H&OHS *Newsletter*, Summer 1971
12. The South-East Regional Sports Council wanted the Parliament Hill athletics track upgraded to full Olympic standard, with 50ft floodlighting towers, grandstand seating, large pavilion with public address equipment, and a large car park (H&OHS annual report 1972)
13. (1985), p 31
14. Heath reports in H&OHS annual reports, 1976 & 1977
15. GLC report, 29 Mar 1977
16. Minutes of walk, H&OHS *Newsletter*, Autumn 1977
17. H&OHS annual report, 1977; SSSI: Sites of Special Scientific Interest
18. *The Times*, 25 Apr 1978, p 20
19. GLC report, 4 July 1978
20. H&OHS *Newsletter*, Autumn 1979
21. H&OHS annual report, 1981
22. Letter, G.A. Barber, Asst Director of GLC Dept of Recreation & the Arts, to Peggy Jay, 1981 (H&HS archive: A/1048/3/4 Ownership of the Heath)
23. H&OHS annual reports, 1982 & 1983
24. GLC Arts & Recreation and Race Relations Committee report, 4 Jul 1984
25. *Evening Standard*, 3 Jul 1984
26. *Ham & High*, 5 Jul 1984
27. H&OHS *Newsletter*, Autumn 1984
28. The booklet was originally commissioned and published by the GLC as part of centenary celebrations for the Hampstead Heath Act in 1971.
29. Letter, Peter Pitt to Peggy Jay, 6 Dec 1984 (H&HS archive)

Chapter 18

# The abolition
# of the Greater London Council

Yet again London faced political upheaval as part of government policy to reform local government nationwide. The role of the strategic London authority had always been problematic. As the London boroughs grew and their powers increased, so did the conflict between them and the London County Council, and its successor, the Greater London Council (GLC). No adequate solution to the difficult working relationship had yet been devised despite several royal commissions and inquiries, from the Ullswater Commission of 1923 to the Herbert Commission, appointed by Harold Macmillan's government in 1960. In between, William Robson of the London School of Economics argued for a Greater London Council in his 1939 polemic *The Government and Misgovernment of London*. The 1965 reform, replacing the LCC with the GLC, shifted the balance further towards strengthening the London boroughs. "The GLC ... was from the outset a pale shadow of its predecessor. ... It had all the panoply and trappings of power, but very few of the services that would justify that power. The GLC has had status without a role".[1]

Neither was it simply a party political question – the parties themselves were deeply divided over the GLC's role. Its plans for house-building in particular set the Conservative outer London boroughs against the Conservative-controlled GLC in the 1970s, and proposals for a new motorway network, the 'London Motorway Box', caused massive London-wide opposition. "There was fundamental disagreement over every element of change in London. There was no common ground – indeed furious dispute – over roads versus communities, or redevelopment versus conservation".[2] Calls for the abolition of the "interfering" GLC had begun well before Margaret Thatcher or Ken Livingstone ever arrived on the scene. According to Patrick Jenkin, Livingstone himself once said: "I feel that the boroughs are the major instruments of local government in London. I very much regret that Mr Cutler has not been really ruthless ... and axed the whole appalling show".[3]

Ironically, Hampstead's MP, Geoffrey Finsberg, was of the 'abolitionist' faction in the Tory party. A former Hampstead Borough councillor, and Conservative leader of Camden Council from 1968 to 1970, he was steeped in local politics, had strong views, and had long been an opponent of both the LCC and the GLC. The 'Abolish the GLC' campaign drew up a 'Policy for London', reviewing the role and purpose of the GLC, gave evidence at the Marshall Inquiry, and advocated stripping the GLC of most of its housing powers. They even fought 31 seats (out of 92) at the GLC elections of 1977, but failed to win any.

These disputes took place against a backdrop of growing dismay at 1960s policies that were destroying heritage assets, and which led to the formation by Duncan Sandys of the Civic Trust. Large numbers of new civic societies and amenity groups formed, outraged at bureaucratic insensitivity to locally familiar and valued townscapes, and the proposed London Motorway Box (see p 231). Before 1940 there were only about a dozen civic societies across London; now they were joined by many others, including, in 1966, a valuable new working partner, the Highgate Society. Moreover, these societies were given increased ability to challenge planning decisions by the Skeffington Committee Report in 1969. It acknowledged that the Town and Country Planning Act was a largely 'top down' system, and proposed that local development plans should be subject to full public scrutiny and debate.[4]

The advent at the GLC in 1981 of Ken Livingstone, who courted controversy on every side, did not help. Amongst many contentious initiatives, an early clash came over an idea from an official in the GLC's Arts and Recreation Committee, that GLC art treasures, including those at Kenwood, might be sold off to support trendier forms of art, even though it was very well known that legally this was not possible. Tony Banks, then Chairman of the Committee, appeared to make a very half-hearted rebuttal, which caused a rift with the Friends of Kenwood. The concern created by this mischievous suggestion led to questions in Parliament about the legal ownership of the paintings at Kenwood. Banks later said that, in the face of cuts to its arts budget, "the GLC was demonstrating ... that if it was forced into extremis it would have no option but to consider selling some of its assets in order to save some threatened [arts] companies".[5] Rumours also circulated that the GLC intended to seek powers to introduce entrance charges, as if this were something new. But the Iveagh Bequest, Kenwood Act of 1929 had already made provision for charges on two days a week, a fact that most people are unaware of.

The stage was set for a battle, and plans to abolish the GLC and metropolitan councils across the country duly appeared as a Tory manifesto commitment in the 1983 election campaign. However, the real point of contention emerged when it became clear that the GLC was not simply going to be reformed or replaced with something better, but abolished altogether, leaving London with no strategic authority – unique among large cities, as many were to point out. There had already been two public meetings in Hampstead, and Alan Greengross (leader of the GLC Conservatives) had published his views in the *Ham & High*. Peggy Jay was in no doubt as to the serious implication of the manifesto commitment for Hampstead Heath and immediately wrote to the *Ham & High*, calling attention to the worrying possible consequences for its future.[6]

The Government issued its White Paper 'Streamlining the Cities' in October 1983, confirming the Society's fears: the elected authority was to be replaced by joint boards and quangos. Mention of parks and open spaces was relegated to a single paragraph in an Appendix, with the terse assumption that the borough councils "will take over the GLC's functions and assets of this kind". Most alarming of all, it appeared to have already been decided to split Kenwood from the Heath, a re-run of the 1965 proposals; it was to be given to the newly formed English Heritage, a quango created by Michael Heseltine from the Historic Buildings and Monuments Commission, a suggestion that came from within the Commission's own Directorate.

The GLC fought back with a major propaganda campaign, with advertising and parliamentary lobbying. Two glossy publications, *Planning for the Future* of *London* and an *Annual Report*, heaping praise upon itself and all its works, made the case for its future. But these, too, scarcely mention parks and open spaces at all, perhaps indicative of the lack of interest in them amongst the GLC leadership. The Society had got through at officer level but not much further.

While there was little love lost for the GLC, there was unease on the Government benches at the way in which it was being abolished. It was widely felt, not just by the Opposition, that the Government's main motivation was party-political. There had been no public inquiries or royal commission, as had preceded past upheavals; the arguments were based on assumptions rather than evidence or research. London would be left with no strategic-level governance. Moreover, GLC elections would have to be cancelled, which many regarded as an attack on the democratic process. Conservative MPs John Wilkinson and Cyril Taylor spoke for many when they wrote to *The Times*, saying that "Unfortunately, the White Paper ... talks vaguely of joint boards and 'voluntary' committees. ... London will be left unique among the world's capital cities without any form of citywide government to provide a voice for Londoners".[7] This failure properly to consider how new arrangements were to work was to cause immense problems for the future of Hampstead Heath and, especially, the Kenwood estate.

Competing with a myriad of political currents and tensions, the future of Hampstead Heath was, as the *Ham & High* said, "but a minor element in the chaos",[8] and might have stood little chance of being noticed. "Amidst all this confusion and amongst all the other battles on subjects ranging from education to waste-disposal, what chance does the Heath have?"[9] There was far more concern about what was to happen to the Inner London Education Authority. The Society had a fight on its hands, not unlike the original battle to preserve the Heath. But then the fight was against only one greedy landowner; now it was taking on the full might of government. All the Society had worked for and achieved would be put at risk. The Heath's London-wide status would be downgraded; it would be dismembered and parcelled out to the boroughs; and such expertise as there was on how to manage it, built up painstakingly over recent years with the GLC, could be lost. It was "the gravest threat to the security and conservation of the Heath since its birth as a public open space for London in 1871".[10]

The eventual outcome is a tribute to the tenacity of the Society's committee in refusing to allow the fate of the Heath to be lost sight of. Led by its redoubtable Chairman Peggy Jay, and its President, Lord Cottesloe, the Society launched a remarkable campaign, using every possible avenue to raise its concerns: it would "seek a chance to give expert evidence to whoever will listen".[11] Gerald Isaaman, widely respected Editor of the *Ham & High*, had joined the Society's committee in 1976 and was now formally appointed its press representative. Parliament was lobbied through its three local members - Geoffrey Finsberg, Hampstead's MP, and Frank Dobson, MP for Holborn and St Pancras; and Lord Cottesloe in the House of Lords.

130. Gerald Isaaman OBE (1933-2019). As Editor of the *Ham & High* for 25 years (retiring in 1994), he set the 'gold standard' for local newspapers. (cartoon by Trog)

Several other members of the Lords who were also Hampstead residents backed the Society's efforts. The plight of Hampstead Heath was raised at every opportunity, with regular questions and interventions in the debates. Finsberg, while sticking to his belief that the GLC was superfluous and should be abolished, nevertheless began to understand that the Heath's management could not be divided up.

And the press also, just as in the 19th-century battle, not only questioned the Government's plans but helped to keep the subject of the future of the Heath to the forefront of public discussion. That quite a number of journalists were local residents cannot have been unhelpful. An early editorial in *The Times*, calling the White Paper "half-baked ... a policy conceived in the haste of the government's failure to find a satisfactory alternative to domestic rates", raised from the outset the question of what was to happen to Hampstead Heath.[12] The *Financial Times* summed up the widespread view that the proposals failed on three essential criteria: they must be an improvement on the old arrangements; accountability must not be reduced; and democracy and democratic principles must be neither weakened nor violated.[13] *Country Life* also ran an editorial, and there was sympathetic coverage in the *Daily Telegraph*, the *Guardian*, and the *Evening Standard* (whose CEO's wife, Irene Hardy, was then the Society's Secretary).

A public meeting, already scheduled for 17 October 1983 at Burgh House, was used by the Society to alert members to the threat. A unanimously supported resolution stated that "this meeting of the Heath and Old Hampstead Society strongly resists any alteration in the way the Heath is administered. A regional open space needs a democratically elected regional authority for its management". It was a widely shared view but it was difficult for the Society to appear apolitical in such a stance. They were accused by some of supporting the GLC; Peggy Jay wrote to the *Ham & High* to refute this.[14] As Michael Norris said, "the Society's stand throughout has been that the future of the Heath is above party politics: but that since we live in a political world we need the support of politicians".

At the beginning of 1984 a highly visible three-week campaign was launched, with stalls at Kenwood and in the streets of Hampstead. A 12,000-signature petition was gathered to send to Downing Street, and a packed public meeting at Burgh House in February was addressed by local politicians of all parties, with MPs Finsberg and Dobson, and GLC members Alan Greengross (Conservative) and Ann Sofer (SDP). Finsberg's conflicted position, at odds with his constituents, turned the meeting into a battle between him and everyone else. All his suggestions for future management of the Heath were shot down by his Tory colleague Greengross, who supported the abolition of the GLC but wanted something better to replace it, and by Dobson, and were greeted with scorn by the audience. On 7 March, Society committee members took their petition to Downing Street.[15]

131. Presenting the Society's petition at 10 Downing Street;    L to R: Mike Norris, Peggy Jay, Ray Softly, Irene Hardy,    Caroline Lee and Kate Springett

The Society set up a Working Party, chaired by its Vice-Chairman Michael Norris, who had joined the Committee in 1980. With a varied background in engineering, social anthropology and economics, he worked at the Tavistock Institute of Human Relations on a wide variety of advisory and research projects relating mainly to government policies and inter-organisational relationships. His minutely detailed reports in the Society's newsletters kept members informed of every twist and turn throughout the campaign. He was joined on the Working Party by representatives from the Highgate Society, and from Hampstead Garden Suburb – Tony Mandelson (father of Peter Mandelson) and Gerard Mansell (who had just retired as Deputy Director General of the BBC). Other local support came from the Finchley Society and the Muswell Hill & Fortis Green Association. A joint letter sent to all London MPs and members of the House of Lords, setting out their concerns, led to the formation of a group from both Houses of Parliament prepared to assist the Society in its campaign.

They were supported by many eminent public figures and local celebrities, the press and media outlets. A letter to the *Ham & High*, arguing for a London-wide democratically elected body to manage the Heath, was signed by Peter Barkworth, Peggy Ashcroft, Professor Peter Medawar, Michael Foot, Robert Dougall and Bill Oddie.[16] London-wide support came from the Blackheath Society, the Civic Trust, the Landscape Institute, Lea Valley Regional Park Authority, the London Sports Council, London Wildlife Trust and the Pedestrians Association. All shared the Society's concern about the future of the green spaces managed by the GLC and how democratic accountability was to be maintained under any new arrangements.

The debates that began following the Queen's Speech in July 1983 put the Government on notice. As these marathon, often heated sessions dragged on, and months turned into years, it became all too obvious that the abolition proposals had been ill-thought through and that no consideration had been given to what would happen to whole swathes of GLC assets. "The abolition bill can be examined in vain for any expression of a general philosophy of the role of government in society. It is a document lacking coherent principles for local administration".[17]

The first serious clash came early in 1984 over the so-called 'Paving Bill' intended to prepare for the main Bill to abolish the GLC and the Metropolitan County Councils; it cancelled the next year's GLC elections. Abolition of the GLC was one thing, but cancelling elections was a step too far for many Conservatives, who were appalled at being asked to pass such legislation. They protested in letters to *The Times* that "... the replacement of a directly elected Labour council by a nominated Conservative council" was "unacceptable". The cumbersome new arrangements would see democratically elected Metropolitan councils replaced by "appointed rate-precepting joint boards, joint committees and joint working arrangements between large numbers of district and borough councils". It was "constitutionally unprecedented", and they urged the House of Lords "to throw out this most improper legislation".[18]

The Lords took their cue and at the second reading in June caused a major upset to the Government's timetable, pushing through an amendment with cross party support, which frustrated the plan to abolish the elections but without actually wrecking the Bill. The crucial issue, said Lord Denham, was not whether any of these councils deserve to be abolished but to protect democracy and the rights of electors. "We have no knowledge of what will be in that Bill or of what is to take the place of these great councils. Indeed, this is why my noble friend Lady Fisher called this the 'crazy-paving' Bill: a way is being paved, but to what destination?"[19]

The scale of the defeat – 191 votes to 143 – astonished the Government. Prime Minister Margaret Thatcher came to the Commons herself to announce that the Government would meet the constitutional objections by extending the whole process for another year, allowing the present members of the GLC to continue in office until 1986 and thus avoiding the need to cancel elections. Prominent among the significant band of Tory rebels who challenged the abolition proposals were former Prime Minister Edward Heath, Geoffrey Rippon, Patrick Cormack, Francis Pym and Sir Ian Gilmour, who, it was quickly noted, had all been members of the Government, led by Heath, that brought in the GLC. "They are prepared to wipe out the GLC and the government of London without any public inquiry; ... the Government have landed themselves in a ghastly mess".[20] But in truth, with its huge majority in the Commons, even the mauling given to the Paving Bill mattered little; the Government could afford to ignore all the hostile comment.

The H&OS's campaign in Parliament intensified. Frank Dobson MP raised the matter directly on the Society's behalf, getting confirmation that the Heath "was to be managed by a joint committee comprised of representatives of Camden and Barnet Borough Councils". He also asked Sir George Young, Secretary of State for the Environment, what discussions he had had with the Heath & Old Hampstead Society about the future of Hampstead Heath. The curt answer was "none".[21] But that was soon to change.

Peggy Jay pointed out yet again, in a letter to *The Times,* that the Heath was recognised in the 1967 London Government Act as "a regional open space ... and therefore not one to be transferred to local councils". The decision on the Heath's future "has been reached without any royal commission or other detailed study of the needs of the Heath".[22] Moreover, the three local authorities, Barnet, Camden and Haringey, made it clear that they did not want this responsibility. The Leader of Barnet – which included the Prime Minister's own constituency – was adamant that the boroughs could not look after the Heath properly. When Lord Cottesloe pointed out to the Department of the Environment minister, Lord Avon, that Barnet and Camden were not even on speaking terms, Avon replied, "Indeed, my Lords, it is quite difficult to get a response from Camden". Lord Tordoff, with pointed sarcasm, suggested: "My Lords, in that case, is it not clear that there ought to be some authority that can bang their heads together; namely, some sort of elected authority to cover the strategic matters of Greater London?"[23]

Another public meeting was held in October at Hampstead Town Hall, when Peggy Jay publicly lectured both Ken Livingstone and Sir Geoffrey Finsberg – whose stance was considered unhelpful to say the least – on the needs of the Heath, to loud applause from a packed hall.[24] Attempts to derail the Bill during its second reading continued through 1984 and 1985, with efforts to get amendments that the GLC should be replaced by a directly elected authority. On one occasion in December 1984, a backbench rebellion saw the government's majority whittled down to 23, described by one MP as a moral defeat for the government. It was a "massive piece of irrelevant legislation ... undertaken merely to deal a political blow at one's political opponents".[25]

Even Finsberg had changed his tune, now saying he did not believe that Hampstead Heath could be taken over by the three boroughs. In a lengthy debate in March 1985, ostensibly over yet another amendment before a packed House of Commons, he and Michael Foot clashed spectacularly, each accusing the other of not caring sufficiently about the future of the Heath. Foot scornfully advised that "no note" should be taken "of what is said by the hon. Member for Hampstead and Highgate, who certainly does not represent his constituents on this matter, if indeed he still represents them on any subject." Dividing control of Hampstead Heath between three boroughs, none of which wanted the responsibility, was "a recipe for the utmost confusion and for a failure to protect the heath". In vain did Finsberg try to protest that the Government had never said it should be physically split up, and that he had always advocated that its management should be properly funded and not be fragmented. MPs, including the Prime Minister, were by now left in no doubt as to the importance of Hampstead Heath.[26]

The Society even managed to use the occasion of a constituency visit to confront Mrs Thatcher personally about the future of the Heath. Tony Mandelson was persuaded by Peggy Jay to ask her directly to "look after the Heath"; she replied, "Ah – the Heath";[27] a letter duly came from Number 10, explaining why the policy could not be changed.[28]

**Notes, Chapter 18**

1. Patrick Jenkin, HC Deb 27 Mar 1985 vol 76 cc545-94
2. Jerry White, LSE seminar, 'The Greater London Council, 1965-1986'. White worked in local government, mainly in London, from 1967-2009 and was Local Government Ombudsmen for England (1995-2009).
3. Ref. 1. Sir Horace Cutler, Conservative GLC leader (1977-81) had set up the Marshall Inquiry, but its recommendations to strengthen the GLC's powers were dropped with a change of government.
4. 'People and Planning: report of the Committee on Public Participation in Planning', prepared by Arthur Skeffington MP and the Ministry of Housing & Local Government, 1969
5. HC 25 May 1984 vol 60 cc1386-94
6. Ham & High, 3 Jun 1983
7. The Times, 1 Dec 1983
8. Ham & High, 3 Feb 1984
9. Mike Norris, H&OHS annual report, 1983-84, p 6
10. H&OHS annual report, 1983-84
11. H&HS archive: A/01048 Box 2
12. 'NO, MINISTER', The Times 1st leader, 8 Oct 1983
13. Financial Times, 12 Dec 1984
14. Ham & High, 27 Jan 1984
15. H&OHS reports and Newsletters, 1983-84 passim
16. Ham & High, 14 Dec 1984. Robert Dougall, MBE, was a senior BBC newsreader and announcer (in 1939 it was he who announced to the world Britain's declaration of war on Germany). A keen amateur ornithologist and President of the Royal Society for the Protection of Birds for five years, he was on the H&OHS committee from 1962 to 1966 and lived in Hampstead until 1989.
17. 'And after abolition?', The Times leader, 24 Nov 1984
18. Letters from Conservative GLC councillors, The Times, 10 Apr 1984
19. HL Deb 28 Jun 1984 vol 453
20. Edward Heath, HC Deb 4 Dec 1984, Local Government Bill
21. HC Deb 11 Jun 1984 vol 61
22. The Times, 21 Jun 1984
23. HL Deb 13 Dec 1984 vol 458 cc391-4
24. H&OHS annual report, 1985
25. Lord Evans of Claughton, HL Deb 15 Apr 1985 vol 462 cc440-591
26. HC Deb 27 Mar 1985
27. Ham & High report, 26 Mar 1985
28. Letter from Downing Street (H&HS archive)

# Chapter 19

# The Heath divided

But despite the Society's petition, and the representations by ten organisations, not to mention all the interventions by MPs, peers and the press, the Local Government Bill moved inexorably on to its committee stage almost unaltered. Kenwood was to be excised from the Heath; it was a betrayal of everything past generations had fought so hard for and this time the Society could not stop it. The declaration in the 1929 Kenwood Act, that Lord Iveagh's bequest should be "part of Hampstead Heath for ever", was brushed aside. The Heath was sliding into limbo, to be managed by whom and in what manner, no-one knew. *The Times* devoted a whole editorial to its fate, castigating the Government for leaving it "high and dry by the haste and expedience" of its abolition proposals. "Attention focuses on Hampstead Heath and not because journalists and politicians live on its borders". The Heath is loved and "used by people from all social strata".[1]

However, by now the Society had made its mark and its campaign had begun to rattle the Government. Up to this point the Department of the Environment had not seen fit to consult anyone on the changes and had certainly not been interested in the views of the Heath and Old Hampstead Society – assuming it even knew who they were. The Society now began to establish a line of communication directly to ministers. In March 1985 Lord Cottesloe and Peggy Jay secured meetings with Lord Avon and with a group of peers, to discuss further amendments to the Bill that might protect the Heath. This resulted in a statement from Lord Whitelaw, Leader of the House of Lords: "… in response to the large number of representations have been made about the future management of Hampstead Heath. The Government recognise the real strength of feeling on this issue and will consider the possibilities for ensuring that the Heath continues to be managed as an entity".[2]. Having once established these contacts, Peggy Jay kept up an unremitting stream of letters and requests for meetings with various ministers, with Environment Secretary, Patrick Jenkin, and with Lord Elton. She also began sounding out the National Trust.

Lord Cottesloe stepped up his campaign in the Lords by tabling a group of four amendments in May 1985, which the Society helped to draft, calling for the 800 acres of Hampstead Heath to be transferred "in their entirety" to a body such as the Royal Parks or the National Trust, or some other public body that could look after it if willing to take it on. It called also for adequate finance, and consultation with amenity groups and other interested bodies, on management and maintenance of the Heath. He had strong support from, among others, Lord Strabolgi, Lord Kilmarnock who lived in Primrose Hill, and Lord Molson, who had served as Treasurer of the Commons Preservation Society (CPS) for ten years. He reminded the House of the origins of the CPS and its role in the campaign to save the Heath: "... eminent Parliamentarians and ... public figures of all parties united to form, spontaneously, the Commons Preservation Society. Anyone who has any interest in legal history and the long fight to establish what were commoners' rights and the rights of the Lord of the Manor can read ... the long litigation which was carried on in order to preserve Hampstead Heath and Wimbledon Common from being developed as building sites. ... it is incumbent upon the Government to consider how these important parts of the heritage of the nation are to be preserved. Therefore, I hope that the Government will be prepared now to go a little further than they have before and to make it quite plain that Hampstead Heath will be preserved under the management of a single body as a public possession and a great amenity to London".[2]

Lord Elton, the Secretary of State, replied that the Government was well aware of these anxieties and those of the Heath and Old Hampstead Society. "We share my noble friend's ambitions, and what we are now discussing is not whether they should be pursued but who should be chosen to pursue them". In reply to a direct question from Lord Strabolgi as to whether the option to divide the Heath among the three local authorities had now been discarded, Elton replied, "It will be managed as an entity; there is no question of partition".[3] But the Government did not seem to have understood that the Kenwood estate was part of that entity; if it was to be hived off, this commitment had already been rendered meaningless. However, having secured this reassurance, and with the Whitelaw statement in mind, Cottesloe withdrew his amendments. Kenwood had been lost; but the fate of the rest of the Heath still had to be settled and the Society now had a chance at least to influence that decision.

*Heath & Old Hampstead Society*

## Enter the City

During his reply, Elton also took the opportunity to press the case for the City of London Corporation, which by now was being regularly mentioned as a contender to run the Heath; he referred to Peggy Jay's "pretty dusty answer" to the suggestion in the letters column of *The Times*.[3] Other options being mentioned, in addition to the National Trust, were the Historic Buildings and Monuments Commission (who now already had Kenwood), the Royal Parks, or an independent Trust.[4]

ANNUAL REPORT for the 88th year            1984 – 1985

132. Front cover of the Society's annual report 1985: "Our all-party, all-star panel of speakers meet on the Heath; [R to L:] Michael Foot, Anne Sofer and Alan Greengross will appear together on May 23 at Hampstead Town Hall".

Unfortunately, the City had a bad reputation locally: its record at Highgate Wood had caused concern from the moment it took it over in the 1880s. Highgate and Epping Forest, which they had rescued from enclosure a century earlier, were their first two forays into the world of open-space management, and like the LCC, the City had not really understood that these needed different management from public parks. Local opinion felt that the beauty of the woods was being destroyed by the laying of asphalt paths. There was an outcry not unlike that in Hampstead in the 1890s when the LCC took over the Heath. A E. Housman, who lived in North Road, Highgate, wrote a letter of protest, in deeply ironic vein, to the *Evening Standard* in March 1894:[5]

> Sir, in August, 1886, Highgate Wood became the property of the Mayor and Commonalty and Citizens of the City of London. It was then in a very sad state. So thickly was it overgrown with brushwood, that if you stood in the centre you could not see the linen of the inhabitants of Archway Road hanging to dry in their gardens. Nor could you see the advertisements for Juggins' stout and porter which surmount the front of the public house at the south corner of the wood.[6]
>
> Therefore the Mayor and Commonalty and Citizens cut down the intervening brushwood, and now when we stand in the centre, we can divide our attention between Juggins' porter and our neighbours' washing. Scarlet flannel petticoats are much worn in Archway Road, and if anyone wishes to feast his eyes on these very bright and picturesque objects, so seldom seen in the streets, let him repair to the centre of Highgate Wood.
>
> Still we were not happy. The wood is bounded on the north by the railway to Muswell Hill, and it was a common subject of complaint that we could not see the railway from the wood without going quite to the edge. At length however the Mayor and Commonalty and Citizens have begun to fell the trees on the north, so that people in the centre of the wood will be able to look at the railway when they are tired of the porter and the petticoats. ...

One hundred years later things seemed not much better. In a survey of managers of open space, the London Wildlife Trust had ranked the City near the bottom; and a report from the London Natural History Society commissioned in 1984 by the Muswell Hill and Fortis Green Society, found that Highgate Wood was deteriorating because of the way it was managed. The local verdict, as reported in the *Ham & High*, was that the City's consultative committee was a mere token gesture.[7] The H&OHS was therefore not impressed by the idea of the City taking over the Heath: it was not "a fitting authority for such a task. On grounds of accountability, standards and attitudes to open space management and finally for reasons of traditional geographical and electoral associations, the City cannot do this job".[3] Nevertheless, ever conscious of one of its founding principles – the necessity for working in harmony with the authorities – the Society accepted that "it is vital for us to make contact with any organisation seriously suggested by the

Government as a 'successor body'", and a deputation was made to the Guildhall.[8] It was received amicably but the Society's anxieties were not allayed.

In September the Government plan to announce that the Heath would go to the City was sabotaged by a leaked report in the *Ham & High*, causing an avalanche of objections on all sides, including a protest that there had been no consultation. Adding to the confusion, Camden and Barnet Councils decided to return to the fray, Camden renewing its bid to take over the Heath and Barnet claiming that Golders Hill Park should go to them. The Society pointed out to the Department of the Environment that the borough boundary ran through the park, putting the bandstand in Camden. A further complication was the deepening financial crisis at Camden Council; it was feared by many that if the rate-capped borough were to be given responsibility for two thirds of the Heath, it might well try to raise the money to pay for it through revenue-raising commercial activities. That did not stop Camden from threatening legal action. Malcolm Holmes recalls being asked by its Chief Executive to produce urgently a raft of legal documents needed about Hampstead Heath. It was at Holmes's suggestion that Kit Ikin was approached to provide expert advice.

Kenneth Baker, the new Secretary of State for the Environment, hastily added a consultation period but the Government's plans were now in disarray, provoking yet another editorial in *The Times*, 'The lonely Heath'. The leaders of Barnet, Camden and Haringey Councils were called in to "review the position" with the Minister. At the same time the row about how much land at Kenwood was to go to English Heritage (EH) was still rumbling on. The Bill to abolish the GLC had been duly altered to avoid "splitting ownership" of the Heath, but this was an empty assurance; it had already been partitioned. The Government still seemed incapable of understanding that the grounds of Kenwood were legally part of the Heath.

1986 opened with nothing yet resolved. Questions about Kenwood in January, by both Finsberg and Lord Moyne (the Earl of Iveagh's grandson), revealed that over 100 acres of land was to be transferred to EH with Kenwood House, including South Wood, and not just the 75 acres of the Iveagh bequest. Unbeknown to anyone, behind the scenes, inspectors from the Historic Buildings and Monuments Commission had decided this, advising that Kenwood House must have an appropriate amount of landscape transferred with it to preserve its historic setting.[9] It was all done without any consultation with, or regard for, the local community. It seemed to be forgotten by those in authority that most of the Kenwood estate was bought by public subscription with the express purpose of adding it to the Heath. Moreover, Lord Iveagh himself had made clear that the ground he had bought with the House was also to be added to the Heath. To carve it up in this way was indeed a betrayal. Kit Ikin pointed out that the new Act stipulating powers of the successor authority failed even to mention the Iveagh Bequest, Kenwood Act of 1929 – "presumably", as Mike Norris suggested, "omitted by DoE officials in an attempt to re-write history". They thus "suppressed Lord Iveagh's plain English statement that his land was to become part of Hampstead Heath in perpetuity".[10]

Peggy Jay wrote to Lord Elton – by now on first name terms – advising him of a public meeting to be held on 19 February to protest at the broken promises and betrayal. She urged him not to take any precipitate steps in respect of the land at Kenwood. Lord Montagu, the Chairman of EH, wrote to the *Ham & High*, publicly promising continuity of management policies and access between "their" land and the Heath.

Meanwhile, the political gyrations over the fate of the 'lonely' Heath continued. Lord Elton summoned the three boroughs to another meeting in February to discuss the possibility of triumvirate management. The controversial proposal of the City was still on the cards and a Mori poll conducted for Camden found that, in fact, more people supported the City to take over in preference to Camden. But time had run out. On 1 April 1986, the Local Government Act came into force. The London Residuary Body (LRB) took charge of GLC assets, including the Heath, the future of which had still not been decided, and was given five years to sort it out. Its Chairman, Sir Godfrey Taylor, summed it up feelingly at the Society's 1986 annual general meeting: "I think the government realises it has a hot potato on its hands".[11]

Despite the political chaos, the LRB set about discharging its duties with a will. It took over the GLC staff and set up a Hampstead Heath Unit; staffing levels were restored to those before the cuts of the 1970s. The work done by Kit Ikin, David Sullivan and Ray Softly, to build a close relationship between the Society and Heath staff and management, was able to continue. They attended quarterly meetings and reported favourably on work programmes in the Society's *Newsletter*. Attention was also turned to finalising a deal on the Pergola with Manor House Hospital.

In July the LRB launched further consultations on options for the Heath's future, which were now the City, a new Hampstead Heath authority, or Camden, hoping to announce the findings in October ready for new management to take over in April 1987. Camden Council immediately complained that the options were unfair: the City would have finance from across London, while Camden would have to find the costs from its own rates. The LRB, trying to mollify them, said that there was room for other options. Camden produced a management proposal, *Blueprint for the Heath*, and called a public meeting. Meetings were also organised by the Highgate Society and the Muswell Hill and Fortis Green Association. Camden claimed that it was "more likely to learn of any opportunities to further extend the Heath, which arise from time to time. Other organisations are not so well placed. The Council sees the tradition of gradual acquisition over the past century as an integral part of the Heath's wellbeing." In response to criticism of its record, Camden declared that it would never make the Heath compete for funds with other services. However, it rashly chose to cite its record on public libraries: "if that were the case Camden's Libraries would not be the best in the country." Barely a year later, in the midst of the borough's deepening financial chaos, it was making plans to sell off library buildings, and to dispose of the Branch Hill sites which could have "further extend[ed] the Heath" (see p 226).

There was also talk of management of the Heath by the National Trust, the Royal Parks or the Department of the Environment itself, and for a while the Society favoured a new dedicated trust with London-wide representation. However, at a meeting with Patrick Jenkin, the Environment Secretary, he made it clear that as a precepting body such a trust would need primary legislation and any solution requiring an act of Parliament was unlikely to be accepted. At one of many meetings between Godfrey Taylor and the Society's representatives – Peggy Jay, Mike Norris and John Carswell – Taylor made clear that there was no support for such a trust from the boroughs, and therefore the LRB could not pursue the option. In an echo of the Metropolitan Board of Works debates a century before, he said at the Society's AGM that people on the other side of London were not interested in the Heath and would not be prepared to contribute money to run it. It was no longer regarded as a London-wide facility – a sign of how times had changed. With so many open spaces preserved all over London, the Heath's London-wide relevance is no longer so significant.[12]

By August the Society finally accepted that the trust option was not viable. It may have sounded fine, but would have involved "a whole complex of constitutional questions about aims, powers, geographical scope, funding and the relationship with other bodies",[13] not to mention what would happen to all the sports facilities.

It was not until February 1987 that the LRB announced the outcome: there were over 100 responses to the consultation, and three contenders emerged. The Society had by now come to the firm conclusion that the City of London Corporation was only viable option; it was "time for everyone to work together for the good of the future of the Heath".[14]  It had also realised this could bring an important advantage which might well be a good thing for the future: the separation of powers. The LCC and GLC had been planning authorities as well as the 'owners' of the Heath.

But the final transfer date was delayed yet again until April 1988, and this in turn later slipped to April 1989. And just as had happened a hundred years before, five parcels of land which were, through Whitehall error, left out of the abolition legislation, had to be sorted out. Negotiations had now "dragged out for so long that everyone has lost interest – probably also the City".[15] Questions were regularly asked in Parliament about when the LRB would make its decision on the ownership and management of the Heath. Some of the replies began to sound like something out of a Gilbert and Sullivan opera: "The first three options in the second consultation paper are there because they are the front runners as a result of the first consultation; and there is the new option that has been added...".[16]

Tony Banks, MP and former GLC councillor, was particularly assiduous in keeping up the pressure, asking questions which the Government had neglected to consider. Who was to be responsible for administering Kenwood House after the abolition; where was funding to come from; what was to happen to the concerts (to which came the vague reply that Lord Montagu "has indicated" that he would like them to continue);[17] how had the minister decided to transfer 112 acres surrounding Kenwood House to the Historic Buildings and Monuments Commission – whom had he consulted;[18] what arrangements were being made for the future management of Hampstead Heath and what consultations have been held?[19]

**Notes, Chapter 19**
1. *The Times*, 30 Apr 1985
2. HL Deb 15 Apr 1985 vol 462 cc440-591
3. *The Times*, 11 May 1985
4. HL Deb 14 May 1985 vol 463 cc1115-46
5. Reprinted by H&OHS in its *Newsletter*, winter 1984-85, as part of its evidence for opposing the City

6. Presumably The Woodman, rebuilt in the early C20 and still trading today as a gastropub
7. *Ham & High*, 16 Nov 1984
8. H&OHS annual report, 1984-85, p 2
9. Julius Bryant, conversation with the author, 27 Nov 2017

10. Michael Norris, 'After the Greater London Council', H&OHS annual report, 1985-86
11. H&OHS AGM, 9 Jun 1986; *Newsletter*, autumn 1986
12. H&HS archive: A/1048/3/4/1/5 - A/1048/3/4/2/4
13. Mike Norris, H&OHS *Newsletter*, winter 85-86, p 11

14. *Ham & High*, 10 Apr 1987
15. *Ham & High*, editorial, Jan 1988
16. HL Deb 2 Apr 1987 vol 486 cc693-5
17. HC Deb 25 Oct 1984 vol 65 cc659-60W
18. HC Deb 13 Feb 1986 vol 91 c513W
19. HC Deb 21 Apr 1986 vol 96 c67W; 21 Oct 1986 vol 102 c836W

Chapter 20

# The final settlement

While other local groups clung to their antipathy to the City of London Corporation, putting forward further unrealistic proposals for a new trust through the pages of the *Ham & High*, the H&OHS worked closely with Ministers, the London Residuary Body and the City, to get the best deal possible. The Society's views on the future management of the Heath were sought and it was consulted and kept informed at every stage. They made their four outstanding concerns clear:

- Unified management,
- Democratic responsibility,
- Adequate finance,
- The Long Term View.

There must be adequate representatives of Heath users and interests on a London-wide basis; the Heath's management must be governed by a balance of specialist and community issues; and there must be a fair deal for staff. The Society's previous antagonism was overcome by the City's willingness to listen and accommodate. Gradually the City expanded its offer, promising to develop a management plan and giving the Society a seat on the Heath policy making committee.

One further obstacle presented itself at the last minute: there were cash problems over the Lido and sports facilities, which were all in poor condition. The City considered that a sum of £4.6m would be needed to do the work but the LRB was willing to provide only £3m. The City issued a press release,[1] saying it could not negotiate any further; if the extra money was not forthcoming then the

133. Peter Rigby (1929-2002) Chairman of the City's Hampstead Heath Management Committee, 1993-97

CITY
OF
LONDON

134. City coat of arms

LRB must close the facilities, as the City did not want to be seen by the public as the body closing them. The *Ham & High* pointed out that the LRB had plenty of money in its coffers because of its sell-off of GLC assets. By April these problems were resolved and the LRB finally announced that the Heath would go to the City. The decision was welcomed by the H&OHS and on 24 June 1988 Peter Rigby, then Chairman of the City's Policy and Resources Committee, attended the Society's AGM. It was he, behind the scenes in his discreet way, who steered the process that rescued Hampstead Heath from the politically created vacuum. Like so many of the protagonists in this story, he was a man with an old-fashioned sense of duty who devoted much of his spare time from his business interests to charitable causes, and local government. Since 1948 he had served first on the old Hornsey Borough Council and on Middlesex County Council, and then on Haringey Borough Council, becoming leader of the Conservative group in 1968. Among his many appointments at the City, he chaired the Bridge House Estates Trust Fund and steered grants towards promoting sustainable development and improving the environment of London.

The new Hampstead Heath Management Committee was announced in December: there were to be 12 City councillors, one from Camden and a representative of the H&OHS. There was also to be a second committee, the Hampstead Heath Consultative Committee, with 20 members, which would meet twice a year, and it was owing to the Society's influence that it included a much wider range of local groups than had first been contemplated.[2]

Peggy Jay became the Society's first representative on the new Management Committee, and John Carswell took over as Chairman of the Society. A civil servant with extensive experience of government, he had been under-secretary to ministers of Education and Science, and Health, and Secretary to the University

135. John Carswell (1918-97)

Grants Committee. He also served as Secretary to the British Academy for five years. His mother was the writer Catherine Carswell, and he grew up at the heart of 1930s literary Hampstead. D.H. Lawrence, Katherine Mansfield, John Middleton Murry, and Ivy and Maxim Litvinoff were all frequent visitors to the Carswell home.[3] His books included histories ranging from *The South Sea Bubble* in 1960 to *The Saving of Kenwood* in 1992.

It was Carswell who realised the significant advantages in the new arrangements. Under all its predecessors the Heath had had no dedicated budget and was simply one of many open spaces vying for funds from the authority's overall budget. Now there was a regime "entirely devoted to the Heath on its own, as, in effect, an endowed open space, with an income in its own right. Its needs were to be met partly from a trust fund derived from former GLC reserves, and partly, under a statutory formula, from the City's independent resources" – the so called 'City's Cash' fund. With its two separate management and consultative committees, "the finance and governance of the Heath are thus ring-fenced from all the City's other responsibilities. ... the voice of the Heath's users now has not only opportunities, but rights to be heard".[4] It would also have, for the first time, a proper management plan, something the Society had pleaded for for nearly a hundred years.

It is possible now with hindsight to see the fears about the City's assumption of responsibility for the Heath as exaggerated; certainly they were lacking an appreciation of historical context. As Ruth Rowntree observed: "The key to the development of Hampstead lies with the City of London".[5] The City had had strong links to Hampstead and its Heath since Tudor times, from creating the ponds, to Hampstead's development as a community, to saving the Heath from Sir Thomas Maryon Wilson, and to extending it with new land. The leading protagonists at every stage had been City men, often liverymen of various City Companies: Sharpe, Freshfield, Powell, Lister, Figgis, the Fields and the Hoares. Several Hampstead men had served as lord mayors of London, including Sir William Ashhurst[6] and Sir Thomas Lane,[7] in the 1690s. There were three in the 18th century: Marshe Dickinson MP, George Nelson and William Beckford. Warren Stormes Hale (Lord Mayor in 1864), who lived in the Vale of Health, was Master of the Tallow Chandlers Company and founder of the City of London School. Even fears of about the much discussed 'democratic deficit' faded away as the Management and Consultative Committees ushered in a new era of co-operation. The City confounded all expectations and responded admirably to the challenge presented by the much-fought over and prized piece of land.

## Problems at Kenwood

It was at Kenwood that real problems emerged, stemming from the Government's total failure to investigate what abolition would involve or to make any preparations for it. They had no understanding of the intricate cross-departmental funding that had developed under the London County Council (LCC) and Greater London Council (GLC), or what Hampstead Heath and Kenwood meant to many Londoners. It simply charged ahead with an abolition bill which, as *The Times* had said, lacked any coherent principle for local administration. On the face of it, English Heritage (EH) was a good choice to run Kenwood. Hived off from the Ancient Monuments and Historic Buildings Directorate as an agency with specific responsibility for the Government's 400 or so historic properties, its team of experts dedicated to the conservation cause was welcomed by conservation bodies.[8] But the National Heritage Act setting it up had only just been passed in 1983, and it was still exploring its new role and relationships, and establishing who did what. As its first Chief Executive, Peter Rumble wrote: "The rationale for the proposed division of responsibilities was not given; nor can I recall that it emerged during debates on the Bill." Staff had mixed feelings, ranging from "constructive welcome through resigned acceptance, to overt hostility". The cynical view was that the change was all about reducing costs and that its real purpose of conservation would be overruled in the drive for efficiency. One of the new expectations was that the monuments were there for public enjoyment and there were fears that "a more commercial approach would bring vulgarity" (a fear later justified by what happened to the Kenwood concerts). "Staff coming from the private sector, especially those from marketing backgrounds ... found the rules arcane, bureaucratic and inhibiting".[9]

Onto this already difficult situation was suddenly bolted responsibility for the GLC's Historic Buildings Division and its three historic house museums. Staff at Kenwood had already spent two years worrying about their future and what was to happen to their jobs and, in some cases, their homes; at Kenwood for instance there were nineteen residential units for staff.[10]. So it was not surprising that some of them came to EH "with a distinct lack of enthusiasm".[9] Unlike the GLC, EH was not a precepting body; it was dependent on a block grant from the Government which was for national conservation, and could not simply be used for the entertainment of local people. No adequate endowment was provided and although its grant was increased in 1986 to take account of the costs of the GLC takeover, it was never enough to cover costs.[10] EH staff were civil servants with no experience of dealing with the public and were certainly not used to a high level of public interest at properties they managed. "Working in a body more directly answerable to the public involved a more responsive attitude than some had been used to in the past".[9] Neither they nor the Government had the faintest comprehension of the deep sense of public ownership at Kenwood; it had, after, all been rescued from destruction by the action of the local community.

While the Friends of Kenwood were at first enthusiastic about EH, the Heath & Old Hampstead Society was much more wary. Whereas in the City the two Committees – Management and Consultative – worked well and helped to establish a good working relationship from the beginning, there were no such arrangements at Kenwood, and the Society felt that EH was prioritising promotional ideas over landscape values. There was no sign of the promised "unified management" between the two authorities. "There was no consultation over major changes to the House and no integration of ideas/policies nor of satisfactory action on the ground. Worst of all its marketing division was using the property to hold too many sponsored money-making events leaving the house and grounds in a mess. ... Kenwood is becoming a visual slum".[11] This was all echoed in letters from the public and reports in the *Ham & High*, complaining about the poor management. John Gummer, the Minister for Local Government, had assured Peggy Jay on more than one occasion that EH and the City would co-operate but this was now publicly contradicted by Peter Rigby (Chairman of the City's Policy and Resources Committee) who said no agreement had been reached with them.[12] The H&OHS declared that unless EH improved, the Society would campaign for Heath land to be handed over to the City, leaving EH with only the Iveagh bequest.[13] They requested an urgent meeting with Christopher Chope, Under-Secretary of State at the Department of the Environment.

In 1989 Gummer wrote again to the EH Chairman, Lord Montagu, with a copy to the Society, reminding him of the agreement that EH would work with the City, so that "visitors to Hampstead Heath should be able to pass from the City to EH land without perceiving a change in the ownership because of different management approaches".[14]

But in the end this was not practicable. EH pointed out that Kenwood was an historic designed landscape and needed to be managed as such; under their "ownership" they had their own statutory duties. This was too much for well-known local campaigner Gene Adams (former Museums Advisor to the Inner London Education Authority who organised educational programmes at Kenwood). She immediately wrote to remind EH that it did not "own" Kenwood: ownership is vested in the public – EH only administers it.[15] But the real stumbling block was the stringent security needed for the world-class collection of old-master paintings. Whereas the Heath was never closed, Kenwood had always had a railing demarcating its grounds from the rest of the Heath, and opening and closing times which were vital for security; it required a different set of operational bylaws. Since the theft of the Vermeer in 1974 security had become an increasing preoccupation. EH, with its devoted conservation staff, set about making its own plans for the future.[10]

## High season for public consultation

Both EH and the City launched consultations on their management plans. The H&OHS found that the City "has been responsive to the Society's ideas and it seems that they share the Society's vision of the Heath. We look forward to constructive discussions with them as they develop the management plan".[16] But at Kenwood it found "the existing management structure of English Heritage a hindrance to meaningful consultation on most major issues".[17]

EH mounted an exhibition of its plans to restore the Kenwood landscape with a questionnaire to which nearly 4,000 people replied. While there was support for conservation works such as dredging the lake and restoring the ornamental bridge, there was opposition to what was seen as an attempt to redraw the landscape and return to the past. Brian Beaumont-Nesbitt, now the Society's Heath sub-committee Chairman, accused EH of behaving "as if they own Kenwood as completely as the Earls of Mansfield, and have not bothered to establish any form of regular consultation with the locals. This means that we, and other organisations like the Highgate Society, can only make our views known after an event by complaining directly to [them] or sounding off in public. We have been particularly worried by the future of the landscape in and around Kenwood".[18]

Julius Bryant, who had just joined EH as Chief Curator and Director of Museums and Collections, replied to these accusations in the next H&OHS *Newsletter*.[19] He insisted that regular local liaison had been in operation since EH took over: it was represented at the Hampstead Heath Management Committee; it participated in a quarterly meeting with the City and the H&OHS; and it was also meeting the Society on site to discuss details of proposed management work. EH wished to consult the public thoroughly on the future management of the estate. Owing to financial constraints, EH would need to launch an appeal to fund these works.

The main issue contributing to this falling-out was a disagreement over the history of the Kenwood landscape. It was always suggested that Humphry Repton had landscaped the grounds but, in the absence of any 'Red Book', still "untraced" in 1990, and scant reference to it in Repton's writings, many doubted his involvement, including John Carswell, then the Society Chairman, who felt that to "impose" such a landscape at Kenwood would be wrong.[20] However, further research in the Mansfield Archive at Scone discovered the Red Book, commissioned in 1793, and EH was keen to start work. Peggy Jay intervened to bring everyone together again and Julius Bryant was invited to write an article in the Society's *Newsletter* about EH's plans. Under the heading 'Management and Myths at Kenwood', he used the opportunity to correct some "basic misunderstandings": English Heritage was not seeking to "turn the clock back to the eighteenth century as if Kenwood might be the private garden of a remote stately home". He also stressed that "contrary to some rumours, Kenwood is not in the hands of distant bureaucrats or myopic historians but is managed by staff who ... share the commitment of the Heath and Old Hampstead Society".[21] The Society gradually developed a much improved working relationship with EH at Kenwood, which included regular meetings with the staff.

### Those trees again

By 1993 management plans were well advanced and being widely consulted on. But any thought of discussing these in a calm manner was overtaken by a tremendous furore which broke out over proposals to manage trees, both at Kenwood and on the Heath. In its consultation document, the City had put forward 'Opportunities for Enhancement' such as clearing some trees to restore heathland and views. They were simply possibilities in response to the many ideas that had been discussed over the years about how the Heath might, or should be managed, and to find out whether the public would want to support them. But several highly vocal activists raised an outcry, misrepresenting the proposals as plans for mass tree-felling, and their views were given inordinate publicity in the local press and wider media, to the dismay of the Society and established ecology experts. It emerged that those promoting this opposition represented few other than themselves. It was not at all clear what their real motives were and

214

some appeared to oppose the idea of any management at all. They made highly misleading claims – that the suggestions under 'Opportunities for Enhancement' were management plans, which they were not, and portrayed the City's tentative suggestion to restore heathland as an attempt to clear the Heath of trees. One opponent made it clear to the *Ham & High* that he did not even accept the wisdom of established ecology groups.[22] Another, who styled himself "Friends of Hampstead Heath", was based in Ladbroke Grove, and was heard on local radio stating that public access to the Heath may have to be restricted. On one occasion several men from the group Outrage invaded the Heath Superintendent's office with whistles and placards, having made sure to alert the press to their plans.

FRIDAY, AUGUST 26, 1994          133rd year          40p weekly

● Members of gay rights group OutRage protest in Heath superintendent Paul Canneaux's Archway office.

136. Outrage invading the Heath Superintendent's office (*Ham & High* front page, 26 August 1994)

Eventually, encouraged by the H&OHS, three local ecologists, Ralph Gaines, David Bevan of the London Natural History Society, and Dr Eric Robinson of London University's Department of Geological Sciences (who was the Society's advisor), sent a joint letter to the *Ham & High*, welcoming the management plan, supporting the City's consultation and deploring the misleading claims that had been bandied about. It was also pointed out to the editor that the massive publicity the paper had given to these one-man-bands was disproportionate. Curiously, vindication of the City's consultation came from a most unexpected source. In 1996, Camden, having taken a battering in the High Court over its failure to consult adequately on a parking scheme at Primrose Hill, set up an Officers' Working Group to examine what went wrong. One of the Group's findings, set out in their report, *We're Listening*, was that the City's consultation on their Heath Management Plan "was most often put forward as exemplary". The questionnaire was good; it was widely distributed and open meetings were held attended by "top City people and consultants".[23]

Gerald Isaaman who had now retired as Editor of the *Ham & High*) praised the City in the H&OHS *Newsletter*: "This is the first time any custodian of the Heath has directly involved the public in this fashion, and in retrospect it was a brave move. ... the outstanding fact remains that the Corporation now has a sound basis of understanding of what the public wants, something that never existed before. So bravo for the City".[24] Peggy Jay, too, completely revised her opinion and was unstinting in her praise and gratitude. "I came to appreciate the depth and concern felt for the Heath by the City", which "has shown itself keenly aware of local feeling and shown that it is willing to consult".[25]

At Kenwood, Sir Jocelyn Stevens, who had taken over as EH Chairman in 1992, had launched an appeal to raise money for the ambitious plans to restore both the landscape and the House. He too faced a highly publicised negative campaign about the number of trees to be cut down, by an organisation called Kenwood Trees. For once Stevens's legendary abrasive style was put on hold: he had to call a halt and begin a new consultation. Eventually mutual agreement was reached and the restoration continued.

An unexpected consequence of this extraordinary period of upheaval is that management of the Heath and Kenwood was actually greatly improved, with proper management plans, dedicated staff, and the public's right to have a say recognised in formal procedures. The Society's views have modified over the years in response to changing public perception of the role of open spaces, and in 2002 the Society's Heath sub-committee published its own ideas on Heath management in a booklet, *Heath Vision*.

137. The Society's *Heath Vision* booklet with the 1780 George Robertson picture across the front and back covers

**Notes, Chapter 20**

1. 25 Jan 1988 (H&HS archive: A/1048/3/4/2/3)
2. Paper, 'Bodies suggested for representation on the Consultative Committee (H&HS archive: A/1048/3/4/2/1 - 3/4/3/1)
3. Obituary by Ruth Gorb, *The Independent*, 18 Nov 1997
4. 'Our right to be heard', H&OHS *Newsletter*, Jan 1991
5. Rowntree (2004), p 17
6. Ashhurst (1647-1720) resided at Ashhurst House in Highgate (built in 1675, demolished in 1830 to make way for St Michael's Church), but was also a Hampstead copyholder with land at Child's Hill.
7. Lane's house, Aldenham or the White House, was in Pond Street
8. The body's official name, the Historic Buildings and Monuments Commission for England, was soon changed to English Heritage by Lord Montague of Beaulieu, its first Chairman, who had long experience in conservation matters as founder member and chairman of the Historic Houses Association.
9. Peter Rumble, 'English Heritage: the first 21 years', Conservation bulletin, issue 49, summer 2005
10. Julius Bryant, conversation with the author, 27 Nov 2017
11. Michael Norris, letter to Peggy Jay, 2 Jan 1988 (H&HS archive)
12. *Ham & High*, 4 Nov 1988
13. *Ham & High*, 18 Nov 1988
14. 8 Mar 1989 (H&HS archive: A/1048/3/8/5/1/3)
15. *Ham & High*, 17 Feb 1989
16. H&OHS *Newslettter*, autumn 1990
17. Summary of Society views, Sep 1991 (H&OHS archive: A/1048/3/8/5/1/3)
18. H&OHS *Newsletter*, autumn 1990
19. Ibid., Jan 1991
20. Bryant & Colson (1990). Repton's plans for his clients were always bound into a book covered in red Morocco leather.
21. H&OHS *Newsletter*, Oct 1992
22. *Ham & High*, 22 Sep 1994
23. LB of Camden, 'We're Listening', final report: 'Examples of good consultation', Jan 1996, para. 7.48
24. H&OHS *Newsletter*, Oct 1994
25. Ibid., autumn 1989, p 45

---

## PART 6          PRESERVING THE RURAL ILLUSION

### Chapter 21

# The rise of town planning

I n 1997 the Heath and Old Hampstead Society celebrated its centenary with a book called *A Constant Vigil* – a selection of extracts from a century of annual reports – and another change of name, to its present one, The Heath & Hampstead Society.

138. Society centenary logo

139. Centenary celebrations. The Lord Mayor opens a children's art competition in a marquee on the Heath in 1997, as part of a year-long programme of events, including an art exhibition at Kenwood sponsored by *The Times*, and various refurbishment schemes. R to L, with the Lord Mayor: Peggy Jay, Peter Rigby and Helen Marcus (H&OHS Chairman)

217

When the Society was founded 100 years before, town planning did not exist, although vestries and manor courts did exert some minimal control. Piecemeal legislation concerned itself mainly with improving the terrible slum conditions. It came as a rude awakening to members of the new Hampstead Heath Protection Society in 1903 when The Pryors in East Heath Road was sold to developers and replaced with two massive blocks of flats. The copyhold, acquired by the Hornsby family,[1] went back to at least the 1750s when East Heath Road was just a track across the Heath. In the 19th century it was closely associated with generations of Heath campaigners. The Pryor family, related by marriage to the Hoares, the Tollers and the Holfords, lived there from the early 1800s;[2] and later residents were Strickland Cookson, and Walter Field, the artist whose petition had launched the Hampstead Heath Protection Society. No legislation existed through which the property could have been saved and all the Society could do was "express great regret at not being able to prevent the disfigurement to the Heath".[3] To make matters worse, a row of eleven elms on the Heath that screened the flats was cut down. As a prescient letter writer to *The Times* complained: "while the trees had been there for at least 50 years, the flats are a thing of yesterday. ... the trees were held in trust by the London County Council for the public, whose interests and property it is no exaggeration to say are being sacrificed to promote private interests. In many parts of Hampstead-heath are displayed notices warning the public against depredations, yet who can expect much heed to be paid to them when the London County Council so flagrantly violates its own regulations?"[4]

140. The Pryors: an "old fashioned mansion" in nearly 2 acres with 15 bedrooms, a billiard room, "brick built detached artist's studio" and "charming and secluded grounds" with tennis courts and vinery, according to the Potter sales advert, 6 June 1902 (The Pryors website)

141. Plan of the Estate, from the Manor Court Book; East Heath Road was still Middle Heath Road

The first attempt at town planning in a broader sense came with the Town Planning Act of 1909, which not only made provision for better housing but gave powers to plan main streets, fix densities and house types and, in particular, to provide and protect open space. It also introduced the idea of a government inspectorate with the power to conduct public inquiries. But the aim was still mostly to improve housing rather than preserve the wider amenity of areas.

The Society, alerted to the new danger by what happened at The Pryors, welcomed the new town planning regulations that followed: the Housing and Town Planning Act of 1919, which separated housing from planning; and, particularly, the Town Planning Act, of 1925, which gave the London County Council (LCC) power to prepare specific Town Planning Schemes across London. In 1929 Scheme No. 3 (Highgate and Hampstead), enthusiastically supported by the Society, introduced a special policy for 'Fringes of the Heath', with proposals to limit the size and height of buildings. A Greater London Regional Planning Committee was established as an advisory board, for which Raymond Unwin (designer of the first Garden City at Letchworth in 1903, and of the Hampstead Garden Suburb) produced plans.

It came not a moment too soon, as the scale of the potential problem began to be realised, with increasing pressure to replace old properties surrounding Whitestone Pond with tall blocks of flats like The Pryors, as they came on the market. With the help of Town Planning Scheme No. 3, proposals for a 7-storey block in 1929 at Bellmoor – Barratt's old home opposite Whitestone Pond – were reduced to four storeys, and plans to redevelop the Old Court House were fought off. The Society recorded that, were it not for the new powers under the LCC's Town Planning Scheme and the "firm attitude" taken by the local authorities, "the Heath would already be dominated by vast blocks of modern flats".[5] The Estate Market correspondent of *The Times* shared these concerns, regularly reporting on potential threats to the Heath from sales of surrounding properties with their large gardens in the "quiet old-fashioned back-waters of Hampstead … The development of private land close to the Heath will not enhance the picturesqueness of its surroundings".[6]

1932 provided a further portent of things to come. The Air Ministry acquired Heath Brow at Littleworth, next to Jack Straw's Castle, which had been empty for three years, intending to turn it into an administrative headquarters and officers' club for No. 60 (Bomber) Squadron of the Auxiliary Air Force.[7] The house was included in the LCC's new Planning Scheme No. 3 but no-one thought to enquire whether there were any planning restrictions – it was a new concept. The Ministry declared its intention to cover the garden with a building tall enough to affect views across the Heath, claiming that as a government body it was exempt from the planning Act, and the Government considered that the interests of national defence were more important than town-planning obligations. But the Ministry had not reckoned with the local sense of proprietorship and determined spirit where the Heath was concerned. There was strong objection on all sides led by the Society: "once any relaxation of the present Town Planning restrictions is permitted, it will be increasingly difficult to enforce the scheme. The Committee particularly deplore that the Air Ministry should insist upon the privileged position which they enjoy as a department of the Government to carry through this scheme in the face of the united opposition of the local authorities ... and the residents".[8] Under pressure

from the LCC and Hampstead Borough Council (HBC), the Ministry was made
to create a mock-up of the structure which was put on public display. Lord Moyne,
the son of Lord Iveagh, who still owned the neighbouring Heath House, and was

"HEATH BROW"
Shaded portion shows the alteration as originally proposed

142. The proposed Air Ministry structure at Heath Brow (HHPS annual report 1932)

a member of the Society, advised: "I think there is something to be said for going
ahead with public opposition before the Air Ministry make up their minds".[9]
The Society was supported by its old allies the Open Spaces Society (the former
Commons Preservation Society which, like the H&OHS, has changed its name
over time), and Lawrence Chubb, along with well-known local residents, Flinders
Petrie, and Edward Duveen, a committee member who lived at Gangmoor.
Although they did not manage to stop the Ministry from putting up the buildings,
they did succeed in getting the heights reduced.

Further legislative progress was made in 1932 when a new Town and
Country Planning Act introduced a power to preserve buildings of special
architectural or historic interest. But the improved financial situation in the 1930s
brought with it a "rising tide of speculative commercial building development"
which the authorities seemed to lack the will to combat. With repeated applications
for large blocks of flats on land adjoining the Heath, the planning legislation was
unequal to the pace of development, and failed on several occasions to provide
safeguards, despite the strongest possible opposition of local residents.

Moreover, the HBC still had no power – all it could do was express an
objection to the LCC, where the final decision on all applications rested. The
Society realised that to protect the Heath they needed to look with equal vigilance
at what was happening around it. "Such development constitutes the principal
menace to the rural character which the Heath still retains".[8] They feared the
Heath would be "overwhelmed and finally swept away by it".[5] They therefore

220

widened their objects and changed their name to reflect this, becoming the Hampstead Heath and Old Hampstead Protection Society (HH&OHPS).[10]

At the same time the Society's Committee was attracting important new members, whose strength it was to need in the coming years: Hutchinson, Brooke and Viscount Knollys, have already been mentioned). There were also Sir Alexander Kaye Butterworth, a railway executive (father of the composer George Butterworth, another casualty of the Great War); and the architect Clough Williams-Ellis,[11] whose 1928 book *England and the Octopus* was a manifesto for the Council for the Preservation of Rural England (CPRE). He had joined the HHPS in 1930 when he bought Romney's House (then being used as Assembly Rooms), making extensive alterations, and living and running his practice there until 1939. Professor Randolph Schwabe, on the Society's Committee from 1934, was Slade Professor of Fine Art at University College London and served as a war artist in both World Wars.

In 1935 a proposal to demolish the old Willow Cottages facing the Heath at the bottom of Willow Road, and replace them with a block of flats, was granted permission by the LCC, against its own policies and in defiance of strong objections by the Society and the Borough Council. Yet again, enforcement of the much-welcomed town planning schemes proved inadequate. The Society's annual report accused the LCC of not paying sufficient regard to public opinion and called for the policies to be "administered with greater courage and firmness than has hitherto been shown".[12] In the event the architect, Ernö Goldfinger, built only three houses, but legend has it that Ian Fleming, who still had Hampstead connections, immortalised this villainy in the person of Goldfinger in the eponymous James Bond novel.

## The road menace – 1: the great god Traffic

New threats were also emerging from another quarter. It is hard to believe that schemes to knock down the historic houses in Heath Street to widen it, and even to expropriate bits of the Heath to make wider roads, appeared as early as the 1920s. As car ownership and use increased, so did the problems they caused; and so did the need for the HHPS to combat damaging proposals for road building and widening. The Society was well ahead of its time in its understanding that the more you widen or build new roads, the more traffic will be attracted to them. They realised that it was the very narrowness of some of the roads in question that had helped to keep heavy traffic away from the Heath.

The Heath itself needed protection from the new motorised traffic. Before the advent of the motorcar the tracks across the Heath were used by carts and horses, and there appeared no reason to change this when it became a public open space. The 1871 Act had reserved two roads across East Heath for the use of the Maryon Wilsons should they develop East Park, but after 1885 when East Park became part of the Heath, these gradually dwindled into footpaths. However, by the 1920s cars were using the Heath tracks as short cuts, and clogging them up by parking for long periods; on one occasion, the Society reported that a charabanc was seen. Firmer action was now needed and in 1924 the Society persuaded the LCC and HBC to close the two tracks at North End, one to West Heath Road and one to Spaniards End, by placing posts at either end.

That same year HBC officials first started eyeing up North End Road with a view to widening it. The deep cutting from the Bull & Bush to Hill House, overhung by trees, although picturesque, was considered dangerous. Lord Clarendon, who lived at Pitt House, was generously prepared to give a 6ft-wide strip of land from his garden along the road frontage, to assist the Borough Council's plan. The Society vigorously opposed the proposal as being not only unnecessary, but impossible without destroying large numbers of beautiful trees. A resolution condemning the scheme was sent to the LCC and HBC. Fortunately, owing to lack of finance, the scheme was dropped. But in 1932 the plans were revived. The LCC asked the HBC to provide a list of proposals for widening streets "which might be taken into consideration"; these included Heath Street from Holly Hill to Hampstead Heath, and a revival of the North End Road scheme. The Society expressed "profound regret that such proposals should ever have been entertained by the Borough Council". It would mean "the destruction of ... the Mount ... familiar as the scene of Maddox [sic] Brown's best known picture".[13]

It was a further vindication of the decision to extend the Society's remit to cover Old Hampstead. Geoffrey Hutchinson, who was then a borough councillor and also the Society's Secretary, tried, but failed, to get the two roads taken out of the list. A trenchant letter of protest was sent to The Times by several distinguished members of the Society, headed by Lord Clarendon, who had now become its President (and, accordingly, changed his view): the scheme would obliterate "those individual and ancient features which still preserve Hampstead from the dreary monotony and unsightliness of modern suburban development." Moreover "it would strike alarum among a wider circle of Londoners when it is realized that its accomplishment will bring into being an almost straight and uninterrupted motor way from Swiss Cottage right across the top of Hampstead Heath to Golders Green Station. All this threatened destruction and expenditure is to be undertaken in order to ensure that the passing motorist shall not be occupied for a few additional moments on his rapid journey through Hampstead. We, as residents and ratepayers in Hampstead, cannot believe that our borough council will ever consider that such an object is worth the price which we are asked to pay".[14] The following day, Sir Reginald Blomfield added his voice to the protest: "Hampstead is one of the few attractive places round London which has not yet been sacrificed to the motorist".[15]

Surprisingly, some members of HBC disparaged the letter writers. Alderman Spriggs "was amazed that there should be any protest against the widening of Heath Street, for the matter had been before the Council as an urgent one for at least 25 years"; while Councillor Townroe objected that "men of distinction" should have such a letter, which was "very ill-informed" published in The Times "simply because they were men of distinction".[16] Wiser counsels prevailed: Lord

Haddo, Chairman of the LCC Town Planning Committee, replied reassuringly that he was "happy to be able to assure your correspondents and others that there is very little danger of either Heath Street or North End Road being widened in the near future".[17] But his optimism was misplaced; much worse threats were to come.

By 1935 things were so bad that a public meeting was called "to demand the preservation of Hampstead from unsightly building developments". At a crowded meeting at Hampstead Town Hall a resolution moved by Hampstead's LCC representatives "was carried by acclamation", calling on "the Ministries of Health and Transport, the LCC, and other responsible authorities to safeguard and preserve the residential character of Hampstead as it exists to-day". The meeting was addressed by Sir Raymond Unwin, and Sir Gilbert Upcott representing Highgate,[18] the Society's Chairman Howard Figgis, and Geoffrey Hutchinson, who had just become the Honorary Secretary. Sir Reginald Blomfield, one of the first members of the Society's Committee and now a Vice-President, protested in words that have an all too familiar ring: the wishes of the residents and of the borough council were being treated with cynical contempt by the higher authorities. He called on them "not to allow Hampstead to be sacrificed to the rapacity of speculators in property". The annual report noted that their stand on these matters "brought a marked increase of public interest" in the Society's work.[19]

## The Bressey Report

Growing traffic problems in the 1930s exposed the inadequacy of London's roads, and in 1934 Charles Bressey[20] and Sir Edwin Lutyens were commissioned by the Government to prepare a thirty-year plan for a new road network in Greater London. The idea of building new ring roads around the capital had begun as far back as 1905, with recommendations of the Royal Commission on London Traffic, proposing a circular road around London (the future North and South Circular Roads) and also a circular road further out (12 miles from Charing Cross). A start was made around 1911, but the Great War intervened and the idea receded for a time. But now it returned with a vengeance. Bressey's Highway Development Survey, for Greater London, was published in 1938, with plans for a series of motorways radiating outwards from the city, triple-storey parking garages, large roundabouts, and recommendations for a series of orbital roads around the city. No part of London would have been left unscathed. It was just the beginning of what was to culminate in a London-wide battle in the 1960s.

The proposals for Hampstead were extraordinary, beginning with "the possibility of a by-pass along the eastern fringe of Hampstead" in order, it was claimed "to avoid drastic alterations in Heath Street, and the consequent loss of its picturesque characteristics". It was to start from Fitzjohn's Avenue, and "follow Lyndhurst Road (widened and improved) to Lyndhurst Gardens where a roundabout would be required". From there a new "cut" would be made to Rosslyn Hill, with another roundabout "and the line would continue along Pilgrim's Lane, to the east end of Carlingford Road. At this point" – it was seriously suggested – "the road would continue on a viaduct clearing Denning Road and Willow Road and coming to earth at Heath Side. Continuing along East Heath Road the route would terminate at Whitestone Pond." The designers of this nightmare were of the opinion that "… although some demolition would be necessary, no building of architectural or historic interest would be threatened", while providing "an unobstructed route discharging clear of the built-up area, near Whitestone Pond".[21] Fortunately, disagreement between the LCC and the Ministry of Transport delayed progress, and then once again war diverted the planners' energies, and the necessary finance.

## The Second World War

In the prelude to the Second World War, the development boom died down. Professor Cyril (C.E.M.) Joad, who lived at 4 East Heath Road, described how the War was "… ushered in by the removal of large tracts of [the Heath] to fill sandbags; lorries rumbled, great pits yawned, more trees were cut down and a hill literally disappeared. … Presently a rifle range was established. … Then came anti-aircraft guns, rocket guns and a search-light station. A large camp appeared, complete with concrete, asphalt, latrines, Nissen huts and all the rest of the paraphernalia of the Army".[22] Some of the debris was still there 3 years later.

The Society noted that "for the second time in its existence, it is being carried on in time of war". Hutchinson joined up again, and Howard Figgis, the Chairman, had to take on the role of Secretary as well. But there was little active work and the Committee only met from time to time. Figgis died in 1944, having moved out of London after his house (Heathlands, at Littleworth) was bombed, and W.J.H. Brodrick took his place as Chairman.[23]

As in the Great War, the Heath was used for allotments as part of the Dig for Victory campaign and sheep were re-introduced on it. While the Society thought it a pity that ground near East Heath Road and The Pryors was dug up, "it is good to know that the [allotments] have all been taken up".[24] According to Kit Ikin, a great lorry park appeared on the Sandy Road near West Heath Road; "bren gun carriers careered around destroying the heather on Sandy Heath" and many trees were killed by oil drips.[25]

The ghost underground station at North End, Hampstead Way (see p 140) suddenly found a use as a secret archive for sensitive government documents; it could be accessed only from the cabs of passing maintenance trains.[26] One of the most popular old music hall songs, sung to keep spirits up in the air-raid shelters, was *Down at the Old Bull and Bush.*

Barrage balloons and ack-ack guns were sited on Parliament Hill.[27] There was a great deal of bomb damage. Bombs rained down on Kenwood until the anti-aircraft battery with its spotlight moved away, but all the windows were blown out. Fortunately, the paintings had been removed to Elveden Hall, Lord Iveagh's country seat in Suffolk. In 1996, records released by the Ministry of Defence revealed that there was still one unexploded bomb beneath the south terrace.[28]

Golders Hill House, some of North End village and the enclave around Jack Straw's Castle were demolished (see pp 167-168).

## The Greater London Plan

In response to the terrible devastation wrought on London by the Blitz, Sir Patrick Abercrombie was commissioned immediately in 1942, to draw up a plan in collaboration with J.H. Forshaw, the LCC's architect, for its rebuilding.[29] In 1943 a new Ministry of Town and Country Planning was created, and out of all these initiatives came the 1947 Town and Country Planning Act, with greatly enhanced planning protections, based on Abercrombie's plan. According to Sir Desmond Heap, lawyer and town planning expert, it was "the Great Watershed in the developing story of planning control. ... Nothing associated with the land was ever to be the same again".[30] The principle was established that owners must get planning permission to develop their land and borough councils were given powers over planning decisions for the first time. A new listing system also gave them power to preserve buildings of historical interest.[32] Another important measure was the creation of a Central Land Board, with compulsory purchase powers recommended by the 1942 Uthwatt Report on Compensation and Betterment; development rights over all undeveloped land were in effect nationalised. This was to have untoward consequences for Hampstead.

Abercrombie's far-reaching ideas included reducing London's population and ensuring there was sufficient green space for every community. But for all his recognition of the importance of respecting London's ancient village communities, his Plan took no cognizance of what had preserved the unique features of a place like Hampstead. Its blanket recommendation, for higher-density development of 75 or 100 persons per acre on high ground and near an open space, would have undone at a stroke the 1929 policies which the Society regarded as essential to preserving the *rus in urbe* quality of the Heath. The LCC took it as a cue for the complete reversal of the Fringes of the Heath policy and it seemed to the Society that the LCC deliberately planned to site buildings of great height and mass in the vicinity of the Heath. The old consensus seemed to be gone.[32] St Pancras Borough Council, its days of staunch support for enlarging the Heath long past, was even rumoured to be considering using part of Parliament Hill Fields for housing, leading to questions being asked in the House of Commons. Fortunately, nothing came of this, but planning problems resumed and increased.[33]

With much of London's housing stock still substandard, and large areas destroyed by bombing, house building claimed priority. The LCC, empowered by the new measures, began searching for any empty-looking spaces on the map to fill with houses or flats. Unfortunately, one such was the old Branch Hill estate, comprising Branch Hill House and grounds, and Oak Hill Park, amounting to over 22 acres. They showed up on the maps as private residential land, giving no hint of the still large areas of green space. The new Development Plan designated the whole lot as building land with compulsory purchase orders under the new Act.

## The battle for Branch Hill

The Branch Hill estate is one of the remarkable survivals of Hampstead's rural past. It began as copyhold enclosures carved out of the Heath from the 1680s, and by 1730 a house known as Bleak Hall or Judges Bench House had been built. Its old oaks were said to be a relic of the Forest of Middlesex and, like all the high sandy ridges of the Heath, the ground is riddled with small streams. The Branch Hill stream flows down into the Redington/Frognal area, joining another tributary from Telegraph Hill to become the Westbourne river, formerly known as the Kilbourne, flowing on to the marshy area which is now the Serpentine at Hyde Park and thence into the Thames. When Sir Thomas Clarke, Master of the Rolls, bought the copyhold of the estate in 1745, Branch Hill was only a track across the Heath, and as late as 1899 the Hampstead Antiquarian Society could still describe how "a continuation of the avenue of trees on Judges' Walk can be traced through the present garden to the old house".[34]

Clarke bequeathed the estate in 1764 to his patron Lord Macclesfield, whose family sold it to Lord Wedderburn. By 1800 it had been bought by the Neave family, who enlarged the estate with more enclosures, securing freeholds and rebuilding and enlarging the house. In the 1840s Sir Thomas Neave divided the estate into two parts, laying out Oak Hill Park, a close of stuccoed villas. He sold Branch Hill Lodge and lived in one of his new houses, Oak Hill Lodge. By 1903 Branch Hill Lodge, still with a large garden, had been acquired by John Nivison, a banker, who later became the first Lord Glendyne; his son was living there in 1947 when the new Development Plan threatened the whole area with a compulsory purchase order.

Talk of the LCC intending to build large blocks of flats of possibly ten or more storeys, at densities of 70 persons per acre, provoked widespread objection. Hampstead Borough Council conveyed its concerns to the LCC, which denied the story about the high-rise flats and gave assurances that only small houses, carefully designed to fit in, were proposed. Oswald Milne, then an Alderman and Chairman of the Borough Planning Committee, who had succeeded Hutchinson as Chairman of the Society in 1953, protested in the columns of the *Ham & High*: the land should be added to the Heath; "… to London as a whole the preservation of the Heath and its leafy environs is of far greater importance in the long view than the insertion of a few hundred flat dwellings in the wrong place". The old heathland, with its waterlogged steep and craggy slopes on unstable sandy subsoil, was wholly unsuitable for such building. Many were the stories of flooding and drainage problems.[35]

It was fortunate that the Society's committee in these immediate postwar years was exceptionally strong and well equipped to deal with the challenges that emerged on every front. In addition to Committee members already mentioned in Chapter 15, there were architects Courtenay Theobald and John Brandon-Jones; Elisabeth Chesterton, a distinguished town planner; and Fred Salfeld, editor of the 'Peterborough' column in the *Daily Telegraph*. Oswald Milne resigned as Chairman in 1959 but remained on the committee, and there was close co-operation between the Society and the Borough Council, which agreed to let them know about any important new planning applications to the LCC for development on the Fringes of the Heath. Milne's successor as Society Chairman was Sir Colin Anderson (grandson of Elizabeth Garrett Anderson), who had joined the committee in 1956. The Andersons were shipping magnates: Sir Colin was a director of the family firm of Anderson Green and of the Orient Line and P&O, and also President of the Chamber of Shipping. His interests were immensely wide and he made

a remarkable contribution to public life. He was devoted to the arts and music and was at various times, Chairman of the Trustees of the Tate Gallery, a director of the Royal Opera House and the English Opera Group; a trustee of the National Gallery; and Chairman of the Royal Fine Art Commission. He produced the Anderson Committee Report on education for the Government. And, as if all that was not enough, he was also a keen gardener and regularly opened his garden at Admiral's House for the National Garden Scheme.

*The Times* weighed in against the plan for Branch Hill with eloquent support: "the semi-rural character of a beautiful and historic

143. Sir Colin Anderson (1904-80)

neighbourhood may be spoilt. A winding, rural lane ... [leads] up to the heath from West Hampstead. ... On either side of it grow ancient elms and oak trees, which stood when Hampstead was a country village".[36] The outcry forced the LCC to think again and it withdrew the Branch Hill plan, citing the weight of local criticism and the technical difficulties of building there. "Subsoil and contours of the ground make it unsuitable".[37] Some of the more damaging 1947 provisions were repealed in 1954, but the threat of the raised densities remained and went to a public inquiry; the Society, led by Hutchinson, raised funds to engage professional counsel to represent them. The Inspector's decision announced in 1955 "upheld almost entirely the Society's point of view"; densities around the Heath would remain at 30 persons per acre.[38] But it was only a temporary reprieve for Branch Hill; the damage was done, and the London County Plan still showed 23 acres in the area as future potential development land, setting in motion a fifty-year battle to preserve it.

It was the death knell for the old Victorian villas at Oak Hill Park. Sir Stanley Unwin, the publisher, lived at No. 4 in the 1930s and, sensing that the estate could not resist attempts to redevelop it much longer, bought seven acres of it from the Neaves in 1936 to try to save it. But wartime bombs and requisitions left several of the properties beyond repair and most of the tenants departed. By 1958, Unwin realised he could hold out no longer and put the estate on the market.[39] It was bought the next year by a private developer, who bombarded HBC with applications for building schemes, each one worse than the last, ending up with several 12-storey blocks of flats which would have compromised Heath views. Strenuous opposition was mounted by the Society, working with neighbouring residents. Eventually they got the heights reduced from 12 to 7 storeys, with clauses written into the leases protecting the trees, the rural features, and the barrier across Oak Hill Way to preserve the character of the footpath to the Heath. But it was a complete departure from 25 years of policy that no such large blocks would be allowed near the Heath. They were out of scale with the rest of Hampstead.

As Hampstead Borough Council began to use its new powers, the Society now had two planning authorities to deal with. When in 1957 it expressed concern about the poor quality of development decisions in old Hampstead, it was met with the disconcerting reply that "providing density and daylighting standards are met, [the HBC] is not prepared to resist the present tendency to build in old established Hampstead gardens; nor does it recognise that the architectural quality of building in the borough is being allowed to drop". This was an astonishing response to a committee with several eminent architects and a distinguished town planner on it, especially in the light of what was happening at Oak Hill Park. Attitudes had changed, as typified by a remark from a newly elected councillor, Roy Shaw, who in a discussion of the proposed new densities in the County of London Development Plan is reported as saying: "The skyline of Hampstead Heath will be improved" if high blocks of flats are allowed to go up round the fringes".[41]

The Society secured a meeting with the Chairman of the LCC Planning Committee, Councillor John Townsend, and his officers, at which Sir Colin Anderson, accompanied by Elizabeth Chesterton and Hutchinson (now Sir Geoffrey), highlighted their concerns about the threat posed by commercial interests. Property developers were "getting away with things", seeking to exploit the charm of the Heath itself by aiming to erect large blocks of flats as near to it as possible. Oak Hill Park and development issues in Hampstead in general were discussed, and in particular the possibility of adding the Branch Hill Estate, and the garden at Witanhurst, to the Heath if ever the opportunity arose.[42]

Oak Hill Park was lost, but the Branch Hill story had by no means ended: it "lay like a submerged log just below the political surface".[43] In 1963 Sir Colin Anderson, and Sir Geoffrey Hutchinson (now Lord Ilford and President of the Society), approached Lord Glendyne to suggest that when he was ready to sell, Branch Hill might be offered to the LCC as an addition to the Heath. The idea was positively received and got as far as discussions with Sir Isaac Hayward, then LCC Chairman. It was also supported by various boroughs but, ominously, not by Councillor Charlie Ratchford of St Pancras. The 1965 political reorganisation (see Chapter 17) saw the LCC become the GLC and Hampstead Borough Council was subsumed into the new Camden Council, with Ratchford as its leader. The change brought with it a new and growing element of political partisanship, which all too often was allowed to influence what should have been disinterested decisions. Although the Branch Hill deal went ahead in May 1965, it became hideously entangled in party politics. With the loss of the borough council, which had provided Hampstead with its own local voice, the role of the Society took on new significance.

The terms of the agreement with Glendyne became a subject of intense controversy. For what purpose did Camden acquire it? Was the price really below market value? Councillor Ratchford initially announced that Branch Hill House was to become an old people's home and the surrounding land kept as open space, because "it is on this understanding that Lord Glendyne has agreed to sell the property to the Council." Barely a few months later he denied ever having said this; the area was zoned as residential and the Council intended to draw up plans for development. The trouble was that he had given the original assurance that the land would not be developed, in no less a place than County Hall, and there was a minute of it. It had not been incorrectly noted by some careless junior reporter, as Ratchford tried to suggest. It came from a press statement signed by Ratchford and sent to the local newspapers.[44]

Through various twists and turns and changes of political leadership, proposals to build council houses, or to sell the land on for development, came and went, depending which political party held power. The Society – its name now shortened again, to Heath and Old Hampstead Society (H&OHS)[45] – continued trying to get the land added to the Heath. The old people's home was opened in Branch Hill House in 1970 and Camden Council then embarked on a protracted effort to build council houses on part of the garden, encouraged and opposed in equal measure by various factions in the community. There were restrictive covenants on the land, and Camden even approached the owners of adjoining property to see if they would waive them. Costs escalated because of the difficulties of the site, further aggravated by the refusal by the DoE, under a Conservative government, to approve any subsidy because the enormous cost could not be justified. Camden decided to plough on regardless, subsidising the cost from its own coffers.[46]

The houses, called Spedan Close, were finally ready for occupation in 1978 – one and a half years late – and were dubbed the most expensive council houses ever built. The *Architects' Journal* report gives a flavour of the debate that raged: "Camden said 'Nothing's too good for the workers' – but is this good enough? Are the workers being used in a half-baked social experiment, in a flawed architectural exercise, providing an ego trip for the politicians and the architects?"[47]

Camden's mounting financial difficulties now became a major element in this seemingly endless saga. Debts incurred over many years were compounded by new government regulations and rate-capping in the 1980s. Selling the remaining Branch Hill land with planning permission was seen as a way to ameliorate the Council's situation. A planning brief was drawn up, dividing it into three separate sites; although two of them were small woodlands, and the third was allotments, all were described as suitable for development, putting the Council in breach of its own Unitary Development Plan (UDP) policies. Unsurprisingly, this attracted widespread objection, but the Council nevertheless proceeded to apply to itself for the necessary planning consents.

The Society mounted a new campaign led by John Carswell, working with various local residents' associations who had called the alarm, and backed by the Open Spaces Society, the CPRE, SAVE Britain's Heritage, the London Ecology Unit and the London Wildlife Trust. In January 1990, Hampstead's MP, now Sir Geoffrey Finsberg, got the Secretary of State, Michael Heseltine, to put the site under an Article 14 direction, blocking Camden from granting itself planning permission without his approval. By this time a further complication had arisen, as parts of the site had been designated a conservation area and, as Carswell amusingly put it, Camden found "they had missed some essential steps in their constitution minuet, causing them to go through the whole dance again". As Camden tried every means to get round the Article 14 direction, Carswell described how "it became one of my regular tasks to ring the DoE to ask if the Order was still there. 'Oh yes', my genial contact at the Department would answer. 'It's still there'. And so far as I know it may be there yet. Successive Ministers remained unmoved by Camden's pleas".[48] In an extraordinary and completely

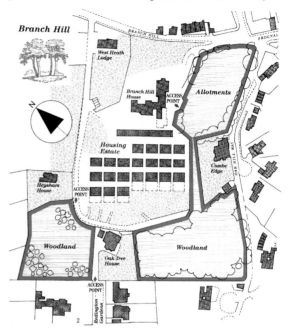

144. Plan of the three sites offered for development at Branch Hill. From a booklet *Branch Hill Combe*, published by the Society as part of its campaign to save the land, the cost having been funded by a "personal donation".

unexpected move, a local resident nobly saved the largest woodland site by buying it from Camden, under covenants forbidding development. Soon after, with growing dissent within its own ranks as a result of the campaign led by the Society, Camden Council was persuaded to drop any further development plans. The whole site was redesignated as private open space in 1995, and this was confirmed in the new UDP. But in June 2018, Camden was reported to be selling Branch Hill House to private developers.

## The road menace – 2: the Motorway Box

Abercrombie's Greater London Plan had also incorporated Bressey's ideas for motorways and road widening, which by 1960 the Society considered to be the greatest threat: "curves must be straightened out, bottlenecks removed and features destroyed in the name of speeding up traffic".[49] The Bressey by-pass plan was dropped, but a succession of damaging proposals – involving either the destruction of Hampstead's historic fabric or taking land from the Heath – came, and fortunately, for the most part, went.

A 1960 plan to widen a section of East Heath Road by Squire's Mount was foiled by the National Trust, which refused to release the required land, but the next year talk of plans to widen Heath Street surfaced again. As Sir Colin Anderson commented: "Mercifully other counsels prevailed but that such a thing can even be contemplated shows that some officials are so dedicated to the god Traffic that they lack any feeling for the importance of the human environment upon which so much happiness depends".[50] Then, in 1962, there were revived rumours of the motorway plans for London, including one across the Heath itself, or a tunnel under it, and it was not long before these were confirmed.

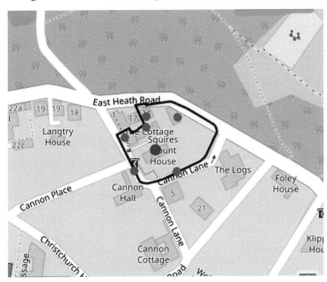

145. Map of the Squire's Mount property left to the National Trust by the Field sisters

Amenity societies, now springing up across London, made common cause to fight these threats which would have blighted whole areas of the capital. HH&OHPS members attended a conference called by the Kensington Society to consider 'London and the Motorways', which attracted 300 representatives of London amenity societies.[51] A resolution called on the Government to reconsider the plans and put the welfare of communities first. "That such a resolution should be necessary suggests a failure of top-level liaison difficult to credit".[52] But when the LCC was replaced by the Greater London Council (GLC) in 1965, the motorway plans were firmly on the agenda. Proposals for a three-ring Motorway System were announced, the innermost of which, Ringway One – the London Motorway Box – was to be a 20-mile route circling the capital, going through Willesden, Hampstead and Islington, and with the possibility of a tunnel under Hampstead. A Hampstead Motorway Action Group was formed, threatening court action against the GLC unless an immediate inquiry was held.

It was just at this moment that the Highways Committee in the newly formed Borough of Camden came up with an astonishing proposal to widen the whole length of East Heath Road, from Whitestone Pond to South End Green, into a dual carriageway by taking land from the Heath. There was a furious outcry and the project immediately became associated in the public mind with the proposed new motorways. The whole idea was quickly dropped and "the issue had the important consequence of swinging the Council against motorways".[53]

But highways engineers continued hatching up new schemes. In 1966 the Society prevented yet another attempt to widen the cutting at North End Road. In 1967, without any consultation, the GLC prepared a plan to turn Whitestone Pond into a traffic roundabout with six sets of traffic lights. Trees and shrubs were to be cut down and replaced by a car park. The Society sent a deputation to Camden Council which, fortunately, refused permission. In 1972 the Council's planners proposed to widen Pond Street but were overruled by the councillors. And over it all hovered the continuing threat of the Motorway Box. Elections in 1967 saw the Conservatives re-elected at the GLC with an increased majority, and they took this as a cue to press on with the motorway programme.

Peggy Jay's former husband, Douglas Jay MP, now relegated to the back benches, led a London-wide campaign to get the Motorway Box stopped. The route would have cut through both his Battersea North constituency and Hampstead, where he lived. With support from a wide range of eminent public figures – including the Bishop of Southwark, Beatrix Lehmann, C. Day Lewis, Jonathan Miller, Henry Moore, J.B. Priestley, John Summerson and Yehudi Menuhin – he formed the London Motorway Action Group and led a delegation to the Minister of Transport to call for a public inquiry. This was promised for the following year and backed by an editorial in *The Times*.

At first the motorway idea was not a party-political issue, having been supported by both Labour and Conservative administrations at government and local authority level. But as public opposition mounted, the (Labour) Government began to doubt the wisdom of this vast project. In November 1968, the Labour opposition on the GLC declared they would fight the proposals, and the Government too began to back-track: the Minister wrote to Douglas Jay, making it clear that the Government was not now committed to the Motorway Box. Throughout 1969 and 1970 there was almost daily correspondence in the letters pages of the national and local press, especially after the opening of Westway, the only part of the proposed network to get built, and it was understood just what the monstrous reality really meant.

The promised inquiry finally opened in October 1970 under the chairmanship of Frank Layfield and finished in May 1972. To everyone's consternation, he found in favour of Ringway One – the Box. But it was already too late; the GLC had begun drastically revising the programme and shelving long stretches of it, and Sir Reginald Goodwin, leader of the GLC Labour group, said his party would go into the following year's elections opposed to it outright. They won with 57 seats and the plan for the Motorway Box was finally seen off. As the H&OHS annual report amusingly commented in 1972, "Hampstead must be the only place in the country where the headline 'Wilson attacks Heath' conjures up thoughts of a nineteenth century land grab rather than a disagreement in the House of Commons".[54]

## Notes, Chapter 21

1. Manor Court Book D, 1744-61 (LMA: E/MW/H/221)
2. Court Book K, 1816-22 (LMA: E/MW/H/228)
3. HHPS annual report, 1903
4. *The Times*, 14 Jun 1904
5. HH&OHPS annual report, 1934
6. *The Times*, 14 Dec 1926; 29 Apr 1925
7. *The Times*, 11 Aug 1932
8. HHPS annual report, 1932
9. Letter from Lord Moyne (H&HS archive: A/1048/3/8/9/2)
10. HH&OHPS annual report, 1933
11. A pioneering conservationist, best remembered today as the architect of Portmeirion village in North Wales
12. HH&OHPS annual report, 1936
13. Ibid., 1933. Begun in 1852, *Work* by Ford Madox Brown depicts navvies at work on Hampstead's main drainage.
14. *The Times*, 27 Jul 1933, letter signed by (among others) Clarendon, Le Quesne, [C.T. Le Quesne, KC], Lord Moyne, Maxwell Ayrton, A.K. Butterworth, Gerald du Maurier, Howard Figgis and E.V. Knox.
15. *The Times*, 29 Jul 1933. Sir Reginald Blomfield RA (b.1856), one of the Society's founder members, architect, garden designer and author, built a pair of houses at 51 Frognal in 1886 and lived there until his death in 1942. Amongst his designs were college buildings for Lady Margaret Hall, Oxford, and part of the Quadrant on Regent Street.
16. Report of HBC General Purposes Committee meeting, *The Times*, 28 Jul 1933
17. *The Times*, 5 Aug 1933
18. A new Highgate Preservation Society was being formed in response to similar development threats; Geoffrey Hutchinson was invited to speak at its inaugural meeting in March 1936 (H&HS archive: A/1048/4/1/47/1). Sir Gilbert Upcott, Government Comptroller and Auditor-General, was its first Chairman. In 1966 it amalgamated with the Save Highgate Committee, to become Highgate Society in response to more destructive road proposals
19. HH&OHPS annual report, 1935; *The Times*, 29 Oct 1935
20. Later Sir Charles Bressey, Chief Engineer to the Roads Department, who during WWI was a military road engineer in France and Belgium
21. Bressey Plan: 'Northern outlet – Swiss Cottage and Spaniards Road'
22. Article by C.E.M. Joad in *Hampstead Music and Arts*, Sep 1948, reprinted in H&OHS *Newsletter*, winter 1987- 88. Prof. Joad, Head of Philosophy Dept at Birkbeck College, became famous in the *Brains Trust* on radio and TV; buried in the Additional Burial Ground, Hampstead Parish Church.
23. W.J.H. Broderick OBE (1874-1964), barrister and Metropolitan Police Magistrate, lived in Frognal Gardens; buried in the Additional Burial Ground, Hampstead Parish Church.
24. HH&OHPS annual report, 1953
25. Ikin (1985), p 26
26. www.urbanghostsmedia.com/2016/06/unfinished-north-end-ghost-station-hampstead-heath-war/
27. Dermot Greene, 'Highgate Men's Pond: a short history', *CHR* 33 (2009)
28. Julius Bryant, 'Kenwood's lost chapter: the forgotten story of the National Gallery's management of the Iveagh Bequest, 1928-49', *Apollo*, 159 (1 Mar 2004), pp 40-46
29. Abercrombie was one of the founders of the Council for the Preservation of Rural England (CPRE) and its Hon. Sec; his 1926 pamphlet *The Preservation of Rural England* became CPRE's manifesto.
30. Sir Desmond Heap (1975), *The land and the development, or, turmoil and the torment* (Sweet & Maxwell, Hamlyn lecture series). Heap was President of both the Planning Institute and the Law Society.
31. Further enhanced in 1967 by the introduction of Conservation Areas under the Civic Amenities Act)
32. HH&OHPS annual report, 1951
33. HC Deb 3 May 1944 vol 399 cc1316-7
34. Hampstead Antiquarian Society, Jun 1899
35. *Ham & High*, 21 Mar 1952
36. *The Times*, 12 Nov 1951
37. *Ham & High*, 8 Aug 1952
38. HH&OHPS annual report, 1955
39. Sir Stanley Unwin (1960), *The truth about a publisher* (Allen & Unwin)
40. HH&OHPS annual report, 1957
41. *Ham & High*, 3 Jul 1959
42. Report of Meeting at County Hall, 5 Aug 1959 (H&HS archive: A/1048/4/1/68/1)
43. Wauchope (2010), p 73
44. Ibid., p 42
45. A change suggested by Sir Hugh Casson at the 1968 AGM
46. 'The history of Branch Hill', paper by the author, prepared for the Public Inquiry 1995 (author's archive)
47. *Architects' Journal*, Jun 1979, p 1269
48. John Carswell, 'Memoirs of Branch Hill' (extracts), H&OHS *Newsletter*, vol. 26 nos 1 & 2 (1996)
49. HH&OHPS annual report, 1960
50. Ibid., 1961
51. H&HS archive: A/1048/4/1/94/2
52. HH&OHPS annual report, 1962
53. Wistrich (1972), p 166
54. Harold Wilson was Leader of the Opposition 1970-74, when Edward Heath was Prime Minister.

## Chapter 22

# The Fringes of the Heath – planning battles

Increasingly turbulent years were to follow as one by one the estates surrounding and overlooking the Heath on the Northern Heights came onto the market. Planning threats loomed all around the Heath. Witanhurst; the three hospitals, Athlone House, St Columba's and Manor House Hospital (Inverforth House); the fairground and other sites in the Vale of Health; the Old Court House, Ivy House at Golders Hill, and Mount Tyndal opposite the Spaniards Inn – all were to come under threat. Persuading the local authorities to keep to the special 'Fringes of the Heath' policy became a never-ending struggle. Where campaigners could not stop development on these valuable old estates, they worked hard to keep densities to a minimum. Some were saved by the generosity of local people; others were modified through local campaigning, and several have been the subjects of running battles lasting decades and still going on. In all of them the Society took the lead, and it has been largely successful in preventing massive developments which would have destroyed the rural character of the Heath. In a letter to *The Times* in 1966, Lord Ilford was joined by other eminent names[1] in pointing out that "much of the extraordinarily rural illusion of size in this remarkable area of London depends upon an unbroken band of splendid landscape gardening in which scarcely any buildings obtrude".

The Society had understood early on the importance of preventing high-rise buildings from surrounding the Heath to protect the distant views of London, and preserve the feeling of openness, and until the 1960s there were none in the immediate vicinity of the Heath. But the Royal Free Hospital tower broke the accord. Government departments were then still not obliged to seek planning approval and could override local opinion – as had happened at Heath Brow in 1933. However, the huge public protest did get the originally proposed 18-storey hospital tower reduced to twelve.[2] But in the 1980s, not only was the whole future of the Heath in doubt with the abolition of the GLC, but the planning problems were also multiplying. The Society's annual report of 1982 commented that it was becoming ever clearer that planning policies were too weak to resist the demands from developers: "Official planning briefs have all too often been taken by developers as the borough's initial bid ... rather than the non-negotiable ceiling that [the Society] thought they were".[3]

## Mount Tyndal

The last little bit of Lord Erskine's property, a 1½-acre freehold plot with a frontage on Spaniards Road, probably where his stables had stood, was sold by the Mansfields in the 1920s as part of their disposal of the whole estate (see Ch. 14).

In 1925 a new house of some 15 or 20 rooms, called Mount Tyndal, designed by architect Cyril E. Power, was built for a Mr. C.H. Bland, of Oakhill Avenue.[4] Viscount Knollys lived there briefly from 1938. After the Second World War part of its garden was sold on to create another new residence, The Cottage. When Mount Tyndal came on the market in the 1960s the Society and Hampstead Borough Council urged the LCC to buy the land and add it to the Heath. But this plan was sabotaged by the Ministry of Housing and Local Government which, as with Pitt House, refused to allow the LCC to take a loan for the purpose. Lord Ilford commented: "It would be most unfortunate if the Ministry took this line over every attempt to safeguard sites on the edge of the Heath".[5] A series of redevelopment plans, for blocks of flats and garages, were refused and at a public inquiry the Inspector upheld the policy that no development should be allowed to intrude on the wooded heathland character. But eventually permission was granted to demolish Mount Tyndal and build the present block of flats in 1970.

### Ivy House

Ivy House, next to Golders Hill Park, dates from 1786 when it was built by John Coore (who had also lived at Golders Hill House). In the 1840s Ivy House was the home of C.R. Cockerell (who drew up the plan for the Hampstead Heath Park; see p 84); it became famous as the residence of the ballerina Pavlova, who lived there from 1912 until her death in 1931. Then bought by Manor House Hospital (p 167), the house became caught up in attempts by the hospital trustees to make some money out of developing the garden with blocks of flats. One proposal was for a block of 11 storeys, which "would have wrecked the views from Golders Hill Park".[6] Hendon Council, supported by Middlesex County Council, refused permission and at a public inquiry at which the Society had legal representation, so did the Inspector. Ivy House was then sold in 1962 to the Royal Academy of Music for the New College of Speech and Drama, but with only part of the garden, the hospital still hoping to get permission for residential development. Eventually, the Academy managed to buy the rest of the garden, which has been largely preserved. They sold the property in 1974, and it has continued in educational use, most recently as St Anthony's School for Girls, sister establishment to the boys' school in Arkwright Road.

### A Tower of Babel in the Vale of Health

The Vale of Health village enclave is part of the extraordinary mix of *rus in urbe*, which makes Hampstead so distinctive, occupying an idyllic spot in the middle of Hampstead Heath itself. Its development dates from 1777 after the Hampstead Water Company had drained the marshy ground to enlarge the pond. It was originally known as Hatches Bottom (sometimes spelt Hatchetts), after Samuel Hatch the horse harness maker, who, with the parish poor houses were the first residents. Its rather more fanciful name, the Vale of Health, is recorded from about 1801. But it has suffered a long catalogue of planning assaults and even an attempted appropriation of land from the Heath. In the 1850s Donald Nicoll, who lived in West End Lane – a highly successful tailor with shops in Regent Street and in several other towns – began speculating in property in the Vale of Health. He took advantage of the 1852 Enfranchisement of Copyholds Act, which allowed copyholders to buy their freeholds, to build the Villas on the Heath in 1862. The following year he built the Vale of Health or Suburban Hotel to cater for the multitudes that descended on the Heath at holiday times. It was a most extraordinary building, totally out of scale with its surroundings, and said to accommodate 2,000 people. It was excoriated by William Howitt as this "monster public-house", which "raised its Tower of Babel bulk in that formerly quiet and favourite spot".[7,8] The hotel was still there – minus its tower – in 1958, but was replaced in 1964 by a large block of flats, Spencer House, despite objections and a public inquiry. The Ministry of Housing and the LCC overruled all objections to its excessive density and unsuitable appearance, including those by Hampstead Borough Council.

146. The "Tower of Babel" and the Fairground site in 1914

Nicoll also rented land adjoining the hotel from the Lord of the Manor, to provide an amusement ground with tea gardens, merry-go-rounds, slot machines, swings and roundabouts. It became a source of contention almost immediately and remains so to this day. Nicoll fell out with Sir Thomas Maryon Wilson, who threatened to invoke the law to stop the amusements, and by 1867 the hotel had closed. But the use of the site as a fairground and tea-rooms continued, and in 1926 it was bought by the Grays; they divided the site between various branches of their family – the Grays, the Bonds and the Abbotts.[8] In recent years there has been a series of attempts to develop the sites, despite their designation as Metropolitan Open Land (MOL), all strongly resisted by the Society, joined by the Vale of Health Society after it was founded in 1973.

Camden Council drew up a planning brief in 1980 which, because the two sites were an eyesore, accepted the principle of some limited development of two or at the most three dwellings. But that did not stop a continuing flow of planning applications, particularly for the North Fairground Site including one, in 1984, for a large block of flats, a 150-seat restaurant and a car park for which, astonishingly, officers recommended approval. The Society, together with the Vale of Health Society and the Hampstead Conservation Area Advisory Committee, succeeded in getting the Council to reject this scheme outright and reaffirm its own planning brief. This decision was upheld at a public inquiry and further attempts in the 1990s were also dismissed by both Camden councillors and Planning Inspectors. Recently, attempts to develop the site have resumed, this time seeking to change its present use for a 'certificate of permitted use', which would allow permanent residential structures on the site. The owners had a developer waiting in the wings to buy the site if successful. But unanimous local opposition saw this off yet again and Camden refused to issue a change of use certificate. At the time of writing the results of an appeal application by the developer are awaited.

The South Fairground Site was also subject to regular attempts to develop it. Former Borough Archivist Malcolm Holmes remembers one particularly farcical occasion when he had representatives of the developer, the Vale of Health Society and Camden Planning Department all demanding at the same time to see the same documents; with difficulty he remained even-handed in helping them to access the items. The site was eventually sold in 2017 to a purchaser who has built a house on it without planning permission. The Heath & Hampstead Society offered £50,000 to buy the site, in the hope that it might be added to the Heath, but the offer was rejected. Camden has commenced enforcement proceedings and this matter also is going to appeal. The future of the sites continues to be a source of anxiety.[9]

## Witanhurst

It is a sad irony that, while Sir Arthur Crosfield worked so hard to save the land at Kenwood, it was not possible to save the grounds of his own house. Described as London's largest private residence, with a vast ballroom, a music room and 17 acres of grounds, Witanhurst was built by the Crosfields in 1913 on the site of Parkfield, an early-18th-century house. By the time of Lady Crosfield's death in 1965, the money had run out. Their adopted son, Paul, struggled to maintain the crumbling mansion, but put it up for sale in 1970. Proposals for demolition of the house and replacement by flats and houses aroused huge opposition locally, with hundreds of letters from objectors and a petition containing over 18,000 signatures. This resulted in a successful public campaign to get the house Grade-II* listed.

The Witanhurst Working Group was set up, drawing together the Heath & Old Hampstead Society, Highgate Society, and other local amenity groups, led by Peggy Jay, Lord Ilford and Ronald Bernstein QC (Highgate). Together they fought the development proposals tooth and nail through every twist and turn, during the next twenty years as the property was passed from one developer and mystery foreign owner to the next, in a stream of rejected planning applications, a bank repossession, and three public inquiries.[10]

Having just celebrated the centenary of the 1871 Act that saved the Heath

147. Witanhurst (line drawing from a Society *Newsletter*, 1979)

for the public, Peggy Jay wrote: "Witanhurst seemed an ideal opportunity to mark the occasion in a way which showed that the imaginative spirit of our Victorian predecessors was still alive. However, economics prevailed over imagination, and although the combined efforts of ourselves and the Highgate Society may yet succeed in tempering the worst of the proposals, it is something of a disappointment to have to celebrate the Centenary of the Hampstead Heath Act with the construction of a luxury housing scheme".[11]

Although all attempts to get any land added to the Heath failed, the battle was not entirely in vain and Lord Ilford's "illusion of size" was saved for yet another day. With the aid of lawyers Michael Mann and Kit Ikin, who represented the two Societies *pro bono*, only 24 houses were allowed to be built instead of the 70 originally proposed, and Witanhurst itself was preserved, as were the many fine trees that were threatened by development. Like so many of these Fringes of the Heath battles, the saga is not yet finished, as the house has been up for sale again in recent years.

## Three hospitals

The three large estates bordering the Heath which became hospitals were all transformed yet again in the 1990s. Manor House Hospital was placed into voluntary liquidation in 1998 and closed the next year. The transition of Inverforth House to residential use was relatively uncontentious, with little alteration to the house externally and most of the garden with the Pergola returned to the Heath (see p 172).

## St Columba's – The Elms

But when St Columba's Hospital closed in 1980 it led to nearly twenty years of uncertainty and threat, as the future of this important site on Spaniards Road, formerly The Elms, was thrown back into contention again. It was sold first to the President of the United Arab Emirates and then in 1987 to a private developer.[12]. This coincided with the controversy over the radio mast at Whitestone Pond (see below), and a deal was done behind the scenes which resulted in permission for the addition of a large block of flats in return for the restoration of the old house, which had been listed, a piece of the garden to be given for the radio mast, and another two acres to be added to the Heath. This hugely contentious decision was strongly opposed but government pressure in connection with the re-siting of the radio mast with, apparently, national security implications, overrode all objections. The site was then sold on again with these various permissions, but it was only ten years later, when new owners began preparations to build the new block of flats in 1996, that the enormity of what had been agreed to so many years before was realised: for the first time in over a hundred years, a new development was to be allowed in what was to all intents and purposes the middle of the Heath. Moreover, the new owners now put in applications to increase the size of the new block of flats still further. The Society did everything in its power to get it stopped, and the then Chair of Camden's Planning Committee admitted that the granting of permission was "the worst decision Camden had ever made".[13] But it was to no avail. The only redeeming elements are that, because the land along the Spaniards Road was so much lower than the road itself, owing to all the gravel extraction in the past, the building is not nearly as obtrusive as everyone had feared, and more land was returned to the Heath.

## Athlone House - Caen Wood Towers

An equally worrying battle began in 1997 at nearby Athlone House which dominates the Northern Heights, overlooking the Heath and the Kenwood estate. Built in 1872 on the site of Lord Dufferin's 1830s Dufferin Lodge, Caen Wood Towers, as the building was then called, was designed by the architect Edward Salomons for Edward Brooke, a dye manufacturer. In 1919 it became the home of Robert Waley-Cohen, one of the many public-spirited local residents who had campaigned to save Kenwood. Its tower has been a familiar landmark on the Heath horizon for well over 100 years, glimpsed relatively unobtrusively through the trees. After the Second World War it became an NHS hospital and home for the elderly, but this was closed down in 1997. Again the Heath & Hampstead Society and the Highgate Society came together in a Working Group, strengthened by the Conservation Area Committees, to press for a suitable planning brief. The Athlone House Working Group (AHWG) has closely monitored proposals for the future use of this historic mansion and estate for twenty years, liaising with the City of London to try to ensure the best outcome with minimal impact on Hampstead Heath and Kenwood. After years of discussion and consultation, planning consent was granted in 2007 for three blocks of luxury apartments on the footprint of the old hospital buildings, in return for the renovation of the old mansion as one large house. As part of the deal the AHWG managed to secure a hectare of land to be added to the Heath. The land was no use to the developers because it was the very land that Robert Waley-Cohen had bought with stringent restrictions against building during the negotiations to secure the Kenwood estate in the 1920s (see p 157). But this vindication of Crosfield's strategy has now been compromised by more recent events – see below.

148. Distant view of Caen Wood Towers (Athlone House); photo: Michael Hammerson

However, having built their flats, the developers sold the site on without having kept the bargain to renovate the house. It then passed though various owners, becoming the subject of several public inquiries and legal challenges. One of the new owners applied to demolish the building and replace it with what was described as a mix of "Stalinist palace and Victorian asylum", which would tower over the landscape, degrading the view. The AHWG successfully mounted a legal challenge which went through several rounds of appeals and court hearings, to hold the developers to the original brief that required them to restore the old house. In the summer of 2015 they won a stunning victory when the Planning Inspector and the High Court completely upheld their view.

It was only in the middle of all these proceedings that the secret wartime history of the House was revealed: it had not been a hospital as everyone had been led to believe. What no-one knew was that, in 1942, the house had been requisitioned from Sir Robert Waley-Cohen by the Air Ministry and used as a base for the RAF Intelligence School, part of MI9, operating under the guise of an RAF convalescence hospital. Escape, evasion, and survival skills were taught, and there were also courses for United States airmen. In 1944, the house was hit twice by German V-1 flying-bombs. It continued in use by the RAF until 1948, when it was de-requisitioned. It was acquired by the Ministry of Health only in 1951, and converted into a hospital specialising in geriatric care. All this wartime information was declassified only in 2005. It explained why all attempts in 1997 to find out if there were any covenants attached to its use as a hospital, that might prevent its sale to developers, drew a mysterious and complete blank, as did a visit to the Records Office at Kew; it was all still classified information shrouded in mystery under the Official Secrets Act. This missing piece of local, and British, military history was uncovered by RAF historian, Flight Lieut. Dan Marshall, who contacted the Society, knowing that it was trying to preserve the building.[14] This saga may now perhaps be over: the most recent new owners are presently restoring the house to its original design with the support of the Heath & Hampstead Society and the Highgate Society.

### West Heath

Two other legacies of the 1980s are over-large blocks of flats opposite West Heath, one on West Heath Road replacing Spedan Towers, the home of John Lewis (the store owner); and another dominating Constable's view of Branch Hill, where Tudor (later Hawthorne) House was owned by W.J. Goode, son of the Mayfair shop founder. It is astonishing that with all the sophisticated planning law that has developed since the Society was founded, that nothing could be done to stop these being built.

### The old Toll Gate House, Spaniards Gate

Another prolonged battle took place over the old Toll Gate House at Spaniards Inn, a relic of the 18th-century turnpike trusts. "Not only is the Toll House part of Hampstead history and landscape, but the Heath would be completely cut in two by the Spaniards Road once this safeguard was removed".[15] Hated by the town hall bureaucrats because it holds up the traffic, and disliked by drivers mortified at having to reduce speed on approaching it, it was under some sort of threat throughout the 20th century.

It first appears in the Society's reports in 1922, when the plans to redevelop the Kenwood estate included proposals to demolish the Toll House and take a strip of land from the Kenwood grounds, so as to widen Hampstead Lane, to take the supposed extra traffic. The Society opposed this but with the saving of Kenwood, the proposal was dropped. In 1930, the plan was revived but the Society successfully fought it off at a public inquiry. The authorities were persuaded instead to create a footpath round the back of the building using a strip of land from North Wood.

149. The old Toll House, from a painting by F.I. Naylor, 1955

There was then a period of respite until 1960 when it all began again, this time in the press, with calls to demolish the Toll House and widen the road because it obstructed traffic. The Society swung into action. A letter from a Society member started a correspondence in *The Times*, BBC-TV News interviewed Geoffrey Hutchinson and Committee member Fred Salfeld used his 'Peterborough' column in the *Daily Telegraph* to deplore the suggestion. An added complication was that the Toll House stood across various shifting borough boundaries – first Finchley and Hampstead, and later Camden and Barnet. Sir Colin Anderson maintained a vigorous campaign to preserve it during his chairmanship throughout the 1960s, as patiently and humorously recorded in the Society's annual reports. He takes up the story "in the days of the LCC, which like ourselves wanted the Toll House kept". By 1964 it was a "lorry-scarred relic of quieter days", being allowed to quietly disintegrate. It would "be left isolated as a sort of super-bollard with a highway on each side and the Spaniards Road thus become a race track many drivers would prefer." This, together with suggestions then circulating that Whitestone Pond should be filled in and made a traffic roundabout,  Sir Colin considered "a matter of social values".[16] Various proposals came and went: Wenlock Brewery offered the Toll House to Finchley

242

Council, who wanted to knock it down. The GLC wished to preserve it, while the new Camden Borough Engineer reportedly favoured widening the road.

In 1965 he returned "to this hardy perennial, this precarious survival of quieter days, wiser in the ways of democratic processes but not thereby much encouraged. We have been publicly misrepresented as wishing to preserve the Toll House solely for architectural and antiquarian motives. In fact, we have never pretended that it had any aesthetic distinction. But we have considered it an inherent part of a composition just as important: an attractive, homogenous group of buildings". But it "means much more than that to very many Hampstead residents. It has become a symbol of our battle against traffic and our desire not to have our environment brutally destroyed in the interests of cars and lorries that ought to be diverted elsewhere". [17]

By then nearly everyone concerned had been taken over by someone else: the Wenlock Brewery by Bass, Mitchells & Butler, Finchley by Barnet, Hampstead by Camden and the LCC by the GLC, adding further bureaucratic complications. According to Peggy Jay, the Barnet Town Clerk once wrote to Camden to complain that Camden rainwater was flowing into Barnet from the Toll House gutters!

Nevertheless, the pace quickened "to an almost perceptible crawl". The Toll House had lost its roof and was "gradually crumbling into sad and disillusioned decay". Bass, Mitchells & Butler proposed to transfer it to the Society which was willing to organize its restoration if it could secure possession. The GLC had now decided against demolishing it to widen the road and it remained only for Barnet to agree to this arrangement. But, according to the Society's 70th annual report (1966), that was when "farce rushed in. Barnet suddenly decided to slap a compulsory purchase order on that two-thirds or so .... within their boundary. This extraordinary piece of what appeared to be petulance" involved a Ministry of Transport inquiry. However, victory was in sight: Society members had already contributed £550 towards the £1000 needed to put the Toll House to rights, and work was started.

The following year Sir Colin was able to conclude "the Old Toll House serial story" which "most of our members must know by heart." They "will no doubt be as relieved as the Committee is, that the fifth successive year in which the 18th-century Toll House has been prominent in the annual report is - or should be - the last. The long fight to save this small but vital symbol of civilisation has been won. Restored at the Society's expense, it is now in the care of the Greater London Council". The brewers had contributed £1,000 to the costs and Mekhonick's, the builders, did some of the work *pro bono*. The Civic Trust gave the Society one of its 1967 awards with the citation: "It is significant that people fought for and saved the quality of this area for traffic as well as for aesthetic reasons – preserving a bottleneck in order to slow down traffic".[18] The Toll House was listed Grade II in 1974. Kit Ikin relates how, when restoration began, motorists thought it was being demolished and cheered the workmen!

But the story was not yet over. The abolition of the GLC in 1986 again put its future in doubt and the game of pass-the-parcel started again. It was transferred to the London Residuary Body, but no-one wanted to take it on. Camden and Barnet declared it should go to the City of London for "nil" consideration; but City officers recommended it should go to English Heritage, who had already rejected it. In 1990 Peggy Jay tried without success to get the City to reconsider; one City councillor said he would rather see it knocked down. Eventually it stayed with Camden, gently disintegrating yet again, until in 2007 the Society began another campaign and raised funds to restore it for a second time.

150. The Mayor of Camden unveiling a plaque at the Toll House after its second restoration by the Society. With the Mayor (L to R), members of the Society's Town sub-committee: Robert Linger, Frank Harding and Juliette Sonabend (photo: Nigel Sutton)

The story of the Toll House's vicissitudes, and its final restoration, illustrates well both sides of the Society's work – not always simply objecting to things, but often taking positive action to restore and enhance the townscape that surrounds the Heath, and the Heath itself. In addition to adding land to the Heath, they have raised money for countless small projects: restoring the original chalybeate well, creating bird sanctuaries, and installing signs such as the one describing the view from Parliament Hill. The Society's work to enhance the streets of Hampstead would require another book.

**Notes, Chapter 22**
1. "Esher" (Lionel Brett, 4th Viscount Esher, architect, town planner, 1st Chairman of the Central Council of Civic Societies and President of the Kensington Society), G. Jellicoe and Peter Shepheard; letter to *The Times*, 15 Sep 1966
2. H&OHS *Newsletter*, summer 1971, p 7
3. H&OHS annual report, 1982-83
4. Hampstead Borough Council, drainage records: application for new domestic dwelling, 22 Jun 1925 (microfiche, CLSAC)
5. *Ham & High*, 19 Oct 1962
6. HH&OPS annual report, 1963
7. Howitt (1869), p 94
8. Dick Weindling & Marianne Colloms, 'Donald Nicoll, tailor, speculator and *bon viveur*', *CHR* 36 & 37 (2012 & 2013)
9. H&HS archive: various reports and *Newsletters*
10. Extensively detailed in H&OHS annual reports and *Newsletters*
11. H&OHS annual report, 1972
12. See Chapters 11, 14, 15.
13. *Ham &High*, 22 Nov 1996, p 5
14. Article by the author, H&HS *Newsletter*, vol. 41 no.1 (Jan 2010)
15. HH&OHPS annual report, 1960
16. Ibid., 1964
17. Ibid., 1965
18. Ibid., 1967

Chapter 23

# The constant vigil

When Thomas Barratt published his great history of Hampstead in 1912, he declared: "It is still necessary to keep a watch over this great breathing space. From time to time even now encroachments are attempted, and but for the safeguarding vigilance of the Hampstead Heath Protection Society, the Heath, in spite of its Act of Parliament, would not long be permitted to remain intact."[1] He spoke from first-hand knowledge of attempts by the Heath's supposed guardians to meddle with its boundaries and even to allow building on it. History has proved him right. It was, above all, the setting of any precedent that had to be guarded against. It seems impossible to believe that appropriations of strips of Heath still have to be challenged, even today.

## The Observatory, 1907

One of the first tests was the proposal of the Hampstead Scientific Society (HSS) to build a new observatory on the Heath. In 1898 Philip Vizard, an enthusiastic amateur astronomer (and a member of the Hampstead Heath Protection Society Committee), accepted the gift of a 10-inch reflecting telescope, and the HSS was founded. The London County Council (LCC) was persuaded to allow the telescope to be set up in a building in the swimming pond enclosure on Hampstead Heath, but after ten years the LCC asked for it to be removed. The HSS requested an alternative site for a permanent observatory and was granted a licence to build in the Flagstaff enclosure behind Whitestone Pond.[2] This caused a public outcry. *The Times* weighed in, publishing letters of objection, and both an article and an editorial, all written more in sorrow than anger because, as the paper put it, "apart from this question, we would speak with all respect and sympathy of the Hampstead Scientific Society".[3a] The paper pointed out that the Heath was not vested in the LCC for it to allow any buildings, public or private to be built on it. "If an observatory can be erected on the Heath, why not a school, or the isolation ward of a hospital?" they asked.[3b] A long letter of objection from Barratt accused this small group of "chiefly Hampstead residents" of seeking "this very coveted position for their own private purposes, at the expense of and to the exclusion of the multitude, to whom every inch of the land rightly belongs, and for whom it was acquired".[4] Lord Meath followed up in support, saying that it would set a precedent and "one and all [could] adduce excellent reasons why they also ought to be granted sites for building purposes on the heath".[5]

151. The Observatory; drawing by A.R. Quinton from Barratt's *Annals*, vol. III

In the face of such hostility, the HSS reluctantly surrendered the licence. Fortunately, a far more suitable site was found nearby on the Metropolitan Water Board's new grass-covered reservoir in Lower Terrace. An agreement was signed in 1909. Peace broke out and Barratt made amends by donating 10 guineas to the HSS.

## An exchange of land at Parliament Hill Fields, 1913

Not long after this, another episode confirmed how prescient were the words of Barratt and *The Times*. The LCC lodged a Parliamentary Bill seeking power to dispose of, or exchange, bits of public common land for various reasons. One clause sought to take more than an acre of Heath for tennis courts for a new school in Highgate Road, in exchange for a smaller piece of land adjoining Grove Farm at Parliament Hill Fields.[6] It was justified on the grounds that it was for educational purposes, and that the smaller piece of land was more valuable. The Society's objection, both on a point of principle, and that the land offered in exchange was not even a proper equivalent, was widely supported by MPs, the Commons and Footpaths Preservation Society, the Kyrle Society, and the London Playing Fields Committee. The Deputy Mayor of Hampstead, Alderman Woodward (who lived in Church Row and was also a member of the HHPS) wrote furiously to *The Times*, publicly accusing the LCC of attempting to "filch" land from the Heath. The plans, which clearly showed that the land offered in exchange was smaller, did not accompany the Bill. "I do not care what 'educational purposes' may mean, ... this is a direct attack upon an open space which we all considered had been dedicated to the public for ever. ... We must arrest the wedge before the insertion of its thinnest edge".[7]

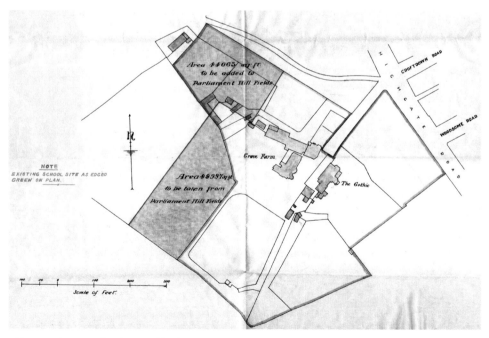

152. Map of proposed exchange of land, 1913

Thomas Barratt linked it to the 1907 events and pointed out that the land being proposed as a substitution was outside the boundaries of the Heath: "... the excuse now being that it is for educational purposes; but neither scientific societies nor educational purposes were contemplated when the public subscribed its money and entrusted it to the Council".[8]

Hampstead MP John Fletcher[9] rejected the LCC's arguments and demanded that the proposals be dropped: "Enthusiasm will be greatly damped and checked" he said "if the public get the idea that the London County Council has the power of snipping off little bits of land here and there". Worse still, the LCC had tried to prevent Hampstead Borough Council's petition to Parliament against the Bill being heard. At one point the debate descended into the minutiae of the flower beds lining the gravel path from Highgate Road: "What are you going to do with the nice set of flower beds ... on the lefthand side? You are going to abolish the greater portion of them".[10] Major Francis Goldsmith, MP for Stowmarket, made the vital point, all too often forgotten, or perhaps not even properly understood by such authorities, even today, that "The county council are not the owners of the land. They are simply the trustees for the public".[10] The MPs voted the clause down and the exchange was stopped.

## The radio mast, 1968-1992

With the development of radio communication it was only a matter of time before someone lighted on the heights of Hampstead Heath as the ideal place to put a mast. The first moves came in the late 1960s when the Greater London Council, as operator of a range of public services (fire, ambulance, and flood warnings), needed to improve its communications networks London-wide. As its 'owner', it saw the Heath as the ideal solution. The H&OHS found itself fighting a rearguard action. They expressed extreme regret that there had to be a mast at all but, given to understand that it was required for essential public services, they took the 'very painful decision' not to oppose it. It was to be 120ft high (40ft higher than the Flagstaff), and Kit Ikin dubbed it a miniature Eiffel Tower.[11] But the Society made clear their unease about the situation, asking in the annual report of 1970: "Can the GLC circumvent the 1871 Act and put the mast wherever it pleases? The Heath is not the proper place for it".[12]

There then ensued several years of negotiations about where it should be put, with the Royal Fine Arts Commission involved in its design. Various sites around Whitestone Pond came under discussion: the tower of Jack Straw's Castle, the covered Reservoir, the grounds of Queen Mary's Nursing Home, Branch Hill Lodge, and, on the Heath itself, the Fern Lodge site, the Flagstaff area (the flagpole to be moved somewhere else), and finally the enclosed triangle of Heath next to Whitestone Pond. These last three would have contravened the 1871 Act and were therefore illegal. Kit Ikin asked the GLC how it was going to get round the Act pointing out that the triangle site is specifically referred to in section 17.[13] The GLC came up with a sleight of hand: invoking the 1967 Greater London

Parks and Open Spaces Act,[14] it claimed that the mast was "reasonably required to serve some purpose related to the Heath": the Heath Ranger would be able to use it in the course of his duties, a trivial justification for a 120-ft mast.

The Society, muzzled by the life and death 'public services' claims, had to content itself with trying to get the least worst option; in particular they wanted to ensure that, whatever site was chosen, it would be shared by everybody so as to avoid a proliferation of other applications and masts  Camden, as the local planning authority, was also in a dilemma, sharing the Society's opposition to some of the proposed sites, and resisting proposals that would damage the Heath. Eventually, the triangle site was chosen and the mast stood there for over 20 years under a sort of compromise whereby it had only temporary planning permission that had to be renewed every few years. The promise that it would be shared by everybody was not kept. The ambulance service did not wish to co-operate and the London Fire and Civil Defence Authority (LFCDA) had another mast in the grounds of Queen Mary's Nursing Home. The Society exerted continuous pressure on GLC to reduce the clutter.

In 1987 it began again, just as the final negotiations to transfer the Heath from the London Residuary Body to the City of London were taking place. The LFCDA, seeing an opportunity to sort out the mast problem once and for all, lodged a Private Bill in Parliament for permission to compulsorily purchase the triangle site and build a replacement mast on it; they did not even discuss it with the LRB. The plans would have completely transformed the area, with an even higher mast, car parking and ancilliary buildings. This attempted expropriation of Heath land was a step too far. Baroness Phillips, who presented the Bill, rather gave the game away from the start, admitting that "without it, the erection of the mast would be unlawful under the provisions of the Hampstead Heath Act". Her snide distortion of the Society's stance – "One asks oneself whether it is more important to have access to vital services or to worry about the effect of a mast overlooking Hampstead residents"[15] – was firmly rebutted by Baroness Birk, who reminded the House that the Heath was not the prerogative of a small or large group of Hampstead residents. It was a London landmark. She also made short shrift of the LFCDA's offer of an equivalent piece of land in exchange for the one to be taken: "I do not have the slightest idea where, when or how the land would be found. Is it suggested that parts of people's gardens around the Heath should be taken? Any other land within the Heath already belongs to the Heath".[15]

Everyone accepted that adequate communications for London's fire service were essential, but felt that the case for it being on Hampstead Heath was not sufficiently made out. Lord Jay went to the heart of the matter: a private act overriding the 1871 Act "would be ... a most dangerous precedent both for the rest of the Heath and other open spaces". Lord Cottesloe condemned the proposal as "vandalism of a public amenity secured for the public in perpetuity by an Act of Parliament of 1871". Lord Birkett made an impassioned plea for the preservation of "one of the glories of the London landscape; ... to propose the compulsory purchase of a piece of public open space in order to erect such an eyesore is, I think, quite beyond the pale".[16]

The Bill was referred to a Select Committee where the LRB put up an extremely strong defence against it, calling many experts to give evidence. Peggy Jay and Kit Ikin were also called and made clear that any appearance of assent by the Society or the local Conservation Area Committee to the proposals was because they were afraid that if they opposed the Bill outright, the Government would step in and impose a mast with no negotiations. The LRB view prevailed: "We regard the Whitestone site as totally inappropriate for a radio installation of any kind. It is far too critical and too important". The Bill was rejected on the preamble.[17] Later, as previously described, the mast was relocated to private land, albeit still on the Heath, as part of the deal done with the developers at St Columba's.

## Vale of Wrath – the road to Manor Cottage

Another notorious case which began in the 1970s was an attempted land grab by a local resident to make a road on the Heath at Manor Cottage in the Vale of Health. It became the subject of an ownership controversy that dragged on for over twenty years. In 1973 the owner of Manor Cottage applied for permission to build five detached houses in his garden, and tried to extend a vehicular right of way across the strip of Heath next to his garden fence to give him access. He was refused permission for the houses by Camden Council, and its decision was upheld at a public inquiry, but for some inexplicable reason he was allowed to continue to use the track he created so long as it remained only gravelled.

Meanwhile, Kit Ikin discovered that the original conveyance of the Heath in 1871 had failed to include this strip of manorial waste next to the Manor Cottage fence, and it apparently still belonged to the Lord of the Manor who was ready to sell to the GLC for a modest sum. Peggy Jay led a deputation to County Hall in 1974 to urge the GLC to purchase the strip from the Maryon Wilson Trust but they refused. She publicly accused the GLC of not fulfilling its trust.[18] To everyone's dismay, the owner began actively to widen the track, cutting a 14-ft swathe across a 50-ft stretch of the Heath in an attempt to establish a right of way. Even a successful action by Camden in the High Court in 1978 did not stop him.

It was not until many years later that it was discovered just how badly the GLC, and the LCC before it, had indeed failed in their trust. The LCC had considered buying the land in 1954 but decided the cost was not justified. Though much more shocking was the revelation that the GLC had in fact registered all the land in that part of the Heath under the new Commons Registration Act in 1965, but then failed to assert its right as the legal owner. Matters came to a head in 1993 after the Heath was transferred to the City of London. The Manor Cottage owner attempted to claim that his right of way was now established after twenty years use, and he put in yet another application to build garages in the garden. It was only then that the Vale of Health Society led by its feisty American Chairwoman, Bobby de Joia, who was also on the H&OHS Committee,[19] made the astonishing discovery of the GLC's forgotten 1965 registration in a thorough search in the Register of Common Land. Instead of asserting its ownership the GLC had corresponded with the Manor Cottage owner over a number of years, sometimes saying it owned the land, and on other occasions suggesting that the Manor Cottage claimant should apply to the Land Registry.[20] The two Societies, with the help of legal advice, succeeded in persuading the City at last to take firm enforcement action. Kit Ikin's involvement was one of his last contributions in the service of the Heath before his death in 1998.

## Cycling on the Heath

In 2001 the cycling lobby began a campaign to get more Heath paths opened up for cycling and to create through routes across it, persuading the City of London to run a special consultation on the matter. The H&HS had a long tradition of opposing cycling on the Heath and believed that it should essentially be for those on foot. As far back as the 1930s the Society championed the pedestrian cause, "a section of the community whose interests are too frequently neglected in these days of the motor-car"; "… the natural and rural conditions which are still to be found on Hampstead Heath must not be impaired by the requirements of traffic, the reconstruction of roads … or in any other way." In 1950 it opposed a new cycle-track on the Heath Extension where "the path there forms a delightful walk for pedestrians".

Several members of the Society's committee, were themselves keen cyclists, including Jeremy Wright, a civil engineer by profession, who carefully researched the issue and co-ordinated the Society's response. "Cycling is green and clean, and we all strongly support it, but not on the Heath", he wrote. It was all too easy to exploit urban green spaces as an alternative for inadequate road provision. "We should not allow the Heath to be used as an easy, cheap substitute for the local highways network". Green spaces are part of the environmental infrastructure in their own right with their own specific purpose; they must not be regarded as subsidiary elements for use by other services.[21]

The Society pointed out to the City in no uncertain terms that the policies in the Heath Management Plan were decided after detailed consultation with expert nature conservation bodies, and wide consultation with the general public. It could not be right to consider changing a policy merely at the behest of one single-issue pressure group. The City's duty should be to take a strategic and objective view; policy must be determined by reference to its remit as the Trustee of the Heath, not as a result of pressure from one group to conduct a separate consultation on a policy for reasons other than its duty to safeguard the Heath under the terms of the 1871 Act. In so doing a dangerous precedent had been set.[22]

The whole exercise raised several legal questions: had the City the power to create cycle tracks if these were to be used as part of the transport system? How would they reconcile statutory requirements on safety and widths of paths, and conversion of existing footways to shared use between cyclists and pedestrians, with its duty to preserve the "natural" Heath? Might it have to compensate Heath users for the land so taken, by adding to the Heath an equal area of contiguous equivalent land? In the event, the Society's carefully reasoned arguments, backed by a wide range of evidence and public support, persuaded the City's Heath Management Committee not to proceed with any new or extended cycle routes.

## A 21st-century squatter

Undoubtedly the most disturbing case in recent times is that of the tramp Harry Hallowes who, notwithstanding all these lessons from history, was allowed in effect to expropriate 7,000 square feet of land at Athlone House that had been intended for the Heath. No-one at the time seemed to be aware that it was the very land bought from Lord Mansfield in 1925 to save it, but rejected by the LCC and bought by the surrounding neighbours to preserve it (see p 157). It only became part of the gardens of Athlone House (then still Caen Wood Towers) to protect it, with stringent covenants specifically to prevent building. It was these covenants that persuaded the developers – Dwyer Investments who had bought Athlone House as a redundant NHS hospital – to cede the land to the City in 2007 to add to the Heath, as a condition of their planning permission to replace hospital buildings in the grounds with new block of flats.

As a letter to the *Camden New Journal* said: Hallowes "was very lucky in his choice of land to squat on as Athlone House was then NHS property and its managers were negligent in failing to evict him";[23] they took little interest in its grounds. Dwyer tried unsuccessfully to evict him in March 2005, but Hallowes went to the courts to challenge his eviction and subsequently obtained a declaration of legal freehold under the rule of adverse possession ("squatters' rights").[24]

Hallowes died in February, 2016. But rather than bequeath the land to be added to the Heath (itself a charity) that he claimed to care so much about, he left it instead to two national homelessness charities. They rejected a generous joint private bid from the Heath & Hampstead Society and the City of London and, claiming compliance with mandatory rules of charity law, put the plot up for public auction where it was sold for £154,000 to a property developer. The train of events, stretching back some ninety years, has culminated in a new threat to a part of the Heath and an effective betrayal of the public-spirited philanthropy of the generation who saved the Kenwood estate. Perhaps the new owner might put an end to this unfortunate situation by generously donating the land to the Heath and have his name added to the illustrious list of its past benefactors.

## Safeguarding the Heath for the future

"It should be emphasised that the battle which Hampstead fought in the 1860s still needs to be fought today. Then it was a question of saving the Heath as a unique open space; today, it is a question of keeping it that way. ... attacks on the Heath continue with great regularity. In the name either of public utility or of private profit, schemes are put forward whose result would be, in one way or another, to diminish the qualities for which the Heath is so celebrated". So wrote Peggy Jay presciently in her Annual Report to the Society in 1973.

In a time when the hard fought for planning system is now being steadily dismantled and the understanding by local authorities of their role as trustees of public assets is diminishing, what will be the future of Hampstead Heath? It is faced with fresh threats in each generation; cherished historic landscapes – and buildings – can be mutilated by careless politicians and planners. Although most of the new skyscrapers rising in the City still form a distant view from the Heath, one other, the Shard, has been allowed to rise in Southwark on the South Bank – with the backing of the then Mayor of London in 2003 – destroying the historic three centuries-old view of St Paul's from Parliament Hill. Another damaging precedent was set in 2015 when the 1871 Act was overridden by the Reservoirs Act 1975 in connection with rebuilding the dams on the Heath Ponds, in order to eliminate a theoretical risk of their sudden collapse in the event of storms of biblical proportions, at the behest of over-zealous health and safety experts. Much of the 1871 Act has, in fact, been overridden by subsequent legislation; these recent episodes demonstrate all too clearly why it is vital that this history must be retold in every generation.

The words of the Preservation Society's longest-serving Chairman, Howard Figgis, are as relevant today as they were when written in the 1930s: "The value of a practically unspoiled tract of country within five minutes of the centre of Charing Cross increases year by year as London becomes more populous and more difficult to escape from, testifying afresh to the wisdom of those who, seventy years ago secured Hampstead Heath as an open space for ever. ... It is thanks to the existence of the Society and to its resistance against every tendency to spoil or formalise

153. The Shard during construction – a 300-year-old view destroyed

the Heath that the open space secured for the public in 1871 has been preserved natural and wild to this day".[25] This wonderful *rus in urbe* must continue to be safeguarded by the people's Constant Vigil.

**Notes, Chapter 23**
1. Barratt (1912), Vol. II, p 211
2. Philip Eden, H&HS *Newsletter*, May 2000; Doug G. Daniels, ibid., Sep 2010
3a. *The Times*, 8 Nov 1907
3b. *The Times*, 18 Oct 1907
4. *The Times*, 19 Oct 1907
5. *The Times*, 29 Oct 1907
6. London County Council (General Powers) Bill, 1913
7. *The Times*, 29 Mar & 4 Jun 1913
8. *The Times*, 5 Jun 1913

9. Sir John Fletcher, elected in 1905, was Hampstead's first local candidate. A wealthy solicitor, and the last occupant of Treherne House in West End Lane, he had been a member of the Hampstead Board of Guardians in 1876 and was later Deputy Chairman of the LCC.
10. HC Deb 2 Jun 1913 vol 53 cc694-717
11. Letter from Kit Ikin, 9 Jan 1970 (H&HS archive: A/1048/3/7/4/7 /1)
12. H&OHS annual report, 1970
13. Letter from Kit Ikin, 1 May 1970 (ref. 11)

14. Ministry of Housing & Local Government, Provisional Order Confirmation (Greater London Parks and Open Spaces) Act 1967, Articles 7(i)(f) & 11
15. HL Deb 24 Mar 1988 vol 495 cc320-38
16. Ibid.; Lord Birkett was former director of the GLC Parks Department
17. Minutes of evidence before the House of Lords Committee, Jun 1988 (H&HS archive: A/1048/3/7/4/1 to -/3)
18. Letter to *The Times*, 2 Apr 1976
19. She went on to set up the Heath Hands volunteers.

20. Paper by Jeremy Wright, Chairman of H&HS Heath Sub-committee, 1998 (author's archive)
21. Jeremy Wright, Michael Welbank, H&HS *Newsletter*, Sep 2002
22. Ibid., Sep 2003
23. *Camden New Journal*, 7 Jun 2007
24. Like the Statute of Merton, its origins go back centuries to an ancient law, the 1275 Statute of Westminster.
25. HH&OHPS, annual reports, 1937 & 1938

# Roll of honour

Heath & Hampstead Society committees and notable members

## CHAIRMEN

| | |
|---|---|
| Ernest Lake | 1897-1916 |
| Howard Figgis | 1917-1944 |
| W.J.H. Brodrick | 1944-1948 |
| Geoffrey Hutchinson | 1948-1953, |
| Oswald Milne | 1953-1959 |
| Sir Colin Anderson | 1959-1967 |
| Peggy Jay | 1967-1989 |
| John Carswell | 1989-1991 |
| Peter Gorb | 1991-1994 |
| Helen Marcus | 1994-1998 |
| Martin Humphery | 1998-2002 |
| Tony Hillier | 2002-2014 |
| Marc Hutchinson | 2014 |

## PRESIDENTS and PATRONS

| | |
|---|---|
| Duke of Westminster | 1897-18 99 |
| E. Brodie Hoare MP | 1897-1902 |
| Earl of Mansfield | 1900-1906 |
| Lord Eversley | 1908-1911, 1920-1927 |
| Sir Robert Hunter | 1911-1913 |
| Sir Colin Anderson | 1974-1980 |
| Lord Cottesloe | 1983-1992 |
| Peggy Jay | 1992-2004 |
| Lord Hoffmann | 2004 |

## NOTABLE MEMBERS  (* indicates committee members)

Sir Colin Anderson*
Sir Ove Arup
Dame Peggy Ashcroft
Maxwell Ayrton*
Sir Leon Bagrit
Peter Barkworth
Dame Henrietta Barnett
Canon Samuel Barnett
Thomas Barratt
Sir Walter Besant*
Sir Arthur Bliss
Sir Reginald Blomfield RA*
Dr J. Bronowski
Rt Hon. Henry Brooke MP
 (later Lord Brooke)*
Sir Bernard and Lady de Bunsen
Sir Alexander Kaye Butterworth*
Lady Byron
Basil Champneys*
Dame Elisabeth Chesterton*
Sir Lawrence Chubb
Sir Kenneth (later Lord) Clarke
Milein Cosman
Jill Craigie
Sir Cornelius Dalton*
Frank Debenham
Robert Dougall*
Gerald du Maurier
Lady du Maurier*
Sir E. Durning-Lawrence MP

Sir Alfred East
Sir Geoffrey Finsberg MP
Valentine Fleming
Michael Foot
John Fremantle (Lord Cottesloe)*
Rt Hon. Earl of Gainsborough
John Galsworthy
Richard Garnett*
Dr William Garnett
Lord Glenconner
Lord Glendyne
Ernö Goldfinger
Hon Rupert Guinness
 (2nd Earl of Iveagh)
Col Walter Guinness
 (Lord Moyne)
Prof. John W. Hales
The Hon. Alan Hare*
Mary Hill*
John Hillaby*
Samuel Hoare MP
 (Viscount Templewood)
Rt Hon. Lord Hobhouse
Sir Julian Huxley
Gerald Isaaman*
Rt Hon. Douglas (Lord) Jay
Viscount Knollys*
E. V. Knox*
Sir J.C. Lamb*
Marghanita Laski

Sir William Lever
 (Lord Leverhulme)
Oswald Lewis MP
5th Earl of Listowel
6th Earl of Mansfield
John Masefield
Tobias Matthay
Prof. Peter Medawar
Yehudi Menuhin
Grand Duke Prince Michael
Oswald Milne*
David Murray ARA
E.S. Nevinson*
J.L. Nevinson
Sir James Peile*
Prof. Sir Nikolaus Pevsner
Sir Ralph Richardson
Frank Salisbury RA
Sir Charles Santley
Norman Shaw
Sir Peter Shepheard*
Kenneth Snowman
Sir John Summerson
Sir Richard Temple
Sir William Hamo Thornycroft
Sir James Thursfield*
Sir Stanley Unwin
Arthur Waugh
Clough Williams-Ellis*
Sir Donald Wolfit

# Bibliography

## PRIMARY SOURCES

### Camden Local Studies & Archives Centre
Hampstead Vestry minute books
Hampstead Borough Council minute books
Greater London Council minute books
Heath & Hampstead Society archive (A/01048)
'The case of Hampstead Heath, by a member of the Metropolitan Board of Works [Thomas Turner]', 1857 (ibid, A/01048/3/2/1/2)
Transcript of court case, Gurney Hoare v Maryon Wilson (ST2/ID/1-14), including copies of parts of Manor
Court Books and Copyholders' minutes (MS and microfilm UTAH 706)
*The Diary of a Heath-Keeper, 1834-39*
Henry Sharpe, Journal (uncatalogued)
Conservation Area Statements

### London Metropolitan Archives
Maryon Wilson family and Hampstead Manor records, catalogued (E/MW/H/) and uncatalogued
Hampstead Manor Court Books A-S (E/MW/H/218-236)
Copyholders' minutes (M/81)
London County Council minutes
Metropolitan Board of Works, minutes of proceedings

### Parliamentary Papers
(www.hansard-archive.parliament. uk/; Proquest website, British Library)
HC Deb: House of Commons debates
HL Deb: House of Lords debates
Select Committee proceedings

### Camden History Society website
Hampstead manorial Court Rolls and Court Books (up to 1743), translated from Latin by Mrs Pauline Sidell DAA, digitised by Dr Peter Woodford and Daniel Croughton

## BOOKS

**Biographies and diaries** (in order of name of subject)
Barbauld, Anna Lætitia – Le Breton, Anna Letitia (1874), *Memoir of Mrs Barbauld: letters and notices of her family and friends, by her great-niece* (G. Bell)
Grosvenor, Hugh Lupus – Huxley, Gervas (1967), *Victorian Duke: the life of the first Duke of Westminster* (Oxford U.P.)
Hill, Octavia – Maurice, Charles Edmund (1913), *Life of Octavia Hill, as told in her letters* (Macmillan)
Hoare, Samuel – Hoare, Sarah & Hannah (daughter and widow, 1825), *Memoirs of Samuel Hoare* (Headley Bros, 1911)
Hoare, Samuel John Gurney, Viscount Templewood (1949), *The unbroken thread* (Collins)
Hunt, Leigh – *The autobiography of Leigh Hunt* (1850, Smith, Elder & Co.); Monkhouse, Cosmo (1893), *Life of Leigh Hunt* (Walter Scott Ltd)
Robinson, Henry Crabb (1860), *Diary, reminiscences, and correspondence* (Macmillan)
Sharpe, Samuel – Clayden, P.W. (1883), *Samuel Sharpe, egyptologist and translator of the Bible* (Kegan Paul & Trench)

**Histories and other books about Hampstead**
Baines F. E. (1890), *Records of the manor, parish and borough of Hampstead* (Whitaker; Hewetson)
Barratt, Thomas J. (1912), *The annals of Hampstead*, 3 vols (A. & C. Black)
Besant, Sir Walter, ed. (1902), *The fascination of London: Hampstead and Marylebone* (A. & C. Black)
Carswell, John (2001), *The saving of Kenwood and the Northern Heights* (Aidan Ellis)
Farmer, Alan (1984), *Hampstead Heath* (Historical Publications)
Hammerson, Michael (2014), *Hampstead Heath from the Thomas Barratt Collection* (Amberley)

Holmes, Malcolm (1995), *Hampstead in old photographs* (Camden Leisure & Community Services)
Howitt, William (1869), *The Northern Heights of London: historical associations of Hampstead, Highgate, Muswell Hill, Hornsey, and Islington* (Longmans)
Ikin, C.W. (1971), *Hampstead Heath centenary* (GLC)
Ikin, C.W. (1985), *Hampstead Heath: how the Heath was saved for the public* (High Hill Press; H&OHS)
Kennedy, J. (1906), *The manor and parish church of Hampstead and its vicars* (S. Mayle)
Jenkins, S. & Ditchburn, J. (1982), *Images of Hampstead* (Ackermann)
Lobley, J. Logan (1889), *Hampstead Hill: its structure, materials and sculpturing* (based on a series of articles appearing in the *Ham & High*)
Monro, F.R.D'O. (1949), *The history of Hampstead Cricket Club* (Home & Van Thal)
Newton, E.E (1910), *Fifty years of progress in Hampstead* (reprinted from the *Ham & High* for private circulation)
Oppé, E.F. (1951), *Hampstead: a London town* (Ham & High)
Park, J.J. (1814, 1818), *The topography and natural history of Hampstead* (Nichols, Son & Bentley)
Potter, George W. (1904), *Hampstead Wells: a short history of their rise and decline* (George Bell & Sons)
Potter, George W. (1907), *Random recollections* (Eyre & Spottiswoode)
Prickett, Frederick (1842), *The history and antiquities of Highgate, Middlesex*
Richardson, John (1986), *Hampstead one thousand* (Historical Publications)
Rowntree, Ruth (2004), *'Religious Devills' of Hampstead: individually respected, collectively reviled* (Oxford: Harris Manchester College)

Soame, John (1734), *Hampstead Wells*

Summerson, Sir John (1962), *The Iveagh Bequest, Kenwood: a short account of its history and architecture* (LCC)

Thompson, F.M.L (1974), *Hampstead: building a borough 1650-1964* (Routledge & Kegan Paul)

*The Victoria History of the County of Middlesex (VCH)*, vol. 9: Hampstead and Paddington parishes (Oxford U.P.; www.british-history.ac.uk/vch/middx)

Wade, Christopher (1989), *Hampstead past* (Historical Publications)

Wade, Christopher (1998), *For the poor of Hampstead for ever* (CHS)

Wade, Christopher (2000), *The Streets of Hampstead* (CHS)

Wauchope, Piers (2010), *Camden: a political history* (Shaw Books)

White, Caroline A. (1900), *Sweet Hampstead and its associations* (Elliot Stock)

### General works

Defoe, Daniel (1724), *A tour thro' the whole island of Great Britain*

Booth, Charles (1886-1903), *Life and labour of the people in London*

Brewer, J.N. (1801-15), *The beauties of England and Wales* (Longman)

Eversley, George Shaw-Lefevre, Baron (1881), *English and Irish land questions: collected essays* (Cassell, Petter, Galpin)

Eversley, George Shaw-Lefevre, Baron (1894), *English commons and forests: the story of the battle for public rights* (Cassell)

Gerarde, John (1597), *The herball, or, Generall historie of plantes* (Norton)

Hoare, Edward (1883), *Some account of the early history and genealogy of the families of Hore and Hoare* (Alfred Russell Smith)

Loudon, John Claudius (1838), *The suburban gardener, and villa companion*

Lysons, Daniel (1795), *The environs of London: an historical account of towns, villages and hamlets within 12 miles of the capital* (Cadell & Davies)

Macky, John (1722), *A journey through England*, 5th ed. (J. Hooke)

Middleton, John (1807), *View of the agriculture of Middlesex* (Board of Agriculture)

Owen, David Edward (1982), *The government of Victorian London, 1855-1889: the Metropolitan Board of Works* (Harvard U.P.)

Patmore, P.G. [Victoire, Count de Soligny, pseud.] (1823), *Letters on England* (H. Colburn & Co.)

Sexby, John James (1898), *Municipal parks, gardens, and open spaces of London* (Elliot Stock)

Seymour, Robert (1735), *Survey of the Cities of London and Westminster* (J. Read)

Smith, John G. (1986), *History of Charlton*, vol. 3

Smith, John Thomas (1797), *Remarks on rural scenery, with twenty etchings of cottages, from nature* (Nathaniel Smith)

Smith, John Thomas (1828), *Nollekens and his times* (H. Colburn)

Sullivan, David (1994), *The Westminster corridor* (Historical Publications)

Sullivan, David (2006), *The Westminster circle* (Historical Publications)

Thorne, James (1876), *Handbook to the environs of London* (Murray)

Vincent, David (1998), *The culture of secrecy: Britain, 1832-1998* (Oxford U.P.)

Wistrich, Enid (1972), *Local government reorganisation: the first years of Camden* (LB of Camden)

### SERIALS

*Camden History Review* passim

*All the Year Round* (Dickens, ed.), vol. XVII, no. 409 (23 Feb 1867)

*Household Words* (Dickens, ed.), vol. IV, no. 79 (27 Sep 1851)

*The Spectator* Archive, online

### Newspapers

*Hampstead & Highgate Express* (CLSAC)

*The Times* Digital Archive, 1785-2013, online

Other papers: British Newspaper Archive, online

### OTHER SOURCES

Hampstead Antiquarian and Historical Society, Transactions 1898 -1905 (Sydney C. Mayle)

Bogart, Dan & Richardson, Gary (2006), 'Parliament, property rights, and public goods in England: 1600 to 1815' (Dept of Economics, Univ. of California-Irvine)

Carter, Paul (1998), 'Enclosure resistance in Middlesex, 1656-1889: a study of common right assertion' (thesis, Middlesex University)

Robinson, Eric, 'Geology in the Vale of Health' (paper, Dept of Geological Sciences, UCL)

Thornton, Neil P. (1988), 'The taming of London's commons' (thesis, Univ. of Adelaide)

# Index

* = illustration
‡ = map or plan
n = note

**A**

Abercrombie, Sir
 Patrick 225, 230
Adams, Annie 112
Adams, Gene 213
Addington, Sir Wm 34
Addison, Joseph 27
Adelaide, Queen 41
Admiral's House
 64, 65, 227
Aiken, Anna Laetitia 65
Ainger, Rev. Thomas 79n
Air Ministry 219-220
Aitchison, George 135
Alcock, Thomas 93, 94
Aldenham 26, 217n
Allen, Lewis 35
Allingham, Mrs 141
allotments 146, 224
Alma-Tadema, Sir
 Lawrence 139, 141
Alvanley, Lord 31
Anderson, Sir Colin
 7, 173, 227*, 228,
 231, 242
Apothecaries' Co. 21
Arbuthnot, John 28
Archway Road 205, 235
Arden, Lord Charles 57
Argyll, Duke of, see Lorne
Arkwright Road 143
Arnold, Christopher 37n
Artists' Rifles 147
Ashcroft, Peggy 200
Ashurst, Sir William 211
Asquith, Herbert 128,
 139, 141
Athlone House (once
 Caen Wood Towers)
 154, 157, 239-241,
 240*, 251; Working
 Group 240
Austin, Edward 122
Auxiliary Air Force 219
Ayrton, Maxwell 169

**B**

Bagshot Sands 15-16
Baines, Frederick E.
 115, 125, 128
Baker, Kenneth 206
Baker, Thomas 27

Balfour, Arthur 154
Bank Holidays 108*,
 109-112, 111*,
 150, 180
Banks, Tony 196, 208
Barbauld, Anna 30,
 65, 122
Barber, Mr 98, 105
Barkworth, Peter 200
Barnes, Thomas 39,
 48n, 60*
Barnet Council 188,
 201, 206, 243, 244
Barnett, Henrietta &
 Samuel 117*, 134,
 142, 144, 160
Barratt, Thomas 7, 41,
 92, 96, 102, 115*, 129,
 137, 138, 144, 219,
 245, 246, 247
Bass, M&B 243
Battery, The 22, 145‡
Bax, Arnold 115, 142
Bax, Ridley 143
beacons 21, 109
Beaumont-Nesbitt, B 213
Beckford, William 211
Bedford, Duke of 128
Beecham, Joseph 143
Beechwood 131n
Bellmoor 115, 166, 219
Belsize 12, 75
Belsize Avenue 140n
Belsize Lane 45, 140n
Belsize Park Gardens 169
Bentham, Jeremy 40
Beresford-Hope, A. 97
Bernal, Ralph 54, 55, 77
Bernstein, Ronald 237
Besant, Sir Walter 11,
 118*, 132, 135, 179
Bevan, David 215
Bickersteth, Rev. E.H. 134
Bill, John 121
birds 182, 183
Birk, Baroness 248
Birkett, Lord 248
Bishops Avenue, The 154
Blackheath 11, 62, 95,
 114, 200
Blackmore, Sir Richard 27
Bland, C.H. 235
Bland, John 37n
Bleak Hall 226
Bliss estate 46
Blomfield, Sir Reginald
 135, 179, 222, 223
Blue House 173
Blunt, Anthony 162

Bodkin, Sir William 22
bogs 185, 188, 191
Bonacina, Leo 169
Bond, Edward 119,
 125, 141, 143
bonfires 109*, 150
Booth, Charles 114,
 139, 187
Bosanquet, Col. 41, 57
botany 20-21
Bowling Green
 House 31, 51‡
Boydell, Josiah 21
Brabazon, Lord (later Earl
 of Meath) 12, 117-118*,
 125, 136, 143, 151, 153,
 179, 245
Branch Hill 59n, 189,
 207, 225-230‡, 241
 House 225, 229, 230
 Lodge 157, 226, 247
 Pond 20
Brandon-Jones, John 226
Bressey, Charles 223, 230
Brett, Lionel 244n
Brewer, Dr William 102
Brian, Havergal 149
brickmaking 49, 119,
 148, 177
British Women's
 Temperance Assoc. 147
Brodrick, W.J.H. 224
Brooke, Edward 239
Brooke, Henry 169, 221
Brougham, Lord 40,
 55, 76
Brown, Ford Madox:
 Work 116*, 222
Browning, Robert 117
Bryant, Julius 162, 214
Buckland caravan 184
Bull & Bush PH 21, 31,
 113, 139, 164, 222, 224
Burdett-Coutts, Baroness
 Angela & William 117,
 125, 126, 127, 128,
 143, 155
Burgh, Rev. Allatson 68
Burgh House 22, 193,
 198, 199
Burke, Edmund 33
Burney, Fanny 33
Burrell, Sir Charles 55
Buss, Frances M. 128
Butterworth, Sir
 Alexander Kaye 221
Buxton, Charles 94, 98
Buxton, Sir Thos F. 37
Byron, Lady Fanny 164

Byron, Lords 34, 40
Byron Cottage 37, 164

**C**

Caen Wood 21, 45,
 57, 121, 182; see
 also Kenwood
Caen Wood Towers
 see Athlone House
Caine, Sir Hall 168
Camden Council 187,
 188, 195, 201, 206,
 207, 228-249 passim
Camden Town 81, 126
Camelford, Lady & Lord
 32-33; Camelford
 Cottage 33‡, 168
Campbell, Lord 76
Campbell, Thomas 39
Campden, Lady E. 22n
Campden Charity 22n
Cannon Hall 98, 169
Cannon Place 154
Carlingford Road 223
Carrington, Lord 139
Carswell, John 6,
 92, 123, 154, 208,
 210*-211, 214, 230
Cathcart, Louisa 45
Cedar Lawn 35,
 166, 167
Central Land Board 225
Chalcots estate 46
Chalybeate Well 30*
Champneys, Basil
 120n, 135
Charlton House 12,
 50, 56, 68, 70, 94,
 95, 96, 99
Chatham. Earl of, see Pitt
Chesterton, Elisabeth
 226, 228
Chevalier, Albert 112
Christ Church 59n, 131
Chubb, Sir Lawrence
 118, 154, 158, 160
Church Row 116, 154*,
 168, 169, 246
City of London
 Corporation 80, 139,
 173, 204-216 passim,
 240, 244, 248-251
 passim; Heath
 Management Plan
 209, 211, 213,
 215, 216, 250
 Parochial Charities
 128, 139, 156
 Royal Field Artillery 147

Civic Trust 136, 196, 200, 243
Civil War 23, 24
Clanricarde, Lord 76
Clapham Common 11, 62
Clarendon, Earl of 171, 222
Clark(e), Frederick James 93, 99, 102, 106
Clarke, Sir Thos 31, 226
Clifton, Lord 56
Clock House, see Fenton House
Cloth Hill 17
Cockerell, C.R. 74*-75, 79n, 84, 85‡, 235
Coleridge, Lord 108
Coleridge, S.T. 39
Collis, Inspector 111
commons 11, 13, 15, 25, 44-45, 62, 108, 126, 249, 250
Commons Preservation Society 11, 94-95, 98, 100, 103, 114, 118, 124, 129, 141, 154, 203-204, 246
Conduit Fields 119
Congreve, William 27
Constable, John 16, 149, 189, 190
Cookson, W.J. Strickland 65, 66, 98, 119, 218
Coore, John 137, 235
copyholders 13, 25, 44, 55-58 passim, 74, 87, 98, 100, 101, 173, 179, 218, 226, 236
Copyholders' Committee 36, 47, 51, 52, 55, 59n, 65, 68, 75
Cottage, The 235
Cottesloe, Lord (John Fremantle) 169*, 198, 201, 203, 204, 248
Council for the Preservation of Rural England 136, 221, 230
County of London Plan 227, 228
Cowper, Henry 92, 94
Cowper, William 98
Crabbe, George 36, 39
Cresswell, Mr Justice 70
Crewe, Lady 32, 33
Crewe Cottage 33‡, 168
cricket 106-108, 119, 164, 182
Cromwell, Richard 64

Crosfield, Arthur 6, 151-160 passim, 151*, 237, 240; plaque 161*
Crown Estate 45, 63
Cruikshank, George 61*
cucking pond 17
Culverhouse, John 119
Curzon, Lord 153
Cutler, Sir Horace 195
cycling 250-251

**D**
dairies 122, 122*
Dalton, Sir Cornelius 135, 163, 179, 181
Dartmouth, Earl of 11, 95, 114
de Brabazon, Sir R. 12
de Joia, Bobby 249
Debenham, Frank 129, 134, 138, 141, 149
Defoe, Daniel 24, 26, 189
Delane, John 60
Denham, Lord 200
Denman, Lord 7, 71
Denning Road 2 24
Devonshire, Duke of 129
Dickens, Charles 37, 43, 72, 74, 75, 81, 86, 117
Dickinson, Marshe 211
Dingley, Charles 137, 171
Dissenters 23-24, 44, 64
Ditchfield, John; courts & copyholds 29, 32, 35, 100, 164
Dobson, Frank 198, 199, 201
donkeys 42*-43, 86, 109-110*
Dougall, Robert 200
Doulton, Frederick 94
Downshire Hill 86, 116, 140n, 180
Drummond, Mrs 73
Du Maurier, George 109, 132; Lady 135, 169
Dufferin Lodge 239
Duffield, John 26
Durning-Lawrence, Sir Edwin 181
Duveen, Edward 174, 220; Joseph 161, 174
Dwyer Investments 251
Dyer, Sir William T. 135

**E**
East Heath 49, 69‡, 90, 102, 113, 119, 148, 171, 180, 189, 193, 221
East Heath Road 20*, 24, 27, 51‡, 140n, 166, 179, 189, 218, 224, 231
East Park 49, 69‡, 71, 73‡, 74, 75, 77, 80, 84, 86, 89, 90, 102, 119, 123, 125, 129, 130, 221
Ebury, Lord see Grosvenor …
Ecclesiastical Commissioners 124
Egmont, Earls of 70, 91n
Eirene Cottage 116
Elgar, Edward 148*-149
Elm Cottage 116
Elms, The (Highgate) 131n, 157 (Spaniards Rd) 161, 174-175, 239
Elton, Lord 203, 204, 207
enclosures 24, 25, 61-62
English Heritage 197, 206, 207, 211-214 passim, 244
Epping Forest 45, 54, 94, 126, 205
Erith, Raymond 171
Erskine, Lord 32, 47, 59n, 100, 123, 125, 173-174, 234
Esher, Lord 244n
Eskhaven 140n
Eton College 13, 46, 63, 102, 142, 143, 144
Evans, Mrs 58
Evelyn, John 60
Evergreen Hill 123, 174
Eversley, Lord, see Shaw-Lefevre
Eyre family 45

**F**
Fairground sites 171, 236-237
fairs 41, 86, 110*-111
Fawkener, William 164
Fellows Road 115
Fenton, James 50
Fenton House 13, 19, 50, 65
Fern Lodge 33‡, 168, 169, 170*, 247

Field family 179, 211
Edwin 64*, 79n, 98, 114, 163
Emily 67n, 134, 137, 143, 182; Henry 64
Rogers 100, 101‡, 105, 135, 137, 138
Walter 132, 218; fountain 144*
Figgis, Howard 33, 163, 166, 168, 170, 171, 211, 223, 224, 252
Figgis, Samuel 137, 138, 141, 164
Finchley Borough Council 143, 159, 243
Finchley Road 43, 45-46, 50, 57, 68, 76, 90, 93, 97, 98, 119, 137
Finchley Society 199
Finsberg, Geoffrey 195, 198, 199, 201, 202, 206, 230
Finsbury Park 82, 84, 93, 103, 115, 116
Firs, The (house) 57
Fisher, Lady 200
Fisher, George 165
Fitzjohn's Avenue 119, 223
Fitzroy Farm 122, 123, 157
Fitzroy Park 66, 115, 116, 154, 157
Flagstaff, The 21, 98, 102, 105, 107, 109, 150, 245, 247
Flask Walk 17, 41
Fleet river 18‡, 19, 122, 187
Fleming, Ian 164, 221
Fleming, Valentine 164
Fletcher, Sir John 247
Foley family 24
Foot, Michael 193-194, 200, 202, 204*
Footpaths Preservation Society 246
Forshaw, J.H. 225
Fox, Charles 33
Fraser, Sir William 94
Fremantle, John, see Cottesloe, Lord
Freshfield, Henry Ray 65, 79n, 103, 211
Friends of Kenwood 196, 212
Frognal 13, 164, 169
Frognal End 118
Frognal Hall 19

**G**

Gaines, Ralph 215
Gainsborough, Earls
of 12, 26, 28
Gainsborough, Thomas
38, 39
Gainsborough Gardens
26, 117, 162n
Games, Wm Langhorn 28
Gangmoor 145, 174, 220
Gardnor House 22
Garnett, William 143
Garrett, V.R. 183
Garvin, James 154
Gasque, Clarence W. 174
Gattaker, Thomas 164
Gay, John 28
geology 14‡, 15-16
George V 152, 161*
Georgian Group 136
Gerard, John 21
Gilberts 53‡
Gilkes, Mr 33
Gillies, Margaret 116
Glendyne, Lord 156,
226, 228, 229
Golders Green 140,
141, 143, 163, 222
Golders Hill Estate 75,
129, 137, 138‡
Golders Hill House 125,
139*, 147, 225, 235
Golders Hill Park 118,
137, 139, 147, 180,
206, 235
Goldfinger, Ernö 221
Goldsmith, Francis 247
Goldring, William 181
Goode, W.J. 241
Goodison, Henry 154;
fountain 161*
Goodwin, Sir R. 232
Gordon, Robert 54, 55
Gospel Oak 119,
123, 146
Grange, The 98
Gray family 236
Greater London Council
172, 173, 175, 187-194
passim, 211, 213, 231,
232, 243, 247, 249,
250; abolition 195-202,
234, 244
Greater London Plan
225, 230
Greengross, Alan 196,
199, 204*
Greening, William 107

Grenville, Lord 32,
33, 36, 44
Grosvenor, Sir Robert
(Lord Ebury) 66*, 77,
80, 81, 88, 103
Grove Farm 246
Guinness, Edward Cecil
see Iveagh, Earl of
Gummer, John 213
Gurney, John 36
Gurney, Louisa 36
Gurney, Sarah 35
Gyll Holt 121
gypsies 193-194

**H**

Haag, Carl 134
Haddo, Lord 222-223
Hale, Warren S. 211
Hales, John W. 124, 128
Hall, Sir Benjamin 77,
80, 83, 103
Hall Oak Farm 45, 49, 83
Hallowes, Harry 251
Ham & High 89, 114,
119, 165, 198
Hampstead Antiquarian
Society 124, 226
Hampstead Bonfire
Club 109
Hampstead Borough
Council 7, 139, 141,
143, 145, 146, 154,
155, 159, 164-170
passim, 179, 181, 187,
198, 220, 221, 222,
226, 227, 228, 235,
247
Hampstead Brook 19
Hampstead Conservation
Area 237, 249
Hampstead Drill Hall 134
Hampstead Fair, see fairs
Hampstead Garden
Suburb 137, 144, 199
Hampstead Grove 20
Hampstead Heath
6-252 passim; see also
specific subjects
Act (1871) 11, 103,
146, 181, 183, 188,
248, 250, 252
Defence Assoc. 107
Extension Committee
124-129 passim, 125‡
Extn Council 143-144
Protection Society, see
Heath & Hampstead

Hampstead Heath
Extension 142‡, 143-
144, 146, 160, 188
'Hampstead Heath Park'
84, 85‡, 235
Hampstead Heath Station
20, 86, 87*, 109
Hampstead Heavies 148
Hampstead Howitzer
Brigade 147, 147*
Hampstead Junction
Railway 123
Hampstead Lane
15, 122, 124, 153,
157, 241
Hampstead Manor
28, 45, 49‡; see also
Wilson family
Hanpstead Manor Court
15, 24, 25, 26, 29, 52
Hampstead Motorway
Action Group 231
Hampstead Museum 22
Hampstead Parish Church
29, 65, 110, 118,
136, 173
Hampstead Ponds
19, 130, 148, 180,
245. 252.
Hampstead Ratepayers'
Association 134
Hampstead Reading
Rooms 64
Hampstead Scientific
Society 245-246
Hampstead Society for
the Protection of
Animals 111
Hampstead Spa, see
Hampstead Wells
Hampstead Tube
140-141, 143
Hampstead Vestry 20,
36, 42, 63, 65, 74,
75, 80, 84, 85, 105,
107, 114, 119, 128,
131, 137, 139, 165
Hampstead Vestry Hall/
Town Hall 115, 128,
166, 201, 223
Hampstead Village
12, 23-24
Hampstead Volunteer
Reserve 149
Hampstead Volunteers
109, 164
Hampstead Water Co.
19-20, 121, 122,
145, 235

Hampstead Way 172
Hampstead Weekly
Express 89
Hampstead Wells
26-29, 31; Wells
Charity/Trust 23n, 24,
26, 28, 29, 36, 96, 136
Harben, Sir Henry
115*, 125, 129, 139,
141, 165
Harding, Frank 244*
Hardy, Irene 198, 199*
Haringey Council
201, 206, 210
Harmsworth, Cecil 154
Harmsworth, Harold (Lord
Rothermere) 138,
143, 164
Harrison, Mr 29
Harrow Lodge 120n
Hart, Alice 138
Hart, Ernest 118, 137
Hatch, Samuel 145, 235
Hatches Bottom 145‡-
146, 165, 235
Hathaway, Charles 98
Haverstock Hill 65, 142
Hawthorne House
37n, 241
Hayward, Sir Isaac 228
Heath, The (house) 98
Heath Action Group
191, 192
Heath & Hampstead
Society (formerly
Hampstead Heath
Protection Society;
Hampstead Heath & Old
Hampstead (Protection)
Society; Heath & Old
Hampstead Society) 5,
7, 11, 64, 66, 130, 134-
252 passim; founding
134-137; Heath Sub-
Committee 181, 185,
189, 190, 192, 216;
centenary 217-218,
217*, 238, 251
Heath Brow 33, 168,
171, 219-220*, 234
Heath Brow Cottage 168
Heath End 29
Heath End House 143
Heath House 35-36,
35*, 37n, 160, 164
Heath Keeper's
Cottage 103*
Heath Lodge 33-34*,
36, 165, 167

Heath Rise 140n
Heath Side 224
Heath Street 27, 43,
  64, 116, 134, 221,
  222. 223, 231
Heathfield 163
Heathlands 32, 33*,
  167, 170, 224
Hemett, Jane 33-34, 165
Hendon Borough Council
  143, 146, 170, 235
Hendon Manor Ho. 171
Henry VIII, King 19
Heseltine, Michael
  197, 230
Hicks, Sir Baptist 12
Highgate Harriers 182
Highgate Lifebuoys 182
Highgate Lit & Sci 152
Highgate Ponds 19, 149,
  130*, 152, 157, 252
Highgate Road 130,
  246, 247
Highgate Society 196,
  199, 207, 213, 237,
  238, 239, 241
Highgate West Hill 22n,
  25, 115
Highgate Wood 122,
  124, 205
highway robbery 44-45
Hiley, J.H. 141
Hill, Emily 116
Hill, Gertrude 116
Hill, Miranda 117
Hill, Octavia 7, 66, 94,
  115-117, 116*, 119,
  126, 130, 132, 136
Hill Garden, The 34, 172
Hill House; The Hill 34,
  35*, 36, 164-167‡, 172
Hillaby, John 184*-185
Hillside 66, 115,
  116, 154
Historic Buildings …
  Commission, see
  English Heritage
Hoare family 35-36,
  43, 65, 74, 179, 211
  E. Brodie 134, 135*,
  141; Hannah 36
  John Gurney 35, 36,
  65*, 75, 79n, 80, 88,
  89, 90, 94, 98, 99,
  100, 102, 105, 114,
  127, 134, 163, 164,
  165; Joseph 79n
  Margaret 135
  Samuel 35-36*, 39,
  68, 94, 164

Samuel jnr 36*, 57, 164
Sir Samuel (later Lord
  Templewood) 36,
  134, 141, 145, 146,
  164, 165
Hobhouse, Lord 135
Hodgson family 174
Hogg, see M'Garel-Hogg
Holford family 47, 65;
  estate 51‡; Charles
  51, 52, 55, 57
Holland, Sydney 135
Holland, Lady 127
Holly Bush Hill 18
Holly Bush Inn 124
Holly Hill 43, 140
Holly Lodge 155
Holmes, Basil 136, 181
Holmes, Malcolm 6,
  192, 206, 237
Holy Trinity Priory
  121, 122
Honeywood family 24
Hornsby family 218
Hornsey Borough Council
  155, 158, 170, 210
horse racing 28, 29
Housman, A.E. 205
Howard, Frank 154,
  158*-159, 160, 166
Howitt, William 115,
  124, 153, 176, 236
Hughes, Thomas 98
Hume, Joseph 62, 66
Hunt, Leigh 39*-40,
  60, 66
Hunter, Robert 7,
  94, 100*, 117, 118,
  124, 127, 136, 143,
  144, 146, 181
Hutchinson, Geoffrey
  (later Lord Ilford)
  168*-169, 170, 171,
  188, 221-228 passim,
  234-238 passim
Huxley, Julian 185

I

Ikin, Kit 6, 175, 188-192
  passim, 189*, 194, 206,
  207, 224, 238, 243,
  247, 249, 250
Ilford, Lord, see
  Hutchinson, Geoffrey
Industrial Orthopaedic
  Society 172, 173
Inverforth, Lord 167, 172
Inverforth House 167, 238

Isaaman, Gerald
  198*, 216
Islington Vestry 82, 98,
  102; Borough Council
  143, 144, 155, 159
Iveagh, Earl of 6, 136,
  141, 143; 160*-161,
  206, 224
Iveagh Bequest 161,
  196, 203, 206
Ivy Bank 142, 143
Ivy House 74, 137,
  172, 188, 235

J

Jack Straw's Castle 21
  28, 31*, 32, 72*, 96,
  105, 140, 145, 148,
  167, 171, 225, 247
James. Edwin 82, 88
Jay, Douglas 232
Jay, Peggy 143,
  172-173*, 188, 190,
  194, 196, 198, 199*,
  201-204 passim, 207,
  213, 214, 216, 217*,
  237, 238, 243, 244,
  249, 251.
Jenkin, Patrick 203, 208
Joad, Cyril E.M. 224
John Street 65
Johnson, Thomas 21
Judges Bench House 226
Judges' Walk 105,
  149*, 226

K

Keats, John 21, 39, 40
Keats Grove 20, 65
Kelly, Mr 56
Kennedy, James 189
Kensington Society 231
Kentish Town Green 123
Kenwood 21, 43, 42,
  45, 50, 57, 118-123
  passim, 123‡, 126, 148,
  151, 160*-161, 174,
  175, 182, 184, 187,
  188, 191, 197, 203-
  208 passim, 211-214,
  216, 224, 237, 240, 241
  Dairy 122*, 188
  House 41, 124, 152*,
  160-161, 162, 196,
  206, 208, 211-214
  Preservation Council
  153, 155-159 passim
  Trees 216; Trust 162
Kilbourne stream 226

Kilmarnock, Lord 203
King, Charles Bean
  155, 158, 159
  offices 154*, 170
King, Dave 191, 192
King Henry's Road 128
King's Meadow 146
Kirk, Thomas 39
Kit-Cat Club 26-27,
  65, 166
Kneller, Sir Godfrey 27
Knight, Charles 98
Knights Templar 12
Knollys, Viscount 163,
  221, 235
Knox, E.V. (Evoe)
  7, 42, 169
Knutsford, Lord 139
Kyrle Society 117,
  118, 124, 129, 246

L

Lake, Ernest 136*,
  137, 141, 163, 179
Lamb, Charles 40
Lamb, Sir J.C. 135
Lane, Rev. Charlton
  97, 105
Lane, Sir Thomas 24,
  26, 211
Langhorn, Sir Wm 12, 28
laundresses 17, 86
Lawrence, P.H. 100
Layfield, Frank 232
Le Breton, Philip Hemery
  65, 66, 80, 85, 93, 94.
  102, 103, 105, 106
Lee, Caroline 199*
Lefevre, Lady C. 127
Lefevre, Shaw
  see Shaw-Lefevre
Leg of Mutton Pond
  19, 176, 180
Lehmann, Beatrix 232
Leighton, Sir Frederick
  117, 129
Leopold, Prince 117
Lessingham, Mrs
  33-34, 100
Lever, William H. (later
  Lord Leverhulme) 34,
  151, 152, 164-167
  passim, 172
Lewes, Charles 116, 125
Lewis, C. Day 232
Lewis, Harvey 97
Lewis, John 241
Liebknecht, Wilhelm 42
Linger, Robert 244*

Linnell, John 47
Linton, Sir James 135
Lister, Isaac Solly 65, 98, 100, 101, 134, 211
Littleworth 29, 32‡, 34, 36, 145, 167, 219, 224
Livingstone, Ken 194, 195, 201
Loaden, William 75, 83, 89, 93
Lobley, Logan 15, 21
Locke, John 27, 94
London Boroughs Association 188
London Cemetery Company 63
London Conduit Act 19
London County Council 61, 112, 116, 130-131, 132-137 passim, 139, 143, 144, 146, 155-169 passim, 172, 175, 177-186 passim, 189, 195, 211, 223-228 passim, 235, 242-247 passim, 251
London Dyeing Co. 86
London Ecology Unit 230
London Fire & Civil Defence Authority 248
London Motorway Action Group 232
London Natural History Society 205, 215
London Playing Fields Committee 246
London Residuary Body 173, 207-210 passim, 244, 248, 249
London Sports Council 200
London Wildlife Trust 200, 205, 230
Lorne, Marquis of 117, 139
Loughborough, Lord, see Wedderburn
Loutherbourg, P.J. de 39
Lover's Walk 106
Lowe, Robert 77-78, 81
Lower Fairground 171
Lower Heath 19
Lower Terrace 246
Loyal Hampstead Association 21
Lutyens, Edwin 223
Lyddon, Mr 58, 68, 70, 94

Lyndhurst Gardens & Road 223

**M**
Macclesfield, Lord 226
M'Garel-Hogg, Sir James 105, 106, 127
MacInnes family 168, 170; Anna Maria 135 General John 79n
MacKean, Muir 156
Mackenzie, Mr 105
Mandelson, Tony 199, 202
Mann, Michael 238
Manning, Cardinal 125
Manor Cottage 249-250
Manor Farm 45, 49, 83
Manor House Hospital 167, 171, 172, 173, 207, 235, 238
Mansell, Gerard 199
Mansfield, Earls of 13 1st Earl 49, 50, 56, 57, 121*-122 3rd Earl 57, 122, 123, 174 4th Earl 71, 87, 89, 90, 94, 119, 123-124, 126, 127, 129, 135-136 5th Earl 41, 143, 151 6th Earl 151, 153-159 passim, 251
Marcus, Helen 217*
Marshall, Dan 241
Marshall, James 98
Marshall Inquiry 195
Marx, Karl 42
Mary, Queen 152, 155, 161*, 166
Marylebone, see St Marylebone
Maryon, Margaret 29
Maryon Wilson family see Wilson family
Masefield, John 149
Matheson, Hugh Mackay 33, 167
Matthews, Bert & Becky 110
Maud, Philip 181-182
Maurice, Charles 116, 117, 124, 125, 128, 129
Maurice, Rev. F.D. 116, 117, 128
Mawson, Thomas 165
May, Phil 112
Meath, Earl of, see

Brabazon, Lord
Medawar, Sir Peter 200
Melbourne, Lord 63
Men's Bathing Pond 130*, 152
Menuhin, Yehudi 232
Metropolitan Board of Works 11, 61, 65, 80-85 passim, 88, 89, 92-108 passim, 114, 125-130 passim, 141, 168, 208
Metropolitan Public Gardens Association 117-118, 136, 137, 139, 141, 143, 146, 148, 151
Metropolitan Railway 140, 180
Metropolitan Water Board 159, 183, 246
Michael, Grand Duke see Romanov …
Middle Heath Road 24, 218‡
Middlesex County Council 139, 144, 146, 154, 159, 170, 210, 235
Middleton, John 44
Midland Railway Co. 97
military activity 21-22, 100, 136-147*, 152*, 164, 224
Mill, John Stuart 94
Millais, Sir John 115, 132
Miller, Jonathan 232
Millfield Farm 19, 121, 122
Millfield Lane 159
Milne, Oswald 169*, 226
Milvain, Thomas 135
Ministry of Health 241
Ministry of Housing 235, 236
Minoprio, F.C. 156
Mixed Bathing Pond 130, 148, 245
Molson, Lord 203
Monro, F.R. D'O. 108
Montagu, Edward 31
Montagu, Lord 207, 209, 213
Montagu Grove 98, 164
Moon, Edward 135
Moore, Henry 232
Moore, Thomas 40
Morgan, Charles 16
Morris, William 117

Mother Huff's PH 123, 174
Motorway Box 195, 196, 231-232
Motte, S. 63
Mount, The 116*, 222
Mount Tyndal 188, 234-235
Moyne, Lord 136, 206, 220
Munyard, Mr 58
Murray, David 134, 141, 176
Murray family, see Mansfield, Earls of
Muswell Hill & Fortis Green Association 199, 205, 207
Myrtle Lodge/Cottage/ Grove 37, 164

**N**
Napoleonic Wars 21, 45
National Gallery 162
National Gardens Scheme 163, 227
National Trust 117, 118, 136, 141, 143, 203, 204, 208, 231
Neave, Sir Thomas 47, 56, 226
Nelson, George 211
Netherhall Gardens 149
Nevinson, E.S. 135
New College of Speech & Drama 235
New End 29
New Georgia 30
New River Company 20, 130, 183
Newbould, Palmer 185
Newton, E.E. 115, 125, 148
NHS 251
Nicoll, Donald 90, 236
Nield, Sir Herbert 154, 155, 158
Nine Elms 123, 174
Nivison, John, see Glendyne, Lord
Noel family 12, 26
Norris, Michael 198, 199*, 206, 208
North End 29, 32, 37, 74, 98, 103*, 105, 137, 164, 167, 171, 180, 222, 225
North End Avenue 164

North End Road 222, 223, 232
North End Station 140, 142, 144, 224
North End Way 32, 164, 171
North Fairground 237
North Road 205
North Wood 122, 124, 242
Northern Heights Footpath Assoc. 164

**O**
Oak Hill Lodge 226
Oak Hill Park 225-228 passim
Oak Hill Way 228
Oak Lodge 102
Oakhill Avenue 235
Oaklands Hall 90
Observatory 245*-246
Oddie, Bill 200
Old Bull & Bush
see Bull & Bush
Old Court House 219
Old Engine House 20*, 108*
Old Wyldes, see Wyldes
Open Spaces Society 11, 220, 230
Oram, William 32, 167
Osborne, Bernal 77
Osmond, Beatrice 154
Ostend 13
Outrage 215*

**P**
Paddington Borough Council 170; Vestry 63, 139
Paddock, The 102, 160, 164-165, 166, 167‡, 170*
Page, Edward 46
Pall Mall Gazette 118, 133
Palmer, George 179
Parke, Baron 70
Parkfield 237
Parkinson, J.C. 79n
Parliament Hill 49, 73, 75, 80, 84, 117, 119, 121-127 passim, 130, 136, 137, 138, 174, 187, 191, 192, 224
view from 244, 252*

Parliament Hill Fields 84, 134, 151, 187, 189, 192, 225, 246‡-247
Parliament Hill Lido 183, 209
Parsons, Samuel 135
Paterson, William 19
Pavlova, Anna 235
Paxon, Mr 57
Pearly King & Queen 110
Pearsall, W.H. 185
Pease, Mr 154
Pedestrians Assoc. 200
Peel, Sir Robert 62
Perceval family 57, 70, 91n; Spencer 32, 55
Pergola, The 172*-173, 207, 239
Petrie, Flinders 154, 220
Phillips, Baroness 248
Pilgrim's Lane 193, 223
Pitt, Peter 194
Pitt, William, the elder 32,, 44, 137, 171
Pitt House (alias Wildwoods) 137, 138, 164, 171*, 222
Platt's Lane 20, 21, 141
pleasure gardens 30-31*
Plowright, Oliver 169
Plummer, Desmond 190
Plymouth, Lord 154
Pollard, John 105
Pollexfen, Sir Henry 31
Pond Street 20, 26, 29, 232
ponds 17, 19‡; see also specific ponds
Pooley, H.F. 125, 154, 163, 181
Pope, Alexander 28
Portland Cemetery Company 62-63
Potter, George Wm 22, 25, 107, 108, 135, 179
Poulter Trust 156
Powell, David 34, 36, 211
Power, Cyril E. 235
Pratt, John 173
Priestley, J.B. 232
Primrose Hill 63, 74, 75, 203, 215
Pryor family 43, 218
Robert 36, 79n
Pryors, The 36, 98, 132, 193, 218*‡

**Q**
Quakers 35-36, 44, 156
Queen Mary's Maternity Home 166, 247, 248
Queen Victoria Rifles 147

**R**
radio mast 188, 189, 239, 247-249
Ratchford, Charlie 228 229
Rawnsley, Canon 143
Red Lion Hill 63
Red Lion Pond 19
Redington Road 143
Reed, William H. 148
Rees, Sir J.D. 147
Regional Hospitals Board 175
Repton, Humphry 137, 214
reservoirs 20, 246, 247
see also ponds
Reynolds, Walter 181
Richardson, John 6
Richardson, Samuel: Clarissa 29-30, 166
Richmond, Sir Wm 135
Riddell, Lady 46
Rigby, Peter 173, 210*, 213, 217*
Ringway One, see Motorway Box
Ripley, Rev. T.H. 52
Ripley, Sydney 191
Ripley, William 52-56 passim, 59n, 88
rivers 17, 18‡, 19, 226
road schemes 189, 221-224, 230-232
Robertson, George 38
Robinson, Eric 22n, 215
Robinson, Hy Crabb 66
Robinson, J.R. 174-175
Robinson, Wm 177-178*
Romanov, Prince Michael (Grand Duke) 151*-154 passim, 182
Romilly, Lord 100-101
Romney's House 221
Rose, Francis 185
Rose, William 94
Rosslyn Hill 116, 223
Rosslyn Hill Band 109
Rosslyn Hill Chapel 63
Rosslyn Park 98
Rothermere, Lord, see Harmsworth, Harold
Rothschilds 129, 143

Rotunda refreshment room 86
Royal Academy of Music 235
Royal Air Force 241
Royal Engineers 147
Royal Fine Arts Commission 247
Royal Free Hospital 234
Royal Horse Artillery 188
Royal Institute of British Architects 136
Royal Life Saving Society 130
Royal Parks 203, 204, 208
Royal Society 154
RSPB 154, 202n
Rumble, Peter 212
Russian Trade Delegation 188

**S**
St Anthony's School 235
St Columba's Hospital 175, 239, 249
St James's Gazette 133
St John's Wood 45, 81
St Marylebone Botough Council 170; Vestry 63, 75, 80, 83, 98, 99, 129, 139
St Pancras Borough Council 143, 144, 155, 157, 159, 170, 179, 181, 187, 225, 228
St Pancras Church Lands 123
St Pancras Vestry 63, 75, 80, 98, 127, 128, 129, 131, 139
Salfeld, Fred 226, 242
Salisbury, William 21
Salomons, Edward 239
sand extraction 16*, 47*, 86*, 97*, 98, 177
Sanderson, John 173
Sandy Heath 142, 188, 189, 224
Sandy Road 224
Sandys, Duncan 196
Santley, Charles 132, 134
SAVE Britain's Heritage 230
Schwabe, Randolph 221
Seedo, Mr 30
Severn, Arthur 135
Severn House 149
Seville, William 35
sewerage 159

Seymour, Ernest 166
Seymour, Robert 31
Shaftesbury, Lord 7, 51, 76
Shakespeare's Head PH 123, 174
Sharpe family 64
  Daniel 64
  Henry 42, 43, 64*, 65, 68, 73,95, 96, 98, 99, 107, 109, 114, 163, 211; William 64
Shaw, Norman 132, 134, 141, 149
Shaw, Roy 228
Shaw-Lefevre, George (later Lord Eversley) 8, 92*, 93, 94, 98, 99, 114, 117, 118, 124-129 passim, 136, 139, 143, 153
Shelley, Percy B. 39, 40
Sheppard, Thomas 56
Sheridan, Richard B. 33
Sherrard, Robert 28, 29
Sinclair, Sir John 63
skating 109
skiing 183-184*
Slaney, Robert 61-62
Smith, John Thomas 38
Smith, Thomas Southwood 66, 115
Smith, Tyson 161
Smith, Walter 138
Snow, Dr John 80
Soame, Dr John 29
Sofer, Ann 199, 204*
Softly, Ray 192, 193, 199*, 207
Soldiers' Allotments 146
Sonabend, Juliette 244*
songs 30, 112*-113
Sotheby, Samuel 33, 168
South End Green 20, 41
South Fairground 237
South Hill Park 75, 84
South Wood 182, 206
Southampton, Lady 122
  Lord 13, 122, 123
  Lodge 131n
Spaniards End 57, 143, 222
Spaniards Gate 241-243, 242*
Spaniards Inn 30, 31*

Spaniards Road 15, 22, 74, 86*, 97*, 123, 130-131, 133 159, 173, 174, 175, 179, 180, 188, 234, 239, 242
Spedan Close 229
Spedan Towers 241
Spencer, Earl 11, 95, 114
Spender, Harold 156
sport 106-107, 182-184
  see also specific sports
Spriggs, Alderman 222
Springett, Kate 199*
squatters 24-25, 32, 157; cottage 25*
Squire's Mount 59n, 64, 67n, 116, 231‡
Stamp, Reginald 185
Stanfield, Clarkson 79n
Steele, Richard 27
Stephens, H.C. 135
Stevens, Sir Jocelyn 216
Stevenson, John 41, 58
Stewart, John 55
Stormont, Lord 45, 122
Strabolgi, Lord 203, 204
Strachey, Lyttonn 162n
Strachey, St Loe 154
Stride, John 47
Stubbs, John 174
Suburban Hotel 236*
Sullivan, David 6, 188-190, 189*, 191, 207
Summerson, John 232
Summit Lodge 37n
swimming 130, 148, 152, 182-183
Swinford, Mrs 33

T

Taylor, Cyril 197
Taylor, Sir Godfrey 207, 208
Taylor, John 53
Telegraph Hill 21*, 75, 80, 84, 113, 119, 139, 146, 226
Temple, Sir Richard 33, 168
Templewood, Viscount see Hoare, Sir Samuel
Tenterden, Lord 57, 71
Thatcher, Margaret 194, 195, 200, 202
Theobald, C. 226
Thompson, F.M.L. 7-8, 79n, 88, 94, 104n, 120n

Thorne, James 106
Thursfield, James 163
Thwaites, Sir John 80*, 98, 99, 102
Tilt, Mrs Jane 17
Times, The 11, 52, 54, 57, 60, 61, 69, 71, 72, 78, 106, 110, 126, 129, 137, 141, 142, 198, 203, 219, 227, 232
Tite, Sir William 102
Toll Gate House 159, 188, 241-244, 242*, 244*
Toller, Edward 65
Toller, Thomas 63, 65, 68, 69, 70, 87, 100, 114
Tordoff, Lord 201
Town (& Country) Planning Acts 218-219, 225
Townroe, Cllr 222
Townsend, John 228
Townsend, Lena 185
Tree, H. Beerbohm 132
tree felling 190, 214-215, 232
tree planting 74, 130-131, 133, 176, 178, 179, 189
Tudor House 37n, 241
Turner, Thomas 65, 80, 83, 84, 85, 88, 93, 105, 114
Turner's Wood 30
Tyburn river 17

U

Unitarians 44, 63-64, 65
University College School 148*
University of London 154
Unwin, Raymond 144, 219, 223
Unwin, Sir Stanley 227
Upcott, Sir Gilbert 223
Upper Bowling Green House 98
Upper Flask Tavern 27*, 30, 31, 166
Upper Heath 22, 65, 86

V

Vale of Health 22, 39, 58, 105, 110, 145-146, 159, 184, 211, 235-237, 249-350

Hotel/PH 188, 236*
Pond 19, 109, 145, 146, 180, 236*
Society 237, 249
Vanbrugh, Sir John 27
Veale, Mr 58
Viaduct, The 72*, 130, 177; view from 177*
Viaduct Pond 178
Victoria, Queen 43
Villas on the Heath 236
Vizard, Philip 245
von Herkomer, H. 132
Vulliamy, George 106

W

Wabe, The 143
Waddilove, Sir J. 174
Wade, Eric 121
Wade, William Thomas 70, 75, 76
Waley-Cohen, Sir Robert 154*, 155, 157, 239, 240, 241
Walford. Cornelius 124
Walpole, Sir Robert 27
Wandsworth Common 11, 45, 54, 62, 136, 140
Ware, Richard 98, 100, 134, 163
Warmington, Eric 185
water supply 17-20, 246, 247
Waterlow, Sir E. 135
Watling Street 12
Webster, Robert 135
Wedderburn, Alexander 31, 32, 226
Wedgwood, Josiah 43
  Frog Service 43*
Weir, Andrew 167, 172
Well Walk 24, 26, 31, 65, 107, 162n
Wells, Sir Spencer 125, 128
Wells Charity, see under Hampstead Wells
Wenlock Brewery 243
Wensleydale, Lord 70
West End Green 96
West Field 185, 191
West Heath 19, 28, 106-118, 103, 177*, 189, 241
West Heath Road 21, 98, 113, 222, 224, 241
West Middlesex Water Company 20

Westbourne 17, 226
Westminster, Duke of
66, 117, 125-129
*passim*, 134, 135*,
136, 139, 151
Westminster Abbey 12
Whinns, The
*see* Paddock
White, Henry 46, 56
White House, The 217n
Whitefield, George 29
Whiteside, James 82
Whitestone Pond 20,
41, 98, 105, 109, 140,
146, 180, 188, 189,
219, 224, 232, 239,
242, 245, 247, 249
Whittingham, Wm 156
Whytebirch 49
Wichells, Abiel 30
Wicks, Arthur 191
Wild Beast Show 179

Wildwood Avenue 105
Wildwoods, *see*
Pitt House
Wilkin, J.B. 134
Wilkinson, John 197
Wilkinson, T.W. 156
Willes, Sir Francis
32, 46, 47
William IV, King 41
triumphal arch for 41*
Williams, Walkyn 112
Williams-Ellis, Clough
135, 162n, 221
Willow Cottages 221
Willow Road 140n,
221, 224
Wilson family 123, 136,
146; Lieutenant 76
Dame Jane 46, 47, 59n
Sir John Maryon *(9th
Bart)* 50, 70, 75, 95,
102, 106, 113, 119

Sir Spencer Maryon-
*(10th Bart)* 102, 119,
125, 126
Sir Thomas Maryon
*(7th Bart)* 12, 46, 96
Sir Thomas Maryon
*(8th Bart)* 6, 7, 11,
12, 32, 45, 46, 49*,
50-58 *passim*, 68-78
*passim*, 81-102 *passim*,
114, 119, 123, 127,
165, 177, 189, 211,
236; Sir Thos Spencer
*(6th Bart)* 12, 46
Wimbledon Common
11, 62, 95, 114, 204
Windmill Hill 13
Windmills 13, 17*
Winfield, C.H. 56
Wistrich, Enid 187, 191
Witanhurst 152,
228, 237-238*

Woodward, Ald. 246
Wordsworth, William 39
World War One
146-150, 152, 153, 155
World War Two 168,
170, 171, 224, 241
Wright, Jeremy 250
Wroth, Sir Thomas 12
Wyldes Farm 47, 71*,
103, 190
Wyndham, William
*see* Grenville, Lord

**Y**
YMCA 147*, 148
Yorke, Sir Joseph 55
Young, Sir George 201

# German Com         s of World War II (1)

## Army

Gordon Williamson · Illustrated by Malcolm McGregor

Series editor Martin Windrow

First published in Great Britain in 2005 by Osprey Publishing
Elms Court, Chapel Way, Botley, Oxford OX2 9LP, United Kingdom
Email: info@ospreypublishing.com

ISBN 1 84176 596 1

CIP Data for this publication is available from the British Library

Editor: Martin Windrow
Design: Alan Hamp
Index by Glyn Sutcliffe
Originated by The Electronic Page Company, Cwmbran UK
Printed in China through World Print Ltd.

05 06 07 08 09   10 9 8 7 6 5 4 3 2 1

FOR A CATALOGUE OF ALL BOOKS PUBLISHED BY
OSPREY MILITARY AND AVIATION PLEASE CONTACT:

NORTH AMERICA
Osprey Direct, 2427 Bond Street, University Park, IL 60466, USA
E-mail: info@ospreydirectusa.com

ALL OTHER REGIONS
Osprey Direct UK, P.O. Box 140, Wellingborough,
Northants, NN8 2FA, UK
E-mail: info@ospreydirect.co.uk

www.ospreypublishing.com

## Artist's Note

I would like to express here my gratitude to the following
individuals and institutions for the generous help I have received
while preparing the illustrations for this book, in the form of
reference material supplied and helpful advice tendered.
My grateful thanks to Brian Davis for allowing me access to his
reference files. Andrew Mollo, Nigel Thomas and Gordon
Williamson supplied reference photographs at critical moments.
The Heeregeschichtliches Museum, Vienna, provided information
on Imperial Austrian medal ribbons. As so often in the past the
Imperial War Museum, London, was a valuable source of both
photographs and wartime German newsreel film. I would like to
record my gratitude to Hi-Speed Photos of West Ealing for their
helpful efficiency, and for finding information for me on the Internet.
Douglas Blann of Landmark Booksellers found and supplied me
with important reference books. Again, my thanks to Ann for her
encouragement at all times.

Readers may care to note that the original paintings from which the
colour plates in this book were prepared are available for private
sale. All reproduction copyright whatsoever is retained by the
Publishers. All enquiries should be addressed to:

Malcolm McGregor,
64 Cavendish Avenue, Ealing, London W13 0JQ, UK

The Publishers regret that they can enter into no correspondence
upon this matter.

## German Army officer ranks
with abbreviations used in this text, and British (US) equivalents

| | |
|---|---|
| Leutnant (Lt) | 2nd Lieutenant |
| Oberleutnant (OLt) | 1st Lieutenant |
| Hauptmann (Hptm) | Captain |
| Major (Maj) | Major |
| Oberstleutnant (ObstLt) | Lieutenant-colonel |
| Oberst (Obst) | Colonel |
| Generalmajor (GenMaj) | Major-general (2-star) |
| Generalleutnant (GenLt) | Lieutenant-general (3-star) |
| General der Infanterie, etc (Gen d.Inf) | General (4-star) |
| Generaloberst (GenObst) | – |
| Generalfeldmarschall (GFM) | Field marshal (5-star) |

OPPOSITE **In 1938 Hitler ensured his grip over the officer corps by promoting the undistinguished but obedient General der Artillerie Wilhelm Keitel to Generaloberst and appointing him Chief-of-Staff of Combined Services at Oberkommando der Wehrmacht (OKW). An unintelligent bureaucrat with no experience of senior command, he was a pliable 'yes-man' for his Führer, who described him as having the brains of a cinema doorman. As the professional head of the armed services he did little to support field commanders plagued by Hitler's unrealistic orders. He also signed without question a wide range of documents, some of which took him to the gallows after the Nuremberg trials.**

# GERMAN COMMANDERS OF WORLD WAR II (1) THE ARMY

## INTRODUCTION

**T**HE NAMES SELECTED for inclusion in this book are purposely diverse. As well as the famous field marshals and army commanders, whose names it would seem perverse to omit, we have included a number of divisional commanders; and also officers of more modest rank whose accomplishments were nonetheless impressive, and who stand as representatives of the mass of combat unit commanders. Their order of arrangement in this book is more or less according to the level of command in which they became most renowned.

The subject of the professional quality – or lack of it – found among the senior German military leadership in World War II could be argued *ad nauseam*. The Wehrmacht's rapid victories in 1939–41, and stubborn defensive fighting in 1944–45, created a conventional wisdom that perhaps tended to over-value the German officer corps without discrimination. Equally, some post-war studies have questioned the 'star

qualities' of many of the most famous German commanders, suggesting that their abilities have been overrated (though it must be said that the same claims have been made, and disputed, in respect of many Allied commanders).

In reality, of course, none of the senior German commanders were superhuman, and all had failings of some sort and to some degree. Many of the most senior commanders were aristocrats, born into families with centuries-long histories of military service. Many of them despised Hitler and the Nazis as gutter demagogues; and yet they acquiesced with many of the Nazi policies when these seemed to be bringing national and military success. The moral code of their class involved a real sense of duty and obligation, particularly since they had sworn a personal oath of allegiance to the head of state by name; the repulsion they felt towards any sign of disloyalty overcame any moral repugnance they may have felt towards the Nazis' behaviour in power.

Some were strictly non-political professional soldiers, whose qualities earned them the loyalty, even the devotion of their officers and men. Erwin Rommel was the best known of these; and Julius Ringel was christened 'Papa' by his troops – a nickname that history proves is only ever given to the most genuinely popular commanders. Some, like Dietl, Model and Schörner, were convinced and dedicated Nazis; yet they were undoubtedly brave and skilful soldiers, who also attracted loyalty, even when – as in the case of Model – they did not flinch from accepting high casualties. Even some of these Nazi 'believers' were among the German generals who earned the grudging respect of their enemies.

Other senior commanders, such as Rundstedt, were generally regarded at the time, even by their enemies, as among the best that Germany possessed; yet in retrospect their achievements seem far less impressive. Despite Rundstedt's personal contempt for Hitler, he was unbending in his adherence to the old Junker code, and was prepared to sit on the 'court of honour' which stripped many officers suspected of complicity in the July 1944 bomb plot of their military rank, in preparation for their torture and execution.

Among the commanders included here are attacking generals like Guderian – known to his men as 'fast Heinz' – who excelled in the energetic and audacious tactics of the Blitzkrieg; and others, like Model – the 'Führer's fireman' – who were supremely able commanders in defensive situations.

It has often been suggested that the German generals were in the main first class commanders, and that their military failures were due to the constant interference by Hitler in decisions that were beyond his competence. While such interference is well documented, it must also be accepted that in some situations Hitler was proved right. There are also examples of senior commanders who had the courage to stand up to Hitler when they believed that his orders were totally wrong, or who simply ignored such orders and did what they felt best. None was ever executed for such rank disobedience; the worst that normally happened was that they were dismissed from their commands, and even then most were later recalled to duty.

It is hoped that the selection of officers in this book will provide the reader with a range of examples covering many of the most significant field commanders, ranging through a variety of character types from the most energetic and innovative to the cautious traditionalists, and from the convinced Nazis to those whom even their enemies considered models of Prussian chivalry.

# ARMY GROUP COMMANDERS

### Generalfeldmarschall Erwin Rommel
### (Plate A2)

Probably Germany's most famous soldier, who gained the devotion of his own troops and the respect of his enemies, Erwin Johannes Eugen Rommel was a Swabian, born at Heidenheim near Ulm in Württemberg on 15 November 1891. The son of a bourgeois schoolteacher, Rommel had no advantages of social rank or military forebears. In 1910 he joined Infanterie Regiment 124 (Württembergisches), and two years later he was commissioned Leutnant from the Danzig military school.

Rommel served throughout World War I with considerable distinction. After being wounded on the Western Front he transferred in October 1915 to the new Württemberg Mountain Battalion, with which he served in the Carpathians and, in 1917, on the Italian front. There he earned the coveted Pour le Mérite for spectacular success in the capture of Monte Matajur during the 12th Battle of the Isonzo (Caporetto) in December 1917. By the end of the war in November 1918 he had risen to the rank of Hauptmann in a staff appointment.

Captain Rommel was retained by the 100,000-man army of the Weimar Republic, the Reichswehr. In 1929 he was posted to the Kriegsschule at Dresden as an infantry instructor, being promoted Major in April 1932. That October he was posted to command Infanterie Regiment 17, remaining with this unit until 1 March 1935, when he was promoted Oberstleutnant and posted to the Kriegsschule at Potsdam. During his time there Rommel published an acclaimed book on infantry tactics, *Infanterie Greift An* ('Infantry Attack'), and in August 1937 he was promoted to the rank of Oberst. Although he never joined the General Staff, Rommel did enjoy the patronage of the Bavarian General List.

Hitler was always on the lookout for talented 'new men' to counter the influence of the old Junker class among the officer corps; and in October 1938, following the annexation of the Sudetenland, he appointed Rommel as temporary commander of the *Führerbegleitbataillon*, his Army personal escort unit, during a visit to the newly seized territory. The following month Rommel was posted to command the Kriegsakademie at Wiener-Neustadt; but in March 1939 he was once again called to command the *Führerbegleitbataillon*, and on 1 June was promoted to Generalmajor. With his choice of commands, he asked for one of the new armoured divisions which were attracting the interest of many ambitious officers; and on 15 February 1940, GenMaj Rommel was given command of 7. Panzer Division for the campaign in the West.

The attack on France and the Low Countries opened on 10 May 1940. As part of XXXIX Panzerkorps, 7. Panzer Division crossed the Meuse and by 21 May had reached Arras. There a British counter-attack briefly unnerved Rommel; he thrust on, however, leading always from the front, often in personal danger and out of contact with his staff – a persistent habit of his. On 26 May Rommel was awarded the Knight's Cross of the Iron Cross; and on 8 June his division reached the coast at Les Petites Dalles. Turning north, 7. Panzer surrounded St Valery, and on 18 June the division reached Cherbourg – on one single day Rommel covered 150 miles. During the campaign 7. Panzer took more than 100,000 prisoners and 300 guns, and captured or destroyed some 450 armoured vehicles.

In January 1941 Rommel was promoted Generalleutnant; and in February he was given command of a German force being sent to assist the Italians in North Africa, where they had been defeated with ease by a much weaker British force. Rommel landed in Tripoli on 14 February;

An informal shot of Erwin Rommel after his elevation to Generalfeldmarschall in June 1942. Here he wears his everyday lightweight tropical uniform, without most of the decorations worn on full dress uniform, but displaying his Knight's Cross with Oakleaves and Swords, and his World War I 'Blue Max' won at Caporetto. Worn above the breast pocket is the blue ribbon of the Italian Bravery Medal in Silver. (Josef Charita)

within days he was in action with his advanced party, successfully engaging British units near El Agheila. A few weeks later he was ordered to return to Berlin, where on 19 March he was invested with the Oakleaves to his Knight's Cross, in retrospective recognition of his achievements in 1940. Before his return to Africa a few days later his troops had captured El Agheila itself. Emboldened by this success, and in defiance of explicit orders not to launch any major attacks, Rommel made a successful surprise assault on positions at Mersa el Brega, and pressed on with a three-pronged advance eastwards, with the intention of seizing the whole of Cyrenaica.

Benghazi and Derna fell to the advancing Afrikakorps, which was soon at the gates of Tobruk; but on 11 April a two-day battle to seize this strategic port ended in failure. A further attack from late April until 2 May also failed to dislodge the British garrison. Rather than delay his advance, Rommel by-passed Tobruk and continued his advance eastwards. On 15 June he fended off a British counter-attack ('Battleaxe') in a battle which saw over 200 outclassed British tanks destroyed for the loss of just 12 of his own. On 1 July 1941, Rommel was promoted to General der Panzertruppe. Running short of supplies, however, he was inevitably forced onto the defensive, and gradually fell back to Mersa el Brega.

This pattern of fast, daring advances and tactical victories, followed by bogging down at the end of long, unsustainable lines of supply across the desert, would become familiar. So too would Rommel's frequent disregard of superior orders; his independence, energy, and talent for sensing and seizing an opportunity, which sometimes led him into failed gambles; and his inability to work smoothly with his Italian allies, of whom his World War I experience had left him with a poor opinion. Rommel was unsophisticated, hard-headed and practical; he made great demands on his staff and troops, but shared every hardship and risk, and inspired their confidence and devoted loyalty.

Another attractive quality was his old-fashioned military chivalry: Rommel would burn Hitler's orders that captured British commandos should be shot, and later in his career would on two occasions demand (in vain) the punishment of SS personnel guilty of atrocities in Italy and France.

On 17 November 1941, the British launched Operation 'Crusader', to punch through the German lines and relieve Tobruk while forces from inside the garrison struck out to attack the Germans from the rear. In the battles that raged over the next few weeks Rommel's forces succeeded in completely disrupting the British attack and inflicting very heavy losses, but by 12 December they were forced back to the Gazala line. Nevertheless, on 20 January 1942, Rommel was decorated with the Swords to his Knight's Cross; and on the 22nd he was promoted Generaloberst. His command was raised to the status of an Armoured Army (though in practice his German units amounted to little more than a reinforced corps).

On 21 January 1942, Rommel made a surprise advance which recaptured the port of Benghazi; his major problems were logistic, as British strength in tanks and aircraft slowly increased, and the Axis failure to eliminate Malta's air and submarine bases continued to expose his own sea supply lanes to interference.

Rommel's renewed attack on the Gazala line on 26 May 1942 cost him heavily in tanks, but he succeeded in out-generalling and out-fighting British 8th Army early in June; on 21 June the South African garrison of Tobruk surrendered. This was the summit of Rommel's achievements; on 22 June Hitler promoted him General-feldmarschall – at 50, the youngest in the German forces. His meteoric rise and the publicity given to him by Goebbels' propaganda machine made him a national hero, but earned him jealous enemies. His contemporaries acknowledged his energy and flair, but several of them regarded him as an adventurer, promoted beyond his natural level as a corps commander.

Despite these laurels, Rommel received only a fraction of the reinforcements and supplies he needed to face the steadily growing 8th Army. He gambled once more on 23 June 1942, capturing Mersa Matruh; but at the end of August his advance into Egypt was solidly blocked at Alam el Halfa by 8th Army's new commander,

This 1944 photo shows Rommel (centre) at a conference with GFM von Rundstedt (right) shortly before the Allied invasion of Normandy. Of interest is the Pilot's Badge with Diamonds worn by Rommel – an honorary award in the gift of Reichsmarschall Göring. (US National Archives)

Gen Bernard Montgomery. The cautious Montgomery maintained his positions on the El Alamein line while systematically building up his forces until they outnumbered the German/Italian army nearly two to one. On 23 October 1942, when Montgomery attacked, Rommel was on sick leave in Germany, and his temporary replacement, Gen Georg Stumme, died of a heart attack the following day. Rommel rushed back to Africa, still not fully recovered; but Montgomery persisted in his assaults despite heavy losses, until the Italian divisions disintegrated and the German armour was ground away. By 3 November, Rommel had only 24 tanks still operational, and Hitler grudgingly gave his approval for a withdrawal.

Hitler's promises of reinforcement proved vain, and Rommel was steadily pushed westwards towards Tunisia. He was ill, exhausted, and handicapped by a divided command structure when, on 4 March 1943, he unwillingly obeyed Hitler's orders for a counter-attack at Medenine. British intelligence were forewarned, and the Germans suffered heavy losses before being forced onto the retreat once again. On 9 March Rommel was summoned home and sent on sick leave; Hitler did not want the German people's favourite field marshal personally associated with the inevitable defeat in Africa, which came on 12 May. On 11 March 1943, Rommel was decorated with the supreme award of the Diamonds to the Knight's Cross.

After a series of largely advisory commands in rear areas, in November 1944 Rommel was named as C-in-C of Army Group B in France, charged with preparing the Atlantic Wall defences against the inevitable Allied invasion attempt. He threw himself into this task; but his control over troop dispositions was strictly limited, and many of his recommendations were turned down. When the Allies finally landed in Normandy on 6 June 1944 he was again absent, having unluckily taken a few days' home leave. Given his inability to deploy the armoured reserves on his own responsibility, it may be argued whether his presence on D-Day would have made much difference. Rommel sought the support of fellow commanders – even such hard-bitten Waffen-SS generals as 'Sepp' Dietrich and Willi Bittrich – in an attempt to reason with Hitler; he was personally convinced that separate peace negotiations with the Western Allies should be attempted. However, Rommel's ability to affect events came to a sudden end on 17 July 1944, when his staff car was strafed by an RAF fighter near Livarot.

Three days later, while he was under treatment for his serious wounds, the bomb attempt on Hitler's life failed. Rommel was on friendly terms with a number of the chief conspirators, and had been sounded out in general terms, but there is no evidence that he was privy to the details of the plot.

Nonetheless, while in hospital after a failed attempt to blow his brains out, Gen von Stulpnagel, one of the ringleaders, was overheard to mutter Rommel's name in his delirium; and a second man may have implicated Rommel under torture.

Hitler had no wish to grant the Allies the propaganda gift of seeing Germany's most famous soldier condemned for treason. Rommel was offered a guarantee of safety for his family if he agreed to take poison, and did so on 7 October 1944. The German people were treated to the spectacle of a state funeral for their greatest hero, 'dead of his wounds'.

# Generalfeldmarschall Erich von Manstein (Plate A1)

While Rommel may have achieved lasting fame, many commentators believe that the most able of all Germany's marshals – combining high intellect with the imagination and decisiveness of a born field commander – was Erich von Manstein. Born Fritz Erich Lewinski on 24 November 1887 in Berlin, he was one of the ten children of a Prussian artillery officer, Gen Eduard von Lewinski; following the death of his parents he was adopted by his uncle Gen Georg von Manstein, whose name he took thereafter. His career as a soldier began in 1906, when he became an Ensign (officer candidate) with the 3rd Foot Guards, in which he was commissioned Leutnant in 1914.

During World War I, Manstein served on both the Western and Russian fronts. Wounded while fighting in the East, he was appointed to the staff of an army group commander; promoted Hauptmann in 1915, he later filled other staff positions for the rest of the war. In the new Reichswehr he served on Gen von Lossberg's staff, and by 1927 had reached the rank of Major. In 1932 he was promoted Oberstleutnant and for a short time commanded a Jäger battalion. Shortly after the Nazis came to power in 1933, Manstein was promoted to Oberst and was subsequently appointed head of the Operations Department on the General Staff of the new Wehrmacht.

A formal portrait of GFM Erich von Manstein. At his throat, below the Knight's Cross, is the Romanian Order of Michael the Brave; in southern Russia he had large Romanian forces under his command. The ribbon in his buttonhole is that of the 1914 Iron Cross 2nd Class.

He was elevated to Generalmajor in 1937, commanding 18. Infanterie Division the next year; and to Generalleutnant by April 1939, becoming Rundstedt's chief-of-staff at Army Group A that August. He excelled in this post during the Polish campaign, and during the preparations for the campaign in the West. Unimpressed by the General Staff's intention to follow the basic plan conceived by Schlieffen in 1914, he contributed his own plans for an attack into France. These involved a powerful armoured force striking through the supposedly impenetrable wooded hills of the Ardennes, and seizing the bridges over the Meuse prior to by-passing the Maginot Line defences and cutting off enemy forces in the north. Hitler was impressed by the audacity of the scheme, and overruled its rejection by the OKH (Oberkommando des Heeres).

Manstein was given command of XXXVIII Armeekorps for the attack in the West; although this was a secondary formation, he handled it extremely well and advanced with impressive speed. Manstein was promoted to General der Infanterie in June 1940 and, on 19 July, was awarded the Knight's Cross for his contribution to the success of the *Westfeldzug*.

In early 1941 Manstein was given command of LVI Panzerkorps on the northern front for the forthcoming invasion of the Soviet Union.

Manstein is seen here during a meeting with Adolf Hitler in March 1943. Manstein's relationship with the Führer grew increasingly stormy, and he ignored Hitler's orders on more than one occasion – a tendency which cost him his appointment in March 1944. (US National Archives)

With the launch of Operation 'Barbarossa' his armoured corps advanced some 200 miles in four days, capturing bridges across the Duna river and coming very close to seizing Leningrad before being ordered to halt and await support. In August his corps was shifted to 16. Armee around Starya Russa, where he got a stalled advance moving again.

In September 1941 Manstein was given command of 11. Armee, part of Rundstedt's Heeresgruppe Süd, and ordered to drive on Rostov with the ultimate aim of capturing the Crimea. Given his weakness in armour this was too ambitious, but by early November he had taken Simferopol and more than 430,000 prisoners. The onset of winter brought massive Soviet counter-attacks, great difficulties, and Manstein's unpopular dismissal of the XLII Korps commander, Gen Graf von Sponeck. Promoted Generaloberst on 1 January 1942, Manstein was forced onto the defensive for four months. On 11 May 1942, he attacked once more, on the Kerch Peninsula; in six days his imaginative plans overcame much stronger defenders for light German casualties. In early June he had a hairsbreadth escape when on reconnaissance in an Italian torpedo boat which was strafed by Russian fighters, killing several members of his immediate staff. A few days later he launched his first attacks on Sevastopol – the strongest fortress in Russia – with an unprecedented five-day barrage. Successive lines of forts were taken, at heavy cost, and the final assaults captured the city on 3 July. In recognition of this brilliant victory Erich von Manstein was elevated to the rank of Generalfeldmarschall dating from 1 July 1942.

He was immediately transferred north once again, and in August took command of the German forces facing Leningrad; but his 11. Armee was weakened, and in September he was forced onto the defensive by Soviet pressure.

On 27 November 1942, Manstein was brought south and given command of the new Heeresgruppe Don; this comprised both the 6. Armee encircled in Stalingrad, and German/Romanian forces of variable quality which were tasked with breaking the siege. Manstein launched his rescue mission on 12 December; by Christmas Eve Gen Hoth's spearhead was within 30 miles of the city when the attempt had to be abandoned, in the face of a new Soviet offensive which smashed through the Italian 8th Army on the Don behind Manstein's left flank. Manstein's subsequent controlled retreat doomed the 200,000 men of 6. Armee, but avoided both the encirclement of Heeresgruppe Don and the cutting off of Kleist's Heeresgruppe A in the Caucasus to the south-east.

Given command of Heeresgruppe Süd in February 1943, Manstein was nearly dismissed by Hitler when he gave up Kharkov, but recaptured it on 15 March – a success swiftly followed by the capture of Belgorod. On 14 March he was decorated with the Oakleaves to the Knight's Cross.

Hitler insisted on a major offensive against the Kursk salient in July 1943, against the judgement of both Manstein and Model, who would command the southern and northern prongs of the attack respectively. Manstein had made the greater progress when Hitler abandoned the costly offensive on 17 July. Manstein's requests both for withdrawals to shorten the front, and a reorganization of the high command in the East (to reduce the malign influence of Hitler and his pliable generals at Oberkommando der Wehrmacht, OKW), put his employment in jeopardy despite his great talents.

Forced during the autumn into a masterly fighting retreat of 250 miles to the west bank of the Dnieper, Manstein concentrated on holding this line during winter 1943/44, while repeating his requests for a rationalized command structure. In February 1944, however, when 60,000 men were cut off in the Cherkassy (Korsun) Pocket, Manstein ignored Hitler's 'stand fast' instructions and ordered a break-out to the west on 16/17 February. On 30 March, after a series of arguments with the field marshal, a furious Hitler dismissed Manstein from his command. Typically of Hitler, on the same day he decorated Manstein with the Swords to his Knight's Cross.

Erich von Manstein retired to his home at Liegnitz, where he remained until January 1945 when the approach of the Red Army obliged him to evacuate his family westwards. Taken prisoner by the British in May 1945, Manstein was transferred to a special POW camp for high-ranking officers in the UK, finally returning to Germany in mid-1948. He died in retirement in Bavaria on 11 June 1973, aged 86.

## Generalfeldmarschall Walter Model (Plate A3)

Born near Magdeburg in 1891, the son of a Lutheran schoolmaster, Model began his military career as a cadet, but only just scraped through his training to gain his commission as a Leutnant in 1910. He saw front line service in World War I with Infanterie Regiment 52, eventually reaching the rank of Hauptmann.

By 1934 he had achieved a regimental command and the rank of Oberst. In 1935 Model was appointed to the Technical Department of the Oberkommando des Heeres. He became a protégé of Propaganda Minister Goebbels; in 1938 he was appointed chief-of-staff of IV Armeekorps, and served in this position during the Polish campaign. In April 1940, just before the offensive in the West, he was appointed chief-of-staff of 16. Armee with the rank of Generalmajor. After the successful conclusion of that campaign he was given command of 3. Panzer Division and promoted Generalleutnant.

Serving under Schweppenburg and Guderian, Model's division performed well during the opening phases of Operation 'Barbarossa'

One of GFM Manstein's greatest achievements was the defence of the Crimea during the crisis of winter 1941/42. In recognition of this campaign a special award was created for participating troops, in the form of a bronzed metal shield to be worn on the upper left sleeve; Manstein himself received a special version in solid gold. As C-in-C of 11. Armee, his signature appeared on the official award document for each shield.

and its commander attracted attention for his aggressive energy. In July 1941 he was awarded the Knight's Cross, and by October he had been promoted to General and given command of XLI Panzerkorps. In early 1942, General der Panzertruppe Model was appointed to command 9. Armee in the central sector of the Eastern Front, at the height of the dangerous Soviet winter counter-offensive. In furious fighting around Rzhev, Model's troops rebuffed at least four major enemy attacks, holding their positions before going over to the offensive and partially destroying the Soviet 29th and 39th Armies. For his part in this campaign Model was promoted Generaloberst and received the Oakleaves to his Knight's Cross on 17 February 1942. This astonishing rise, from colonel to four-star general in just three years, was a tribute to Model's dash in the attack, determination in defence, and talent for improvisation. Although he never hesitated to expend their lives, he was popular with his troops; he often showed himself in the front lines, and was thought to be lucky.

Throughout 1942 and early 1943 the short-handed 9. Armee further distinguished itself in a series of basically defensive battles around Rzhev and Viazma, and the army commander received the Swords to his Knight's Cross on 2 April 1943. In July of that year, Model commanded the forces in the northern pincer of Operation 'Zitadel', intended to nip off the huge Soviet salient around Kursk. Despite having under command five corps (21 divisions, including 900 tanks, plus 730 aircraft), Model argued in vain against this operation. In the event his forces made good early progress, but soon bogged down with heavy losses due to the great depth of the enemy defences. From 13 July to 5 August Model commanded not only 9. Armee but also 2. Panzerarmee.

After 'Zitadel' was abandoned Model, despite high losses in men and equipment, once again showed considerable flair and skill in defence as the inevitable Soviet counter-attacks developed along the central sector of the Eastern Front. In late January 1944 he was appointed to command Heeresgruppe Nord. He was one of the few senior commanders whom Hitler trusted sufficiently to allow him to make tactical withdrawals in order to stabilize his front line, something that Model achieved with considerable success. On 30 March 1944, Model was given command of Heeresgruppen Nordu-

Walter Model often appears grim-faced and solemn in his portraits. Here, in a portrait of him in the rank of Generaloberst after the award of the Oakleaves to his Knight's Cross, he appears to be in an unusually buoyant mood. Despite the monocle he affected in his right eye, Model was no Prussian aristocrat, but from relatively humble origins – one of the 'new men' who owed their rise to Hitler and who repaid him with loyalty. Note the astrakhan facing added to the collar of his regulation general's greatcoat.

kraine and Süd, replacing Manstein, and one day later he was promoted Generalfeldmarschall – at 53, Germany's youngest.

In June 1944 Gen Busch's Heeresgruppe Mitte collapsed under a massive offensive by several Russian armies – Operation 'Bagration'. Model was given the order to 'save whatever can be saved'; still officially in command of Heeresgruppe Nordukraine as well, he was now the most powerful German commander ever to serve on the Eastern Front. He sprang into action, and began to organize the shattered remnants of the army group. It is said that when Model arrived to take command of the situation, and was asked by GenLt Krebs what reinforcements he was bringing, he replied 'Myself!' He built 'scratch' units from stragglers, organized defensive positions, transformed a panicked rabble into a cohesive fighting force once more, and restored supplies of ammunition and equipment. Gradually the German resistance stiffened, and by mid-August 1944 the Red Army had finally been halted – though on the very borders of German territory.

A delighted Hitler declared Model to be 'the saviour of the Eastern Front', and on 17 August awarded him the Diamonds to his Knight's Cross, as one of only 28 recipients of this decoration. That month Model was sent to replace Kluge as commander-in-chief of Heeresgruppe B as well as Commander-in-Chief (Oberbefehlshaber) West, in the hope that the genius of the Eastern Front could help stem the Allied advance in Normandy.

Model was abrasive and unpopular with other officers both as a commander and a subordinate, but his tactical talents were respected; and as a loyal Nazi he was able to stand up to Hitler as very few other generals dared to do. Within three months, however, his troops had been forced out of France; he was subsequently replaced as Oberbefehlshaber West by GFM von Rundstedt, although retaining command of Heeresgruppe B.

LEFT **GFM Model with officers of his staff, in a photo whose autograph is dated 4 February 1945, only a couple of months before he shot himself. He wears the 'Diamonds' – the Oakleaves clasp studded with small diamond chips – and the Swords to his Knight's Cross.**

ABOVE **In this grainy photo Model emerges from a field conference; to his left is SS-Stubaf Heinrich Springer, his orderly officer. Although Springer was a decorated combat veteran, many Army officers were dismayed at Model's appointment of a member of the Waffen-SS to this role. Model rated the major very highly, however, and recommended him for further promotion.**

His mastery of defensive fighting came to the fore again as he withdrew his army group northwards through Belgium and into Holland and stabilized the central front. His troops held the Allies at bay for over 80 days as they attempted to take the Scheldt estuary, and the defeat of the British airborne attack at Arnhem in September owed something to his rapid reactions. In December 1944 he took a major part – despite his misgivings – in the ill-fated Ardennes offensive, where his command included both 5. Panzerarmee (Manteuffel) and 6. Panzerarmee (Dietrich).

Model also argued for a withdrawal east of the Rhine to build up the Siegfried Line defences, but Hitler remained obsessed with holding every yard of ground at whatever cost.

When the Allies crossed the Rhine, Model's 21 remaining divisions, numbering some 325,000 men, became trapped in the Ruhr Pocket in April 1945 by the advance of three US armies, and morale began to collapse. The only possible relief force was diverted towards Berlin in the forlorn hope of saving the capital. Model's attempts to break out both to the north and the south failed, and on 14 April the pocket was split in two when US forces met at Hagen on the Ruhr river. With any hope of saving his command gone, and having no wish to face the consequences of final defeat and capture, Walter Model shot himself in a wood near Duisburg on 21 April 1945.

### Generalfeldmarschall Ferdinand Schörner (Plate B1)

Ferdinand Schörner was born in Munich on 12 June 1892, the son of a police official. In 1911 he served briefly as a volunteer with the Bavarian Army, before commencing studies to become a schoolteacher. With the outbreak of war in 1914 he returned to the military and served as a Leutnant of the reserve. Schörner saw a great deal of combat, both on the Western Front (including Verdun), and with the Bavarian regiment of the Alpine Corps on the Italian front. At Caporetto in October 1917 he led his platoon in attacks on Italian positions on the Kolorat Ridge and Hill 1114, earning the Pour le Mérite decoration. Accepted by the Reichswehr after the Armistice, he later became a convinced supporter of the Nazi regime; by 1937 he had achieved the rank of Oberstleutnant and command of Gebirgsjäger Regiment 98.

Schörner's troops fought well during the Polish campaign, participating in the capture of the Zbolska Heights and the city of Lemberg; and again in the 1940 *Westfeldzug*. In August 1940 Oberst Schörner was promoted Generalmajor and given command of 6. Gebirgs Division. His division distinguished itself in Greece and later on Crete, earning its commander the Knight's Cross on 20 April 1941.

Schörner's division subsequently served on the northern sector of the Russian Front, opposite Murmansk. A promotion to Generalleutnant followed in January 1942 when he was appointed to command XIX Gebirgskorps. In the hard defensive fighting of that winter Schörner's troops held off repeated heavy attacks; he earned a reputation as a forceful and determined commander, driving his men hard, but always right at the front with his troops. Although a ruthless disciplinarian he showed care for the welfare of his men when he could. He was promoted General der Gebirgstruppe on 1 June 1942, to command all German troops on the northern Norwegian front.

Despite his mountain infantry background, in October 1943 Schörner was appointed to command XL Panzerkorps on the Dnieper sector of the central Russian Front. He was soon leading a temporary army of three corps – Gruppe Schörner, or Armeeabteilung Nikopol – holding a 75-mile front against heavy odds. He once again showed himself extremely able in defensive actions, rebuffing several major Soviet attacks. When in January/February 1944 positions flanking Schörner's command were overrun, he conducted a skilful fighting withdrawal from the so-called Nikopol Pocket bridgehead on the east bank of the Dnieper, saving most of his men – an example of outstanding generalship which earned him the admiration of his troops and, on 17 February 1944, the Oakleaves to his Knight's Cross. He was also appointed head of the National Socialist Political Guidance Corps, a group broadly analogous to the political commissars of the Soviet regime.

Two weeks later Schörner was promoted Generaloberst, with command of Heeresgruppe Süd Ukraine in succession to Kleist. In April 1944 he flew to Germany to argue in vain against Hitler's order to hold the Crimea. When further defence became impossible in May, Hitler agreed to his repeated request for an evacuation, but too late to save most of the troops involved.

Schörner was appointed on 24 July 1944 to command Heeresgruppe Nord. Hard pressed in the Baltic states, he eventually ignored 'stand fast' orders from Führer Headquarters and withdrew his armies from hopeless positions north of Riga, where they were under threat of being swamped fully by 20 Soviet corps. Despite his disobedience he was decorated with the Swords to his Knight's Cross on 28 August 1944.

Ultimately, his 16. and 18. Armee were cut off on land after withdrawing into Kurland. Hitler refused to countenance a general evacuation by sea, and this time Schörner did not demur: although their position was all but hopeless, these troops were tying down over 100 enemy divisions that would otherwise be free to turn south against the German armies battling desperately on the central front.

On 1 January 1945, Schörner was decorated with the Diamonds to his Knight's Cross, and took command of Heeresgruppe A (1. & 4. Panzerarmee, 9. & 17. Armee), holding a line from north of Warsaw in Poland down to the Czechoslovakian Carpathians. Driven back to the Oder river line by late January, his command was retitled Heeresgruppe Mitte; it had the battered remnants of 24 divisions, to hold a 300-mile front. Despite a masterly defence that blunted the next Soviet offensive and inflicted huge losses, Schörner could not prevent the loss of Upper Silesia by the end of March. On 3 April 1945, he was promoted Generalfeldmarschall, the last German soldier ever to reach that

Gen Ferdinand Schörner, in a typically unsmiling portrait. Although Schörner developed a reputation as a stern disciplinarian, he did show care for the welfare of his men; he was more likely to behave harshly towards rear echelon elements, often sending divisional or corps staff who earned his displeasure for a spell in the front line. He was even known to refuse or ignore orders that he felt would cause unnecessarily high levels of casualties. (Josef Charita)

rank. In late April he inflicted another setback on Soviet forces advancing south of Berlin. Before Hitler committed suicide he appointed Schörner his successor as Commander-in-Chief of the Army (Oberbefehlshaber des Heeres), a reflection of his continuing trust.

Schörner flew from the Eastern Front to the Tyrol in May 1945, and surrendered himself to US troops – an act which brought him lasting unpopularity among many Eastern Front soldiers. He was handed over to the Soviets, who sentenced him to 25 years for war crimes. Nevertheless, he was released in 1955 – and on his return to Germany was re-arrested, for the murder of German soldiers who had been executed on his orders during the closing days of the war. A court in Munich found him guilty of manslaughter in 1957, and he served another four and a half years in prison. Schörner lived in relative obscurity after his release, and died of a heart attack in Munich on 6 July 1973.

**Schörner pictured in the field, somewhere on the Eastern Front in winter. His Knight's Cross with Oakleaves and Swords is clearly visible at his throat, dating the picture to after August 1944. Of interest are the tinted spectacles worn in place of his normal glasses, presumably to protect against the glare from snow. (Josef Charita)**

### Generalfeldmarschall Gerd von Rundstedt (Plate B2)

Karl Rudolf Gerd von Rundstedt was born at Aschersleben, near Halle, on 12 December 1875, the son of a major-general of aristocratic Prussian stock. In March 1892 he joined the army as an Ensign with Infanterie Regiment 83, gaining his commission as Leutnant with Infanterie Regiment 121 on 17 June 1893. He was promoted Oberleutnant in 1902, and Hauptmann in March 1907.

On the outbreak of World War I, Rundstedt was posted as operations officer with 22. Reserve Infanterie Division. Between November 1914 and spring 1915, Major von Rundstedt served on the staff of the military governor of occupied Belgium. In the summer of 1916 he was posted as a chief-of-staff in Armeegruppe Grossherzog Karl, a joint Austro-Hungarian/German formation on the Eastern Front. In the second half of 1917 he became chief-of-staff first of LIII Armeekorps in the East, then of XV Armeekorps on the Western Front; he ended the war as a highly experienced and well-regarded staff officer.

After the war Rundstedt was appointed chief-of-staff to 3. Kavallerie Division; he rose steadily in the small post-war army, and in February 1923 was given command of Infanterie Regiment 18 in the rank of Oberst – a command in which he took part in the ruthless suppression of left-wing uprisings in Thuringia. Promotion to Generalmajor and chief-of-staff of Military District (Wehrkreis) II at Stettin followed in November 1927. As a protégé of GenLt von Schleicher (who was briefly Chancellor of Germany), by March 1929 Rundstedt had been appointed commander of 2. Kavallerie Division and promoted Generalleutnant. In January 1932, Rundstedt was appointed to the important command of Military District III based in Berlin, and that October he was promoted

A formal portrait of GFM Gerd von Rundstedt, in the regulation greatcoat with the scarlet lapel facings of a general officer. Despite his lofty rank, Rundstedt preferred to wear the collar patches and shoulder straps of an infantry officer, an entitlement derived from his position as colonel-in-chief of Infanterie Regiment 18.

General der Infanterie with command of 1. Armeegruppe – effectively giving him control of almost half of the entire army.

As a typical member of the traditional Junker class he was disdainful of the Nazis who took power in 1933; but he took full advantage of their rearmament programmes to build the new Wehrmacht and equip it for mobile warfare. He was promoted Generaloberst in March 1938, becoming the second most senior officer in the Army. Disgusted with the Nazis' political interference with the senior ranks of the Army (which extended to false criminal charges against, and even assassination of, generals who resisted them), in October 1938 GenObst von Rundstedt resigned, a couple of months before his 63rd birthday.

With the approach of war, Rundstedt – one of the Wehrmacht's most experienced and respected officers – was recalled from retirement on 1 June 1939. He was given command of Heeresgruppe Süd – three armies, over half a million strong – for the attack on Poland. (From then on, throughout his active career, Rundstedt always held the title of 'Oberbefehlshaber' or Commander-in-Chief of various army groups, or indeed entire fronts.) His part in the Polish campaign of September

A later photograph of Rundstedt taken some time after February 1945, displaying the Oakleaves with Swords to his Knight's Cross; again, note the characteristic uniform as *Chef* of Inf Regt 18. He was furious that the obviously doomed Ardennes offensive of December 1944 was associated with his name, when his powers to influence its planning, as 'Commander-in-Chief West', were purely nominal. Rundstedt yielded to nobody in his contempt for Hitler, as a man and as a military strategist; nevertheless, throughout the war this doyen of the German professional officer corps did nothing to resist or remove the Führer. (Josef Charita)

1939 was almost flawlessly conducted, and Rundstedt was decorated with the Knight's Cross on 30 September. He was also appointed as Oberbefehlshaber Ost, effectively in command of all German forces in Poland. His outspoken condemnation of the behaviour of SS and other security units in occupied Poland resulted in his being removed from this post and reassigned to the West. There he was given command of Heeresgruppe A, on the south central sector of the front, for the attack on France and the Low Countries – his greatest campaign.

In this command Rundstedt enthusiastically backed the plan devised by his chief-of-staff, Manstein, for a thrust through the Ardennes to Sedan to unhinge the French defence. The stubborn promotion of this plan eventually secured Hitler's support, and Gen von Bock's forces for a northern thrust by Heeresgruppe B were greatly reduced to Rundstedt's benefit. Given control of 44 divisions, including Gen

Guderian's armoured corps, in May 1940 Rundstedt was able to put Manstein's plan into practice with stunning success. His brief pause to consolidate in the last week of May, specifically endorsed by Hitler, would later cause controversy for contributing to the escape from Dunkirk of the British Expeditionary Corps.

Following the successful conclusion of the campaign, on 19 July 1940 Rundstedt was promoted Generalfeldmarschall. Subsequently he took command of the occupation forces in France, and would have been responsible for the invasion of Britain if it had been ordered (though he never believed in 'this Sealion rubbish').

For Operation 'Barbarossa' in June 1941, Rundstedt was appointed to command Heeresgruppe Süd: three armies (6., 11. & 17.) plus Kleist's Panzergruppe and allied formations, totalling nearly 60 divisions – though weakened by the distraction of the Balkan campaign in the spring. Rundstedt's front was between the Pripet Marshes and the Carpathians, his objectives the Dnieper crossings, Kiev and Kharkov. His troops made relatively slow progress at first, but Kleist's tanks were reinforced with Guderian's Panzergruppe in August; after a huge battle of encirclement on the lower Dnieper, which cost the Red Army some 665,000 prisoners alone, Kiev fell to 6. Armee on 19 September. Rundstedt's armies were ordered to sweep on across the Ukraine, past Kharkov and then on towards the Crimea and Rostov on the River Don. Rundstedt advised consolidation of the front with the onset of winter, but Hitler was both fixated on the strategic importance of the Crimea and Russia's distant southern oilfields, and determined that his northern armies should capture Moscow. Despite suffering a heart attack in early November, Rundstedt succeeded in taking Rostov, but was soon thrown out again by a Soviet counter-attack. Hitler was enraged when his field marshal demanded permission to carry out a tactical withdrawal of 60 miles to the River Mius, and dismissed Rundstedt from his command on 1 December 1941. (His successor, GFM von Reichenau, soon had to withdraw to the Mius in his turn.)

Just over three months later, however, GFM Rundstedt was recalled to duty once again and given command of occupation forces in France as Oberbefehlshaber West. This was a quiet backwater command, and Rundstedt was content to take a passive role, watching events unfold with an attitude of sardonic detachment. Although he rejected all approaches from the 'bomb plotters', he had no illusions about the ultimate outcome of the war under the national leadership of 'the Bohemian corporal'. Despite his title he had very little control over the deployment of forces; in any case, he judged the Pas de Calais the most likely invasion site, and favoured holding the Panzer reserves back from the coast – both mistaken judgements.

When the invasion came and the Allies secured their beachhead in Normandy, in mid-June 1944 Rundstedt advocated abandoning France south of the Loire and moving all forces north for a battle of manoeuvre. Hitler naturally rejected this idea; and when, after the failure of the counter-attack at Caen on 1 July, GFM Keitel at OKW moaned over the telephone 'What shall we do?', the 69-year-old field marshal replied, 'Make peace, you fools.' The enraged Hitler dismissed him once again the next day, though Rundstedt was nevertheless awarded the Oakleaves to his Knight's Cross on 1 July.

On 4 September 1944, Rundstedt was recalled yet again to serve as Oberbefehlshaber West; but by now Hitler was insisting on taking virtually all decisions, and Rundstedt's actual input into the planning of the doomed Ardennes offensive in December – ostensibly his operation – was minimal. He was finally replaced with GFM Kesselring on 10 March 1945, and went into final retirement. At the end of the war Rundstedt was captured by US forces and handed over to the British. During his captivity he suffered a further heart attack; he was released in 1948, and lived quietly in Hannover until his death in 1953.

## Generalfeldmarschall Ewald von Kleist (Plate B3)

Born in Brauenfels on 8 August 1881, Paul Ludwig Ewald von Kleist was the son of a schoolmaster; however, his family was steeped in military tradition, and had produced more than 30 generals over the centuries. Ewald von Kleist joined the artillery in 1900 as an officer cadet, and in August 1901 was commissioned Leutnant. Promoted Oberleutnant in January 1910, he was posted later that year to the Kriegsakademie, where he stayed for three years. His next regimental posting was to the cavalry, in Liebhusaren Regiment 1, where he was soon promoted Rittmeister (Captain).

Kleist saw intense action early in World War I, serving with his regiment at the battle of Tannenberg in August 1914. Various staff positions followed, and he became chief-of-staff of the elite Garde Kavallerie Division in 1917. From 1922 to 1926 Major von Kleist was a tactics instructor at the Kavallerieschule in Hanover, rising to command the school and being promoted Oberstleutnant in December 1926. He held other staff appointments before being promoted Oberst in 1929 as commander of Infanterie Regiment 9 at Potsdam. In January 1932 he achieved the rank of Generalmajor, with command of 2. Kavallerie Division based at Breslau. Promotion to Generalleutnant came on 1 October 1933, and to General der Kavallerie on 1 August 1936.

In February 1938, Kleist was one of those who were retired as part of the Nazis' drive to replace all senior officers of whose loyalty they were not certain; but in August 1939 he was recalled to duty, and appointed commander of XXII Armeekorps (mot). The following month this corps formed part of Rundstedt's Heeresgruppe Süd in the southern half of a massive pincer movement to divide the Polish armies and isolate Warsaw.

For the 1940 campaign in the West, Kleist was given command of a huge armoured force, Panzergruppe Kleist – in effect an armoured army, comprising XIX & XLI Panzerkorps and XIV Armeekorps: a total of five Panzer and three motorized infantry divisions, with almost 3,000 tanks. Kleist's forces struck through Luxembourg

GenObst Ewald von Kleist, shown here in a formal portrait before his elevation to Generalfeldmarschall. It is quite common to encounter in such photos only the minimum of military decorations being worn; here Kleist wears only his Knight's Cross and 1914 Iron Cross 1st Class with 1939 clasp. Visible on the left breast of his tunic is a long row of thread loops to take an extensive ribbon bar for the other awards to which he was entitled. (Josef Charita)

**Besitzzeugnis**

Im Namen

des Führers

wurde dem ...... Obergefreiten ......
(Dienstgrad)

...... Otto Bergner ......
(Vor- und Familienname)

...... 2./Nachr.Abt. 173 ......
(Truppenteil)

der **Kubanschild** verliehen.

H.Qu., den *1.10.1944.*

*[signature]*

Generalfeldmarschall

Ewald von Kleist was responsible for the defence of the Kuban bridgehead in February–October 1943. Like the defence of the Crimea, this was commemorated by a campaign shield, and as C-in-C of that sector he signed all award documents. Unlike Manstein's gold Crimea Shield, no special version of the Kuban decoration was created for Kleist.

and on through the Ardennes to reach the River Meuse. On 12 May he crossed into France and struck westwards for the English Channel, reaching the Aire-St Omer Canal on 22 May, but being halted there on Rundstedt's orders. At the successful conclusion of the first phase of the campaign, Kleist was decorated with the Knight's Cross on 15 May. His Panzergruppe won further victories against the French before reaching the Atlantic on the Spanish border on 29 June. For his considerable contribution to the victory Kleist was promoted Generaloberst on 19 July 1940.

In April 1941, Kleist led his Panzergruppe into Yugoslavia, forcing that country's surrender in just nine days; he was then moved to allied Romania in preparation for the invasion of the USSR. Attached to Heeresgruppe Süd, Kleist's Panzergruppe 1 struck into the Ukraine; by the end of September, Kiev had fallen to a huge pincer movement of which Kleist's Panzergruppe formed the southern claw. On 6 October, Kleist's formation was upgraded to become 1. Panzerarmee. Kleist's next objective was Rostov on the Don.

The advance deep into Russia had taken its toll, however; combat attrition, mechanical breakdowns and overstretched supply lines all conspired to leave him greatly weakened by the time he reached the approaches to Rostov in mid November 1941. After a three-day battle his troops seized the city on 20 November, but were unable to hold it against powerful counter-attacks. Rundstedt, Kleist's immediate superior, was dismissed, and Hitler sent Kleist himself an insulting signal. Nevertheless, he received the Oakleaves to his Knight's Cross on 17 February 1942.

In May 1942 Kleist played a significant role in the battle for Kharkov, where two Panzer armies under his command halted Timoshenko's spring offensive and captured almost a quarter of a million Soviet troops. After this success he returned to command 1. Panzerarmee with eight divisions, as part of Heeresgruppe A for the drive through southern Russia towards the Caucasus oilfields. His spearhead reached Maikop in early August, but the next month the advance bogged down on the Terek river; Kleist was faced by much stronger forces, his supply lines were overstretched, and troops, aircraft and fuel were steadily diverted northwards to Stalingrad. On 5 November, 13. Panzer Division got to within three miles of Ordzhonikidze in northern Ossetia, but that was the furthest east the Wehrmacht ever got.

On 21 November 1942, Kleist was appointed to command Heeresgruppe A. Hitler was still mesmerized by the unreachable oilfields, and while the battle for Stalingrad raged Kleist had to cling to his exposed positions far to the south, with his rear lines constantly threatened by a Soviet break-through. On 1 February 1943, Kleist was promoted Generalfeldmarschall; and later that month, after the fall of Stalingrad, he was at last authorized to withdraw his 400,000 men. His conduct of the retreat from the Caucasus to the Dnieper was masterly, and by March

1943 he was able to launch counter-attacks. Kleist maintained a determined defence of the Kuban bridgehead for several more months, finally being given permission to transport most of his forces by sea over the Straits of Kerch to the Crimea. Despite Kleist's repeated requests Hitler refused to countenance any further withdrawals, and on 1 November 1943 the German forces in the Crimea were cut off.

In March 1944, Kleist allowed his 8. Armee commander, Gen Wöhler, to withdraw behind the Dniester river. On 30 March, Hitler had Kleist flown to his headquarters at the Obersalzburg, where he was first decorated with the Swords to his Knight's Cross, and then relieved of his command. Kleist was a phlegmatic, unexcitable character; he was also a realist, very popular, and an old-fashioned gentleman. In 1944 Hitler wanted ruthless senior commanders of absolute loyalty, and he replaced Kleist with Schörner. Kleist lived in retirement until the Soviet advance in 1945 obliged him to evacuate his family to Bavaria. Taken prisoner by US forces on 25 April, Kleist was held in England before being handed over to the Yugoslavs, who charged him with unspecified war crimes in 1941 and sentenced him to 15 years' imprisonment. Three years later he was handed over to the USSR, and tried on the incredible charge of 'alienating the population through mildness and kindness' – i.e. he was charged with the crime of treating the Russian population better than the Soviet regime itself, and thus encouraging them to side with the Germans. Ewald von Kleist died in solitary confinement in Soviet captivity on 15 October 1954.

# ARMY COMMANDERS

### Generaloberst Eduard Dietl
### (Plate C2)
Born in Bad Aibling on 1 July 1890, Eduard Dietl was the son of a Bavarian finance official. In 1909, at his second attempt, he joined Bavarian Infanterie Regiment 5 as an officer cadet, and was commissioned Leutnant in October 1911 after studying at the Kriegsschule in Munich. He was promoted Oberleutnant in October 1915, and served as a company commander with his regiment. Promoted Hauptmann in March 1918, Dietl was wounded in action four times during the war, and was in hospital at the time of the Armistice.

A member of the Epp Freikorps in 1919, Dietl joined the Nazi Party as early as 1920.[1] Dietl served as a company commander with Infanterie Regiment 19 before staff appointments, and a spell as an instructor at the Infanterieschule in Munich, before being given command of his regiment's III (Gebirgsjäger) Bataillon with the rank of Major. On 1 January 1933, he achieved the rank of Oberstleutnant and regimental command. Promotion to Oberst followed in 1935, with command of the newly formed Gebirgsjäger Regiment 99. In April 1938 he was promoted Generalmajor and given command of 3. Gebirgs Division, based at Graz in Austria; the following year he led it during the Polish campaign.

On 9 April 1940, he and his mountain troops were landed at Narvik during the invasion of Norway, although his division was weakened by the detachment of one regiment to seize Trondheim. The initial capture

1 See Elite 76 *The German Freikorps 1918–23*

OPPOSITE **Gen Eduard Dietl, in a portrait photograph taken after he won renown at Narvik in April–June 1940. Note that he wears the Oakleaves to the Knight's Cross, Dietl being the first soldier of the Wehrmacht to be awarded this newly created decoration. This Bavarian officer was always a convinced National Socialist; in the Reichswehr of the 1920s he was a conduit of information to the young Nazi Party, and he was a supporter of Hitler's attempted** *putsch* **in Munich in 1923. (Josef Charita)**

OPPOSITE **Dietl's signature on the award document for the Narvik Shield, created in honour of his defence of that town. This was the first of a number of such battle decorations. Although such documents often bear only a facsimile stamped signature, this example has a genuine autograph.**

General der Infanterie DIETL

of the port went well, but the arrival of a powerful British naval force saw the destruction of most of the German destroyers in Narvik Fjord. This left Dietl's force on shore in a perilous position, with the nearest friendly units over 700 miles to the south. On the positive side, some 2,000 sailors were now available to Dietl to bolster his force, and plenty of food, ammunition and weapons were salvaged from ships which had been run aground. A limited number of small artillery pieces were also landed by Luftwaffe transport planes on a nearby frozen lake.

Dietl concentrated his force to defend a limited perimeter around Narvik against determined attacks by British, French, Polish and Norwegian troops supported by heavy gunfire from British warships. On 9 May, during the battle for Narvik, Dietl was promoted to General-leutnant and decorated with the Knight's Cross. Although he was successful in fending off attacks, steady combat attrition reduced his strength. On 27 May, French Foreign Legion troops with naval support landed in the town, and after bitter fighting seized Narvik port. Although a small number of reinforcements were dropped by parachute, they were too few to make a significant difference.

A two-pronged attempt was then launched to relieve Dietl's force, with reinforcements travelling both by sea and overland. British submarines torpedoed two of the German transports; and those travelling overland faced a trek of over 700 miles across the most barren and inhospitable terrain. The land column then received an order cancelling the operation when they were only a few days' march away – but the reason was good news for the Germans. A patrol sent out by Dietl had reported that the enemy appeared to have abandoned the port. Unknown to the beleaguered Germans in Narvik, the campaign elsewhere in Norway had gone well, and on 9 June Norway surrendered. Dietl was the hero of the hour for his determined defence, but later admitted that he

had been seriously considering withdrawing his forces over the border into neutral Sweden and internment. So great was the impact of this narrow victory on German morale that a special campaign decoration, the Narvik Shield, was created to commemorate the battle.

On 19 July 1940, Dietl was promoted to General der Gebirgstruppe and appointed as commander of Gebirgskorps Norwegen; on the same day he became the first German soldier to win the newly instituted Oakleaves to the Knight's Cross.

In June 1941, GenLt Dietl, as commander of 20. Gebirgsarmee, took two mountain divisions across the far northern sector of the Russian Front along the Finnish-Soviet border, with the task of seizing the vital port of Murmansk with the co-operation of Finnish forces. In the swampy tundra, cut by numerous lakes, progress was difficult and resistance stubborn, and by 19 September Dietl was forced to withdraw into defensive lines behind the Litsa river in front of Petsamo. In January 1942 he was appointed commander of all German forces in Lappland, and in June that year was promoted to Generaloberst.

Dietl's impeccable Nazi credentials kept him in Hitler's favour, and Goebbels' propaganda machine promoted him vigorously. Nevertheless, he failed to achieve any signficant advances on this far northern front. On 23 June 1944, Dietl was summoned to a meeting with Hitler at the Obersalzberg to discuss relations with the Finns, who had become unenthusiastic allies; his aircraft crashed en route, and he was killed. Dietl was posthumously decorated with the Swords to his Knight's Cross on 1 July 1944.

Gen Heinz Guderian, seen here during a field conference. He is wearing the older and slightly more elaborate M1920 form of the general officer's tunic, with eight-button fastening and red piping to the front edge. (Josef Charita)

### Generaloberst Heinz Guderian (Plate C3)

Heinz Wilhelm Guderian was born at Kulm on 17 June 1888, into a family of West Prussian landowners. Although Guderian's father was a humble Leutnant and the family had no great tradition of soldiering, he developed a passionate interest in the military. Enrolled at the cadet school at Berlin-Lichterfelde, he graduated in 1907 and joined his father's unit, Jäger Bataillon 10. After a year at the Kriegsakademie he served throughout World War I mainly as a wireless communications specialist, as signals officer of 5. Kavallerie Division and later assistant signals officer at 4. Armee headquarters. Guderian proved a tough, determined and energetic officer; impatient to learn and apply new skills, he took the opportunity to fly as an observer on reconnaissance missions. He also briefly commanded II Btl, Infanterie Regiment 14, and this experience of the horrors of static trench warfare would confirm him as an exponent of fast, mobile warfare. On 28 February 1918, he was appointed to the General Staff, and during the last great spring offensives on the Western Front he gained valuable experience in the movement of large formations.

‘Fast Heinz’ Guderian with tank officers on the scene of perhaps his greatest triumph – his thrust, at the head of his own XIX Panzerkorps, right across France from the River Meuse to the Channel coast at Boulogne in just over a week during May 1940. (US National Archives)

At the end of World War I, Guderian served with the newly formed frontier force – Grenzschutz Ost – created by Gen von Seeckt to defend the eastern territories from Russian and Polish incursions; he later joined Maj Bischoff's 'Iron Division' Freikorps, which fought in Kurland in 1919. Guderian's interest in mobile warfare was to be given expression when in 1922 he was tasked with studying the possibilities for motorization of the Reichswehr, given the tight restrictions imposed upon it by the terms of the Treaty of Versailles. He investigated the most up-to-date developments in mechanized and armoured warfare, including command and control by radio communications. Guderian could see the potential for the use of armour not merely for infantry support, but as a breakthrough weapon in its own right. In his long struggle against more traditionally minded officers he had a champion in Oberst Oswald Lutz, chief-of-staff to the Inspectorate of Motorized Troops and the true father of the Panzer force. In 1929 Guderian was

Guderian displaying the Oakleaves to his Knight's Cross, as well as the ribbon of his 1914 Iron Cross with the 1939 clasp attached. This portrait perhaps hints at Guderian's impatient and hot-tempered nature, which gave him the courage (shown by very few, if any, others) to contradict Hitler face to face and with raised voice. (Josef Charita)

given command of a motorized infantry battalion; and two years later Oberstleutnant Guderian became Lutz's chief-of-staff. From 1933 the climate of opinion swung behind the armour enthusiasts. Hitler himself exclaimed, after seeing a demonstration of mechanized troops organized by Guderian at the Kummersdorf training grounds, 'That's what I need! That's what I want to have!'

Guderian's hard work eventually bore fruit when, in 1935, Gen Lutz won approval for the creation of three armoured divisions, and Guderian was given command of 2. Panzer Division – though initially there were precious few tanks available. In 1936 Guderian was promoted Generalmajor; and in 1938, after Lutz fell foul of the Nazis, Guderian was raised to Generalleutnant and given command of XVI Korps, comprising the three armoured divisions. Hitler wished to give his new armoured formations a high profile, and Guderian began to be seen regularly at the Führer's side – to the chagrin of those who opposed him. In November 1938, Guderian was promoted General and appointed commander of mobile troops (Chef der Schnelltruppe). Just prior to the outbreak of war he was given command of XIX Panzerkorps, a formation with one armoured and two motorized divisions.

Although the tanks committed to the Polish campaign were predominantly light and obsolescent PzKw I and II models, and despite a high level of mechanical breakdowns, the Panzers' performance in 1939 dispelled any remaining doubts over their use as a fast breakthrough weapon to be deployed en masse, in co-operation with tactical aircraft. On 27 October 1939, Guderian was decorated with the Knight's Cross.

Guderian's star was in the ascendant; he was consulted closely by Manstein during the planning of the Western offensive, and his reputation was enhanced even further during that campaign. In the *Westfeldzug* he led XIX Panzerkorps of three Panzer and some motorized divisions, which attacked through the Ardennes – a route thought by many to be impossible for armour – to cross the Meuse at Sedan and drive for the Channel Coast at Abbeville and Calais. However, there were still those who feared the risks of allowing the tanks to run too far ahead of the following infantry support, and Hitler was persuaded to order the tanks to halt to allow the infantry to catch up. The impatient and choleric Guderian, unaware that the halt order had come from Hitler, offered his resignation, and was only persuaded to reconsider by being allowed to continue his advance under the guise of a 'reconnaissance in force'. Guderian was subsequently given command of his own Panzergruppe, comprising two Panzerkorps each with two Panzer and one motorized divisions. At the successful conclusion of the campaign he was promoted Generaloberst.

For the invasion of the Soviet Union in June 1941 (against which he had argued) Guderian was given command of Panzergruppe 2, with five armoured, three motorized and one cavalry division. As part of Heeresgruppe Mitte, Guderian's 850 tanks slashed through the Soviet western armies towards Smolensk at remarkable speed, reaching the Dnieper in just 15 days. Just as it seemed that Heeresgruppe Mitte could indeed attain its goal of reaching Moscow, Hitler ordered the main thrust of the advance to shift southwards into the Ukraine on 21 August. Guderian played a leading part in the great encirclement battle around Kiev; but by October, when the advance was refocused on Moscow, it was too late – about half Guderian's vehicles had been lost in action or had broken down under the demands of the huge mileages achieved over bad roads.

Facing increasing enemy resistance, and the onset of the Russian winter (for which the Wehrmacht was ill equipped), Guderian managed to advance as far as Tula, 110 miles south of Moscow, before his units ground to a halt. Concerned for the welfare of his thinly clad troops, and handicapped by serious shortages in ammunition and food, Guderian simply ignored orders refusing him permission to make withdrawals, and pulled back his troops wherever he saw fit. His persistent refusal to obey 'stand fast' orders resulted in his dismissal from command on 25 December 1941, just after suffering a minor heart attack.

Guderian remained in enforced retirement, recuperating from his ill health, until March 1943, when he was persuaded to accept the post of Generalinspekteur der Panzertruppe (Inspector General of Armoured Troops). This new role brought Guderian, as the senior officer of the armoured corps, a status equal to that of a commander-in-chief of an army; and with it came direct access to Hitler, in order to argue his opinions on tank design and production (and, since he was both opinionated and fearless, on operational questions which were now beyond his remit). However, while the advisory and trouble-shooting powers of such inspectorates was great, their direct authority to give orders was ambiguous.

During 1943 tentative approaches were made to Guderian by those plotting against Hitler. A straightforward patriot, Guderian would never consider breaking his military oath; but he remained silent about these approaches. On 21 July 1944, in the immediate aftermath of the failed bomb attempt, the raging Führer showed his continuing trust by appointing Guderian as Chief of the Army General Staff. This was a post stripped of much of its real authority; but although the blunt and fearless Guderian repeatedly became involved in furious arguments against Hitler's increasingly dogmatic and ill-judged interference in military decisions, he remained loyal to his duty. Finally, on 27 March

A fine portrait study of GenObst Hans Hube. Nicknamed 'Clever Hans' by the troops, Hube was a courageous, popular and most able commander, whose career deserves to be more widely known. The multitude of medal ribbons worn in addition to his Knight's Cross with Oakleaves and Swords is testimony to his long military service.
(Josef Charita)

The cropping of Hube's portraits may be deliberate, to conceal the loss of his left arm in the early weeks of World War I – a handicap which did not prevent him returning to the front line as an infantry company commander. After various staff jobs he was back in the trenches facing British infantry and tanks at the very end of the war, and narrowly missed an award of the *Pour le Mérite*. (Josef Charita)

1945, Hitler had had enough of his insolent general, and ordered Guderian to go on six weeks' sick leave. Long before his leave was up, Hitler had committed suicide and the war was over.

Guderian surrendered to US forces; he was finally released in 1950, and died in retirement in May 1954 at the age of 66.

### Generaloberst Hans Hube (Plate C1)

Hans Valentin Hube was born on 29 October 1890 at Naumburg. He enrolled as an officer cadet in Infanterie Regiment 26, being commissioned Leutnant in 1910. A platoon commander on the outbreak of World War I, Hube was appointed as battalion adjutant within days of going into action on the Western Front. Scarcely a month later he was seriously wounded during the battle for Fontenay, and his left arm was amputated. However, the young Hube was a fiercely determined soldier, and somehow persuaded his superiors to allow him to return to front line duty in January 1916, as Oberleutnant commanding 7 Kompanie, Infanterie Regiment 26. Later in that year he was appointed as an orderly officer to the high command of IV Armeekorps; but by the end of the year he had returned to his old regiment as its adjutant. Various staff postings followed, with Hube moving back and forth between his regiment and higher formations. In the closing stages of the war Hauptmann Hube was recommended for the Pour le Mérite for his part in defeating a major British attack with tank support, but the war ended before the award could be approved.

Despite his injuries, Hube was a supremely fit young man and his determination to succeed impressed those charged with building the new Reichswehr. Accepted in October 1919, this keen student of tactics threw himself energetically into his duties, taking a particular interest in realistic field training. Hube was promoted Major in 1932, with command of I Btl, Infanterie Regiment 3. Two years later he was promoted Oberstleutnant, and on 1 May 1935 he was appointed commander of the Infanterieschule at Döberitz. Here Hube wrote a two-volume work entitled *Der Infanterist* ('The Infantryman'), which was to become a standard training text.

Hube did not see action during the Polish campaign, but in October 1939 was appointed to command Infanterie Regiment 3 with the rank of Oberst. He led this unit in the early weeks of the 1940 campaign in the West, and its performance brought him, in May, promotion to Generalmajor and command of 16. Infanterie Division (mot). Later that year his command was re-formed as 16. Panzer Division, and was sent in December to allied Romania as a demonstration unit. It served as part of Panzergruppe Kleist with Rundstedt's Heeresgruppe Süd during Operation 'Barbarossa' in June 1941.

Hube's division distinguished itself for aggression and spirit in the breaking of the so-called 'Stalin Line', and its commander was decorated with the Knight's Cross on 1 August 1941. In subsequent fighting in the Ukraine, 16. Panzer took part in the smashing of two entire Soviet armies around Kiev, bringing Hube the Oakleaves on 16 January 1942. On 16 September 1942, Hube was promoted Generalleutnant and given command of XIV Panzerkorps, then located in Stalingrad; and on 21 December he was awarded the Swords to his Knight's Cross. Refused permission to attempt a break-out from the winter siege, Hube resigned himself to a soldier's death alongside his men; but on 18 January 1943 he was ordered to fly out of the pocket and report to Führer Headquarters.

Hube was subsequently charged with forming a new XIV Panzerkorps to replace the formation lost at Stalingrad. This corps was then deployed in the defence of Sicily, where Hube was given command of all Army and Flak troops on the island. Promoted General der Panzertruppe, Hube made the Allies pay dearly for their advance across Sicily in July 1943; and despite their air and sea superiority, he subsequently organized the withdrawal of the surviving units across the straits to the Italian mainland with remarkable success. He repeated this stubborn defensive battle in September after the Salerno landings, but Allied airpower and naval gunfire support tipped the balance.

In November 1943, Hube was transferred eastwards once again to command 1. Panzerarmee with Heeresgruppe Süd, holding positions on the northern flank of the threatened 'Dnieper bend' salient. In March 1944 deep Soviet advances to the north and south encircled Hube's army nearly 50 miles east of the enemy front line. Hube wanted to break out to the south, and that was where the Red Army expected him; but on 26 March, his army group commander GFM von Manstein ordered him to head west, while Gen Raus's 4. Panzerarmee, reinforced by II SS-Panzerkorps rushed from France, pushed east to meet him. Led by 7. Panzer Division, Hube's army struck westwards out of the pocket, taking the enemy by surprise and destroying nearly 700 armoured vehicles and 200 artillery pieces. On 6 April his spearhead linked up with the SS Panzers, and by 9 April the whole of 1. Panzerarmee had rejoined safely. On 1 April 1944, Hube was promoted Generaloberst; and in recognition of this outstanding success he was personally awarded the Diamonds by Hitler in a ceremony at the Obersalzberg on 20 April.

On the following day, 21 April, Hube was returning to Berlin in a Heinkel He 111 when the aircraft crashed; Hube was seriously injured, and died in hospital. He was buried with full military honours in the Invalidenfriedhof in Berlin.

## General der Panzertruppe Hasso von Manteuffel (Plate D2)

Hasso von Manteuffel was born in Potsdam on 14 January 1897, into a family with a centuries-long tradition of Prussian military service. In

Gen Hasso von Manteuffel, who showed heroism as an infantry officer before proving himself one of Germany's best Panzer generals. He is pictured in the leather greatcoat he often favoured, and the so-called 'old style officer's field cap'; the Oakleaves and Swords at his throat date the photo to after 2 February 1944, at which date GenLt von Manteuffel was commanding the Army's premier mechanized division, the 'Grossdeutschland'. (Josef Charita)

1908 he joined the Kadetenanstalt (Cadet Institute) at Naumburg, moving to the Senior Cadet Institute in Berlin in 1911. He joined the Army officially in February 1916, as an officer candidate with Husaren Regiment 3 at Rathenow. Manteuffel served on both Eastern and Western Fronts during World War I; he was commissioned Leutnant in April 1916, and was wounded for the first time that October.

Like many of his contemporaries, Manteuffel served with the Freikorps in the immediate post-war period – in his case, as adjutant to Freikorps von Oven in Berlin – before joining the Reichswehr in May 1919. He served with Kavallerie Regiment 25 until 1920, when he joined Reiter Regiment 3; after three years as a squadron commander he became the regimental adjutant.

An accomplished horseman, Manteuffel won several sporting awards; and was promoted Rittmeister (Captain) with Reiter Regiment 17, a Bavarian unit. Promoted Major in 1936, he was appointed to the staff of 2. Panzer Division, and the following year to that of the Kommando der Panzertruppe – the office of Gen Guderian.

In February 1939 he was appointed to command Panzertruppe Schule II at Berlin-Krampnitz, and that April he was promoted Oberstleutnant. In this position, Manteuffel missed seeing action during the early campaigns of the war.

In May 1941, Manteuffel took command – at his own request – of II Btl, Jäger Regiment 7, a distinctly junior posting for an officer of his rank. Three months later, however, he took command of Jäger (Panzergrenadier) Regiment 6 when its commander was killed in action, and he led this unit of 7. Panzer Division during the opening phase of Operation 'Barbarossa'. The daring cavalryman gained a considerable reputation for dash and courage in these infantry battles. His troops entered Vyazma on the road to Moscow on 6 October, encircling a considerable number of enemy troops and resisting all their attempts to break out. In December, rifle in hand, the 44-year-old ObstLt Manteuffel personally led an attack which resulted in the capture of a bridge over the Volga-Moscow canal, and of the adjacent Yakhroma power station (which served the Kremlin). For his heroism he was decorated with the Knight's Cross on the last day of 1941, and promoted Oberst.

Manteuffel remained on the Eastern Front until May 1942, when his division was pulled back for rest and refitting in occupied France. Here Manteuffel remained until he was posted to North Africa in February 1943, to take command of an ad hoc division comprising a mix of German Army, Luftwaffe and Italian troops. This Division von Manteuffel, was involved in extremely heavy fighting in Tunisia as part of LXXXX Armeekorps. Manteuffel collapsed from exhaustion and became seriously ill; evacuated to a German hospital, he was promoted Generalmajor on 1 May 1943.

Three months later he was given command of his old 7. Panzer Division in Russia. On top form once again, Manteuffel led this division on the southern sector of the front, at first resisting the Soviet offensives which followed the fall of Stalingrad, including the defence of Kharkov, and then fighting in the Kursk offensive. During the defensive campaign which followed its failure 7. Panzer was moved back and forth from crisis point to crisis point, acting as a fire brigade. His capture of Zhitomir during a night attack brought Manteuffel the Oakleaves to his Knight's Cross on 23 November 1943. In December 1943, Manteuffel was summoned to Hitler's headquarters, where he was honoured by being appointed to command the elite 'Grossdeutschland' Division, the Army's premier combat formation, with the rank of Generalleutnant. On 2 February 1944, Manteuffel was awarded the Swords to his Knight's Cross in recognition of his inspired command of 7. Panzer Division; at this date he was only the seventh divisional commander to be so decorated.

While fighting a series of desperate defensive battles Manteuffel oversaw the expansion of 'Grossdeutschland' from a mechanized infantry division into one of the most powerful Panzer divisions Germany possessed. He led his new command to great effect, often drawing the Soviets into rapid advances that exposed them to flanking attacks that cut off their forward elements. 'Grossdeutschland' saw intense combat at Korsun (Cherkassy) in February, losing much of its tank strength for months afterwards. In March–April 1944 the 'GD' was forced back into Romania, fighting around Jassy, and in May 1944 defeated an offensive that threatened the Romanian oilfields. In August the division was transferred north to the East Prussian/Latvian front. On 1 September 1944, Manteuffel was promoted to the rank of General der Panzertruppe, and appointed to command 5. Panzerarmee on the Western Front.

Manteuffel's welcome to the West involved immediate heavy combat in Lorraine, where his scratch force, hastily cobbled together and short of infantry and artillery, was committed to a counter-attack against Patton's US 3rd Army. During a four-day battle – which opened the eyes of Russian Front veterans to the very different capabilities of the US Army – Manteuffel's forces took a terrible pounding from Allied fighter-bombers and suffered heavy losses in armour. The 5. Panzerarmee was withdrawn to the woods of the Eifel sector, and rebuilt in preparation for the forthcoming Ardennes offensive.

Hitler's ill-conceived plan was to strike across the Meuse and onwards to the impossibly ambitious objective of Antwerp, cutting the Allied armies in two. The northern flank was formed by SS-Obstgruf 'Sepp' Dietrich's 6. SS-Panzerarmee; Gen Brandenberger's weak, mainly infantry 7. Armee operated on the southern flank, while Manteuffel's 5. Panzerarmee delivered the central thrust. All these commands were short of vital supplies, and manned by a mixture of half-trained boys and exhausted survivors of earlier defeats. When the advance began on 16 December the Americans were initially taken by surprise, and the parallel columns made reasonable progress; bad weather helped the attackers by grounding Allied air support. The German divisions were hampered by fuel shortages, however, and by the problems of moving large numbers of vehicles, including heavy tanks, along narrow, snowbound roads through difficult wooded terrain. The 7. Armee failed to take Bastogne, which later tied down considerable numbers of troops, including some of Manteuffel's armour; this significantly delayed his progress towards his own objectives. By 24 December the spearheads had advanced about 65 miles, but were still short of the River Meuse; and on that day the clearing weather allowed the Allies to begin employing their overwhelming air superiority. Rapidly running out of fuel and ammunition, the German divisions were forced first onto the defensive and, by 9 January, into general retreat.

On 18 February 1945, Manteuffel was decorated with the Diamonds to the Knight's Cross. He was appointed to command 3. Panzerarmee on the Eastern Front, defending positions in Pomerania; but the end was in sight, and his troops were pushed westwards towards Mecklenburg. Hitler had ordered him to strike towards Berlin and attempt to relieve the capital, but Manteuffel knew that this would be a futile gesture that would cost tens of thousands of his soldiers' lives. He negotiated the surrender of his forces to the British who were approaching Mecklenburg from the west.

Released after two years, in 1953 Manteuffel was elected to the Bundestag as a member of the Free Democratic Party, sitting as a member of parliament until 1957. Hasso von Manteuffel died on 24 September 1978 at the age of 81, deeply admired by the men he had led and respected by those he had fought against.

### General der Panzertruppe Ludwig Crüwell (Plate D1)

Ludwig Crüwell was born on 20 March 1892 in Dortmund. In 1911 he became an officer candidate in a dragoon regiment, gaining his commission in August 1912. He was sent on temporary detachment to the Kriegsschule at Hersfeld before rejoining his unit, where he became regimental adjutant. He spent most of World War I with Dragoner Regiment 9, but with several periods of detachment, including a spell on the staff of 233. Infanterie Division and a brief command of an infantry company. He ended the war as an Oberleutnant on the staff of 33. Infanterie Division.

Crüwell returned to his old dragoon regiment in January 1919, and served on detachment to the Army General Staff. In October 1920 he transferred to the staff of 1. Kavallerie Division, and over the next two years alternated between service with mounted units and with the Defence Ministry; in May 1922 he was promoted Rittmeister (Captain). In October 1925 he joined 2. Kavallerie Division,

Gen Ludwig Crüwell, whose capture in October 1942 meant that he appears much less often in wartime photographs than many of his peers; he was, nevertheless, a senior and respected tank officer who would doubtless have been given even more senior commands if he had returned from Africa. This shot was taken in late 1941 after the award of his Oakleaves and appointment as commanding general of the *Afrikakorps.*

*(continued on page 41)*

1: GFM Erich von Manstein; Sebastopol, July 1942
2: GFM Erwin Rommel; French coast, spring 1944
3: GFM Walter Model; Holland, September 1944

A

1: Gen Ferdinand Schörner; Finland, spring 1943
2: GFM Gerd von Rundstedt, autumn 1944
3: GFM Ewald von Kleist; Ukraine, spring 1943

B

1: GenLt Hans Hube; Sicily, August 1943
2: GenObst Eduard Dietl; Soviet/Finnish border, June 1942
3: GenObst Heinz Guderian, c.1943–44

1: Gen Ludwig Crüwell; Libya, May 1942
2: Gen Hasso von Manteuffel; Ardennes, December 1944
3: GenMaj Julius Ringel; Crete, 1941

D

1: Gen Heinrich Eberbach; France, August 1944
2: GenMaj Theodor Scherer; Cholm, early 1942
3: GenLt Fritz Bayerlein; Normandy, June 1944

E

1: GenMaj Dr Franz Bäke; Eastern Front, April 1945
2: GenMaj Horst Niemack; Ruhr Pocket, March 1945
3: GenMaj Hermann von Oppeln-Bronikowski; Silesia, 1945

F

1: Hptm Waldemar von Gazen; Caucasus, January 1943
2: Obst Heinz von Brese-Winiary; Lithuania, September 1944
3: GenMaj Otto Remer; Eastern Front, spring 1945

1: Maj Willy Jähde; Leningrad front, March 1944
2: Maj Peter Frantz; Eastern Front, spring 1943
3: ObstLt Josef Bremm; Ruhr Pocket, spring 1945

H

and three years later 3. Kavallerie Division, being promoted Major on 1 October 1931. Further staff appointments included spells with the General Staff and the staff of the Oberbefehlshaber des Heeres, bringing promotion to Oberstleutnant on 1 April 1934 and to Oberst on 1 March 1936. For just two months from February 1938 Crüwell commanded Panzer Regiment 6, taking part in the occupation of Austria before returning to staff postings, ultimately with the Oberkommando des Heeres.

Shortly after the outbreak of war, Crüwell was appointed as chief quartermaster to 16. Armee, and on 1 December 1939 he was promoted Generalmajor. Assigned to 5. Panzer Division on 6 June 1940 on temporary attachment for one month, on 1 August he was finally given command of his own formation: 11. Panzer Division, the famous 'Ghost Division'. Crüwell led 11. Panzer during the spring 1941 Balkan campaign, spearheading the advance of XIV Panzerkorps into Yugoslavia; and on 14 May he was decorated with the Knight's Cross. His division remained with 1. Panzergruppe for the June attack on the Soviet Union, where it formed part of XXXXVIII Armeekorps in Heeresgruppe Süd. It took part in the drive through Zhitomir to Uman; by 8 August the latter had been taken, with over 100,000 prisoners from the 25 divisions that had made up the Soviet 6th and 12th Armies.

In September 1941, promoted Generalleutnant and decorated with the Oakleaves, Crüwell was appointed commanding general of the Deutsches Afrikakorps (15. & 21. Panzer Divisions) subordinate to Rommel's enlarged command, now designated Panzergruppe Afrika. Crüwell led the Afrikakorps through the battles around Tobruk, El Duda and Sidi Rezegh, which resulted in the destruction of much of the British 7th Armoured Division and the South African 5th Brigade.

Further promoted to General der Panzertruppe in December 1941, Crüwell was appointed commander of Panzergruppe Afrika in March 1942 – a temporary command while Rommel was on sick leave. By the time Rommel returned, Crüwell had contracted jaundice and was himself evacuated to Europe for treatment. Command of the DAK passed to GenLt Nehring; and when Crüwell eventually returned to Africa he was given command of the so-called 'Italian Front', which comprised four divisions of Italian troops and one of German.

This force was designated as Gruppe Crüwell for the assault on the British positions around Gazala in May 1942. On the 27th of that month the light aircraft in which he was a passenger was brought down by the British and Crüwell was taken prisoner. He remained in captivity until 1947, and died in retirement in Essen on 25 September 1958.

## General der Panzertruppe Heinrich Eberbach (Plate E1)

Heinrich Kurt Alfons Willy Eberbach was born in Stuttgart on 24 November 1895. He joined the Army as a 19-year-old officer cadet in 1914, being commissioned Leutnant in an infantry regiment the next year. Not long after joining his unit at the front he was seriously wounded in the face, having part of his nose blown away, and was taken prisoner by the French. He was repatriated in 1916 due to his wounds; after undergoing plastic surgery he returned to military service in 1918.

Gen Heinrich Eberbach, seen here in the black uniform for tank crews, displaying his Knight's Cross with the Oakleaves suspension clasp awarded in December 1941, shortly before he took over 4. Panzer Division. The facial wound that Eberbach suffered during the early stages of World War I still leaves its mark. (Josef Charita)

Assigned as a liaison officer to the Turkish forces, he was captured once again, this time by the British. He was promoted Oberleutnant in October 1918 while in captivity.

After the war Eberbach joined the Police, serving until 1935 when, on 1 August, he returned to the Army in the rank of Major. A year later he was posted to Panzer Regiment 6, beginning his long association with the armoured troops. Promoted Oberstleutnant in October 1937, Eberbach went on to command Panzer Regiment 35 in 4. Panzer Division, with which he took part in the invasion of Poland. During the campaign in the West in June 1940 Eberbach seized the crossings of the River Seine near Romilly, and then captured the town itself, taking several thousand prisoners. In recognition of this feat Eberbach was decorated with the Knight's Cross on 4 July 1940, and promoted Oberst on 1 August.

Eberbach led his regiment through the opening phases of the invasion of the USSR, receiving the Oakleaves to his Knight's Cross on 31 December 1941. Taking temporary command of 4. Panzer Division in January 1942, in March he was promoted to Generalmajor and confirmed as divisional commander. Subsequently assigned command of XXXXVIII Panzer Corps, Eberbach was wounded once more on 1 December 1942. During his convalescence he was promoted Generalleutnant in January 1943, and in August of that year to General der Panzertruppe. On returning to duty Eberbach held various staff postings until October 1943 when, over a three-month period, he commanded XXXXVII Panzer Corps, XXXXVIII Panzer Corps and then XXXX Panzer Corps on the Russian Front. In all these commands he showed great energy and skill.

With an Allied invasion of France imminent, Eberbach was transferred to the West and ultimately given command of the so-called 5. Panzerarmee in Normandy – with an actual strength of about 120 tanks, of a single division mixed with battered survivors of several other SS and Army formations. Eberbach's luck ran out on 31 August 1944, when he once again became a prisoner of the British. This time he was captured by 3rd Royal Tank Regiment, 11th Armoured Division, while on a reconnaissance near the River Seine.

Heinrich Eberbach died in retirement at Notzingen in July 1992.

# DIVISIONAL COMMANDERS

### General der Gebirgstruppe Julius Ringel (Plate D3)

Born at Völkermarkt in the mountainous Kärnten area of Austria on 16 November 1889, Julius Ringel became an officer cadet in the Austro-Hungarian Army in August 1909, and was commissioned Leutnant in

November 1910. He was promoted Oberleutnant in August 1914, days before the outbreak of World War I, and Hauptmann on 8 July 1917. After decorated combat service with the Tiroler Kaiser-Jäger during the war, Ringel rose steadily through the ranks of the post-war Austrian Army, to Major on 15 May 1921 and Oberstleutnant on 15 December 1932. Two years later he was appointed chief-of-staff of the Austrian 5. Gebirgs Brigade. After the Anschluss with Germany he was confirmed in his rank with the Wehrmacht in 1938, and appointed chief-of-staff of 3. Gebirgs Division.

In September 1939, Ringel moved from the mountain troops to the line infantry when he was promoted Oberst and became chief-of-staff of the Bavarian 268. Infanterie Division; a month later he was given his own command, Infanterie Regiment 266. In April 1940 he returned to the mountain troops, joining the newly formed 5. Gebirgs Division based at Salzburg; unlike Ringel, most of its soldiers were in fact Bavarians. In late 1940 Ringel was promoted Generalmajor and appointed to command the division.

After intensive training in the Bavarian Alps, where it formed part of 2. Armee on the home front, in March 1941 the division moved into the Balkans. Here it played a major role in breaking the Greek 'Metaxas Line' defences after four days of intensive fighting, fending off numerous enemy counter-attacks. Soon afterwards, Ringel's men were committed to one of the war's greatest gambles – the invasion of Crete.

Once again Ringel's mountain troopers played a pivotal role, coming to the assistance of the beleaguered paratroops during the fighting for Maleme airfield, the turning point of the whole battle. Many of the Gebirgsjäger were killed when a convoy of fishing vessels transporting them to the island was intercepted by the Royal Navy. A later landing, under fire, by Ju52 transport aircraft on Maleme airfield was successful, and between them the Fallschirmjäger and Gebirgsjäger drove the bulk of the British Commonwealth garrison from the island, the remainder surrendering on 31 May 1941. On 13 June 1941, Ringel was decorated with the Knight's Cross, and became for a time the military commander of Crete.

After a rest as occupation troops in Norway from September 1941, in January 1942 Ringel and his men were despatched to the Eastern Front to help stem the Soviet winter counter-offensive. The division fought under 18. Armee, in Heeresgruppe Nord, between Lake Ladoga and Novgorod on the Leningrad front. Ringel's Gebirgsjäger took part in the capture of over 33,000 prisoners in the Volkhov pocket, before being employed as a mobile 'fire brigade' at various crisis points on the Leningrad and Finnish fronts. During 20 months on the northern front Ringel's division gained an enviable reputation for steadfastness in defence and élan in the

A formal portrait of the Austrian Mountain Troops general Julius Ringel, painted in oils. Although somewhat eclipsed by Dietl, he showed himself an extremely able commander on Crete, in Russia and in Italy; and the nickname 'Papa' Ringel given him by his men was a sign of real affection and trust. (Josef Charita)

attack. In recognition of the achievements of his division, Ringel was promoted Generalleutnant on 1 December 1942.

In mid-1943 the division were transferred to the Italian Front, taking part in the defensive fighting on the Gustav Line as part of 10. Armee. On 25 October 1943, Ringel was awarded the Oakleaves to his Knight's Cross. His division took over the positions of the 305. Infanterie Division just before the first battle of Cassino in January 1944, and soon afterwards elements were sent to help resist the Allied landings at Anzio, before 5. Gebirgs pulled back to help defend the Gothic Line. Ringel was appointed to command LXIX Gebirgskorps in April 1944, moving briefly to take command of XVIII Gebirgskorps in June, when he was promoted to General der Gebirgstruppe. He left the front to become commanding general of Military District XVII (based at Salzburg) in late July 1944.

In February 1945 one of the ad hoc formations scrambled together in Austria in the face of the approaching Red Army was given the title Korps Ringel, and he helped organize the defence of the Steiermark region. In desperate fighting the various battlegroups formed by Ringel managed to halt – albeit temporarily – the Soviet advance. Despite the overwhelming superiority of the enemy, Ringel's determined Gebirgsjäger held their ground, and these hills remained in German hands until the last days of the war.

After the war Ringel lived in retirement, publishing in 1956 an account of his wartime experiences, *Hurra die Gams*. He died in Bavaria on 10 February 1967 at the age of 78.

As evidenced by his many medal ribbons, Ringel had enjoyed a long and successful career in the Austro-Hungarian and later Austrian armies before being taken into the Deutsches Heer after his country's annexation. The white-enamelled award worn below his Knight's Cross is the Bulgarian Order of St Alexander; his Austrian ribbons are the Order of the Iron Crown, Military Merit Medal (Silver & Bronze), Karl Troops Cross, and Tyrol Commemorative Medal 1914–18; his German medals are the Army Long Service, Austrian Anschluss 1938, Occupation of Czechoslovakia 1938, and Great War Cross of Honour – retrospectively awarded by Chancellor Hindenburg in 1934. (Josef Charita)

### Generalleutnant Theodor Scherer (Plate E2)

Theodor Scherer was born on 17 September 1889 at Hoechstädt, Bavaria, the son of a schoolteacher. Joining Bavarian Infanterie Regiment 12 as an officer candidate, he was commissioned Leutnant in October 1910. Scherer served throughout World War I in machine gun detachments, ending the war as a Hauptmann. He joined the Bavarian Police, and spent 15 years as a police officer; he was an Oberstleutnant by 1935, when he rejoined the Army in that same rank. Scherer initially served on the staff of Infanterie Regiment 111; he was promoted Oberst in January 1937, and in April 1938 was given command of Infanterie Regiment 56 in Ulm. After two years Scherer was transferred to take command of the newly formed Infanterie Regiment 507, which he led throughout the campaign in the West and until September 1940. In November of that year he was promoted Generalmajor.

In October 1941, Scherer was chosen – no doubt because of his police experience – to take command of 281. Sicherungs Division. These 'security divisions' were not front line combat formations, but lightly equipped for ensuring the security of the areas behind the front, which were often infested with partisans and Red Army stragglers. Despite this modest divisional command, Scherer was destined to be in the right place at the right time to find fame, in one of the most dramatic actions of the winter 1941/42 crisis on the Eastern Front.

Cholm is a small town on the River Lovat, between Wilikije Luki and Demjansk, and one of the few areas of firm terrain in a region with more than its fair share of swampland. By January 1942 the region was under severe pressure from the Soviet counter-offensive; the area held by the Wehrmacht at Cholm was gradually compressed into a perimeter barely a mile across, and by 21 January the town was completely surrounded. Inside this 'cauldron' were a number of disparate units including elements of Infanterie Regiments 218 & 329, a battalion from a Luftwaffe field regiment, a Police Reserve battalion, transport units, and even some Navy personnel from river craft, plus Scherer's 281. Sicherungs Division headquarters: in all, around 5,500 men.

This 'Kampfgruppe Scherer' at first possessed no anti-tank guns; and artillery bombardments destroyed most of the houses, leaving the Germans without shelter in the bitter cold. The lack of cover was also important in that enemy snipers took a regular toll of German soldiers. Fortunately for Scherer, there was no flexibility to the enemy tactics; the Germans were able to predict accurately where and when each new assault would be made, allowing them to concentrate their meagre resources in that sector. Crucially, they were also able to radio for supporting artillery fire from outside the pocket. Eventually a flight of Ju52 transports succeeded in flying in a handful of anti-tank guns and some medical supplies.

As the siege wore on, overwhelming pressure of numbers allowed the Soviets to capture and maintain a foothold in the eastern outskirts of the town. Ambushes were laid, and as the Soviet troops advanced through the narrow streets, in which their supporting tanks were unable to manoeuvre, they were scythed down or forced to withdraw in disarray. With the advent of better weather in the early spring further Luftwaffe supply missions were mounted, although the position remained precarious. Finally, on 5 May 1942, supported by a massive artillery barrage and Stuka dive-bombers, a relief force broke through to the garrison, which by then numbered only 1,200 men still fit for action. For 107 days Scherer's troops had held off all enemy attempts to sieze the town, although the Red Army had launched almost 2,000 individual assault actions during the siege. On 1 July 1942 a special 'battle shield' award was instituted for veterans of the battle to display on their left sleeve.

For this achievement, Scherer was decorated with the Knight's Cross on 20

Facial hair was usually restricted to moustaches. While 'Papa' Ringel's neat beard was the kind of dandified affectation tolerated in an admired officer from a non-German military tradition, they were normally only allowed in the German Army to disguise disfiguring facial wounds. Theodor Scherer – shown here in the uniform of a Generalmajor after the award of the Oakleaves to his Knight's Cross – was for a time an exception to this rule, but such portraits date from the harsh Russian winter of 1941/42 when his division won renown in the Cholm Pocket. (Josef Charita)

February 1942, and on 5 May with the Oakleaves. In September 1942 he was appointed to command 34. Infanterie Division, and two months later was promoted to Generalleutnant. His new division fought in Heeresgruppe Mitte's defensive battles during 1942–43, at Kharkov in January 1943 and particularly well in the third battle for that city in August 1943. After the spring 1944 retreat across the northern Ukraine, by July it was good for nothing but transfer to a rear area behind the Italian front.

In April 1944, GenLt Scherer had been appointed to the rather unglamorous role of inspector of coastal defences on the Eastern Front. The final ignominy came in late 1944, when his C-in-C GenObst Schörner posted Scherer back to Germany with the comment that he had 'no further use for him and his staff within my sector'.

Theodor Scherer survived the war, but was killed in an accident at Ludwigsburg in May 1951.

### Generalleutnant Fritz Bayerlein (Plate E3)

Fritz Hermann Michael Bayerlein was born on 14 January 1899 in Würzburg. In June 1917 he joined Infanterie Regiment 9 as an officer cadet; however, the war ended before he was comissioned. He became a Leutnant in January 1922, after nearly three years in the ranks of the Reichswehr; thereafter he gradually progressed

This later photo of the gaunt-featured Scherer, clean-shaven this time, shows him wearing on his left sleeve the Cholm Shield created as a campaign award for the personnel who held – or landed aircraft to supply – that surrounded position. It is also interesting to note that he wears the Wound Badge in both its 1918 Imperial and 1939 versions, side by side. It was much more common for servicemen to 'consolidate' their total number of wounds into the relevant class of the World War II award. (Josef Charita)

through the ranks, reaching Major in June 1938.

In April 1939 Bayerlein was assigned to the staff of 10. Panzer Division, with which he served during the Polish campaign. Throughout 1940 and most of 1941 Bayerlein held various staff positions, being promoted Oberstleutnant. His next major posting was as chief-of-staff to the Deutsches Afrikakorps in October 1941. Bayerlein was decorated with the Knight's Cross on 26 December 1941.

In April 1942 Bayerlein was promoted Oberst. During the period when Gen Nehring was recovering from wounds received at Alam Halfa in August 1942, Bayerlein briefly held command of the DAK. When Gen von Thoma was captured at El Alamein on 4 November, Bayerlein once again resumed control of the Afrikakorps during the subsequent retreat. On 7 December 1942, Obst Bayerlein was appointed chief-of-staff to Panzerarmee Afrika. On 1 March 1943, he was promoted Generalmajor; but like Rommel – whose loyal admirer he was – Bayerlein was by now in poor health. He developed rheumatism and hepatitis, and was evacuated from North Africa on 7 May 1943 just before the final surrender. On 6 July 1943, Bayerlein was decorated with the Oakleaves to his Knight's Cross.

From October 1943 to January 1944, Bayerlein commanded 3. Panzer Division, serving under Guderian on the Eastern Front. In January 1944 he took command of the elite Panzer Lehr Division, many of whose

personnel were highly experienced soldiers who had served as instructors. Bayerlein's appointment to this command was apparently on the personal recommendation of Guderian, and was a tribute to his outstanding abilities. On 1 May 1944, Bayerlein was promoted Generalleutnant.

Panzer Lehr saw heavy combat in Normandy, but under conditions which prevented Bayerlein or his division from fulfilling their potential. Even before being committed to the fighting around Caen on 8 June it had suffered badly from Allied air attacks en route, during one of which Bayerlein himself was wounded, but he led his division into battle the next day. The German armoured reserves in Normandy were greatly handicapped by a muddled chain of command and contradictory orders. After some initial successes Panzer Lehr was unable to throw back the British units it faced, which were supported by heavy naval gunfire. For several days the division held off repeated attacks, suffering heavy attrition in the process. Bayerlein was decorated with the Swords to his Knight's Cross on 20 July 1944. Five days later his division's area suffered 'carpet bombing' by the USAAF of such devastating effect that up to 70 per cent of its strength was destroyed. The remnant was committed to the failed Mortain–Avranches counter-attack in early August.

Gradually withdrawing over the Seine, the survivors of Panzer Lehr returned to Germany, where the division was rebuilt during October 1944. The renewed division fought at Bastogne during the Ardennes offensive in December, before being committed to the defence of the Ruhr the following spring; it was finally surrounded in the Ruhr Pocket. In late March 1945, Bayerlein was appointed to command LIII Armeekorps, and was forced to surrender to US forces on 16 April.

LEFT **Fritz Bayerlein, shown here in a photo from early 1942 as an Oberstleutnant, in tropical service dress, wearing the Knight's Cross he was awarded in December 1941 for his very able work as chief-of-staff to the** *Afrikakorps* **under Rommel's command.**

ABOVE **Bayerlein, now a Generalmajor, wears the Oakleaves and Swords, the latter awarded on 20 July 1944. Although now leading the Panzer Lehr Division in France he still wears the lightweight tropical tunic. Illness and unremitting hard service on two failing fronts have aged him visibly in two-and-a-half years. (Josef Charita)**

Held prisoner until April 1947, Bayerlein retired to his home in Würzburg. He died in January 1970.

### Generalmajor Dr Franz Bäke
### (Plate F1)

Franz Bäke was born at Schwarzenfels on 28 February 1898, and while still a teenager was decorated for gallantry in World War I. After serving in the Reichswehr as an NCO he was commissioned Leutnant in December 1937, and promoted Oberleutnant in November 1939 while serving with Panzer Abteilung 65. In May 1941, serving with Panzer Regiment 11 in 6. Panzer Division, he was promoted to Hauptmann.

The 6. Panzer was soon advancing deep into Russia; the armoured regiment's ageing Skoda PzKw 35(t) tanks reached the outskirts of Leningrad, before being shifted south in September to join the push on

ObstLt Dr Franz Bäke, seen here in the turret cupola of a Tiger tank; the remnant of the Tiger battalion sPzAbt 503 formed part of his powerful Kampfgruppe in early 1944. On the right sleeve of his black Panzer vehicle uniform he displays three Tank Destruction badges, each awarded for the single-handed destruction of an enemy tank with hand-held weapons.

Moscow. It suffered severe losses during the Soviet winter counter-offensive; in December 1941 Bäke rose to command I Btl of his regiment, moving to II Btl in April 1942, when it was withdrawn to France for rebuilding. That August he was promoted to Major; and Bäke continued to prove himself a first class battalion commander after returning to Russia in November 1942, when 6. Panzer Division formed part of 4. Panzerarmee in the vain attempt to relieve Stalingrad. Major Bäke was awarded the Knight's Cross on 11 January 1943; the Oakleaves were added on 1 August 1943, after he showed great gallantry at Kursk, where his regiment fought in the southern pincer of the offensive. It was in this campaign that he personally knocked out three Russian tanks with hand-held weapons while dismounted from his tank.

Bäke was promoted Oberstleutnant in November 1943, subsequently taking command of Panzer Regiment 11. During the defensive fighting of late 1943 and early 1944 he showed intiative and determination at the head of an ad hoc regimental group comprising a PzKw V Panther battalion, some SP guns and engineers, and the remaining few PzKw VI Tigers of sPzAbt 503. In one five-day action in the 'Balabanovka Pocket' they destroyed 267 Soviet AFVs for the loss of one Tiger and four Panthers; ObstLt Bäke received the Swords to the Knight's Cross on 21 February 1944, the award being personally presented by Hitler. Bäke was promoted Oberst in May 1944; and on 3 July that year he was given command of Panzerbrigade 106 'Feldherrnhalle'.

On 9 March 1945, he took command of the so-called Panzer Division 'Feldherrnhalle 2', a makeshift formation cobbled together from the remnants of 13. Panzer Division and 60. Panzergrenadier Division 'Feldherrnhalle', both of which had been virtually wiped out defending Budapest that January. Bäke was promoted to the rank of Generalmajor on 20 April 1945, leading his command on the collapsing Hungarian/ Czechoslovakian/Austrian front.

This remarkable officer survived the war, to die in an automobile accident at Hagen on 12 December 1978.

### Generalmajor Horst Niemack (Plate F2)

Horst Niemack was born in Hannover on 10 March 1909. He joined the Reichswehr in 1927 as an officer cadet and was commissioned Leutnant in 1931. Serving with Reiter Regiment 18, Niemack became an accomplished horseman, and took part in many equestrian competitions. He later served as an instructor at the Kavallerieschule, finally transferring to a reconnaissance unit, Divisions Aufklärungsabteilung 5, in October 1939. He commanded this unit through the Western campaign; it was the first to reach the River Marne, an achievement which brought Rittmeister Niemack the Knight's Cross on 13 July 1940.

Major Horst Niemack, a distinguished cavalry officer and prize-winning horseman, seen here shortly after the award of the Oakleaves to his Knight's Cross in August 1941. The decoration in this case recognized considerable personal gallantry in action as well as skilled leadership of his armoured reconnaissance battalion during the invasion of Russia.

At the beginning of Operation 'Barbarossa', Niemack's unit struck out towards Orla, where the Soviets were thrown back with heavy losses. Niemack continued to pursue the enemy, cutting their main route of retreat. Here his battalion's anti-tank guns and light artillery denied passage along the road for fully five days, and Niemack's troopers fought off several desperate attacks. In recognition of this feat, during which he was seriously wounded, Major Niemack was awarded the Oakleaves on 10 August 1941.

Niemack served as commander of the cavalry section of the school for mobile troops at Potsdam-Krampnitz while recovering from his wounds. He returned to combat duties with Panzergrenadier Regiment 26, 24. Panzer Division, in February 1943 with the rank of Oberstleutnant. In mid-October he took command of Fusilier Regiment 'Grossdeutschland', one of that crack division's two mechanized infantry regiments; from May 1944 it took the prefix 'Panzer' when it was completely equipped with armoured half-tracks. Niemack led his new unit in many hard-fought actions, which often came down to hand-to-hand combat; and on 4 June 1944 he was decorated with the Swords to the Knight's Cross for his regiment's part in successful attacks north of Jassy in Romania. In late August, Niemack's command half-track received a direct hit; he was dragged from the blazing wreckage at the last moment, and immediately evacuated to a Berlin hospital, where surgeons only narrowly avoided having to amputate his left arm.

Niemack returned to duty in January 1945, taking over command of the Panzer Lehr Division from Gen Bayerlein in the rank of Oberst on 5 February (a month short of his 36th birthday), and was subsequently promoted Generalmajor. He was involved in the battles in the Ruhr Pocket, until severely wounded once again at Winterburg on 2 April during fighting against the US 9th Division. Niemack was recovering in hospital when the war ended.

After the war he resumed his passion for equestrian sports, and was chairman of the German Olympic Committee. He also became the President of the Association of Holders of the Knight's Cross in 1954; and served in the West German Army as a Generalmajor of armoured troops. Niemack was decorated with the Grand Cross of the Merit Cross of the Federal German Republic. He died in April 1992 in Hannover.

### Generalmajor Hermann von Oppeln-Bronikowski (Plate F3)

Born in Berlin in 1899, Oppeln-Bronikowski was a Prussian aristocrat. Volunteering for Uhlan Regiment 10 in 1916, he served during th e second half of World War I as a Leutnant platoon commander in Infanterie Regiment 118, winning the Iron Cross 1st Class. After the war he returned to the 10th Cavalry of the Reichswehr, and – like Hasso von Manteuffel and Horst Niemack – made a name for himself as a competition horseman; he represented his country at the 1936 Olympic Games, winning a Gold Medal in the dressage event. Progressing through the ranks, by the outbreak of war in 1939

Oberst von Oppeln-Bronikowski, displaying the Oakleaves to his Knight's Cross, awarded on 28 July 1944 for the stubborn – though doomed – resistance of his 21. Pz Div in Normandy. Note that he also wears in his lapel buttonhole the ribbon of the campaign medal for the first winter on the Eastern Front; this reminder of the grim *'Winterschlacht 1941/42'* was proudly worn thereafter by all survivors, from general to private. (Josef Charita)

Maj Hermann von Oppeln-Bronikowski; as well as the Knight's Cross, he wears the German Cross in Gold on his right breast. Like Niemack a keen equestrian, Oppeln-Bronikowski was also an Olympic Gold Medallist. (Josef Charita)

Oppeln-Bronikowski was a Major commanding the reconnaissance battalion of 24. Infanterie Division.

He served with this unit during the Polish campaign, winning the 1939 clasp to his 1914 Iron Cross; and subsequently was appointed to the staff of Oberkommando des Heeres in 1940. In this appointment he gained valuable knowledge and experience during the campaign in the West. Promoted Oberstleutnant on 1 August 1940, Oppeln-Bronikowski remained with the OKH; his specialist area was the conversion of traditional cavalry into armoured reconnaissance units. After again missing front line service in the Balkan campaign and the early phases of the invasion of the USSR, ObstLt Oppeln-Bronikowski was finally assigned to a combat unit in October 1941 when he joined the staff of 4. Panzer Division, briefly commanding Panzer Regiment 35 in succession to Obst Eberbach in January 1942.

In February 1942 he was promoted Oberst, and took command of Panzer Regiment 204 in 22. Panzer Division on the southern sector of the Russian Front. Mauled at Parpach in March, the division went on to fight extremely effectively on the Kerch Peninsula in May. It advanced to the Don, fighting at Rostov in July, and Oppeln-Bronikowski's tanks accounted for at least 500 Soviet AFVs – an achievement which retrospectively brought him the Knight's Cross in January 1943. By that time, however, 22. Panzer – part of XLVIII Panzerkorps – had been reduced to a wreck during the failed attempts in November-December 1942 to prevent the encirclement of 6. Armee at Stalingrad.

Transferred to command Panzer Regiment 11 in 6. Panzer Division, Oppeln-Bronikowski took part in the ill-fated offensive at Kursk. During the huge tank battle at Prokhorovka, Oppeln-Bronikowski and other officers holding a field conference were mistakenly bombed by Luftwaffe aircraft, and he was seriously wounded. On his recovery he was appointed commander of Panzer Regiment 22 in 21. Panzer Division in France. Destroyed in Tunisia, the division still had a number of Afrikakorps veterans, but had only one battalion of PzKw IV tanks and two dozen ancient French Somuas.

When the Allies landed on 6 June 1944, Oppeln-Bronikowski was ordered to attack immediately in an attempt to destroy the Normandy beachheads. As is notorious, the delays due to a dysfunctional chain of command, and the Allies' total air superiority, robbed the German armoured reserve of their brief chance of achieving this. Panzer Regiment 22 suffered numerous attacks from Allied fighter-bombers on its way towards the British 'Sword' beachhead, before becoming embroiled in furious fighting at Ranville and Caen. On 28 July 1944, Oppeln-Bronikowski received the Oakleaves to his Knight's Cross in recognition of his men's efforts: they had held their positions for over 30 days under severe pressure, at the cost of at least 50 per cent of their armour. Subsequently the remnants of 21. Panzer were fortunate to avoid annihilation in the Falaise Pocket.

In January 1945, Oppeln-Bronikowski was promoted Generalmajor, with command of 20 Panzer Division. He saw action in Silesia, Hungary, Czechoslovakia and Austria, where his division was steadily destroyed in desperate defensive actions. In April 1945 GenMaj Oppeln-Bronikowski was awarded the Swords to his Knight's Cross. He finally disbanded the remnants of his division in the area around Dresden on 8 May 1945, and was captured by US forces.

After the war, Oppeln-Bronikowski once again took up his interest in equestrian sports, coaching the Canadian team for the Tokyo Olympics. He died in retirement in 1966.

### Generalmajor Otto Remer
### (Plate G3)
The character and abilities of this dedicated Nazi stand in contrast to those of previous entries, on officers of long experience who had seen battle in World War I. (Nazi beliefs did not in themselves preclude real military talent, of course – viz. Dietl, Model and Schörner.)

Born on 18 August 1912, Otto Ernst Remer joined the Army at the age of 20. He enjoyed a steady but unspectacular rise through the ranks over the next ten years, reaching the rank of Major by

ObstLt Otto Remer, posing shortly after the award of his Oakleaves in November 1943. The personal bravery of this officer of the 'Grossdeutschland' mechanized infantry was never in question; note the Close Combat Clasp among his many decorations. However, it would become clear that Remer's later promotion to senior command – due to his fanatical loyalty to the Nazis and the accident of his being in a position to help suppress the July 1944 coup attempt – outstripped his competence.

1942, when he rose to command the half-track battalion of the elite Grenadier Regiment 'Grossdeutschland'. At the head of I (gep.) Btl, Panzergrenadier Regiment 'GD', he showed considerable energy during the German counter-attacks which recaptured Kharkov in March 1943 and then pursued the retreating enemy as far as Belgorod. For his part in these actions Remer was decorated with the Knight's Cross on 18 May 1943. He continued to lead his battalion during the great armoured offensive at Kursk, and later at Krivoi Rog, its achievements bringing him the Oakleaves in November 1943.

Remer might well have been forgotten by history as just another brave and competent battalion commander; however, in March 1944 he was posted to take command of the elite Berlin guard detachment Wachregiment Berlin, which was a satellite unit of the 'GD' (and had been its original pre-war parent). On 20 July 1944, when ObstLt von Stauffenberg made the bomb attempt on Hitler's life at his Rastenburg headquarters, Remer was at first ordered by the plotters in the capital to arrest Propaganda Minister Goebbels and to secure the ministry

The Panzergrenadier battalion commander Maj Waldemar von Gazen, in regulation infantry officer's service dress and wearing his Knight's Cross with Oakleaves and Swords.

buildings. However, Goebbels enabled Remer to speak to the Führer by telephone; Hitler promoted Remer to Oberst on the spot, and ordered him to crush the mutiny. Remer acted immediately, and by the end of the day most of the conspirators were either dead or in custody.

Remer's reward was command of the elite Führer Begleit Brigade on the Eastern Front in August, and subsequent promotion to Generalmajor when the brigade was up-graded to a division within the so-called Panzerkorps 'Grossdeutschland' on 31 January 1945. Although the brigade fought well in the Ardennes, reaching St Vith on 21 December, the limitations of an officer promoted beyond his competence steadily became obvious. Throughout Remer's period of command the formation's casualties were heavy, and often blamed upon his incompetence.

Remer was fortunate enough to avoid Soviet captivity, and after the war entered politics, his extreme right wing beliefs unchanged. Although his party gained several seats in parliament it was subsequently banned, and Remer was forced to live in exile for a considerable time. After returning to Germany, in 1992 he was imprisoned for 22 months – when in his 80s – for making inflamatory speeches which amounted to Holocaust denial. Forced into exile once again, Remer died in Spain in 1997.

# REGIMENTAL & BATTALION COMMANDERS

### Oberst Waldemar von Gazen
### (Plate G1)

Born in Hamburg on 6 December 1917, Gazen joined the Wehrmacht as an officer candidate in 1936 and was commissioned Leutnant with Infanterie Regiment 66 in 1938. This unit evolved into Panzergrenadier Regiment 66, which served with 13. Panzer Division. During the attack on Rostov in June 1942, Gazen led his Grenadiers into the city, entering the northern sector where he seized and held an important bridge against enemy counter-attacks, thus ensuring a passage for the units following. For this action he was decorated with the Knight's Cross on 18 September.

In January 1943 Hauptmann von Gazen was in command of a small battlegroup during the fighting in the Caucasus. In a two-day battle of great intensity he and his men held off numerous enemy attacks and knocked out 22 Soviet tanks. On the following day, the enemy succeeded in breaking into the German lines, but were thrown back when Gazen led an immediate counter-attack. For these actions he was awarded the Oakleaves to his Knight's Cross on 18 January 1943. Gazen was promoted Major the following month. Still serving with Panzergrenadier Regiment 66, Maj von Gazen was decorated with the Swords to his Knight's Cross on 3 October 1943. In August 1944 he was assigned to the General Staff, remaining in this post until the end of the war and reaching the rank of Oberst. Released from captivity in 1946, in civilian life he became a lawyer and notary.

### Oberst Heinz Wittchow von Brese-Winiary
### (Plate G2)

Born on 13 January 1914 in Dresden, von Brese-Winiary joined the Army in April 1934, being commissioned Leutnant in 1936. In May 1939 he was promoted Oberleutnant and served as a battalion adjutant with Infanterie Regiment 10, seeing action during the campaign in Poland. He

The studious image of Heinz von Brese-Winiary concealed an extremely tough soldier, a holder of the Close Combat Clasp who was decorated for conspicuous personal gallantry. The Oakleaves to his Knight's Cross were awarded in April 1944; he had already been in almost unbroken combat service since the Polish campaign of 1939, and would fight on until the end.

remained with the regiment during the campaign in the West, earning the Iron Cross 1st Class. For bravery during the first winter of the war on the Eastern Front he was decorated with the German Cross in Gold in December 1941, as one of the early recipients of this newly introduced decoration.

Promoted Hauptmann in March 1942, von Brese-Winiary commanded 6 Kompanie of his regiment. Throughout 1942 he saw continuous action on the southern sector of the Eastern Front during the drive to Stalingrad, being wounded in action several times. In April 1943 he was decorated with the Knight's Cross and promoted to Major. Von Brese had been tasked with defending a bridge over the River Don which was vital for the supply of the German forward units. Despite the fact that he had only a scratch group under his command, made up of stragglers of all types, the bridge was held. Subsequently he was given command of Panzergrenadier Regiment 108 with 14. Panzer Division, and fought with distinction in the Cherkassy Pocket, earning the Oakleaves to his Knight's Cross on 6 April 1944, five days after his promotion to Oberstleutnant.

In September 1944 he was promoted Oberst and given command of the elite Panzer Fusilier Regiment 'Grossdeutschland' in succession to the wounded Obst Niemack, which he led until the unit finally surrendered to the Soviets in February 1945. He survived Soviet captivity, and died in retirement in Freiburg in 1991.

### Oberstleutnant Josef Bremm (Plate H3)

Josef Bremm was born on 3 May 1914 at Mannebach. He joined the Army in 1935, and by the outbreak of war he was a Leutnant with Infanterie Regiment 425. Bremm saw service in the West during the invasion of France, where he earned the Iron Cross in both classes.

With the opening of Operation 'Barbarossa', Bremm served on the northern sector as a platoon commander with Infanterie Regiment 426, 126. Infanterie Division, and was wounded in action a few weeks after the start of the campaign. Given command of 5 Kompanie of his regiment in early August 1941, he was promoted to Oberleutnant in October. During the winter battles of 1941/42, Bremm led his company in repulsing a Soviet attack and then in a furious counter-attack which destroyed an enemy battalion. He was decorated with the Knight's Cross on 18 February 1942. Again wounded in action shortly afterwards, he was evacuated for treatment, and on his recovery was promoted Hauptmann and given command of II Btl of the regiment, still serving on the Leningrad front. In September 1942 Bremm's battalion succeeded in blocking a Soviet attack south-east of Lake Ilmen, which brought him the Oakleaves to his Knight's Cross on 23 December 1942.

Josef Bremm, seen here as a Major, in a formal portrait taken after the award of his Oakleaves in December 1942 for gallantry and leadership at the head of an infantry battalion on the Leningrad front. Already this much-wounded officer looks rather older than his 28 years. On 9 May 1945, on the Western Front, ObstLt Bremm became the final German soldier of World War II to be awarded the Swords to the Knight's Cross.

In January 1943 Bremm was seriously wounded once again during operations to relieve the Demjansk Pocket, and was evacuated to Germany. He was posted to a training school as an infantry tactics instructor, and in February was promoted Major. This was only the briefest of rests, however; in March 1943, at his own request, he was reassigned to a combat unit, with command of a fusilier battalion in 712. Infanterie Division, a static formation then stationed on the Belgian/Dutch coast.

In 1944 Bremm saw heavy combat during the later fighting in Normandy, being given command of Infanterie Regiment 990, 277. Infanterie Division in August 1944. This partly Austrian formation had been sent into the line in mid-June to replace the battered 9. SS-Panzer Division 'Hohenstaufen'; it was heavily engaged against the British around Caen, and the disaster of the Falaise Pocket reduced it to about 1,000 combat troops and 1,500 others. On 1 November 1944, Maj Bremm was promoted to Oberstleutnant.

The 277. Division, rebuilt as a Volksgrenadier formation, saw action again during the Ardennes offensive; ObstLt Bremm was once more seriously wounded, but remained with his Grenadier Regiment 990 through the final retreat into Germany. Bremm would become the last soldier of the German Army to be decorated with the Swords to the Knight's Cross, on 9 May 1945. He survived the war, and died in retirement in 1998 at the age of 84.

## Major Peter Frantz
## (Plate H2)

Born in Leipzig on 22 July 1917, Peter Frantz joined Artillerie Regiment 4 in Dresden as an officer candidate in 1936, gaining his commission two years later. As a Leutnant, he was posted to the artillery regiment of the largely Austrian 2. Panzer Division, and served in the regimental headquarters during the Polish campaign. Frantz then attended the artillery school at Jüterbog where the Army was forming its first battery of Sturmgeschützen (self-propelled assault guns), and was posted as a platoon commander when Batterie 640 was assigned to Infanterie Regiment 'Grossdeutschland' in time to participate in the campaign in the West. Promotion to Oberleutnant came just after the end of the campaign in France.

In June 1941 only the armoured and artillery elements of the 'GD' were initially deployed in the invasion of the USSR, operating with 7. Panzer Division, but the remainder soon followed. OLt Frantz was commanding the assault gun company (designated 16. Kompanie) of the regiment, which saw extremely bitter fighting around Tula in December 1941 during the last push towards Moscow, destroying 15 enemy tanks in one day. For this achievement Frantz was decorated with the Knight's Cross. By March 1942 he had been promoted to command one of the three batteries in what was now the Sturmgeschütz Abteilung 'Grossdeutschland'.

Hptm Peter Frantz, a highly decorated commander of armoured assault guns, in a posed studio portrait taken shortly after the award of the Oakleaves in April 1943. Note the 'Grossdeutschland' divisional cuffband on his right sleeve and the gilt 'GD' cipher on his shoulder straps.

On 14 March 1943, resisting the major Soviet counter-offensive in the region of Kursk, Hptm Frantz (by now the Sturmgeschütz battalion commander in the Panzergrenadier Division 'GD') was leading a detachment of assault guns that destroyed 43 enemy T-34 tanks from a 60-strong force, even calling down artillery fire on their own position when their ammunition began to run low. Hitler personally decorated Frantz with the Oakleaves which he was awarded on 14 April.

Frantz served on with the 'GD' Division until January 1944, when he was assigned to the Kriegsakademie for general staff training. He was promoted Major in the General Staff (Major i.G) in August 1944. In the latter part of the war Frantz served on a corps headquarters staff on the Western Front; he was captured by US forces in May 1945.

### Major Willy Jähde
### (Plate H1)

Willy Jähde was born at Helmsdorf on 18 January 1908. Joining the Reichswehr in 1927, he was assigned to a transport unit, and eventually gained his commission as a Leutnant in 1934.

By the outbreak of war he had been promoted Oberleutnant and was serving as a company commander in Panzer Abteilung 66 of 7. Panzer Division. Jähde served during both the Polish and French campaigns, earning the Iron Cross in both classes; he was promoted Hauptmann in 1940, before being transferred to the Unterführerschule at Putloss as an instructor.

He returned to combat duty in mid 1942 with Panzer Regiment 29, 12. Panzer Division on the Leningrad front, and the following summer he saw action during the Kursk offensive. In late October 1943, Hptm Jähde returned to the Leningrad front as commander of the Tiger tank battalion schwere Panzer Abteilung 502. For about six weeks from the beginning of November 1943 the unit was involved in furious defensive battles near Nevel, where it became encircled and was forced to fight its way out. More defensive battles around Voronovo followed, the massive Tigers being used as a mobile 'fire brigade' whose appearance on the battlefield often proved decisive. By late February 1944 the Abteilung had run up a score of over 500 enemy tanks destroyed. For this achievement Jähde was decorated with the Knight's Cross on 16 March 1944.

From May of that year until the closing stages of the war Jähde commanded the school for Panzer NCOs at Eisenach, returning briefly to combat duty when he took command of a small Kampfgruppe just before the end. He was captured by US forces but released within a couple of months, returning to civilian life. His home was now in the Soviet zone (DDR), from which Jähde and his family escaped in 1961. In retirement he lived at Tutzing.

Major Willy Jähde of sPzAbt 502 is seen here in a snapshot taken on the Leningrad front. This Tiger tank commander habitually wore a sheepskin jacket over his black Panzer uniform during the Russian winter.

# THE PLATES

## A1: Generalfeldmarschall Erich von Manstein; Sebastopol, July 1942

As commander of Army Group South during the siege of Sebastopol, von Manstein wears a field uniform with the general officers' field-grey *Feldmütze* of the M1938 'new style'. This cap bears the gold general officers' national eagle-and-swastika insignia, and gold piping on the crown seam, the front 'scallop' of the turn-up flap, and in an inverted 'V' around the national cockade. The all field-grey tunic (i.e. without dark green badge cloth facing to the collar) appears in a photograph to be of lightweight material; it is worn with plain grey breeches (without the regulation generals' scarlet *Lampassen* double stripes and seam piping), and officers' riding boots. The gold breast eagle, 'Alt Larisch' collar patches, and shoulder straps are those of all general officers, the latter distinguished by the silver crossed batons of field marshal. His decorations are the Knight's Cross (awarded 19 July 1940, as Gen der Inf commanding XXXVIII Corps in France), and the ribbon of his World War I Iron Cross 2nd Class with a crossed swords clasp. After the institution on 25 July of the Crimea battle shield, awarded to all ranks for operations on that front between 21 September 1941 and 4 July 1942 **(see detail, right)**, von Manstein apparently displayed a gold version on his upper left sleeve. His brown officers' field belt supports a holstered Walther PPK semi-automatic pistol.

## A2: Generalfeldmarschall Erwin Rommel; French coast, spring 1944

Inspecting the coastal defences as Oberbefehlshaber West, Rommel carries the field marshal's *Interimstab* baton. His *Schirmmütze* service cap has generals' gold piping and chin cords, but the silver national eagle and wreath which were regulation before 1 January 1943. His generals' field-grey greatcoat has dark green collar facing and scarlet lapel facing; the exposed dark green tunic collar bears scarlet generals' patches with abbreviated 'Alt Larisch' embroidery, with only two 'leaves' instead of three. Almost obscured here are field-grey breeches complete with scarlet *Lampassen*. His throat decorations are the Knight's Cross with Oakleaves, Swords and Diamonds (awarded, respectively, 26 March 1940, 20 March 1941, 20 January 1942 & 11 March 1943), above the *Pour le Mérite* awarded in December 1917 for bravery on the Italian front during the Caporetto campaign.

## A3: Generalfeldmarschall Walter Model; Holland, September 1944

The commander of Heeresgruppe B during the Allied Operation 'Market Garden', Model wears his characteristic monocle, and a light cellophane British anti-gas 'eye protector' on his service cap, which bears the gold insignia ordered on 1 January 1943. His field-grey service tunic with green collar facing, and grey breeches with scarlet double stripes flanking scarlet seam piping, are conventional; the

latter have light grey suede cavalry-style reinforcement on the inner leg. He wears regulation insignia for his rank on collar, breast and shoulder straps. At the throat he displays the Knight's Cross with Oakleaves, Swords and Diamonds (awarded, respectively, 9 July 1941, 17 February 1942, 2 April 1943 & 17 August 1944). He wears the buttonhole ribbon of the 1941/42 Eastern Winter Campaign medal; and on his left breast, his World War I Iron Cross 1st Class below the clasp of a World War II repeat award. In the same cluster are his Tank Battle Badge, and a Wound Badge in Gold signifying a total of five separate awards.

## B1: General der Gebirgstruppe Ferdinand Schörner; Finland, spring 1943

As commander of Heeresgruppe Nord in northern Finland, April–May 1943, General of Mountain Troops Schörner wears a field uniform assembled to personal taste. The field-grey *Bergmütze* bears no indication of his rank apart from gold buttons; the Edelweiss badge worn by all ranks of the mountain troops **(see detail right)** is obscured here, but was worn on the left side of the flap, stem forward. His field-grey service tunic is an old M1928 model, with scarlet general officers' piping on the lower and front edges of the green-faced collar, down the front edge and round the cuffs. His insignia of rank are conventional; on his right upper sleeve he displays the mountain troops' Edelweiss patch. His throat decorations are the Knight's Cross (awarded 20 April 1941, as general commanding 6th Mountain Division), and the *Pour le Mérite*, which he was awarded – like Rommel – for bravery in the Caporetto fighting of autumn 1917. On his left breast pocket is the large Gold Party Badge, awarded to

Ferdinand Schörner's portrait, as executed by the famous war artist Wolfgang Willrich. Almost all the leading field commanders sat for such portraits by Willrich, which were then mass-produced in postcard form for sale to the public. Note that the rank shown on his shoulder straps is the two stars of a general. (Josef Charita)

Nazi Party members with numbers below 100,000. Photos show the loose trousers of mountain troops, gathered at the ankle, in a paler shade than his tunic; they are worn with heavily cleated regulation mountain boots.

## B2: Generalfeldmarschall Gerd von Rundstedt, autumn 1944

Von Rundstedt was often photographed in this uniform, which emphasized his background in the Imperial army and his pride in his appointment as honorary colonel (Chef) of Infanterie Regiment 18. It displays a combination of regimental and field marshal's rank features: the M1920 eight-button officers' service tunic has infantry-white frontal piping; the regimental officers' silver bars (Litzen) on infantry-white collar patches; and field marshal's shoulder straps on infantry-white underlay, bearing both the batons and the regimental number. The cap has pre-1943 insignia; the striped field-grey breeches, riding boots, grey kid gloves and Interimstab are all conventional. His decorations include both World War I and II awards of the Iron Cross 1st Class, and the Knight's Cross with Oakleaves (respectively, 30 September 1939 & 1 July 1944).

## B3: Generalfeldmarschall Ewald von Kleist; Ukraine, spring 1943

The commander of Heeresgruppe Süd wears a pair of motoring goggles over the 1943 insignia on his service cap. His clothing is as regulations, apart from the fur collar added to his generals' greatcoat. His Knight's Cross and Oakleaves

**Ewald von Kleist receives his marshal's baton from Adolf Hitler at a special ceremony at the Führerhauptquartier following his elevation to Generalfeldmarschall in February 1943. Note that Kleist carries a sidearm (probably a Walther PPK) even in the Führer's presence; this would later be prohibited out of fear of assassination attempts. (US National Archives)**

were awarded, respectively, on 15 May 1940 and 17 February 1942.

## C1: Generalleutnant Hans Hube; Sicily, August 1943

The most obvious feature of the commander of XIV Panzerkorps is the odd-looking false left arm; this replaced the limb which he lost in 1914. The combination of the olive cotton tropical uniform with white shirt and black tie is unusual, but not unique in wartime photographs. The cap bears plain all-ranks' insignia but has generals' gold piping at the crown, front scallop and in an inverted 'V'. Tunic insignia and breeches are regulation; note the gold-on-black breast eagle of a General der Panzertruppe. Unusually, Gen Hube displays his 1914 and 1939 Iron Crosses 1st Class and his Tank Battle Badge, but not his Knight's Cross with Oakleaves and Swords (awarded, respectively, 1 August 1941, 16 January 1942 & 21 December 1942).

## C2: Generaloberst Eduard Dietl; Soviet/Finnish border, June 1942

The commander of 20th Mountain Army, and Oberbefehlshaber Lapland, displays a dazzling array of insignia and awards on this uniform – basically the field-grey Bergmütze and M1935 'piped field service tunic' (Feldblüse mit Vorstössen), and stone-grey generals' breeches worn with puttees and mountain boots. The cap is unpiped at this date and bears silver national insignia, with the Edelweiss

**Gen Eduard Dietl, in a leather greatcoat of the type favoured by many senior officers, greets one of his soldiers decorated with the Knight's Cross, Uffz Helmut Valtiner, temporarily serving in the military police while recovering from wounds received during the action which earned him the award. Dietl's modest social background and friendly manner made him well liked by his troops and by the Finnish population alike. (Josef Charita)**

badge pinned to the left side. The insignia of rank on the shoulders and red-piped collar, and the gold breast eagle, are regulation. Dietl was awarded the Knight's Cross on 9 May 1940, and the first-ever award of the Oakleaves on 19 July 1940. The Edelweiss right sleeve patch is balanced by the Narvik battle shield on the left **(see detail, left)**. On his right breast pocket is the prestigious mountain guides' (*Bergführer*) qualification badge – an honorary award, as was the Luftwaffe's Pilot/Observer badge pinned to his left breast alongside his Wound Badge in Silver, and Iron Crosses 1st Class of both World Wars. A final presentation piece is the Navy's 'honour dagger' which Dietl received after the battle of Narvik, engraved with the names of the ten destroyers of the Narvik squadron.

**C3: Generaloberst Heinz Guderian, c.1943–44**
This figure is chosen to illustrate Gen Guderian wearing the black 'special uniform for armoured troops' with generals' distinctions – which is only rarely seen in photographs of the Inspector of Armoured Troops. He wears the service cap with pre-1943 insignia; his rank is otherwise indicated only by the gold breast eagle and the shoulder straps, since he follows regulations in wearing the all-ranks pink-piped death's-head collar patches of the Panzertruppe. Awards of both classes of Iron Cross in both World Wars are displayed – in the buttonhole (2nd Class), and on the left breast (1st Class), beside his Tank Battle Badge.

**D1: General der Panzertruppe Ludwig Crüwell; Libya, May 1942**
The temporary commander of Panzerarmee Afrika in Rommel's absence, Gen Crüwell was photographed in this uniform shortly after being captured by British forces. Just visible under the goggles is gold generals' piping on his tropical field cap. This, his tunic and shorts all show differing shades, as was common with the frequently washed tropical cotton clothing; they are worn with high, first-pattern laced tropical boots of canvas and leather. All insignia are conventional; note on his right sleeve the 'AFRIKAKORPS' formation cuff title introduced on 18 July 1941. At his throat are his Knight's Cross (4 May 1941) and Oakleaves (1 September 1941). Just visible above his belt buckle, a monocle hangs on a fine cord.

**D2: General der Panzertruppe Hasso von Manteuffel; Ardennes, December 1944**
The commander of 5th Armoured Army wears the popular 'old style officers' field cap', with no cords, a soft leather peak, gold piping, but with non-regulation gilt metal

**Wolfgang Willrich's portrait study of Gen Ludwig Crüwell, executed in charcoal. Note at top left the insignia of the *Gespenster* or 'Ghost' Division (11. Panzer Division, which Crüwell had commanded); and a facsimile of his signature at top right, above Willrich's own runic logo. (Josef Charita)**

wreathed cockade instead of the regulation flat-woven badge. The collar patches of rank are visible on a late war field-grey tunic collar. His shoulder straps (on which he sometimes displayed the 'Grossdeutschland' Division's 'GD' cipher) are attached to a privately purchased leather greatcoat, to the right forearm of which – very unusually – Gen von Manteuffel has added two cuff titles: the commemorative 'AFRIKA' band, prescribed by regulation for the other sleeve, above the 'Grossdeutschland' title of his former division. His Knight's Cross, Oakleaves and Swords were awarded respectively on 27 November 1941, 19 November 1943 & 22 February 1944.

**D3: Generalmajor Julius Ringel; Crete, 1941**
The commanding general of 5th Mountain Division, instantly recognizable by his beard, wears the M1930 field-grey *Bergmütze* with single-piece insignia (the eagle still silver) and the Edelweiss side badge. The tropical tunic (of a more faded olive shade than the breeches) is shown in different photographs with both closed collar and generals' collar patches, and with this plain open collar – perhaps the latter style dated from the award of the Knight's Cross on 13 June 1941? It bears rank shoulder straps, a pin-on gilt metal breast eagle, the Edelweiss right sleeve patch, the Iron Cross 1st and 2nd Classes, a Wound Badge, and a long ribbon bar displaying 'Papa' Ringel's Austro-Hungarian World War I and German awards.

**E1: General der Panzertruppe Heinrich Eberbach; France, August 1944**
The commander of 7th Army was one of the relatively few

A portrait study of Obst Franz Bäke wearing the Swords added to his Knight's Cross with Oakleaves on 21 February 1944. Of particular interest is the Tank Battle Badge worn under the Iron Cross 1st Class on his left breast. This is the special version awarded to those who had taken part in at least 100 separate tank battles; it is rarely seen in photographs. (Josef Charita)

Panzer generals who retained the black tank uniform after reaching senior rank. This seems to follow the original M1934 pattern, with a very broad collar piped all round in pink *Waffenfarbe*, bearing the regulation all-ranks patches. It is worn with the black version of the officers' M1938 'new style field cap' with an inverted 'V' of pink piping round the cockade. Generals' rank is indicated by his shoulder straps, gold eagles on cap and breast, and gold cap piping. His decorations are the buttonhole ribbons of the 1941/42 Eastern Winter Campaign medal and 1914 Iron Cross 2nd Class with 1939 clasp; the 1914 Iron Cross 1st Class with 1939 clasp; the Tank Battle Badge, and a Wound Badge in Silver. Eberbach's face shows evidence of the severe wound he suffered in 1915, after which his nose had to be partially reconstructed.

### E2: Generalmajor Theodor Scherer; Cholm, early 1942

Another of the tiny handful of German senior officers who wore beards, Scherer wears against the cold of the Russian winter an example of the long, loose, reinforced M1934 watchcoat or surcoat *(Übermantel)*, with in this case

sheepskin lining added to its broad collar, and shoulder straps of his rank. His 'old style' officers' field cap has gold piping and regulation flat-woven silver insignia. His issue ski boots are protected by canvas 'Styrian' gaiters. On 1 July 1942 a battle shield **(see detail, right)** was instituted for veterans of the Cholm Pocket.

### E3: Generalleutnant Fritz Bayerlein; Normandy, June 1944

The commander of the Panzer Lehr Division wears the M1943 'universal field cap', which became increasingly popular among senior officers in the last two years of the war; this example lacks either generals' or even officers' piping, and only the pin-on gold eagle from a service cap betrays Bayerlein's status. His service dress is otherwise entirely conventional for his rank, though he displays the gilt 'L' cipher of his division on the shoulder straps **(see detail, Plate F)**. His Knight's Cross was awarded on 26 December 1941 when he was Rommel's chief-of-staff in North Africa; the Oakleaves, on 6 July 1943 for staff service in Italy.

### F1: Generalmajor Dr Franz Bäke; Eastern Front, April 1945

The black tank uniform and M1943 cap are illustrated here with gold insignia and piping, although this officer could only have worn major-general's distinctions in the last two weeks of the war, when he was promoted to command Panzer Division 'Feldherrnhalle 2' (formerly 13. Panzer Division) on the Hungarian/Czechoslovakian/Austrian front. However, several photographs confirm his former uniform as the colonel commanding Panzer Brigade 106 'Feldherrnhalle', and he wears the silver-on-brown cuff band with that honour title. His most noticeable decorations – remarkable for such a senior officer – are the three right-sleeve badges each for single-handed destruction of a tank with hand-held weapons, which he won at Kursk. Apart from his Iron Crosses and 1941/42 Winter Campaign ribbon, he also displays the bi-metal Tank Battle Badge for 100 engagements, and a Wound Badge in Gold for five or more wounds. His Knight's Cross, Oakleaves and Swords were awarded on 11 January 1943, 1 August 1943, and 21 February 1944 respectively.

### F2: Generalmajor Horst Niemack; Ruhr, March 1945

Another distinguished colonel who only attained general rank in the final weeks of the war, Niemack took over command of the Panzer Lehr Division from Gen Bayerlein on 5 February 1945, but only held the post until being wounded once again on 2 April. He is illustrated in completely conventional M1936 service dress, though with leather-reinforced cavalry breeches; the Pz Lehr Div officers' gilt 'L' cipher **(see detail, above)** is pinned to his shoulder straps. Surprisingly, he does not display a Wound Badge, only his Iron Cross 1st Class, and Knight's Cross with Oakleaves and Swords.

### F3: Generalmajor Hermann von Oppeln-Bronikowski; Silesia, early 1945

The last commander of 20. Panzer Division, this aristocratic cavalryman wears black tank uniform with gold insignia and piping and the shoulder straps of the general rank he finally attained in January 1945. He displays the usual decorations and Battle Badge; note on his right breast the German Cross in Gold.

## G1: Hauptmann Waldemar von Gazen; Caucasus, January 1943

Illustrated as a captain commanding a Kampfgruppe of PzGren Regt 66, 13. Pz Div, von Gazen wears the 'old style' officers' field cap; and a motorcyclist's rubberized fabric coat (*Kradschutzmantel*) with cloth-faced collar. Cap and shoulder straps of rank show the green *Waffenfarbe* piping and underlay of Panzergrenadiers. His Knight's Cross and Oakleaves show at his shirt collar.

## G2: Oberst Heinz Wittchow von Brese-Winiary; Lithuania, September 1944

The newly promoted colonel commanding Panzer Fusilier Regiment 'Grossdeutschland' (in practice, simply this large division's second mechanized infantry regiment) is portrayed in full service dress, with decorations that represent almost a history of the German infantryman's war. He was awarded his Iron Cross 2nd Class in Poland, 1939; the 1st Class in France, 1940; the German Cross in Gold for the 1941/42 winter campaign in Russia; his Knight's Cross for leading a battlegroup in the aftermath of Stalingrad in spring 1943, and the Oakleaves for commanding a regiment in the Cherkassy Pocket in April 1944. In the meantime he had earned the Infantry Assault Badge (bronze, for mechanized troops); the Close Combat Clasp in Gold; and a Wound Badge in Gold – in all von Brese was wounded no fewer than nine times.

## G3: Generalmajor Otto Remer; Eastern Front, spring 1945

Newly promoted to command the Führer Begliet Division (nominally expanded to that status from its true identity as a badly mauled brigade), this fanatical Nazi officer gives the Party salute – which compulsorily replaced the old military salute for all personnel after the 20 July 1944 coup which he helped suppress. Like Obst von Brese, his unit forms part of the 'Grossdeutschland' Corps, so he wears the 'GD' cipher on his shoulder straps; unlike von Brese, who was newly transferred to that corps, the long-serving Remer also wears its cuff title on his right sleeve. Remer's uniform and insignia are conventional. His decorations include the Knight's Cross, which he received in May 1943 when commanding the halftrack-equipped I Btl/ PzGren Regt 'GD' at Kharkov, and the Oakleaves, which followed that November for his command of the regiment. He also displays the Iron Cross, German Cross in Gold, General Assault Badge, Close Combat Clasp in Silver, and Wound Badge in Silver; and the ribbons of the Iron Cross 2nd Class, Winter 1941/42 and 4 Years' Service medals.

## H1: Major Willy Jähde; Leningrad front, March 1944

The commander of the Tiger tank battalion sPz Abt 502 was photographed wearing this sheepskin jacket over his black tank uniform. The system of sleeve ranking, in green oakleaves and bars printed on black, was introduced in February 1942 for all clothing that was not supposed to bear shoulder straps; in practice, it is not much seen in wartime photographs.

## H2: Major Peter Frantz; Eastern Front, spring 1943

The commander of the 'Grossdeutschland' Division's Sturmgeschütz Abteilung is pictured during the rest period in the rear which followed his unit's distinguished fighting in

Maj Willy Jähde, seen here in the distinctive black Panzer jacket, which was more usually worn with the lapels pressed open. This portrait study was taken not long after the award of his Knight's Cross in March 1944. (Josef Charita)

early March, for which he was awarded the Oakleaves to his Knight's Cross. The field-grey 'special uniform' for assault gun crews is conventional, but note the divisional cuff band worn high on the right forearm. Frantz's shoulder straps have the usual artillery-red *Waffenfarbe* underlay and 'GD' ciphers (see detail, right), and his collar *Litzen* have matching red 'lights' on the silver lace bars. Most unusually, the silver officers' piping on his M1938 'new style' field cap extends to the soutache of braid around the cockade.

## H3: Oberstleutnant Josef Bremm; Ruhr Pocket, spring 1945

This much wounded and highly decorated infantry officer is included for symbolic reasons: he was the last man to be awarded the Swords to the Knight's Cross, on 9 May 1945 – 24 hours after the European war ended. We reconstruct the commander of Gren Regt 990, 277. VolksGren Div as wearing a helmet without insignia; and a field-grey leather greatcoat, to which he has added his lieutenant-colonel's shoulder straps with infantry white underlay.

# INDEX

Figures in **bold** refer to illustrations.

1. Panzerarmee 21, 29
2. Panzerarmee 12
3. Gebirgs Division 22
3. Panzer Division 46
4. Panzer Division 51
5. Panzerarmee 31, 42
6. Armee 52
6. Gebirgs Division 14
6. Panzer Division 48, 49, 52
7. Panzer Division 30, 31, 57, 58
9. Armee 12
11. Panzer Division, 'Ghost' 41
13. Panzer Division 55
14. Panzer Division 56
XIV Panzerkorps 29, 41
15. Panzer Division 41
16. Panzer Division 28, 29
XVI Korps 26
18. Armee 43
XIX Gebirgskorps 14
XIX Panzerkorps 26
20. Panzer Division 52
21. Panzer Division 41, 52
22. Panzer Division 52
XXII Armeekorps 20
XXXVIII Armeekorps 9
XXXX Panzerkorps 42
XLII Korps 10
XXXXVII Panzerkorps 42
XLVIII Panzerkorps 52
XXXXVIII Armeekorps 41
XXXXVIII Panzerkorps 42
LIII Armeekorps 47
LVI Panzerkorps 9
281. Sicherungs Division 44, 45

Afrikakorps 5–6, 41, 46, 52
Ardennes offensives
    (1940) 9
    (1944) 31–2, 47, 54, 57

Bäke, Generalmajor Dr. Franz **F1, 48,**
    48–9, 62, **62**
Balabanovka Pocket 49
*Barbarossa*, operation 11–12, 19, 28, 50,
    56
Bayerlein, Generalleutnant Fritz **E3,**
    46–8, **47,** 62
Blitzkreig 24, 25
Bremm, Oberstleutnant Josef **H3, 56,**
    56–7, 63
Brese-Winiary, Oberst Heinz Wittchow
    **G2, 55,** 55–6, 63

Cherkassy Pocket 11
Cholm Pocket 45
Crete, invasion of 43
Crimea 10, 15
Crüwell, General der Panzertruppe
    Ludwig 32, **32, D1,** 41, 61, **61**

Austrian **44**
Bulgarian Order of St. Alexander **44**
Cholm campaign shield 45
Crimea campaign shield **11**
German Cross in Gold 56
Grand Cross of the Merit Cross of the
    Federal German Republic 50
Iron Cross **20,** 51, 56
Knight's Cross 5, **5,** 6, 7, 9, **9,** 10, 11, **11,**
    13, 14, 15, 16, 18, 19, **20,** 21, 22, 23, **23,**
    26, **26,** 29, 30, 31, 32, 41, 43, 45–6, 47,
    49, 50, 52, 53, 55, 56, 57, 58
    Association of Holders of the 50
Kuban campaign shield **21**
Narvik campaign shield **23,** 24
Romanian Order of Michael **9**
Demjansk Pocket 57
*Der Infanterist* (Hube) 28
Dietl, Generaloberst Eduard 4, 22–4, **23,**
    **C2, 60,** 60–1
Dnieper sector, Eastern Front 15, 19, 29
Dunkirk evacuation 19

Eastern Front *see* Russian campaign
Eberbach, General der Panzertruppe
    Heinrich **E1,** 41–2, **42,** 61–2

Falaise Pocket 52, 57
Finnish campaign 24
Fortune, General Victor **6**
Frantz, Major Peter **H2, 57,** 57–8, 63

Gazen, Oberst Waldemar von **G1, 54,** 55,
    63
German commanders, characteristics of
    3–4
Goebbels, Joseph 7, 11, 53–4
Grossdeutschland Division 31, 50, 53, 57
Guderian, Generaloberst Heinz 4, 19, **24,**
    24–8, **25, 26, C3,** 47, 61

Heeresgruppe A 15, 18, 21
Heeresgruppe Mitte 27, 46
Heeresgruppe Nord 12, 15, 43
Heeresgruppe Süd 17, 19, 29, 41
Hitler, Adolf 3, 4, **10,** 12, 13, 18, 19, 26,
    27, 31
    assassination plot (July 1944) 4, 8, 27,
    53–4
    and Rommel 5, 8
Hube, Generaloberst Hans **27, 28,** 28–9,
    **C1,** 60
*Hurra die Gams* (Ringel) 44

*Infanterie Greift An* (Rommel) 5
Italian campaign 29

Jähde, Major Willy **H1,** 58, **58,** 63, **63**

Keitel, Generaloberst Wilhelm **3,** 19
Kesselring, Generalfeldmarschall Albert
    20
Kharkov 10, 19, 21, 31, 46, 53
Kiev 19, 21, 27, 29
Kleist, Generaloberst Ewald von 19, **20,**

20–2, **B3,** 60, **60**
Korsun Pocket 11
Kursk 11, 12, 31, 49, 52, 53, 58

Leningrad 10
Lutz, Oberst Oswald 25–6

Manstein, Generalfeldmarschall Erich von
    **9,** 9–11, **10,** 18, 29, **A1,** 59
Manteuffel, General der Panzertruppe
    Hasso von **29,** 29–32, **30, D2,** 61
Model, Generalfeldmarschall Walter 4,
    11–14, **12, 13, A3,** 59
Montgomery, General Bernard 8

Narvik 22, 23
Niemack, Generalmajor Horst **F2, 49,**
    49–50, 62
Nikopol Pocket 15
Normandy invasion 19
North Africa campaign 5–6, 41, 46, 52
Norwegian campaign 22–4

Olympic games 50, 52
Oppeln-Bronikowski, Generalmajor
    Herman von **F3, 50,** 50–2, **51,** 62

Panzer Division Feldherrnhalle 2 49
Panzer Lehr Division 46, 50
Panzergruppe 2 27
Panzergruppe Kleist 20
Polish campaign 14, 17–18, 20, 51

Remer, Generalmajor Otto **G3,** 52–5, **53,**
    63
Ringel, General der Gebirstruppe Julius
    3, **D3,** 42–4, **43, 44,** 61
Rommel, Generalfeldmarschall Erwin 3,
    4–8, **5, 6, 7, A2,** 59
Ruhr Pocket 14, 47, 50
Rundstedt, Generalfeldmarschall Gerd
    von 4, **7,** 16–20, **17, 18, B2,** 60
Russian campaign 10, 11–12, 15, 19, 21,
    27, 28–9, 30, 31, 41, 42, 43, 45, 46,
    48–9, 50, 52, 53, 55, 56, 57, 58

Scherer, Generalleutnant Theodor **E2,**
    44–6, **45, 46,** 62
Schleicher, Generalleutnant Kurt von 16
Schörner, Generalfeldmarschall
    Ferdinand 4, 14–16, **15, 16, B1,** 46,
    59–60, **60**
Sevastopol 10
Sicily campaign 29
Sponeck, General Graf von 10
Springer, SS-Sturmbannführer Heinrich
    **13**
Stalingrad 10, 21, 31, 49, 52

Volkhov Pocket 43

Western Europe campaign 5, 9, 18, 19,
    20, 21, 26, 28, 42, 47, 52, 56, 57

*Zitadel*, operation 12

**64** | decorations

EDITOR: LEE JOH

**OSPREY MILITARY**  **MEN-AT-ARM**

# AXIS FORCES
# IN YUGOSLAVIA 1941-5

*Text by*
## N. THOMAS &
## K. MIKULAN
*Colour plates by*
## D. PAVELIC

First published in Great Britain in 1995 by
Osprey, an imprint of Reed Consumer Books Ltd.
Michelin House, 81 Fulham Road,
London SW3 6RB
and Auckland, Melbourne, Singapore and
Toronto

ISBN 1 85532 473 3

Filmset in Great Britain by Keyspools Ltd
Printed through Bookbuilders Ltd, Hong Kong

## Publisher's Note

Readers may wish to study this title in conjunction with
the following Osprey publications:

MAA142 *Partisan Warfare 1941–45*
MAA147 *Wehrmacht Foreign Volunteers*
MAA254 *Wehrmacht Auxiliary Forces*

If you would like to receive more information about
Osprey Military books, The Osprey Messenger is a regular
newsletter which contains articles, new title information
and special offers. To join free of charge
please write to:

**Osprey Military Messenger,
PO Box 5, Rushden,
Northants NN10 6YX**

## Acknowledgements

This book would not have been possible without the
generous assistance of many knowledgeable correspon-
dents, friends and agencies. The author would like to
thank Peter Abbott; Phillip Buss (MA); Josef Charita;
Frano Glavina; Croatian State Archives, Zagreb; Mrs.
Rhea Ivanuš (Chief Custodian), and Mrs. Bosa
Komadina (Custodian) of the Croatian History
Museum, Zagreb; Franjo Jančikić; Dr. Marc Landry;
David Littlejohn; Stjepan Marcijuš; Stane Mrvič
(Director), and Matija Žgajnar (Curator) of the
Modern History Museum, Ljubljana; Antonio Muñoz;
Staff of the National University Library, Zagreb; Josip
M. Novak; Jan-Poul Petersen; Horia Vladimir Şerb-
ănescu Frank Steff; Pierre C. T. Verheye; Sergei Vrišer;
with special thanks to Henry L. de Zeng IV. Nigel
Thomas would like to thank his family, Heather, Alex-
ander and Dominick, for their patience and support.
Krunoslav Mikulan would like to thank his parents,
Zlata and Josip, for their support and encouragement.

## Author's Note

This book is intended to expand on, and to correct,
information contained in Men-at-Arms 142 *Partisan
Warfare 1941–45*, to which readers are referred for
extra detail. Any corrections or additional information
would be welcomed, and may be addressed to the
authors via the publisher's address.

## Artist's note

## INTRODUCTION

On 1 December 1918, the 'Kingdom of the Serbs, Croats and Slovenes' was established, uniting the ex-Austro-Hungarian provinces of Slovenia, Croatia-Slavonia, Dalmatia, Bosnia and Herzegovina with the kingdoms of Serbia – including Macedonia, Vojvodina and Kosovo – and Montenegro. The Serbian King assumed the crown. In October 1929, his kingdom was renamed 'Yugoslavia'.

Yugoslavia had 16 million inhabitants in 1941. These comprised 6½ million Serbs, 3¾ million Croats, 1½ million Slovenes, 900,000 Macedonians, 800,000 Albanians, 800,000 Moslems, 400,000 Hungarians, 250,000 Germans, 400,000 Montenegrins and some 400,000 Czechs, Slovaks, Rumanians, Jews and Gypsies. Heavy-handed Serbian political control was especially resented by the Croats, and in October 1934 Croatian Fascists, the Ustashas (or Ustashe) had King Alexander assassinated in Marseilles during a state visit to France.

To prevent British forces in Greece threatening Italian troops in Albania and the Italian-German Army in North Africa, Adolf Hitler ordered Operation Marita, the invasion of Yugoslavia and Greece, on 27 March 1941. On 6 April, the German 2nd and 12th Armies (15 divisions, including five armoured), Italian 2nd and 9th Armies (23 divisions), and the Hungarian 4th, 5th and Mobile Corps (8 brigades) invaded Yugoslavia from Italy, Germany, Rumania, Bulgaria and Albania. Few of the Royal Yugoslav Army's 30 divisions actively resisted – most Croat and many Slovene units deserted to the invader – and after 11 days the Yugoslav High Command surrendered.

Hitler immediately dismembered the Yugoslav state. Germany annexed the central Slovene districts of Carinthia, Upper Carniola and Southern Styria. Italy annexed Western Slovenia, as Lubiana Province, and the Dalmatian coastal districts, occupied Montenegro and awarded Kosovo and Western Mac-

*A German Rifle unit on campaign in Dalmatia, 1943. (Roba Archive via J. Charita)*

edonia to its Albanian client-state. Hungary annexed the districts of Prekmurje, Medjimurje, Baranja and Bačka in Northern Yugoslavia, and Bulgaria annexed Eastern Serbian, Macedonia and, in January 1942, South-Eastern Serbia. Croatia-Slavonia, Dalmatia, Bosnia and Herzegovina formed the 'Independent State of Croatia'. Serbia, reduced to its 1912 borders, came under German military government, while the Banat region of Serbia was administered by the local German population.

Some Yugoslav troops escaped to Egypt to join King Petar II, but the principal resistance to the Axis devolved to two guerilla armies. In mid-April 1941, Colonel Dragoljub 'Draža' Mihailović formed Chetnik Detachments, later recognized by King Petar as the Yugoslav Army of the Homeland with 72,000 active combatants and perhaps 200,000 reserves. These detachments were based at Ravna Gora, Central Serbia, and operated mainly in Serbia, Bosnia, Herzegovina, Montenegro, Slovenia and Macedonia. The Chetniks were royalist, pro-Allies and anti-Communist, but local commanders were prepared to form temporary alliances with the enemy, especially the Italians, against their arch-enemies, the Partisans.

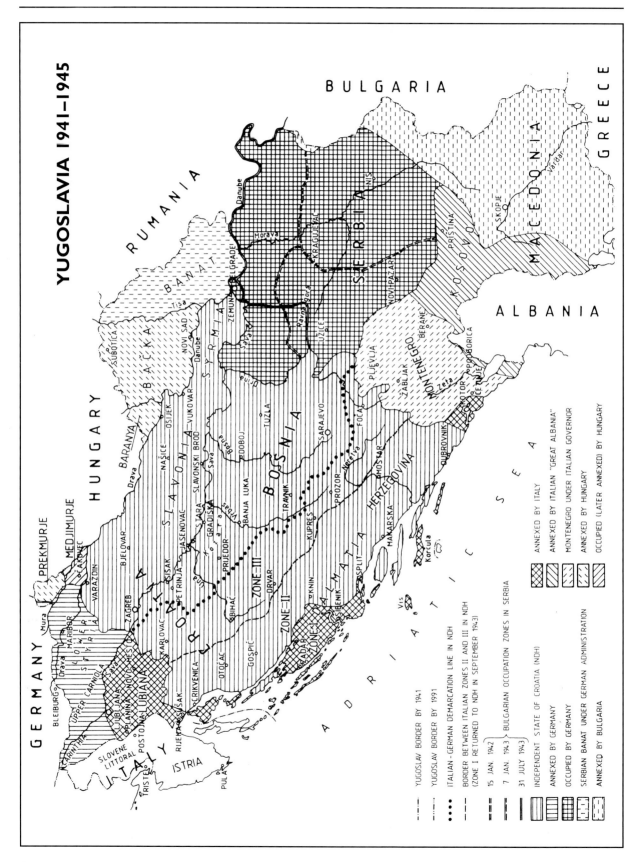

# YUGOSLAVIA 1941–1945

BULGARIA

GREECE

RUMANIA

ALBANIA

MACEDONIA

HUNGARY

GERMANY

ITALY

BANAT

BAČKA

BARANYA

PREKMURJE

MEDJIMURJE

SLAVONIA

CROATIA

BOSNIA

HERZEGOVINA

DALMATIA

SERBIA

KOSOVO

MONTENEGRO

ZONE-I
ZONE-II
ZONE-III

SLOVENE LITTORAL

ISTRIA

UPPER CARNIOLA

LOWER STYRIA

SYRMIA

A D R I A T I C   S E A

Subotica, Novi Sad, Zemun, Belgrade, Morava, Kragujevac, Niš, Priština, Skopje, Novipazar, Berane, Pljevlja, Žabljak, Podgorica, Cetinje, Kotor, Dubrovnik, Makarska, Šibenik, Split, Zadar, Knin, Gospić, Otočac, Bihać, Drvar, Banja Luka, Travnik, Kupres, Prozor, Foča, Sarajevo, Tuzla, Doboj, Slavonski Brod, Vukovar, Osijek, Našice, Bjelovar, Varaždin, Čakovec, Zagreb, Karlovac, Sisak, Petrinja, Jasenovac, Gradiška, Prijedor, Crikvenica, Rijeka, Postojna, Ljubljana, Novo Mesto, Maribor, Bleiburg, Korčula, Vis, Trieste, Pula

Rivers: Danube, Tisa, Drava, Mura, Sava, Drina, Bosna, Una, Vrbas, Neretva, Zeta, Ravna, Morava, Vardar, Ibar

YUGOSLAV BORDER BY 1941

YUGOSLAV BORDER BY 1991

ITALIAN-GERMAN DEMARCATION LINE IN NDH

BORDER BETWEEN ITALIAN ZONES II AND III IN NDH
(ZONE I RETURNED TO NDH IN SEPTEMBER 1943)

15 JAN. 1942
7 JAN. 1943 } BULGARIAN OCCUPATION ZONES IN SERBIA
31 JULY 1943

INDEPENDENT STATE OF CROATIA (NDH)

ANNEXED BY GERMANY

OCCUPIED BY GERMANY

SERBIAN BANAT UNDER GERMAN ADMINISTRATION

ANNEXED BY BULGARIA

ANNEXED BY ITALY

ANNEXED BY ITALIAN "GREAT ALBANIA"

MONTENEGRO UNDER ITALIAN GOVERNOR

ANNEXED BY HUNGARY

OCCUPIED (LATER ANNEXED) BY HUNGARY

In June 1941, Josip 'Tito' Broz, a Croatian communist, established the Partisan Detachments, in November 1942 renamed the Yugoslav National Liberation Army. The struggle between Tito's Partisans and the Chetniks added civil war to bloody resistance to the Axis. Guerilla war and civil conflict, always vicious, reached new heights of horror in Yugoslavia.

Axis forces occupied the principal towns and patrolled the main road and rail links, abandoning the villages and countryside, with its craggy mountains, deep river-valleys and impenetrable forests, to the guerillas. Guerilla bands included men of all ages, women and even children, all driven from their homes. Dressed in makeshift uniforms, they avoided concentrations of superior enemy forces, picking off soldiers, policemen and collaborators, individually or in small groups. Axis forces responded by killing civilians or captured guerillas out of hand, burning villages suspected of harbouring or supplying the guerillas. The Germans executed 100 hostages for every German soldier killed.

*Six* Wachtmeister *(corporals) and one* Oberwachtmeister *(lance-sergeant, seated far left) of a German Police unit in Upper Carniola, Slovenia, wearing the Police grey-green field uniform with M1943 peaked field-cap or* *the M1936 service-uniform with grey-green tunic with brown cuffs and collar, peaked cap with brown cap-band, and rank insignia modifications introduced late 1942. (Modern History Museum, Ljubljana)*

## Axis Offensives

The 3¼-year guerilla war, from June 1941 to September 1944, was characterized by successive Axis drives against Partisan and sometimes Chetnik strongholds. Yugoslav historians call these 'Enemy Offensives One to Seven'.

In June 1941, Serbs in Eastern Herzegovina rose up against the new Croatian regime and, in July, a general uprising led by Communists and supported by the Chetniks broke out in Western Serbia. It soon spread to Montenegro and Western Bosnia.

In the First Enemy Offensive, of September to December 1941, the Germans and Italians recovered all this liberated territory. In November, Partisans and Chetniks had ceased to co-operate and turned on each other, Mihailović based on Ravna Gora mountain, Tito in Užice, Western Serbia.

On 15 January 1942, in the Second Enemy Offensive, 35,000 German and Croatian troops advanced through Eastern Bosnia, forcing Tito to retreat southwards to Foča, where he formed mobile 'Proletarian brigades', controlling Eastern Bosnia, Northern Herzegovina and Western Montenegro. In the Third Enemy Offensive, April to June 1942, German, Croatian, Italian and Chetnik forces attacked Foča, but Tito marched 200 miles north-westwards to Western Bosnia, where, in November, he established a liberated 'Titoland' based at Bihać, just south of the Kozara plateau where German and Croat forces had dislodged local Partisans in Operation *Kozara* the previous July.

On 15 January 1943, in the Fourth Enemy Offensive, Operation *Weiss I*, *II* and *III*, German, Croatian and Italian units overran 'Titoland'. But Tito broke through the weak Italian-Chetnik link in the encircling ring. He conducted an epic fighting retreat south-eastwards back across the Neretva, Drina and Lim rivers – capturing Prozor and Konjic but suffering 16,000 casualties – before reaching the safety of Žabljak, on Mount Durmitor, Western Montenegro, at the end of March. On 20 May, he was surrounded there by German, Italian and Bulgarian forces in the Fifth Enemy Offensive (Operation *Schwarz*), but slipped back to Eastern Bosnia with 3,000 men, leaving 13,000 dead. There he ordered his troops to disperse throughout Bosnia, Serbia and Croatia, and fan the flames of a general revolt.

The Italian Armistice of September 1943 netted Tito huge supplies of equipment, some Italian Partisan recruits and access to Allied bases in Italy to supply his army, now 200,000 strong. However, in the Sixth Enemy Offensive (Operation *Kugelblitz*), beginning 2 December 1943, Axis troops captured Tuzla, Eastern Bosnia, and Bihać, Western Bosnia. In Operation *Herbstgewitter*, in December 1943, the Partisans lost their key supply base on Korčula island and, in Operation *Schneesturm*, Tito's HQ at Jajce. In January 1944, Tito escaped to Drvar, Central Bosnia, where, on 25 May 1944, he narrowly escaped capture by German paratroopers in Operation *Rösselsprung*, the Seventh, and last, Enemy Offensive. Now, in June 1944, strong Partisan forces headed into Serbia to meet the Soviet Red Army advancing through the Eastern Balkans. In Operation *Roeslein*, in July, the Germans prevented the Partisans reaching Northern Macedonia. Operation *Feuerwehr*, however, failed to stop their infiltration into Eastern Serbia and Operation *Ruebezahl* forced them back into Western Serbia. Finally, in Operation *Treubruch*, in September 1944, German forces checked an advance by the Partisans and Bulgarians, now allies, into Macedonia. At this stage, King Petar urged all patriotic Yugoslavs to support Tito.

### Axis Defeat

On 29 September 1944, the Red Army entered Serbia and liberated Belgrade in October. Now guerilla war graduated to conventional war. The Germans, having retreated from Albania and Greece, abandoned Serbia, forming a defensive line on the Bosnian border. Finally, on 20 March 1945, the 800,000-strong Partisan army (redesignated the 'Yugoslav National Army') began a general offensive. On 15 May, a week after VE-Day, all Yugoslav territory had been retaken. Tito then took a terrible

revenge on thousands of Axis troops who, prevented by British 8th Army from seeking refuge in Southern Austria, surrendered to his forces.

Tito's charisma, brutal secret police and efficient communist organization, prevented nationalist conflicts erupting again in the post-war period, and it was not until June 1991, eleven years after his death, that Yugoslavia, always a fragile creation, began once more to disintegrate.

# GERMANY

### Ground Forces

In June 1941, Field-Marshal List of the German 12th Army, whose headquarters were in Athens, assigned Lieutenant-General Bader's 65 Corps to occupy Serbia and the German occupation zone of Croatia. Headquartered in Belgrade, Bader had four '15th Wave' infantry divisions – the 704, 714 and 717 in Serbia, and the 718 at Banja Luka, Bosnia, with five second-line *Landesschützen* battalions (447, 823, 923–5) guarding the Croatian section of the Vienna-Salonika railway vital for supplying to North Africa.

The 700-series divisions were smaller – only 8,000 men – less well-trained and well-equipped than front-line divisions. They contained two three-battalion regiments (instead of three); a three-battery artillery battalion (instead of a regiment); cycle-reconnaissance, engineer and signals companies (instead of battalions); and a few logistical and motorized services. Their personnel were too old for front-line duty and were intended for static occupation tasks. However, they provided the backbone of the German forces until late 1942.

In the First Offensive into Montenegro, Serbia, Herzegovina, Bosnia, September to December 1941, 704 and 714 were reinforced by the front-line 113 and 342 Infantry Divisions from France and Russia respectively, and the 125 Infantry Regiment from Salonika. 342 and 718 fought in the Second Offensive in Eastern Bosnia in January and February 1942. But in January, 113 left for the Russian Front, and in February, 342 and the Bulgarian 1st Army occupied South-Eastern Serbia to fill the vacuum.

On 1 March 1942, 65 Corps was redesignated

*Three Chetniks pose with two German Customs officers, 1944. (Modern History Museum, Ljubljana)*

Serbia Command (*Militärbefehlshaber Serbien*). For the Third Offensive in Eastern Bosnia, in April and May 1942, Bader formed Task-Force Bader (*Kampfgruppe Bader*) with 714, 718, Italian and Croatian forces. And in July, 714 fought in Western Bosnia in Operation *Kozara*.

By late 1942, guerilla activity was increasing steadily in Bosnia, but decreasing in Serbia. Accordingly in October, 'Croatia Command' (*Befehlshaber der deutschen Truppen in Kroatien*) was formed under Major-General Lueters at Slavonski Brod. In November, it was assigned 'Railway Security Staff Croatia' (*Deutscher Eisenbahnsicherungsstab Kroatien*, known from late 1943 as *Eisenbahnsicherungsstab* 6) supervising *Landesschützen* and German-Croatian police-battalions guarding the railways.

Unwilling to divert front-line units from Russia to Yugoslavia, the German High Command explored local sources of manpower. In August 1942, the 369th Infantry Division, the 'Devil's Division', was established as a Legionary Division with Croatian troops under a German cadre. It had two infantry regiments (369 and 370), an artillery regiment (369), anti-tank, reconnaissance, engineer and signals battalions. 369 Infantry Regiment and 1st Battalion, 369 Artillery Regiment, formed earlier in July 1941, served as the Croatian Legion in Russia. It was replaced in the Division by the 969 Infantry Regiment and 969 Artillery Battalion. These units adopted their predecessors' numbers when the Croation Legion was destroyed at Stalingrad in December 1942. In January 1943 a second Legionary Division, the 373 'Tiger Division', was formed.

In October 1942, the 'Prinz Eugen' SS-Mountain Division joined Serbia Command. Led by the charismatic Lieutenant-General Arthur Phleps, it contained 19,000 ethnic Germans from Banat, Rumania and Croatia, illegally conscripted into the Waffen-SS. With two mountain infantry regiments; a mountain artillery regiment; reconnaissance, engineer and signals battalions, a company-strength battalion of French Hotchkiss H-38 light tanks and an attached *Luftwaffe* squadron of *Fieseler Storch* spotter aircraft, 'Prinz Eugen' was probably the toughest and most feared German division in Yugoslavia.

In December 1942, the 187 Reserve Division, with Austrian recruits undergoing basic training, arrived in Serbia. It had three infantry regiments,

'Prinz Eugen' SS troops advance behind a Hotchkiss tank of the Divisional Armoured Company, 1943, wearing snow-smocks and coloured sleeve field-signs (Roba Archive via J. Charita)

artillery and engineer battalions, and signals and medical companies.

On 1 January 1943, 12th Army, whose headquarters had moved to Salonika, was redesignated 'Army Group E' (*Heeresgruppe* E), under *Luftwaffe* General Löhr. It then controlled Serbia Command (704 Division and the 1st Bulgarian Army) and Croatia Command (187 Reserve; 369, 373, 714, 717, 718 Infantry Divisions; and the 'Prinz Eugen' Division).

Most of Croatia Command fought in the Fourth Offensive in Western Bosnia, January to March 1943. Later, on 1 April 1943, 704, 714, 717 and 718 were revitalized with younger personnel and redesignated 104, 114, 117 and 118 *Jäger* (Rifle) Divisions. Trained for hilly terrain, they had two three-battalion rifle regiments; a three-battalion artillery regiment; reconnaissance, anti-tank, engineer and signals battalions. And in December 1943, 187 Reserve became the 42 Rifle Division.

For the Fifth Offensive in Herzegovina and Western Montenegro, in May and June 1943, 'Prinz Eugen', 118 and 369 were reinforced by the élite 1st Mountain Division in Army Group Reserve in Serbia, and the 4th Regiment of the Brandenburg Commando Division. In June 1943, 100 *Jäger* Division was assigned to Croatia Command and, in July, 28 Infantry Division joined Serbia Command before both were transferred to Albania.

The Allied landings in Sicily in July 1943 convinced the Germans of the imminent collapse of Italy, and so the German forces in Yugoslavia were strengthened to repel the expected Allied invasion of

Members of SS-Parachute Battalion 500 at Drvar, during Operation Rösselsprung ('Knight's Move'), May 1944. (Roba Archive via J. Charita)

Dalmatia from the Italian coast. In August 1943, Army Group F, headquartered in Belgrade under Field-Marshal von Weichs, assumed command of all Axis forces in the Balkans with 2 Armoured Army (2.*Panzerarmee*) from the Russian Front; 'South-East Command' (*Militärbefehlshaber Südost*), formerly Serbia Command, now almost entirely Bulgarian; and Army Group E in Greece.

The 2 Armoured Army, with HQ at Kragujevac, Serbia, under Lieutenant-General Rendulić and paradoxically without any armoured divisions, was the main strike-force, with 15 Mountain Corps (114, 369, 373 and 'Prinz Eugen' Divisions) and 69 Reserve Corps (187 and 173 Reserve – formerly Croatia Command); 21 Mountain Corps (100, 118 *Jäger* and

Croatian dictator Ante Pavelić visiting troops of a Croatian Legion Division, wearing German Army uniforms with the Croatian chequerboard on the right upper arm (Croatian Legion in Russia, left arm), June 1944. (Croatian History Museum, Zagreb)

297 Infantry Divisions) and, from September to November 1943, III (Germanic) SS Armoured Corps, with the German-Danish-Norwegian mechanized division, *Nordland*, and the Dutch *Nederland* Mechanized Brigade.

On 9 September 1943, the day of the Italian Armistice, Rendulić, with seven divisions (114, 118 *Jäger*; 297, 369, 373 Infantry; 187 Reserve and 'Prinz Eugen' Divisions), disarmed the Italian divisions in Croatia and Montenegro and secured the Adriatic coastline. Only 'Prinz Eugen' encountered serious resistance, at Split.

Meanwhile 2 Armoured Army continued its buildup. In October 1943, the 1st Cossack Division, formed in August from anti-Soviet Russians, arrived. With two mounted brigades, each with three mounted regiments, a mounted artillery battalion and logistical services, the cossacks had fought Soviet partisans in Russia and left a string of burned villages and terror-stricken peasants while with 69 Reserve Corps in Eastern Croatia. In November, V SS-Mountain Corps HQ and the 181, 264, 367 and 371 Infantry Divisions arrived to boost German strength.

V SS-Mountain Corps (118 *Jäger*; 181, 369 Infantry; 1 Mountain; 'Prinz Eugen' Divisions) fought in the Sixth Offensive in Bosnia in December 1943, with the Bosnian–Moslem 13th SS-Mountain Division *Handschar*. It had been formed in March 1943, and returned in January 1944 from Le Puy, Central France, to join the new 'Syrmia Command' (*Befehlshaber Syrmien*) in Eastern Croatia. Meanwhile, XV Mountain Corps, with 264 and 373 Infantry and 392 'Blue Division', the third Legionary Division, formed 17 August 1943, cleared Korčula Island in Dalmatia of Partisans.

Anxious to regain the tactical initiative, the Germans launched the Seventh, and last, Offensive in May 1944 in Western Bosnia. 202 Armoured Battalion, 92 Motorized Regiment, elements of the 'Brandenburg' and 1st Mountain Divisions, and Croatian units supported SS-Parachute Battalion 500's unsuccessful attempt to capture Tito at Drvar.

In August 1944, a reinforced Corps called Army

Section Serbia (*Armeeabteilung Serbien*) was formed from South-East Command with two Corps-status groups, to defend Serbia from the advancing Red Army. *Korpsgruppe Schneckenburger* (117 and Brandenburg Divisions, and 92 Infantry Brigade) defended Belgrade, surrendering on 27 October. *Korpsgruppe Müller* guarded the flank of General Löhr's 340,000-strong Army Group E in its epic 1,000-mile retreat from Greece through Macedonia into Bosnia where, in November 1944, it absorbed Army Section Serbia.

In December 1944, the 2 Armoured Army joined Army Group South in Southern Hungary, leaving Army Group F (abolished as a Staff in March 1945) with the four weak Corps of Army Group E to defend Northern Yugoslavia. These were 15 Mountain Corps (373 and 392 Infantry Divisions); 21 Mountain Corps (963, 966, 969 and 1017 Fortress Brigades); 34 Corps (41 Infantry and 117 *Jäger* Divisions) and 91 Corps (11 *Luftwaffe* Field, 297 Infantry, 104 *Jäger* and 'Prinz Eugen' Divisions; 967 Fortress Brigade). Fortress Brigades (*Festungsbrigaden*) were Fortress Regiments manning static coastal fortifications in Greece, redesignated brigades in July 1944. Later, 69 Corps arrived, along with 15 Cossack Cavalry Corps (under Major-General von Pannwitz), formed in February 1945 from the 1st and 2nd Cossack Cavalry Divisions (formerly Brigades), 11 *Luftwaffe* Field and 22 Infantry Divisions.

Four other noteworthy Waffen-SS units served in Yugoslavia. The Ukrainian 14 Infantry Division fought briefly in Slovenia in March and April 1945. The Bosnian-Moslem 23 Mountain Division *Kama* was formed in June 1944 but disbanded in October in Southern Hungary. The Albanian 21 Mountain Division *Skanderbeg*, formed May 1944, served in October and November in Kosovo and Macedonia, and fro m December 1944 to May 1945 as a Regimental Task-Force with 'Prinz Eugen'. And the Commando Battalion 'SS-*Jagdverband Südost*', was based in Zagreb. It had seven companies, of which two – the *Serbien-Kroatien* and *Albanien* – operated in Croatia from January to February 1945.

On 20 March 1945, Tito's Yugoslav National Army launched an offensive against Army Group E. 15 Mountain Corps retreated up the coast until it was reinforced in Istria by 97 Corps (188, 237 and 392

*Members of the 13th SS-Mountain Division Handschar, in German mountain infantry uniform with a scarlet (service-dress) or grey-green (field uniform) fez with SS insignia, and the scimitar (Handschar) on the right collar-patch. January 1944. (J. Charita)*

Infantry Divisions). Central Bosnia and Eastern Croatia held until 10 April, then the Army Group was in headlong retreat towards Southern Austria. Most units surrendered to the British in Austria on 15 May. The Cossacks were handed over to the Red Army by the British, and suffered imprisonment and death. 104 *Jäger*; 181, 297, 373 and 392 Infantry and 'Prinz Eugen' Divisions capitulated to Tito and were appallingly mistreated as prisoners-of-war – 50,000 lost their lives in captivity.

### Air and Sea Forces

German Naval and Air Forces in Yugoslavia were modest. The Corps-level Staff 'Admiral Adria' (HQ Belgrade) controlled two brigade-status coastal units – *Seekommandant Norddalmatien* (HQ Šibenik) and

*Seekommandant Süddalmatien* (HQ Mostar) with three Naval Artillery and four Naval Infantry Battalions from September 1943 to December 1944.

In 1941, the Corps-level 'Air District XVII' (*Luftgaukommando XVII*), headquartered in Vienna, supervised training squadrons in Croatia and Serbia. From January 1943, the Army-Group status 'Air Force Command Southeast' (*Luftwaffenkommando Südost*) operated 20 *Flakdivision* and brigade-level 'Air Command Croatia' (*Fliegerführer Kroatien*), attacking 15 USAAF bombers from Italy. Most aircraft were destroyed in September 1944 in Operation Ratweek, leaving a few to defend Zagreb until May 1945.

German police units are covered under 'Croatia', 'Serbia', 'Montenegro' and 'Slovenia'.

# ITALY

### Ground Forces

The Italian High Command assigned 24 divisions and three coastal brigades to occupation duties in Yugoslavia.

The 2nd Army was headquartered in Sušak, Northern Dalmatia, from March 1942 to May 1943. Designated the Slovenia-Dalmatia Command (*Supersloda*), it was commanded by Acting General Ambrosio from April 1941. Acting General Roatta took over in February 1942 and Acting General Robotti in February 1943. *Supersloda* comprised 12 infantry, two mobile divisions and, from 1942, three coastal brigades. These were allocated to four corps (XI, V, XVIII and VI) covering Western Slovenia; the

coastal provinces of Zara (Zadar), Spalato (Split) and Cattaro (Kotor) – annexed by Italy as the Governorship of Dalmatia and the western half of the Independent State of Croatia, with Western Croatia proper, Western Bosnia, Dalmatia and Herzegovina. These regions, excluding Slovenia, were divided into three zones: the Annexed Zone – the Governorship; the Demilitarized Zone – a 40-mile wide coastal strip with Italian garrisons; and the Occupied Zone – a 40-mile strip adjacent to the German Occupation Zone, with Croatian and weak Italian garrisons.

The 9th Army was headquartered in Tirana, Albania, from July 1941 to May 1943. Designated the Albania Armed Forces Command (*Superalba*), it deployed two infantry divisions in Yugoslavia, in districts annexed to Albania. XIV Corps – with four infantry, one infantry (mountain) and three mountain (*Alpini*) divisions – garrisoned Montenegro. On 15 May 1943, the 9th Army, XIV Corps and 2nd Army's VI Corps were reorganized as 'Army Group East'.

An M1940 'binary' Infantry Division, 14,300 strong, had two three-battalion infantry regiments, one three-battalion artillery regiment, a mortar and an engineer battalion. Some divisions received, as a third infantry regiment, a Blackshirt Assault Legion, volunteers from the Fascist Voluntary Militia for National Security (MVSN), with two infantry battalions and a support company. An Infantry Division (Mountain), intended for hilly terrain, had extra pack-horse transport. A 7,750-strong Mobile (*Celere*) Division had two cavalry regiments, each with one machine-gun and four mounted squadrons, a three-battalion *Bersaglieri* cyclist regiment, a three-battalion artillery regiment, a 61-tank light-tank battalion and *Bersaglieri* motorcycle, anti-tank and engineer companies. A 13,000-strong Mountain Division had two three-battalion mountain regiments, a three-battalion artillery regiment, engineer battalion and anti-tank platoon. A Coastal Brigade had one coastal infantry regiment and supporting units.

Sixteen Independent Blackshirt Battalions (3, 4, 8, 16, 29, 33, 54, 58, 61, 71, 81, 85, 115, 144, 162,

*A colonel* (console) *commanding the 98th MVSN Assault Legion, with fellow-officers, a German Police officer and lance-corporal* (Rottwachtmeister) *and Slovene Village Guards, South-Eastern Slovenia, 1942. (Modern History Museum, Ljubljana)*

215) operated in Yugoslavia and six (8, 16, 29, 71, 81, 85) were redesignated as elite M (Mussolini) Battalions for distinction in combat. There were also organic Army and Corps troops.

When concentrated in viable units, Italian troops were a match for the Partisans, but usually they were dispersed in isolated garrisons or escort columns vulnerable to attacks and ambushes. Occupation duty was unpopular, and the fragile morale plummeted in July 1943 with the Allied invasion of Sicily and the fall of Mussolini.

XI Corps, headquartered in Ljubljana, garrisoned Western Slovenia and Karlovac District in Northern Croatia with three infantry divisions – the 14th *Isonzo*; the 153rd *Macerata* from June 1942, replaced in May 1943 by the 57th *Lombardia*; and the 21st *Granatieri di Sardegna*, repatriated to Italy in September 1942 after replacement, in July, by the 22nd *Cacciatori delle Alpi*. They contained Partisan activity, especially after a successful campaign from July to November 1942.

The 1st Mobile Division *Eugenio di Savoia* operated in 2nd Army reserve in Karlovac, and from October 1941 on the Northern Dalmatian coast.

V Corps, headquartered in Crikvenica, garrisoned Northern Dalmatia, Western Croatia proper and Western Bosnia with three infantry divisions – the 13th *Re*; the 57th *Lombardia*, replaced in May 1943 by the 153rd *Macerata*; and, from February 1943, the 154th *Murge*; and the 14th Coastal Brigade. The 2nd Mobile Division *Emanuele Filiberto Testa di Ferro* returned to Italy in November 1941, after service with the Corps.

XVIII Corps, headquartered in Split, took over Central Dalmatia and Central Bosnia from the overstretched VI Corps in February 1942. It inherited three infantry divisions from VI Corps – the 12th *Sassari*, repatriated in April 1943; the 15th *Bergamo*; and, from November 1941 to July 1942, the 151st *Perugia*, the 158th *Zara*, formed in September 1942, and the 12th Coastal Brigade were added.

VI Corps, headquartered initially in Split and from February 1942 in Dubrovnik, garrisoned Southern Dalmatia and Herzegovina with three infantry divisions – the 32nd *Marche*; from August 1942, the 18th *Messina*; and from September 1941 to July 1942 the 22nd *Cacciatori delle Alpi* – plus the 28th Coastal Brigade.

*An MVSN captain (centurione) of the 16th 'M' Battalion (left), compares notes with an official (Segretario federale) of the Italian National Fascist party (PNF) with a member of the 2nd Grenadier Regiment, 21st Infantry Division, looking on. Slovenia, 1942. (Modern History Museum, Ljubljana)*

In the First Offensive, September to December 1941, the *Marche* division reoccupied Eastern Herzegovina and the *Cacciatori delle Alpi* division fought in Eastern Bosnia in the Third Offensive (Italian codename *Trio*) from April to May 1942. Partisan pressure forced the evacuation of Zone 3 in late 1942. *Lombardi*, *Re*, *Sassari* and elements of the *Murge*, *Bergamo* and *Marche* fought in the Fourth Offensive, from January to March 1943.

XIV Corps, headquartered in Podgorica from December 1941 to June 1943, became 'Montenegro Command'. It controlled two mountain divisions – the 5th *Pusteria*, replaced in August 1942 by 1st *Taurinense* (previously in 2nd Army reserve); and, from March to December 1942, the 6th *Alpi Graie* – along with four Infantry Divisions – the 19th (Mountain) *Venezia*; the 48th *Taro*, replaced from July 1942 to August 1943 by the 151st *Perugia*; from July to September 1941, the 22nd *Cacciatori delle Alpi*; and from May 1942, the 23rd *Ferrara*. The 18th *Messina*, replaced in April 1942 by 155th *Emilia*, garrisoned Kotor for the 2nd Army under XIV Corps control.

The communist-led revolt of 13 July to 12 August 1941 was suppressed by the *Venezia*, *Messina*,

*Pusteria*, *Taro* and *Cacciatori delle Alpi* divisions, and all contained local attacks in the First Offensive in September to December 1941. The *Taurinense* and *Pusteria* divisions fought in Operation *Trio* in April 1942 and the *Ferrara*, *Venezia* and *Taurinense* divisions participated in the Fifth Offensive, in May and June 1943.

The 9th Army allocated the 38th Puglie division to Sector Z, the Kosovo Region of Serbia, and the 41st *Firenze* to the Debar and Struga Districts of Western Macedonia. Partisan activity there was minimal, allowing *Firenze*'s 127 Infantry Regiment to fight in the Fifth Offensive in Montenegro.

### Italy Surrenders

On 8 September 1943, the Italians concluded an armistice with the Allies, leaving seventeen Italian divisions stranded in Yugoslavia. All divisional commanders refused to join the Germans. The *Taurinense* and *Venezia* divisions joined the Montenegrin Partisans as complete units. *Firenze* joined the Albanian Partisans. Other units surrendered to the Germans, to face imprisonment in Germany or summary execution. Others surrendered to the Croats or the Partisans, simply disintegrated, or reached Italy on foot via Trieste or by ship across the Adriatic.

### Air and Sea Forces

Until September 1943, Dalmatia Maritime Command (*Maridalmazia*) controlled the Yugoslav coast with Zadar, Split, Ploče and Dubrovnik Naval Commands and Rijeka-Sušak Independent Command. Kotor Naval Command came under Albania Maritime Command.

Slovenia-Dalmatia Air-Force Command, head-quartered in Mostar, controlled six Air-Force Wings and eleven squadrons. There were ten *Carabinieri* (Rural and Military Police) battalions; seven regimental-status Frontier Guard 'sectors' and eight Customs Guard battalions.

# CROATIA

On 10 April 1941, the Ustasha underground leader in Croatia, Slavko Kvaternik, proclaimed the 'Independent State of Croatia' (*Nezavisna Država Hrvatska*, or NDH), and on the 16th Dr Ante Pavelić returned from exile in Italy as *Poglavnik* (Leader) of the new state.

Croatia, technically a kingdom under the absentee King Tomislav II, the Italian Duke of Spoleto, had 6.1 million inhabitants – 3.2 million Croats, 1.8 million Serbs, 700,000 Moslems, 100,000 Germans and 300,000 Czechs, Slovaks, Jews and Gypsies. The Government was strongly nationalistic/Roman Catholic, pro-Axis, anti-Serb, anti-semitic and anti-communist, yet the existence of Italian and German occupation-zones belied Croatia's independence. Furthermore the large Serb minority and many Croats rejected the Ustashe and turned to Tito, plunging the country into civil war.

On 16 April 1941, the 'Croatian Home Defence Force' (*Hrvatsko Domobranstvo*) was formed by Field-Marshal Kvaternik, with an Army, Navy, Air-Force, National Guard, Gendarmerie and Labour Service. In January 1943, the Force was redesignated the 'Croatian Armed Forces' (*Oružane snage NDH*), incorporating the Ustasha Army.

### The Croatian Army

The Army (called the *Kopnena vojska*, and from January 1943, the *Domobranstvo*) was commanded, from August 1941, by Lieutenant-General August Marić as Chief of Staff. He was replaced in November by Lieutenant-General Vladimir Laxa. General Slavko Štancer was Army Inspector. There were 55,000 men organized in the old Yugoslav Divisional Districts, each district comprising three infantry regiments with two to three battalions each. *Sava* in

*Newly promoted Croatian Army second lieutenants in parade-uniform, with two air-force officers far right in Zagreb, 13 June 1941. (Croatian History Museum, Zagreb)*

Left: Members of the Croatian NCO School, 1944, in summer uniforms, the gold collar-patch braid bars indicating NCO Candidates. (Croatian History Museum, Zagreb)

Right: A Croatian anti-aircraft artilleryman, wearing an ex-Yugoslav Army field tunic with Croatian collar-patches, air-force breast-badge and M1941 peaked field-cap. (Josip M. Novak)

Croatia proper and Dalmatia had 1 to 3 Infantry Regiments. *Osijek* in Slavonia had 4 to 6. *Bosna* in Southern Bosnia had 7 to 9; *Vrbas* in Northern Bosnia had 10 to 12. And *Jadran* in Herzegovina had 13 to 15. There were also two artillery battalions with two batteries each, one medical, one labour and three replacement battalions per district. There was also the Zagreb Cavalry Regiment with two battalions and an independent cavalry battalion; an engineer regiment of three battalions; I–V Frontier Battalions on the Serbia-Montenegro border; a railway security and a signals battalion; and Motor Transport Battalions 1–2. From December 1941, ethnic Germans formed the 1st and 2nd Rifle Battalions and a local militia, absorbed into the 'Prinz Eugen' SS-Division in April 1943; and three railway Security Battalions (11–13), reformed as German-Croatian Police Volunteer Regiment 3 in December 1943.

The fledgling Army crushed the revolt by Serbs in Eastern Herzegovina in June, and fought in July in Eastern and Western Bosnia. They fought in Eastern Herzegovina again, when Croatia-Dalmatian and Slavonian battalions reinforced local units.

In November 1941, the Army reorganized into three Corps Regions, each with a Corps – I (Croatia proper, Northern Dalmatia); II (Slavonia, Northern Bosnia); III (Southern Bosnia, Herzegovina), each with two infantry divisions. A Division – with only 4,000 men, so really a Brigade – had 2–3 Infantry Regiments and 1–2 Artillery Battalions, all in Bosnia.

## Mountain Division

Soon more units were formed. The most important was the 17,000-strong 1st Mountain Division, acti-

vated in April 1942 with four mountain brigades, each with a three-battalion mountain infantry regiment, a rifle battalion, a mountain artillery battery and support services. There were the *Banja Luka*, *Srijem* and *Tuzla* Independent Brigades, I Bicycle Battalion, I Assault Battalion, and 18 Railway Security Battalions under the German Railway Security Staff Croatia. Total Army strength was about 100,000.

The 4th and 5th Infantry Divisions fought in the Second Offensive in Eastern Bosnia in January 1942, and 1st–3rd Mountain Brigades in Operation *Kozara* in Western Bosnia in July. In October 1942, the 1st Mountain Division fought in Slavonia and, in early 1943, the 1st–3rd Mountain Brigades were in Western Bosnia for the Fourth Offensive. In October, Pavelić dismissed Kvaternik and appointed himself Armed Forces Commander, with Lieutenant-General Ivan Prpić as Army Chief of Staff.

On 1 May 1943, the six Divisions were reorganized into four mountain and four rifle brigades, an operation mostly completed in January 1944 (6th Division survived until December). A mountain brigade (*Gorski Sdrug*) had two mountain regiments (ex-Mountain Division brigades or divisional infantry regiments) and 1–2 Artillery Battalions. A rifle brigade (*Lovački Sdrug*) had two rifle regiments (ex-infantry regiments) and one or two artillery battalions. In February 1944, each Corps received a replacement brigade (*Doknadni Sdrug*) and in March 11 garrison brigades (*Posadni Sdrugovi*) were established from existing garrison and *Domdo* village militia battalions. In Autumn 1943, the Mobile Brigade (*Brzi Sdrug*) was formed from the Zagreb Cavalry Regiment, and I and II Bicycle Battalions. The 23

Railway Security Battalions were organized in five sectors grouped in I Region (Sectors A–C) and II Region (Sectors D–E). There were also three labour regiments.

## Armoured Units

Croatian Armoured Forces consisted of three Corps armoured-car battalions – I (Zagreb), II (Slavonski Brod) and III (Sarajevo). By 1943, these were attached to the appropriate Replacement Brigades. A 41-man Armoured Platoon formed in November 1941 and by 1943 Ustasha Active Service Brigades I–V had an army tank company in support, and the rifle and mountain brigades had support platoons of two light and three medium tanks. There were also Armoured Train Companies 1–3.

The 4th Rifle Brigade fought in the Fifth Offensive in May 1943 in Herzegovina. In September

*Italian and Croatian Army, and Ustasha officers, 1943, in Bosnia. The Ustasha officer standing fourth from the left is Major Rafael Boban, the notorious commander of Ustasha V Active Service Brigade. The officer far right is a military chaplain (captain equivalent) with special collar-patches and sleeve rank rings. Moslem Imams wore a fez and different collar-patches. (Croatian History Museum, Zagreb)*

# BATTLE ORDER OF CROATION FORCES

**Army (1 November 1941 - 30 April 1943)**

I Corps (Sisak)
| | |
|---|---|
| 1 Inf. Div | 1, 2, 11 Inf. Rgt, 1, 2 Art. Bn |
| 2 Inf. Div | 3, 12, 15 Inf. Rgt, 8, 10 Art. Bn |
| | Zagreb Cav. Rgt, 1 Bicycle Bn, 1, 3 Eng. Bn. |

II Corps (vonskSlavonski Brod)
| | |
|---|---|
| 3 Inf. Div | 4, 6 Inf. Rgt, 3, 4 Art. Bn. |
| 4 Inf. Div | 5, 8, 10 Inf. Rgt, 6, & 7 Art. Bn. |
| Banjaluka Bde | 10 Inf.Rgt, 8 Art. & 1 Asst. Bn, 2 Domdo Bns. |
| Srijem Bde | 5 Front, 2, 4 Eng. Bn. |

III Corps (Sarajevo)
| | |
|---|---|
| 5 Inf. , 5 Art. Div | 7,9 Inf.Rgt, 5 Art. Bn |
| 6 Inf. Div | 13,14 Inf. Rgt, 9 Art.Bn. 1-4 Front. Bn. |
| 1 Mtn. Div | 1-4 Mtn. Bde, 1-18 Rail Sec. Bn. |
| | 21 Domdo Bns. |

**Army (1 May 1943 - 20 November 1944)**

I Corps (Zagreb)
| | |
|---|---|
| 1 Mtn. Bde | 1rps (Zagreb) |
| 1 Mtn. Bde | 1, 5 Mtn. Rgt, 11/ 3, 6 Art. Bn. |
| 3 Mtn. Bde | 3, 11 Mtn. Rgt, 3/2 Art. Bn. |
| 4 Mtn. Bde | 4, 8 Mtn. Rgt, 1, 12 Art. Bn. |
| 2 Rifle Bde | 1, 10 Rfl. Rgt, 4, 8  Art. Bn |
| 1 Garr.Bde | 1-4 Bn |
| 2 Garr.Bde | 1-5 Bn |
| 3 Garr.Bde | 1-3 Bn |
| 4 Garr.Bde | 1-3 Bn |
| Zagreb Garr.Bde | 1-3 Bn |
| 1 Repl. Bde | Pokuplje, Kvarner, Velebit Reg. Commd. Istrian Def. Rgt |
| Zenica Bde | 1 Armd. Car  Bn. |

II Corps (Slavonski Brod)
| | |
|---|---|
| 1 Rfl. Bde | 4, Rfl. Rgt ; 5, 16 Art. Bn |
| 3 Rfl. Bde | 5, 8 Rfl. Rgt; 7, 18 Art. B |
| 4 Rfl. Bde | 7, 13 Rfl. Rgt; 6/11, 22 Art. Bn |
| 5 Garr. Bde | 1-4 Bn |
| 6 Garr. Bde | 1-5 Bn |
| 7 Garr. Bde | 1-4 Bn |
| 10 Garr. Bde | 1-10 Bn |
| 2 Repl, Srijem, Tuzla Bdes | 2 Armd. Car Bn |

III Corps (Sarajevo)
| | |
|---|---|
| 2 Mtn. Bde | 2, 9/6  Mtn. Rgt; 9/13, 20 Art. Bn |
| 8 Garr. Bde | 1-5 Bn |
| 9 Garr. Bde | 1-6 Bn |
| 3 Repl. Bde | 3 Armd. Car Bn |
| Mob. Bde | 1-3 Bn |
| Rail Sect. | A(4-7 Bn), B(1-3, 8-10 Bn), C(1-3, 18-9 Bn) |
| | D(14-7 Bn), E(1-4 Bn ), |
| | Armd. Train Coy, 1-3 Lab. Rgt |

**Ustasha Army (1 June - 31 December 1943)**

| | |
|---|---|
| PTS | 1,2 Rgt; Cav, Mob, Art, Gd, Eng, 1,2 Repl. Bn |
| 1 Bde | 2,3,14,21-3,28 Bn |
| 2 Bde | 4,6,8,15-6,18-9,36,1 Rail Sec. Bn, 2 Mtn. Batt |
| 3 Bde | 5,10-3,30,33,35,37 Bn |
| 4 Bde | 9,17,19,31-2,34 Bn, 4 Mtn Bn |
| 5 Bde | 1,7,20,24-7 Bn, Eng. Coy, 1 Mtn Bn |
| 6 Bde | 1-4 Bn |
| 1 Comm. Bde | 1-4 Bn |
| 2 Comm. Bde | 1-4 Bn |
| 1 Def. Bde | Rgt, Mob. Bn, 3-5 Gd. Bns |
| 2 Def. Bde | |

1943, following the Italian Armistice, Croatian troops occupied Italian-annexed Dalmatia (Zone 1), establishing three regional commands to defend this territory and the Istrian Home-Defence Regiment at Sušak. There was also a *Zenica* Brigade. Lieutenant-General Fedor Dragoljov was Chief of Staff. He was succeeded in Autumn 1944 by Ustasha Colonel Tomislav Sertić. By late 1944, the performance of the Croatian Army, by then only 70,000 strong, had deteriorated sharply. Many recruits avoided enlistment. Others were creamed off into Ustasha Brigades or Croatian Legion Divisions, and whole units were deserting to the Partisans.

In November 1941, the Italians formed their own 'Motorized Croatian Legion' (*Legione Croata Autotrasportabile*), comparable to the German-sponsored Croatian Legion. It had 1,320 men in two infantry, one replacement and one artillery battalion,

and one mortar company. They were dressed in Italian Army uniforms with *fasces* collar-badges and a national armshield. In March 1942, the Legion joined Italian 8th Army in Russia, and was destroyed at Stalingrad in December 1942. It reformed in May 1943 at Lake Garda as the 2nd Legion, then disbanded in September, its personnel joining 373 and 392 Legion Divisions.

## Ustasha Units

The Ustasha Army (*Ustaška Vojnica*) was established on 10 May 1941 from the Ustasha Penetration Detachment – 300 emigrés from the Fontenecchio and San Demetrio camps in Italy and the Yanka-Puzta camp in Hungary, formed in 1932 as the Ustasha Forces (*Ustaška vojska*) – and the Ustasha Detachments, which had sprung up in April 1941. On 27 May the Ustasha High Command was formed in

### Ustasha Army (1 January - 20 November 1944)

| | |
|---|---|
| PTS | 1,2 Rgt; Mob, Armd, Art, Gd, Eng. Bn |
| 1 Bde | 2,24,29 Bn |
| 2 Bde | 6,15-6,18, Repl.Bn |
| 3 Bde | 5,10,13,30,33, Repl.Bn |
| 4 Bde | 9,19,20,31-2,34-5,Otacac Def. Bn |
| 5 Bde | 1,7,20,35 Bn |
| 6 Bde | 1-4, 26 Bn |
| 7 Bde | 1-6 Bn |
| 8 Bde | 1-4,6,8,11 Bn |
| 9 Bde | 1-5 Bn |
| 10 Bde | 1-6 Bn |
| 11 Bde | 1,3,4,6 Bn |
| 12 Bde | 14,23,25-6,29 Bn |
| 13 Bde | 6,16 Bn |
| 14 Bde | 1 Rail.Sec, Repl.Sec, Moslavac Rail.Sec.Bn |
| 15 Bde | 5-7 Bn |
| 16 Bde | Brod,Derventa Garr.Bn; 2 Rail.Sec.Bn |
| 17 Bde | Ogudin, Vrbovska, Susak, Rijecica, Ozalj, Karlovac Garr.Bn |
| 18 Bde | Otacac, Brinje, Senj,Lovinac Garr.Bn |
| Zagreb Garr.Bde | 1-4 Bn |
| Camp Def.Bde | 1-4,Mob,Art.Bn |

### Croatian Armed Forces (21 November 1944 - 15 May 1945)

| | |
|---|---|
| I Pog.Bodyg.Corps | |
| Pbd | 1,2 Boddyg.Rgt; Repl.Rgt; Art,Cav,Mob,Eng,Gd Bn |
| 1 Asst.Div | 20-2 Inf Rgt; 20-1 Art Bn; Mob.Bn |
| 5 Div | 5 Ust, 11 Inf Bde; 2 Art.batts/April 1945 23-5 Inf.Asst.Rgt, Mob.Brig |

| | |
|---|---|
| II Corps | |
| 2 Div | 15,20, Ust, 20 Inf.Bde; 3 Eng.Repl.Bn |
| 12 Div | 3 Mtn, 12 Ustt Bde; 2 Eng.Repl.Bn; 3 Art.batts |
| 14 Div | 14 Ust,19 Inf. Bde |
| 17 Div | |
| 18 Asst.Div (inc. 30 Asst.Rgt) | |
| | |
| III Corps | |
| 3 Div | 1 Rfl,2,13 Ust Bde; 7,18 Art.Bn |
| 7 Mtn.Div | 1,14 Mtn.Bde; 1,6 Art.Bn |
| 8 Div | 1,11 Ust, 18 Inf.Bde, 1 Art.batt |
| 9 Mtn Div | 2 Mtn, 9 Ust.Bde; 3 Art.batts |
| | |
| IV Corps | |
| 4 Div | 7 Rfl,8,19 Ust, 14 Inf Bde, 12 Art.Bn |
| 6 Div | 10 Ust, 15 Inf.Bde; 2 Art.batts |
| 15 Div | 16 Ust, 16 Inf.Bde |
| | |
| V Corps | |
| 10 Div | 10 Rfl, 7 Ust.Bde, 8 Art.Bn; 2 Art.batts |
| 11 Div | 4,18 Ust, 13 Inf.Bde, 1 Art.batt |
| 13 Div | 3,17 Ust, 12 Inf.Bde; 1 Art.Bn/April 1945, 28-9 Inf.Rgt; 5 Corps Recce.Bn; Ust.Repl.Bn; Ust.Eng.Bn; 1 Art.Bn |
| 16 Repl.Div | 21,23 Repl, 21 Ust.Repl.Bde, 4 Repl.batts; April 1945 |
| 16 Ust.Train.Repl.Div | Ust.Repl.Brig; Ust.Repl.Eng.Bn; Ust.Student Coy |
| 1 Ust.Def.Bde | 1-4 Inf,Gd,Mob,Art,Garr,3 Recruit bns; 1 Peopl.Upr.Rgt |
| Peopl.Upr.Corps | Baranja, Vuka, Posavje Rgt Coy |

concentrated in the Armoured Battalion (comprising two armoured, two infantry assault and one support company) and a Mobile Battalion (with one armoured, one motorized and one support company). The unit was based in Zagreb, conducting military operations north of the City.

## Defensive Battalion

The Defensive Battalion, formed in 1941 by Colonel Vjekoslav 'Maks' Luburić, was part of his *Ustaška obrana* service, which organized the concentration camps. This itself was a part of the 15,000-strong Ustasha Control Service (UNS), the Croatian Gestapo/SD apparatus, under Lieutenant-Colonel Eugen 'Dido' Kvaternik, son of Slavko Kvaternik. In January 1942, the Battalion became a brigade (*1.Ustaški Obrambeni Sdrug*), and in summer a 2nd Brigade was established. It disbanded December 1943. From December 1943 to March 1945, the 1st Brigade was known as Camp Defence Brigade (LOS) before reverting to its original title. By 1944, it had 10,000 personnel, guarding the notorious Jasenovac and Stara Gradiska death-camps for Serbs, Jews, Gypsies and anti-fascist Croatians, and acting as an élite combat unit. In January 1945, 13,000 strong, it joined 18th Croatian Assault Division and in April became 30th Assault Regiment.

## Ustasha Regiments

The 1st Ustasha Regiment was formed in September 1941 in Sarajevo by Major Jure Francetić for service in Eastern Bosnia. In December, then 1,500 strong, it was unofficially designated the Black Legion (*Crna Legija*) after adopting black uniforms. It had already become the most ruthless Croatian unit, killing Chetniks, Partisans and Serb civilians indiscriminately, eventually prompting German protests. Its four battalions fought in the First to Third Offensives and Operation *Kozara* in 1942, and its proudest hour was the defence of Kupres in August 1942, just before Francetić's transfer and the Legion's disbandment.

*Above: Ustasha emigrés return to Zagreb from Italy, April 1941. Note the distinctive field-cap and tricolour collar-patches. (Croatian History Museum, Zagreb)*

*A corporal of the Croatian Black Legion by the Drina River, Eastern Bosnia, October 1941. Note the black field-cap. (Croatian History Museum, Zagreb)*

Zagreb, with Colonel Tomislav Sertić as Chief of Staff. From Autumn 1944 Colonel Ivica Herenčić took over. Colonel was the highest active Ustasha rank – the title *Krilnik*, held by Slavko Kvaternik and in 1944 by Ante Vokić, was more of an honorary rank. Total Ustasha strength grew from 15,000 in 1941 to 76,000 in December 1944. It was a volunteer force until 1942, when garrison battalions were conscripted.

## Bodyguard Battalion

The élite Poglavnik Bodyguard Battalion (*Poglavnikova Tjelesna Bojna*, or PTB), under Colonel Ante Moškov, reported directly to Pavelić, and comprised one infantry and one mobile battalion. On 10 May 1942, it became a brigade (called the *Poglavnikov Tjelesni Sdrug*, or PTS) with guard, cavalry and mobile battalions, expanding in late 1943 to two regiments, seven battalions and one tank company. In January 1945, it became a Division (*Poglavnikova Tjelesna Divizija*), with almost all Croatian armour

## Active Battalions

The backbone of the Ustasha Army were the Ustasha Active Battalions (*Ustaške Djelatne Bojne*), each comprising 400–1,000 men. Battalions I–XII were formed in 1941. Battalions XIII–XXXVII and 27

*Left to right: Eugen Kvaternik, Chief of the infamous Croatian UNS Security Service; Colonel Jure Francetić, Black*

*Legion commander; Mladen Lorković, Minister of Internal Affairs. 1942. (Croatian History Museum, Zagreb)*

*Ustasha junior officers of the Poglavnik Bodyguard Battalion, Sarajevo, March 1942, wearing the first*

*pattern Ustasha tunic introduced May 1941. (Croatian History Museum, Zagreb)*

Preparatory Battalions (*Ustaške Pripremne Bojne*), numbered I–XXXIV with gaps – part-time guard units with older reservists and Ustasha Youth undergoing pre-military training – were formed in 1942. In late 1942, the 39 Active Battalions then constituted were formed into Active Service Brigades I–VI. Later 12 more – VII–XVIII – and the Zagreb Garrison Brigade were formed. Each brigade (*Ustaški Stajaći Djelatni Sdrug*) had four to nine battalions and, usually, artillery support. By then there were 19 brigades with 89 battalions – 66 active, two replacement, one defensive, four railway security and 16 garrison. The garrison battalions (*Posadne Bojne*) were conscripts from the former Preparatory Battalions.

## Railway Troops

The Ustasha Railway Troops (*Željeznička Vojnica*) were established in October 1941 for railway security duties. In 1942, the eight battalions were reorganized into Communications Brigades (*Prometni sdrugovi*) I and II, and in 1944 the remaining four battalions joined the Active Service Brigades.

## German Units

In October 1941, the ethnic German community formed an Ustasha Active Unit (*Einsatzstaffel*), and by September 1942 there were four battalions – 'Prinz Eugen', 'Ludwig von Baden', 'General Laudon' and 'Emanuel von Bayern', wearing

Waffen-SS style uniforms and insignia, in action in Syrmia and Slavonia. In April 1943, they joined 'Prinz Eugen' SS-Division.

The Ustasha Army earned a reputation for fanatical bravery and brutality, but never matched the systematic savagery of the Partisan mass-executions. Captured Ustashas neither asked for, nor received, mercy.

On 21 November 1944, Croatian Army and Ustasha units were combined into the Croatian Armed Forces (*Hrvatske Oružane Snage*), in order to create a more effective fighting machine. Pavelić was Supreme Commander, assisted by Army General Gjuro Gjurić, with Ustasha Colonel Sertić as Chief of Staff.

## New Units

The army's 19 mountain, rifle and garrison brigades were reorganized into four mountain (1–4), three rifle (1, 7 and 10), ten infantry (11–20) and two replacement (21 and 23) brigades. The Ustasha Zagreb Garrison and 18 Active Service Brigades became one replacement (XXI) and 22 Ustasha brigades (I–XX, XXII–XXIII). All these units were grouped into 13 infantry, two mountain, two assault and one replacement Croatian Divisions (from 20 April 1945, Ustasha Divisions) and the Poglavnik Bodyguard Division. Each division, often only 5,000 strong, had one to three brigades (in March–April 1945, redesignated as regiments), one or two artillery battalions and minimal support units. The Army Mobile Brigade became an Ustasha unit.

In January 1945, the Poglavnik Bodyguard Corps (*Poglavnikov Tjelesni Sbor*, or PTS) was formed from the Poglavnik Bodyguard Division, 1st Croatian Assault and 5th Croatian Division. From 5 February, this comprised the 1st Bodyguard Division – which from 5 March included the Ustasha Mobile Brigade – and the 1st and 5th Croatian Assault Divisions. In April 1945, Croatian Corps (from 20 April, Ustasha Corps) 2 to 5 were formed from the remaining 14 Divisions, leaving the replacement division in Zagreb.

From early 1945, the Croatian Divisions were allocated to various German Corps, and by March were holding the Southern Front. By 1 May, much reduced by casualties, they crowded into the Zagreb region. On the 6th, 200,000 troops and civilians retreated through Slovenia into Austria while Pavelić and his top officials fled abroad. At Bleiburg, the British forced the Croatians back, insisting they surrender to the Partisans. Some 20,000 escaped, leaving the rest to Tito's revenge. About 100,000 were shot or died from exhaustion on death-marches to camps in Banat.

## Air and Sea Units

The small Croatian Navy (*Hrvatska Mornarica*) was commanded by Rear-Admiral Djuro Jakčin until late 1943. Commodore Edgar Angeli took over until 1944, and Rear-Admiral Nikola Steinfl commanded until May 1945. The three Naval Commands – North Adriatic (based at Crikvenica, later Sušak), Central Adriatic (at Makarska, later Split) and South Adriatic (at Dubrovnik) undertook coastguard and customs duties until September 1943, when the Italian Armistice nullified the veto on Croatian sea-going forces. A river flotilla (based at Zemun) patrolled the Danube and Sava, and there was a Naval Infantry Battalion at Zemun, later Zagreb.

The Croatian Naval Legion, eventually about 1,000 strong, under Commander Andro Vrkljan and later Captain Stjepan Rumenović, served as the German 23rd Minesweeping Flotilla in Crimea, Black Sea and Sea of Azov. In 1943, a Coastal Artillery Battery was added. The Legion repatriated to Trieste in May 1944 as a torpedo-boat flotilla under German 11th Escort Flotilla. The Germans disbanded it in December 1944 to prevent defection to the Allies.

The Croatian Air Force (*Hrvatsko Zrakoplovstvo*), formed 12 April 1941, was 9,775 strong in 1943. It was commanded by Major General Vladimir Kren until 14 September 1943 and Colonel Adalbert Rogulja until 4 June 1944, when Kren took over again. The four airbases controlled seven Wings (*Skupina*), subdivided into squadrons (*Jato*). There were 19 squadrons in 1943, operating Italian, German and obsolete French aircraft. 1st Airbase (Zagreb) had 1st, 5th Bomber and 11th Fighter Wings; 2nd (Sarajevo) had 2nd Wing; 3rd (Mostar) had 3rd Wing; and 5th (Banja Luka) had 6th Wing.

From July 1941, the Croatian Air-Force Legion fought in Russia. The 4th Fighter Wing operated as 15th Squadron, 52nd *Luftwaffe* Fighter Group (15./J.G.52), scoring 263 kills over Ukraine up to July 1944, when it returned to Croatia. Then it absorbed the Pilot Training School, which had been redesignated in December 1943 1st Air Force Legion Fighter Wing. The 5th Bomber Wing fought as 10th Squadron, later 15th Squadron, 53rd *Luftwaffe* Bomber Group (10-15/K.G.53) over Leningrad until repatriation in December 1942.

The Air-Force Parachute Company, formed January 1942, became 1st Parachute Battalion (*1.Padobranska Lovačka Bojna*), fighting Partisans

AFV personnel attached to the Ustasha Black Legion, on the road from Gornji Vakuf to Jajce, Bosnia, summer 1942. Note the CV Fiat Ansaldo L38 tankette and the German black M1935 AFV tunic worn by two of the soldiers. (Croatian History Museum, Zagreb)

*Members of the Ustasha V Brigade, 27 February 1943, wearing ex-Yugoslav greenish-grey greatcoats, German M1916 and ex-Yugoslav French M1915 helmets, and the black 'Black Legion' field-caps. (Croatian History Museum, Zagreb)*

*Below: A Croatian Naval Lieutenant leads a squad of sailors, Dubrovnik 1943. Note the title 'Mornarica' on the cap-tallies. (National and University Library, Zagreb)*

east of Zagreb under 1st Airbase. The Anti-Aircraft Artillery was divided into two regions – I (Zagreb) with 1, 2, 4 and 6 AA Wings, and II (Sarajevo) with 3, 5 and 7 Wings. From early 1943, the Croatian Flak Legion, mainly Moslem, provided anti-aircraft batteries for the *Luftwaffe*. The National Guard (*Narodna Zaštita*) was responsible for air-raid precautions.

## The Labour Service

On 30 July 1941, the State Honorary Labour Service (*Država Časna Radna Sluzba* or DČRS) was formed on the German model under Labour Major-General F. Halla, to give Croatian citizens aged 19 to 25 one year's labour duties and pre-military training. In 1942, it was redesignated State Labour Service (DRS) under Labour Major-General Palčić, but by September 1943 there were still only 6,000 personnel

in labour companies on military fortification and air-raid clean-up duties. In January 1945, they were absorbed into the 18th Croatian Assault Division.

## State Reserve Units

In Summer 1944, older armed forces reservists were formed into the independent People's Uprising Corps (*Pučko Ustaški Sbor*), with army or Ustasha officers, under Major-General Josip Metzger. There were four regiments – *Vuka*, *Baranja*, *Posavje* and *Livac-Zapolje*. The last joined the Camp Defensive Brigades in December 1944 as the 1st People's Uprising Regiment. The other units were disbanded in March 1945.

The various Croatian armed forces established village militias in Bosnia-Herzegovina. The army's Home Defence-Force Volunteers (*Domdo* units) eventually comprised 21 battalions. The Ustashas organized the Ustasha Militia (*Ustaška Milicija*) and Ustasha Peasants' Protection Force. The Gendarmerie had a 7,500-strong Moslem Militia (*Milicija*). And the German Army formed the South Dalmatian Legion. From 1943, the UNS organized a Serbian militia, the Serbian Self-Protection units (*Srpske Samozaštitne Postrojbe*) in the Banija Region south of Zagreb.

There were also some semi-autonomous village militias, including the Husko Legion (*Huskina Legija*). This comprised 3,000 men in 11 battalions in Western Bosnia under Husko Miljković. It was formed in Summer 1943, defecting to the Partisans in February 1944. Hadžiefendić's Legion (*Hadžiefendića Legija*) operated in several detachments in North-Eastern Bosnia.

## Police Units

The Croatian Gendarmerie (*Hrvatsko Oružništvo*) was formed on 30 April 1941 as rural police under Major-General Milan Miesler, then Major-General Tartaglia, and from August 1942 Ustasha Colonel Viljko Pećnikar. By September 1943, there were 18,000 men in seven regiments – 1 (Zagreb), 2 (Split), 3 (Banja Luka), 4 (Sarajevo), 5 (Mostar), 6 (Knin), 7 (Zemun). These were divided into 23 companies (one per county plus one for Zagreb). The companies were subdivided into 142 district platoons, each with several posts. In early 1942, a three-battalion Combined Gendarmerie Regiment, in July redesignated Petrinja Brigade, was established for anti-partisan operations in Slavonia.

The Croatian Urban Police (*Redarstvena Straža*) was established in April 1941 with 5,000 personnel covering the 142 Districts. It was controlled by the Ministry of Interior's Public Order and Security Directorate (*Ravsigur*) until June 1942, when the Police joined the Ustasha Army, transferring back in January 1943.

No German police regiments operated in Croatia, but on 10 March 1943 a German-Croatian Police (*Deutsch-Kroatische Polizei*) was established by SS-Police Major-General Konstantin Kammerhofer, manned by German Police, ethnic Germans and Croatians, for internal security duties. It was deeply mistrusted by the Croatian authorities. By December 1944 there were 32,000 men in Police Volunteer Regiments 1–5 (with three battalions each) and independent Police Volunteer Regiments (Croatia) 1–15, twelve of which formed the Croatian Gendarmerie

Division in 1945. German Einsatzgruppe E (Action Group E) of the SS Security Service, with battalion-sized Commands 1–5, and other units, were included. The German Police also supervised a village militia, the *Ortswehr*, in Bosnia.

Following the military co-operation agreement of 11 January 1942 between the Italian 2nd Army and Trifunović-Birčanin, the Italian Zones' Chetnik Commander, most Chetniks, about 22,000 in all, joined the Italian Voluntary Anti-Communist Militia (MVAC), with Italian weapons and maroon-dyed uniforms. It was organized in battalions and companies and included some Croats and Moslems. Most Bosnian Chetniks in the German Zone signed one of

*Above: A Croatian paratrooper corporal, already sporting the German infantry assault badge and two Croatian bravery medals, receives a third Medal, 1943. Note that the collar-patch rank wings are thinner and flatter than those in the German Air-Force. (Josip M. Novak)*

*Croatian paratroopers in 1943, showing a good range of uniforms and insignia. Note the parachute sleeve-badge. (Josip M. Novak)*

three agreements with the Croatian authorities in May and June 1942. These 'legal' Chetniks fought the Partisans in the Third to Fifth Offensives, and in September 1943 reverted to their former 'illegal' status or joined the Germans.

The Croatian Forces, established to protect legitimate national aspirations for independence, were compromised by association with the Axis cause and an authoritarian Ustasha regime lacking wide-spread popular support. Their military defeat led to the Bleiburg massacres, and 46 more years of political discrimination until their independence was achieved again on 25 June 1991.

*Lieutenant Dušan Dojčinović, company commander in 4 Regiment, Serbian Volunteer Corps, 1943, wearing ex-Yugoslav uniform with two gold pips on a silver braid shoulder-board with dark-blue underlay and collar-patches. Chetniks wore Yugoslav uniforms, usually with peakless field-cap and M1939 cap insignia, and often bushy beards*

# SERBIA

The German Military Command (*Befehlshaber Serbien*), established 25 April 1941, controlled four regimental-status Sub-Area Commands – *Feldkommandantur* 509 (based in Belgrade), 610 (Pančevo), 809 (Niš), 816 (Užice). Each had 1–3 battalion-status District Commands (*Kreiskommandanturen*) and a *Landesschützen* Garrison Battalion (562, 592, 920, 266 respectively, in 1941). On 13 August 1943, it was absorbed by South-East Military Command.

### Serbian State Guard

Milan Aćimović's Serbian Administration, established 30 April 1941, was superseded on 29 August by General Milan Nedić's 'Government of National Salvation'. On 10 February 1942 Nedić expanded the ex-Yugoslav *Drinski* and *Dunavski* Gendarmerie Regiments into a 17,000-strong static security force, the Serbian State Guard (*Srpska Državna Straža*), under Colonel Jovan Trišić, and later Major-General Borivoje Jonić. It was deployed as Municipal Police (*Gradska Straža*), Rural Police (*Poljska Straža*), Village Guard (*Seljačka Straža*) and a 2,500-strong Frontier Guard (*Srpska Granična Straža*), organized in five regions (Belgrade, Kraljevo, Niš, Valjevo and Zaječar). Each region (*oblast*) had one battalion. Each region was divided into three districts. Each district (*Okrug*) had several companies. The Guard was royalist, pro-Chetnik and, despite desertions, initially performed creditably against the Partisans.

On 6 October 1944, 5,000 Guards, under Lieutenant-General Stefan Radovanović, joined the Chetniks in Bosnia as 1st Serbian Assault Corps (*1.Srpski Udarni Korpus*), with 1st and 2nd Assault, and 3rd Frontier Guard Divisions. The Germans sent 3,000 to Austria as *Organization Todt* workers. The remaining 2,000 joined the Chetnik Šumadija Division in Slovenia under Lieutenant-General Miodrag Damjanović in March 1945 and surrendered to the British in Southern Austria in May.

### Serbian Volunteer Command

On 15 September 1941, the conservative politician Dimitrije Ljotić formed a Serbian Volunteer Command from Chetniks and his Zbor Movement activists. It had twelve 120–150-strong detachments. In January 1943, it became the 7,000-strong Serbian Volunteer Corps (*Srpski Dobrovoljački Korpus*) with five 500-man battalions, expanding in early 1944 to five 1,200-man regiments (1–5) and a 500-man Artillery Battalion, under German tactical command but reporting to General Nedić. The pro-Chetnik, royalist Corps was admired by the Germans for its effective performance in combat. In October 1944, it retreated to Slovenia where, on 9 November it became, nominally, a Waffen-SS unit. On 30 March 1945, it joined the Chetnik Šumadija Division. The three regiments surrendering to the British in Austria in May were sent back to Tito; two others surrendering in Italy remained in the West.

### The Russian Defence Corps

On 12 September 1941, the Independent Russian Corps – redesignated the Russian Defence Corps on 2 October – was formed from Russian Imperial Army

A 2nd lieutenant (Podporuchik) of the Russian Protection Corps' Artillery Battalion, wearing Imperial Russian insignia (sometimes with Yugoslav pips). These were worn from 12 September 1941 to 30 November 1942 concurrently with special Corps collar rank insignia. On 1 December 1942, German Army uniforms and insignia were adopted. (US National Archives)

veterans exiled to Serbia in 1921. Lieutenant-General Boris Alexandrovich Shteyfon took over command on 15 September 1941 and expanded the Corps to an 11,197-strong force in September 1944. It comprised one Cavalry Regiment – 1st Cossack Regiment *Generala Zborovskogo* – and four infantry regiments (2–5). The veterans were reinforced by younger emigrés and former Soviet POWs, and deployed by the Germans as factory guards. Later they fought against the Partisans. In September 1944, the Corps helped defend Belgrade against the advancing Soviet Army, before transferring to anti-Partisan duties in Bosnia. There, on 10 October, it became the Russian Corps in Serbia (*Russkiy Korpus v Serbii*). Colonel Anatoliy Ivanovich Rogozhin assumed command on 30 April 1945 and, in May, surrendered to the British, who allowed the pre-Soviet era emigrés to settle in the West.

## Other Units

Nedić formed a Serbian labour service, the 'Reconstruction Service', claiming 16,000 members in 1942. In August 1941, Konstantin 'Kosta' Pećanac placed

his 8,000 Chetnik troops under German command as 'legalized Chetniks', followed in November by 2,000 Mihailović Chetniks. In February 1943, the Germans dismissed them, but in November concluded new agreements with Mihailović's 16,000 'loyal Chetniks'. Mihailović retreated in October 1944 to the Vučjak Mountain, Derventa, Northern Bosnia, with a 12,000-man force. It was destroyed by the Partisans near Kalinovik, Eastern Bosnia, in May 1945. Mihailović was captured near Višegrad in March 1946.

Banat military units were under German Police control. The 1,500-strong Banat State Guard (*Banater Staatswache*), nicknamed the Black Police, was commanded by Colonel Ernest Pelikan, reporting to Franz Reit, the Police Commissioner. It was formed in February 1942 as municipal and rural police. The Auxiliary Police (*Hilfspolizei*) was formed September 1941 as a mobile anti-partisan force for Serbia. It comprised ten Battalions (1–10), 5,800 men organized in June 1944 into Police Volunteer Regiment (Serbia) 1–3, in German Police uniforms. Decimated in October–November 1944, the survivors joined the German-Croatian Police in Croatia.

In April 1941, the 6,000-strong SS-style German Force (*Deutsche Mannschaft*) was formed for village security. Six battalions were raised. Each Battalion (*Sturmbann*) had four to seven companies (*Stürme*). The Force, under Lieutenant Michael Reiser and from spring 1942 Captain Hein, defended the Banat in October 1944, before withdrawing to Croatia.

# MONTENEGRO

### Ground Forces

Anti-Partisan forces in Montenegro comprised the Greens – separatists wishing to restore the pre-1918 Kingdom; Whites – Nationalists wanting union or federation with Serbia; and the Chetniks.

In August 1941, the Italians formed separatist Voluntary Anti-Communist Militia (MVAC) companies, superseded, in January 1942, by Krsto

*Serbian Volunteer Corps marching to the front, 1944, wearing Italian helmets, uniforms and webbing. (Jan-Poul Petersen)*

Popović's Montenegrin Troops, renamed Katun Troops. In February 1942, Colonel Bajo Stanišić formed a Nationalist National Army of Montenegro and Herzegovina in six battalions with some Nationalist Chetnik battalions. Meanwhile, in October 1941, Mihailović appointed Major Djordjije Lašić as Montenegrin Chetnik Commander.

In July 1942, the Montenegrin National Troops were established as Italian auxiliaries, with the 1,700-strong separatist *Lovćen* Brigade, the 1,500-strong Nationalist *Zeta* Flying Detachment, and 1,500 Chetniks in the *Lim-Sandžak* Flying Detachment, leaving the new Chetnik Commander, Blažo Djukanović, with 17,300 Chetniks and 5,000 nationalists.

Some 4,000 Chetniks and Nationalists fought at the Neretva in the Fourth Offensive in February 1943, but in June the Germans and Italians disbanded almost all anti-partisan units.

In September, the Germans succeeded the Italians in Montenegro, establishing *Feldkommandantur 1040*. In November, they formed the 2,000-strong nationalist-separatist National Militia. In December, Major Jovo Djukanović reformed the Chetnik-nationalist-separatist Montenegrin National Troops. 7,000 strong, it was badly mauled by the Partisans in March 1944.

In June 1944, Lieutenant-Colonel Pavle Djurišić, perhaps the finest Yugoslav Chetnik leader, became Montenegrin Chetnik Commander, with 7,000 Chetniks under his command. He formed the 2nd Serbian (Montenegrin) Volunteer Corps – 5,650 men in 6th, 7th and 8th Volunteer Regiments. From August to December 1944, the Chetnik Sanjak Commander, Major Vojislav Lukačević, operated a breakaway Independent National Resistance Group, which attacked German units.

On 6 December 1944, Djurišić retreated with Chetniks, the Volunteer Corps and Montenegrin National Troops to Eastern Bosnia. These reformed in January 1945 as the 10,000-strong Chetnik 8th Montenegrin Army, with 1st, 5th, 8th and 9th (Herzegovina) Divisions. This force was defeated by Croatian Ustashas near Banja Luka, and Djurišić was killed. The survivors formed a new separatist Montenegrin National Army, under Boško Agram. It reached Austria in May 1945, only to be handed back to the Partisans.

## Police Units

Police duties were discharged from April 1941 by the ex-Yugoslav *Zeta* Gendarmerie Regiment, superseded in July 1942 by the 3,000-strong National Gendarmerie. The Germans formed a Banat-German Police Volunteer Battalion Montenegro in June 1944, and a Police Volunteer Battalion Sanjak in July.

In Sanjak, the border region between South-West Serbia and Northern Montenegro, the Italians formed a 3,000-strong anti-Partisan Moslem Militia, under Hoxha Patchariz, reformed in early 1944 as the Moslem Legion, under SS-Major Karl von Krempler.

# BULGARIA AND MACEDONIA

## Ground Units

In 1935, Bulgaria expanded its Armed Forces. By 1939, the Army (*Bulgarska Voyska*) had ten line infantry divisions (1–10), two Mobile (ex-Cavalry) Divisions (1–2) and a Mountain Brigade. There were also 24 Frontier Battalions, organized into regiments.

A 15,500-strong Infantry Division had three to four three-battalion infantry regiments, one three-battalion artillery regiment, a reconnaissance battalion (with one cyclist, one heavy machine-gun and two mounted companies), an anti-aircraft artillery battalion, a machine-gun battalion, an engineer battalion, a signals battalion, a labour battalion and logistical services. A Mobile Division had two mounted cavalry brigades, each with two five-squadron regiments, one two-battalion motorized infantry regiment, one artillery regiment (one motorized and one mounted battalion), an anti-aircraft artillery battery, a motorized engineer company, a signals company and logistical services. The Mountain Brigade was disbanded 1942 and reformed early 1943. It had two infantry regiments and a mountain artillery battalion.

The 1st Tank Company, formed in March 1935, became the Armoured Vehicle Battalion in April 1939 (with 1, 2 Tank Companies and a repair battalion). In early 1941, it became the Tank Group, with 1–4 Tank Companies. On 15 August 1941, it was

*Bulgarian paratrooper NCOs and men are briefed by an officer, Macedonia, 1943. Note the Bulgarian-manufactured grenades and the German-style diving-eagle parachute qualification breast-badge. (Varna Military Museum)*

redesignated the Armoured Regiment and, on 1 October 1943, the Armoured Brigade. This had 4,226 men in an armoured regiment (with two armoured, one anti-tank and an anti-aircraft artillery battalion), a reconnaissance battalion with light tanks, a two-battalion motorized infantry regiment and an artillery regiment.

## Organization

All divisions and brigades were grouped into four corps-sized Armies (I–IV Armiya). The 1st Army (based in Sofia) guarded Western Bulgaria with 1 and 7 Infantry and 1 Mobile Division and the Mountain Brigade; the 2nd Army (Plovdiv) guarded Southern Bulgaria with 2, 8 and 10 Infantry Divisions; the 3rd Army (Varna) guarded Eastern Bulgaria with 3, 4 Infantry Divisions, 2 Mobile Division; and the 4th Army (Pleven) guarded Northern Bulgaria with 5, 6 and 9 Infantry Divisions.

Germany forced the cession of Southern Dobrudja by Rumania on 21 August 1940 under the Treaty of Craiova, and on 1 March 1941 Bulgaria confirmed its Axis status by signing the Tripartite Pact. King Boris III avoided committing troops to the invasions of Greece and Yugoslavia, claiming that all battleworthy divisions were in 3rd Army guarding the German flank against Turkey, but German 12th Army was permitted to use Bulgaria as a springboard to attack Greece and Yugoslavia on 6 April 1941.

In 1941, four line (12 and 14–16) and four reserve (11, 13, 17 and 21) divisions were formed, in early 1943 six reserve (22–27) were added and, later, two more reserve (28–9) divisions were formed. Only the 12th Infantry Division (3rd Army, Southern Dobrudja) was a true line division. The other fifteen, including the locally recruited 14–16 Divisions, were units raised during the war for occupation duties. They drew cadres from line divisions whose numbers they usually carried as duplicates (for example, 11 and 21 from 1st Infantry Division). Lacking a metropolitan recruiting district or continuous existence, they were usually understrength in men and equipment. The High Command retained the best line divisions in Bulgaria proper.

Army Chiefs of Staff were Lieutenant-General Gheorgi Popov (from 1938), Nikola Hadzhi-Petrov (from 1940) and Konstantin Lukash (from December 1941).

On 19 April 1941, Bulgaria occupied Macedonia and some districts of Eastern Serbia, which, with Western Thrace and Eastern Greek Macedonia (the Aegean Province), were annexed by Bulgaria on 14 May.

The 1st Army (1, 7, 9, 11, 13 and 16 Infantry Divisions) garrisoned the Aegean Province. Its policy of forcible 'Bulgarianization' drove the Greek puppet government in Athens to consider mass evacuation of Greeks to German-occupied territory. In

German Units
1: Gefreiter, German Army, Eastern Herzegovina, May 1943
2: SS-Hauptsturmführer, Dalmatia, September 1943
3: Paratrooper, Western Bosnia, May 1944

A

Italian Units
1: Colonnello titolare, Eastern Montenegro, 1942
2: Vicecaposquadra, Slovenia, August 1942
3: Sergente-Maggiore, Western Croatia, September 1941

B

**Croatian Army Units**
1: General Zagreb, Croatia, February 1943
2: Poručnik, Bosnia, January 1944
3: Bojnik, Zagreb, February 1945

C

1: Razvodnik, Tuzla, Bosnia, December 1941
2: Stožerni Narednik, Western Bosnia, June 1943
3: Domobran, Eastern Bosnia, December 1943

D

Croatian Naval/Artillery Units
1: Bojnik, Bosnia, October 1942
2: Narednik, Koprivnica, September 1943
3: Vodnik, Dubrovnik, February 1944

Ustasha Units
1: Dupukovnik, Croatia, 1942
2: Rojnik, Croatia, January 1944
3: Porucnik, Central Bosnia, March 1942

F

Bulgarian Units
1: Rotmistr, Macedonia, 1942
2: Podofitser, August 1943
3: Officer, Macedonia, 1943

**G**

Slovene Units
1: Nadporočnik, Slovenia, December 1943
2: Podnarednik, Slovenia, November 1944
3: Stražmojster, North-East Italy, May 1944

H

February 1942, the 1st Army transferred to Serbia, leaving 16th Infantry Division, bolstered by elements of 1st and 10th Infantry Divisions as an embryonic Aegean Command. In July 1943, the 7th Infantry Division was posted to Salonika under the German Salonika-Aegean Command. Later 2nd Corps (7, 26 and 28 Infantry Divisions) garrisoned Aegean Province against expected Allied landings, and in February 1944 it occupied Greek Western Macedonia.

The 5th Army, headquartered in Skopje, was formed to garrison Macedonia with the 14th Infantry Division in the North, the 15th in the South-West, the 4th Cavalry Brigade and later the 27th Infantry Division. The Macedonians had initially welcomed the Bulgarians as liberators from Serb oppression, but soon resented Bulgarian assimilation policies. Resulting partisan activity was ruthlessly suppressed and had virtually ceased until early 1943. Meanwhile the Italians, hoping to extend their Western Macedonia occupation zone into Bulgarian territory, in order to reach valuable mineral deposits, caused serious clashes between the Axis partners in August and October 1942.

On 15 January 1942 the 1st Army (7, 9 and 21 Infantry Divisions) transferred to South-East Serbia. Headquartered at Niš, under German Serbia Command, it replaced German divisions needed in Croatia and Russia. On 7 January 1943, it also occupied South-West Serbia. Savage pacification measures reduced Partisan activity appreciably. This allowed the 1st Army to return to Bulgaria in spring 1943, leaving 1st (Occupation) Corps, with five reserve divisions (22–5 and 27). On 31 July 1943, the corps garrisoned all of Serbia, with the exception of the North-West and Belgrade. From mid-1943, Partisan attacks reintensified and in May 1943 the 23rd Infantry Division moved into Northern Montenegro, blocking the Partisan escape-route to Serbia during the Fifth Offensive. In December 1943, the 24th Infantry Division moved to Eastern Bosnia for the Sixth Offensive.

King Boris died suddenly on 28 August 1943, having avoided Bulgarian involvement on the Eastern Front. He had claimed his russophile troops would desert. He had also vetoed the 1942 German proposals for the formation of a Bulgarian SS-Legion, although a Regiment was established by emigrés in Germany in November 1944.

## Bulgaria joins the Allies

On 10 September 1944, Bulgaria changed sides and declared war on Germany as an Allied Power. The Germans swiftly disarmed the 1st Occupation Corps, but 5th Army resisted tenaciously Operation *Treubruch*. Survivors of both armies retreated to Bulgaria, joining the new 450,000-strong Bulgarian National Armed Forces (*Bulgarska Narodna Armiya*) under Lieutenant-General Ivan Marinov. On 8 October, the 1st and 4th Armies occupied Serb Macedonia with Partisan permission. The 2nd Army occupied South-Eastern Serbia. The 1st Army then swung north with the Soviet 3rd Ukrainian Front, through Eastern Yugoslavia and South-Western Hungary, and linked up with British 8th Army in Austria in May 1945. The 3rd Army remained on the Turkish frontier.

*Bulgarian troops handling machine-gun ammunition, 1942. Note that the rank insignia of the Corporal far right consists of two yellow shoulder-loops with central branch-colour stripes probably intended for fatigue uniforms. (Varna Military Museum)*

## Air, Sea and Police Units

The Bulgarian Navy (*Morski Voyski*) had Black Sea, Danube and Aegean (headquartered in Kavala, Greek Macedonia) fleets; four coastal artillery regiments (two in Greece, at Kavala and Alexandropolis) and a 630-man Naval Infantry Battalion, formed 1942, on the Aegean islands of Thassos (with two companies) and Samothraki (one company).

The 5,000-strong Air Force (*Vazdushni Voyski*), under Major-General Airanov, had eight wings. Each wing (*orlyak*) had three or four squadrons. Deployed on Black Sea coastal patrols, they formed a defence against USAAF bombers from August 1943. From April 1944, they were used against Partisans in Serb Macedonia. And they supported the 1st Army from October 1944. The Parachute Battalion, formed early 1943, fought in Serb Macedonia under the 5th Army and with the 1st Army from October 1944.

The Military Police (*Voenna Politsia*) also functioned as Security Police. It had a fearsome reputation. By July 1944, each army had an MP Battalion (1–5) attached to it.

The National Police (*Darjavna Politsia*) under Director Hristo Dragalov, then from October 1942 Anton Kozarov, deployed 4,000 uniformed personnel in Serbia and Serb Macedonia in two regional, three municipal and 21 district commands. There were motorized units and at least one combat battalion, at Skopje.

From August 1941, the National Police controlled Anti-Partisan Units (*Kontračete*) in Serb Macedonia. These had about 2,000 men, recruited from the Internal Macedonian Revolutionary Organization (VRMO). The units – each *Kontračeta* comprised about 30 men – were dispersed across the twelve Macedonian district commands: Bitola, Gevgelija, Kačanik, Kavadarci, Kočani, Kratovo, Prečevo, Prilep, Skopje, Skopska crna gora, and Veles. There were also Albanian units and units in Greek Macedonia, but virtually all were destroyed by Partisans in summer 1944.

Bulgaria also had a 24-battalion Labour Corps (*Trudovi voyski*) under Colonel Konstantin Avramov, for Jews and Bulgarians not liable for military service. From January 1941 to September 1944, there was a 200,000-strong *Brannik* ('Defender') compulsory Youth Organization.

# SLOVENIA

## Ground Forces

In April and May 1941, Slovenia – *Drava* Province – was divided amongst the Axis belligerents. Western Slovenia was annexed by Italy as Lubiana (Ljubljana) Province and an extended Fiume (Rijeka) Province. Central Slovenia was incorporated into the German Reich – Carinthia (*Kärnten*) and Upper Carniol (*Oberkrain*) joining Carinthia Province, Lower Styria (*Untersteiermark*) joining Styria. The Prekmurje District of Eastern Slovenia became Hungarian. There was also a substantial Slovene minority in the North-East Italian provinces of Gorizia and Trieste.

In April 1941, the *Drava* Governor, Dr Marko Natlačen of the Catholic Slovene People's Party formed a National Committee for an independent Slovenia, and his Slovene Legion (*Slovenska Legija*) began disarming defeated Yugoslav Army units. Independence denied, the Legion continued in Western Slovenia as Italian auxiliaries.

In March 1942, the outlawed Slovene political parties formed the Slovene National Alliance with the Slovene Legion, 10,000 former University Student Guards (*Stražari*) and High School Fighters (*Borci*), organizations of the pre-war 'Catholic Action' movement. These were joined by the Sokol Legion (*Sokolska Legija*) – 1,000 Liberals and Socialists in the 'Sokol' gymnastic organization – and the 1,000-strong National Legion (*Narodna Legija*) made up of smaller parties. These legions considered themselves part of Mihailović's Chetniks and in September 1942 were largely absorbed into Voluntary Anti-Communist Militia (MVAC), leaving three to four hundred men organized in early 1943 as four Chetnik detachments unofficially named the Blue Guard (*Plava Garda*), operating in Eastern Lubiana Province under Major Karlo Novak.

On 6 August 1942 the Italians formed the MVAC in Slovenia – a thousand men under the command of Lieutenant-Colonel Ernest Peterlin. These had originally been Village Guards (*Vaške Straže*) formed in May 1942 as a village protection force widely known as the White Guard (*Bela Garda*). The MVAC companies formed bore the name of the locality. By December 1942, there were 4,500 guards in 41 companies with 71 posts. By July 1943, 6,000 in

Members of the Slovene Legion of Death parade in Mokronog, in September 1942, wearing civilian clothes and Italian Army uniform items, with ex-Yugoslav Czech M1934 and French M1915 steel helmets. (Modern History Museum, Ljubljana)

107 Posts. In February 1943, four élite mixed Italian-MVAC Special Battalions (*Posebni bataljon št.* 1–4) were formed.

In May 1942, Major Novak's Slovene Chetnik Detachment, formed July 1941, joined the MVAC as the 'Legion of Death' (*Legija Smrti*). It comprised intially 640, and by February 1943 1,687, mobile hot-pursuit troops in 11 companies. These were formed as the 1st Battalion (Vrnika), who were mainly Chetnik; and the 2nd (Gorjanci) and 3rd Battalion (Mokronog), ex-Slovene Legion and Sokol Legion, deployed around Ljubljana.

On 1 November 1942, a 210-strong MVAC Ljubljana Security Guard was formed as security police, but proved too zealous and was disbanded in January 1943.

In July 1943, the Slovene National Alliance decided to reorganize the MVAC into a 19-battalion Slovene National Army (*Slovenska Narodna Vojska*) to support anticipated Allied landings, but the plan was not completed. However in September, Captain Albin Cerkvenik organized 60 White Chetniks and 1,600 MVAC troops into the 1st *Triglav* and 2nd *Krim* Mountain Brigades of the Chetnik Slovene Army.

Following the Italian Armistice on 8 September 1943, the Partisans launched a general offensive in Slovenia, smashing Cerkvenik's brigades at Turjak Castle and most of the Blue Guard at Kočevje. The Partisans overran many MVAC garrisons, but failed to defeat the Legion of Death Battalions.

On 10 September 1943, German-occupied 'Ljubljana Province' joined the 'Adriatic Coastal Area' (*Adriatisches Küstenland*) of North-East Italy. On 24 September the Governor, ex-Yugoslav army Lieutenant-General Leon Rupnik, formed the 'Slovene Defence Legion' (*Slovenska Domobranska Legija*) with three Battalions (1–3 *bataljon*) formed from 2,000 former MVAC troops. On 30 September, the Germans took it over as the Slovene Home Defence Force (*Slovensko Domobranstvo*) under German Police control, with Rupnik as nominal Commander-in-Chief and Colonel Franc Krener as tactical commander.

The Force comprised 63 infantry companies (1–7, 11–29, 31–48, 51–6, 61–3, 65–7, 71–2 and 111–5) – 43 as local garrisons, the others grouped into battalions. There were also engineers, signals, medical and labour companies, and four artillery batteries, with a fifth operating five armoured trains.

The battalions underwent many reorganizations. In October 1943, Battalions 1–5 were formed, with 4th Battalion as a Training Battalion. In December, compulsory military service was introduced. This brought the strength up to 10,500 men. The Battalions were reformed as seven combat groups (1–7 *Bojna Skupina*) and Training Groups 1 and 2.

On 25 February 1944, it reorganized again into four groups (*Skupine*) – the 1st Training Group (ex-1st Group); the 2nd Railway Security Group (ex-Groups 4 and 5); the 3rd Operational Group (ex-2, 6 and 7) including Assault Battalion *Kriz*; and 4th *Novo Mesto* Protection Group.

On 16 May 1944 the Force, now 12,000 strong, was divided into four Operational Zones, each recruiting an Assault Battalion (*Udarni bataljon*). On 5 July 1944, these were designated N (*Nord*) – 1st Battalion; W (*West*) – 2nd Battalion; M (*Mitte*) – 3rd Battalion, disbanded March 1945; and O (*Ost*) – 4th Battalion. The 5th Battalion was formed in August 1944; the 6th in March 1945. In December 1944, as desertions increased, German 14th and 17th Police Regiments contributed a company to each battalion (except the 2nd) and German officers took command.

Finally, on 28 March 1945 the Battalions were renumbered: 1 remaining as 1; 2 became 5; 4 became 2; 5 became 6; 6 became 10. By this time there was also a 12th Battalion.

A State Security Service (*Državna Varnostna Služba*) was formed on 29 October 1943 by Lovco

*After the Italian Armistice in September 1943, Slovene Village Guards replaced their black MVAC berets with coloured triangle rank insignia and ex-Yugoslav uniforms dyed brown, grey-green Italian uniforms and leather equipment, with Yugoslav Army grey-green field-caps (also worn by the Chetniks). The cap-badge was a cloth triangle with the Slovene colours, white, blue and red horizontal stripes, or a Chetnik silver metal skull and crossbones. (Modern History Museum, Ljubljana)*

Hacin with a uniformed police force (*Policijski Zbor*) under Lieutenant Colonel Stanko Palčič. On 3 January 1944, a Railway Police was formed. And on 29 October 1944 a civilian Labour pool, the *Narodni Pionirji*, and a paramilitary Labour Service, the *Delovna Služba*, under German officers, were created.

In Styria, ethnic Germans not liable for *Wehrmacht* service joined the SA-*Wehrmannschaft* (SA-Defence Force) for static guard duties. By 1942 it claimed 105,000 members. Later a *Wehrmann-schaftsregiment Untersteiermark* (Defence Regiment Lower Styria) was formed with the 1st to 5th Battalions as a mobile strike-force.

Carniolan Slovenes also joined the *Wehrmannschaft* and some enlisted in its *Selbstschutz* platoons. At least seven were formed, operating from May–Autumn 1942 under German Gendarmerie command. From 2 November 1942 to 20 April 1943 some Village Guards units were operational, but the most effective anti-partisan units were the five mobile Anti-Guerilla units (*Protibande*) – 'Martin' 'Ludvig', 'Filip', 'Stefan' and 'Lux'. These were formed in July–August 1942 from ex-Yugoslav *Dravski* Regiment Gendarmes, volunteers and Partisan deserters. From July 1942, Slovenes were liable for German military service. Slovenes in Eastern Slovenia were liable for Hungarian Army conscription.

On 9 January 1944, 1,000 Slovenes in Upper Carniola formed a Home Defence Force (*Gorenjsko domobranstvo*) as a local guard force on the Western Slovene model. By May 1945 there were 2,600 men in about 46 Posts and a mobile assault company, headquartered at Kranj. Nominally commanded by Slavko Krek, later Franc Erpič, it was under the Gestapo control of Sergeant Erich Dichtl. The Black Hand (*Črna roka*), formed early 1944, tracked down, tortured and killed about 1,000 Partisans and their civilian sympathizers.

German Police Regiments 13, 14, 25 and 28 served from February 1944 in Upper Carniola.

On 12 November 1943, Colonel Anton Kokalj formed the Slovene National Security Corps (*Slovenski Narodni Varnostni Zbor* or SNVZ) from Slovenes in three North-East Italian Provinces. There were few volunteers. Many Slovenes conscripted into the Italian Army had been taken prisoner in North Africa and had joined the Royal Yugoslav Forces in Egypt. As a result, compulsory military service was introduced, but the desertion rate was so high, that the SNVZ never exceeded 2,000 men.

A Headquarters Reserve at Trieste and 16 Rifle Companies were formed. These were divided into posts to guard individual villages. These Companies were organized into the following Groups (*Skupine*): *Postojna* (Trieste Province); *Gorica* (Gorizia Province); *Ilirska Bistrica* and *Idria* (Rijeka Province). On

*A Slovene Home Defence Force Company parades in Ljubljana in December 1943, wearing Italian helmets, equipment, and distinctive greatcoats. (Modern History Museum, Ljubljana)*

24 October 1944, these were reorganized as 1st to 4th Battalions of the 1st Slovene Coast Assault Regiment, with the 1st to 16th Companies allotted sequentially. SS-Major Georg Michalsen took over command in February 1945 when Kokalj was killed in action, and was himself succeeded in April 1945 by Major Janko Debeljak.

The SNVZ established three sub-units – the Urban Police (*Policija*), formed March 1944 and eventually comprising two security companies and five platoons: a Rural Police (*Orožniški Zbor*) formed February 1945; and the Reserve Defence Force (*Rezavna Dežełna Bramba*). This was formed in early 1945, under Major Šinkovec, to train SNVZ reservists.

On 3 May 1945, the Slovene National Alliance proclaimed Slovene independence, and on the 4th revived the Slovene National Army, which had been stillborn in July 1943. This time it had three Divisions – *Ljubljanska* (Slovene Home Defence Force), *Gorenjska* (Upper Carniola Home Defence Force) and *Primorska* (SNVZ). The commander was Major-General Krener. Most of *Primorska* surrendered to the British 8th Army near Gorizia on 3 May. On 7 May, *Ljubljanska* and *Gorenjska* retreated with the Germans and Croats into Southern Austria, only to be handed back to Tito's concentration-camps and firing-squads.

# THE PLATES

## A1: Gefreiter, 738 Jägerregiment, 118 Jägerdivision, German Army, Eastern Herzegovina, May 1943

The M1943 tunic differed from the M1935, being brownish-grey rather than greenish-grey. It had a brownish-grey collar, shoulder-straps and arm-badge backings (rather than dark blue-green), squared off pocket-flaps and no pleats. And there were six (not five) front buttons. Since 25 April 1940, NCO collar and shoulder-strap braid, shoulder-loops (here for an NCO Candidate) and chevrons were in matt-grey artificial silk, not aluminium braid. The plain mouse-grey silk collar-patches were introduced 9 May 1940. Special *Jäger* distinctions were adopted 2 October 1942. These comprised Mountain Troops' light-green branch-colour and peaked field-cap; oak-

Lieutenant-General Leon Rupnik, the only Slovene Home Defence Force General Officer, inspects troops of the Upper Carniola Home Defence Force, wearing German and Italian uniforms and equipment. Note the SS cap-badge. Behind Rupnik are three Slovene Home Defence Force officers – Colonel Vizjak (wearing spectacles), Colonel Franc Krener, Force Commander, and a third officer – Polhov Gradec, Western Slovenia, 4 June 1944. (Modern History Museum, Ljubljana)

leaf cap-badge (here with unofficial branch-colour backing for Austrian units); and right arm-badge. This Lance-Corporal wears the Iron Cross 2nd Class ribbon, Signaller's arm-badge, and black wound-badge, signifying one or two wounds.

## A2: SS-Hauptsturmführer, Armoured Battalion, SS-Freiwilligen-Gebirgs-Division 'Prinz Eugen', Waffen-SS, Split, Dalmatia, September 1943

This Captain wears the M1938 SS version of the Army M1935 black AFV uniform, distinguished by a straighter-cut front flap and shallower collar, but has omitted the usual officer's aluminium cord collar-piping. Against regulations he wears the M1938 NCO's field cap often favoured by officers. Rank is on Army shoulder-boards with 'Panzer pink' and 'SS-black' underlays, and the left collar-patch. 'Prinz Eugen' affiliation is indicated by the Odal Rune on the right collar-patch (theoretically SS runes were not permitted to the ethnic Germans), cuff-title and Mountain-Troops' arm-badge – the only German Armoured unit so entitled. Breast decorations comprise (clockwise) the Iron Cross 1st Class, a bronze commemoration badge for six months *Einsatzstaffel* service, runes indicating full SS membership and the M1939 tank battle badge. The unofficial Croatian armshield indicates past 'Einsatzstaffel' service.

## A3: Paratrooper, SS-Fallschirmjägerbataillon 500, Waffen-SS, Drvar, Western Bosnia, May 1944

A member of the sole Waffen-SS parachute unit, this trooper wears Air-Force equipment – the M1937 paratrooper's helmet with Air-Force eagle decal, the M1941 camouflage smock still showing the Air-Force breast eagle and Air-Force parachute webbing. His SS membership is only revealed by the peakless field-cap for NCOs and Men (officers had aluminium wire badges and flap-piping) introduced November 1940.

## B1: Colonnello titolare, 83 Infantry Regiment, 19 Infantry Division 'Venezia', Italian Army, Eastern Montenegro, 1942

The grey-green officers' field uniform, introduced 5 June 1940, adapted the M1934 uniform by substituting a plain collar (instead of coloured) and plain shoulder-straps (instead of pipings, braids and branch-badge). Branch-colour collar and cuff pipings were also omitted, only breeches piping remaining. Cuff rank-bars were of yellow rayon, and shorter. The M1942 peaked field-cap had a yellow infantry branch-badge, with regimental number, and the cloth rank-rectangle with yellow stars and braid. The smaller collar-patches indicate the division, as does the 'St. Mark of Venice' tradition breast-badge, introduced 6 November 1940. This replaced the divisional arm-shield, which was abolished July 1940. The Colonel's position as Regimental Commander (*titolare*) is indicated by scarlet underlay on cap and cuff insignia.

## B2: Vicecaposquadra, 81 'M' Blackshirt Battalion, Italian Blackshirt Militia, 21 Infantry Division 'Granatieri di Sardegna', Novo Mesto, Slovenia, August 1942

MVSN troops wore the standard Army M1934 grey-green Other Ranks field uniform (also recommended for officers) with the *Bersaglieri* undress fez in black, or the M1933 helmet; black tie; and M1939 arm-chevrons, modified 1940, silver for Junior NCOs, red for Privates. This Senior Lance-Corporal wears the black collar-patches (derived from *Arditi* assault troops in the First World War) with silver fasces and 'M' monogram, introduced 1941. He also wears M1934 webbing and the traditional Blackshirt dagger.

## B3: Sergente-Maggiore, Motorcyclist Company, 11 Bersaglieri Regiment, 1 Mobile Division 'Eugenio di Savoia', Italian Army, Karlovac, Western Croatia, September 1941

The élite *Bersaglieri*, originally light infantry, then cyclist, motorcycle and lorried infantry, had worn the traditional dark-green cockerel feathers on headdress since 1936. Here they appear on the M1933 steel helmet. This soldier wears the black 'Motorcycle' helmet decal stencil, introduced in 1937 for members of Corps motorcycle companies. The greatcoat has no insignia, except the metal collar 'activity star', worn by all Italian Armed Forces personnel. Gold was worn by generals; silver metal by other officers; and aluminium by NCOs and men. Sleeve rank chevrons were introduced on 4 October 1939. They were gold for junior NCOs and red for privates. From 5 June 1940, they were in plain yellow or red rayon. Note the M91 *Moschetto* carbine.

## C1: General, Croatian Army, Zagreb, Croatia, February 1943

Croatian Army uniforms, introduced 24 May 1941, show German influence. The officers' greenish-grey service tunic had a dark-brown collar with gold buttons for generals and greenish-grey buttons for other officers. They had a pattern of ornamental 'troplet' edging and a trefoil. The peaked-cap had a dark-brown band and branch-colour piping. The 1st Pattern cap-badges, worn May 1941 to November 1942, were a gold 'NHD' in an oval, above a tricolour cockade in a gold or silver wreath. Generals had a double gold knotted chin-cord. Field-Officers had the same in silver. Captains and Subalterns had a

*Pts (1–3) and NCO's (4–7) wore white metal or bone badges and silver braid. Jnr officers (8–12) wore silver metal badges and silver piping Field officers (13–15) gold metal, badges and silver braid, Generals (16–18) silver badges and gold braid. Field Marshal Kvaternik (19) wore gold braid leaves on silver braid. Officer's cap badges: First-pattern (20–1) gold metal above blue-white-red (centre) cockade with silver (gold–Generals) metal leaves. Second pattern (22–23) silver*

*(gold–Generals). Collar patch cloth: scarlet–Generals; scarlet, black, velvet inset – General Staff; light -red – Infantry, Mtn. Infantry, Railway Security; grass-green – Riflemen; dark-yellow – Cavalry; black (until Nov. 1943) – armour; bright -red – Artillery; dark-green – Eng./Signals; light-beige – Medical Officers; dark-brown – Medical orderlies. (13, 17) – braid worn May 1941–March 1942; (14–16, 18) – worn March 1942–Januaryt 1945.*

# THE CROATIAN ARMY (KOPNENA VOJSKA/DOMOBRANSTVO)
## 24 MAY 1941–12 JANUARY 1945

### 1. DOMOBRAN
(Private)

### 2. DESETNIK
(Lance-Corporal–Engineers)

### 3. RAZVODNIK
(Corporal–Signals)

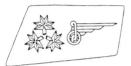

### 4. VODNIK
(Lance-Sergeant–Railway Security)

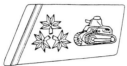

### 5. NAREDNIK
(Sergeant–Armour)

### 6. STOŽERNI NAREDNIK
(Warrant Officer II–Medical Corps)

### 7. June 1941 ČASTNIČKI NAMJESTNIK
(Warrant Officer I)

### 20. Cap-badge 1941-42

### 22. Cap-badge 1942–45

### 8. Sept 1941 ZASTAVNIK
(Junior 2nd Lieutenant)

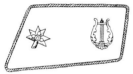

### 9. PORUČNIK
(2nd Lieutenant–Band)

### 21. Cap-badge 1941–42

### 23. Cap-badge 1942–45

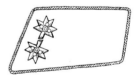

### 10. NADPORUČNIK
(Lieutenant)

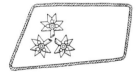

### 11. SATNIK
(Captain)

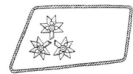

### 12. Sept 1941 NADSATNIK
(Senior Captain)

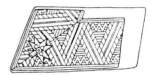

### 13. BOJNIK
(Major)

### 14. PODPUKOVNIK
(Lieutenant-Colonel)

### 15. PUKOVNIK
(Colonel–General Staff)

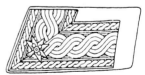

### 16. GENERAL
(Major-General)

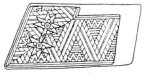

### 17. PODMARŠAL
Aug 1942 GENERAL-PORUČNIK
(Lieutenant-General)

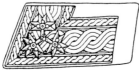

### 18. GENERAL PJEŠAŠTVA,
TOPNIŠTVA, KONJANIŠTVA
(General of Infantry, Artillery, Cavalry)

### 19. VOJSKOVODJA
(Field-Marshal)

A Croatian urban police cadet, Zagreb, 1943. Police wore ex-Yugoslav uniforms and insignia from April 1941, changing in June 1942 to Ustasha rank insignia, in December 1943 adopting new uniforms, probably with collar rank-insignia. (Croatian History Museum, Zagreb)

single silver knotted cord. The 2nd Pattern, worn November 1942 to January 1945, was a 'U' in a patterned square above 'NDH' in a wreathed oval, in gold braid or metal for generals, or silver metal for other officers. NCOs' peaked-caps, adopted 1943, omitted the oak wreath. Black trousers were worn for ceremonials. They had branch-colour piping. Generals had two wide scarlet stripes. In service, dress breeches and riding-boots were worn. Austrian-style collar-insignia commemorates the original *Hrvatsko Domobranstvo*, which was part of the Austro-Hungarian Army 1868–1918.

### C2: Poručnik, Croatian Army Armoured Units, Bosnia, January 1944

From November 1943, AFV personnel wore an Air-Force style uniform and cap in black (grey in summer) with Air-Force shoulder-boards (see plates E1 and E2) with red piping and black underlay. Privates wore a silver tank on a black collar-patch with 2mm red patch piping. NCOs added 0.8cm silver collar braid (like Air-Force NCOs). Officers had 2mm

silver patch-piping and collar-piping. And generals had a gold patch and gold collar-piping. The black AFV helmet had a national shield on the right side. The peakless field-cap had a gilt 'NHD' in an oval from November 1942 a bronze or aluminium 'NDH' in an oval.

### C3: Bojnik, Croatian Infantry, Zagreb, February 1945

The January 1945 combined Army and Ustasha uniform comprised a modified German M1943 greenish-grey tunic with gold/silver plain or patterned buttons. Trefoils on intricately plaited shoulder-boards indicated officer rank, flat shoulder-boards NCO rank, and arm-chevrons privates. Branch-colour collar-patches had army, Ustasha or PTS badges. The peaked-cap had dark-red piping and dark-brown cap-band, with an 'AP' (*Ante Pavelić*) above oval Ustasha or army badges for officers. NCOs and men had 'AP' above 'U' and chequerboard or 'U' and grenade respectively. This insignia was also worn on the army peaked or Ustasha peakless field-cap. On the peaked-cap, generals had gold knotted cap-cords, field-officers dark-red and silver, captains and subalterns dark-red, senior NCOs black leather. Note the M1944 officers' sabre and the 'Armed-Forces' badges on the right breast – 'U' and chequerboard on the tricolour flag, equivalent to the German breast-eagle. Personnel of the 1, 5 and 18 Assault Divisions wore 'H', large Ustasha 'U' and 'D' on a tricolour flag on the left breast. Wartime shortages necessitated limited issue of this uniform so most troops retained the 1941 version.

### D1: Razvodnik, 4 Infantry Regiment, 3 Infantry Division, Croatian Army, Tuzla, Bosnia, December 1941

At first, the Croatian Army wore greenish-grey Yugoslav uniforms, which often faded to a brownish colour. Dark-green collars and shoulder-straps, and fly-front buttons were added. These uniforms were worn until at least 1944, as were Italian M1934 and some German M1935 uniforms. Rank was indicated

*Collar-patches: (1, 2, 4, 5) red-white-blue cotton, worn red inwards, silver metal insignia; (6) red cloth, (7) red metal; large silver badge (shown) – NCO's & men, small–officers. (8–9) red metal, silver metal (badges. Cap-badge (3) silver metal. Arm (10–16) and cuff (17–25) rank (insignia – red*

*braid spirals. Senior Capt. wore Capt.'s insignia shown (August 1942–44; otherwise Capt.'s insignia. 'Zbornik' (Lt.Gen.), 'Vojskovodja' (Gen.), 'Ratovofja' (Field Marshal) existed 1 April, 1941–21 June 1941, but no insignia prescribed, and no officer held the rank.*

# THE USTASHA ARMY (USTAŠKA VOJNICA)
## APRIL 1941–12 JANUARY 1945

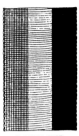

1. UV & PTB
1 April–21 June 1941

2. PTB
22 June 1941–
9 May 1942

3. Cap-badge

4. PTB officers
1942–1945

5. PTB NCOs & men
1942–1945

6. UV
22 June 1941–12 Jan 1945

7. PTS
10 May 1942–mid. 1944

8. PTS
mid. 1944–12 Jan 1945

9. Ustasha Railway
Troops

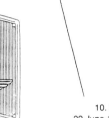

10. USTAŠA
22 June 1941 ČARKAR
Aug 1942 VOJNIČAR
(Private)

11. ROJNIK
22 June 1941 DOROJNIK
(Lance-Corporal)

12. RAZVODNIK
22 June 1941 ROJNIK
(Corporal)

13. VODNIK
22 June 1941 DOVODNIK
(Lance-Sergeant)

14 STRAŽARNIK
22 June 1941 VODNIK
(Sergeant)

15. ČAST NAMJESTNIK
Aug 1942 STOŽ VODNIK
(Warrant Officer II)

16. Aug 1942
ČASTNIČKI NAMJESTNIK
(Warrant Officer I)

NCOs & men     Officers
(10–16)        (17–25)

17. ZASTAVNIK
(Junior 2nd Lieutenant)

18. PORUČNIK
(2nd Lieutenant)

19. NADPORUČNIK
(Lieutenant)

20. SATNIK
(Captain)

21. Aug 1942 NADSATNIK
(Senior Captain)

22. BOJNIK
(Major)

23. PODPUKOVNIK
Aug 1942 DOPUKOVNIK
(Lieutenant-Colonel)

24. PUKOVNIK
(Colonel)

25. KRILNIK
(Major-General)

on branch-colour collar-patches. Engineers, Signals, Railway Security, Medical Corps personnel and Bandsmen added special badges. Other ex-Yugoslav badges were worn unofficially. No unit badges or numerals were worn. Moslems wore a scarlet fez. Other troops wore the M1941 peaked field-cap, with the 1st pattern cap-badge – a gold 'NHD' in an oval – or 2nd pattern – a bronze or aluminium 'NDH' in an oval. Moslem personnel were represented throughout the armed forces but to forestall Moslem nationalism, they were not concentrated in separate units. Only the 1st–4th, 6th and 9th Infantry Regiments had significant proportions of Moslems.

### D2: Stožerni Narednik, Croatian Artillery, Western Bosnia, June 1943

The greenish-grey M1941 field tunic, with a dark-green collar (dark-brown for generals) and dark-green shoulder-straps for NCOs and men, with plain greenish-grey buttons, was similar to the German Army M1935, but had distinctive pocket-pleats. As a veteran of the Croatian Legion 1941–2, this senior NCO wears a linden-leaf badge on the left side of the field-cap, although wearing it on the left breast-pocket was more normal. Members of Mountain Brigades wore Roman numerals I–IV between two Edelweiss flowers on the left side of the cap. From 1944, the German army M1943 uniform was issued. Ethnic German troops wore a white-wreathed swastika badge on the upper left sleeve. Gendarmerie wore dark-red collar-patches (lowest rank was *Oružnik*, equivalent to *Razvodnik*) and special gold, silver or grey aiguillettes. New dark-brown uniforms and rank insignia were introduced in 1944.

### D3: Domobran, 7 Rifle Regt, 4 Rifle Brigade, Croatian Army, Eastern Bosnia, December 1943

Initially Croats wore ex-Yugoslav greenish-grey greatcoats, but the Croatian greenish-grey version was issued from mid-1941. Generals had a dark-brown collar with scarlet spearhead collar-patches with a gold patterned button, and scarlet collar, cuff, pocket-flap and front edge piping. Officers wore the dark-brown service-dress and dark-green field-uniform collars with greenish-grey patterned buttons on branch-colour patches, and branch-colour pipings. NCOs and men had dark-green collars and shoulder-straps, branch-colour collar-patches without buttons, cuffs or pipings. There was no specific rank insignia. Rifle Brigade personnel wore an Edelweiss on a black triangle piped silver on the left upper sleeve. German M1935 and Italian M1933 helmets were worn; also ex-Yugoslav French M1915 'Adrian' and Czech M1934 models.

### E1: Bojnik, Croatian Air Force, Bosnia, October 1942

The grey-blue officer's uniform had rank on German Air-Force-style branch-coloured collar-patches piped silver (gold for generals), a peakless field-cap or peaked service-cap with a silver 'NHD' in an oval over a silver eagle and half-wreath. Generals had double gold knotted peaked-cap chin-cords. Field-officers wore silver. Captains and subalterns had two intertwined plain silver cords. The Air-Force badge was worn above the right breast-pocket.

In November 1941, German-style shoulder-boards on branch-colour underlay were added. Field-Marshal Kvaternik wore collar-patch with gold eagle, wreath and chequerboard shield, gold-silver-gold knotted shoulder braids and crossed silver batons. General-Officers had 3–1 gold wings and wreath with 3–1 gold trefoils on gold-silver-gold knotted shoulder-braids. Field-Officers had 3–1 silver wings and wreath with 3–1 gold trefoils on silver knotted braids. Captains and subalterns had 3–0 silver wings above half-wreath with 4-0 gold trefoils on silver flat braids. A senior captain had captain's collar insignia in gold. In November 1942, peaked-caps had a silver 'U' in a patterned square above a silver eagle above a wreathed 'NHD' in an oval. Field-cap insignia was as before. In December 1944, peaked-caps had a tricolour cockade with 'AP' monogram above a

# THE CROATIAN ARMED FORCES (HRVATSKE ORUŽANE SNAGE)
## 13 JANUARY 1945–15 MAY 1945

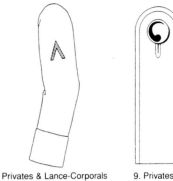

1. Ustasha and PTS NCOs and men

2. Army NCOs and men

3. Ustasha and PTS officers

4. Army officers

Privates & Lance-Corporals (8,10,11)

9. Privates & Lance-Corporals

5. PTS officers

6. Ustasha officers

7. Army officers

8. VOJNIK (Army)/VOJNIČAR (PTS & Ustasha) (Private)

10. STRIELAC (Senior Private)

11. DOROJNIK (Lance-Corporal)

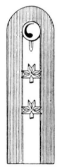

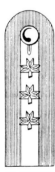

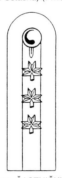

12. ROJNIK (Corporal)

13. VODNIK (Lance-Sergeant)

14. STRAŽNIK (Sergeant)

15. STOŽERNI STRAŽNIK (Warrant Officer II)

16. ČASTNIČKI NAMJESTNIK (Warrant Officer I)

17. ZASTAVNIK (Junior 2nd Lieutenant)

18. PORUČNIK (2nd Lieutenant)

19. NADPORUČNIK (Lieutenant)

20. SATNIK (Captain)

21. NADSATNIK (Senior Captain)

22. BOJNIK (Major)

23. DOPUKOVNIK (Lieutenant-Colonel)

24. PUKOVNIK (Colonel)

25. GENERAL (Major-General)

26. GENERAL-PORUČNIK (Lieut.-General)

27. GENERAL-PUKOVNIK (General)

# THE BULGARIAN ARMY (BULGARSKA VOYSKA)
## 1941–1945

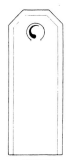

1. REDNIK
(Private)

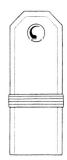

2. EFREYTOR
(Lance-Corporal)

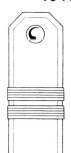

3. KANDIDAT
PODOFITSER
(Corporal)

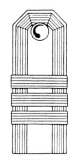

4. PODOFITSER
(Sergeant)

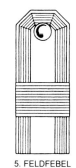

5. FELDFEBEL
(VACHMISTER – Cav.)
(Warrant Officer)

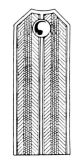

6. OFITSERSKI
KANDIDAT
(Junior 2nd Lieutenant)

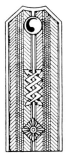

7. PODPORUCHIK
(2nd Lieutenant)
(Signals)

8. PORUCHIK
(Lieutenant)
(Cavalry)

9. KAPITAN
(ROTMISTER – Cav.)
(Captain – Medical Corps)

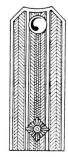

10. MAYOR
(Major)

11. PODPOLKOVNIK
(Lieutenant-Colonel)

12. POLKOVNIK
(Colonel)

13. GENERAL-MAYOR
(Major-General)
(Air Force)

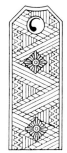

14. GENERAL-
LEYTENANT
(Lieutenant-General)

15. GENERAL
(General)

16. MARSHAL
NA BULGARIA
(Field-Marshal)

17. Generals (13–16)

18. Officers (7–12)

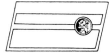

19. Junior 2nd Lieutenant (6)

20. NCOs (4–5)

21. Privates (1–3)

silver winged chequerboard. On field-caps, there was the winged chequerboard only. Finally in March 1945, army shoulder-straps were prescribed (see C3).

The branch-colours were: light-blue – flying and parachute troops; light-red – anti-aircraft artillery; dark-red – technical; brown – medical; and light-grey – auxiliaries. Pilots and radio-operators wore a German-style wreathed silver eagle badge on the left breast-pocket.

The National Guard wore a grey uniform with black facings, and air-force collar-patches with trefoils instead of wings.

## E2: Narednik, 1st Parachute Company, Croatian Air Force, Koprivnica, September 1943

In May 1941, NCOs and men wore a grey-blue tunic with silver wings and braids on branch-colour collar-patches with a silver 'NDH' in oval on the peakless field-cap. From November 1941, they also wore German-style shoulder-straps with branch-colour piping and silver insignia. Senior NCOs and sergeants had 3–1 wings on the collar-patch with 0.8cm silver collar-braid, with 3–1 trefoils on the strap with silver braid encircling the strap. Lance-sergeants and privates had 3–0 wings – lance-sergeant had braid around strap edge, privates plain straps. In November 1942, silver 'NDH' in an oval appeared on the field-cap.

From 1942–3, paratroops wore ex-Yugoslav greenish-grey uniforms with army collar-insignia and a silver metal parachute on the left upper arm, and a wreathed diving eagle on the left breast-pocket. In 1943, camouflaged field uniforms were introduced. As a company sergeant major (*Stegovni Dočastnik*), this NCO wears German-style double cuff braids.

## E3: Vodnik, South Adriatic Command, Croatian Navy, Dubrovnik, February 1944

In April 1941, Royal Yugoslav uniforms and rank insignia were worn. Officers adopted a tricolour cockade above a gold 'NDH' on a wreathed anchor cap-badge. NCOs wore an anchor in an oval. Seamen had a gold 'NHD'. From November 1942, the 'NDH' appeared in an oval. In July 1941, new rank insignia appeared, with officers wearing a gold trefoil above rank rings. And in January 1944, all ranks adopted Croatian air-force-style shoulder-boards on navy-blue backing. Finally in December 1944, the officer's cockade was replaced by a 'U' on a chequerboard badge with 'wavy wings', also worn on the seaman's cap. Seamen also wore a navy-blue beret.

## F1: Dopukovnik, Croatian Ustasha Army, Croatia, 1942

In May 1941, Ustasha troops adopted greenish-grey tunics and trousers or breeches with a distinctive peakless field-cap with an aluminium grenade and chequerboard within a 'U', and the pre-war tricolour rectangular collar patches changed to red with an aluminium 'U' and grenade. In December 1941, a yellowish-brown uniform was adopted, with a peaked-cap with a tricolour cockade with the 'AP' monogram (which was now added to the field-cap) above a wreathed 'U' and grenade in an oval. Officers wore red braid rank spirals and bars on both cuffs and the left side of the field-cap, NCOs and Men insignia on both upper sleeves only. Ex-Yugoslav Army, Croatian Army M1941, German Army M1943 and Italian M1940 uniforms were also worn, and occasionally locally produced versions.

In January 1945, the combined Army-Ustasha uniform was introduced, Ustasha officers retaining their cuff rank-insignia. Officers commanding Divisions or Corps were given dual army and Ustasha rank to compensate for the lack of Ustasha active General-Officer ranks – for example, *General-poručnik i Ustaški Pukovnik*.

## F2: Rojnik, 2 Regiment, Poglavnik Bodyguard Brigade, Zagorje, Croatia, January 1944

The PTB wore standard Ustasha tricolour collar-patches, adding a large aluminium 'U' and grenade in June 1941. In February 1942 they adopted pent

*Other ranks' shoulder-straps (1–5) are uniform colour piped in branch-colour with yellow or white medium bars, gold or silver NCO braid edging, and a gold or silver wide bar. Gold or silver braid officers' straps (6–15) with branch-solour piping and centre stripes, silver or gold pips and branch-badge. Rank 16, intended for Tzar Boris for October 1943 (he died in August) had a gold strap piped red with silver*

*insignia. Collar patches were branch-colour (Generals – red for Army, light-blue for Airforce) with gold or silver braids and buttons. Branch-colour: Infantry – red /gold; Cavalry – red & white/silver; Armour – red & yellow/silver; Artillery – black & red/gold; Gen. Staff – red & black, silver; Eng. & Signals – black & white/silver; Medical – black & dark blue/silver; Airforce – light-blue/gold.*

angular patches with small badges for officers or large badges for NCOs and men. In May 1942, the PTS changed to a red metal pentangular patch, but old 'PTB Hands' kept their tricolour patches until May 1945.

In mid-1944, a red metal collar-patch with a 'U' in a patterned square was adopted for German M1943 uniforms. In December a new grey-blue uniform was introduced, with special shoulder-strap rank insignia. The design is unknown. PTS armoured personnel wore a black uniform with a tank-badge above the left breast-pocket. Note the *Zbrojkovka* machine-gun.

### F3: Poručnik, 1 Battalion, Black Legion, Croatian Ustasha Army, Han Pijesak, Central Bosnia, March 1942

Black Legion troops wore standard Ustasha insignia on a black tunic and field-cap, which they adopted January 1942. On their disbandment in August 1942, some men joined II Communications Brigade, but most retained their black uniforms and joined V Ustasha Active Service Brigade, which continued the name 'Black Legion' until May 1945.

### G1: Rotmistr, 2 Cavalry Regiment, 4 Cavalry Brigade, Bulgarian 5 Army, Macedonia, 1942

Bulgarian officers wore the M1935 grey-green tunic, breeches and greatcoat, with dark-green collars, and peaked caps. Branch-colours were shown on the cap-band and cap-piping, underlays to the German-style

tunic collar-patches and the Russian-style overcoat collar-patches, breeches stripes, greatcoat cuff and collar-pipings, and shoulder-board pipings. The buttons carried a branch-badge. Labour Corps officers had special tunic collar-patches. Regimental monograms and numerals were omitted in wartime, and officers could wear field shoulder-boards of grey-green cloth, but branch-badges were retained. General-officers, regimental commanders and general-staff officers wore a double breeches-stripe. The distinctive M1936 helmet, with a national shield on the right side, replaced the German M1916, which was still encountered in reserve units. This Cavalry Officer, easily identifiable from his silver shoulder-boards, white pipings and cavalry-boots, carries a German M1908 9mm Parabellum pistol.

### G2: Podofitser, 63 Infantry Regiment, 22 Infantry Division, 1 Occupation Corps, Bulgarian Army, Niš, August 1943

Bulgarian NCOs and men wore a tobacco-brown tunic and trousers, with a peaked service-cap with branch-colour cap-band and Russian-style cockade in white, green and red with gold Bulgarian lion, or peakless field-cap. The pre-war branch-colour shoulder-straps, with yellow/white unit numerals or monogram, were replaced by plain straps piped in branch-colour, and collar-patches lost their button. NCOs added gold/silver shoulder-strap and collar-braids. The field-cap (grey-green for officers) had a gilt Bulgarian lion on the front and tricolour national shield on the right side, and officers added rank-class braid stripes. Generals had one thick gold stripe. Field-officers had one thin one and one medium one in silver. Captains and subalterns had one single thin silver stripe. Armoured Corps wore the German black double-breasted tunic with a red collar-patch piped yellow and a silver skull and crossbones for officers and NCOs, black peaked field-cap and long trousers tucked into ankle-boots. Motorized Infantry wore a grey-green version. Labour Corps wore a black 'T' on an oval – striped horizontally white, green and red – on the left upper arm.

*Croatian labour service troops in summer 1942 wearing German-style insignia, introduced 30 July 1941, replaced in 1942 by coloured shoulder-strap bars, with new German RAD-style insignia adopted on 20 July 1944. (National and University Library, Zagreb)*

### G3: Officer, Parachute Battalion, Bulgarian Air Force, Macedonia, 1943

The Battalion wore Italian camouflage field-smocks over grey-blue field tunics and trousers. The field-cap had the silver metal air-force winged cockade, a national shield on the right side and silver rank-class braid. This officer carries the MP38 German *Schmeisser* sub-machine-gun and magazine pouches. The M1938 Air-Force uniform was grey-blue, with light-blue collar-patches and pipings and silver braid.

### H1: Nadporočnik, 3 Assault Battalion, Slovene Home Defence Force, Ljubljana, Slovenia, August 1944

Officers wore a light grey-green tunic and breeches or trousers with riding-boots or ankle-boots. The Force badge, on the left upper arm, was a dark-blue eagle on a white shield edged dark-blue. General-officers (*Divizijski General* and *Brigadni General*) had 1–0 silver pips on German gold-silver-gold plaited shoulder-boards with red underlay piped in gold wire. Field-Officers (*Polkovnik*, *Podpolkovnik* and *Major*) had 3–1 silver pips on flat gold braid shoulder-boards piped red. Captains and subalterns and warrant officer IIs (*Stotnik*, *Nadporočnik*, *Poročnik* and *Štabni Narednik*) had 3–0 gold pips on flat silver braid boards piped red. There was no branch insignia. The peakless field-cap had the Slovene tricolour cockade, adding a white eagle to it in mid-1944.

The grey-green peaked cap had a silver eagle with outstretched wings. AFV crews had black overalls.

### H2: Podnarednik, 2 Assault Battalion, Slovene Home Defence Force, Rakek, Slovenia, November 1944

NCOs and men wore a light grey-green tunic with peakless field-cap with tricolour cockade, or the Italian M1933 helmet with a national shield on the left side. NCOs (*Višji Narednik*, *Narednik*, *Podnarednik* and *Kaplar*) wore dark-green shoulder-boards completely edged in silver braid and 3–0 silver bars. Privates (*Domobranec*) had a plain strap. Roman battalion numerals were sometimes worn on the shoulder-boards and straps.

The Upper Carniola Home Defence Force regulations of 4 December 1944 prescribed German

*Troops of the Upper Carniola Home Defence Force in Lesce, near Lake Bled, wearing German SIPO uniforms and insignia introduced December 1944. (Modern History Museum, Ljubljana)*

SIPO uniforms with an M1943 field-cap with a German eagle on the right side. The arm-badge was a dark-blue eagle on a red (left) and white (right) shield edged dark-blue. On the right cuff, 10cm wide braids indicated rank. Officers (*Poveljnik Centra Gorenjskega Domobranstva*, *Nacelnik* and *Namestnik Načelnika*) had 3–1 gold bars. NCOs (*Poveljnik Postojanke*, *Vodnik* and *Desetar*) 3–1 silver bars. The Assault Company ('Udarna četa') wore a silver skull on the left collar.

### H3: Stražmojster, 8 Company, Postojna Group, Slovene National Security Corps, Postojna, North-East Italy, May 1944

The SNVZ wore Italian uniforms, Slovene Home Defence Force cap-cockades and helmet decals. They also sometimes wore Italian camouflage field-uniforms. The Force arm-badge was a red Illyrian galley on a white (upper) and waved dark-blue (lower) shield, piped dark-blue. Rank insignia and officers' rank titles (highest rank *Polkovnik*) were as the Home Defence Force, but NCOs and Men initially adopted translations of German Police titles – *Glavni Stražmojster*, *Stražmojster Vodnik*, *Nadstražmojster*, *Stražmojster*, *Krdelni stražmojster*, *Podstražmojster* (July 1944, *Nadstražar*), *Pripravnik* (July 1944, *Stražar*). They adopted Home Defence Force titles in October 1944 (*Nadstražar* and *Stražar* became *Stražar* – Private).

## Notes sur les planches en couleur

**A1** Tunique, col, épaulettes et doublure des badges de manche marron-gris, revers de poche carrés et pas de plis. Les écussons de col en soie unie gris souris furent introduits en avril 1940. **A2** Il s'agit de la version M1938 SS de l'uniforme AFV noir M1935, distingué par un revers avant plus drit et un col moins large mais pas de passepoil de col en galon d'aluminium pour les officiers. **A3** Casque de parachutiste M1937, smock de camouflage M1941 et équipement en toile de parachutisme Air Force.

**B1** Uniforme d'officier gris-vert avec col uni et épaulettes, seul le passepoil de la culotte reste. La casquette de campagne à visière M1942 portait un badge jaune de branche d'infanterie avec le numéro du régiment. **B2** Uniforme gris-vert standard M1934 avec le fez de petite tenue 'Bersaglieri' en noir ou le casque M1933 et l'équipement en toile M1934. **B3** Vert foncé traditionnel sur coiffure, manteau uni sans insignes sauf 'l'étoile d'activité' sur le col portée par tout le personnel italien.

**C1** Tunique gris-vert, col marron foncé, casquette à visière avec passepoil de la couleur de la branche. Les généraux avaient une double mentonnière nouée dorée et deux larges rayures écarlates sur le pantalon de service pour indiquer leur rang. **C2** Le personnel AVF portait un uniforme et une casquette de style Air Force gris-noir en été avec des épaulettes Air-Force au passepoil rouge et doublure noire. Le casque AVF noir portait l'écusson national du côté droit. **C3** Tunique allemande gris-vert M1934 modifiée avec boutons dorés/argent unis ou à motifs. Épaulettes, chevrons sur manche indiquaient le rang, comme les insignes sur le badge de casquette.

**D1** Jusqu'à 1944 au moins, l'uniforme yougoslave gris-vert était porté avec un col vert foncé ajouté et des épaulettes et des boutons sur la braguette. Les musulmans portaient un fez écarlate etles autres la casquette à visière M1941. **D2** La tunique de combat M1941 se portait avec un col vert foncé et des boutons gris unis, assez similaire au M1935 de l'armée allemande mais avait des plis de poche distinctifs. **D3** Initialement, les Croates portaient le manteau gris-vert exYougoslave. On leur en distribua un qui leur était propre en mai 1941. Col et épaulettes vert foncé, écussons de col de branches sans boutons, pas de manchettes ni de passepoils. Il n'y avait pas d'insignes de rang spécifiques.

**E1** L'uniforme gris-bleu des officiers portait le rang sur des écussons de col de style allemand portant la couleur de la branche et passepoilés d'argent, une casquette de campagne sans visière ou une casquette de service avec visière avec un 'NHD' argent dans un ovale au dessus d'un aigle d'argent et d'une demicouronne. **E2** Les NCO et les hommes portaient une tunique bleu-gris avec ailes et ailes sur des écussons de col de la couleur des branches et un 'NHD' argent dans un ovale sur la casquette de campagne sans visière. Ils portaient aussi des épaulettes de style allemand avec un pessepoil de la couleur de la branche et des insignes argent. **E3** On portait les uniformes et insignes de rang royaux yougoslaves. Les officiers adoptèrent une cocarde tricolore au dessus d'un 'NHD' doré. Les marins portaient également un béret bleu marine.

**F1** Tunique et pantalon ou culotte gris-vert avec casquette de campagne sans visière caractéristique portant une grenade aluminium et un échiquier dans un 'U', des écussons de col rectangulaires rouges avec le 'U' et la grenade aluminium. **F2** Le PTB portait des écursons de col tricolores Utashi standard et ajouta un gros 'U' et une grenade aluminium en juin 1941. **F3** Tunique et casquette de campagne noires avec insignes Utashi standard.

**G1** Les officiers bulgares portaient la tunique, la culotte et le manteau gris-vert M1935 avec un col vert foncé et une casquette à visière. **G2** Les NCO et les hommes bulgares portaient une tunique et un pantalon tabac avec une casquette de service à visière portant une bande de la couleur de la branche et une cocarde de style russe en blanc, vert et rouge avec un lion bulgare doré, ou une casquette de campagne sans visière. **G3** - Le bataillon portait des smocks de campagne italiens de camouflage par dessus une tunique et un pantalon de campagne gris-bleu. La casquette de campagne avait la cocarde ailée argentée de l'Air Force, un écusson national sur la droite et un galon argent de rang. L'uniforme M1938 de l'Air Force était gris bleu avec des écussons de col et passepoils bleu clair et un galon argent.

**H1** Les officiers portaient une tunique et une culotte ou un pantalon gris-vert clair avec des bottes de cheval ou des bottines. Le badge Force, sur le bras gauche, était un aigle bleu foncé sur un écusson blanc bordé de bleu foncé. **H2** Les NCO et les hommes portaient une tunique gris-vert clair avec une casquette de campagne sans visière et une cocarde tricolore ou bien le casque italien M1933 avec un écusson national sur la gauche. Quelquefois les numéros romains des bataillons étaient portés sur les épaulettes. **H3** Les SNVZ portaient des uniformes italiens, des cocardes de casquettes de la force défensive slovaque et des décalcomanies de casque. Ils portaient aussi quelquefois des uniformes de campagne de camouflage italiens.

## Farbtafeln

**A1** Bräunlich-grüner Waffenrock, Kragen, Schulterklappen und Unterlagen für das Ärmelabzeichen, abgeflachte Taschenklappen ohn Falten. Die einfachen, mausgrauen Kragenspiegel aus Seide wurden im April 1940 eingeführt. **A2** Es ist die M1938er SS-Version der schwarzen AFV-Uniform M1935 der Armee, die sich durch eine gerade geschnittene Frontleiste und einen kleineren Kragen auszeichnet, jedoch am Kragen nicht die aluminiumfarbene Kordeleinfassung der Offiziere hat. **A3** Fallschirmjägerhelm M1937, Tarnkittel M1941 und Fallschirm-Gurtzeug der Luftwaffe.

**B1** Graugrüne Offiziersuniform mit einfachem Kragen und Schulterstücken, nur die Vorstöße an den Breeches bleiben. Die Feldmütze mit Schirm M1942 hatte das gelbe Waffengat tungsabzeichen der Infanterie mit der Regimentsnummer. **B2** Graugrüne Armee-Uniform M1934 in Standardausführung mit dem Ausgeh-Fes "Bersaglieri" in schwarz, beziehungsweise dem Helm M1933 und M1934-Gurtzeug. **B3** Diese Figur trägt das traditionelle Dunkelgrün auf der Kopfbedeckung, dem einfarbigen Mantel ohn Abzeichen, abgesehen vom "Activity Star" am Kragen, den alle italienischen Militärangehörigen trugen.

**C1** Grünlich-grauer Waffenrock, dunkelbrauner Kragen, Schirmmütze mit Vorstößen in der Waffenfarbe. Generäle hatten eine doppelte, verknotete Goldkordel am Kinn und zwei breite scharlachrote Streifen auf den Diensthosen, die den Rang bezeichnete. **C2** Die Angehörigen der AFV trugen eine Uniform im Stil der Luftwaffe und im Sommer eine schwarz-graue Mütze mit den Schulterstücken der Luftwaffe mit roten Vorstößen und schwarzer Unterlage. Der schwarze AFV-Helm hatte ein Nationalschild auf der rechten Seite. **C3** Modifizierter deutscher grünlich-grauer Waffenrock M1934 mit gold-/silberfarbenen, einfachen beziehungsweise gemusterten Knöpfen. Schulterstücke, die Winkel an der Armbinde gaben wie das Mützenabzeichen den Rang an.

**D1** Bis mindestens 1944 wurde die grünlich-graue jugoslawische Uniform mit zusätzlichem dunkelgrünen Kragen und Schulterklappen getragen sowie Knöpfen an der Vorderseite. Moslems trugen einen scharlachroten Fes, die anderen Truppen die Feldmütze mit Schirm M1941. **D2** Der Feldmütze M1941 wurde mit dunkelgrünem Kragen und einfachen grauen Knöpfen getragen und glich weitgehend dem M1935 der deutschen Armee, hatte jedoch charakteristische Taschenfalten. **D3** Anfangs trugen die Kroaten die ehemaligen jugoslawischen grünlich-grauen Mäntel, im Mai 1941 wurden ihnen eigene ausgegeben. Dunkelgrüne Kragen und Schulterklappen, Kragenspiegel der Waffengattung ohne Knöpfe, Manschetten oder Vorstöße. Es gab keine spezifischen Rangabzeichen.

**E1** Die grau-blaue Offiziersuniform zeigt auf den Kragenspiegeln in der Waffenfarbe mit silbernen Vorstößen im deutschen Stil den Rang an, eine Feldmütze ohn Schirm oder eine beschirmte Dienstmütze mit einem silbernen "NHD" in einem Oval über einem Silberader und einem Halbkranz. **E2** Unteroffiziere und Gefreite trugen einen blau-grauen Waffenrock mit Flügeln und Litzen auf den Kragenspiegeln in der Waffenfarbe mit einem silbernen "NHD" in einem Oval auf der Feldmütze ohne Schirm. Außerdem trugen sie Schulterklappen im deutschen Stil und Vorstöße in der Waffenfarbe sowie silberne Abzeichen. **E3** Man trug die königliche-jugoslawische Uniform und Rangabzeichen. Die Offiziere übernahmen eine dreifarbige Kokarde über einem goldenen "NHD". Matrosen trugen auch eine dunkelblaues Barett.

**F1** Grünlich-grauer Waffenrock und Hosen beziehungsweise Breeches mit der charakteristischen Feldmütze ohne Schirm mit einer aluminiumfarbenen Granate und Schachbrett innerhalb eines "U", rote, rechteckige Kragenspiegel mit einem aluminiumfarbenen "U" und Granate. **F2** Das PTB trug die aluminiumfarbenen dreifarbigen Kragenspiegel der Utashi, denen im Juni 1941 ein großes Aluminium–"U" und eine Granate Hinzugefügt wurde. **F3** Schwarzer Waffenrock und Feldmütze mit den standardmäßigen Utashi-Abzeichen.

**G1** Bulgarische Offiziere trugen den grau-grünen Waffenrock M1945, Breeches und Mäntel mit dunkelgrünen Kragen sowie Schirmmützen. **G2** Bulgarische Unteroffiziere und Gefreite trugen einen tabakbraunen Waffenrock und Hosen und eine Dienstmütze mit Schirm und Mützenband in Waffenfarbe sowie einer Kikarde im russischen Stil in weiß, grün und rot mit einem goldenen bulgarischen Löwen, oder eine Feldmütze ohne Schirm. **G3** Dieses Bataillon trug italienische Tarnfeldkittel über den grau-blauen Feldwaffenrock und Hosen. Die Feldmütze wies die silberne Kikarde der Luftwaffe mit Flügeln aus Metall auf, eine Nationalschild auf der rechten Seite sowie dilberne Ranglitzen. Die Luftwaffen-Uniform M1938 war grau-blau mit hellblauen Kragenspiegeln, Vorstößen und Silberlitze.

**H1** Offiziere trugen einen hellgrau-grünen Waffenrock und Breeches oder Hosen mit Reitstiefeln oder Kurzstiefeln. Das Abzeichen der Streitkräfte auf dem linken Oberarm war ein dunkelblauer Adler auf einem dunkelblauen eingefaßten weißen Feld. **H2** Unteroffiziere und Gefreite trugen enien hellgrau-grünen Waffenrock und eine Feldmütze ohn Schirm mit einer dreifarbigen Kikarde, oder den italienischen Helm M1933 mit einem Nationalschild auf der linken Seite. Battaillonsnummern in römischen Ziffern wurden manchmal auf den Schulterstücken und -klappen getragen. **H3** Die SNVZ trug itlienische Uniformen, die Mützen-Kokarde der Slovene Home Defence Force und Helmabzeichen. Manchmal trugen sie auch italienische Felduniformen mit Tarnmuster.